THE MAKING OF THE JEWISH MIDDLE CLASS

STUDIES IN JEWISH HISTORY

Jehuda Reinharz, *General Editor*

THE JEWS OF PARIS AND THE FINAL SOLUTION
Communal Response and Internal Conflicts, 1940–1944
Jacques Adler

ATLAS OF MODERN JEWISH HISTORY
Evyatar Friesel

A SIGN AND A WITNESS
2,000 Years of Hebrew Books and Illuminated Manuscripts
Paperback edition (copublished with The New York Public Library)
Edited by Leonard Singer Gold

A CLASH OF HEROES
Brandeis, Weizmann, and American Zionism
Ben Halpern

THE MAKING OF CZECH JEWRY
National Conflict and Jewish Society in Bohemia, 1870–1918
Hillel J. Kieval

THE ROAD TO MODERN JEWISH POLITICS
Political Tradition and Political Reconstruction in the Jewish Community of Tsarist Russia
Eli Lederhendler

RESPONSE TO MODERNITY
A History of the Reform Movement in Judaism
Michael A. Meyer

THE VATICAN AND ZIONISM
Conflict in the Holy Land, 1895–1925
Sergio Minerbi

ESCAPING THE HOLOCAUST
Illegal Immigration to the Land of Israel, 1939–1944
Dalia Ofer

CHAIM WEIZMANN
The Making of a Zionist Leader, paperback edition
Jehuda Reinharz

THE TRANSFORMATION OF GERMAN JEWRY: 1780–1840
David Sorkin

FOR WHOM DO I TOIL?
Judah Leib Gordon and the Crisis of Russian Jewry
Michael F. Stanislawski

UNWELCOME STRANGERS
East European Jews in Imperial Germany
Jack Wertheimer

THE HOLOCAUST
The Fate of European Jewry, 1932–1945
Leni Yahil

WILHELM MARR
The Patriarch of Antisemitism
Moshe Zimmerman

OTHER VOLUMES ARE IN PREPARATION

The Making of the Jewish Middle Class

Women, Family, and Identity in Imperial Germany

MARION A. KAPLAN

New York *Oxford*
OXFORD UNIVERSITY PRESS
1991

The author wishes to thank the Leo Baeck Institute
for its support in the research and writing of this work.

Oxford University Press

Oxford New York Toronto
Delhi Bombay Calcutta Madras Karachi
Petaling Jaya Singapore Hong Kong Tokyo
Nairobi Dar es Salaam Cape Town
Melbourne Auckland

and associated companies in
Berlin Ibadan

Published by Oxford University Press, Inc.,
200 Madison Avenue, New York, New York 10016

Oxford is a registerd trademark of Oxford University Press

Library of Congress Cataloging-in-Publication Data
Kaplan, Marion A.
The making of the Jewish middle class : women, family, and
identity in Imperial Germany / Marion A. Kaplan.
p. cm. (Studies in Jewish history)
Includes bibliographical references and index.
ISBN 0-19-503952-1
1. Jews—Germany—History—1800–1933. 2. Women, Jewish—Germany.
3. Germany—Ethnic relations. I. Title. II. Series.
DS135.G33K292 1991
943'.004924—dc20 90-45234

1 3 5 7 9 8 6 4 2

Printed in the United States of America
on acid-free paper

Recent Title in War, Technology, and History

Thunder over the Horizon: From V2 Rockets to Ballistic Missiles
Clayton K. S. Chun

About the Author

NORMAN YOUNGBLOOD is Assistant Professor in the College of Mass Communications at Texas Tech University and has written on public relations aspects of the International Campaign to Ban Landmines. His research areas include the history of technology and communication about technology.

For Ruth, Douglas, and Joshua

PREFACE

This study of Jewish women in Imperial Germany attempts to integrate German history, women's history, and Jewish history. It arose from the growing disparity I found between what I read in the fields of Jewish and German history and what I knew about women's history. The absence of women in Jewish and German history books has biased our ideas concerning what history "was" and the conclusions we have drawn from it. Their presence will make a difference not only in how we evaluate them, but in how we view the past in its entirety. Historians have only recently and haltingly begun to incorporate women's studies into German history. In Jewish history, masculine actors and male arenas have been virtually the only ones that mattered. Similarly, Jews have been absent in most chronicles of modern Germany, including German women's history. When they appear, they still figure primarily as victims of the Nazis rather than as active participants in the social, economic, and political processes of nineteenth- and twentieth-century Germany. Therefore, in addressing three fields—German, Jewish, and women's history—this book points to the importance of ethnicity in women's history, attempts to merge women and Jews into German history, and reassesses Jewish history in light of women's experiences.

Importantly, in the tradition of the women's movement and women's history, I have tried to make women "visible."[1] I have sought to uncover their successes and disappointments, their rebellions and submissions, their dynamism and the obstacles they faced. Therefore the primary goal of this book is to show how Jewish women made their own history, within the confines of gender, ethnicity, religion, and class. It describes the changing lives and roles of women who were part of an urbanizing, economically mobile, but socially spurned minority. It looks at their "double burden" as females and as Jews and also examines the advantages they drew from these and from their middle-class status. In addition, it points out the ambiguous role that Jewish women played: they were powerful agents of class formation and acculturation on the one hand, and determined upholders of tradition on the other.

Another goal of this book—implicit in its title—is to make women central to the writing of Jewish history and the history of the middle class. There is an unfortunate tendency among historians to view a history of Jewish men as Jewish history but a history of Jewish women as women's history. This book consciously avoids such marginalization of women's lives and history. It documents how the making of the Jewish middle class is incomprehensible without focusing on women and, more broadly, how women are central to a social history of German Jews.

In examining the history of a specific minority of women, I hope to make the writing of German women's history more inclusive. Historians of German women's history, which has recently come into its own as a field of scholarly inquiry in the former Federal Republic of Germany, the United States, and England, have largely neglected Jewish women. Studies in German women's history have, up to now, concentrated on "German" women rather than on women in Germany. They have assumed—rather than inquired into—the homogeneity that German society so rigidly sought to impose on ethnic or religious groups (whether Jews, Poles, or Huguenots, and in certain regions, Catholics). Furthermore, most German scholars have allowed Jewish women to disappear from German history as Jews, either because those scholars feel troubled and uneasy about their country's history with regard to Jews, are simply oblivious to Jewish history before 1933, or have made a political decision to view Jews as Germans (fearing that the alternative—to see them as a distinct group—might be considered racist). It is, perhaps, not surprising that the two books in German women's history which devote the most serious consideration to Jewish women are written by an American and a French woman.[2] This book should help those who study German women's history to incorporate Jewish women into the story.

In addition to showing the place Jewish women had in the history of German women, I have questioned the facile assumption of all too many historians of modern Jewry that a study of male Jews suffices, that women are somehow subsumed in that category.[3] In particular, this assumption has led to a skewed analysis of Jewish "assimilation." By ignoring women, but stressing the political and intellectual accomplishments of men, historians have inadvertently overestimated both the desire of Jews to assimilate and even their capacity to do so. Including women in the story helps us not only to complete the picture, but to alter it as well. Moreover, by analyzing German-Jewish women, I hope to add comparative material to the emerging field of Jewish women's history. While most work in Jewish women's history has focused on the American experience, attention to Western Europe can enrich our knowledge of Jewish women, families, and communities.[4] Further, in exploring women's history, particularly their private relationships and feelings, this study can augment our general understanding of minority relations by clarifying such issues as a minority's desire to retain its ethnic distinctiveness versus its need to integrate. Shifting the focus to women allows us to uncover Jews who were both intent on integrating and insistent on maintaining a dynamic, relatively encapsulated Jewish familial and social life.

Since German-Jewish women considered themselves Germans (as well as Jews), and since the great majority acculturated to German bourgeois standards—even setting a few themselves—this study presents an inquiry into the social history of German bourgeois women between 1871 and 1918. As such, it adds to the growing field of bourgeois women's history in the United States and Europe.[5] It highlights the commonalities shared by bourgeois Jewish women and their Christian counterparts: their educational backgrounds and career options, attitudes toward marriage and family, and patterns of "leisured" behavior. Despite these gender and class similarities, however, ethnic and religious differences clearly separated women. Jewish women had to negotiate their lives within racist boundaries which were often more relentless than the sexist ones.

German historiography, too, may gain from an understanding of Jewish women's history. In the Imperial period, 85 percent of Jews were considered middle-class (25 percent of whom were lower-middle-class).[6] By examining the lives of Jewish women and, through them, the Jewish family, we can look into the private lives of the German *Bürgertum*, or bourgeoisie, a group which has attracted the interest of social historians.[7] While, in comparison to other German middle-class families, Jewish families were more liberal politically (less xenophobic, more tolerant of pluralism, more supportive of one of the liberal parties[8]), many of their social and familial customs, from the role of the *Hausfrau* to the emphasis on *Bildung* (education and cultivation), paralleled those of their Christian counterparts. A case study of Jewish bourgeois life, alluding to its similarities with and differences from that of other Germans, can enrich our understanding of the German bourgeoisie as a whole.

Studying the linkages between Germans and Jews and their perceptions of each other not only reveals their ambivalent relationship, but also exposes some of the internal social dynamics in Imperial Germany. Granted legal and civic equality by 1871, Jews nevertheless continued to face anti-Semitism. Whereas most studies have examined the spread of anti-Semitism within the highest echelons of government and society, this one examines its pervasiveness in informal or small-scale interactions. Jewish women met other German women in many arenas (in the neighborhood, schools, university, and workplace, to name only a few), and on occasion Jewish and non-Jewish women chose to work or relax with each other (for example, in feminist or social welfare organizations, in university women's groups, or at spas); yet social barriers remained. We find genuine cooperation, but also friction; earnest communication, but also rigid barriers, prohibiting even toleration. The material presented here thus undermines two common stereotypes: the first, that no coexistence was possible between Jews and Germans, and its opposite, that Jews were accepted as Germans, that they "were" Germans.

In short, in Germany Jewish women could never simply locate their identity as female. They were constantly aware of—and were reminded of—their Jewishness. Yet there was no universal Jewish experience either, for they belonged to a sex-segregated religion and a sex-segregated society. Furthermore, their lives reflected their middle-class status and aspirations: most were not simply Jews, but bourgeois Jews; not simply women, but bourgeois women. Although at certain times one factor may have been temporarily of overriding importance, in considering the variables of ethnicity, gender, and class, we can evaluate their intersections and interconnections, rather than the primacy of any one of them.

It is the historian's task to contest conventional wisdom, and women's historians embark on this venture with intellectual and political enthusiasm. However, finding women's voices and evidence of their actions takes a great deal of detective work. This effort is often difficult and frustrating because women left so few traces of their lives. Apparently, they were not aware of the importance of their lives or had less time for reflection. For example, women wrote fewer memoirs than men, and the purpose of the memoirs they did write was often to describe the lives of their fathers or husbands. "The autobiographical form of these notes," apologized one woman, "is only an expedient. Not *my* life, but Ernst's personality shall be depicted."[9] Another submitted: "if one has the luck, as I do, to be a link in a chain to which men like my . . . grandfather . . . and father . . . belonged, then one feels right to bring back the memory of such personalities."[10] (Fortunately, neither author remained true to her introduction.) Similarly, women's associations as well left far fewer documents than did equally or less important men's organizations. This was due, in part, to lack of funds, smaller office staffs, and the voluntary, sporadic assistance that women's groups had at their disposal, compared to the wealthier and professionally run male groups. But again, it was also due to the women's lack of appreciation of their own work and historical worth.

Despite the scarcity and arbitrary nature of the sources, what follows is an overview of the materials, scattered and incomplete, that contributed to this study. My sources have included Jewish newspapers and organizational literature and records; *Gemeinde* (Jewish communal) records and school reports; various statistical data for women's employment, marriages, conversions, fertility, and schooling; letters by and to women; diaries by women and men; prescriptive literature (including cookbooks) detailing how women "should" behave; rabbinical essays, conference speeches, and resolutions; oral interviews; novels and short stories written by Jews; and assorted archival and memoir collections, particularly those at the Leo Baeck Institute in New York.

Memoirs have provided my richest sources. They come closest to revealing women as whole persons engaged in private and public life. Moreover, although they are more selective than other sources, memoirs are also more eloquent than most. While I cannot argue that they are absolutely "representative" of German–Jewish middle-class women, I do feel they reflect certain collective social and cultural processes that affected many, if not most, of my subjects. Still, memoirs suffer from certain serious limitations. They often describe an ideal as much as a reality, reporting the way family life was supposed to be while repressing or reinterpreting actual experiences. In these memoirs the division of labor is invariably the same. They do not capture nuances in the role divisions possible even in Imperial Germany. As a result, the father is respected and loved from a distance while the mother emerges as a giant, the central figure, the heart of family life. It is she who cultivates the family, with her husband's approval and sometimes guidance. Further, in the uppermost strata of the bourgeoisie—those with several servants and governesses—children often had limited contact with their mothers. The memoirs of these children may convey a yearning for, rather than the actual experience of, the mother. Memoirs often describe how family feeling was created and ritualized as much as they convey an accurate state of affairs.

Another drawback of memoirs is that the most accessible ones are those that have been saved and donated to libraries by families that have maintained a connection to Judaism. Thus I have come across few, if any, memoirs that describe the complete rejection of a Jewish heritage. The available memoirs often discuss the writer's relationship to Judaism and the Jewish community, outline family rituals, and describe changes in attitudes toward religion which occurred over time. In general, these sources must be read cautiously and, as regards outlook toward religion, one may even have to "read between the lines." For example, memoirs which proudly proclaim total integration and "assimilation" into German society frequently, albeit inadvertently, disclose continuing Jewish connections and allegiances. Thus they often argue one point but provide information that contradicts the assertion. Nevertheless, in general most memoirs reveal an ongoing tension between the desire to acculturate and the need to maintain some sense of Jewish identity—a tension found in many other sources as well.

As a result of the kind of material I have uncovered, this study focuses on urban bourgeois housewives and families. I have found few traces of Jewish working-class women or Eastern European Jewish immigrant women (often overlapping groups), aside from some employment and immigration statistics and sporadic references.[11] Memoirs, a rich source for middle-class women's lives, do not exist for their working-class sisters. Working-class women had neither time nor wherewithal to write memoirs. Moreover, I was unable to find adequate material on Zionist and Orthodox women or their organizations. Zionism originated in 1897, but women played only a tangential role in its early years. In Germany a women's Zionist organization, the Cultural Association of Jewish Women for Palestine (Kulturverband Jüdischer Frauen für Palästina), was founded in 1909, and youth groups a few years earlier.[12] The Orthodox organization Agudat Israel, created in 1912, also had a women's branch, but that, too, proved difficult to trace.[13] Female converts and those who chose interfaith marriages are not represented in this work either. Though a small minority, they suggest the wide range of possible Jewish identities in Germany encompassed between the extremes of Orthodoxy and conversion to Christianity. With a few exceptions (the autobiographies of female professionals and some statistics on divorce), I have found almost no material about independent single women or widows and nothing about lesbians or divorced women. Also, the literature about rural Jews is less extensive than that referring to their upwardly mobile urban relatives. The result is that a differentiated analysis of Jewish women, one reflective of wealth, geography, cohort, and life cycle, is elusive. I hope that my work will encourage others to uncover the lives and life cycles of a greater variety of women, so that together we may weave the strands of Jewish women's experiences into a satisfying whole.

New York M.A.K.
January 1991

ACKNOWLEDGMENTS

In the course of researching and writing this book, I have been extraordinarily lucky to have had the intellectual and moral support of many friends and colleagues. I am deeply grateful for their good-humored encouragement, astute advice, and tactful critiques.

I would like to thank my friends in the German Women's History Study Group of New York—Bonnie Anderson, Renate Bridenthal, Jane Caplan, Atina Grossmann, Amy Hackett, Deborah Hertz, Claudia Koonz, Molly Nolan, Catherine Prelinger, Sibylle Quack, Joan Reutershan, and Hanna Schissler—who have painstakingly critiqued almost every chapter of the book. I am indebted to their intelligence and probing questions as well as their generosity and patience. Our monthly meetings over the last ten years, in which we debated the burning issues in German and women's history, read one another's manuscripts, gave one another professional advice, and exchanged baby clothes have been a delight and inspiration to me.

I am also grateful to the members of the Institute for Research in History's Study Group on Women's History—Jean Christie, Ellen Ervin, Naomi Goodman, Sue Gronewald, Nancy Hennigsen, Nancy Sokoloff, and Sydney Weinberg. They have provided not only a thoughtful reading of the introduction to this volume, but also more than twelve years of animated monthly discussions about women's history, enriching my scholarly and social life.

Friends and colleagues in the fields of women's history, Jewish history, and German history contributed invaluable advice on a range of issues in various chapters. My gratitude goes to Avraham Barkai, John Foster, Ute Frevert, Karin Hausen, Rolf Landwehr, Robert Liberles, Arnold Paucker, and Norma Pratt. Particular thanks go also to Jay Kaplan for his support at the beginning of this project and his continued enthusiasm throughout. I am grateful to my editor at Oxford, Nancy Lane, who remained consistent in her enthusiasm and optimism. Also, as series editor, Jehuda Reinharz provided sound advice and kind encouragement when it was most needed.

Of all the people who devoted their time and effort, three dear friends, Renate Bridenthal, Paula Hyman, and Monika Richarz, deserve special mention. They have read this manuscript more times than either they or I care to remember. I am indebted to them for sharing their expertise in discussions of earlier drafts, for their reassurance and support, which is so important in a long process such as this one, and for their friendship, which has given me so much joy.

I could never have completed my research and writing without substantial aid. Special thanks go to Peter Freimark, director of the Institut für die Geschichte der Deutschen Juden in Hamburg, for encouraging me to embark on this project and for organizing support from the Deutsche Forschungsgemeinschaft. Its generosity supported three years of research and writing.

The Leo Baeck Institute in New York granted me a summer fellowship in the early stages of research and, while I was its associate director between 1983 and 1985, time off for writing. At the time I was working on the book, its director, Fred Grubel, its president, Max Gruenewald, and his successor, Ismar Schorsch, encouraged me with their interest, advice, and enthusiasm. I also appreciate the practical help and advice of its librarians and archivists, past and present. Alan Divack, Evelyn Ehrlich, Frank Mecklenburg, Sybil Milton, Diane Spielman, and the late Ilse Blumenthal-Weiss were always ready to assist in the most friendly and professional manner. Without the meticulously kept archives and library of the Leo Baeck Institute, this project would have been impossible. Archivists in the Federal Republic of Germany, particularly those in Berlin, Frankfurt, and Hamburg, also deserve thanks, as do the kind people at the Central Archives for the History of the Jewish People in Jerusalem.

As a member of the faculty of Queens College of The City University of New York, I have received a Professional Staff Congress–City University of New York Research Grant and a Scholar Incentive Award to facilitate the research and writing of this book. A Queens College Faculty-in-Residence Award relieved me of one course obligation at a crucial point in the writing process. Finally, the National Endowment for the Humanities generously sponsored a Travel to Collections Grant and a College Teachers and Independent Scholars Fellowship to complete my project. I hope this book merits, to some extent, the generous support of those to whom I owe my sincere appreciation.

Last, but certainly not least, I want to thank my family for the love and support they have shown. My husband, Douglas Morris, sustained me with his sense of humor, moral support, friendship, and love. Moreover, his interest in the subject was matched by his editing skills. To my daughter, Ruth Kaplan, I offer my apologies for seeming distracted at times, my thanks for diverting my attention from German history, my gratitude for putting up with a mom who sat at her typewriter, and later at her computer, for what must have seemed an eternity to a child, and my deepest admiration and love for the wonderful person she is. And, finally, to tiny Joshua Kaplan-Morris, who considerately arrived one week after I handed in my manuscript, I look forward to the much-needed diversion he is certain to provide during my future projects—and to many hugs.

CONTENTS

THE MAKING OF THE JEWISH MIDDLE CLASS

Introduction

> Every Friday evening, after she lit the candles, mother blessed us. She laid her hands on our heads and said words in Hebrew. . . . A warm kiss ended this small, solemn ceremony. . . . [Afterward] we had dinner. A beautifully set table, with the Sabbath candles burning. . . . [On Saturdays] our parents always had lots of company. . . . We . . . played, . . . read, and if there were enough of us . . . we read from the classics, dividing up the roles [for] *Don Carlos*, the *Maiden of Orleans*, *Iphigenia* or another.[1] (1880s)

> We kept a kosher home. Every Friday evening we went to the synagogue. . . . Our circle was really all Jewish. We had lots of relatives and we didn't mix much with other people. Family life was very strong. . . . We all had music lessons at home. That was the done thing. . . . I was the fourth [daughter] and . . . learned the cello . . . and the piano. . . . Then in 1914 the war came. We had the biggest . . . flag in the whole street. When Germany had a victory on the battlefield everybody hung out flags . . . and ours was perhaps three storeys high![2]

> Mother . . . came from a religious background, though she rebelled against it. . . . I was absolutely smitten with the royal family. . . .But in the [1918] revolution . . . when I was thirteen, I remember looking at the portraits of the Kaiser and Queen Luise in the drawing room, . . . and saying to Mother, "What are they doing here? They are ridiculous. They ought to go." Mother simply said, "What a shame. They are so nicely *framed*."[3]

The Sabbath and German classics, synagogue and piano lessons, carefully crafted furnishings and German patriotism, Jewish friends and family—these were the separate threads which composed the fabric of middle-class Jewish women's lives in Imperial Germany. Jewish women wove intricate and complicated patterns in designing their environments, choosing from modern bourgeois practice and traditional familial and communal customs. Paradoxically for historians, but perfectly consistently and reasonably for themselves, they were agents of acculturation and tradition, of integration and apartness. On the one hand, many joined the German feminist movement in demanding women's rights, helped develop the field of modern social work, and pioneered women's role in higher education and the professions. They urged their Jewish communities to keep pace with changing attitudes toward women's place in the home and society. They made sure that their families, especially their children, adapted to the manners, speech, clothing, and education of the German bourgeoisie. On the other hand, many demonstrated their feeling of fellowship with other Jews and their Jewish self-consciousness by insisting on Jewish rituals and holidays in the home, sometimes long after their husbands and children found these quaint at best; by maintaining familial and Jewish communal networks; and by organizing Jewish women's societies. Often the same individuals expressed many of these loyalties at the same time. Although painfully aware of their position in an increasingly intolerant society, most Jewish women saw no conflict between affirming their German heritage and retaining their religious and cultural legacy.[4] Jewish women created a varied and dynamic Jewish community while simultaneously adding cultural heterogeneity to German society. Thus they forged a modern Jewish identity.

This exploration of the Jewish experience in the years between 1871 and 1918 looks beyond the intellectual and political history of German Jewry.[5] Instead, I have examined the private, day-to-day basis of Jewish identity: how seemingly contradictory tendencies were actually perceived in everyday life. To do this, I have surveyed the unexamined territory of women's and family history and have underlined the significance of family and community as a locus for understanding Jewish self-awareness and the ambiguities of acculturation. Consequently I have emphasized the importance of gender—the "socially imposed division of the sexes"[6]—as a vital analytic tool in approaching Jewish history. Finally, this study situates the lives of Jewish women in the context of bourgeois class formation in Germany. By this I am referring not only to the relations of both women and men to the economy or to class society, but even more to their interests, values, and relationships with each other.

Germany's industrializing, urbanizing society and the Jewish middle classes' economic successes and aspirations affected traditional expectations regarding family life and women's roles. Jewish women's work within the home and family—from bearing and raising children to doing or directing housework and consumption—changed in ways similar to the work of other German women of their class. By the 1890s tedious and grueling household toil and comanaging or helping out in the business increasingly gave way to the cultural and social aspects of housewifery and marriage. Women's work changed—from helpmate and housewife to cultural connoisseur and mother par excellence. However, even for the relatively privileged, women's work was still "never done." Their new responsibilities required time and attention. As in the past, women's economic contribution as housewives remained a significant determinant of their husband's and the family's social status. In addition, women often clung to old roles and values in an effort to steady the family against the instabilities of the era and to sustain their role in it.

While husbands improved their occupational status and increased their incomes, often entering the professions, it was in the household and family—where people tried to "live decently"[7]—that the most marked *embourgeoisement* took place. The bourgeoisie set itself apart from other classes by devising and promulgating a culture of domesticity, one which was dominated by women and set off from the marketplace, the habitat of men. The household is therefore a key location for probing class formation and gender relations. It is crucial to both the private and public identities formed by the bourgeoisie. The household was both a private and a public phenomenon, touched by and affecting the public sphere. In fact, it epitomized the interactions between the private and public spheres; it was shaped by the husband's occupation and need to keep up appearances, and it was instrumental in maintaining present and molding future public participants.[8] Integrating household and child rearing into recent concepts of bourgeois class formation and Jewish acculturation will give us a more complex and also a more tangible image of the way women and men defined their own membership in the Imperial bourgeoisie.

Background

Because this study encompasses the converging spheres of German, women's, and Jewish history, this introduction is intended to furnish an overview to those with limited background in one or more of these fields. The first part provides an outline of German-Jewish history. It describes the demographic and social characteristics of German Jews and their attempt to go beyond emancipation and the achievement of civic and political equality toward social acceptance. The second part surveys developments in the lives of nineteenth-century German bourgeois women. It depicts changes in women's roles and expectations, the new opportunities slowly opening to them, and the persistence of barriers to their progress.

German Jews: Population, Acculturation, and Anti-Semitism

When the final restrictions against the full political emancipation of Jews were removed at the beginning of the Imperial era,[9] Jews and their liberal supporters generally believed that Jews had acquired certain of the social, cultural, and economic attributes of their neighbors and that their integration into bourgeois society was advancing. It was also clear, however, that this integration had not succeeded completely, that Jews were still a distinct subgroup and somehow more than a religion.[10]

The demographic characteristics of German Jews help to locate the contours of their lives. In 1871, 512,000 Jews made up 1.25% of the German population. By 1910, their numbers had grown to 615,000, but their proportion had dropped to 0.95%. In comparison to the rest of the German population, which expanded by 58%, the Jewish portion of the population grew by only about 20%.[11] The sex ratio among Jews tended toward what Germans termed an "oversupply of women" (*Frauenüberschuss*). Less severe than the "oversupply" in the general population, this imbalance was particularly acute in smaller towns, limiting marriage opportunities and raising the financial stakes of marriage. Only among Eastern European Jewish immigrants were there more men than women, leading to "intermarriages" between German and Eastern European Jews.[12] In general, statistics indicate that Jews had a lower frequency of marriage than non-Jews, and when they did marry, they did so at a later age.[13] Thus middle-class Jewish women faced an uncertain marriage market, making jobs or careers a serious alternative for some.

Well before other Germans, Jews began to limit their fertility to about two children. By the first decade of the twentieth century, the Jewish birth rate in Prussia was only half that of the general population.[14] Since Jews had fewer children and a lower mortality rate than other Germans, the Jewish population profile was an aging one: Jews were older than other Germans.[15] This fact had repercussions in such diverse areas as widowhood, crime rates, and job choices. For Jewish women, fewer pregnancies and offspring freed them to pursue other interests and to take on the increasing duties of "class representation" such as dinner parties, social calls, and stylish home decoration. Moreover, as we shall see in a later chapter, with fewer children to support, Jewish families could more easily provide advanced education for their daughters.

Interfaith marriage and conversion threatened the Jewish population with losses, although a gender analysis reveals that fewer women than men left the fold. After 1880 Jewish conversions climbed; between 1880 and 1919 about 23,000 Jews converted.[16] Interfaith marriages also mounted. Between 1911 and 1915, 22 percent of Jewish men and 13 percent of Jewish women entered a marriage with a non-Jew.[17] Those who left or married out may have seen themselves as very distant from Judaism, but were often still considered to be Jews by their neighbors. For the most part there was no "escaping" their Jewish heritage in Imperial Germany. They might hope that their children would become entirely "acceptable" to Christian society, but they themselves often remained on the fringes of two worlds.

The influx of Eastern European Jewish immigrants from the Austro-Hungarian and Russian Empires increased the numbers of Jews in Germany, lowered their average age, raised their fertility rate, and created a significant proletarian minority. Beginning in 1881, as a result of economic boycotts, pogroms, and general poverty in Eastern Europe, Eastern Jews sought refuge in Western lands. By 1910 nearly 70,000 Eastern Jews had settled in German cities, accounting for slightly under 13 percent of the Jewish population. In terms of employment, Eastern Jewish women probably provided a greater proportion of the Jewish female work force than their proportion of the Jewish population.

German Jews had distinctive social and economic characteristics. At the beginning of the Imperial era, most of them could be described as securely bourgeois.[18] Jewish social mobility began to progress significantly long before Germany's industrial "takeoff."[19] This was a mixed blessing. It raised their standard of living but also contributed to an image, exploited by anti-Semites, of Jews as the epitome of bourgeois society and bourgeois–capitalist competition. Their work profile added grist to the mill of those who conflated Jews with capitalist exploitation. Both Jewish women and men tended to concentrate in commercial fields, frequently in higher status positions, and disproportionately in the professions.[20]

Some of the differences between the demographic characteristics of Jews and those of other Germans can be explained by class status; other differences relate to Jewish concentration in urban areas. Historically forced to cede agriculture and the crafts to Christians, Jews were hardly interested in becoming peasants and artisans when these declining sectors of the economy finally opened to them. With fewer ties to the land, Jews fled the countryside for career and educational opportunities several decades before other Germans.[21] In 1871 about 20% of all Jews lived in cities with populations of over 100,000. This figure leaped to 58.3% by 1910. The corresponding statistics for the general population were 4.8% in urban areas in 1871 and 21.3% in 1910. Berlin, in particular, had attracted over a quarter of all Jews by

1910. Urbanization was linked with economic and social ascent. It also had important positive repercussions for Jewish women. Jews tended to take on the characteristics of urban populations, engaging in urban enterprises, valuing the cultural offerings found in cities, and benefiting from urban educational institutions to a greater extent than the overall population. Urbanization and Jewish internal migration not only underscored differences between Jews and other Germans, but also profoundly influenced Jewish life. In fact, according to Avraham Barkai, geographic mobility "was the most outstanding feature of German-Jewish history in the nineteenth and early twentieth centuries."[22] Since whole families moved, it fell to Jewish women to facilitate the physical and social accommodation to new urban surroundings.[23]

Legal emancipation, financial success, and the benefits of urban life were only halfway measures. Jews needed and desired admittance to bourgeois society—their ticket, they believed, to acceptance as "Germans." To become part of a German *Volk*, a separate people and/or nation identifying with ancient Germans, a Germanic soul, and a national consciousness verging on a racial community, was impossible. A bourgeois life-style, however, was tangible and achievable. Jews not only internalized the economic and cultural standards of the bourgeoisie but also became ardent admirers and promoters of many of its values.[24] However, Jews did not merely imitate the Imperial bourgeoisie. Their political posture remained more liberal and some of their habits and styles probably preceded those of their Christian counterparts, particularly in small towns.

In the early nineteenth century the German middle class consisted of civil servants (a broad category encompassing high public officials and university teachers as well as state bureaucrats) and other educated groups. Although Jews in the early part of the century were mainly petty tradesmen, barely able to make a living, by 1848 many had achieved middle-class incomes. They were barred, however, from state posts such as the civil service and entrance into the fields of law and medicine.[25] Jewish prosperity had resulted largely from commercial successes. Their familiarity with trade and credit, two vocations permitted them in the German states, expedited their success in the new areas of retailing, wholesaling, import, and export. Moreover, "free from the deadly grip of genteel values, [Jews were] able and willing to pick up the opportunities opened by industrial, financial and technological revolutions."[26] In fact—as indicated, for example, by the representation of Jews in commerce and their rate of urbanization—the Jewish capitalist bourgeoisie actually "arrived" shortly before its German counterpart. Thus commercially successful, upwardly mobile Jews were there, waiting to be absorbed into a newly forming German capitalist bourgeoisie (and consequently bore the brunt of hostility from those who held capitalism and money-making in contempt). On the one hand, they tried to adapt to the earlier bourgeois life-style of the (noncapitalist) educated upper middle class: solid respectability, which covered insecurities over with a decent income and the hope of an even brighter future for the children. On the other hand, by the very nature of their commercial, rather than civil-service or professional, identities, Jews also realized a more consumer-oriented, culturally active, wealthier variant of bourgeois existence. Even when academic and professional careers opened to Jews during the Imperial era, university-educated Jewish males often married the daughters of Jewish businessmen and therefore had the means to maintain a substantial existence.

Peter Gay has noted that Germans carefully distinguished between *Bürgertum*, which designated the citizen of a state or the member of a class, and "the fashionable import 'bourgeoisie.'"[27] Notwithstanding their long history on German soil, Jews were seen by many as the personification of the "fashionable import." This included, in particular, the nouveau riche aspects of their behavior and tended to overlook their genuine appreciation of the cultural benefits of wealth and their desire to be accepted by others of their class. Finally, as the German capitalist bourgeoisie grew, late nineteenth-century styles emerged, combining elements of cultivation (*Bildung*) with new aspirations to wealth and display (*Besitz*). Arriving between the earlier and later bourgeoisie, Jews appropriated some traits and introduced others. They found themselves in the paradoxical position of epitomizing the avant-garde while trying to catch up to it.

The changes in structure of the German bourgeoisie made culture a defining character of class. Thus, during the struggle for Jewish legal emancipation, nineteenth-century bourgeois liberals urged Jews to develop intellectually as a way of integrating into class and nation, and Jews adapted eagerly.[28] "Jews had been emancipated simultaneously into the age of *Bildung* and middle class respectability."[29] For newly emancipated German Jews, the educated bourgeoisie (*Bildungsbürger*) became the ideal. The German word *Bildung* combined the concepts embodied in the English word "education" with a belief in the primacy of culture and the potential of humanity. In merging education with character formation, moral growth, and self-improvement, it described a cultured, well-bred personality, an autonomous, harmonious person of refined manners, aesthetic appreciation, politeness, and gentility.[30] *Bildung* appealed to Jews because it could transcend differences of religion or nationality through the development of the individual personality. Moreover, *Bildung* denoted learning through interpretive interaction with venerated texts, and extolled the evaluative insight that came from theoretical, as opposed to practical, knowledge.[31] (Male) Jews could acquire the attributes of *Bildung* by adopting the German intellectual and scholarly traditions of the nineteenth century—that is, by attending schools and universities, by showing appreciation of intellectual and cultural pursuits, and by cultivating their own personalities. Jews clung to this interpretation of *Bildung* long after it had become nationalized and narrowed. They believed their own display of *Bildung* would enhance their roles as citizens and allow them to associate with their equally respectable middle-class neighbors.

Although it enticed them, this version of *Bildung* left women out. Jews then, and historians ever since, placed great emphasis on the educational and intellectual elements of *Bildung* rather than on its more subtle cultural and familial side, which will be stressed here. In his recent elegant study of the ideology of Jewish emancipation, David Sorkin describes *Bildung* as the "integral self-development by which the whole *man* would develop his inherent form by transforming all of his faculties, mind and body, into a harmonious unit."[32] [Emphasis added.] "Man achieved a unity of essence and existence through a self-initiated process for which he was his own model."[33] Neither Sorkin's work nor George Mosse's original and profound contribution to our understanding of Jewish identity include, because nineteenth-century liberals did not consider, women in a concept of the individual. Mosse writes:

> Wilhelm von Humboldt provided the model for German citizenship for newly emancipated Jews: through fostering the growth of reason and aesthetic taste, each *man* would cultivate his own personality until he became an autonomous, harmonious individual. This was a process of education and character building in which everyone could join regardless of religion or background; only the individual mattered.[34] [Emphasis added.]

Only the male individual. Much as nineteenth-century liberals overlooked women, with the extraordinary exceptions of a John Stuart Mill or a Theodor von Hippel, so too did German governments and educators. They ignored women's intellectual needs, excluding them from the universities (with some exceptions) until 1908. Ute Frevert has noted: "It was never intended that female persons would take part in either a general or specialized *Bildung*. All . . . reform energies and theoretical insights stopped short before the barriers of gender."[35]

"Everyone" could not join the process of education and character building, since women were barred from serious study, and character was based on a male model. Serious self-cultivation, too, was a perilous path, offensive to a society that expected a smattering of intelligence and polish—but no more—from its women. Moreover, the respect accorded the theoretical features of *Bildung* engendered misgivings about practical knowledge and intervention in the physical or social world,[36] precisely those areas in which women exhibited competence. Nevertheless, as was the case with so many liberal concepts, *Bildung* too expanded beyond its original limitations. *Bildung* appealed to the universal, encouraging the self-cultivation of the individual—a clear invitation to women. In addition, *Bildung* implied far more than an appropriate intellectual stance or an appreciation of high culture. It also meant manners and breeding and thus included women in a subtle but powerful way: they were to raise a family of *Bildung*.

The middle classes (both women and men) had legitimized themselves, compared to those above and below them, through their *Bildung* and its display in the family. In fact, the very notion of a "bourgeois family" implied the combination of *Bildung* and family. Typical of the European and American bourgeoisie—although perhaps exaggerated in its German rendition—*Bildung* signified authentic respectability.[37] It was a form of intellectual and social capital, a means of upward mobility. Symbolically and practically, *Bildung* as family and breeding was as important as an advanced education to bourgeois Germans of all faiths. It was of particular importance to most German Jews, male and female, who could not achieve the academic and professional heights open to a small (though growing) number of Jewish men. Their social and cultural education, however, could proceed apace within an exemplary and refined family. Culture did not begin and end with the university or the German classics. It included the creation of a model home life, a model family.[38] Women were central to this family incarnation of *Bildung*.

Both consciously and unconsciously, Jewish women set the tone and style of this way of life, affirming—and sometimes contesting—its values, roles, and relationships. They contributed to the highly prized tranquility and steadiness of the bourgeois family, to its *Gemütlichkeit*, manners, and pretensions. They created cultivated and respectable families, displaying their similarity with others of their class. Thus Jewish women—like their non-Jewish counterparts—were crucial to bourgeois class formation. It was inconceivable without them. Simultaneously—but in contrast to their non-Jewish counterparts—Jewish women helped the family to acculturate to German norms. To examine women's role, then, is to emphasize the molding and sculpting of the family as essential both to upward social mobility and also to acculturation, since a bourgeois profile was synonymous with the only "German" identity available to Jews.

Bildung served not only as the entrée of Jews into cultured German society. Paradoxically, for many Jews it also became "synonymous with their Jewishness."[39] It merged Jewish traditions with German forms. For example, *Bildung* blended the Jewish tradition of learning with the secularization of that tradition into an appreciation of German language,[40] literature, and etiquette. George Mosse has underlined the importance of *Bildung* to German Jews as a symbol of both their Germanness *and* their Jewishness.[41] "With the passage of time, *Bildung* [was] detached from the individual . . . and was transformed into a kind of religion—the worship of the true, the good, and the beautiful."[42]

The Jewish family—albeit a cultivated, middle-class one—was also an essential part of being Jewish. It was often an extension of religious life and, as we shall see, increasingly a substitute for it. Among Jews, images of an intimate family life preceded the making of the German bourgeoisie but also complemented it. The portrait of a comfortable family life became not only a class emblem and vehicle toward integration, but an important element of Jewish ethnic identity. Like the German middle class, Jews developed their dual identities as Jews and Germans around domestic values and private family life. A family of *Bildung* exemplified both "Germanness" and "Jewishness" to its members.

Thus adapting to German bourgeois standards and setting some themselves, Jews "acculturated" to German society. By the term "acculturation," I mean the acceptance of the external, objective behavior and standards of the dominant culture. They adopted styles of dress and manners of speech, they moved out of predominantly Jewish neighborhoods into newer ones (often forming new enclaves), they accommodated to contemporary middle-class attitudes toward work and achievement, and they developed a deep loyalty to the fatherland. They saw no contradiction between their *Deutschtum* (Germanness) and their *Judentum* (Jewishness).

Still, their sentiments and perceptions often separated them from other Germans.[43] Their celebration of holidays and life-cycle events, their antipathy toward conversion and intermarriage, and their social contacts further set them apart. Although Christians often excluded them, Jews too had "an emotional affinity with each other, which drew them together and tended to exclude Gentiles."[44] Moreover, a gender analysis of religious observance in the home (chapter 2) calls attention to the continuation of Judaism in the private sphere long after public worship had waned. When Abraham Geiger, the founder of the Reform movement, lamented that "deadly silence reigns"[45] in the Jewish community, he directed his gaze toward the synagogue, not the living room.

Thus German Jews acculturated to German society, but they did not "assimilate," nor did most ever intend to do so. The term "assimilation" implies that the vast majority of Jews sought to fuse with other Germans in the desire to give up their religious or cultural distinctiveness. It suggests a kind of submission, an exchange of "Jewishness" for "Germanness,"[46] and perpetuates contemporary negative stereotypes that German Jews felt no Jewish solidarity. Moreover, historical debates about assimilation—which was successful according to some, disastrous according to others—overstate the magnitude and understate the contradictions of assimilation.[47] Historians of assimilation point to the fervor with which Jews cultivated the German classics and their deep identification with the German state. They also highlight the participation of (male) Jews in public life and their relatively elevated status in economic and cultural spheres.

This use of the term "assimilation" provides an inaccurate picture of German Jews. It focuses exclusively on public conduct and conscious identity ("we were so German"), taking both at face value. It ignores unconscious identity[48] and important emotional and behavioral factors, particularly in the private sphere. It tends to overlook what is meant by "family" and "friendship." Moreover, it slights what anthropologists call "culture"—"the totality of socially transmitted behavior patterns, arts, beliefs, institutions, and all other products of work and thought characteristic of a community."[49]

"Assimilation" becomes especially problematic when we study women whose lives focused on the cultural domain and whose ties to customs and community remained strong. In telling only men's story, historians have neglected women's powerful and sustained influence on German-Jewish identity. As a result, they have frequently overestimated the extent to which Jews—*women* and men—"assimilated" at all. To put the question of Jewish identity into perspective, one might rephrase the words of Judah Leib Gordon, a proponent of the Jewish Enlightenment in Eastern Europe: Jews were men and women on the street and Jews at home. They displayed their Germanness while they privatized their Jewishness. Women formed the core of this process, striving for integration on the one hand and the preservation of their cultural or religious identities on the other.

In evaluating women's—and men's—sense of Jewish identity, the theoretical insights and oral interviews of Marion Berghahn with German Jews in Britain are particularly enlightening. Using tools from social anthropology and history, she emphasizes mental structures, feelings, and perceptions, rather than certain practices or institutions, when characterizing ethnic differentiation. In other words, sentiments count as much as—perhaps more than—actions. This may be particularly true for Jewish women, barred from participation in Jewish learning and synagogue ritual. Berghahn also suggests that German Jews redefined Jewish identity, transforming what it meant to be Jewish rather than disavowing former loyalties, sentiments, and perceptions: "Jewish and German elements were integrated in such a way that a form of German-Jewish ethnicity emerged which was not identical with either culture."[50] This new culture "possessed a character entirely of its own" which was not always immediately apparent to participants or observers.[51] German-Jewish society was not a way station en route to homogenization. While undergoing evident changes, it was still a "form of social life capable of renewing itself."[52]

Thus Berghahn uncovers the persistence of ethnicity in modern societies. My study of Jewish women in Imperial Germany unearths the roots of this persistence and highlights its dynamics: the permeability as well as impenetrability of the boundaries between German-Jewish culture and German society. Although we may stress the contradictions and tensions of their quest more than Uriel Tal did, Berghahn's work as well as my own reaffirm his conclusion that Jews strove for integration *and identity*. The former included efforts to achieve political and social equality. The latter was the desire to exist as individuals, remaining faithful to themselves and their heritage.[53]

"Ethnicity" is, of course, a contemporary word with which Jews in Imperial Germany would have been unfamiliar. Yet the study of women shows its usefulness to modern scholars. For while Jewish women shared behavioral similarities and national pride with other German women of their class, they also shared a sense of community and an emotional attachment with other Jews, even those not of their class.[54] The overt cultural traits of German Jews became increasingly bourgeois. For example, middle-class Jewish women took on the attributes of the leisured bourgeoise and often forced an onerous degree of decorum on their children. Indeed, Eastern European Jews often described their German coreligionists as "too German." However, the personal, affective relationship among Jews—even of different classes—remained. Emotional needs and shared values combined with structural and institutional forces to maintain Jewish life.[55]

Institutions such as the social welfare organizations and programs associated with the *Gemeinde* (Jewish community) reinforced affective bonds. The *Gemeinde* was a legal entity, corresponding to similar legal arrangements for Catholics and Protestants in a Protestant-dominated German Empire. Created and empowered by the states, the *Gemeinde* was a compulsory community which embraced all Jews within certain territorial limits, levied taxes on members, and organized Jewish communal and ritual affairs.[56] Each *Gemeinde* had a life of its own and an important history of its own. Jewish communal autonomy harked back to the eleventh and twelfth centuries, with the emergence of feudalism, although the origins of that communal form can be traced to the Second Temple period. By the Imperial era, the *Gemeinde* had been stripped of most of its earlier civic autonomy by the state. Its transformation, however, may have intensified its importance in Jewish cultural and social life. Led by elected male officials, the *Gemeinde* ran various communal institutions, including social associations, libraries, newspapers, charities, and health arrangements. Women played vital roles in these endeavors, despite their relegation to insignificance in religious and political matters. Women contributed continuity and coherence to the national and local cultural, educational, and social welfare aspects of Jewish communal life. Further, they organized sociability for themselves and their coreligionists. Ultimately, the communal networks and sense of affinity fostered and expanded by women gave Jews a sense of identity which resisted dissolution, long after strict religious observance had waned.

Judaism, too, adjusted to nineteenth-century norms. In Germany its "response to modernity"[57]—in the form of Reform, Conservative, and neo-Orthodox movements and the scholarly study of the Jewish religion and people (*Wissenschaft des Judentums*)—embraced contradictory tendencies and attempted to maintain the loyalties of its flock. The predominance of Reform by 1900 had significance for women both practically, since only about 15 percent of Jews could still be called Orthodox by the turn of the century, and also theologically, because Reform leaders raised issues and introduced practical innovations regarding women's role in the religion.

Jewish social mobility and acculturation took place in a nation in which the "Jewish question"—whether or how Jews were to be integrated into polity and society—had never been answered. Moreover, it occurred in the context of a major resurgence of anti-Semitism which raised the stakes of the "Jewish question," permitting it neither to disappear nor to be resolved. Thus anti-Semitism is crucial to an understanding of Jewish life in Germany. In addition, the history of German Jewry and of anti-Semitism is fundamental to an understanding of the successes and weaknesses of the German Empire. Complex and fraught, the "Jewish question" was "part of, and a clue to, the larger question: the German Question."[58]

In embarking on a discussion of anti-Semitism and its effect in Imperial Germany, it is necessary to heed Richard Evans's admonition not to read German history "from Hitler to Bismarck."[59] It is important to trace receptivity as well as hostility to Jews, the striking successes of Jewish integration as well as the omens of disaster. Imperial Germany, seen through the eyes of its Jewish contemporaries, rather than with the genocide of the twentieth century in mind, provides an intriguing example of Jewish successes, failures, hopes, and fears.

Histories of anti-Semitism and anti-Semitic parties are readily available.[60] Consequently, here we focus on the mentality and interactions of ordinary people, on the social history of their experience.[61] Specifically, we will encounter some of the attitudes and behaviors—friendly and exclusionary—of Jews and other Germans as perceived by Jewish memoirists. We will note the extent to which anti-Semitism touched the lives of Jews and raised their anxieties. We should be aware, however, that Jewish observers frequently used the terms "Germans," "Gentiles," or "Christians" interchangeably. Yet "Germans," like "Jews," were diverse. Regionalism and local consciousness played significant roles for both. Religious upbringing, too, determined loyalties and affiliations. Substantial Catholic minorities, persecuted by the state in the *Kulturkampf* of the 1870s, often differed from the Protestant majority in their attitudes toward Jews. In this study the majority of memoir material is from Protestant areas where most Jews lived.[62] Scattered references to rural Jews in Bavaria and Baden refer to predominantly Catholic states. Sometimes, where Protestants and Catholics lived in close proximity, Jews actually benefited from intra-Christian rivalries. One Jewish woman recalled a sunny childhood in southern Germany where the antagonism between Protestants and Catholics resulted in members of both groups trying to win her friendship![63]

German Jews assumed a certain minimum of anti-Semitism. They focused on its eruptions. Jewish newspapers reported on anti-Semitic incidents and political movements. Jews chose jobs and careers in hopes of minimizing anti-Semitic obstacles. Families routinely avoided anti-Semitic schools, neighborhoods, and vacation resorts. Moreover, people who wrote memoirs and diaries—including those who delighted in their non-Jewish friendships—recalled anxieties about anti-Semitism as well as its reality, much of which they *took for granted and overcame*.[64] Still, publicly, most Jews rejected all talk of a "Jewish question" as a survival of primitive politics. Dubbing themselves "German citizens of the Jewish faith" (*deutsche Staatsbürger jüdischen Glaubens*), they "hovered uneasily between . . . 'we are Germans like everyone else' and a frank recognition that there could and should not be only one kind of German."[65]

On a practical level they were citizens (Jewish males voted before any women did), but equal opportunity in the civil service, officers' corps, judiciary, and professoriate, to name a few, remained remote. The "failure of the German state to arrive at a satisfactory relationship between nationality and citizenship," and the "contradiction between the secular Empire and [its] Christian member states," led to the perpetuation of barriers to social and political integration.[66] The era of the first Great Depression (1873–96) further threatened the completeness of Jewish emancipation. Economic crises helped create a climate in which anti-Jewish prejudices found new expression in racism and anticosmopolitanism. Moreover the Dreyfus Affair, raging in France at the turn of the century, cast its shadow over Germany as well. Jack Wertheimer's meticulous analysis of the debates about and expulsions of Eastern European Jews from the Empire has provided a rich backdrop to what we know about the increase in anti-Semitic agitation in the Imperial era.[67] The 1880s witnessed the circulation of anti-Semitic petitions,[68] the mass expulsion of ten thousand Eastern European immigrants from Prussia, and the first "international" congress of anti-Semites held in Dresden (1882). In 1892 the Conservative Party officially adopted an anti-Semitic plank in its Tivoli Program. Every year from 1893 to 1902 anti-Semites in the Reichstag introduced restrictionist legislation against all Jews. Although these proposals did not pass, they caused consternation in the Jewish community. Anti-Semitic movements, like Court Preacher Stoecker's Christian Social Movement (1878), and parties like the Anti-Semitic People's Party[69] (1890), achieved sufficient popularity to alarm Jews. Among intellectuals, too, the anti-Semitic movement gained advocates. Between 1904 and 1906 more mass expulsions of Eastern European immigrants occurred, while agitation against Russian Jewish students in Germany continued unabated. By 1912 the right-wing parties shared anti-Semitism as a common denominator, exploiting it as a political tactic. At the outset of World War I, Germany expelled thousands of Russian Jews or interned them as enemy aliens, although many had lived in Germany most of their lives.

German Jews empathized with the plight of their coreligionists from the East, even if they sometimes shared a German distaste for Eastern European customs or manners.[70] Moreover, they realized that the broad attacks on Eastern European immigrants included them, too. Anti-Semites did not draw fine distinctions among Jews. When the influential historian Heinrich von Treitschke called Jews "our national misfortune," he met with approval and, like Stoecker, made anti-Semitism respectable. Other anti-Semites accused German Jewry of dishonesty, cupidity, and foreignness and linked them with the "trouser-peddlars" from the East. "By repeatedly harping on the identity of character between native and foreign Jews, anti-

Semitic propagandists strove to use Eastern Jews as pawns in their far larger struggle against German Jewry."[71]

Jews fought anti-Semitism politically and organized in self-defense.[72] But their institutional response was only a part of their overall approach. Individuals and families also reacted to the constant pressure of a hostile environment. Many Jews tried to placate anti-Jewish sentiment by modifying their religion and their own behavior. Mothers were crucial to the latter process, shaping their children to German bourgeois customs and ways. *Embourgeoisement*, then, was not only a positive choice based on economic and political improvements, but a defensive strategy as well. Nevertheless, Jews found it a great deal easier to memorize the German classics than to reduce anti-Semitism or integrate into Christian social circles. A study of Jewish women underlines the difficulties of a social symbiosis with other Germans. It highlights the centripetal forces which supported Jewish identity. With few exceptions, Jewish women had less opportunity than men to leave the home, family, and immediate community, to meet and merge with the majority. Conversely, they had more occasion to cultivate family, friendship, and communal ties, the few arenas in which Jewishness could still be expressed without interference. Socially prescribed roles thus reinforced their allegiances.

Bourgeois Women in Germany

Jewish women acted within the boundaries established not only by their class and religious/ethnic group, as shown above, but also—and in some ways even more—by their gender. Analyzing social history in terms of gender can help us understand more clearly not only a set of roles but also an entire system of meanings that differentiates between masculine and feminine. Gender analyses suggest that the differences between the sexes, their relationships with each other, and male and female identities are culturally and hierarchically constructed. Gender analyses raise questions about how these socially determined hierarchies came into being, changed over time, and varied according to class, race, ethnicity, and locale. A society's gender definitions change along with its structural transformations, but often those definitions also reinforce cultural patterns of male dominance long after they have become anachronistic. A gender analysis of the Jewish experience in Germany highlights the varieties of that experience and sharpens our understanding of a past that has been interpreted without any reference to women at all.

Historians sensitive to gender issues have found that women frequently experienced historical changes differently from men. Historical "turning points" were not necessarily the same for women as for men,[73] because popular historical periodization is derived from political history, an arena from which women have been excluded. This is not to say that political decisions did not impinge on women. Some political dates were especially important for women, such as the new German Civil Code of 1900, which changed the legal status of women; the vast educational reforms of 1908; and the abolition, in 1908, of laws banning women's political participation. Time frames of even more relevance to women's lives are tied to changes in the mode of production, in health care, in household and office technology, in the availability of birth control, and in attitudes toward sexuality and childbearing. For Jewish women in particular, the precipitous decline in Jewish fertility (starting in the 1880s) and improvements in infant health (beginning around 1900) must have influenced the quality of both male and female lives, but affected women more immediately. Indeed, even when men and women simultaneously weathered the same process, such as urbanization, new experiences did not always bring contemporaneous changes for both sexes. Jewish wives, for example, moved with their husbands both geographically socially, but generally appeared more "traditional" than men to themselves, to the men around them, and to historians today. "Traditional" is not a term of endorsement or censure; it describes a time lag resulting from gender limitations. Women approached changes from their home base and often from a disadvantageous position in comparison to the men in their group. Yet the barriers to women's equality often shielded them, as well, from the onslaught of modernity.

With these concepts in mind, we can begin to place women in the context of Imperial Germany. Industrialization had come late to Germany, but once under way, it unfolded at an exceptionally quick pace. Middle-class men reacted to the stresses of this new and maddening industrialized world in part by expecting wives to provide islands of tranquillity. While this also occurred in other European countries and in the United States, Germany's extremely rapid industrialization, unlike that of these other nations, caused the stages of social development to accelerate. The contradictions between bourgeois serenity on the one hand, and the needs and aspirations of middle-class women on the other, intensified. The image of the family as a haven became an integral component of bourgeois class consciousness, even if actually achieved only by some.[74] The family was the place where men were to be loved, consoled, and refreshed (usually by wives whom they had married for financial and status reasons). It was also the place where children were to be nurtured, loved, educated, and cultivated (usually in the hope of presenting a public facade which reflected favorably on the father's business fortunes and the family's status). More than ever before, women were defined through the family. A value system which described women as domestic, weak, modest, dependent, self-denying, emotional, religious, and virtuous gained currency. Increasingly, woman's "natural" profession was "the preservation and cultivation of traditional morality, the defense of the family, and the furtherance of a spirit of self-discipline, moderation, and self-sacrifice."[75] At the same time, men under pressure to succeed in the outside world viewed these traits as encumbrances.[76]

Despite an ideology which revered domesticity, the family became the arena in which women's new opportunities for freedom confronted impediments that restrained them. The social landscape of the bourgeois woman centered on the cultivated and orderly home, a domestic life modeled on the notion of *Bildung*. Yet fewer children, greater wealth, and women's new role as consumers rather than producers might have meant more freedom and less work for married women and their daughters. However, women increasingly encountered new demands for "representation," or showing off the bourgeois family, binding them ever more closely to the home. They became the new cultural administrators, devoting considerable time to mediating class values and practice.[77] Still, as we shall see, even though the cult of domesticity emphatically relegated women to home and family, women used domestic ideology to exert considerable influence on their community from their private stations.

Perched rather precariously on a pedestal, married women remained respected, protected, and powerless. Although under the new German Civil Code married women received full legal status, the right to contract for jobs without permission of the husband, and the right to keep the money that they had earned, the Code maintained men's privileged position in the family. Men had the right to make all decisions affecting the family. They could determine educational matters, were the children's legal guardians, could dispose of any wealth that their wives brought into the marriage, and could force their wives to stop working outside the home, if they felt such work interfered with their wives' primary duties to the household.[78]

Despite an emphasis on women's place in the home during the Imperial era, the entry of single women of the urban middle classes into the world of work became more and more noticeable. The "woman question" confronted polite society. In 1898 the *Brockhaus* encyclopedia's presentation of this "question" contended that middle-class women had to work because men seemed increasingly averse to marriage or, at least, were marrying at a later age.[79] Young women often had to wait as long as ten years after finishing their schooling before marrying. Also, as a result of the so-called "oversupply of women," some would not secure a husband at all. Moreover, industrialization and urbanization meant smaller living quarters that no longer required the housework of countless grown daughters or maiden aunts, nor provided the space to accommodate them. The "answer" to the "question," then, appeared to indicate that more and more young women would have to work.

Regardless of these new demographic and economic reasons for women to work outside the home, social prejudice hampered middle-class women who sought employment. Some sort of "appropriate" women's occupations became essential. Organizations such as the Lette Association developed courses for middle-class women in nursing, midwifery, engraving, pattern making, drawing, telegraph operations, bookkeeping, stenography, sales, and library skills. In addition, despite extraordinary difficulty (see chapter 6), middle-class women succeeded in entering the teaching profession, particularly at the lower levels.

The Imperial era also saw the evolution of women's associations and an organized women's movement. A multitude of women's groups—including trade associations and societies dedicated to women's welfare issues, legal protection, career advice, athletics, clothing reform, and the fight against state regulation of prostitution—flourished at the local and national levels.[80] In 1894 the German women's movement, known as the Federation of German Women's Associations (Bund Deutscher Frauenvereine), formed a loose federation of many of these existing associations as well as others dedicated to improving women's education and employment options. Flanked on the left by a Social Democratic women's movement and on the right by a Patriotic Women's Association, the Federation became the strongest force in middle-class German feminism. Gearing its main efforts toward improving work and educational opportunities for women, it turned toward the suffrage issue only after 1902. This was, in part, a necessary strategy in response to laws which denied women the right to join political parties or attend public meetings at which participants debated political concerns. In most parts of the Empire, women could be barred from discussions and activities which the authorities construed as "political." Until 1908, when a unified Imperial Law of Association finally permitted women's participation in politics, German women's political activities were possible only in certain cities or states.[81]

The Federation of German Women's Associations indulged in a rhetoric of domesticity, glorifying the innate difference between man and woman, praising marriage and motherhood, and characterizing sexuality exclusively as a means for reproduction. This rhetoric perpetuated the traditional role of women at the same time that it opened new room for women in public life. By insisting on women's "natural vocation" as wives and mothers, movement leaders argued that women's feminine nature would influence male politics and smooth the rough edges of economic and social policies. Just as motherhood humanized the family, so too should motherhood in its larger social dimension temper a male-dominated industrial system.

Jewish women participated in both the leadership and the rank and file of the German women's movement as well as founding the League of Jewish Women (Jüdischer Frauenbund), a popular and articulate advocate of their own. Established in 1904, the League joined the Federation of German Women's Associations in 1907. By 1913 the League had grown to 32,000 members who belonged to approximately 160 affiliated societies.[82] While maintaining its separate institutions and goals, the League supported the demands of the Federation, working closely with its locals during World War I. Jewish women shared many of the prevailing attitudes toward marriage and motherhood. Still, many Jewish women, like some of their Christian counterparts, took an interest in communal activities and charity or social welfare organizations. Community activism—in both traditional, religious societies and activist feminist associations—provided an outlet for Jewish women's energies, raised their curiosity and consciousness regarding women's issues, and provided invaluable services to the Jewish communities. Increasingly, Jewish women also sought temporary jobs and permanent, often professional, careers.

Despite an often constricting climate, the Imperial era was a heady—if anxiety-provoking—epoch for Jewish women. Like other bourgeois women, they experienced increased urbanization, a higher standard of living, a loosening of religious strictures, the beginnings of birth control, greater chances for education and careers, and the first organizational efforts to attain political equality.[83] They also shared general middle-class concerns about a growing and politically active working class, were politically powerless themselves, feared rapid secularization, and faced the anxieties inherent in their newly acquired status. Unlike other bourgeois women, Jewish women's experience of urbanization, high-school and university education, and birth control came sooner and more intensely. Also, their vulnerability to anti-Semitism heightened their political powerlessness in contrast to that of their bourgeois sisters.

In sum, a double dilemma confronted Jewish women: they could reach for new goals opened up by Jewish emancipation and integration into bourgeois society, and they could strive beyond boundaries that once limited women. Yet they still suffered from double discrimination based on gender and religion. For example, the Imperial era saw the admission of women to the universities, and Jewish women took advantage of this in percentages that well exceeded their proportion of the female population. Furthermore, as professions opened up to women, a dynamic minority of Jewish women seized the chance to build careers. Moreover, a general increase in female employment allowed more middle-class women to develop beyond the confines of the home. Such "progress," however, took its toll. Employment, for example, was a mixed blessing. It produced the dual burdens of running the home and performing at the workplace. Further, the increase in Jewish women's employment took place not only because more women wanted to work, but also because more women *had* to work. Higher education also bore disappointments for women who sought the social advantages of *Bildung* at a time when it was being transformed into *Ausbildung* (a more technical, less prestigious education). Acculturation too had silent internal costs. Women had to negotiate with tradition. They tried to reconcile the tensions of maintaining Jewish traditions even as they recast them. They attempted to accommodate to the majority culture even as it continually changed.

Ultimately, it is the contradictions of Jewish women's lives which stand out: they enjoyed benefits from the opportunities extended to them as women and as Jews, but they also faced harsh limits. As women they never received full legal equality and suffered from economic, political, and social discrimination; as Jews they saw the fruits of emancipation dwindle dramatically with the recurrence of anti-Semitism.

Scope of the Present Study

Women's historians have often conceptualized their research in terms of such seeming dichotomies as public and private spheres, state and family, or productive and reproductive realms. There was, and still is, a certain sense in this method. In fact, the rough outline of this book reflects such a pattern. Women's lives were frequently veiled in domestic privacy, in reproducing the home and family. When they ventured "out," their encroachment on the public sphere was recognized as such by the trailblazers and by their detractors.

This paradigm, however, has its limits and can lead to misconceptions. It does not describe historical reality as much as it replicates ideological categories imposed upon women. Also, it can serve to further women's segregation and exclusion from the "center" of the historical record, which has usually been defined as the site of male politics and endeavors.[84] In addition, as already noted above, it understates the convergence between public and private realms of life. More recently, historians have preferred a "double vision" which situates women in a more complex social reality, one which emphasizes "connecting spheres."[85]

Such connecting spheres become increasingly apparent as we delve into the daily lives of German-Jewish women. Public and private as well as distinct male/female domains overlap and blend. For example, women's charitable endeavors, generally viewed as extensions of their (private) housekeeping functions, can be reinterpreted as public and even political as well, despite women's own conventional protestations to the contrary. Also, as will be demonstrated, wives backed middle-class husbands with both dowries and housework. Beyond their income or profession, men "counted" because of the wealth, status, and culture of their families. Conversely, political structures and ideas, particularly those which sought to define gender roles, shaped all aspects of intimate life: "the private sphere is a public creation."[86] Personal relations and domestic rules followed the terms established in political realms.

These insights notwithstanding, the words and overt behavior of individual women in Imperial Germany manifest their adherence to the conceptual division of the world into public and domestic. Moreover, women were aware that for them the current between private and public generally flowed in one direction: from the private to the public. That is, women increasingly and persistently tended to "overstep" their boundaries, whether by seeking paid work or by affecting public space from the privacy of their homes.[87] In this regard it is noteworthy that men rarely hazarded the reverse course from public to private. In fact, in controlling the domestic sphere through public policy, men made sure that they would never be confined to it.

Consequently, although my study follows the apparent organization of women's lives into public and private, my underlying theme is the interconnections and tensions between these realms of life.

The first part describes the home life of Jewish women. It reflects on prevailing norms regarding women's "place" and how these were contested and often reaffirmed. The chapters examine how women raised their children, preserved religious and familial customs, and reached out to family and friends. They show how women maintained extensive kin and social networks and hence consolidated interfamilial and class relations. These chapters also present the cross-fertilizations that occurred between German and Jewish cultures. Both groups had to adapt to dislocations which reached deeply into the family. The Imperial era offers an opportunity to explore the ways in which Jews and other Germans confronted traditions which had become outmoded, while accommodating to new environments and challenges.

The first chapter focuses on women as housewives and mothers. If there is one generalization that can be made about Jewish women in Imperial Germany, it is that the overwhelming majority of them were housewives or future housewives. Single, married, widowed, divorced, working for pay or not, they performed the tasks associated with running a home. Thus their homemaking and child-rearing roles are an essential and primary part of their various stories. These duties and the perception of what was woman's "proper" place shifted from helpmate, where house and business often merged, to "leisured" lady, an indication of and an accouterment to her husband's status. It was she who choreographed the bourgeois family. Central to a discussion of the family is women's allegiance to religious practice, addressed in the second chapter. Women attempted to maintain customs within the family, and eventually the family itself, as a secular version of religion. They transformed ritual into modern familial forms, shaping a new Jewish ethnicity.

This ethnicity was also formed by the marriage strategies of Jews, detailed in the third chapter. These reveal the extent of allegiance to the religion and community as well as the evolution of Jewish expectations regarding "love or money." The discussion addresses Jewish and Christian criticisms of the "dowry chase," and explores the marriage patterns common among the commercial classes and the *Bildungsbürgertum* at this time, including the more "modern" ways in which people met and married. The final chapter in this section, focusing on women's leisure, first explores the very concept of "leisure" itself. It emphasizes the "Labor of Leisure" which encompassed exhausting feats as well as class-appropriate amusements necessary to build and extend social contacts and status. This chapter is shorter than the others, accurately reflecting the proportion of women's lives available for leisure.

Even though women focused on their families, opportunities for diversion and even independence increased in this era. The second half of the book discusses women outside the home: their education, their employment, and their public, charitable activities. In considering women's entry into the hallowed halls of the university, chapter 5 describes the sexist and racist prejudices and practices faced by this pioneer generation. It analyzes the choices they made in their academic careers and compares these with the career paths of other women. Chapter 6 examines the unofficial and official employment of Jewish women using, respectively, memoirs and census materials. It also reflects on women's attitudes and those of their families toward paid work and behind-the-scenes work. It compares women's occupational profile and job status to those of Jewish men and to other German women, noting their disadvantages compared to the former and their advantages compared to the latter. Lastly, it portrays the career paths and personal life choices of women in the vanguard: teachers, lawyers, and doctors.

Turning to women's social work, the last chapter portrays its evolution and variety. It surveys the archaic but very active burial societies; the modernizing benevolent associations; twentieth-century social welfare organizations; and the Jewish women's movement. It emphasizes the activities of several exemplary individuals whose creativity enlarged the scope of Jewish women's concerns and rewards, and highlights a few leaders who reached out beyond the Jewish community to work in secular social welfare organizations.

Jewish tradition maintains that Judaism is a composite of three elements: education, worship, and philanthropy. Jewish education (Torah study) and public worship, however, were predominantly male monopolies, leaving women less scope than men for public action and recognition. In taking women as a vantage point, I have argued for a far broader picture of Judaism, one that encompasses home, family, and community. It is the task of future scholarship, mine and others', to integrate our findings about Jewish women and the significance of gender into general histories.[88] Until then, our history books can claim to depict only the history of Jewish men—half the Jewish population in Imperial Germany.

I

WOMEN AND THE CONSTRUCTION OF BOURGEOIS CULTURE

1

Cultivating Respectability: A Family Enterprise

Jews built the walls around their homes to be highly permeable, allowing German bourgeois modes to penetrate intimate familial relationships as well as the decor and atmosphere of their interiors, and permitting the display of Jewish acculturation to flow to the exterior. The home was where they experienced the ambivalences and contradictions inherent in the dual desires to maintain their family, Jewish community, and heritage, and to integrate into social and cultural life with other Germans. It was where boys and girls were raised to fit the role of religiously observant or secular men and women, and where new options for girls and women were first explored. It was where Jews absorbed the impact of their economic success and prepared to achieve the social status commensurate with it. The home was the juncture at which gender, class, and ethnicity confronted one another.

Despite differences in time, place of residence, religious observance, and wealth, one common aspect can be seen in the behavior of Jewish families in Imperial Germany. Jews were intent upon acculturating. Outwardly they tried to look, speak, and act like other Germans. Inwardly they accepted middle-class mores for their family and made them their own. In a society in which proper behavior, public and private, differed according to class, it was the task of the mother and housewife to act as cultural mediator between the intimate sphere of the family and society at large. She had to raise children according to proper bourgeois criteria, confronting the pressures to negotiate and accommodate in family life. She was to maintain a household positively "Germanic" in its cleanliness and orderliness, virtues deemed necessary to produce a hardworking moral citizenry. Also she had to mediate between German popular culture, in the forms of music, literature, and social engagements, and her family. Mothers were responsible for the behavioral and cultural attainment of the family, for its *Bildung*.

Housework and Household

Notwithstanding their retroactive image of Imperial Germany as a time of peace, harmony, and stability for the middle classes, "the golden age of security,"[1] for Jews it was also a time of flux. Only when measured against later periods of war and

Mothers and children playing a circle game while on vacation in Friedrichsroda (Thuringian Forest), 1913. *Schild-Scheier family Collection. Courtesy of the Leo Baeck Institute, New York.*

disaster does the turn of the century take on an air of quiet security for Jews. As regards the changing role of Jewish women in the household during this period, class position, more than geographic location or religious adherence, produced the most profound differences among Jewish women. The wealthy hired domestic servants and acquired modern technology such as electrical appliances and indoor plumbing first. New consumer goods provided the material comfort, and new wealth created the "lady of leisure." The newly rich bourgeoisie could thus emulate the nobility through the seeming indolence of its women. The middle class in general, and the poorer or petty bourgeoisie in particular, placed great value on the "nonworking" mother and wife. In fact, by the 1890s, as soon as they could afford to live without the wife's participation in economic activity or her wages—and sometimes before—many of the lower middle class made do without it. So deeply was middle-class status signified by the non-wage-earning and leisured woman, and so deeply was Jewish acculturation identified with the bourgeoisie, that even those Jewish women who continued to work in family businesses or around the house often hid from public view while performing their chores.

Among poor Jews there was little opportunity or wherewithal to imitate the customs of the rich. In the countryside poorer German Jews relied for economic survival on the entire family. Wives and daughters remained important as producers and helpmates, taking on the role of consumers more slowly. In the cities, where the Jewish poor often stemmed from Eastern Europe, the family's sustenance depended on the wage earning of the entire family. Mothers might leave work temporarily, but many returned to work as industrial or domestic laborers, and others took in needlework. Daughters who remained at home also brought in wages to support the family and to save up a small dowry. Although the urban environment did not allow women the option of direct production for the family—for example, gardening and canning—poorer women found ways as wage earners and consumers to help make ends meet.

The Early Decades, 1870–1890

The sentimentalization of the home and the housewife, the image of the leisured lady of the *haute bourgeoisie,* and the mistaken conclusion that modern technology necessarily made for less housework, have obscured the actual work and tedium involved in running a household and the economic value of that work to the family and to the economy. Although the years 1870–90 witnessed a flood of emotion which transported women's image to the top of pedestals, down below their housework did not disappear. The technological innovations in household appliances, fixtures, and conveniences came slowly to individual households, even the economically successful ones. Among the Jewish lower middle and middle classes, only 20 percent of whom lived in large urban centers in 1871, women performed myriad tasks, with and without the assistance of servants, while some worked in family businesses as well. Their own memoirs rarely described housework, so much did they take it for granted and so little did they think it would matter to posterity. Their sons and daughters occasionally noted the details of their mothers' exhausting days, often from the vantage point of "modern" urbanites writing at the turn of the century.

In Bismarckian Germany, running a household could absorb the energies of several women, the housewife, her daughters, permanent and day helpers, and often, single female relatives. By this time many households, even in small towns, benefited from new local industry, the expanding domestic marketplace, and the German railroad system. They could purchase rather than produce their own soap and candles. Petroleum lamps, refrigeration through ice blocks, bakers, butchers, grocers, a monthly washwoman (who stayed for two to three days) and ironer, an occasional seamstress, hired help for spring cleaning, and a live-in domestic were boons to such households. In urban homes one might also find running water in bourgeois kitchens.[2] Nevertheless, most housewives still had to produce their own clothing (from bought dry goods) and bedroom and kitchen linens. Jewish women, like other German housewives, shopped, cooked, baked, preserved, and canned, but many also maintained a kosher home (see chapter 2) and performed the extra tasks which that involved. Further, all women cleaned homes grimy from coal or wood-burning stoves and oil lamps, and, except in cities, they also gardened. Large basements contained storage areas for winter provisions, from fruit to goose fat (a butter substitute for those who kept kosher homes).[3] Mothers and grandmothers mended children's clothing and knitted socks.[4] Where household help was available, female employers still exerted considerable energy. For example, one woman who could afford kitchen help and a tutor for her children spent any extra time with her children—all twelve of them. She instructed them in botany and helped with their homework. Child rearing was exclusively her responsibility: "Mother always said that father would hardly have noticed, had his two or three-year-olds been switched with others."[5] Furthermore, this woman shopped and cooked alongside her domestic help. Large families demanded constant, hard work even with household servants available. Also among the wealthiest families, women filled their days with ceaseless activity, even when they carefully avoided heavy physical labor, a sign of lower-class status.[6] In the 1870s, for example, the wife of a Berlin Jewish banker did all the shopping, managed the kitchen help, tailored the clothing for her eight children, and gave them piano lessons. She maintained all social and familial networks which involved time-consuming formal visits and letter writing in the absence of quick phone conversations or a car or bus ride to a friend's home.[7]

Compared to rural and poorer Jews, this was a relatively luxurious set of responsibilities. The lives of urban and rural Jews of the same class and in the same decade gave the impression of a time lag. Even though their peasant neighbors often considered rural Jews to be "modern and urban," their pace of modernization—particularly in the area of female behavior—was slower than that of urban Jews. They had, on the average, more children to care for and fewer modern conveniences to rely upon. Rural Jews also maintained Orthodox traditions longer. The more Orthodox her family, the more children a woman would have, the more tied she felt to daily, weekly, and cyclical religious rituals, and the more housework she had to do.[8]

In the 1870s a young Jewish woman living in a tiny Westphalian village rose before dawn. She milked the goats, prepared the coffee by lighting a wood fire which heated the kettle that hung over it, kindled the furnace in the living room which warmed the entire small house, swept the room, brought water in from the town well, and set the breakfast table. The nine-person family ate eight loaves of homemade bread a week. Since the father, a butcher, earned so little, the family depended on its own garden for fruits and vegetables and on its goats for milk and butter. The women cared for these vital areas. Carefully observing the Sabbath, the mother and daughters could not refrain from working on Sundays. Respectful of their Christian neighbors' day of rest, they closed their doors so as not to offend them and did the wash on Sundays.[9] Primitive conditions were the norm in rural areas. The family of an Alsatian businessman used its wood-burning stove for cooking and heating the house. The family took baths in a community bath which received its water from a brook.[10] The mother prepared bread at home and sent it to the baker's for baking. She readied the Sabbath meal one day in advance—since one could not work on the Sabbath—and sent it, too, to the baker's, where it could be baked or heated slowly until the Sabbath.[11] This was a common practice in rural areas, and it was not unusual to see groups of women or children picking up their Sabbath meal at the bakery. Most Jewish rural shopowners and cattle or horse dealers owned stables, storage bins, and small plots of land which the wife tended by herself or with hired help. House and business were combined.[12] The home usually contained storage areas where business and personal items stood side by side, where the family took up the front part of the residence or only the first floor of the house.[13] Many rural Jewish men engaged in peddling and trade, spending Mondays through Thursdays on business trips. Jewish wives remained behind in charge of the home, family, storage rooms, and often the shop. The novelist Jacob

Picard recalled that his mother ran everything with the help of one maid. She also did all the cooking and baking for her large family, including special baked goods for Sabbath treats.[14] The Sabbath required particular preparations. One woman (born in 1879 in the village of Oberaula) recalled that her mother cleaned and cooked for two days prior to every Sabbath.[15] Yet on this holy "day of rest," the work of even religiously observant women was never done. Although forbidden to cook or clean, they still served and cleared meals and fed and entertained guests who dropped in for the customary Sabbath visit.

The absent husband was not only a rural phenomenon. Urban small businessmen (as late as the prewar years) visited customers away from home during the week. One man left all his office work and correspondence to his wife, who preferred this kind of hidden activity to sitting exposed at the cash register. She considered overt work demeaning.[16] She ran her household along with her other responsibilities. Whereas some women took charge of home and business in their husbands' absences, others worked as partners in the family stores while also running their households. Describing his mother, who was absolutely essential to their small-town store, one son pointed out her economic value to the family as well as her gentility and bourgeois bearing: "Pretty, delicate and fine . . . [she] could work like a peasant and comport herself like a lady . . . could advise like an intelligent woman and help . . . like a man. With her one could begin to fulfill one's plans."[17] In many cases, middle-class Jewish women left much of the housework to hired help and spent evenings catching up with household chores. Still others ran their own businesses along with their housewifely duties. A man born in 1868 in West Prussia recalled that his father was a traveling peddler, while his mother ran a tavern and a household including twelve children. With the help of an unmarried sister-in-law, she cared for the house, the barnyard animals, her customers, and her business. She spent her evenings darning and knitting, and willingly incurred the extra work of remaining religiously observant.[18]

As Jews strove to attain the economic and social mobility promised them by legal emancipation and tempting them through industrial progress, women played an important economic function which reached beyond the home. They had to mediate between the lures of the marketplace and the needs of the family, between outer display and inner frugality. They had to consume enough while economizing and managing. Their consumer functions have often been trivialized in comparison to earlier producer functions. Yet general guide books to good housewifery stressed that careful consumption was a form of income conservation. Thrift contributed to the family's welfare and was taken as seriously as the husband's capacity to earn. Thrift could ease the tensions between social aspirations and what one's income could actually support. Importantly, it could cushion financial instabilities. For Jews in particular, since they were disproportionately involved in commerce, careful money management could compensate for an uneven economy and moderate the results of fluctuating business profits.

Although women in Bismarckian Germany may have produced less than their mothers had, their economic function was to remain thrifty and thus to accumulate capital for their family's needs. Women kept detailed household account books.[19] They carefully registered every last cent of their expenses. Savings provided the funds for children's education,[20] for daughters' dowries, for business investments. Housewives learned to buy in large quantities to avoid overpaying for smaller amounts. Many continued to finish their children's clothing, even in later years when they had become wealthier. Among the wealthy, too, thrift was a virtue. This was a trait carried forward from earlier generations of Jews who saved money to help them through turbulent times, as well as an attitude adopted from a Protestant bourgeoisie which saw extravagance as sinful. Luxuries were appreciated and treated as such. Southern fruits, a rarity in Germany of the 1870s, came to the rich first. In a banker's family, ten people shared two oranges on special Sabbaths.[21]

For the middle classes, necessities rather than luxuries had to be divided. Middle-class women tried to mediate between the needs of individual family members and the family's overall needs. Time too was a commodity to be apportioned carefully. Bourgeois society expected women to exhibit efficiency and time management, to devise routines for their servants, to create people with "built-in clocks."[22] Lina Morgenstern, the Jewish leader of the German Housewives' Association, admonished her members to be prudent with their money and time. Wastefulness was a housewife's worst enemy, for then she would forfeit her savings as well as the spare time she could use for her children or for "sensible enjoyment"[23] (*vernünftigen Lebensgenuss*). Prodigal behavior might even forfeit her right to the kitchen, like one woman whose marriage contract stated that in the "case of excessive wastefulness" her husband would have the right to "encroach in the kitchen, which, as a rule, is normally out of bounds to him."[24] Women drilled thriftiness into their children and could only compensate them with family closeness—if they had saved enough time for it—when individual needs could not be met. Mothers served as examples to their children of "self-discipline, moderation, and self-sacrifice."[25] Thrift, hard work, and a mentality that budgeted time—virtues of necessity in this early period—became ends in themselves later on.

Entering the "Modern" Era, 1890–1918

The Jewish housewife of the Wilhelmine era took on other roles beyond the productive, thrifty, and efficient *Hausfrau*. Gradually relegated to the home by the 1890s, she had to create and mold the bourgeois family. Like other women, she was also responsible for emotional housework. The home was to be a "retreat, [a] refueling station to which the family members return periodically for spiritual, physical and psychological sustenance."[26] In theory, and often in practice, the home was off limits to conflict. Women were to ensure peace and tranquility for family members.[27] The home would assuage the pain of men embroiled in an aggressive, competitive, status-conscious, and achievement-oriented world. The wife and family would not only soothe and comfort, they would also be the reward—and excuse—for the battles of the day. As one male educator, a propagator of this ideology, noted: "On one side of the threshold of his house he belongs to work, on the other side is peaceful pleasure. His second life begins there, the rewards of his day."[28] Thus while men's work evolved into a career or job, women's work remained a calling, defined in terms of its contribution to the common good. It was the housewife's "unselfish love" for husband and children, the production of homeyness, as evidenced by her cozy, clean home and tidy, orderly offspring, which was praised as an example of morality itself.

If the middle class was indeed a "family of desires and anxieties" worrying about its identity, status, political future and moral character,[29] then Jews were the very embodiment of such apprehensions. Concerned about all the issues confronting other bourgeois, they also suffered from the recency of their political emancipation and from their extra social and economic vulnerabilities. Jewish women had to smooth things over at home. As Jewishness became more and more privatized, something one spoke about, felt, or acted upon only inside the family, mothers' tasks as cultural mediators became more complicated. They had to help the family maintain its cohesion and traditions as it acculturated to a bourgeois Protestant society (from bringing up children "properly," to buying the "right" magazines or theater tickets, to living in the "right" neighborhoods). Likewise they had to prepare children for the world and salve the pain of an alienatingly conformist, ruthlessly competitive, frequently hostile environment. Also women needed to raise the family to a new social level to exhibit and maintain its economic achievements. Since class formation demanded visible means of distinguishing those belonging to different classes, Jews needed to be visibly middle-class. But they also needed to be invisibly Jewish. It took a deft sleight of hand to juggle these requirements, and mothers confronted this challenge daily. Faced with contradictions and constant flux, mothers had to raise proper German children while affirming (and redefining) Jewishness, to present a family in the appropriate light to a society intolerant of differences, and to create a refuge for a minority to come home to.

Not only the psychosocial but also the economic functions of bourgeois women were redefined. Before, women's reproductive work, including all aspects of childbearing, child rearing, and housework, had been essential to the family economy, but by the end of the nineteenth century most bourgeois homes—as in other industrializing countries—had become consumption units removed from productive economic activity. Women's work became less physical and more administrative and cultural. The ideal of housewifery, of a spotless home run by a *tüchtig* (efficient and capable) home manager who carefully instructed and regulated her servants, came to replace women's former productive work. By adopting the norms of the cultured family and the sparkling *Haushalt* ("the main duty was to be a *tüchtige Hausfrau*"), Jewish women helped their families fit in.[30] They introduced popular and classical German literature and modeled their home decoration and furnishings, and the style and tone of the household and family, to prevailing bourgeois standards. Responsible for clothing their children and themselves, they often had to advise husbands, too. In small villages, rural women considered Jewish women to be in the "avant-garde of fashion," because they purchased their clothing from the city.[31] In the cities, too, Jewish women were often fashion-conscious, although in a carefully understated way. Anti-Semites had taken notice of the fashion industry, in which Jews played a prominent role, and railed against "judaicized fashion."[32] The granddaughter of the Orthodox Rabbi Hildesheimer remembered how her mother dressed her and her siblings like the Kaiser's children, particularly the sailor suits and middies.[33] Furniture styles and home decorations also announced the family's arrival in the bourgeoisie.

Rural society viewed Jewish women as trend setters. While this may be attributed to higher income levels, it also reflected a conscious effort by Jews to emulate bourgeois standards. This was made easier by contacts with urban relatives and by frequent visits to neighboring cities. For example, the wife of a small-town businessman, who still minded the shop during his lengthy absences, traveled to the nearest city to buy her dining-room furniture and wallpaper, and ordered her living-room and bedroom sets from Berlin (1883–92).[34] Jewish homes physically resembled those of the German bourgeoisie: "nothing was missing from the piano to the asparagus knives."[35] To the curiosity and puzzlement of their neighbors, they brought in city furniture and styles, including plush sofas and chairs, arranged the rooms in a "city manner," and frequently included a piano and a telephone among the basic requirements. Often, Christian neighbors availed themselves of the telephone in Jewish homes.[36] This interaction provided both a moment of friendly exchange as well as a glimpse by the villagers of the different life-style of their Jewish neighbors.

In a highly mobile population streaming to urban areas, many Jewish women had the responsibility of redecorating a home at least once beyond their original domicile.[37] Gas (around 1890) and electricity (at the turn of the century) were rapidly introduced in towns and cities. Although furniture generally remained with the family, furnishing might change to reflect newer styles, and kitchens were generally modernized. Women set the style and tone of the household through careful selection of its furnishings. This included both the latest in decorative brocades as well as hand-embroidered or tatted tablecloths or furniture covers and wall decorations. These handmade decorations signified a woman's usefulness, but they served a very practical purpose as well. In middle-class homes they refurbished and brought "style" to furniture when the family could not afford new purchases. In general, "few bourgeois households were complete without pictures on the wall, music in the parlor, classics in the glassed-in bookcase."[38] In Jewish homes, too, these items were on prominent display. A special decoration to be found in many Jewish homes was a portrait of the Kaiser. One man noted that one such portrait always hung in his grandmother's home, demonstrating her—and the family's—allegiance to a German bourgeois identity. She was *Kaisertreu* (insisting that the portrait remain even in the 1920s) as well as religious. At every Passover, when the family repeated the ritual sentence "next year in Jerusalem," she would reply, "next year in Berlin."[39]

As important as the mahogany table and the atmosphere of solid comfort were to all bourgeois Germans, Jews in particular valued understatement and quality. This restraint may have been the result of insecurity, the fear that anti-Semites might single out Jewish wealth, and the attempt by Jews to control such damage. Hannah Arendt noted that Jews were depicted as a "'principle' of philistine and upstart society,"[40] and anti-Semites did use those families who bought villas in Berlin's fanciest neighborhoods or who dressed luxuriously as favorite targets, to the dismay of most Jews. Further, their studied understatement may have been a sign of Jewish social aspirations and financial success, a disdain for the behavior and showiness of the nouveaux riches from whom they were barely graduating. Finally, their choice of style was in harmony with the general clothing and furnishing tastes of the respectable middle classes of Germany, who were solid but not careless about money.

Like the modest strata of German civil servants and the *Bildungsbürgertum*, Jews measured their respectability more and more in terms of their consumption patterns and their private lives. Not only manners, exemplary family lives, and literate conversations, but cleanliness and orderliness were paramount virtues. These model homemakers decorated and polished their homes incessantly. Every aspect of daily life was governed by order.[41] Women's work allowed even a modest income to support a home which was a shrine to German domesticity and to middle-class gentility. Unlike their French or British counterparts, German women did not minimize housework when their economic and social status would have allowed it. Only the smallest range of the upper bourgeoisie did this. Most middle-class women simply raised the stakes of housework: they became professional household managers. An English visitor noted in 1908, "It was a new idea to me that any women in the world except the Germans kept house at all." She continued: "The extreme tidiness of German rooms is a constant source of surprise. They are as guiltless of 'litter' as the showrooms of a furniture emporium. . . . Every bit of embroidery has its use and its own corner. . . . Each chair has its place. . . . Even where there are children German rooms never look disarranged." Peeking into the husband's room in one house, she remarked to the wife, "He must be a very tidy man. Do you never have to set things to rights here?" "Every half hour," was the response.[42] Extra leisure could turn housewives into *Putznärrinnen* (mad housewives) who tidied the home from dawn to dusk. Such was the case among many Jewish women as well, whose relatives and neighbors recalled their incessant cleaning compulsion. "Our peasant women didn't have time for that," remarked one observer.[43] Bourgeois class formation, eagerly emulated by German Jews, hinged on familial and household order amid massive social–structural changes and in direct contrast to the "disorderly" lower classes.

Although this is not the place to analyze the German proclivity toward housework, it is worth noting the longevity of the tradition as well as its institutionalization and regulation by the state. Housewives could look back to Germanic legends in which female spirits threatened to kidnap a housewife's children if her home were not clean enough. Also the Virgin Mary, the embodiment of pristine purity, was thought to watch over the *Spinnstube* and check to see if the floors had been carefully swept.[44] In Imperial Germany about one million families of civil servants (*Beamten*) had to observe a "respectable" family life exhibiting moral and financial behavior beyond suspicion. Debts or a disorderly family life were situations unbefitting an Imperial civil servant. Husbands were not only economic providers, but were responsible as state officials for a "moral mode of life" (*moralischen Lebenswandel*).[45] They depended on their wives to present the family in an acceptable light as well as to balance a budget. State files repeatedly stress "solid home life" and "exemplary family life" when documenting civil servants' overall performance.[46] Ironically, even as privatization was stressed, this privacy was subject to greater supervision and admonition than ever. Hence these wives felt the state's power directly within the household and set an example for other—including Jewish—housewives to follow. Part of middle-class life-style, then, was a sparkling floor and luminescent glassware enforced by an ever watchful state.

Peers and advice literature assured German housewives that women were responsible for cleanliness and happiness. Housewives in fact seemed to believe that the former was a prerequisite for the latter.[47] Their organizations presented lectures on household chemistry, and exhibitions of the latest household inventions and paraphernalia, and promoted housework as a profession (*Beruf*). Housewives' periodicals printed painstakingly intricate articles entitled "the linen closet" or "how do I teach my servants to wash and rinse the dishes?"[48] Even when she had less to do, or servants to do it for her, the housewife had to know how to do housework so as to set a good example. Advice manuals suggested a variety of ways to clean copper kettles, iron pots, and tin plates.[49] Trousseaus included "cover towels" which one placed over the used dish towels with the embroidered motto: "sparkling bright and tidy is how your kitchen should always be."[50] How-to manuals invaded the private sphere, organizing a housewife's day down to the last minute and smallest detail.[51]

Jewish women possessed a cultural heritage—a religiously grounded compatibility—which blended well with becoming a model housewife. The Talmud lists housework among the wife's obligations to her husband. Even if he can afford servants, the husband cannot let his wife be idle, for idleness could lead to boredom, and boredom to promiscuity.[52] In the prayer traditionally recited by husbands to their wives on the Sabbath, women are praised for devotion to their families as expressed in tireless work and domestic productivity. Women were responsible for maintaining a "Jewish" house. "All the intricate apparatus of domestic religious observance" was under their purview. Men depended on female vigilance to keep them "good Jews" in the "daily mechanics of living." For this, women had to be efficient, skilled housekeepers as well as knowledgeable in the complexities of Jewish dietary and holiday rituals.[53] Thus the strong tradition of careful housewifery among Jews—also among those one or two generations removed from serious religious observance—supported, even exacerbated, the German mania for housekeeping.

Jewish advice manuals, too, cautioned that the well-being and happiness of the family depended on the efficiency of the housewife.[54] Further, a clean house and the knowledge of how to achieve this were signs of the importance of domesticity and of the housewife.[55] Women enhanced their own status in this way, using cleanliness, busyness, and thrift as symbols of their indispensability. Needlework, for example—the pastime of those with less arduous chores—symbolized thrift and industriousness, despite its unproductive and decorative nature. One woman never knitted or mended, she "didn't need to do that," but she did need to keep busy and look useful, so she embroidered. Another woman from a very wealthy family insisted on sewing all her childrens' clothing herself, but from astronomically expensive Liberty of London materials![56] And even when incessant toil was no longer necessary, as when all the children had left home and a woman was widowed, a nephew recalls his aunt "as a small, white-haired woman . . . cleaning her house from morning till night."[57]

Jewish women, like other German housewives, had even nobler duties to fulfill in their endless campaign against dirt and disorder. According to the *General Anzeiger*, the industrious management of the household not only provided for the family, but for the economy, the society, and the state:

> In the last years, it has become apparent that the proper management of a household not only serves the welfare of the home and the prosperity of the family, but the economic prosperity of communities, even the state. For this reason the wife and mother has a noble and important duty. She is responsible for the physical and emotional well-being of all family members, for order, cleanliness, punctuality in the household, for the hygienic arrangement of the living quarters, for the healthy, practical nourishment of the household members, and, simultaneously, has to understand how to guide the servants under her authority, to distribute their work. If she is capable of fulfilling this work entirely . . . she is also contributing her part to solving the social question.[58]

German Jews also had unique motives for maintaining a spic-and-span home. In the midst of rapid economic and geographic mobility, they may have longed for domestic order to compensate for the changes in their lives: "If only the little part of the world over which one has control is neat and tidy, this is enough to instill some security."[59] Also, as has already been noted, Jewish women strove to have their families accepted by the Gentile bourgeoisie. A well-run household, carefully chosen furniture, and well-pressed clothing were marks of gentility, of cultivation, of *Bildung*. Respectable middle-class homes announced that Jews had the moral fiber to be equal citizens in the new state. Finally, sparkling domesticity served not only to confirm their bourgeois credentials, but to create a huge distance between themselves and their more "backward" Eastern European coreligionists. Non-Jews as well as German Jews stressed the filth in which East European Jews ostensibly lived. Marx's description of Polish Jews as the "dirtiest of all races" voiced a general prejudice which lingered on.[60] Theodor Lessing, the diagnostician and leading example of Jewish self-hatred, portrayed them as dirty and decadent.[61] Anti-Semites complained of a "Jewish garlic smell." Echoing a general German distaste for garlic (and for people to the east with whom Germans associated the herb), even Jews with no particularly harsh feelings toward their Eastern coreligionists cringed at the thought of garlic. Remarking on the general filth he encountered when billeted as a soldier in the East during World War I, a German-Jewish physician described his Jewish host as: "a shy, tiny honest man. . . . His home was filthy. . . . A repulsive odor . . . of garlic made it particularly distasteful."[62] It is no wonder, then, that German-Jewish housewives exhibited a true horror of garlic[63] and scrubbed and polished their "Jewishness" away. Both Gentiles and Jews believed that dirt could lead to decadence, but for Jews it could also lead to the dreaded identification with their proletarian, Eastern, nonacculturated brothers and sisters living in the ghettos of Berlin and other major cities. German Jews focused on eliminating dirt and smell—class symbols—from their lives. That is, to some extent they tried to translate anti-Semitism against Eastern Jews into class terms, assuming—and hoping—that their own spotless middle-class behavior (and hence, their Jewishness) would be acceptable to bourgeois Germans.

Domestic Servants

Domestics were essential to many households. Middle-class women have emphasized their contribution, both to stress the necessity of domestic help and to present themselves as above heavy housework in order to raise their class status in their own eyes and in the eyes of others. Historians of the "leisured lady" have taken the values and attitudes of the middle classes more seriously than the actual state of their material existence, assuming that if a household employed a maid, the housewife was ipso facto idle. But a brief overview of the servant situation in Germany shows that even women with servants apparently worked hard. Further, it seems that not all middle-class families could even avail themselves of domestic help.

In 1895 the *Reichstatistik* counted 1,339,316 live-in servants (*Dienstboten*), about 2.6 percent of the population. This was in an era when about three million German families were considered either "aristocratic and wealthy" (0.25 million) or "upper-middle-class" (2.75 million). Even assuming only one maid per family (and many families hired more than one), the result would still indicate that not every upper-middle-class—let alone middle-class—family had a maid. Much more statistical work needs to be done, but at first glance it would appear that upper-middle-class and middle-class women were probably busier in the household—particularly in a country where the *Hausfrau* became legendary—than we have previously thought. Furthermore, the number of servants in general declined in the Imperial era. Between 1882 and 1907 the *Dienstbotenfrage* (servant question) developed into a national "crisis": the number of servants registered in the census dropped from 2.9% of the population to 2%, a 33% loss at a time when the number of employed persons in the total population rose from 41% to 45.5%.[64] In general, after 1850 the lure of industrial work thinned the ranks of servants.[65] The decrease in supply spurred an increase in wages: the wages of untrained servants rose to the level of unskilled workers. Servants' wages took up a larger part of household budgets than ever before. This meant that fewer people could afford servants, and that even those who could, hired fewer per household. In Berlin for example, this meant there were servants in 17.3% of households in 1871, but only in 12.4% in 1900. In Hamburg in 1871, 21.6% of households employed servants, whereas only 12.3% did so in 1900.[66]

Even when maids were available, however, they were most often young, untrained maids-of-all-work (*Mädchen für Alles*) with whom housewives shared work. Furthermore, these young women did not remain in one household for long. In Berlin in 1882, a servant stayed with one employer fifteen months on the average, in 1900 only seven months.[67] Both their lack of training and their turnover meant that one had to train and work with them. Finally, in an era of primitive household technology and few (although increasing) consumer goods, the class status that a maid conferred—important as that was—was outweighed by the practical necessity of hiring her. Memoirs, novels, and diaries often declare: "we had a maid." This statement asserts the writer's class consciousness and helps the historian establish her or his self-defined class position. Until World War I, domestic help, representing the ostensible delegation of housework, was the measure of a class-appropriate life-style.[68] This, however, does not help to unravel the actual, practical reality of the middle-class woman's life, in particular the daily drudgery of her workday. We have already noted the commonplace realities of cooking, shopping, washing, and sewing, and can assume that heavier scrubbing, cleaning, or tending fires may have been done by maids. This would still be a far cry from the idle leisured lady. As one woman reminisced about her middle-class Jewish colleagues: "I remember that only one woman . . . was mentioned as doing housework and I'm sure she had SOME help, also. With heating, laundry, preserving, no bourgeois home could be run without help: even when my maids married they took some youngster they trained to become a maid or a cook."[69]

If, indeed, every middle-class family could not have had full-time help, then what about Jewish families? An educated guess, rather than statistical data, has to suffice at present. By 1871, 60% of Jews were already middle-class and upper-middle-class.[70] By 1914, Berlin Jews, who made up over 4% of the Berlin population (almost 30% of the entire German-Jewish population) paid over one-third of the city taxes.[71] Furthermore, a disproportionate number of Jews lived in commercial centers where the proportion of servants in the population was higher than in other parts of Germany. Probably a majority of middle-class urban Jews and many of their lower-middle-class counterparts had live-in, paid help, usually one maid-of-all-work. In rural areas the Jewish middle class also hired live-in help, generally one maid. In Württemberg, for example, roughly 60 percent of Jewish households hired one maid.[72] The others paid an occasional cleaning woman for heavier housework. Among the small minority that hired Jewish maids, some also hired day help on the Sabbaṭh (*Schabbesmagd*), so that the Jewish maid did not have to work.[73] It was most likely to find Jewish domestics in rural areas. (In cities working-class Jewish women preferred industrial to domestic work.[74]) Even Jews who had no regular household help might hire a Sabbath maid if they were very religious and could perform no work such as cooking, dishwashing, or lighting lamps or fires on the Sabbath. Some Jews even shared the costs of a communal Sabbath maid. In his small town, one man recalled: "Bedtime was regulated by the *Schabbos Goye* [Sabbath non-Jew]. In households that had no maids, or employed Jewish ones, the *Schabbos Goye* made the rounds, extinguishing lights and keeping fires going, and she had to cover a large territory."[75]

By the end of the nineteenth century, as their number shrank, domestics became even more important indicators of status.[76] Moreover, at precisely this time the number of households which could sustain a bourgeois or petty bourgeois standard of living declined. Nevertheless, this insecure middle strata preferred to give up almost anything but its servant. In his novel *Poggenpuhls*, for example, Theodor Fontane described a family in which the mother and daughters earned money by teaching piano and painting porcelain in order to maintain their servants. The lower middle class, too, in order to distinguish itself from those below it, hired a maid or at least day help. Those who could not did the demeaning physical work out of public view. Jewish memoirs portray this phenomenon. The wife and daughter of a Jewish civil servant, for example, rose at four in the morning in order to scrub the doors and windows, clean floors, and do the laundry. "No one could see this, it would have been a scandal. They called this the 'hour of humiliation.'" But "they carried this shame with dignity. The rawness of their hands could be smoothed out with skin creams."[77]

Servants not only signified class status in a highly class-conscious and newly forming middle class. They also provided a hierarchy within the home. It was the woman's duty and privilege to run the home, to decide on the work to be done, and to divide the chores according to her ideas. In wealthier homes she carried the "basket of keys" (*Schlüsselkorb*) with her, a symbol of her authority.[78] It was she who unlocked the various bureaus and cabinets from which her maid would take out the necessary linens, dinnerware, or food supplies. Toward the end of the nineteenth century, in the midst of the servant shortage, some maids demanded access to the foods, linens, and silverware themselves, seeing the key basket as an indication of mistrust, and would not work for women who locked their cabinets.[79] The housewife also commented upon and organized the lives of her servants, placing their wages in bank accounts for their dowries, reprimanding them for unseemly language, and playing the parent-in-absentia for servants sometimes even older than herself.[80] It was not unusual for Jewish housewives to send their maids to church as well.[81]

Hierarchy had its drawbacks for the woman at the top. Household manuals warned that if the housewife was indifferent, even the most diligent servant would slow down.[82] In order to gain respect, she had to earn it. Jewish advice manuals cautioned that if women did not learn about the details of their households, their servants would not take them seriously and might even turn the tables on them: "She has to cook and bake well . . . know how to shop and distribute, love order and cleanliness, . . . if she is not to become the pitiable slave of her servant and cook."[83]

Jewish newspapers took note of the servant shortage, admitting that factory work gave women more freedom than domestic service. Sparing their own daughters, German Jews tried to convince Eastern European Jewish immigrants to train their daughters for domestic service.[84] At the opening of a school for immigrant children, a Berlin Jewish leader admonished: "we need not ladies, but maids. And if you can promise me that girl students will become domestics, then I can pledge you 100,000 marks!"[85] In the face of a lackluster response, Jewish leaders warned that Jewish women would shortly need to run their homes entirely on their own.[86] Commentators cautioned that it paid to be nice to domestics in order to keep them. They expressed particular concern that Christian domestics would refuse to work for Jews, not only because of the complicated rituals affecting the preparation of food, but more so because of anti-Semitism. The *Israelitisches Gemeindeblatt* feared that "the Jewish woman would have to apologize to her maid for her religion."[87] In fact, this undercurrent may have made some Jewish employers more sensitive to the prejudices or needs of their domestics. When a new maid came for an interview, one woman recalled that her mother always mentioned four things: "(1) You don't need to cook, I'll do that; (2) Do you know that we are Jews? ("Wissen Sie . . ." [the polite form]); (3) Do you have a fiancé? He may not visit you here; (4) You must be home at 10 p.m. on Sundays."[88] In Württemberg, servants from Jewish homes spoke highly of their working conditions; remembered the presents they received, including entire trousseaus; commented on the friendly, familial tone in the home; and remarked that invectives were usually in Hebrew.[89] "I ate at the table with them, they treated me like a daughter," recalled one domestic, and there were many domestics who remained loyal to "their" families into the 1940s. Nevertheless, servants understood—or were made to understand—their "place."[90]

Concern with the "servant shortage" and with the "quality" of household help notwithstanding, the majority of Jews in Wilhelmine Germany hired such help. Still, in spite of household assistance, the lady-of-complete-leisure was the exception. We do find the nineteen-room doctor's home in Cologne in which a family of six employed a cook, a cook's helper, a maid, a second maid (for scullery and heavy cleaning), a washwoman (who came to the house every two weeks), a third maid (who took care of the sewing, mending, ironing), and a governess. The woman in charge of this home had "never learned how to cook even an egg."[91] Frequently the offspring of the very wealthy were consciously kept from learning the basics of running a home. The wife of the first Jewish *Oberlandsgerichtsrat* in Prussia (1903) asked her daughter, "Why should you learn to cook? One only has to know how to assign." When her daughter learned to cook a bit as a student, her mother fretted, "but you will never have to learn how to peel potatoes, right?"[92] One woman wrote:

> It is embarrassing to me to tell . . . all the things I did *not* know. . . . I wore dresses made by Frau Baumgarten . . . it was the same with my fine, hand-embroidered underwear. . . . The maid washed my things, the maid ironed them, they were examined and mended by Sissi, I had to do nothing but wear them. . . . The cook, a (male) servant, a maid, a chambermaid and a maid-of-all-service . . . sufficed to keep the house in the most painstaking order. It would have been neither desired nor appropriate for the small daughter of the house to reach for a broom or dust cloth. . . . So I . . . would have been helplessly lost if someone had asked me to make some oatmeal or to fry an egg.[93]

Another woman, less privileged, remembered how hard her mother worked around the home, but would not let her daughters help. "You have more intelligent things to do. When you are forced to learn how to cook, you will be able to do it."[94] Self-imposed self-abnegation as well as status aspirations for her daughters made her encourage their ignorance in household chores. Hedwig Dohm, an early feminist and the daughter of a Jewish tobacco manufacturer, wrote, with her usually acerbic pen: "Isn't today's housewifery a caricature of the past? Because housewives who no longer spin or weave, brew, bake or plant, play with the kitchen, the children and life."[95]

These women were the exceptions to the rule. Although women attempted to appear leisured to the outside world, even wealthier housewives endured long days of work for a variety of reasons: the relatively primitive nature of the household (despite the increasing use of gas lamps, the occasional running-water bathtub or toilet, the new gas stoves and ovens); the few or part-time servants; the ideology of true womanhood and housewifery; the desire to seem indispensable to the family; and the belief that one had to set a good example and work with the servants. Although Margarete Freudenthal, a careful analyst of bourgeois households, might have agreed in part with Dohm's assessment, suggesting that by 1860 it was possible for rich women with few children to abstain from most housework, this was not the case for even most upper-middle-class women until much later.[96] In describing the home of her wealthy (banker's) family (in Mainz in the 1890s), the daughter wrote: "We had two servants who worked in our home all those years. But, what work the household of that era caused." Besides six children, her mother cared for an eight-room apartment (plus five attic rooms) which had no running water and no plumbing. Every few months the toilets were pumped out. Once a week a truck arrived with a bathtub and tanks of hot water (certainly a privilege, compared to heating the tanks themselves). By the turn of the century this family had installed electric lights and prided itself on having one of the first telephones in town.[97]

Another wealthy housewife, the wife of a Berlin judge, did no heavy housework and even had a hairdresser come to her home every day.[98] Still, she carefully supervised the maids and always did her own marketing, walking a substantial distance and purchasing provisions for a large household. She also participated in the wash days by ironing with the hired help, while the maids carried the dirty linens to the basement to be boiled and then to the attic to be dried.[99] She organized and stacked her linen closet, her "pride and joy," by herself. She mended the family wash and linens, "and was always busy with sewing and needlework."[100] She hired a seamstress to make dresses for the family, since ready-made clothing was still in its infancy in the 1880s and wealthier families preferred more careful tailoring. Twice a year she organized dinner parties with ten courses for about twenty-four people. She also kept a meticulous record of household expenses, entering the costs of food, general household services, entertainment, and clothing.[101] When her children had grown up, she volunteered these bookkeeping skills to several welfare agencies, acting as their treasurer.[102] Commenting on her managerial abilities, her daughter, one of three children, noted: "My mother was an excellent housekeeper. Everything ran so smoothly that you did not notice that she kept the strings in her hands."[103]

While wealthy women supervised and pitched in, middle-class women worked a full day despite servants. The daughter of a well-to-do middle-class family (her father was director of the Berlin gas works) recalled that her mother had a maid and at many points in her life also hired a "perfect cook." Yet she traced her own intense dislike of housework to her mother's life:

> I knew how smart mama was and how receptive she was to all education. Because I was conscious at an early age of how this woman worked herself to death with shopping, cooking and the daily duties of the household [she had seven children and ten pregnancies], I developed a certain antipathy, almost a hatred, toward this fruitless . . . waste of energy.

Despite the cook, her mother continued to work in the kitchen:

> She would have seen [her absence from the kitchen] as a transgression against . . . the health of her husband and children. [Her] blue apron and worn out hands (how nice they looked when she was sick) were a hated symbol . . . to me. Mama, herself, always saw her work as a sacrifice of love for her family.[104]

Rural life was still more difficult, partly because of the geographical limitations and partly because poorer Jews remained in villages. Wealthier Jews migrated to larger towns and cities. Born in 1893, one southern villager described her four-room apartment, consisting of a living room, one large and one smaller bedroom, and a kitchen. The bathroom had neither a bath nor running water. To take a bath, one had to heat water on the stove and fill a wooden tub. Iron stoves heated the rooms; "it was a nuisance and hard work to carry the firewood and coal from the cellar every day all winter long, to keep the place warm."[105] Members of the household included a maid and a groom who took care of the cows, horses, and goat. The women prepared breads, cakes, and cookies at home but brought them to the baker's for baking. Clothing was homemade, and the mother and grandmother planted and raised their own vegetables. This was a middle-class household: the father imported Belgian horses, and the mother had been sent to a Parisian relative for five years of schooling in France. Besides her household chores, the mother had raised three children and had managed to teach her daughter to speak French fluently. Her daughter wrote that in the evenings "we had dinner and afterwards while mother did the dishes, [father] played with me." Hardly a life of leisure, despite two servants.

Until 1920 all water for drinking, cooking, and washing had to be drawn from a well in the small town of Niederstettin.[106] Only in 1921 did the family of a merchant have its own bathroom built. The water heater (*Badeofen*) burned wood and coal, and was far more convenient than the open fire that had heated water in the courtyard in previous years.[107] Women had to work very hard to maintain a "decent" (*anständiges*) home. Mostly middle-class and lower-middle-class, Jewish men were small shopowners who sold textiles, paints, or groceries, or they were cattle, wine, or hide dealers. Their wives often had one maid and many hired a charwoman or washwoman. Still, according to one author, his mother milked their cow herself (since the maids often did not know how to do this), gardened, and made the family's bread, cakes, wine, and applesauce. Those who had no oven of their own had to arrange to bring their unbaked goods to the baker's. Newspapers served a dual purpose, first to educate and then as toilet paper.[108] The relative primitiveness of rural life, despite middle-class incomes and aspirations, kept most women exceptionally busy. Even with domestic help, many households needed more than one family member to run them, often drafting unmarried daughters, maiden aunts, and grandmothers into service. The granddaughter of Rabbi Hildesheimer wrote that her mother required various kinds of help to run her large household including six children, their parents and grandfather, two uncles, one aunt, and the rabbi's constant, unexpected visitors. The housewife made use of a cook, maid, baby nurse, governess, and her unmarried sister-in-law. On holidays she called upon extra day help.[109]

Motherhood: Bringing Up German-Jewish Children

Jewish tradition defined women by their primary work, childbearing. Excluded from the metaphysical covenant between God and man as well as from the earthly synagogue community, women's only access to God and to the holy community was in their function as mothers. The Old Testament advanced the position of women over that in previous societies, enjoining children to honor their father and mother and exalting women as teachers of the young.[110] The confluence of this tradition with the economic and social changes in the late nineteenth century combined to make motherhood central to the definition of Jewish womanhood. A consumer society, modern transportation, and a wealthier standard of living allowed more Jewish women freedom from remunerative work and from hard physical labor in the home. Perhaps a generation earlier than among most middle-class Germans, Jewish women's relegation to the home contributed to their increasing concentration on child rearing. Since a woman was no longer primarily a "helpmate," and not yet a "companion" or love mate, popular ideology focused on motherhood. The role of housewife, however, held fast, since an orderly household was, among other things, crucial to good mothering. Jewish families, and particularly women, used the opportunities created by greater wealth and fewer children to acculturate into the German middle class. In discussing fertility among Jews, and the pregnancy, childbirth, and child-rearing experiences of Jewish women, we can observe this development, tracing the shape and style assumed by the Jewish family in Imperial Germany.

Fertility

Jews began to limit their families a generation earlier than other Germans. In preceding what would become a general bourgeois trend by more than two decades, they acted less in conformity with prevailing national standards and more in line with the behavior of a financially rising urban middle class.[111] While careful to conform to the mores of the surrounding society in most cases, in this instance they set the trend, bringing the "two-child system" into being.

All through the nineteenth century Jews had fewer children than the population at large.[112] After the 1880s the rate and actual numbers dropped dramatically: between 1880 and 1900 the absolute number of births decreased by one-third; it continued to do so, lagging far behind that of the general population.[113] This was partly the result of a lower Jewish mortality rate a generation earlier, which had been followed by a lower birth rate. The birth cohorts of the 1850s had fewer children of their own in the 1880s.[114] The drop was also the result of an increase in mixed marriages, which produced fewer offspring. However, in marriages between two Jews the rate declined precipitously as well. For example, in 1866 Jews had 33 births per 1,000 of population in Prussia, compared to the general population figure of 41.1. By 1890 Jews produced 23.75 offspring to the general Prussian figure of 36.6. Between 1905 and 1910 Jews had only half as many children as other Prussians: 16.6 children per 1,000, compared to 33.[115] In the cities both groups had fewer children, but Jews again had the fewest. In Berlin, between 1871 and 1875, Jews had 27.5 compared to the general figure of 40.4. Between 1891 and 1900, Berlin Jews had 18 children per 1,000 population, compared to the non-Jewish figure of 29. By 1910 the Jewish figure in Berlin had dropped to 16 and the non-Jewish to 24.4.[116]

This can be related to the class composition of Jews as well as to the types of occupations Jews entered. John Knodel has found, for example, that areas with higher levels of savings accounts had lower fertility.[117] Since Jews were largely a middle-class and upper-middle-class group, they should not be compared to the general German population, but to their middle-class cohort. When we do this—a difficult and inexact task, because the censuses were not collected that way—we see that the gap narrows, but that Jewish families still had smaller families first. Studies of the German population indicate that families of independent academics in West Prussia limited their families to two children after 1890.[118] In the city of Hannover, for example, they had two to three children as early as 1860. These families were smaller than those of tenured civil servants of the same social position, probably because of the less secure economic position of the independent academics. Knodel found that civil servants, independent professionals, and persons in trade and transportation (all urban economic activities) led the decline,[119] and that those with secure positions still had more children than the "independents." Since Jews could not be civil servants before 1867 and were rarely accepted thereafter, many fell into the category of "independent." Thus their fertility was similar to Germans in this category. Furthermore, since most Jews engaged in commerce, they may have felt the vicissitudes of the depression of 1873–96 in their businesses more immediately than other middle-class Germans (many of whom were protected by their civil-service or army status), and limited their family size accordingly.

The Jewish occupational profile also contributed to later marriages—a form of family planning. Families expected young men to establish businesses before they married. Their later marriage age meant fewer offspring. Moreover, the importance of dowries, particularly to a group intent on expanding businesses or setting up private practices, forced parents to limit their offspring in order to provide sufficient dowries for their daughters. Thus property relations significantly influenced demographic behavior. Further, occupations in commerce and the professions increasingly steered Jews toward urban centers. In 1900, 24% of Prussian Jews lived in Berlin and 64% in cities with over 20,000 inhabitants. But only 7% and 32%, respectively, of Protestants lived in these environments.[120] Smaller city quarters often precluded large families, but it is also likely that couples limited the size of their families in order to move to the city. Large families could be a hindrance to those who hoped to take advantage of the mobility and the educational and economic advances that the final emancipation laws had promised. Although we do not know *how* the modern mentality arose, whereby couples decided whether they "could afford" another child, we can quite specifically point to the 1880s as the time when this first began to happen on a broad scale among Jews.

Cultural traditions may have been a factor in attitudes toward birth control. Jewish tradition (unlike the teachings of the Church) never prohibited birth control in an all-encompassing way. The duty of procreation was primary in Jewish law, but where conception had to be prevented for the sake of the wife's health, contraception was mandated. Abstinence was not an alternative, because it could interfere with marital happiness. Therefore Jews did not have to defy an absolute taboo.[121] Psychological factors probably also played a decisive role in family limitation. Jews must have had second thoughts about having large families in a society in which a racist anti-Semitism reminded them ever more stridently, only a few years after their final, legal emancipation, that they remained outsiders. Further, they consciously strove to avoid identification with Eastern European immigrant Jews, who bore the brunt of racist attacks. A common German stereotype held that Polish Jews, to quote Marx, "multiply like lice."[122] German Jews denounced these stereotypes, though they may have believed them, and tried to avoid similar behavior.[123]

Anti-Semitism was not alone in contributing toward a psychological predisposition to limit family size. As already mentioned, the Jewish population, far more than the Christian one, was in constant flux.[124] Jews moved from villages to towns to cities to the capital city and, unlike their neighbors, they mostly moved in family units. Sometimes the same family made several such moves. This general migration and instability may have caused a feeling of uprootedness not conducive to considering a large family or raising one. Modern demographers further stress "social isolation" as a factor in the fertility decline. Their close cultural and social ties resulted in Jews being a more self-contained, closed community. This "provided a situation in which changing norms regarding family . . . limitation could spread rapidly and relatively independently of the rest of German society."[125] Moreover, since the German bourgeoisie considered large families disorderly and disreputable—the satirical periodical *Simplicissimus*, for example, rarely depicted families above a certain social level with more than three children and often with only one or two[126]—the established German-Jewish bourgeoisie, already limiting their own offspring, could feel validated in their decisions.

Finally, women's initiatives may have played a crucial role in family limitation. Within the couple, it is likely that the woman was more conscious of the dangers of childbirth and sensitive to issues of birth control. Although the Jewish female death rate in childbearing years was lower than that of the overall population, Jewish women still ran considerable risks.[127] Also, as we shall see in chapter 3, marriage was often an occasion for migration. Women, particularly those without adequate dowries, frequently "married down" into smaller cities, towns, or villages. In the case of Nonnenweier, for example, over half of all wives married before 1880 had been born elsewhere.[128] These wives may have brought "city" ideas regarding fewer children with them, influencing their husbands to limit family size in hopes of joining the general Jewish flight from the countryside. Further, when they married, Jewish women were on the average older and better educated than their non-Jewish counterparts.[129] Many could count on a dowry as a power lever. For these reasons, they may have exerted more power within the family and have pushed to lighten the strains and hazards of repeated pregnancies and childbirths. Still, it is impossible to prove conclusively what role most women played in the decision to limit fertility. Despite the general condemnation of all women as "lazy" or "selfish," and specific admonitions in Jewish periodicals, all we really know is that couples practiced birth control and that some women took the initiative.[130]

The memoir of one husband, married in 1909, is suggestive: "Before our wedding, she was able to make me agree that the first year of the marriage should be a *Schonjahr* [protected year] and sought to justify this with youth, frailty and other things. Before this year was over she suggested a 'vacation trip' [by herself] to Berlin." After the birth of their daughter in 1911, his wife wanted a *Schonzeit* of at least five years—"which, alas, I had to agree to." From the context, several things are evident. First, the wife used no contraception, because when she tried to do so without her husband's knowledge her doctor "sensibly did not fulfill her wishes, but instead set her head straight." The manner of birth control was therefore either abstinence or coitus interruptus or a mixture of both, the most commonly used strategies of Wilhelmine society. Second, the wife was candid and forceful about her requirements, much to her husband's dismay. He makes much of his own frustration and his previously (premarital) passionate nature in reporting on these *Schonjahre*. Third, the idea of a *Schonjahr* was a rather common notion, since the writer does not explain it or comment on it the way other memoir writers do when they suspect their children or future generations will not understand a particular phenomenon. He assumes the reader will recognize the concept.[131] Some women, then, could and did take birth control into their own hands. In fact, some husbands preferred that their wives assume the responsibility. Rahel Straus, a medical doctor who started her practice in 1908, told of a rabbi's wife who came to her for birth-control information. The rabbi had made it explicitly clear that what his wife did was not his business (nor, one supposes, his sin).[132] Finally, we cannot rule out the famous migraine headaches of this era or notions of female purity and asexuality as forms of conscious or unconscious birth control.

When birth control did not work, women resorted to illegal abortions as a last resort. An "appendicitis" operation could end an unwanted pregnancy, as could a brief "vacation" away from home.[133] One man discovered that his mother's death from a "heart attack" had really been the result of an abortion. His mother, close to forty years old, had been warned against having another child after a long pause since the birth of her four other children. Also, her son surmised that "social apprehensions may have played a role, especially the worry that an increase in expenses would affect the other children." Still, this did not ameliorate his blanket condemnation of his mother. He concluded that the "main reasons" for the abortion had been "comfort, pleasure-seeking and fear."[134]

Owing to the illegal nature of abortions, only those convicted counted in the abortion statistics. It is therefore difficult to judge the extent to which Jewish women made use of this method to limit their family size. Jewish demographers suggested that contraception was the main form of birth control, arguing that Jews had fewer abortions than non-Jews.[135] This may be true despite the poor sources, since middle-class and upper-middle-class women in general had greater success with contraception than did the poor. Middle-class women, including the vast majority of the German-Jewish population, could have relied on more expensive birth-control measures, including pessaries, syringes, and condoms, which, like abortifacients, could be found advertised in women's magazines, in doctors' health manuals, and even on soap wrappers.

Pregnancy, Birth, and Nursing

Pregnancy still carried many myths and taboos with it. When a woman was "expecting" (*in guter Hoffnung*), doctors and parents admonished her to refrain from any and all exertion. A train ride could be considered too risky. While many middle-class women took such advice to heart, the more modern ones resisted. For example Agatha Bleichröder, the niece of Bismarck's banker, opposed her gynecologist's advice. Her "modern attitudes" determined her decisions to take a long train ride from Breslau to Berlin to care for a sick sister and to accompany her husband to the Alps for some mountain hiking. For 1897 this was "very unusual."[136]

Most childbirths took place at home. In the smaller towns and cities of southern and western Germany, home births occurred well into the 1920s for Jews and other Germans.[137] In Jewish homes midwives, frequently Jewish ones, prepared for and assisted with the birth. In the years immediately preceding World War I, doctors might be called in at the very last moment. Usually they came to check on the baby, rather than to assist the mother. In some villages female friends assisted the mother and decorated her room with amulets and cabalistic drawings to fend off evil spirits (see chapter 2).[138]

In cities, too, women generally gave birth at home. A man from Breslau reported (in 1911) that, although "it was not usual for people from bourgeois circles to go to clinics," when his wife's labor began, "we pulled our beds apart in the best of moods, and set up a bed for me in the guest room. I didn't sleep a wink that night even though I only had to get the midwife in the morning." Most husbands considered the birth a purely female event and made themselves scarce during labor and delivery. A few husbands attended the births. Our Breslau diarist stayed for the birth partly because his wife wanted him there, but also out of curiosity, to see his child's "entrance into life." He remained with his wife during the entire delivery, "sat and stood next to this suffering woman all these painful hours, and probably suffered emotionally as much as the woman physically."[139] Even in Berlin, the custom was home deliveries. In the 1880s an upper-middle-class Berlin Jewish woman had her six children at home with a Jewish midwife's help. Her daughter recalled the midwife telling her mother after one birth, "Why do you say 'thank God?' Once you have it behind you, you have it ahead of you again."[140]

Jewish bourgeois women began to use hospitals only in the first decade of the twentieth century. Yet even where they provided an accessible alternative, women chose home births. For example, Rahel Straus, herself a doctor, had all her four children at home. She preferred the tradition of bringing children into the world

> in their own home. . . . A normal birth is not a disease. It belongs to the life of the family. I understand it well: for the doctor it is more convenient to direct a birth in a . . . hospital, but for a woman in normal condition it is a much different feeling to be in her own home. One is not a number as in the hospital. . . . I . . . directed my household from bed.[141]

Still, a few middle-class women did venture into clinics. In 1906 Elisabeth Bab, the (Protestant) wife of the Jewish theater critic Julius Bab, gave birth to her daughter in the Clinic of Women Doctors in Berlin, where, in contrast to the university clinic, babies remained in the mother's room at night.[142]

Immediately after childbirth, most middle-class women, in town and city alike, stayed in bed for three to four weeks. Thereafter, the religiously observant made their first excursion a visit to the synagogue. Three to four weeks was an artificially imposed rest period, one dictated by contemporary medical standards and applied to the middle classes only. Nevertheless,it is apparent that bed rest, despite its weakening effect, was a welcome hiatus. During their confinement most women could rely on some help. Poor women helped one another or depended upon charitable or familial assistance; middle-class women hired temporary help or welcomed assistance from female relatives[143]; wealthy women and career women hired long-term baby nurses. One religious middle-class woman referred to her convalescence after ten childbirths in as many years as "her yearly vacation and recuperation trip."[144]

In families that could afford to hire one, a Jewish nurse (*Wärterin*) or a temporary, practical nurse (*Wochenpflegerin*) cared for the mother and baby. Among poorer Jews only the birth of a boy merited such help. The preparations leading to his circumcision a week later and the party that followed it, the Brith Milah, were too strenuous for the convalescing mother.[145] An urban couple (1911) with a "modest" middle-class household kept the practical nurse an extra two weeks. The young mother breast-fed, but did not feel sure of herself with her first baby.[146] In fact, the nurse often taught new mothers how to care for their infants. More privileged women hired long-term help and some even took vacations by themselves shortly after childbirth. Nine weeks after the birth of her first baby and soon after the birth of the second, the wife of a lawyer took an extended mountain vacation to "recuperate" from childbirth. Both times she left the infants with her husband and the baby nurse, and in neither case does she seem to have experienced the slightest qualms about it. Obviously the babies would survive and thrive, and her social milieu, which defined middle-class women as frail and fragile, would accept—perhaps encourage—her vacations.[147] Upon her return, her schedule consisted of spending mornings with the babies. In the afternoons the maid baby-sat while she attended to her other responsibilities. Still, this is an exceptional case, one in which some women benefited from their supposed fragility—the wealthier they were, the more fragile—with a certain amount of ease and freedom. Ironically, this behavior flew in the face of the emerging cult of motherhood, but no one seemed to notice.

For the few Jewish women with professional careers, help with their infants was essential. Still, their worries and their guilt at their unusual life-style compelled them to be "supermothers." These concerns—and the relatively new notion of "scientific motherhood"—may explain the compulsive care with which Jenny Apolant, a feminist journalist, kept her infant's health records. For over one year (1900–1901) she noted, in painstaking detail down to the last half Zwieback and the exact time of day, the baby's meals, snacks, and digestive habits as well as its weight and its teething development.[148] In her autobiography Rahel Straus recalled the times when she had to attend medical emergencies while still breast-feeding her infants. The baby nurse had to give the babies bottles of tea to hold them over. She also emphasized the extreme difficulties of trying to balance her career with motherhood: "I was never free again. The best maid did not really calm me and the thought of the child always accompanied me. . . . I always knew that I, who wanted to have a full-time career, had to be doubly certain that the child lacked nothing and missed nothing."[149]

Women could choose among several alternatives to nourish their infants: breast-feeding, bottle-feeding, and wet-nursing. Jewish women generally breast-fed their babies, although bottle-feeding gained increasing acceptance by the end of the Imperial era. In the early decades neither pasteurization nor sterilization were widespread, and the danger of infant mortality loomed large if one resorted to bottles during the early months of the first year.[150] In Germany there were sharp regional differences in breast-feeding.[151] Nevertheless, the middle and lower-middle classes generally continued to breast-feed, especially in rural areas but also in the cities, through World War I, although improvements in hygiene gradually made bottle-feeding an acceptable alternative.

Despite their heavy representation in urban areas, where breast-feeding declined between 1885 and 1910,[152] infant mortality statistics were always lower for Jews than for other Germans.[153] Jewish customs conceivably played a significant role in maintaining breast-feeding and reducing infant mortality. Traditional patterns among Jews had been beneficial to health, for example the custom of hand washing and the rarity of alcoholism and venereal disease. Also, concern for the well-being of nursing mothers was an age-old tradition, the sources of which could be found in the earliest Jewish codes and laws. In the Talmud, for example, nursing mothers were supposed to work less and eat more; they could nurse even against their husbands' wishes; and they had to nurse against their own desires, if their husbands wanted them to do so. Husbands also had to support divorced wives who decided to nurse, though divorcees could not be compelled to nurse.

Fewer cases of illegitimacy also help explain the lower rates of infant mortality.[154] Illegitimate children suffered from higher rates of disease and death than legitimate children. Further, wealth and middle-class amenities allowed for better nutrition and medical care. Yet class factors are at best ambiguous. Even when comparisons are made within the same social class, Jewish rates are lower. Among poor Jews in the rural German countryside as well as among proletarian Jews in major urban centers (of England and the United States), infant mortality was dramatically lower than in similar groups.[155] Doctors credited greater frequency of breast-feeding by Jewish mothers with reducing infant diseases.

Individual memoirs also testified to the importance of breast-feeding among Jews.[156] Rosa Vogelstein, a feminist activist and the wife of a rabbi, breast-fed all five of her children throughout the 1870s and 1880s (Stettin).[157] Still, some Jewish women used cow's or goat's milk successfully. One woman, the only Jewish woman in Constance when she first moved there in the 1860s, recalled that few of the women she knew nursed their babies: "the natural nourishment for a child [was] cow's milk." [158] She, too, bottle-fed. Although breast-feeding predominated, the decision was ultimately a highly personal one. Jenny Apolant and Rahel Straus, for example, two extremely prolific professionals, chose opposite solutions. The former decided to bottle-feed her only child around 1900, documenting every gram the baby consumed, while the latter breast-fed all her children between 1909 and 1914.

Only the wealthiest families hired wet nurses. Statistics from Berlin, shortly before 1900, indicate that about 1,000 wet nurses found employment there.[159] Memoirs, statistics, and Jewish newspapers verify that the wet nurse was an exceptional phenomenon. Wealthy Jewish women who hired a wet nurse (*Amme*) frequently did so because they could not nurse and still distrusted bottle-feeding.[160] Julchen Herzfeld, for example, tried breast-feeding but only succeeded with her second, third, and ninth children. The other seven infants had wet nurses (1868–86, Posen).[161] Agathe Bleichröder failed to nurse despite all her efforts, and hired a wet nurse for her first child.[162] She tried again with her second baby and resorted to a wet nurse only when she developed a serious infection.[163]

Some women chose not to nurse. A gendered class consciousness which depicted wealthy women as fragile, and breast-feeding as unattractive, unfeminine, and lower-class, played a major role in the decision to hire a wet nurse. "Because it was uncomely," the young mother in the novel *Jenny Treibel* refused to nurse.[164] A wet nurse signified status and leisure to an upper middle class eager to see its women as ornaments. Doctors who catered to an upper-middle-class clientele often discouraged their patients from breast-feeding, which they considered too exhausting and unattractive for such women. One Jewish woman recorded: "In those days, doctors did not find it advantageous for a 'lady' to nurse. Her fragile health could suffer, she could lose her good figure. Nursing women had to eat huge quantities of meal-pap, so that they expanded like yeast dumplings. So [breast-feeding] was not pushed. . . . Also, doctors always had a few wet nurses on hand."[165] Even those who needed a wet nurse frequently attached status consciousness to her hiring. The reasons they gave for maintaining a wet nurse were not always the actual reasons, but the "acceptable" ones. One memoir recorded that a mother of seven children (1860s) used a wet nurse because nursing was considered "too strenuous" for women of the "better classes."[166] What the writer failed to weigh was that this mother ran a large household, always had ten or more people to dinner, and also worked in the family business.[167]

The wet nurse was usually a single mother or one whose own baby had recently died and who was still capable of nursing. She almost always lived with the family, slept near the baby, and took primary care of "her" charge. Sometimes she came with her own baby and breast-fed both infants.[168] She was often financially desperate. In one case a wet nurse continued breast-feeding long after she had stopped producing milk. As the infant grew thinner, the family discovered the situation and fed the infant donkey's milk.[169] The wet nurse was usually treated better than the other servants. In Berlin wet nurses stemming from the Spreewald region, renowned for their robust country health and dressed in traditional folk costumes, became status symbols.[170] The wet nurse and baby were usually inseparable. The nurse accompanied the family on all holidays and trips.[171] She stayed about a year, sometimes longer. Charlotte Wolff (born 1901, Riesenburg), who later became a doctor, recalled the profound influence of her wet nurse: "A Polish woman had been the most important person in my babyhood. She was my wetnurse, and her milk fed me for a year, if not longer. She stayed with us until I was two, and my mother later said I was never the same again after she left."[172]

Whereas bourgeois circles generally accepted wet-nursing as a healthy alternative to a mother's breast-feeding, some Jewish critics rejected it. One Jewish newspaper read by a lower-middle-class and working population published a story denouncing wet-nursing and other upper-class child-rearing habits. In 1912 the *Israelitisches Wochenblatt* serialized a story about a "selfish," "egocentric" Jewish woman who hired a wet nurse from the Spreewald. "Under the influence of . . . luxury and cynical modern ideas . . . she watched her child drink another's maternal milk."[173]

Child Rearing: Class Formation and German-Jewish Identity

After infancy, wealthier women hired children's nurses to care for their babies. Others relied on maids-of-all-work to help out. Relatives, grandmothers, unmarried

Mother, nanny, and children out for a stroll. Leipzig, 1901. *Schild-Scheier Collection. Courtesy of the Leo Baeck Institute, New York.*

sisters, and maiden aunts took active part in bringing up children. Some lived with the family, particularly in the first decades of the Imperial period. Others came for extended visits of up to a year. Although the baby was ultimately the mother's charge, responsibility for it remained more diffuse, divided among many interested parties.

In the early years of the Imperial era, when many women still worked with their husbands, they divided their time between mothering and all other duties. Motherhood was not their exclusive job. Whereas most still breast-fed, and therefore devoted a considerable portion of time to their infants, they attended to household and business chores as well. As in traditional Judaism, women attended to religious, economic, and maternal obligations. Only as religious and economic duties became less onerous, did children take on more importance. Commenting on her own childhood (1860s) and that of her siblings, a woman pointed out that her mother worked in the family store: "We three grew up, mostly left to ourselves, without a governess and our mother having rarely time for us, all went well. We had a subscription to a lending library and used to read several children's tales every day."[174]

By the third decade of the Imperial era, most Jewish bourgeois women focused on child rearing as their primary function. Just as Jewish families began to practice birth control, the sentimentalization of the mother/child dyad reached its height in the surrounding culture, perpetuated as well by Jewish circles. Motherhood, that cluster of shifting behaviors and ideas about women's role in the family and child care, was being redefined once again. Women now gained social power as mothers and socializers of children, whereas previous generations had acquired prestige as helpmates in business. Although the household, as we have seen, was extremely important to women, their relegation to the home contributed toward their increasing concentration on child care. A generation before other Germans, Jewish mothers had fewer children and more time to devote to them. In an age in which family planning became a reality, and Jews in particular had fewer offspring, the sentimentalization of childhood grew inversely and motherhood became central to the definition of womanhood. Increasingly, advice literature and popular ideology addressed mothers as the primary socializers of their offspring and suggested gentler methods of child rearing, ostensibly more compatible with "female nature." Still, traditional values regarding men as "head of the family" persisted, perhaps to mask the transition to new conditions and to make these more palatable. By the 1890s the sentimentalization of childhood and the "century of the child" were in their early stages.

The German legal code gave fathers complete control over their children. The father's opinion ranked over his wife's, and he had the right to use whatever financial assets the children owned.[175] Only after her husband's death did the wife have rights over her children, and these could be limited as well.[176] Jewish tradition was more ambivalent than German law. Excluded from the important public function of synagogue participation, women were expected to fulfill a moral and ethical role within the family as well as to perpetuate gender roles. This gave rise to a rigid stereotype of women as inherently closer to the physical, material, and secular world, while men remained in the spiritual one. In Eastern Europe this went so far that many women ran the home entirely on their own—often earning a livelihood as well—while husbands remained relatively remote from all practical details. Thus women's role—more assertive in the home, in contrast to their minor role in the organized religion—was sanctified by time and custom.

Outside observers as well as memoirs tend to confirm this image of the mother as one with direct, not delegated, authority over the children.[177] It is always difficult to dissect the complex interactions between husbands and wives, and all the more so from the perspective of their children, who are usually the memoir writers and who are also affected by the gender-role expectations of their own times. Yet from memoirs, contemporary observers, and novels, one can posit that Jewish women had more power in the family, and particularly over their children, than did other German women. Despite the general sexist norms which preached obedience to the husband, Jewish wives probably demanded and received more respect and authority from their mates than was typical in other middle-class families. This may have been the result of the older marriage age or better education of Jewish women, or the wealth women brought into the marriage partnership. Furthermore, the traditions of a high-sex-ratio society—in which there were more males than females, and females were therefore a valued commodity and treated commensurately[178]—lay not far behind them. Also, most Jews were newly rich. Even in the 1890s they had grandmothers or mothers who had been partners in family enterprises, or had supported their families themselves. These women had maintained the authority which went along with their contributions as helpmates and partners, and younger couples noticed the esteem in which older women were still held. Moreover, and importantly, where husbands were absent, the wife's centrality to the family was a source of influence for women.[179] Although no longer itinerant peddlers, as they had been for the most part before midcentury, Jewish fathers remained absorbed in business and commercial travels or long shop hours. Other men of the same class, many of whom held civil-service posts, spent more time at home and therefore had the opportunity to enforce their domestic authority. Also, civil servants, secure in their careers, may have been less dependent upon their wives' help and cooperation than Jewish businessmen and traders, and hence may have been less deferential.

Finally, Jewish men may have chosen to abdicate power in the home. Confronting an aggressive, often anti-Semitic world, they themselves may have needed support, bartering some authority in exchange for peace and friendship. Others refused to deal with household issues. The daughter of a manufacturer recalled that "mother ruled in our home," but added that it was because her father could not be bothered by its petty goings-on.[180] Sigmund Freud's letters to his fiancée hint at yet another kind of accommodation. Writing about the "absurd" ideas of John Stuart Mill on women, he asked: "Am I to think of my delicate, sweet *girl* as a competitor? . . . I will make every effort to get her out of the competitive role into the quiet, undisturbed activity of *my* home." (Emphases added.) Anxious about her seeming lack of "yielding docility," he later wrote, "I know after all how sweet you are, . . . I will let you rule the house as much as you wish, and you will reward me with your sweet love and by rising above all those weaknesses for which women are so often despised."[181]

It is unusual to discover in Jewish memoirs what came to be a cliché in German literature and cartoons, the "angel in the street, but devil at home," or the husband/tyrant who, meek at work, lorded over his wife and children as soon as he entered the front door.[182] Nor are there significant examples of the father as main disciplinarian, as in other German families,[183] or of Jewish mothers waiting for their husbands to mete out justice or retribution. And while fathers were respected, they were neither omnipresent nor overbearing, as in the civil servant's family in Gabrielle Reuter's novel *Aus guter Familie*, "where one perpetually had to take Papa's opinion into account."[184] Rural observers noted that Jewish women raised the children and that, in general, they had a more respected and independent position than their Christian counterparts.[185] In fact in Jewish homes, as a result of this distribution of responsibility, the strict mother and mild father may have predominated. Of her childhood, one woman related: "When my father slapped me, she [her mother] did not talk to him for a week. But she slapped me."[186] Although the father's strictness may be mentioned, the mother's actual behavior is more often described. She enforced parental decisions and rules and arbitrated immediate events.

In memoirs written by Jews who grew up in Imperial Germany, fathers take a secondary role in the home. Their children acknowledge their business or intellectual pursuits. In fact, these achievements often take up the greater part of the memoirs. Nevertheless, the fathers' personal contact with their offspring is not particularly lauded. One daughter noted: "What did he really know about his many children? He certainly loved them, but he did not find the right path to them. . . . And I loved [him] very much, but he was . . . an object of respect."[187] Another woman reflected on her father's strictness, but added that she rarely saw him: "Contradictions were not allowed. . . . During my childhood I hardly ever spoke with my father, except on those holidays when he took an excursion with us."[188]

A father's many absences modified his impact, even if he was domineering. One father spent one-third of the year on business trips, and "even when he was in Breslau, we children did not see much of him, mostly only at the midday meal." They also saw him on Sunday afternoons when the whole family ate dinner at their grandmother's home.[189] Describing her husband, whom she considered a good father, Rahel Straus depicted a mental rather than a physical absence: "For a man, his career is the main content of his life, everything else is secondary. The entire house is set up to give the man of the house peace and comfort so that he can pursue his career undisturbed."[190] She continued:

> I have often found that in the biography of a man, even in an autobiography, his children are hardly mentioned. And that is easy to explain. For the father, the child is a new, great moment of happiness, but it stands next to his life, which changes in no way. He has greater responsibilities as a result of his children. . . . These lead him even more deeply . . . into his career. Nothing changes in his daily life, in the way he organizes his day, in his work.[191]

Fathers did not play a prominent role in the daily lives of their children and may not have been as emotionally accessible to them as their mothers. It does not follow, however, that fathers played insignificant roles. In particular, daughters who later pursued professions or became feminists often either credited their fathers with their own intellectual development, or identified with them (even when the father had opposed the daughter's ambitions), rejecting the role model of their thoroughly conventional mothers.[192]

Fewer children and increasing wealth meant that the physical work of mothering eased. However, the cultural job expanded. Greater maternal attention, or interference, was required to present well-behaved children, products of a *gute Kinderstube* (literally a "good children's room," but actually a proper bourgeois upbringing).[193] While men earned money, women prepared children not only for the class into which they had been born, but also for the class to which their parents aspired. Training for social mobility, with its obvious economic repercussions, lay in the hands of women.

Jewish mothers attempted to be arbiters of German culture, instructing their children in the gender-specific ways and manners of the male and female bourgeoisie—in fact, creating a Jewish bourgeoisie every bit as stylized as its Christian counterpart. They were uniquely equipped to do so. Excluded from religious learning, women had acquainted themselves with secular culture even before the ghetto walls came down. In this way they preserved their cultural presence in the family, enhancing it with very high attendance in advanced secular schools. They imparted both high culture and the ideas and customs of the social classes they emulated (and to which they also belonged). Their education, and the appreciation of German culture which they shared with their offspring, enhanced their family's status as much as their heavy furniture, fancy salons, and decorative accessories. Further, the Jewish middle class, like other members of the bourgeoisie, was dependent on character and on intellectual (rather than manual) skills. Its children would likely live by their wits and temperament. Mothers therefore inculcated values of responsibility, dependability, and trustworthiness in their children. Character formation and moral education were essential goals of good parenting.

Jews also had special issues to confront as they settled into the bourgeoisie. They were convinced that their emancipation had been earned by their *Bildung*, their eager acceptance of German Enlightenment ideals. Because they continued to link the improvement of their status to their own self-betterment, it was essential to them to impart these ideas and behaviors to their children, to display the "good tone" and cultivation necessary to distinguish themselves from lower social classes.

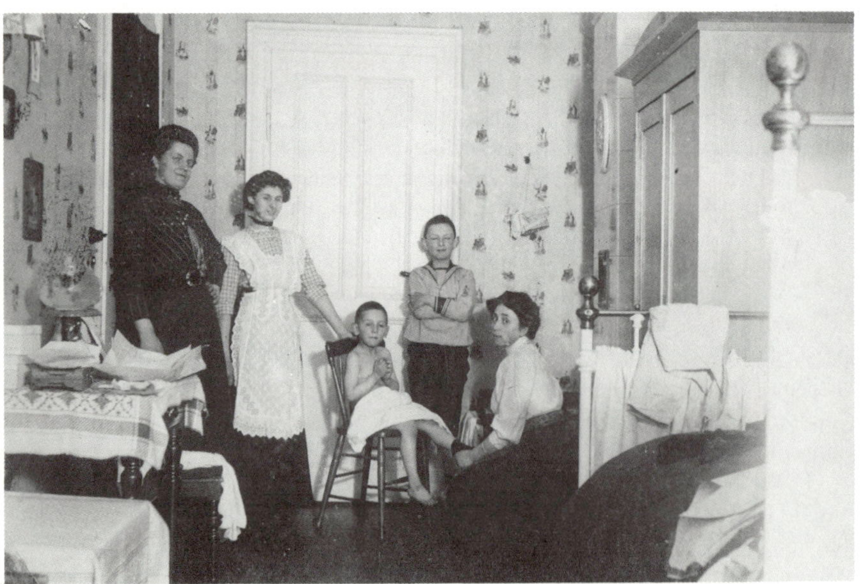

The *Kinderzimmer,* or nursery. Mother, governess, servant, and children. Leipzig, 1911. *Schild-Scheier Collection. Courtesy of the Leo Baeck Institute, New York.*

Moreover, they had to restrain their children from behavior attributed to Jewish children by anti-Semites. The latter depicted Eastern European Jewish children, but by implication all Jewish children, as noisy, dirty, undisciplined, unhealthy, unathletic, and unmannerly—in other words, *ungebildet*. Anti-Semites castigated "Jewish" national or cultural attributes. They were quick to hurl the epithet "just like in a Jewish school" or "Jewish haste" in their disdain, and Jews were eager to show by their calm and mannerly bearing that these slurs had no semblance of reality. The Central Verein Deutscher Staatsbürger Jüdischen Glaubens, the major Jewish defense organization, reminded parents and children to display greater caution and self-control than other Germans, and others warned them not to use *Jargon* (Yiddish) or gesticulate "too wildly."[194] Niceness, gentility, and civility—"the very medium of Western social interaction"—became the shibboleth of the Jew seeking admission to a "world of strangers."[195] When a friend of Freud's complained that Jews had bad manners, Freud agreed. "That is true, they are not always adapted to social life. Before . . . emancipation in 1818 . . . they did not go out in mixed society. Since then, they have had much to learn."[196] It is no wonder that in asserting their claim to German culture, in an era in which the popular historian Heinrich von Treitschke could depict them as "nothing else but German-speaking Orientals,"[197] Jews enforced "a modulation of tone, a lowering of the decibel level"[198] upon themselves and their children.

Jews embedded their claims to Germanness in their family life. To be a middle-class family was an essential part of their Jewish identity (as will be shown in the next chapter), but it was also integral to their German identity. According to a prominent liberal rabbi, who was arguing that Jewishness complemented German culture, a belief in God's system meant "concern for the welfare of the state, . . . the cultivation of loyalty, reverence and family feeling."[199] Moritz Oppenheim's paintings of Jewish family life, immensely popular among German Jews, emulated German middle-class *Gemütlichkeit*[200] and enclosed Judaism and German patriotism in scenes of middle-class family life. Jews admired and copied the "tranquil and steady life" of the middle classes.[201] Their own cultured, respectable bourgeois families announced they were at one with other Germans.

Bourgeois Jewish women encouraged their children to enjoy the attributes of a cultured and "modern" life. In the cities mothers spent more structured time with their children than in the countryside, where children played outdoors and indoors and where time and space flowed more casually. Women organized the day for urban children. "The timing of meals and walks was regulated by the woman."[202] Walks were important activities for children, who seemed especially to enjoy accompanying their mothers to the markets.[203] These walks also provided "educational" opportunities. One woman recalled how her mother made botany lessons out of simple strolls, much to the delight of her children. Others have less favorable memories of walks. Their parents constantly reminded them of their posture and demeanor.[204] Of such walks, one writer despaired:

> Naturally one expected that we children would behave ourselves like the offspring of a well-behaved middle class family. What torture these Saturday or Sunday walks through the old park [were] . . . with the . . . lake upon which very snobbish looking swans swam, which looked as class-conscious as many of the people

> who admired them! We were all dressed very carefully and were expected to return as neatly as when we left. What a chain [*Fessel*] for a lively child![205]

These criticisms remind us of the silent, internal costs of class formation. Middle-class children learned that even their bodies expressed class and gender boundaries.[206] Parents demanded bourgeois respectability of themselves and their offspring; acculturating Jewish parents may have insisted on even greater public decorum in their desire to fit in.

Walks represented only one aspect of children's physical education. Mothers saw to it that children took part in sporting and other physical activities from hiking to swimming, ice skating, and gymnastics. Even daughters participated in the more strenuous exercises, remarking on the newness of these physical ventures for girls and the role of chaperones at some of them. Well-mannered young ladies had to be accompanied, even on ice-skating excursions, where their mothers sat around fires, "turning themselves as if on a spit." Bike riding was the one sport mothers could not chaperone.[207] Jews also tried to harden their children to the elements, much like other Germans. In response to her query regarding child rearing, Jenny Apolant's cousin, a doctor, sent her the following poem:

> So that you can bring her up better,
> Send her outdoors in all kinds of weather,
> If it rains, freezes or snows, . . .
> And, in fact, in light-weight clothes.[208]

Children complained of their rigorous encounters with the German climate. One mother made her daughter walk to school every day (1912): "by rain or shine, ice or snow, which for a six-year-old, took about an hour each way. I suffered. But—perhaps it was good training for difficult times to come."[209]

In Imperial Germany health was equated with patriotism. Germans placed great value on physical upbringing, on the bearing, fortitude, and sports abilities of young people. Jews strove to achieve standards set by their society. They also desired to appear robust and "German" in contrast to the pale, unhealthy image which anti-Semites foisted upon them. Whereas Goethe had commented on the wan, sickly ghetto Jews of Frankfurt, one generation after Emancipation German Jews strained every muscle to distance themselves from that stereotype. Most likely, they also hoped to avoid being associated with the Eastern European Jewish immigrant, cast as work-worn and sickly. Finally, anti-Semitism caused Jews to worry about future physical (as well as emotional) privations. The Central Verein, for example, urged Jewish mothers not to spoil their children but to bring up strong children capable of physical and emotional endurance:

> Mothers must raise a hearty . . . stock that does not suffer from too soft an upbringing. . . . It would not hurt to have more strictness, more naturalness, more simplicity in the guidance and education of our children. The person who does not learn to do without in childhood will have a difficult time being satisfied with little in later life. And who has more reason than we Jews to accustom our children to privation?[210]

Mothers took charge of educating healthy minds as well as bodies. In their gender-specific tasks of putting children to bed or entertaining them, for example,

By the end of the century, bourgeois women could ride bicycles without provoking outrage. Here Martha Kästner stands behind her bicycle in a photograph taken in 1899. *Schild-Scheier Collection. Courtesy of the Leo Baeck Institute, New York.*

women transmitted German (and other favorite European) folktales, fairy tales, and literature. It was her mother who loved *Hermann und Dorothea*, Walter Scott, Dickens, and Heine, according to one woman.[211] Jacob Picard recalled that at the same time he was learning his first Hebrew bedtime prayer, his grandmother read Grimm's fairy tales to him.[212] Another favorite form of entertainment before the advent of the gramophone or radio was reading aloud. Many read the German classics or took roles in German classical plays. Henriette Hirsch recalled taking part in *Don Carlos, The Maiden of Orleans*, and *Iphigenia*. This was a common and popular pastime in many families who adopted Schiller, Goethe, and Lessing for their general renown,[213] and because, as symbols of an Enlightenment tradition and *Bildung*, Jews could read progressive messages in their works. When German Jews remarked, "Quotations from Goethe were part of every meal,"[214] they were not only emphasizing a Jewish allegiance to Goethe as "a bridge toward acceptance through identification with Germany's cultural hero"[215]; they were also explicitly acknowledging the family context—the meal—in which cultural transmission took place. *Bildung* and family, Goethe at mealtime, constituted a German-Jewish identity fostered by parents and implemented by women.

Jews also enjoyed Theodor Fontane and "lighter" authors.[216] Further, young women and girls read the popular "low-brow" literature. While their brothers had to concentrate on the ancient classics as part of their *Gymnasium* education, girls could indulge in popular romances (the "*Backfisch*" *Romane*) which transported them "to a second world."[217] Although her brother admonished her for reading "junk," one woman recalled her enjoyment and noted that she also learned about social customs this way.[218] This was certainly the case for Fontane novels. His depiction of the bourgeois milieu, its habits and foibles, was probably read as much for information and careful emulation as for entertainment.

Women also eagerly subscribed to newspapers and periodicals, probably as much for the fashion and style they endorsed as for the news they conveyed. Many memoir writers recall that their mothers eagerly read the newspapers.[219] The *Gartenlaube* gave advice to housewives regarding style and culture as well as, for example, information on the newest vogue in domestics' uniforms.[220] Jacob Picard wrote that his mother subscribed to the *Gartenlaube*, which "typified the cultural and social level of bourgeois society at the end of the nineteenth century. It was . . . my first introduction to the world of arts. . . . Until I was 13 . . . [I] was fascinated by this reading matter."[221] While his father read the local news and his grandfather subscribed to the Orthodox *Israelit*, it was his mother's reading matter which facilitated his introduction to the German bourgeois world.

Mothers bought the toys, subscribed to the children's journals, and supervised the children's play. Mothers with some musical talent gave music lessons to their children. One woman recalled: "When we were two years old, we had a daily music lesson. With great care, she [the mother] taught us the story and the music of . . . 'Hansel and Gretel,' before she took us to see it. I was four."[222] To play an instrument—usually the piano, for girls—and to have an appreciation for music in general were essential attributes of a bourgeois child's education, one for which the mother was not only responsible but often an active contributor.

Most Jewish children enjoyed the games and toys that absorbed other German children, except at Hanukkah and Purim, when they played special games. Dolls, doll houses, and miniature kitchens occupied girls, and drums, guns, toy horses, and trains entertained boys.[223] Mothers shared the scraps from their sewing baskets with their daughters and let them bake meals for their dolls (*Puppenmahlzeit*) as well as cookies for themselves.[224] Most women looked back on their girlhood play experiences fondly. A few commented upon their dislike of dolls and preference for a brother's or boy cousin's train set.[225] With few exceptions, even later feminists ignored the socialization to motherhood and women's role that was so deeply ingrained in childhood play. Children's journals were also segregated by sex: boys read *Der gute Kamerad*; girls, *Das junge Mädchen*.[226] Jewish journals promoted themes similar to those in other German journals. Children learned that "the highest praise that one can give a child is to call it an obedient child."[227] "More mature female youth" learned that "to help others and to do good, gives every loving woman's soul a boundless treasure of satisfaction."[228]

Amusements with patriotic themes were more overt and more consciously recalled than gender-segregated play. Mothers dressed their children in patriotic garb and decorated the children's rooms with favorite toys, and often with historical pictures and portraits. Adele Rosenzweig, the mother of the philosopher Franz Rosenzweig, knew the important German leaders because she was given hankies embroidered with the profiles of General Albrecht von Roon and the Crown Prince, and because her bedroom was decorated with popular historical paintings.[229] Others recalled waiting for the Kaiser's entourage to drive past on Berlin's Unter den Linden boulevard. They viewed military parades, placed candles in their windows in honor of the Kaiser's birthday, or recited poems about him.[230]

Reading material also followed patriotic themes. The *Israelitischer Jugendfreund*, for example, combined Old Testament stories (poetry, riddles, book reviews, and biographical sketches of male historical figures) with attention to the Kaiser and patriotism. It presented short stories about the Kaiser's family and his children, who "feared, respected and loved" their father and who loved their mother.[231] The journal hailed all the Kaiser's birthdays. Such patriotism was not uniquely Jewish. However, Jewish children received an extra message: that Jews in particular had reason to be grateful to the Kaiser, because "the Kaiser's heart envelops all his subjects in equal love, without regarding religious differences!"[232] Jewish children read: "we will never let ourselves be outdone in our love of Kaiser and Reich. Not despite, but because we are Jews, we are faithful and upright Germans."[233] Echoing a belief held by most German Jews, the journal argued: "A lack of patriotic feelings or national sentiment is as damnable as indifference in religious matters."

Although physical and educational activities dominated children's upbringing, manners, and obedience, bourgeois respectability, in its feminine and masculine varieties, remained omnipresent requirements. These "cultural measures of gentility" were the work of housewives.[234] Children had to be polite at all times. This included curtsies from girls and bows from boys. In a few families the polite form *Sie* may have still been used to address parents as late as the 1890s, although this form was already considered old-fashioned in the 1860s.[235] When company arrived, children were to be seen briefly, but not heard. Writing of being confined to a side room when her parents had a dinner party, one woman observed: "We did not mind a bit, because we got all the delicacies without having to watch our manners. After dinner, we were called in to greet the guests and to make a curtsy in our best party dresses. But we stayed only a few minutes."[236] Children had to eat the foods placed before them and were punished for inquiring about their meals.[237] Only on birthdays did many children have a right to request a special treat. Children of the nobility were not even allowed to discuss food.[238] The feigned disinterest in such topics clashed with the rich banquets in *haut bourgeois* households. Nevertheless, children were not to take notice of the richness of the table or make requests.

In the cities many parents prohibited noisy street play and class mixing, and mothers enforced these rules. Toni Sender (born 1888, Frankfurt/Main) recalled that, although she would have preferred to, she was forbidden to play with "less well-off" children.[239] Johanna Meyer Loevinson (born 1874, Berlin) watched the proletarian children playing on the street. From her second-floor balcony, "one could literally look down upon the children who played in the courtyard, which we were not allowed to do."[240] Like adults, they had to observe decorous behavior. Rowdiness was anathema and children were punished for it; gentility was a must. One daughter commented on her mother's example: her mother had "unlearned an audible laugh . . . smiling in her quiet way."[241] She further noted: "With mother everything was as quiet and unobtrusive as possible, her appearance, her dress, the way she acted and spoke. She could have passed for the wife of a Christian minister."[242] Gentility signified class to bourgeois Germans. To Jews it denoted class *and* Germanness—since for Jews these were one and the same thing.

In Jewish advice literature, mothers read that it was their duty to give children the understanding and thoughtfulness of maturity and that childlike qualities—newly recognized as positive traits—would not be ruined.[243] Hence these childlike qualities were sometimes forcibly repressed. Parents punished children for minor transgressions by denying them a desert, a walk along the river, or a Sunday outing.[244] Corporal punishment for what seem to be petty infractions by today's standards was not uncommon. Children were spanked for taking food without permission[245] and for not getting along with one another. Recalling her mother's reaction to a sibling squabble, one woman wrote: "First each of us got a hearty slap, which she always believed to be the proper beginning."[246]

Many contemporary writers, including as prominent a social observer as Ellen Key, complained that rich women ignored their children. Despite such admonitions, mothers were more present in their children's lives than before. The rich and alienated Jewish mother was an exception (as may well have been her Christian counterpart). When Hedwig Wachenheim criticized her mother's day—consisting of self-absorption and, to Wachenheim, trivial pursuits (coffee visits and concerts) supplemented by an occasional migraine—she described a relatively rare situation and justified her own decision to do something "useful" with her life. By the turn of the century, Jewish mothers began to note the psychological development of their children as well as other developmental traits. They commented in letters and diaries on their children's personalities, moods, health, and habits. They saved children's letters and momentos.[247] Even in novels mothers were shown as trying to be less distant, like the wealthy Jewish woman in Arnold Zweig's *Die junge Frau von 1914* who begged for her daughter's confidence and offered her sympathy and trust.[248] While mothers still devoted considerable time to their representational and household duties—possibly as much as previous generations of women had spent working in businesses—they studied their fewer children more closely, asking advice of one another and sharing child rearing strategies. Jewish advice literature assured—and warned—mothers that nothing was beyond their domain, whether the physical and educational or the emotional and sexual lives of their children. They were to be particularly watchful of their adolescent sons, but daughters too needed a guiding eye: "Even her son's secrets do not remain easily hidden from an attentive mother. She surveys all of the rooms and corridors of her house, all of her sons' and daughters' clothing and linens pass through her hands, she reads her loved ones' happiness and worries, openness and secretiveness on their brows."[249]

That Jewish parents were strict and intrusive with their children should come as no surprise. In their attempt to achieve respectability, they observed the child-rearing practices of the age. Yet in the later decades of the nineteenth century, Jews, like other bourgeois Germans, slowly began to accept the idea of "childhood" and the individuality of children and modified child-rearing accordingly. In a letter to her friend, one Jewish woman reported that she had asked her husband not to slap their child, but then confided that she "could not raise Käthe . . . because I find her so sweet, that despite all the wisdom with which I recognize good upbringing, I'm not capable of being strict . . . I'm too afraid of destroying that irreplaceable, godly spontaneity."[250] In another memoir a daughter reported that her mother respected children as people and that there were no punishments in her home, "a very unusual situation for those times [1890s]." "She didn't raise us, she lived with us and accepted us as we were. But, unconsciously, her example influenced us." In contrast to her home, this young woman was shocked some years later when her teacher told her that she would *not* be punished for a misdeed. "I had never dreamt of punishment," she recalled.[251]

Memoirs suggest that while Jewish parents indeed tended to be strict, they may have been less so than their Gentile urban or rural counterparts. Käte Frankenthal wrote of the atmosphere in her home, which her non-Jewish friends preferred to their own:

> The girls [from noble families] liked coming to my house, and that was understandable. Our home was a kind of children's paradise. It was a large house and the top floor was exclusively a children's empire. . . . Nothing was forbidden, something I became conscious of as a result of the other children's questions. I heard the astonished question, "may we do that?" when I suggested picking fruit. . . . "Yes, why not?" I would not have been able to give a different response. Sometimes I visited my girlfriends. I felt constrained there. . . . Grown ups were in the next room, so we were not allowed to make much noise. We were called in for coffee hour and had to sit at the table responding to friendly questions with courteous answers. There was no doubt that it was a hundred times nicer at our house. I completely understood that my friendship was desired and that I offered children a favor when I suggested going to my house.[252]

Even Toni Sender, who complained of her strict mother, failed to appreciate that her upbringing had enabled her to rebel and that her parents had allowed it, whereas many women of her generation were forced into total submission.

One reads nowhere of the physical constraints that some German parents placed on their children or of the severe corporal punishment meted out by others. Elizabeth Bab, who grew up in a Protestant family in the 1880s in Kiel, described the *Gradehalter* (two sticks attached at right angles and placed down a child's back and through her sleeves) that she had to wear to straighten her posture at the dinner table, and the chin rest (*Kinnstütze*) that prevented her from bending her head. If children spoke to each other during meals at her home, they might be forced to sit with their backs to the table. Bab described these procedures as hateful and demeaning. Her Protestant upbringing generated a demanding superego and large amounts of guilt. "The nicest part about being naughty," she recalled, "were the long letters of apology."[253] Certainly we do not find mothers like the pious Protestant civil servant's wife in Gabriele Reuter's novel *Aus guter Familie*, who forced herself to beat her adolescent daughter with a stick for behavior she considered unladylike. "She knew she should not upset herself, that her nerves would be shattered, . . . [but] it was her duty. The child could not challenge all authority like that."[254] Nor is the making of an *Untertan* (a submissive, subordinate individual), as described by Heinrich Mann, duplicated in any Jewish memoir material available. After a misdeed, Mann's Diederich Hessling:

> would come cringing shyly like a dog to his father's desk, until Herr Hessling noticed that something was wrong and took his stick from the wall. . . . His father had always used the stick methodically, his weather-beaten face reflecting an old soldier's sense of honor and duty. . . . Frau Hessling tried to compel Diederich to fall on his knees before his father and beg his pardon. . . .[255]

Perhaps, as in the above case, the allure and experience of the military, never particularly attractive or hospitable to Jews, influenced the behavior of Gentile men, especially toward sons who would be expected to exhibit discipline and toughness during their own stint in the service. But just as likely, broader cultural and social elements were also evident here.

Outside observers commented on the intensity of feelings between Jewish mothers and their offspring. Theodor Fontane witnessed a reunion between a mother and her children in the Hamburg railroad station. He wrote his wife: "I have never in my life seen such a loving reception." The children ran alongside the train, and "from time to time two lips squeezed through the window opening in defiance of death and caught a kiss from . . . the mother who was quivering with joy. It was ridiculous, but still lovely."[256] Scholars have noted Fontane's mixed feelings about Jews. In this case, "since it is Jewish, what appeals to him as lovely must be ridiculous."[257] However, of interest here is the possibility that such displays of affection were quite unusual among other Germans, and that Fontane both appreciated the intensity of the sentiment and belittled it as unmannerly and hence Jewish.

More comparative work is necessary before we can prove my hypothesis that Jewish parents were less strict—and possibly more affectionate—or at least gave their children a certain resiliency and ability to resist. Clearly they would have had cause enough to adjust their child-rearing practices, perhaps in an attempt to shield their offspring from what they perceived as an unfriendly environment. The Central Verein, for example, cautioned Jewish mothers to be especially supportive of their children: "It is the woman who brings up her children . . . and equips them with armor against which the poison arrows of vile slanderers will rebound. . . . from whom we may expect that she will also raise those battle-worn, disheartened spirits."[258] Admonitions to toughen as well as restore wounded egos could lead to overprotectiveness. Charlotte Wolff, describing her parents, wrote: "My parents pampered, spoiled and over-protected their children. Discipline had no proper place in their educational code. But it had advantages: it gave me trust in people, and considerable self-confidence. . . . I had the naive idea that everybody should be inclined to like me."[259] Such children might be rudely surprised by the real world, but they would have been given a strong, positive self-image with which to handle later rebuffs.

On the other hand, in attempting to shield their children from rejection by the outside world, Jewish mothers may have passed on the not-so-hidden message that children were safest at home and that their family would be their haven. The result, then, could have been an immediate return to the family after experiencing the inevitable snub from outside. Unlike in Wolff's case, this nurturing environment may have made others suspicious and fearful of outsiders, trustful only of kin and perhaps of other Jews, who were often seen as extended kin. Child-rearing habits were certainly an element (along with minority status and occupational profile) in the perpetuation of intense family bonds. In sum, a supportive childhood environment, despite its restrictive tone and high expectations, gave Jewish children the personal wherewithal to venture out, as well as the quiet understanding that it was safest at home.

Women who did not work outside the home and women who had domestic help were the de facto symbols of having "made it" into the bourgeoisie. Their role was essential to the social and economic position of Jews and to their sense of class and, hence, "Germanness." Even the most hardworking woman could consider herself "middle-class" if she could afford some domestic help. Those who could not worked incessantly to maintain an impeccable household and appear unharried. Significantly, they may have made all the difference between a scanty existence and one that—through thrift and good management—exhibited the refinement necessary to pass as middle-class.

Moreover, women cultivated their families. They did not simply bring German culture into the home in the form of high culture, or *Kultur*, which children also learned at school. They made their homes and children "respectable," "middle-class," orderly, and mannerly. They helped their families to act and feel like other Germans by promoting a culture of domesticity, transforming the home into the model German *Haushalt*.

Active agents in the acculturation process, mothers were also inhibitors of complete assimilation. Many continued to perform rituals, cook special Jewish dishes, and think and act in terms of Jewish life cycles, family networks, and the Jewish calendar. Jewish religious customs and German accouterments were not perceived as, nor were they, contradictory. As we shall see in the following chapter, women coupled faith with domesticity.

2

Domestic Judaism: Religion and German-Jewish Ethnicity

"The modern Jewish woman is everything but a Jewess."[1] Throughout the Imperial era, religious leaders and popular myth alike reproached women for the decline of Judaism in terms of population as well as religiosity. Editorials, serial stories, and selective news items in Jewish newspapers depicted women as pushing their families to move to the cities, where they could enjoy a more luxurious life; showed women marrying out of the faith and converting for frivolous reasons; and described them as interested in all sorts of secular activities, but not in their own Jewish community.[2] All implied that Judaism depended, to a large extent, on the role of women, because Jewish home life itself had a religious character: "The . . . Hausfrau emerges as a "priestess [*Priesterin*] of the home. Women are giants who carry the world on their shoulders by caring for the home. . . . If the religious home falls, so does the world of religion."[3] Since women were supposed to imbue the home with its piety, the demise of religion was seen as their fault.

In challenging the belief that women led the way toward assimilation—a belief which persisted well into the twentieth century—we will examine the actual role women played in the maintenance of Jewish tradition and the Jewish family. Moreover, in assessing the extent to which female-specific conditions—women's primary role in the home and family, as a result of their exclusion from formal religious practice, from most forms of public employment, and from politics and higher education—influenced their behavior and attitudes, we will posit that women, for reasons beyond their control, actually remained the guardians of Jewish traditions.

Women in Judaism: Personal Piety, Synagogue, and Community

In Judaism, as in most patriarchal cultures, social roles and character traits are ascribed according to sex, with the valued characteristics and positions reserved for men.[4] Jewish law (*halakhah*) exempts women from all time-bound, positive commandments (*mitzvot*) because of their duties as housewives and mothers. They are not required to participate in communal prayer three times daily, and therefore cannot be counted in a quorum (*minyan*) or lead a service. Further, they are exempt from reading and studying the Torah. Thus they are effectively excluded from synagogue rituals, the fundamental duties of public religious life, which therefore centers on men.[5] Conversely, Jewish law and practice favor the roles of wife and mother, and limit women's sacred responsibilities. They are required to fulfill three positive commandments, all of which underline their location in the home: the separation of a bit of dough to prepare the Sabbath bread; kindling the Sabbath candles; and maintaining the laws of family purity regarding menstruation.

The exclusion of women from essential ritual activities and their assignment to the home had legal, communal, and social ramifications. Women had no independent legal status, thus communal decision-making bodies excluded them. They also did not receive the same education as men. When they did attend synagogue, they sat segregated in a gallery or rear area apart from the men. Relegated to second-class citizenship and prohibited from "the heart and soul of traditional Judaism . . . communal prayer and study,"[6] women not surprisingly found their most effective field of Jewish endeavor in the home. Within that sphere, as "virtuous women" or "women of valor" (*eshet hayil* hailed in Proverbs) they received rewards for their self-sacrificing service in enabling men to pray and study.

This gender hierarchy served to maintain Jewish tradition. "Tradition" as used here is not only Jewish law and custom as religious scholars may interpret it. It is the totality of "little traditions" as well.[7] Interdependent with the "great tradition," these are not simply handed down, but created anew in the process of transmission. Women played a central role in negotiating with tradition, recasting what they had received in the context of their own lives. Thus, even as it stifled Jewish women's public religious expression, sex-role differentiation permitted women to sustain a chain of transmission within the family. As scholars have recently noted: "The family is—and always has been—a crucial institution in Judaism. Woman was identified with, and given primary responsibility for the family. Thus, maintenance of sex-role differentiation has been linked (through the family) to the survival of the Jewish people and tradition."[8] Women were linked inextricably with the family. Both were considered crucial to the raising of children to full Jewish adulthood, and hence to the preservation of Judaism.

This tradition continued essentially unchanged into the modern era. The *Brandspigl*, a popular guide for Jewish women in the seventeenth century, portrayed mothers as facilitators in their children's (though here it meant sons') study of the Torah. Good wives urged their husbands to study the Torah by placing a book on the table when they finished their Friday night meals.[9] The *Brandspigl* advised women to keep the house tidy and the clothes orderly, and to pray for their husbands when they were absent from home.[10] Despite this preponderant domestic focus, Jewish women did engage seriously in reading and practicing a popular nonelite religion. Beginning in the late sixteenth century, a separate woman's vernacular literature of *tkhines*, voluntary, supplicatory prayers directed toward women's needs, began to be written, sometimes even by women. The popular devotional literature of the late seventeenth through early nineteenth centuries also included pious tales, guides to a righteous life, and the women's bible, or *Tsenerene*. This last was a collection of homilies on the biblical portion of the week which was reprinted frequently and read widely. Both the *tkhines* and the *Tsenerene* maintained their popularity well into the twentieth century.[11] The evidence suggests that even as women concentrated on the home, they prayed in their own way in their own space.[12]

With Emancipation, the majority of Jewish women continued to relate to their religion as they had previously—privately and personally. The daughters of the well-to-do, however, benefited first from the new secular education and Enlightenment, since men continued to spend much of their free time on religious study. Thus upper-class Jewish women learned the language of the society beyond the ghetto and became familiar with social graces and foreign languages and literature before men of their class did. Between 1780 and 1806, princes, nobles, and upwardly mobile writers flocked to the salons of Rahel Varnhagen and Henriette Herz, among others. For these Jewish women, salon leadership offered not only an escape from a restricted home life, but also social and personal power and, frequently, interfaith marriages.[13] Jewish men, on the other hand, found it more difficult. "It is on record from the time of the literary salons that some of those men whose wives were the life and soul of social gatherings were too embarrassed to put in an appearance."[14] It is the stereotype of the apostate salon Jewess which haunted Jewish women, although, as will be seen, women generally converted and married out of the faith far less than men and maintained their traditional practices longer.

At midcentury, women's religious education was minimal, consisting of a mixture of morals, religion, reading, and writing (German and Judeo-German).[15] One woman (born in 1844) recalled that, when she borrowed a prayer book in the women's gallery, she found notations in the margins suggesting the emotion or reaction appropriate to certain sections, such as "cry at this passage." She commented: "The majority of women prayed without understanding what was meant."[16] This generalization was no longer entirely true during the Imperial era, when girls learned some Hebrew.[17]

The full extent of women's interest or participation in the formal study of Judaism has yet to be discovered. By the Imperial era, a formal Jewish education proceeded in several ways. Private tutors came to the homes of some girls; others went to a Jewish *Volksschule* or *Töchterschule* (which included the higher grade), where they received between three and four hours a week of religious instruction[18]; still others attended about four hours a week of religious lessons or religious school after the normal school day.[19] Compared to their brothers, Jewish girls were more likely to attend an elementary school (either a *Volksschule* or a Jewish *Volksschule*) which stressed religion, but boys received far more intense religious and Hebrew instruction to prepare them for the Bar Mitzvah. It was not uncommon, therefore, while services went on below them, for women to read the *tkhines* or German prayers and translations of the Hebrew services and to chat with other women.[20] Witnesses and participants decried the lack of decorum in the galleries, where the "second-class citizens of God" sat.[21] One woman remembered "being disgusted at the amount of chatter going on and . . . a 'goy' having to go round constantly to try and stop them."[22] Another recalled hearing the word "parsley" ring out loudly over a sudden lull in the services, and still another reported with some amusement, "The women came home from services inspired and with new recipes."[23]

During the nineteenth century some leaders of Reform (Liberal) Judaism, sensitive to the issue of women in the organized religion, attempted to rectify women's situation. In part, they sought to maintain women's allegiance, but mostly they felt embarrassed that Christian society might observe the Oriental customs evident in the relegation of Jewish women to second-class status. As early as 1837 Abraham Geiger, the scholar and religious reformer, wrote: "Judaism as it exists vigorously rejects women and stifles their receptive feelings for religion. Women are absolved from public synagogue services, the most salutary support for religious ardor, and what incentive should lure [women] to services, where one prays in a foreign language which is indeed supposed to remain foreign to them!" Geiger concluded: "No separation [should] occur between the duties of men and women, unless they arise from the natural laws of both sexes; [there should be] no assumption of women's immaturity, . . . no shaping of public worship, in form or content, that closes the doors of the Temple to women."[24]

The leaders of Reform placed the status of women on the agenda of their synod at Breslau in 1846. They proclaimed as atavistic, and "an insult to the free personality of woman," the segregation of women, the absence of confirmation, the male blessing thanking God "for not having been born a woman," and the ban on women in choirs.[25] A special commission recommended that women be obligated to perform only time-related duties considered still binding, like prayer. It recognized women as members of the prayer forum (*minyan*) and agreed that women's vows could not be negated by their husbands or fathers. Discussion of these recommendations, however, had to be postponed, seemingly for "lack of time."[26] The conference made few practical improvements in women's status in the synagogue, except in the tiny Reform congregation in Berlin.

Still, Reformers did acculturate to some of the practices of the majority. They offered combined religious instruction for boys and girls and introduced sermons which aimed to appeal to both sexes.[27] Confirmation and the double-ring wedding ceremony caught on in Liberal congregations. Confirmation, as practiced in Protestant churches, completed the covenant of baptism. Reform rabbis argued that boys and girls should be confirmed, although they denied that confirmation meant the same thing in both religions. In Judaism there was no definite age at which girls began their obligation to obey the laws; thus, rabbis argued,"once again, [women are] treated as less capable, as in Oriental custom."[28] Rabbinic and lay leaders suggested that the education of both boys and girls "should climax with a solemn act in a sacred place."[29] This custom gained wider acceptance during the last decades of the Imperial era and was supported by Jewish feminists who insisted that girls should receive equal religious preparation.[30]

Another Christian tradition, the double-ring ceremony, may have been forced upon the rabbinate at the initiative of young women. In 1871 Rabbi Joseph Aub remarked to the Augsburg synod of rabbis that young brides who belonged to "the most cultured families . . . did not wish to be passive at the altar, as if they were objects and as though the marriage ceremony could be performed without their equal participation."[31] The synod bowed to this custom, already in vogue in several congregations in Berlin and Frankfurt/Main. Moreover, the rabbis urged that the bride as well as the groom be allowed to make a wedding vow.[32] In addition, the rabbis agreed that the *halitzah* ritual (which demanded a brother-in-law's permission for the remarriage of a widow) should no longer block a widow's remarriage, and that a widow should be free to remarry once the death of her husband had been verified by a non-Jewish judicial authority or the missing husband was generally presumed dead.[33]

Orthodox women also took initiatives, although these met with firmer resistance. In 1893 an inquiry to the chief rabbi of Hamburg from the chief rabbi of Marienbad asking whether women could be permitted to sing in the choir received a negative response. "Jewish law . . . forbade hearing women's voices during the services in the synagogue."[34] Thus there is some evidence that women tried to modify religious practices themselves. This may have been particularly true outside the institutional setting of the synagogue. In rural regions, as we shall see, women frequently imbued certain Jewish home rituals with elements of local customs.

Despite some changes, Jewish law and Jewish tradition, reinforced by the sexism of German society, remained remarkably resistant to female intrusion. Jewish men simply sought to Westernize. This meant appropriating the German gender system—not a terribly radical break. Thus the good intentions of reformers and some superficial modifications did not alter woman's role in the synagogue. She still sat in a women's section, read a women's bible, and more often than not did not even attend, but prayed at home. In 1908 the newly established Union for Liberal Judaism (Vereinigung für das Liberale Judentum in Deutschland) formulated a platform which placed special emphasis on the greater participation of women in the religion and community.[35] Its guidelines added that the participation of women was indispensable and that they should receive an equal share of religious duties as well as rights. Yet theory did not quickly translate into practice. For example, women continued to be segregated in the synagogue.[36] In the years before World War I there was no whisper of religious equality from any quarter, and male leaders even ignored women's demands for the right to vote in communal elections within the *Gemeinde*.

Women's exclusion from the synagogue did not extend to Jewish communal activities, and this is where they found work, demonstrated competence, and maintained a Jewish community network and spirit. Even as the ghetto disappeared and Jews no longer operated in an exclusively Jewish framework, Jewish women continued traditional charitable societies. Men rigidly excluded them from the management of communal affairs, but allowed them to extend their practical housekeeping to the community at large. They donated their spare time to women's charitable groups, ranging from those deeply rooted in Jewish tradition (*chevra kaddisha*) to modern social welfare organizations. An entire chapter (chapter 7) is devoted to such activities, but it should be noted here that many women viewed these benevolent groups as fulfilling a *religious* duty, not simply a charitable or social endeavor. For others, their participation resulted from a general concern for the Jewish community or from a Jewish social welfare tradition, both connected to their understanding of what it meant to be Jewish.

Jewish women also contributed to Jewish political organizations. In 1908, with the abolition of the law banning women's political activities, the *Vereinsgesetz*, many Jewish organizations suddenly became aware of a pool of potential new members. The Central Verein, for example, sponsored its first women's meeting a few months after the ban on women's involvement in politics had been lifted. The C.V. leadership envisioned women's role as "supporting men in their battle against a culturally hostile movement [anti-Semitism], to encourage them and save them from demoralization, to bring up their children to be people of character." The most important job for women members was "to work with their husbands in the spirit of love." The C.V. relegated women to the home, to "strive for self-discipline and self-improvement." Despite a few token spokeswomen (Henriette May, Ernestine Eschelbacher, and Henriette Fürth, all members of the Jewish women's movement as well), the C.V. sought the membership rather than the leadership of women.[37] Women contributed constancy and organization to the national, local, cultural, educational, and social welfare aspects of Jewish life, but remained far from the centers of power and decision making.

Women in the Home: The Tenacity and Decline of Jewish Traditions

The overwhelming majority of Jewish women in Imperial Germany were housewives or future housewives. Single, married, widowed, divorced, whether they held paid or unpaid jobs or not, they performed the tasks associated with running a home. Even if they hired other women to do the more menial chores, the responsibility of the home was theirs. The housewife's job was (and is) gender-linked, and it is clear that any understanding of the religiosity of Jewish women must take this into account.

Affected by *embourgeoisement* as well as by the dominant cultural attitudes toward bourgeois women which expected them to be domestic, dependent, religious, and emotional, Jewish women experienced the contradictions of their new position. They had to maintain the sanctity of the home in a period in which husbands and children were increasingly drawn outside, in which "home" and "world" became increasingly polarized.[38] Furthermore, they had to smooth the way for acculturation, but in so doing became the target of those Jews who sought to protect religious feelings and practice in the face of increasing secularization.

The development of the new bourgeois family occurred at the same time as general trends toward secularization and, for Jews in particular, acculturation and integration. The nineteenth century witnessed the disengagement of society from religion, the "downgrading of religion to a denominational category and concomitantly the end of the primacy of Judaism and Jewishness as an all-embracing influence dominating both social life and the conduct of the individual."[39] Jews experienced the uneven and uneasy process of secularization along with other Germans. By 1900 the Liberal branch of German Jewry, which had grown out of the Reform movement led by Abraham Geiger in the mid-nineteenth century, was predominant.[40] There is no doubt that Orthodox religious observance declined in the Imperial period. (As was already noted in the introduction, only 15 percent of Jews could still be classified as Orthodox by 1900.) Furthermore, there was an absolute and relative drop in Jewish education and Jewish schools as well as lackluster synagogue attendance, all particularly apparent in the cities.[41] Eager to acculturate, some Jews modernized their religious practice to minimize their embarrassment at non-Western customs. Others attempted to shed their ethnic, social, and in some cases religious distinctiveness entirely.

The family, however, remained a central focus for the expression of Jewish feeling and commitment, and Jewish women experienced the effects of secularization from (and may have been sheltered by) their primary position in it. Jewish observance, more than that of other religions, took place in the home in a familial setting. Goitein's observation of medieval Jews held true—perhaps more so—for their modern counterparts: "Without a proper home no Jewish religious life was feasible. The benedictions and elaborate grace accompanying the meals on working days, Saturdays, and holidays, and many other religious duties, such as hospitality and care for the wayfarer and the poor, were best fulfilled in the atmosphere provided by a household."[42] For women, in fact, *religion and family were one totality*. Whereas Judaism relegated women to a peripheral role in the synagogue, it placed them on a pedestal in the home. While this perch kept them safely removed from the centers of public and religious life, it had its compensatory side. Women practiced a domestic religion which intertwined with their daily lives. Family life and the observance of the Sabbath, holidays, and dietary laws were clearly women's domain. Their relationship to family and customs was intimate: "The God women prayed to in the kitchen seemed to have a more personal nature that the deity men invoked" in synagogue.[43]

Women's bond to their religion, then, should be analyzed differently from men's, that is, by the extent of their maintenance of "Jewishness" in the home, both in specific practices and in sentimental attachment.[44] Even when we recognize that successive generations dropped certain rituals, so that we find grandmothers, mothers, and daughters responding in varying degrees to the same religious event, we can only intuit their sentiments. Whereas a granddaughter's Hebrew and religious education might have been far better than her grandmother's, the latter was probably more pious, even though she recited prayers and performed rituals she may not have understood. Each practiced in her own way, negotiating with customs and defining her personal Jewishness with elasticity.

Mothers had a special role to play. Medieval Responsa literature depicted their mission as "supervis[ing] the religious and moral upbringing of their children, send[ing] their boys off to school, . . . urging them to . . . study . . . the Torah." Religion teachers counted on them to transmit a moral and religious education to their offspring. While formal transmission of Judaism took place within the institutional framework of the synagogue and religious lessons or school, mothers were expected to pray with their children and to tell them religious tales. On the other hand, fathers simply had to fulfill their own religious duties to be considered good examples. Thus women had to transmit Judaism actively, whereas fathers only had to be religious.[45]

For the Imperial era, it is difficult to determine who decided upon religious tutoring or schooling or who took more interest in the children's progress and homework in their religious lessons. Moreover, more research is needed to discover what else was involved in the formal and informal transmission of religious knowledge and feeling and how it was divided between parents. It is clear, however, that the informal transmission of Judaism—affective, private, and personal, including foods, family, and hearth—was in large measure women's domain, and that, among traditional families, women were accorded social power and status for their religious adherence. Women fashioned the fabric of daily life which enveloped their children. They shaped the social and cultural milieu in which traditional sentiments were reinforced.

In fact, these sentiments often seem more important than women's actual behavior. Both men and women perceived female-specific ritual as being less significant than male public observance. Men typically slighted women's private rites, and women too accepted the hegemonic values which placed greater importance on the public sphere. Appreciated according to their culturally prescribed role as sentimental, emotional, and religious, women impressed their offspring more with the homely details of their lives and with their feelings about religion than with their loyalty to (private, hence "less" important) religious forms. Looking back over a lifetime, children seem to have been more affected by their mother's faith as revealed in the home and kitchen (whether positive or negative) than by their fathers' attendance at synagogue or their own religious instruction or synagogue participation.[46]

One of the most obvious manifestations of their mother's religious feeling was whether or not she kept a kosher kitchen. The Jewish dietary laws, the laws of *kashrut*, dictated that meat be slaughtered and prepared in a special way and that foods made up of milk products be kept strictly separated from those consisting of meat. This implied not only separate dishes, silverware, kitchen linens, pots, pans, soaps, and cooking utensils, but careful menu planning. It involved seeking kosher butchers and preparing the Sabbath meal in advance (so as not to cook on the day of rest). It meant two entirely different sets of dishes and kitchenware and a massive cleaning (and two more sets of everything) for Passover. Housewives had to instruct their children and helpers in the intricacies of the kitchen, to avoid mixing those items designated for meat with those designated for dairy products.

Religious observers believed that Judaism could be preserved through the kitchen. One suggested that women could give a spiritual aura to "the seemingly mechanical and dull functions in the kitchen," so that the preparation of foods "would serve as more than a means of feeding the hungry." The family would view it as "a religious activity," and the housewife would have prepared a "table that pleased God." Such care, it was argued, could prevent the decline of Judaism, the decay of the family, and interfaith marriage. Should the housewife balk at all the extra work, Jewish cooks should be hired to do the job.[47] Although kitchen methods can become routinized in any household, it is clear from the observations of secular Jews that they saw *kashrut* as a time-consuming extra effort and eagerly relieved themselves of its burdens. Nevertheless, even though the observation of strict *kashrut* declined throughout the Imperial era, probably a majority of Jews still kept a kosher kitchen while others, as we shall see, observed *kashrut* in the breach.

Gershom Scholem has suggested that "not an inconsiderable number of families kept kosher kitchens only out of respect for relatives, mainly of the older generation, who otherwise would not have touched any food in their homes."[48] Although this may have been the way in which Jews articulated their feelings about a custom which many maintained past the war years, I would suggest that far more complex and intimate allegiances were at play. In fact, when Jews commented on their religious background or feeling, their own and their mothers' kitchens became oft-used yardsticks of ethnic and religious identity. Thus Jewish foodways may be seen as "ethnic emblems."[49]

Recent ethnological studies have used Jewish cookbooks as cultural artifacts, as tools for studying identity and ethnicity, family life, community, and the role of women. A monograph on Alsatian Jewry, for example, describes how meal schedules, food rituals within the weekly and annual ceremonial calendar, cooking utensils and techniques, and the ingredients used in family cuisine articulated the social and cultural identity of the Jewish minority in Alsace. "In the materiality and privacy of foodways, a socio-cultural minority defines its boundaries and finds an efficient means of reproducing its traditional values in urban society." Foodways appear to be governed by a form of "policy in which important social and historical challenges are involved."[50] Often food rules, deeply embedded in daily life, became food habits and could be found in nonobservant families as a "nostalgic vestige of a lost tradition."[51] For example, a German-Jewish woman could write in her memoirs about Christmas pudding and special Sabbath meals without exhibiting any sense of contradiction.[52] Others would eat nonkosher meats but shrink from tasting pork. Ethnologists suggest that "certain tabooed foods were rejected on aesthetic grounds."[53] Some people refused to drink milk with meat dishes because "they didn't taste good together." Both instances display "culturally formed thresholds of disgust"[54] which de facto continued an allegiance to traditional Jewish foodways.

Jews in German-speaking lands were the first and most prolific publishers of Jewish cookbooks in the nineteenth century.[55] The earliest of these appeared in 1815.[56] Between 1815 and 1900, ten titles appeared in the major German cities, with each book containing between 300 and 4,000 recipes.[57] Several went through multiple editions, some so quickly that the authors had no opportunity to rewrite or add entries, and several won prizes at international culinary arts competitions.[58] They are useful sources for tracing the continuities and changes in Jewish cuisine. Very popular, "best sellers" of sorts, all respected dietary laws and included regional and/or international specialties. Jewish cookbooks gave recipes for foods appropriate for particular holidays: Passover required preparations made with matzo (unleavened bread); Purim necessitated dishes made with raisins, sugar, and cinnamon; the New Year called for sweet apples, fatty meat (an expensive cut), and sweets.[59] Cookbooks contained recipes for "typical" Jewish foods such as *Berches*, the bread served on the Sabbath. They incorporated fish recipes as well, such as herring, because of their spicy tastes and because they were symbols of fertility, usually eaten on Friday nights.[60] They also introduced new products which could be used in kosher kitchens, for example, *Palmin,* a coconut fat that replaced butter.[61]

These cookbooks offered menus for the Sabbath and multiple varieties of the traditional Saturday dish, called *Schalet* in Germany (and *cholent* in Eastern Europe). Heinrich Heine, the German-Jewish poet who converted to Christianity, immortalized the *Schalet* in a parody of Schiller's *Ode to Joy,* the text sung in Beethoven's Ninth Symphony.

Schalet, wondrous sparkle of the gods,
daughter of Elysium!
That's how Schiller's Ode would have sounded,
had he ever tasted Schalet.

. . . .

Schalet is the true God's
kosher Ambrosia.[62]

The preparation of this one-pot dish had to be completed late Friday afternoon, before the Sabbath—a day when even the housewife was supposed to rest—began. From then on the covered dish cooked slowly for about twenty hours, until it was eaten as the main Sabbath meal. *Schalet* usually consisted of noodles with eggs, raisins, and flour, but sometimes contained meat or apples. It could be a pudding of baked grated potatoes. In Bavaria (where Jews often called it *Kugel*), it frequently included matzos and apples. Most Jews no longer took the Sabbath restrictions quite literally and enjoyed variations of *Schalet*. In fact, only in the cookbooks of the 1870s do we find the sixteen- to twenty-hour *Schalet*. By 1900 *Schalet*, still extremely popular, took far less time to bake. Recipes adhered to traditional tastes, but assumed a *Hausfrau* would be working in the kitchen on the Sabbath—even if for only a short time.

Jewish cookbooks concentrated on bourgeois style and cuisine. The earlier ones offered simple, "thrifty" fare with recipes for fancier or holiday events. Later ones continued to provide traditional recipes, but prided themselves on their "finer" kitchens and international dishes, such as "English plum pudding," "French almond cake," or "French pudding (milk product)" (a warning to those who maintained kosher kitchens).[63] Cookbooks instructed wives preparing dinner parties on style, including information on table setting, serving, menus, seating arrangements, and decorations. They ranged from simple explanations of *kashrut* for "daughters who do not have the opportunity to become acquainted with these religious procedures in their parents' homes and therefore may become embarrassed if religious men desire them as wives" (1875), to detailed methods of further koshering and porging meats that had already been ritually slaughtered.[64] One very popular book added an essay, "Hygienic Reasons for Jewish Dietary Laws," by a medical doctor—probably to reassure those skeptics who began to see no reason for *kashrut*. Surprisingly, many of these books contained special recipes for Easter (*Oster*) meals. However, these turned out to be foods intended for Passover. In fact, the Hebrew letters for Passover appeared in parenthesis after the word "Easter," and the recipes include matzo. This confusion may be seen in the context of linguistic acculturation. "Easter" appeared in books with the most detailed instructions for maintaining a ritually Jewish household, replete with recipes as well as prayers (in Hebrew) to be spoken on the Sabbath and holidays.[65]

Food habits, like other folk customs, passed back and forth between majority and minority cultures. Peasant women baked *Bubele* (plum cake), considered a southern Jewish recipe. In a village in Hesse the peasants enjoyed a stewlike bean soup (probably a form of *Schalet*). When questioned about what they were eating, they would laugh and say, "Today, I'm a Jew."[66] Researchers have found that Swabian Jews enjoyed *Spätzle* (dumplings) and prided themselves on how well they cooked them. "Successful *Spätzle* testified not only to a southern German housewife's skill as a cook, but to her identity as a 'real' Swabian."[67] By the 1920s in southern Germany the Saturday meal, with the exception of *Berches*, often resembled the middle-class Sunday dinner of non-Jewish Germans.[68] Nowhere is this exchange of food habits clearer than in the German-Jewish relish for cakes and the ritual—one might almost say religious—observance of the German coffee hour. A social occasion among ladies, coffee hour was one of the main forms of social activity among German-speaking Jews (as among other Germans) in the late nineteenth century. One Jewish cookbook recommended four to five pies and two platters of assorted baked goods for a gathering of twenty-four women![69] It is no wonder that a researcher found the majority of orally transmitted recipes in her grandmother's cookbook to be cookies, cakes, and *Torten*.[70]

Food customs also distinguished Jews from their neighbors. The same people who enjoyed imitating Jewish foods noticed that Jews ate differently. In Württemberg, villagers pointed to herring, sour cream and potatoes, and bean soup as Jewish specialties. Others mentioned that Jews ate certain regional and local specialties in unusual combinations, because of the milk/meat rules.[71] And Jews, too, felt the difference, particularly those who observed *kashrut*. Rahel Straus recalled that her kosher eating habits set her apart from her school friends.[72]

Thus foods and cookbooks reveal not only culinary delights, but social habits; they show how women shaped the culture of the home and adapted to German bourgeois table manners and tastes. Most importantly for our purposes, they testify to an ongoing culinary commitment to Jewish foods. Foods underline the asymmetry between structural and intellectual secularization and the emotional realm which lagged behind. In fact, foods preserved ethnic identity and religious sentiments well beyond even formal secession from Judaism. Jews continued to enjoy traditional meals and to a lesser extent observed dietary rules disguised as preferences, while they reached out to a cosmopolitan menu to enrich their tastes and display their newly acquired status. Cookbooks testify to the *embourgeoisement* of the Jewish palate, which saw no contradiction in a "French pudding (milk product)."

Closely related to Jewish foodways, but with special attributes of their own, the Sabbath and holidays offered Jews other occasions to acknowledge adherence to their faith. Rural Jews throughout the entire Imperial era waxed almost elegiac when they described the family Sabbaths and holidays.[73] Mothers and grandmothers (with the help of servants) prepared the home and cooked traditional meals. The distinctive Sabbath atmosphere—certain foods, white tablecloth and finer tableware, candles, special clothing, and family gatherings—was attributed to the hard work of the mother. Women and men *benscht* (blessed) the children, and the lighting of the candles by the women signified that the spirit of Sabbath was in the home. This spirit, again, had everything to do with family union: "The peacefulness and ceremony of a traditional Friday evening . . . was unique. It was an evening in which the whole family sat together. The business and sorrows of the work week were forgotten. It was as if one had stepped into another world."[74]

Women also took special care in the arrangements for the major holidays.[75] Passover required the most arduous work. Housecleaning often began in January, climaxing in March or April with an all-night exchange of kitchenware and a carefully executed replacement of the year-round dishes with the Passover ones. Recalled a man born in 1901 in a southern village:

> Once Hanukkah had passed . . . some over-zealous women would start cleaning out the attic to make it the *chametz* bin [for foods and utensils, etc., forbidden on Passover]. . . . Some women in the village were reputed to have only a few *chametz* dishes left in their kitchen a few weeks after Hanukkah. . . . This attitude kept the cleaning process alive and *Pesach* [Passover] in mind. . . . After Purim . . . turning everything upside-down and inside out would begin in earnest. . . . No wonder that the approaching holiday aroused mixed feelings; the housewife balanced the work still to be done against the dwindling number of days ahead. . . . For the week or two before *Pesach*, we ate in the entrance hall, since the living room had to be free of *chametz*. During the last few days, too, the hallway became the last refuge for *chametzdige* dishes and pots, while the kitchen took on the final aspect of becoming *pesachdig*.

On the day before the holiday began, the men left the house entirely to the women for a final cleaning and inspection. They retired to the inn to fulfill the '*mitzvah*' [a commandment or a good or pious deed] of consuming *chametzdige* beer until the last moment that was allowed." After the final, joint inspection and the sale or donation of *chametz* to Gentile neighbors, "our mother's cheek had taken on a red glow . . . from preparing the *Pesach* food on the red-hot kitchen fire."[76] While both parents participated in the final ritual, the symbolic search for *chametz*, the women had actually prepared the family for the holiday.

On the Jewish New Year, or Rosh Hashanah, rural Jews combined religious and familial customs. Aside from synagogue attendance, for which women generally dressed in white, housewives did a special housecleaning, bought or sewed new clothing for the children, and cooked holiday meals. Families visited one another to share New Year's greetings, and children wrote their parents letters thanking them for their generosity and kindness.[77] Religious customs often took on a local flavor as well. For example Purim, a time to recall the drama of Queen Esther, acquired the character of the immediate surroundings. Jacob Picard described Purim balls which reminded him of Catholic celebrations of Mardi Gras, or of the costumes of the Black Forest region, far more than of the Purim story.[78]

Urban Jews also celebrated holidays. In the cities, where secular culture predominated, memoirs indicate that Jews—particularly women—took note of the Jewish calendar and the tradition of particular rituals and foods on holidays. They experienced the Sabbath and holidays as unified religious and familial celebrations. The two elements reinforced each other and were impossible to disentangle. In fact, even as the family functioned to maintain religious practice, religion functioned to affirm family connectedness. One woman wrote of the 1880s in Berlin: "Besides the ceremony of Friday nights there was a strict rule [*ein strenges Gebot*] of family togetherness [*Familienzusammengehörigkeit*]."[79] She continued: "This was not always easy, but proved itself to be the right thing to do." When it was impossible for all her siblings to appear on the Sabbath, her father recited the blessing over bread for those children present at the table and for those absent. Scholars note that "the sharing of cooked food is a relational idiom whose emphasis is on inclusion, on being part of a close and interdependent group."[80] The holidays and Sabbath provided occasions for Jews to reaffirm the family and the group.

Urban Jews, especially second-generation city dwellers, often reduced the number of holidays they celebrated and minimized the religious content. Yet in all but a small minority of families (those conspicuous for their Christmas trees and Easter egg hunts), Jews were aware of, and attempted to commemorate, the major holidays, if only by a family reunion and a traditional meal. Symbolically, the holidays meant family—a way, perhaps, of accommodating to a society still geared to Christian feast and holy days in which Jews represented such a small minority. Whereas old rituals were slowly replaced or forgotten, family ties—supported by Jewish heritage and minority status as well as by the socioeconomic forces affecting most bourgeois Germans—were reinforced. As Jewish religious tradition and identity blended with an urban, bourgeois, secular life-style, the family became the cornerstone of a more secular version of Judaism. In other words, many Jews used the family to fill a religious or ethnic vacuum.[81] For these Jews, family provided the meaning that religion and tradition once had. It became visible testimony to the "*embourgeoisement* of Jewish piety."[82] According to George Mosse, "Religious feeling itself had become identified with . . . the proper bourgeois morality. . . . This . . . Jewishness . . . was set within an ideal of life that was shared by most Germans . . . a bourgeois utopia."[83] I would suggest that the family was the concrete embodiment of this bourgeois morality.

This was apparently also the case for the Protestant bourgeoisie. Public celebrations, many of which had taken place in churches,[84] became privatized in this era. The German Christmas, for example, once focused on the church, now became famous for its emphasis on familial intimacy. Christmas evolved into a celebration of the family.[85] Within this family context, secular Germans attempting to find some sort of common substitute for traditional religion reached for cultivation and culture—*Bildung*—to replace piety. For many, Goethe became a substitute for religion. One observer remarked that for her spouse's (Protestant) father

> the idealists, but more so Goethe and occasionally Wagner, substituted for religion. [He] used to summon the family on Good Friday and read *Faust* or play *Parzifal*. When I was a student I stayed . . . at the home of a theologian . . . [who was] in his writings a non-believer. Every morning we would start the day with sitting silently at the breakfast table and listening to him play a Bach chorale.[86]

The family became the cornerstone of a piety being transformed into middle-class morality and cultivation.

The mundane everyday also centered on the family. German Jews made weekends, vacations, and special outings into family occasions. Entertainment too took place primarily within the family. The German bourgeoisie carefully allocated its limited resources, interspersing hikes on Sundays and regular family gatherings with infrequent concert or theater visits. While maintaining "appearances" (house, servant, yearly vacation, membership in clubs and charities), these families demanded thrift and self-denial from their members. Such a family strategy, which included long-term savings for a son's education or a daughter's dowry, took precedence over individuals' short-term desires. Intensive family ties were the reward for self-disciplining personal needs. These family ties were not only necessitated by the demands of the family economy, but required by the Prussian state. As we have seen in chapter 1, civil servants had to demonstrate an irreproachable family life or face dismissal. The state's interest in an impeccable family life was common knowledge. The theme was echoed widely in popular culture. For example, in Georg Hermann's novel about a Jewish woman, *Jettchen Gebert*, a civil servant loses his job because the authorities suspect that Gebert has left her husband for him.[87] The success of a "social collectivism" within the family, which allowed it to maintain its life-style and secure its future, attests not only to the exigencies but also to the ideology of "family solidarity." Intimate, cultured family life became a means as well as an end for bourgeois Germans of all faiths, who endowed it with spiritual significance.

Among German Christians, women were acknowledged to be the more religious sex (although the differences between male and female religiosity varied according to denomination and region.)[88] Women clung to religion longer, in part because they did not acquire the advanced, scientific education of men, whose world views gradually rejected all or parts of spiritual thinking.[89] Also, they had fewer options to choose from. Men could join political as well as a wide variety of secular organizations. Further, as already noted, a rigid division of roles ascribed spirituality and emotions to women and knowledge, reason, and intellect to men.[90] Women attended church and joined religious clubs more readily than men, and among Catholics tended to home rituals such as maintaining the home shrine and eternal light. Weeks in advance, women cleaned and baked for major holidays—although these activities were prescribed not by the religion but by family tradition. Men were excluded from such activities. Observers of German peasant customs noted that those holidays, which were family festivals—that is, ones where women participated—remained intact, whereas predominantly male holidays fell into neglect.[91]

Ritual waned more slowly among Jewish women as well. First, they experienced less dissonance between religious practice and their daily routines than men. Their private world was more traditional than modern, timed to childbirth, anniversaries, deaths, and the rituals that went with these, as well as to seasonal and sacred holidays. Their sense of time had emotional associations. Certain times of the week or year carried specific meanings and feelings with them: for many, "the year followed the pattern of religious festivals."[92] Second, women could exert some control in the privacy of the family and home, whereas Jewish men faced obstacles to the performance of their religious duties resulting from business obligations and travel. In some cases, men and women might have *felt* similarly about their religion, but women's traditional role within the home permitted them to be more observant. Women's control over their domestic environment, for example, could extend to the maintenance of kosher ritual even against a husband's preference: "What you do in the kitchen is your own business," declared one husband.[93] In fact, in some cases it may have forced them to defend their religious loyalty under new and difficult circumstances—with husbands no longer willing or able to support their efforts.[94] Third, popular ideology permitted, condoned, or encouraged female religiosity. Even unreligious husbands usually did not mind religious wives—or tolerated them—since a certain measure of piety suited bourgeois standards.[95] Among the traditionally religious, women's religiosity provided them with a measure of social power that they could achieve nowhere else. They were loath to give this up.

Finally, Jewish women found it easier to consider themselves religious than did Jewish men. Judaism excluded women from many public rituals to begin with—they had fewer positive commandments to fulfill—therefore their actions had less relationship to religious sentiment than did those of men. For example, the daughter of the Orthodox leader Esriel Hildesheimer wrote that while the men prayed at sunset, the women read short stories to one another while finishing their mending.[96] When men began to neglect their observances, it may have indicated some degree of declining religiosity. Women, for whom religion was less formalized, more domestic, and more internalized, could surrender certain customs without any break in their previous loyalties or feelings. Fritz Stern has reminded us that "a good deal of religious consciousness and sentiment can live on without necessarily finding expression in socially observable conduct."[97] This was especially so for Jewish women.

Women were the last holdouts in practicing laws and traditions in the home, even among secular Jews who no longer observed dietary laws or the Sabbath. The wealthy scion of a Berlin Jewish family, born in 1876, wrote that he had no religious schooling or training, but "it is true that my mother taught me to pray every night." And his grandmother, who lived with him, left him with memories of carefully observed religious practice and daily morning prayers.[98] Another grandmother gave her grandson her two most precious possessions upon his entering medical school in 1902: a ring she had worn for fifty years, and a prayer book that she had read daily since she was a young girl. When he looked in the first section, expecting to find a dedication to himself, and found none, he asked her about it. She replied, "I thought about it, just look and you will find it." He finally found it under "Kol Nidre" (the eve of Yom Kippur, the Day of Atonement and holiest day of the year). When he asked why she had placed it there, she responded: "Perhaps later when you are around fifty or so, you might not keep your religious habits as strictly as you do now, but you always will go to 'Kol Nidre' and to 'Yiskor' [the service for the deceased]. Then you will think of me and that is why I wrote it in this particular place." He recalled this event over sixty years later.[99]

Another young man (born in 1876) noted the totally unreligious behavior of his *parents*. His father would not attend synagogue, and he knew when Christmas, not when Hanukkah, was to be celebrated. Yet "every Friday night, I saw my mother praying conscientiously, standing at the prescribed passages."[100] Charlotte Wolff (born in 1901, Riesenburg) recalled similar situations. She described the excitement of Christmas, the "festive meal of goose, red cabbage," then wrote of "a special day of the week to look forward to—the Sabbath. . . . On Friday evenings my mother put two silver candlesticks on the dinner table; food was special and plentiful, and we had a small glass of port wine afterwards."[101] Another woman (born in 1880, Breslau) recalled that her *family* observed only Yom Kippur, yet she remembered her mother praying at home every Saturday morning.[102] Memoirs typically skirt over women's private prayers. Thus the historian knows far more about the perceived inferiority of women's private rituals than about their actual neglect of them.

Even when women abandoned certain rituals, there seems to have been a time lag between when husbands and wives gave them up. One woman remembered how her fiancé told her she would have to compromise her religious scruples:

> He took me . . . to a restaurant that was not kosher. "You can not always eat kosher," he said, because he . . . wanted to travel a lot. I thought the roof would fall in or the building would collapse, but it didn't; and the chicken that he ordered was not so very different from the kosher chicken. But naturally I had to have a kosher home because I wanted my parents to be able to eat at my place.

He then agreed that the kitchen was her domain.[103] The daughter (born in 1862, Posen) of an observant woman noted that while her mother fasted and prayed on Yom Kippur, for her father "it was easier to fast after a hearty breakfast."[104] Another woman recalled that her father ate pork with no compunction, while her mother prayed fervently that her daughters would not neglect their religion when they grew up.[105] Pauline Wengeroff, who lived in Kovno (near the Prussian border) and St. Petersburg in the 1860s and 1870s, reported similar situations in Russia. She cherished religious traditions, whereas her husband abandoned them and ultimately forced her to do so. She noted, "The wife, clinging tenaciously to the traditions, used to light the Sabbath candles, but her enlightened husband lit his cigarette."[106]

Furthermore, even when a couple gave up certain practices at the same time, women may have been more troubled by this. Sigmund Freud, for example, persuaded his wife to drop all religious practice. She did so, but to the end of their days husband and wife still bickered over Martha Freud's wish to light candles on the Sabbath.[107] Women missed the daily customs that had become second nature to them. The American author Mary Antin alluded to this when she wrote: "My mother gradually divested herself, at my father's bidding, of the mantle of orthodox observance, but the process cost her many a pang, because the fabric of that venerable garment was interwoven with the fabric of her soul."[108] Finally, in some cases husbands simply ignored their wives' wishes. In 1904 the father of newborn twins decided not to have them circumcised and never even consulted his wife. (Interestingly, since both boys later insisted on a Bar Mitzvah, their mother may have prevailed in the end.)[109] These and many more examples suggest that women resisted the complete abandonment of their religious heritage—not always successfully—in the only acceptable form of female opposition: quietly, within the shelter of the home. Such gender-specific private observance was probably perceived as less important by both women and men, since men defined status and prestige in terms of public observance.

Beyond women's involvement in the rituals of the weekly and annual Jewish calendar, we know that a small percentage of women continued their private observance of the laws of family purity by using the *mikveh*, or ritual bath. In 1906 about 55 percent of Jewish communities in Germany maintained a *mikveh* and probably about 15 percent of Jewish women still adhered to this Orthodox ritual. The percentage of women who regularly visited a *mikveh* was larger in the villages, where Jews were more observant, than in the cities.[110] In southern Germany the communal *mikveh*, usually consisting of a one-room building erected near a stream or river, was a commonplace phenomenon. Some communities rebuilt or improved the *mikveh* as late as the 1920s, testifying to its continued importance to a minority of Jews.[111] Whereas a visit to a *mikveh* could in most cases occur in privacy, and was certainly not apparent to outside observers, the use of the more visible *Scheitel,* or wig, required by Orthodox ritual to cover a married woman's head, declined precipitously. Although in the 1870s some grandmothers living in the cities still wore wigs—the custom persisting for at least one more generation in small towns—and although ads for fancy "perukes" continued to appear in metropolitan Jewish newspapers through 1910, the vast majority of younger women had abandoned this custom by the Imperial era. In 1918 even Orthodox rabbis bemoaned the neglect of the *Scheitel,* "even in circles which otherwise take religious duties seriously."[112]

Folklore studies of southern and western Germany have uncovered women's active involvement in rituals surrounding childbed and baby naming. These rituals often ran parallel to the public ceremonies which took place in the synagogue. Since women had traditionally been barred from leadership of public ritual and relegated to observer status in the synagogue, women's initiation of life-cycle ceremonies, such as those surrounding birth, indicated their determination to participate in a separate sphere. In the case of birth rituals, women would sew and hang amulets around the room where the baby was to be delivered. They believed these would ward off evil spirits which could hurt mother and child. In a small town in Württemberg, they encircled the bed while one woman used a knife to cut a circle in the air around the bed, then stuck the knife into the headboard. This was to ensure the safety of the woman and baby inside the circle, for whom "as many angels kept watch as there were shingles on the roof."[113] More elaborate ceremonies attended the mother's return to the synagogue. On a Sabbath, approximately four weeks after the birth, when her state of "impurity" (postnatal bleeding) had drawn to a close, the mother could reenter the synagogue. Her female friends accompanied her on this day, guarding her from any danger while she was still impure. Once she was blessed in the synagogue, she was as safe as any "pure" woman and was reintegrated into the community.

On the same day the community welcomed her daughter or son (who would already have been circumcised) through the baby-naming ceremony, Holekrash. The mother invited every child of the locality to her home. The children surrounded and lifted the cradle, calling, "Holekrash, what should the child be named?" They then shouted its secular (as opposed to Hebrew) name, repeating this ceremony three times. They were rewarded with fruit or candy. To bring these rituals into line with official religion, the cantor or Jewish teacher read biblical verses during the event. Elements of Holekrash appear in rabbinical literature as early as 1100, but anthropologists dispute whether the ceremony was essentially a Jewish one or one that Jews picked up from pagan and Christian sources.[114] In terms of women's history, however, the important point is that women believed they were fulfilling religious prescripts by guarding mother and infant and welcoming them into the community. In terms of Jewish family history, we recognize women's agency in defining and enacting religious family rituals.

It would be useful to discover the extent to which women initiated or practiced other rites of passage. Did they perform private, ceremonial roles in confirmations or marriages? In the case of death rituals, for example, women (like men) formally and traditionally belonged to (sex-segregated) burial societies where they washed and dressed the deceased. They watched over the bodies before interment and offered aid and solace to the bereaved family.[115] Were there informal, female rituals which accompanied these activities? More research is necessary to determine where and how long traditional and/or folk rituals remained intact, among which classes and in which geographical areas, and the role of women in their maintenance or neglect.

Of course some women dropped rituals and observance. Some preferred a more secular approach, others a more convenient one. One woman found that she "could be religious selectively, according to convenience," and convinced her husband that it was foolish to forgo lunch on Yom Kippur.[116] Also, some women assumed that a denial of their Jewish identity—religious and otherwise—would improve their position in Gentile society, yet these were a distinct minority.

Conversion and interfaith marriage statistics show Jewish men to have been the group more prone to cut their ties with Judaism and Jewish society. In the Empire in 1904, 9.3% of Jewish men and 7.7% of women intermarried; between 1910 and 1913 these figures averaged respectively 13.15% and 10.92%; and the war years, 1914–18, saw them leap to 29.86% and 21% respectively.[117] When women intermarried, economic necessity and lack of available Jewish partners were primary causes. Thus one finds that more Jewish males in mixed marriages had middle-class incomes than Jewish females. In Berlin in 1910, for example, far more Jewish women who entered into mixed marriages had been employed before their marriage (attesting to their economic need) than Jewish women who married Jewish husbands. Jewish demographers noted that Jewish men chose wealthier Jewish women who did not have to work for a living.[118] In marriages between non-Jewish men and Jewish women, commentators remarked that the latter most often (*ausserordentlich oft*) came from the lower classes.[119] In Hamburg at the turn of the century, Jewish men who married non-Jewish women belonged to the middle classes, whereas among Jewish women who intermarried, "the Jewish cook who married the Christian guard" was typical.[120] In contrast, the wealthy Jewish woman who married the penniless Prussian aristocrat or officer was a well-known but not particularly representative type. Although Jewish demographers have suggested that between 1874 and 1884 it was "particularly fashionable" for poor Prussian nobles to marry wealthy Jewish women, with the growth of anti-Semitism in the early 1880s, these marriages, despite the attractiveness of wealth, were seen as racial misalliances and declined in frequency.[121]

In rural districts where Jewish women outnumbered eligible Jewish men, there was a slightly greater tendency for women to marry out of their religion than in urban areas.[122] However, rural provinces in general witnessed proportionally fewer interfaith marriages than the more urban industrial regions.[123] As the Jewish population shifted to urban settings, experiencing the secularization that often accompanied such moves, the number of those marrying out increased among both females and males. But as the sex ratio improved for women,[124] their rate of intermarriage fell behind that of men. Large cities provided the arena for the greatest number of interfaith marriages. Berlin and the province of Brandenburg accounted for 43% of all mixed marriages in Germany in 1904: 198 men and 122 women. In this city and its surrounding area, 19.4% of Jewish men and 12.9% of women intermarried, as compared to 9.3% and 7.75%, respectively, in all of Germany.[125]

Within a mixed marriage, Jewish women were more likely than Jewish men to forgo all traces of their religious heritage. This was probably due to their clear disadvantage, compared to Jewish men (and often to non-Jewish women) in similar marriages. The chances of divorce, which were higher among mixed marriages than among those of the same religion, were even higher for those in which a Jewish woman was involved.[126] The number of children born of these marriages, and the number of stillbirths, provide further clues to the position of Jewish women. In general, Jewish women in such marriages bore more children and experienced more stillbirths than non-Jewish women married to Jewish men,[127] leading to the conclusion that intermarried couples with a Jewish wife lived at a "significantly lower standard of living" than those with a Jewish husband.[128] Importantly, the offspring of Jewish fathers were more likely to be brought up within the Jewish faith than those of Jewish mothers (although, in general, children of mixed marriages did not grow up as Jews).[129] One commentator noted: "the cultural structure of the marriage is determined . . . by the man," and this appeared to be particularly true of those with Jewish wives.[130] Thus one can conclude that when Jewish women married out, they most often did so from a more disadvantageous economic and social position than their male counterparts, lived in more meager circumstances, and had few or no resources to maintain their own heritage. The extent to which these women did give up on Jewish traditions suggests that class status influenced women's allegiance to their religion and community. Without middle-class means it may have become increasingly difficult to maintain traditional loyalties.

As in the case of interfaith marriage, female conversion was more often necessitated by serious economic need than was male conversion, which was a means toward achieving job promotion and social acceptance rather than assuring one's basic sustenance. Tax records of Berlin converts in the years 1873–1906, for example, indicate that 84 percent of female converts, as compared to 44 percent of male converts, fell in the lowest income categories.[131] Until 1880, comparatively few women converted. Between 1873 and 1906 women were one-fourth of all converts. By 1908 their share had increased to 37 percent and by 1912 to 40 percent of all conversions.[132] The entrance of women into paid employment and the growth of anti-Semitism contributed to this sudden increase. Analyses in the Jewish press suggested that because more women sought employment, they came into contact with economic anti-Semitism and believed they would not survive unless they dropped their Jewish liability. One could read of the Jewish teacher or domestic, for example, who sought positions in vain until she converted.[133]

Despite increasing rates of conversions and interfaith marriages, most middle-class Jewish women associated with a small group of Jewish friends and remained enclosed in a family circle. Their relegation to the private sphere, despite its increasingly malleable boundaries,[134] inhibited women more than men in assimilatory behavior. It has been suggested that the family was particularly important to Jews, an itinerant people forced to move from country to country, with no history of permanence or belonging. Heinrich Heine referred to it as the "portable homeland" of the Jew. Hannah Arendt noted: "In the preservation of the Jewish people the family had played a far greater role than in any Western political or social body except the nobility. Family ties were among the most potent and stubborn elements with which the Jewish people resisted assimilation and dissolution."[135] Placed in a foreign culture amid different religions, Jews looked toward the family to provide the roots and security they often lacked. Even Jewish feminists, who sought women's emancipation from traditional sociocultural constraints, clung to the notion of the family as the cornerstone of Judaism.[136]

Did Jewish families in fact provide stronger human ties and support than other families of similar class and place? If the family was more central, to what extent did wider family ties hamper contact with Germans and even with other Jews? And to what extent did the family serve as a buffer between Jews and an often unfriendly society? Did this lead to a more tenacious hold over the individuals, particularly the women, by the family?[137] Was this hold more likely to force the acquiescence or foster the rebellion of women?

We have yet to discover in a comparative manner the importance of the family to Jews relative to their German bourgeois counterparts, or the degree to which the centrality of the Jewish family was a result of internal or external circumstances. Internal circumstances include religious and cultural traditions and a positive group identity. External circumstances encompass class status and economic necessity (for example, the close connection between business life and family life among many Jews), the pressures of an anti-Semitic environment, and the high moral value placed on family life by the German bourgeoisie. What is clear is that the *ideology* of the family was very important to all Jews, simultaneously proclaiming their Jewishness and their Germanness. What further role this ideology played, whose interests it served, and who was most affected by it, are areas for further research.

For Jewish women it appears undeniable that the family was the crucial center of activity and one that they actively sought to maintain. It provided them with communality and sociability, a respite from their daily responsibilities. It also made up for their exclusion from many Gentile circles. Jewish women took responsibility for family networks, for the care of grandparents and orphans—in short, for the moral and material support, the continuity and organization, of an often geographically dispersed family system.[138] Frequently the oldest woman in the family orchestrated family events until she was no longer able. One woman recalled that when her grandmother died, her mother assumed the obligation of maintaining the family network, "so that the connections remain."[139] Grown children generally treated the aged as family responsibilities, and memoirs of grandchildren portray the elderly as family assets. Grandparents often lived within walking distance of their grandchildren in towns and big cities alike. They frequently moved in with their children when they became widowed. Single women also lived with an aging mother or father, often giving up their own ambitions to care for a parent.[140]

Jewish women participated in *Kusinenkreise* (cousins' clubs), and planned regular family gatherings to coincide with Jewish holidays or birthdays and anniversaries. Naturally it was easier to maintain contact in the towns. Yet when heightened mobility threatened to tear family ties apart, women in particular traveled to visit relatives. Families with the financial means to allow their daughters to travel sent them to care for or visit relatives.[141] In a society barely tolerant of Jews and Judaism, Jewish families who had become disproportionately mobile in a very short time nourished their ties.

The family was both a richer field of activity and a more constricting boundary for women than for men. Men spent more of their time in non-Jewish surroundings, making acquaintances of a wider circle of non-Jews. They were often unable to fulfill religious obligations in the face of anti-Semitism, or unwilling to fulfill them if they were to compete successfully. Ensconced in—and restricted to—the family, Jewish women had far less access to non-Jewish environments, less opportunity to meet non-Jews, and less occasion to experience anti-Semitism. When they did come face to face with it, they could withdraw further into the family. Even for the few who ventured out into the new world of women's careers, the family persisted as an important haven. While class, geographical location, the bonds and vitality of the local *Gemeinde*, the hostility of the non-Jewish world, and male attitudes surely played their part in shaping women's religious and ethnic identification, it may be suggested that women's socially reinforced familial preoccupations gave them the unique potential to maintain Jewish traditions as they acculturated to the norms of the German majority.

In commenting upon the decline of Judaism in this era, a historian has written: "For the large majority of Jews in Germany, . . . religion had long ceased to be the great regulator of daily life."[142] This statement is true in an overall sense, but it is less true for Jewish women. Their daily lives and monthly calendars acknowledged and marked Jewish traditions, dressing them in secular (family) forms. Jewish family rituals had given women a sense of importance and power. As their economic role in the family economy shrank and religion became less relevant to modern status aspirations, women hung on—at the very least—to traditional family gatherings, most of which marked Jewish holidays or personal anniversaries, and to their socially and culturally respected family position. Thus they effected a gentle transition to modern times, recasting traditional piety and linking it to contemporary familial practice.

In a period of rapid social transition, a gender-based division of labor in religious observance shifted the locus of religious life to the family. As male participation in Judaism declined, women's domestic observance gave a "Jewish" cast to the household. One could still feel "Jewish" without fulfilling all the formal requisites of "Judaism." When Jewish identity increasingly became a matter of choice rather than a way of life, women's traditional practices acquired a new centrality. As one scholar has noted, with the development of "optional ethnicity . . . the significance of women's religious practices moved from periphery to core."[143]

3

For Love or Money: Jewish Marriage Strategies

> A Roman woman once asked Rabbi Jose, "In how many days did the Holy One . . . create His world?" "In six days," he answered. "Then what has He been doing since . . . ?" "He sits and makes matches," came the response, "assigning this man to that woman, and this woman to that man."
>
> [*Midrash Rabbah* Genesis, section 68]

The customs surrounding the arrangement of Jewish marriages in Imperial Germany reflected ancient Jewish traditions, but also mirrored prevailing practices among the German bourgeoisie. Jewish attitudes toward love, marriage, financial security, and parental control were in many ways quite typical. A predominantly middle-class Jewry, like its non-Jewish counterparts in an industrializing capitalist economy, sought to concentrate capital through dowries and to create economic and social alliances through marriage. Jewish expectations and habits revealed the tensions between the commonplace reality of arranged marriages of convenience and the emerging ideal of romantic, companionate marriage. By the beginning of the twentieth century, Jews and other Germans increasingly acknowledged a more sentimental interpretation of the marital relationship. Yet it was only after World War I that the confluence of structural and postwar economic conditions—not the least of which were the entry of middle-class women into the labor force, and the damage to middle-class savings caused by the inflation—successfully challenged the control middle-class parents had over their children's decisions and permitted young people to "fall in love."

The Jewish experience was also distinctive, shaped by the status, aspirations, and fears of a minority. Jews differed from the majority in their emphasis on endogamy and their frank concern with financial security. As a distinct religious and ethnic group, they were committed to the perpetuation of the Jewish family as an indispensable social institution for maintaining their religion and community. As a minority in a society which increasingly practiced racial discrimination, most Jews sought endogamy and in fact had little other choice. Finally, as a group highly concentrated in business, economic interests markedly influenced their marriage decisions. Thus a study of Jews will highlight the particular concerns of a minority as it typifies socially prevalent attitudes toward "love or money."

To the Highest Bidder: Arranged Marriages and Dowries, 1871–1918

The socialization and education of women in Imperial Germany had prepared most of them for, and limited them to, marriage. Marriage was a serious business, too serious to be left to the whims of the individuals involved. Among Jews, her parents, family, friends, and matchmakers served to find the appropriate partner for a young woman. Marriages were contracts between families: material factors were of primary importance.[1] This varied according to class, with the upper strata, where marriages involved substantial property transfers, exerting the greatest control over love and courtship behavior. Families saw their goal as providing young women with economic security and a socially acceptable role, that of wife. Women in turn had to provide for their own happiness by controlling their behavior and emotions so as not to interfere with their status and duties.

Although new attitudes toward love as the foundation of marriage had received public attention in Germany with the development of the Romantic school of the early nineteenth century, it took over one hundred years for these ideas to become widely accepted. Toward the end of the nineteenth century, middle-class families began to pay lip service to notions of sentiment and love. Some parents, bowing to modern convention, arranged situations rather than marriages. As Peter Gay has noted, "If one refused to marry for money or good family, it became proverbial that one might be persuaded to go where money or good family could be predicted."[2] Finally, as memoirs and interfaith marriage statistics[3] imply, more opportunities existed for a minority of young people to respond to romance, as did more occasions when they announced their intentions to their parents. However, as we shall see, this was the exception rather than the rule; even then, couples sought parental consent and understood the importance of financial considerations. The majority, those involved in arranged marriages, resolved the conflict between an impossible and irrelevant romantic ideal and a more practical reality, by covering up arrangements to make it look as though the partners had met by coincidence. When this was not possible, participants attempted to solve the contradiction between "love" and "marriage" by "falling in love" during the engagement or shortly after the wedding.

The incongruity between ideal and reality could be found in the popular literature and social criticism of the era. In the cliché-ridden popular books of Elise Polko (1860s), German women read of conventional roles for women, of subservience to men, of motherhood and housewifery, only to be transported into the realm of "love at first sight." "When his eyes struck her, her soul underwent the most meaningful changes . . . and as the desired and feared hour neared, in which . . . the words 'I love you' fell . . . the golden doors of a new world opened."[4] The satirical weekly *Simplicissimus* debunked such romantic nonsense as a figment of bourgeois imagination and contrasted it with a reality which forced middle-class women into mercenary marriages: "The Chinese are certainly barbarous . . . they sell their girls openly in the marketplace!" a man informed a woman at a party. The woman replied, "Why, isn't that awful! How long will it take them to learn to sell their girls in private, as we do?"[5] Not surprisingly, socialist critics took a harsh view of the marriage market. August Bebel denounced a market in which people frantically sought money and status rather than a relationship based on companionship, respect, and love.[6]

For Jews, as for other bourgeois Germans, marriages of convenience (*Vernunftehen, Versorgungsehen*) were commonplace. Yet, Bebel and *Simplicissimus* notwithstanding, arranged marriages did not necessarily preclude love. Many partners grew to care deeply for each other. It would be inaccurate to assume that their feelings were stunted simply because they also acted upon their economic interests.[7] Moreover, marriage patterns as well as attitudes toward marital partnership did not remain static. A slow evolution from traditional attitudes prepared the way for the more modern courting and marriage patterns brought about by long-term structural changes and by World War I and postwar economic dislocations.

Definitions: Dowry, Trousseau, Arranged Marriage

To analyze the various forms of marriage and the changes in marriage customs, we must define what is meant by "dowry," "trousseau," and "arranged marriage." For purposes of definition, a dowry (*Mitgift*) was a transfer of property to the bride from her family as she entered marriage. This property could consist of cash, real estate, jewels, stocks, or other transferable wealth. Dowries predominated among bourgeois and propertied peasant marriages in the period from 1870 until 1918, and not only in Germany.[8]

Dowry was already known to the ancient Hebrews, among whom it remained the woman's property, although bride-price (*môhar*), or payment to the woman's family, was still the legally required settlement. Concern about the dowry can be found in the Talmud, which disapproved of marrying for money (Kiddushin 70a). During the Middle Ages rabbis expressed the belief that dowries were a form of unjust enrichment,[9] although by the thirteenth century a dowry had become the chief marriage gift in parts of Europe.[10] Its underlying assumption was that women could not contribute to the family's upkeep. By the Imperial period, the dowry's persistence underscored class differences, allowing a small middle class to accumulate capital while those below—and often above—scrambled for similar means of creating and perpetuating wealth. For women, the dowry weakened the social situation of the unmarried, particularly those in the lower ranks, while it continued to bolster the social status of a relatively small group of women of means by adding to their economic weight and hence familial status. Most German-Jewish women could be counted among those with some means, a result of their predominantly middle-class status. For women too poor to accumulate capital, their capacity to work and their own savings became their dowry.

Along with a dowry, grooms and brides expected German middle-class women and propertied peasant women to bring an extensive trousseau (*Aussteuer, Ausstattung*) to the marriage.[11] This often included linens, clothing, tableware, kitchen utensils, and furniture. Among peasants the trousseau, particularly one of hand-embroidered linen, was of great importance: "when a young woman married, she often possessed far more linen than she needed for her household."[12] Families invited their neighbors in to examine the linen and needlework, to everyone's delight and admiration.[13] The trousseau became the pride of middle-class *höhere*

Töchter as well. Confined to the home after their meager education, they stitched away the "waiting period," the time between graduation and marriage, on the linen and finery that would "last them a lifetime."[14] By the turn of the century, even this pastime became superfluous as more middle-class families bought extensive linen trousseaus in stores which began to specialize in these items.[15] As stores began to carry lines of trousseau furniture, costs mounted. The trousseau was as expensive as it was extensive: a bill could run from 2,000 to 3,000 Marks for all necessary linen, kitchenware and a bedroom set. Another 2,500 to 3,000 Marks would buy dining-room, living-room, and kitchen furniture.[16] In *Die Familie*, the conservative writer Wilhelm Riehl bemoaned the expansion of the trousseau in the mid- and late nineteenth century. He complained that, whereas the trousseau used to be made up of a few trusty old pieces of the family's furniture, it now had to be brand-new.[17]

Equipped with a substantial dowry and trousseau, a young woman could expect to have her future, that is, her marriage, arranged for her. Formal, arranged marriages, with rare exception, presupposed dowries. These unions involved a substantial exchange of wealth for security. While, as we shall see, a complex combination of age, status, looks, education, religiosity, and geographical location was factored into the equation, the primary transaction was one in which parents bartered dowries and trousseaus for a bridegroom's financial position. The partners met on the initiative of others for the express purpose of matrimony. In an arranged marriage, the union was determined far more by economic concerns than by personal inclinations. Mutual attraction and personal affinity were not ignored, but these marriages were grounded in considerations of wealth, family, and class. Although parents invariably asked the prospective bride and groom if they found their intended partner suited to them, before the turn of the century it was the rare individual who answered in the negative: "That would have been a gross insult, for in truth one married . . . 'into a family'" (Posen, 1870).[18]

Such an officially arranged marriage must be distinguished from a relationship in which the couple met as a result of others' intervention, but where marriage was not the openly acknowledged goal. A marriage resulting from an informal or coincidental situation—although possibly foreseen by those involved—was not in a strict sense arranged. Although this union proceeded within social and economic parameters—often including dowry considerations—which were consciously or unconsciously respected, the couple involved took some initiative and expressed individual desires.

Before the 1870s Jewish marriages had, with few exceptions, been arranged.[19] In her memoirs Glückl von Hameln, born in 1646, described her own two arranged marriages as well as those of her twelve children, noting the significance of financial considerations. Families respected a "good name" and religiosity, but dowries (often both for boys and girls) were essential. Money was the only insurance Jews had against political and social insecurity. Barely tolerated by local rulers, Jews paid extortionate sums for residential permits and the right to eke out an existence. Dowries enabled families to finance investments and extend the businesses which paid for limited tolerance. Also, dowries served as the basis for establishing a home and family. Partners who came from different cities, and sometimes from different countries, did not see each other before the wedding, but that did not seem necessary to Glückl. She rested assured that "forty days before the birth of every child, a call goes forth in Heaven: 'Such-and-such a child shall be given the daughter of So-and-so.'"[20] If the financial negotiations for a proposed match did not work out, then it had not "found favor with God." If the couple married, then it had been foreordained. Marriage brokers took an active role in facilitating this predestined union. Their contacts reached across national boundaries, particularly when seeking matches for the wealthy. But even the poorest could anticipate an arranged marriage, although this often took longer. If a young woman had no dowry, she waited until a wealthy person or a communal organization provided a modest gift.

Throughout the seventeenth and eighteenth centuries, arranged marriages and the need for dowries remained much as in Glückl's day. However, the bride and bridegroom generally met each other before the wedding, and parents respected strong dislikes despite the financial penalties for breaking an engagement.[21] Henriette Herz's engagement (although not her age) typified the decision-making process of many families of her class. In 1779, when she was fifteen, her parents engaged her to a thirty-year-old doctor.

> At the noon meal my father asked me if I would rather marry a doctor or a rabbi. My heart pounded strongly and I answered that I would be satisfied with anything he decided for me. After the meal, my mother told me I would get engaged to Dr. Markus Herz that evening. . . . I knew little about my fiancé, he was fifteen years older than me, small and ugly, but had an intelligent face.[22]

Even as reformers challenged Orthodox assumptions and rituals in the mid-nineteenth century, Orthodox traditions regarding marriage arrangements continued to be observed by many families. In 1900, over one hundred years after Henriette Herz's engagement, another young woman found it perfectly normal for her father to announce: "Put on a white pinafore, today you are getting engaged!"[23]

The Art of Arranging a Marriage

Families took the lead in finding suitable partners for their eligible members and in working out the details of the engagement and marriage contracts. They did this as a family service and/or as a *mitzvah* (a commandment, a good or pious deed). Women used kin and friendship networks for informal brokering, and men conducted the financial discussions which preceded any formal encounter. Whereas prospective brides remained passive, often unaware of their family's project, grooms, particularly older ones, also took initiatives. Furthermore, parents or relatives often pressed young women into marrying. One reluctant young woman married at the age of nineteen (1865), because it was a relief for her parents to have one less daughter to support. She had not married out of love but "grew to love him," according to her daughter.[24] The Friedmann family of Mannheim serves to illustrate the typical arrangements of the era. In 1889 a young businessman sent his friend to Mr. Friedmann to arrange a marriage with Mr. Friedmann's nineteen-year-old daughter, Eugenie. She had never met the man, but had noticed him when she shopped in his store. Her father told her that a wealthy businessman had asked for her hand. Father, grandmother, and several aunts urged her to accept; she did. Next, in 1894 twenty-three-year-old Martha Friedmann was informed by her parents that a young suitor (*Freier*) would come to visit her. The young couple met and agreed on the spot to marry. Financial arrangements had already been discussed prior to their meeting and the individuals approved of each other's appearance and manners. Beyond this, they knew nothing of each other, assuming only that each would fulfill well-defined roles and duties. Thereafter, the last two Friedmann daughters met their future husbands through the intercession of friends and distant relatives in 1903 and 1906 respectively.[25]

Parents frequently arranged marriages after making formal inquiries with respected families or after coincidentally meeting a prospective partner for one of their children. The future in-laws of Flora Goldschmidt encountered her on a train journey. Vaguely aware of her family's favorable status and position, they enjoyed her company and decided they would like her as a daughter-in-law. The groom's family asked their friend, Flora's uncle, to introduce the young people. The young man visited her home in Breslau on May 14, 1872. They announced their engagement on June 1. Then "he brought me to his parents. . . . I wish to all my female descendants the way I was received at the old family house [of her in-laws] and their joy and fuss."[26] It had been love at first sight between the in-laws and the bride. Formal inquiries were also common. The future father-in-law of Jacob Rosenheim wrote a formal letter to Rosenheim's parents asking if their twenty-seven-year-old son would marry his seventeen-year-old daughter. The families had corresponded about Jewish and philanthropic concerns but did not know each other personally. Young Rosenheim was engaged to his bride several days after they met; they got married a few weeks later.[27] Rosenheim later became the founder of the Orthodox Agudat Israel. Whereas Liberal Jews permitted some individual initiatives, among the Orthodox strictly arranged marriages continued to be the rule throughout the Imperial period. According to one observer (born in 1880), "in the Orthodox tradition, every girl was suited to every man. She had so little individual personality that she could adjust to every man."[28]

Brothers, particularly when they were their sisters' formal guardians, often arranged marriages. In 1862 a seventeen-year-old was talked into marriage by a brother who was also her guardian. She and her contemporaries considered seventeen to be a very young age, but she dutifully submitted.[29] Another brother persuaded his sister to marry by assuring her that, if she consented, "it will be as if you have bought yourself life insurance."[30] Brothers drafted friends as well as casual acquaintances in their pursuit of partners for their sisters. Some of these marriages in turn provided business opportunities for the brothers. In 1878 in Meseritz, a polite discussion between two strangers on the way home from synagogue ended with one man inviting the other to consider a match with his sister. The prospective bridegroom spoke with the mother of the bride and her other brothers, agreeing that if all went well, they would open a business together. Then the young man visited the bride, commented on her "goodness," and concentrated on the details of the financial arrangements.[31] Throughout the Imperial period brothers placed matrimonial advertisements in newspapers for their sisters. Ads and initiatives beginning with the formula "Seeking for my sister . . ."[32] may have been particularly numerous in a society in which responsibility for the family fell to the eldest male when both parents were deceased. Furthermore, according to a Jewish source, "Brothers only married when their sisters had been settled. They were brought up to regard this as a necessary moral preliminary to their own marriages."[33] While this assertion remains to be proved, for the town of Nonnenweier, at least, Jewish marriage patterns suggest that brothers might have postponed their marriages in order to contribute to their sisters' dowries and see them married off.[34]

Thus family members helped each other find appropriate partners, ones who would suit the personal and financial requirements of the individual and the family. With family business goals in mind, for example, the Hirschfeld brothers of Hamburg arranged each other's marriages. Having just opened a new store in 1894, both men decided to vacation in fashionable spas where they could "be seen," and where a "young woman with money might fall in love with us." Each man traveled to a different resort to make useful business and social contacts. Shortly thereafter, both were invited to a fancy wedding. "Coincidentally," one of them was seated next to a woman whom he had met at the spa. One's *Tischdame* (table partner) was usually an eligible young lady, and, as we will see, marriages occasionally ensued from these seating arrangements. After the wedding, Joseph mentioned that he had liked the young woman. His brother immediately arranged a meeting with her relatives. Financial negotiations ensued, and the woman's parents asked the brothers to submit their accounting records. The family offered a 25,000-Mark dowry, a satisfactory equivalent to the groom's share of profits during the preceding year (20,000 Marks) and to the size and prospects of his business. With the negotiations behind him, Joseph embarked on a trip to visit the woman, promising his brother that he just wanted to become acquainted with her. "The train arrived in Hannover at 11:30. At 12 o'clock they announced their engagement to me on the phone."[35]

Parents made use of professional, business, and friendship networks when their familial contacts were limited. Jewish villagers in southern and southwestern Germany, for example, had many ties with other Jews across the borders in France, Switzerland, and Belgium, and used these connections when they sought mates for their relatives or friends.[36] Needless to say, such marriages furthered business, professional, and social contacts as well. In 1870 the well-known Jewish historian Heinrich Graetz asked a former student, Joseph Perles, whom he also considered a friend, to find a suitable husband for his daughter Flora. He suggested that Perles's wife be consulted, informed them that Flora would receive a 1,000-Thaler dowry, and noted that she did not want to marry a rabbi. With those conditions in mind, his friends were to find him a son-in-law. In 1873 Graetz again took his friend into his confidence, asking him to check into the intentions and job prospects of a young scholar who had recently met Flora. Graetz preferred the academic to a wealthy businessman who had indicated his interest but might not have been educated enough for his daughter. Trusting in the "carefulness and intelligence" of a close friend, and keeping his daughter's preferences in mind, the father had not yet asked the daughter's opinion.[37] Friends thus served important functions of information gathering, providing gossip and news about a potential spouse's reputation and income. At other times they helped with introductions, and at still other times they introduced potential partners without having been asked to do so.

When the efforts of family, business contacts, and friends failed to produce a marriage partner, parents hired professional marriage brokers (*Heiratsvermittler* in German, *shadkhan* in Hebrew). These men, and sometimes women, specialized in a particular financial class and in certain geographic territories. After a successful union, the broker received a percentage of the dowry.[38] In a letter to a Jewish father in 1873, one such broker offered his assistance in finding a partner among the wealthy Berlin bourgeoisie: "I know many Jewish families, for example, *Sanitätsrat* Hymann, Dr. Mendel, Dr. Jakobsohn . . . and many others. I have bankers, factory owners, doctors, lawyers, etc."[39] Brokers placed their own marriage advertisements in Jewish newspapers, or responded to the ads placed by individuals.[40] Also, satisfied customers recommended them to friends.[41] While most brokers provided detailed information on a family's history and fortune, detective services offered more sensitive information. They warned their target audiences: "Don't marry or become engaged before you know exact details about . . . the person, family, dowry, reputation, previous history. Discreet special information available."[42] One detective's "highly confidential" report, intended for the father of a young woman, described the health and wealth of the prospective groom. The detective reported on the financial fortunes of the suitor's parents, married brothers and sisters, and their in-laws. He delved into the sporting and athletic activities of the young man as well as his friends and acquaintances. He would not predict the young law student's career success, but could say with confidence that a previous malady was no longer of medical concern and that the family was socially and economically highly recommended.[43]

Urban Jews were by no means the only Jews who called upon the services of professionals. Scattered about small towns and villages at a time when Jews made up only 1 percent of Germany's population, provincial Jews found it difficult to meet suitable partners. This geographic hardship was worsened by economic and social mobility. Young men chose to migrate to larger urban centers to pursue more lucrative careers. They did this around the time they embarked on a career path, at precisely marrying age. Since Jewish men migrated in greater numbers than women, the latter had particular difficulty in finding Jewish mates in their hometowns. Thus rural Jews made substantial use of the broker. In rural Württemberg, for example, brokered marriages were the rule.[44] In Hesse, too, a memoir reveals, "Jewish marriages in the countryside (also in the city) were, as with the peasant population, not made in heaven."[45] Local Jewish teachers frequently served as marriage brokers, using networks of teachers in other villages and towns. This enabled them to earn an extra income to bolster their meager salaries. Whereas all brokers knew the finances of their customers, teachers could often comment on the personalities of their former pupils as well. One teacher who brokered many marriages in Baden around the turn of the century, passed on both of his professions to his son. The young man (born in 1897) continued to broker marriages until his salary reached the level of other local teachers.[46] Despite their general usefulness, brokers were suspected for their mercenary motives and were not usually well respected; "but in families with many daughters and few contacts, one willingly let him in the back door."[47]

Those who could not afford or who mistrusted marriage brokers, those whose connections did not provide sufficient choice, or those who opted to make their own arrangements placed advertisements in local Jewish newspapers. These ads mirrored similar phenomena in German local and regional newspapers, where they could—and still can—be found in abundance. They filled a role which had traditionally been the function of a community or social group. In fact, they attest to the rapid geographic mobility as well as the changing social positions and aspirations of individuals, many of whom found themselves cut off from communal and local roots and connections. Many Jewish newspapers reserved sections for those seeking marriage partners. Samples of these ads can provide an indication of the range of dowries and of their relative importance, although we cannot of course know if these ads resulted in a match. It is likely that, if they did, one or both partners would have denied it. In one case the bride's family, which had placed the successful ad, insisted that the marriage had been a coincidence, whereas the groom's side recalled the ad in the *Frankfurter Zeitung*.[48]

Components of the Marriage Market

Families specified various characteristics of their daughters in the ads they placed, such as age, appearance, education, health, geographic location, previous marital status, ability to engage in paid labor (if the dowry was small), and sometimes religiosity ("pretty, educated girl, religious but not Orthodox").[49] Money, however, was the most important factor. In 1912 the editor of a Berlin Jewish newspaper could still comment that in marriage ads "in the first place, the main thing, the dowry and then the accessory, the gracious bride, is examined."[50] A sample of Jewish newspaper advertisements from Berlin, Cologne, Frankfurt/Main, and Ansbach/Strassburg, as well as memoirs and interviews, offer some insights into the marriage market and the going rate for brides in Imperial Germany. To marry into the upper bourgeoisie in Berlin, for example, a woman had to possess substantial wealth and position. In 1904 a woman with 75,000 Marks sought a lawyer, doctor, or independent businessman. The woman was described as pretty and from the "finest of families" (*aus vornehmster Familie*).[51] Another ad that same year offered a dowry of 50,000 Marks and "more later" for a doctor or lawyer.[52] The price for professionals probably rose in the first decades of the twentieth century, so that the family of another woman had to offer 100,000 Marks for a Berlin dentist in 1920.[53] Assets could be used to set up a home, expand a business, or begin a professional practice. As late as the 1920s, the wealthy Berlin Jewish bourgeoisie still exchanged substantial dowries. "Married couples established themselves with the dowry," recalled one woman. Commenting on her sisters' marriages in 1920 and 1921, she observed: "You could almost buy people. If you had so much you could buy a doctor or a lawyer, or if you didn't have so much you might only get a businessman." She saw no difference between the customs of her grandmother's generation—"sometimes the man married only the dowry"—and those of her own. A girlfriend (born in 1905) had seen her engagement shattered when her seemingly wealthy father died, leaving no inheritance. She compared this incident to her grandmother's constant admonition: "Love is nothing." Even in the 1920s her friends married "to have a nice home, . . . to bring up children."[54]

Dowries were not confined to the *haute bourgeoisie*, although the custom may have continued longest in this class. The Jewish middle strata of well-to-do shopkeepers, tradespeople, and business people were equally dependent on financial arrangements. In Berlin a woman with a dowry of 30,000 could hope to attract a partner with an income of about 10,000, the annual profit margin for a successful shopkeeper or businessman. However, the woman also had to possess other attributes. A thirty-four-year-old men's clothing store owner sought a 30,000-Mark dowry with a woman "no older than twenty-three."[55] The family of one eligible young woman embellished her 30,000-Mark dowry by advertising her youth (twenty years old), looks ("very pretty"), education and family reputation ("from distinguished Israelite family").[56] Thirty thousand marks appears to have been the mean dowry advertised in Berlin. This figure would have been considered very high in a small town or village.

A less substantial dowry would attract a man of even more modest means. For 20,000 Marks a Berlin woman could hope for a husband who would earn about 6,000 yearly, the salary of a mid-level civil servant.[57] Women with from 8,000 to 10,000 Marks could expect suitors who were independent craftsmen or white-collar workers (*Angestellte*).[58] Anything less might attract a craftsman, especially if the woman indicated that she was willing to work outside the home.[59] The lowest amount offered in the Berlin papers was 5,000 Marks in search of a craftsman. There was one exception: a "simple and domestic" young woman with 2,000 Marks sought an "elderly, well-situated gentleman."[60] At the bottom end of the dowry scale, it was more likely for interfaith marriages to occur: thus the example of the daughter of a Jewish cattle dealer whose 4,000-Mark dowry bought her a Catholic husband who was a butcher.[61] Jewish men preferred wealthier Jewish women, and since a "surplus" of women (*Frauenüberschuss*) existed in this period, some Jewish women had to look elsewhere for husbands. As already seen in chapter 2, poverty and the lack of available Jewish partners caused Jewish women to marry out.[62] In fact, generally it was at the bottom end of the dowry scale that women were allowed to "fall in love," for the dictates of parents who could not offer dowries were not as compelling. And despite grave reservations about intermarriage, some parents acquiesced in the belief that their penniless daughter had found someone to provide for her.

Although dowries reached the highest levels in Berlin, other large cities did not lag far behind. In Hamburg, a desirable city because of its business and cultural life and its large Jewish community, the wealthy owner of a very profitable, expanding business received 100,000 Marks with his bride in 1912.[63] As in Berlin, each spouse tried to approximate the other's contribution. For example, in 1909 in Breslau, a couple matched the groom's "worth" of 13,333 Marks (a one-third partnership in his family's business) with the woman's 15,000 Marks (10,000 in cash and 5,000 worth of furniture).[64] In Cologne and Frankfurt, women with only 10,000 to 12,000 Marks suffered a clear disadvantage: they might have to be willing to work outside the home or to marry older, less desirable men, even widowers. One brother's ad referred to his sister's commercial education, an indication that she could help out in a family business or work outside the home. The relative of another woman advertised that she was ready to consider marriage to a widower, even one with a child.[65]

Outside the major cities, Jewish men and/or their families demanded relatively smaller sums. In 1902 a twenty-eight-year-old doctor from a "big city" in Silesia could require around 50,000 Marks from a bride.[66] In 1914 a wealthy man (*Grosskaufmann . . . mit grösserem Vermögen*) who lived in a small village expressed interest in a woman with money, but was willing to settle for no dowry at all.[67] Nevertheless, in the rural countryside, among peddlers and cattle and horse dealers, dowries were essential to the vast majority of marriage transactions. In one case the wife brought 500 Thaler (1857) into the marriage in order to buy a house with a barn for her husband's horses.[68] Where cash was lacking, the bride's father could offer financially valuable substitutes. This was the case in Silesia, where one father-in-law gave the groom three districts in which he could have a monopoly of peddling rights, and in Bavaria, where the father-in-law of a cattle dealer gave a house valued at 25,000 Marks.[69]

Sometimes the dowry became the goal and the bride simply the means to the end. Advertisements were seen such as, "Young man . . . in manufacturing . . . with 10,000 Marks, seeks to marry into business or similar branch," or even more directly, "Cutter wishes to marry into a business" (*Einheirat: Zuschneider wünscht Einheirat*).[70] It was, indeed, the strikingly rare advertisement which made no mention of a dowry. One such ad, placed in 1902 by a woman, rather than under the usual auspices of her parents or brother, ignored financial considerations entirely, noting: "have not stood apart from the women's movement, would like very much to marry now, in order to achieve happiness through mutual work."[71] Such an ad, seeking an egalitarian relationship on a noncommercial basis, stood in stark contrast to those in which men sought "marriage into a business."

Dowries determined not only the partner and economic future a woman might expect, but also her life-style. For example, a substantial dowry gave parents the leverage necessary to insist on certain conditions in the new household. In one case, both fathers-in-law appeared pleased with the prospective couple (arranged through an ad) as well as the financial negotiations. However, the groom's father had one absolute requirement:

> "What about Kosher," he asked. "Who would keep a Kosher kitchen? Without the assurance that my son's household will uphold the Jewish dietary traditions, I cannot give my complete consent." Silence. "Liesl can do the Kosher cooking," Julia [the bride's mother] offered. . . . "I will send her to . . . live with [them]." . . . Liesl had served in the . . . household for more than twenty years. . . . Although she was not Jewish, she had been trained . . . in all the details of keeping a Kosher kitchen. She was the solution. Thereupon, Jakob H. dropped a glass to the floor, stepped on it and said, "Good luck."[72]

The size of the dowry also regulated the geographic area in which a woman would settle. With a generous endowment, women could hope to remain in or move to attractive locations, usually cities. The fewer resources a woman had, the more likely it was that she might have to move to a smaller town. In 1906, for example, a young woman with a substantial dowry of 30,000 Marks could leave her tiny village (of 900 people) and "move up" to a small town where her marriage had been arranged to a man with a "solid middle-class income," a trader in vinegar and dyes.

In 1910 a woman from Regensburg with only 12,000 Marks had to relocate to a tiny village. Her dowry could interest only a man of middling means in a less desirable location. It was commonly concluded that when a city woman moved into a village, it was due to a small dowry.[73] This "downward" geographical mobility was unique to brides: it was the price they paid to maintain their class position, when dowries were inadequate. Men rarely moved from larger to smaller towns for any reason.[74] They either imported wives to their small towns or migrated to larger cities in search of better business and marriage opportunities. Conversely, while brides moved to smaller places, single Jewish women rarely moved to larger cities on their own. As a result, many more women than men of marriageable age lived in the small towns and villages. This probably caused an inflation in the size of dowries needed to lure a diminishing supply of men. It is also likely that many families decided to migrate to urban centers, when it became clear that daughters could not find suitable partners in their hometown. Thus property relations affected the family's geographic mobility: not only business, educational, and cultural opportunities, but family marriage strategies as well, contributed to the lure of urban life for Jews.

Aside from money and geographical location, age played a significant role in a woman's ability to marry. Men demanded that brides be no older than twenty-five; some set the limit at twenty-three. The average age of Berlin bourgeois Jewish brides in 1909, for example, was twenty-two to twenty-three for those marrying academics, and twenty-three to twenty-four for those marrying businessmen. Poorer women were slightly older, but twenty-five was often considered "too old" for any woman.[75] Hence the ad placed for a twenty-eight-year-old woman stated that she "looked young."[76] By that age, most women were considered "old maids" and had resigned themselves to a life of spinsterhood with its financial insecurity and low social status.[77]

The exchange of dowries among Jewish families with some means was an almost universal phenomenon which declined only slowly in the 1920s.[78] Dowries were taken for granted not only for the financial security they promised, but also for the power and status they conferred on the wife and her family.[79] Anthropologists have long identified gift giving—for example, in marriage exchanges—as a means of exerting power,[80] and Jewish families were certainly aware of this. Consequently, the remark of a young man about his sisters' marriages—"the economic base of marriage was highly valued by Jews"—must be interpreted broadly.[81] The dowry preserved women's status in marriage. It was a woman's only psychological counterpoint to total dependency on her husband. In the fifty-four years that followed their marriage in 1912, for example, the wife of a Jewish cattle dealer often reminded him of her large dowry. It was taken for granted that her property preserved a respected position for her.[82] Wives and their parents easily recalled their contributions to husbands' businesses or practices and did not hesitate to recount these details if husbands acted too proudly or if family quarrels developed. Similarly, a substantial dowry increased a bride's authority vis à vis her in-laws. And of course, the dowry served as an economic counterpoint. It is still common today for those women who were told the value of their own dowry, and that of their relatives and friends, to remember them. They insist that these sums made just as important a contribution to their marriages as their husbands' earnings. Further, the dowry was the wife's only financial recourse, if the marriage were to fail. Although German law gave the husband the right to manage and use his wife's dowry, it was not his possession. In most cases, the dowry reverted to the woman if the marriage ended.[83]

All participants understood that a family staked its prestige during dowry negotiations. For a bourgeois family, the dowry was a measure of its reputation. For the petty bourgeoisie, in particular, the dowry was a source of parental pride. Some, in fact, had refused to allow their daughters to invest even part of their dowry in a career, even an "acceptable" one like teaching.[84] Parents had often scrimped and saved in order to accumulate their daughters' dowries. The following exchange from the novel *Moritzchens Tagebuch* by Karl Ettlinger (1908) illustrates this. Moritzchen and his childhood sweetheart had agreed to marry. Just before the wedding the bride's father, a man of humble means, reproached the groom for not inquiring about the dowry. "Am I marrying the dowry, or am I marrying Rahel?" asked the groom. The father replied angrily: "Do you want to introduce an innovation in the world? There's no place for pride in financial matters. D'ya think I saved my whole life long so that my son-in-law should come and be more generous than I? No way! My Rahel gets her trousseau and 10,000 Marks in cash!"[85]

By the time of *Moritzchen*'s publication, it was possible for such informal financial understandings, particularly those involving smaller amounts, to occur. In prior decades, however, parents engaged in formal negotiations, and witnesses and notaries attended the writing of the contract. A typical marriage contract of the 1870s stipulated the exact amount of the bride's dowry and a description of the trousseau; the dates when these had to be delivered; the right of the bride's family to the dowry and her portion of the wedding gifts if she died childless within the first two years of marriage; the bride's rights if the groom died childless within the first two years; and the bride's right to her dowry, trousseau, and wedding gifts in case of a divorce in which she was blameless. The groom usually renounced any further demands on the bride's family and promised to sign a formal receipt when he received the dowry and trousseau. Thereupon, wealthy families would duly enter the dowry in the profit column of their financial ledger.[86] Sometimes the contracts included agreements between parents and children, such as one which promised 30,000 Marks with the understanding that this was part of the daughter's inheritance. An arrangement between the groom and his business partners, providing for his widow's participation in the business, might also appear in a contract.[87] Further, the groom could free his wife from the Jewish ritual of *halitzah* (the law by which a childless widow had to marry her brother-in-law), by stating that he would give her a letter from his brother freeing her to marry whomever she chose, if she became widowed.[88] Although most documents contained the individuals' promises to "remain true in marriage," to remain wedded for the length of their lives, or to engage in "mutually respectful treatment," and some even included a declaration of love, they were stamped by a notary and signed by from two to four official witnesses.[89] Begun with an invocation to God, they ended as a legal business document.

It is unclear when verbal agreements and a handshake began to replace these formally notarized statements. In the 1880s some parents accepted verbal commitments in front of witnesses.[90] By the mid-1890s other families still demanded legal documents. However, in 1895 the groom's side of a 25,000-Mark negotiation "took this as a vote of no confidence, but consented."[91] Most likely, the formal contracts lasted longest where the greatest property was involved. The extent of the negotiations which preceded the legal transactions is also unclear from the available literature. We can only suggest that by the end of the Imperial era, as a result of the further *embourgoisement* of German Jews and their acculturation to German styles of behavior, real bargaining and negotiating seems to have given way to a general agreement regarding a sum understood by both families to be socially acceptable.

Since dowries were an essential ingredient in most Jewish marriages in Imperial Germany, parents, relatives, and the Jewish community sought to ensure that young women might have at least modest means at their disposal when they reached adulthood. In some cases middle-class parents bought dowry insurance which matured when girls reached the age of eighteen.[92] Wealthy relatives might be found to provide a sum if parents could not.[93] Jewish dowry clubs, too, donated funds to needy brides. Giving gifts to poor brides was a holy duty among the ancient Hebrews and medieval Jews. This custom was reinforced by a European (Christian) tradition harking back to the fourteenth century, in which public and private charities dowered the poverty-stricken.[94] The dowering of brides was written into Jewish law. For example, in 1726 the Hamburg Jewish community stipulated that public collections be scheduled to assist needy young women. Financial aid for prospective brides took precedence over most forms of charity.[95] By the nineteenth century, dowry giving was most often organized by women's societies or wealthy families. One such family maintained a book with the names of all the brides to whom it gave donations from 1810 through 1914.[96] Aaron Hirsch Heymann, born in Berlin in 1873, wrote that his family brought forty-four couples together and gave even more donations to needy brides.[97] Traditional women's charities as well as more modern ones focused on the needs of poor brides. The Brautausstattung Stiftung in Hamburg, for example, functioned from 1814 until 1913, and the Israelitischer Brautausstattung Verein, also in Hamburg, lasted from 1840 to 1934. New dowry clubs formed in the Imperial era: in Altona one was founded in 1880 and lasted until World War I; in Würzburg the dowry endowment was also founded in 1880 and existed until 1938; and in Lübeck one was reconstituted as late as 1903.[98] The ubiquity and longevity of these charities testified to their continued and renewed importance, despite their modest donations.[99]

Avoiding Spinsterhood

Women without recourse to any financial assistance had a few options. In contrast to the "oversupply" of women in the German-Jewish community, men outnumbered women among Eastern European immigrants. Despite severe penalties paid by women who married foreigners (they lost their citizenship and could be expelled with their husbands), by the early 1880s German-Jewish women increasingly married Eastern European men. Prussian officials claimed this was part of an effort on the part of poor Jews in Posen to find Russian immigrant Jewish husbands for their unmarried daughters.[100] A more risky venture to avoid spinsterhood was emigration, undertaken by only a few. Some women emigrated as a result of a marriage proposal, others in pursuit of marriage possibilities. "Only poor girls accepted American marriage proposals," noted one woman.[101] Even without proposals, some families were desperate enough to send daughters abroad to make their own way. In the 1890s three daughters from a village family of nine children fled to the United States rather than remain single in Germany. In 1900, when a father of ten children could not afford a dowry for two of his five daughters, they also emigrated to America in hopes of finding work and a marriage partner there.[102]

There was one last opportunity to save oneself from spinsterhood. A woman could marry a widower, widely acknowledged to be a less than optimal match. Generally, widowers were a great deal older than their second brides (and this in an era when a five-to-seven-year age gap was considered normal). Often, they had children and hoped to find a mother and housekeeper for them. Left with four children when his wife died in 1890, one man remarried within a year. When his second wife died in 1901, leaving him with an additional five children, he again remarried within the year. His son recalled, "My father left the care of the children entirely to my stepmother."[103] In order to avoid the necessity of such a match, one brother married his sister off at twenty-one, afraid that at an older age she would be forced to marry a widower.[104] After losing her dowry, another young woman married a widower "who spoke of duty, not of love."[105]

As women reached their late twenties, it was clear to outsiders that their chances had dwindled to nothing. People assumed that, had they had money, they would have been married off. Not only were they aging, but they were also poor. The family of a "maiden aunt" who had reached the ripe old age of twenty-eight considered her "saved" by a fifty-two-year-old widower.[106] Another woman married a widower whose first wife had referred to her as one of those "*Mädchen* . . . who awaited the deaths of women in order to marry widowers."[107] To marry off women in danger of being "left behind" and to help widowers in their endeavors, the prescriptive literature of the period, particularly short stories written for Jewish family magazines, encouraged such marriages of convenience. The young governess who married the rich, old widower with children and lived happily ever after—"it is better . . . to face reality . . . ideals don't bring much"—typified this genre.[108]

Thus the Jewish bourgeoisie attached extraordinary importance to marriage decisions. Marriages, arranged for the most part, were economic transactions expected to provide both partners with reciprocal benefits. They were also social contracts intended to reproduce the Jewish family and maintain the Jewish community. An elaborate network of parents, relatives, friends, associates, marriage brokers, and insurance and charity organizations stood ready to facilitate and control marriages in order to avoid unfavorable alliances, emigration, or spinsterhood. Brides remained primarily passive, part of—but not always the most significant part of—the traffic in dowries. As we shall see, in a period of rapid capital accumulation the interdependence of the traditional gender system with the economic system gave a preeminence to dowries.

The Dowry Chase: Critical Perspectives

Jewish Self-Criticism

Although financial prerequisites for marriages were universally taken for granted, attacks upon the commercialization of marriage proliferated. Dowries were the object of persistent and serious criticism within the Jewish community. Many Jews disparaged the questionable ethics involved in marrying money. They worried that women sought paid employment and postponed marriage in order to accumulate adequate or grandiose dowries. They feared that later marriages would produce fewer offspring for the Jewish community. They also expressed concern that Jews were not living up to German norms. Moreover, they were anxious over the fact that Jewish women were being "left behind"—which they were[109]—as a result of population imbalances caused by male migration, emigration, conversion, and interfaith marriages, but also as a consequence of the pursuit of dowries. If dowries were insufficient, suitors looked elsewhere. One man reported that, despite mutual affection, his mother's engagement had fallen through "because the dowry was not large enough for the young man's family."[110] Conversely, the more it appeared that bridegrooms were shopping and daughters might not marry, the greater the effort to increase dowry sizes became.

As early as 1849, one could read a critique of money marriages in the broadly circulated *Allgemeine Zeitung des Judentums*. The newspaper suggested (as did feminists then and later) that Jewish women learn a trade or the skills with which to contribute toward a family's existence. In that way, love and not money could be the deciding factor. "Why is it that so many marriage candidates of the Jewish [*israelitisch*] middle class strive for economic gain rather than let personal inclinations alone decide their choice?" The journal located this "evil" among the "numerically preponderant middle class," not among the Jewish poor. Aware that Jews had been severely circumscribed to fields of business and commerce, and that their recent emancipation from economic strictures would take years to realize, the *Allgemeine* acknowledged the desire of most young men to combine a favorable financial marriage settlement with the establishment of an independent enterprise. However, it urged Jews to recognize that a woman who could help out in the business, or who could do without servants at home, would be just as useful as a young heiress, the more so, since a badly invested dowry could be lost forever. The newspaper chided parents that women's education was faulty: piano playing, singing, and dancing were hardly as useful as being able to support themselves. "Why don't we see this chasing after money marriages among our Christian fellow citizens? Do not think they like money any less than Jews do: that would be a big mistake. But, [there is a] significant difference. . . . If a Christian middle class father has six daughters, then, for example, one is a teacher, governess or companion, another is a milliner . . . , a third teaches music." The *Allgemeine* concluded that men's demands could not change until young women had a more practical education.[111]

Orthodox spokesmen also spoke out against the deleterious consequence of dowry-centered marriages. In 1895 an editorial in the Orthodox family weekly *Die Laubhütte* stated: "Dowries are getting higher every year. . . . Soon, middle-class girls will no longer be able to buy men, and poor girls already have no chance to get married." The journal censured girls who wanted luxurious life-styles: men could not afford to marry such wives without huge dowries. Echoing male complaints which can be traced back as far as the Renaissance, the *Laubhütte* also repeated age-old solutions: women had to lower their expectations.[112] Unfortunately, neither the causes of, nor the solutions for, money marriages were so simple. Unable to change social conditions, the *Laubhütte* could only promote a novel vision of marriage through its serial stories. In a love story published in 1903, a young man unknown to the family came to the father of the women he admired to ask for her hand. He avoided the use of the customary middleman, an initial break with tradition. The father immediately apprised the suitor that his daughter had no dowry. The prospective groom already knew this—obviously, no reader would have believed that the suitor could possibly have been ignorant of the family's finances—and was willing to forgo all financial prerequisites—a radical break with tradition.[113] Thus the *Laubhütte* disseminated a highly unlikely scenario in its growing awareness of a social dilemma.

A generation later, in 1919, a letter to the *Israelitisches Familienblatt*, the most widely read German-Jewish newspaper, reiterated earlier concerns. The correspondent bemoaned the "tendency, among us Jews, to put the dowry in first place in the choice of a wife." The letter suggested that the situation could be improved, if academically trained men—doctors or lawyers—married for idealistic rather than mercenary reasons. Businessmen of course needed dowries to invest in their businesses. Hence even those who spoke out against marriages for money bowed to their "necessity" in most cases.[114] Jewish feminists, who denounced the "dowry chase" (*Mitgiftjägerei*), had no immediate solutions either. Beyond demanding economic independence for future generations of women, they could only criticize the emphasis on dowries, which was "not limited to Jewish circles."[115]

Surprisingly, discussions of the divorce rate, higher for Jews than for Christians, did not enter the debate about dowries.[116] Most often Jewish demographers simply attributed increasing rates of divorce to the stresses of an increasingly urban life, since arranged marriages had been the norm well before the divorce rates began to cause concern. However, the primary reason for divorce among the Jewish population, adultery (*Ehebruch*), with men ten times more likely than women to seek liaisons outside the marriage, may have had roots in the large number of Jewish arranged "convenience" marriages in a period in which there was both more discussion of love and more opportunities (for men) to roam in search of it.[117]

Tensions between the ideal of a companionate "love" marriage and the financial realities of a "responsible" money marriage were often played out in literature. Jewish writers assailed the "Jewish" proclivity to emphasize dowries, although money marriages were not at all unique to Jewish circles. Jewish literature was replete with tales of and attacks upon arranged money marriages. In a series of Jewish joke books published in the 1860s and 1870s, for example, the jokes and satires both reflected and criticized the pursuit of financial gain through marriage. There was the man who married an unattractive woman, thinking she was wealthy, only to discover that she was poor.[118] For other characters, the brides' looks, simplicity, and thrift were too meager. "Where will that get me?" they wondered.[119] Arranged marriages between the children of business associates were held up to ridicule. In a series of satirical letters, grain merchants discussed business and the possible union of their offspring. In the spirit of their dickering over the prices of wheat and rye, they wrangled with each other over the size of the dowry. The engagement was announced twenty-five days after the start of the grain negotiations.[120]

In *Jettchen Gebert*, first serialized in the *Vossische Zeitung* in 1906 and one of the most popular novels of German-Jewish life, Georg Hermann dramatized the dilemma of an arranged marriage of convenience.[121] The heroine agreed to marry a man she did not love, although she was infatuated with another. She went through with the wedding, but then ran away and found refuge with her uncle. Her aunt, a member of the older generation, tried to talk sense into her by explaining that marriage was, after all, only security: "You have to try to get used to each other. If divorce were as easy as the wedding, no marriage would last longer than half a year. . . . My child . . . I don't understand you. What do you expect from men? After all, they're all alike."[122] Both *Jettchen* and its sequel, *Henriette Jacoby* (1915), contained mixed messages. Hermann acknowledged the importance of love and woman's right to make a decision regarding marriage. The family "encouraged"—never overtly forced—Jettchen to marry. They supported her divorce—reluctantly. Yet Jettchen's romantic feelings were shown to be fleeting and had disastrous consequences. As a result of her escapades, the object of her affection lost his civil-service post. Her family had to negotiate a settlement with her husband for his consent to the divorce, and Jettchen fell in love with yet another man. *Jettchen Gebert* went into its ninetieth reprinting in 1920 with many of its themes still of current interest.

Ettlinger's novel *Moritzchens Tagebuch*, a less ambivalent literary treatment of the subject, clearly advocated love over money. Moritzchen, a young Jew from a small southern German town, set out to make his fortune in Berlin. An efficient and skillful salesman, the young man attracted the attention of his employer. The latter tried to tie Moritzchen to his business by offering him his daughter and 40,000 to 50,000 Marks. When Moritzchen explained that he was already engaged, the employer simply raised the bid to a partnership in the business. The young man mused:

> He is not as dumb as he looks . . . tying me to his business for a lifetime through a marriage with his ugly daughter. . . . That's the thing with money marriages. Every young man eventually gets one opportunity to sell himself to a rich monster. A man can be ugly, stupid, dishonorable—a man is a man! He is a sought-after commodity on the marriage-hawking market and is dearly paid for, depending on the quality. A Christian is more expensive than a Jew, and a noble is almost impossible to pay for![123]

Georg Hirschfeld painted an even more unattractive picture of the marriage market in his play *Agnes Jordan* (1898). What seemed to be a favorable match for a romantic young woman turned into a disaster. The heroine suffered through a miserable relationship with an authoritarian husband who had married her only for her money.[124] The crassest characters of all appeared in Artur Landsberger's *Millionäre* (1913), a critique of the Berlin Jewish nouveaux riches. In danger of being publicly exposed as a swindler, a millionaire agreed to give his daughter as booty to his blackmailer:

> "How much?" asked Leopold.
> "This time it isn't about money . . . "
> "Then?"
> "About your daughter!" . . . My son has never come too close to your daughter. . . . I have . . . the feeling, that the two detest each other. . . ."

"I'm indeed convinced of that."
"That does not change the necessity that they marry each other."[125]

Landsberger also reminded Jewish parvenus that intermarriage with the nobility did not indicate approval of Jews: his nobleman pursued rich Jewish heiresses in alphabetical order.

German Charges and German/Jewish Contrasts

The self-criticism of German Jews was matched, if not exceeded, by the comments of non-Jews. The latter complained that Jews extended "business-as-usual" into the arena of "love" and claimed that this was a peculiarly "Jewish" trait. In Posen, for example, a county court judge commented (around 1905) to a Jewish counsel: "Jewish families are very strict in seeing that the dowry is paid out before the marriage. I have seen the wedding buffet cleared away, because the dowry had not been paid first."[126] In the countryside, peasants observed that Jews "traded their daughters like cattle. Marriage [was] more a thing of the money pouch than of the heart. Often it seemed like the cattle trade."[127] Popular humor journals scoffed at a stereotype that they themselves perpetuated, equating marriage and mammon among Jews. The *Fliegende Blätter*, for example, described a Jewish arranged marriage in a lengthy three-part series. After carefully considering all the economic advantages, the parents ended up discovering that their children were of the same sex.[128] *Simplicissimus* also delighted in debunking the marriages of wealthy Jewish women with impoverished aristocrats. While Junkers looked none too good in these cartoons, Jewish wealth and Jewish arranged marriages for social prestige were held up to universal scorn.[129] It seemed particularly distasteful when Jewish money achieved social "respectability" by marrying into the nobility.

Whereas *Simplicissimus* spotlighted a statistically insignificant but, for some, socially unsettling phenomenon, the county court judge and many peasants took the economics of marriage very seriously. Most probably, they had been married according to financial requirements themselves. Although arranged marriages for economic motives were commonplace among the German bourgeoisie and prevalent among the upper strata of peasants, these very same groups attacked Jews for practices deemed cynical and materialistic, anachronistic and "foreign." Careful to shield their own marital motives, these commentators vented their hostility toward Jews as business people, middlemen, "exploiters," or social climbers.

These observations lead to the difficult question of how representative money marriages were among non-Jewish Germans, and to its corollary: to what extent had Jewish practices remained distinct from those of their neighbors, and to what extent had Jews merely maintained the norms of their class and region? Further, they suggest an inquiry into the discourse surrounding Jewish marriage strategies. Whether or not Jews were actually involved in more money marriages than non-Jews, why were they singled out with vehemence as flagrant offenders?

Although a comprehensive study of German marriage customs has yet to be written, we do know that in the nineteenth century the bourgeoisie and peasantry customarily arranged marriages.[130] An example of bourgeois expectations can be discerned in the work of Theodor Fontane. He assigned love a very important part in his novels, but his characters' sense of social order and social requirements predominated.[131] When the son of Jenny Treibel announced his engagement to an "inappropriate" woman, a woman without money, Jenny responded furiously:

> A son comes up to his mother and simply declares, "I've become engaged." That's not the way it's done in our circles. . . . Whatever you might be planning . . . don't forget that the blessing of the parents builds the houses of the children. If I may advise you, be sensible, and don't deprive yourself of life's foundations, without which there is no real happiness, for the sake of a . . . fleeting whim.[132]

With sadness—and common sense—he broke off the engagement. That dowries continued to be salient factors in many bourgeois marriages well into the 1920s can be seen in Erich Marie Remarque's *Der schwarze Obelisk*. In this novel a stepfather commits suicide when his daughter's fiancé cancels their engagement because her dowry has dwindled to nothing in the runaway inflation.[133] These families would have agreed with their British counterparts who believed that "a good marriage required good money."[134]

German families depended on kin and friends to introduce young people to each other. When these means failed, they used more "modern" forms to arrange marriages, such as newspaper ads and brokers. The first marriage newspapers (*Heiratszeitungen*) appeared at the beginning of the century. One such journal, the *Heiratstempel*, included ads for inheritances and dowries. A man "with good prospects" sought a woman with 1,500 Thaler.[135] By the end of the century, ads still appeared in the personal columns, directly after the "business opportunities" and "jobs wanted" sections of general newspapers. As late as 1914, one man pursued a business venture, preferring a marriage into a business; another demanded a slim, cheerful woman with 200,000 Marks; and still another described his income and university degree, asking for a photo and the financial résumé of any respondents.[136] Ads placed by the families of women immediately referred to their dowries ("Christian woman with . . . 300,000 Marks," or "landowner's daughter with 300,000 Marks"),[137] and even anti-Semites might accept a Jewish woman with money ("Christian, thirty-seven, owner of a good, old firm . . . [seeks] minimum of 40,000 Marks . . . if necessary, a pretty, but clean [*reinliche*] Jewish woman"). If she had no money, a woman might express her modest desires: "my own hearth at the side of an honored and beloved husband."[138] The non-Jewish bourgeoisie also used brokers and detectives. The brokers often specialized in a particular group, such as industrialists, government officials, or spa visitors, and the detectives promised strictest discretion in their pursuit of dowry and personal information.[139] In the midst of these traditional assumptions and institutions, a reader could encounter the contradictions provoked by modern expectations: the mother of an army officer, for example, sought a Protestant woman of "appropriate" status for a marriage of affection (*Neigungsheirat*) with her son.[140]

The German middle class was not alone in arranging its marriages. Well into the twentieth century, most propertied peasants insisted on arrangements which included dowries. In the popular novel *Barfüssele* (1862, reprinted through 1912), Berthold Auerbach's peasant heroine and all who knew her believed she could never marry because she had no dowry. Poetic license alone brought her to the altar.[141] The characters as well as the readers understood how lucky she had been. Contemporary observers stressed the importance of dowry issues for north German peasants in the mid- and late nineteenth century.[142] Recent demographic surveys corroborate the importance of dowries for the Bavarian peasantry as well.[143] In Hesse, too, current studies testify to the continued significance of dowries in the 1920s. Well-to-do horse farmers used matchmakers who were usually cattle or grain dealers, people "who got around in the district and [were] familiar with the financial and social situation of the various farms with sons and daughters of marriageable age. . . . Material factors were to the fore." Here, too, the marriage was a contract between two households.[144] Love matches occurred more commonly among the poorer cow farmers and most commonly among the impecunious goat farmers.

Peasants were not the only rural residents to seek arranged marriages. Village teachers, whose incomes were low but who hoped to maintain a status appropriate to that of a *Beamter* (tenured civil servant), sought "suitable" wives. In the 1880s the Jewish teacher in a small Hessian village helped to arrange the marriage of his Protestant friend, the village elementary schoolteacher. Offering to find "a rich woman . . . so that the peasants will respect you," the Jewish man eventually came up with a woman who was "educated, [had] good manners and [was] a good cook."[145] In the countryside, then, most wealthy peasants as well as the rural bourgeoisie continued to arrange marriages with dowries, while poorer residents allowed children to meet each other at religious festivals, village occasions (*Spinnstuben*, sporting events, harvests), and holidays. All such meetings took place in public, for "social control was vital and choosing one's partner for life a public process."[146] Even though these marriages may not have been formally arranged, they were still unlikely to take place if parents disapproved. Nonarranged but "approved" love matches prevailed among the poorest rural population.

Rural Jews lived in a group apart. Although they maintained social and business relations with their neighbors, they remained separate from non-Jews as a result of their religion, class, and life-style.[147] Their business needs and desire for endogamy contributed to the preservation of arranged money marriages long after the rural poor began to exert independent choice. Small shopkeepers, merchants, and grain and cattle dealers, Jews tended to approximate bourgeois mores rather than adopt peasant customs. Dowries provided the necessary capital with which young men furthered their business interests and supported new families. Also, on the whole, rural Jews were religious. They sought endogamy at all costs and tended to arrange a marriage before an offspring developed her or his own tastes. Since, as noted earlier, rural areas offered an increasingly limited pool of Jewish men, it was all the more urgent to arrange alliances with Jews from outside the village.[148] Arranged marriages prevailed where religiously and class-appropriate mates were in shortest supply, diminishing in frequency in cities with large Jewish populations where religious and class endogamy could be achieved without formal arrangements. In an era of somewhat greater freedom of choice for certain rural residents, Jews were conspicuous in their heavy reliance on arrangements.

So striking a difference between marriage practices of Jews and other Germans was not apparent in the cities. In the 1860s British observers noted that they had never heard of a single love match in the German city in which they lived, and that in the provinces the dowry of every girl was known to the last penny.[149] At least through the turn of the century, most urban bourgeois parents attempted to arrange, formally or informally, the financially satisfactory marriages of their offspring. Although notions of "love" began to enter the equation, few families based their decision on this alone. In Hamburg in 1903, the eighteen-year-old Karen Horney confided to her diary: "It is bad . . . when one comes to know how few marriages are really good ones. . . . Will it ever change? . . . Perhaps even the next generation . . . will already be stronger than we are because more of them stem from a union of love."[150]

Love notwithstanding, novels, marriage ads, and social histories of bourgeois marriages attest not only to the importance of financially based marriages in Imperial Germany, but to the *growing* importance of dowries in the prosperous years after 1890. In the period between 1860 and 1890, most academically educated *Beamten* had jealously guarded their *Stand* (estate), their social status and privilege. In a period of rapid commercial and industrial development, their allegiances shifted: they dropped the static concept of *Stand* in favor of the class privilege and status conferred by capitalism. They married the daughters of businessmen. A study of Westphalia notes: "The attempt to achieve property through marriage was dominant."[151] Still convinced of their own importance, *Beamten* nevertheless appeared more willing to trade their status for their brides' wealth, so as to assure themselves a standard of living beyond their own small salaries and in line with their expectations of their positions.[152] Any luxury in the life-style of a civil servant, such as building his own home or buying property, could be attributed to his wife's dowry.[153]

Much like their counterparts in the civil service, those in the liberal professions such as doctors, lawyers, notaries, and pharmacists also depended on their wives' dowries. They preferred the daughters of industrialists and businessmen in order to secure their insecure incomes. The dowry supported comfort and luxury, while the husband's salary paid for the rent, food, and servants.[154] These men also wedded their education and status to the wealth of their wives' families. In turn, parents became even more conscious of the need to save up for their daughters' dowries, as opportunities to "marry up" increased.[155] The stakes were high. Daughters without large dowries found no partners willing to marry them. Those single women who first entered the civil service in 1882—as ticket clerks and telegraph operators for the railroad—came from middle-class families. They had some education, but neither the "obligatory dowry" nor parents with the means to provide for them.[156] Dowries—or the lack of them—precipitated women's upward or downward social and economic mobility. Neither class, status, education, or personal traits could compensate for the lack of a dowry. Dowries ranked among the most salient concerns in the lives of all German bourgeois women at least until World War I.[157]

Money, Marriage, and Symbols

We have noted that money marriages among Jews were similar to those among propertied Christians as well as propertied peasants up to World War I. However,

Jewish arrangements stood out for several reasons. Jews were a predominantly commercial middle class for whom endogamous marriages made business sense. In some ways they were similar to the old Dissenting sects (Quakers, Unitarians, Baptists) in England who also stood apart from the majority in their religious beliefs and business dealings. For this British nonconformist middle class, endogamous strategies had "considerable business advantages at a time when trading and dealing depended a great deal on personal knowledge and contacts and mutual confidence, and when it was difficult to tell how far strangers could be trusted."[158] This seems likely for the Jewish minority as well. Consequently Jewish practices, like those of the sects, stood in sharp contrast to those of the urban working classes and much of the poorer rural populations. Also, as a result of their minority position, geographic dispersion, and religious desire for endogamy, Jews may have engaged in more energetic forms of marriage brokerage than other Germans of their class or region. Still, Jewish customs were far from unique. In fact, they typified bourgeois expectations and behavior. Why, then, were Jewish arranged marriages condemned and Jewish dowries disdained?

Dowries are generally more important where wealth and status are not balanced.[159] In Germany's rapidly industrializing economy, a great deal of status anxiety and tension surrounding economic dislocation found poignant expression in complaints about marriages arranged for financial mobility. While bourgeois economic fortunes rose, those below them suffered economic disruption and psychic and social dislocation. Above them a "greedy warrior-agrarian class," which denied the importance of money and longed for an imaginary past where honor determined one's social position, faced economic decline.[160] The traditional concept of *Stand* had been undermined by achievement (*Leistung*) and its embodiment, wealth: the size of the dowry, and not only the group to which one was born, determined one's place in society.[161] Those who watched their status slip, as well as those with rising expectations, found the dowry dilemma particularly painful, because it so clearly symbolized the power of money over the lives of their children and the future of their families.

Jewish financial prowess—the result of discrimination and acquired skills—appeared particularly irksome to those who saw their own position slipping or whose daughters could not marry. In an era shaken by the crash of 1873 and increasingly anxious over the deficiencies of capitalism and liberalism—both associated in the popular mind with Jews—much of the disparagement of Jewish marriage strategies may be attributed to growing anti-Semitism. Whereas it is clear that the wealth of the industrial and commercial bourgeoisie in general, not of Jews in particular, undermined traditional social relations, the "pariah capitalists" of a previous era were excoriated.[162]

Ironically, anti-Semitism was also the cause of the overtly economic orientation of German Jews toward marriage. The Christian middle class, aping the nobility's hypocritical contempt of money, avoided talk of what it felt to be base, material motives by stressing the social status a marriage could offer. Jews could partake of no such camouflage. Non-Jewish families used dowries, ostensibly, to cement new social alliances. Jews, on the other hand, were ostracized from "good society" and could not pretend that social alliances took precedence over all else. They concentrated instead on consolidating their financial worth by marrying into their own wealthier strata. Jews were not as likely—nor could they afford—to deny the significance of financial arrangements.[163] For them, money traditionally signified security in a hostile environment. Lucrative marriages meant increased security for their children. Thus while all bourgeois parents attempted to arrange financially auspicious marriages, Jews were more overt and others more covert in their acknowledgment of this issue.

In an age which was beginning to reassess the terms of marriage, a bourgeoisie loath to criticize its own assumptions and practices regarding marriage castigated Jews as the incarnation of marriage-as-business. Only through wealth could the industrial and commercial bourgeoisie, vilified as vulgar upstarts by those they admired, achieve the higher status they sought. Caught between the desire for respectability and their embarrassment at their own mean materialism, they insisted on the superiority of love or social-status marriages, denied the extent to which their dowries bought status, and denigrated Jews who avowed the consequence of money. Peasants, too—both those for whom such marriages may have begun to lose their economic rationale, as well as those who continued to pursue financial goals—deprecated Jews as the beneficiaries of such relationships. Jews seemed as much the issue as the customs surrounding their marriages. That Jews were singled out disparagingly as particularly adept at arranging marriages for money in a society in which dowries were part of an old Christian and Jewish tradition, and in which the vast majority of the middle classes and propertied peasantry aspired to financial advancement through marriage, may tell us more about rising anti-Semitism than about a particularly "Jewish" proclivity. It elucidates the anxieties, jealousies, and disdain of Germans caught first in a severe depression and then in a period of phenomenal growth toward the real and imagined successes of a predominantly middle-class Jewry, and toward the real and imagined importance of money to these outsiders. In the discourse surrounding dowries and arranged marriages, one can discern the conjunction of anticapitalism and anti-Semitism.

"Modern" Marriages in Imperial Germany

Historians have recently suggested that changes in marriage patterns took place in the nineteenth century, including greater freedom in the choice of marital partners, less parental control over marriages, and a more companionate relationship within marriage.[164] Families developed, based on sentiment, affection, and free choice rather than on obligation or material considerations. Many bourgeois Jewish families in this study no longer met or married in the *strictly* traditional mode, but they were not in the forefront of the "free choice" group either. Jews in Imperial Germany represented a transitional stage.

Traditional Judaism recognized the concept of a "successful marriage," not a "happy" one. Economic and social realities took precedence. They were the practical basis for a "successful" marriage, with "success" defined as a "normal" sex life and a harmonious, as opposed to quarrelsome, relationship.[165] By the later part of the nineteenth century, however, individuals increasingly acknowledged the social discourse concerning sentiment and affection (the basis for a "happy" relationship). Between 1870 and 1900 expressions of affection between partners gradually became common. Even though marriage was still a duty, social convention permitted—in fact, encouraged—a young couple to "fall in love." Elders had selected the eligible mate and, under their supervision, the betrothed could engage in courting behavior. For those who lived far apart, this might include an extensive correspondence (the *Brautbriefe*) in which partners discussed their likes and dislikes, their observations and opinions.[166] For those within traveling distance, this usually involved chaperoned visits by the groom, public promenades walking "arm-in-arm" (a sign to the community that they were engaged),[167] and other formal family and community occasions. A complicated interaction between what was supposed to happen ("love") and what was actually happening (anticipation of marriage, common curiosity, and an attempt to be cooperative and pleasing) took place. Social expectations brought about predictable results in some cases: letters between fiancés frequently announced their "love" of each other, although they had barely met. Also, romantic notions may have been easier to conjure up when partners hardly knew each other. Unfortunately, memoirs give a rather one-sided, positive view of the engagement period. Intended for the children and grandchildren of the author, they rarely disclose the fears, anxieties, or anger that might have accompanied such marriage transactions and engagement rituals. It is from Franz Kafka that we discover how an unhappy engagement felt—as though he were "tied hand and foot like a criminal. Had they sat me down in a corner bound in real chains, placed policemen in front of me, and let me look on simply like that, it could not have been worse. And that was my engagement." He broke it off.[168]

"Coincidence": A Fine Art

Conscious of the growing contradictions between social ideology and social reality, some parents "covered up" traditional, arranged marriages. Others arranged circumstances where certain young people could meet each other. Still others allowed their children to fall in love without any familial control over the immediate situation. By the turn of the century, but in some cases even earlier, Jewish families began to pay lip service to "coincidence," or to camouflage actual arrangements in order to accommodate to modern sensibilities and protect the feelings of the young couple. Probably Jews also attempted to adapt to what they considered the changing norms of the era as a result of their own desire to acculturate, and in order to avoid criticism by Gentiles and anti-Semites. Spontaneity and coincidence developed into a fine art in the cities (where more opportunities for spontaneity existed) and among the non-Orthodox.

Memoirs and popular literature described both the arrangements and the pretense of spontaneity—ritual spontaneity—that had to be observed.[169] One father contrived to have a distant relative arrange the marriage of his daughter. The couple met "coincidentally" at a flower show where the young man was introduced as a business acquaintance of the father.[170] Some participants either never discovered that their meetings had been arranged or never admitted it. In Breslau in 1911, for example, the father of a thirty-year-old widower hired a marriage broker for his son.

The woman found an appropriate partner and arranged, through mutual associates, for the young couple to meet with friends at a café. Much later, a close relative wrote: "To this day, A . . . and E . . . do not know that they were brought together by a professional marriage broker. They believe the matter was initiated by F . . . and I hope that this . . . more elevated version is maintained their whole life long."[171]

In other cases the man, but not the woman, knew that the marriage had been arranged. A daughter reported: "One day, my grandmother called after one of her sons: 'Find someone for Trude!' And so my father was found. . . . He knew that my mother had been chosen for him, but my mother had been left 'in the dark'. . . . They were introduced to each other in a theater. Ten days later they got engaged while in a museum, and married within three months on June 19, 1910."[172]

In the countryside, too, where arranged marriages became ever more necessary as Jews migrated to urban regions, such marriages began to be disguised. During the prewar years families would often arrange marriages by orchestrating a chaperoned meeting of the intended couple. This took place at a restaurant, at a friend's home, or at markets and fairs (including horse markets). If the young people liked each other, negotiations followed. If an engagement was announced, "one heard everywhere that the young people had met there or there by 'coincidence' and that it was a real love match."[173] "Die Liebesheirat" (The Love Match), a poem in a book of Jewish humor, portrayed a similar event. At a wedding reception an uncle proceeded to make a toast to "love," while the marriage broker shared his thoughts with the reader:

> [the uncle]
> "My dear guests":
> He said loudly and stroked his beard,
> "Today Amor decided
> That these two would be paired.
> Only lord Amor could ordain
> This marriage we adore
> because the groom could have gotten
> Seven hundred Thalers more".
>
> [the broker]
> "Yes," the *shadkhan* thinks today
> "It took enough struggle,
> Before I brought these two people
> Happily together as a couple."[174]

Such cover-ups could cause embarrassing situations like the one in Posen where the rabbi's wedding speech about the young "love match" he was sanctifying caused general hilarity in the audience.[175]

Alongside the formal arrangement of coincidences, a more modern pattern emerged around the turn of the century. It became more common for parents to influence the informal social contacts[176] of their children so that they would meet only suitable peers. One strategy was to plan propitious circumstances, such as vacations, for meeting eligible partners. Many a marriageable young person met a future spouse on a family vacation at a resort carefully selected by the parents. This was the case for one couple who "fell in love at first sight" at a mountain hotel in 1898. Their courtship was a peculiar, but not unrepresentative, mixture of traditional and modern forms. Emma Goitein's interest had been aroused by physical attraction: "his brown eyes have bewitched me," she told her sister. His feelings must have been reciprocal, for without exchanging so much as one word with his future wife, he discussed his intentions with her mother. The "bride" was dismayed at his behavior—"we were much too modern [for that]"—but waited until he visited her at home, again with only her mother's permission.[177] A little over twenty years earlier (the late 1870s), Emma's mother had been married off in the more traditional manner: both sets of parents had arranged all the details, and the bridegroom had come to a "viewing" (*Beschau*) of the bride. A little over seven years later (1905), her sister Rahel entered a love marriage, but one frowned upon by her Orthodox future father-in-law. The elderly man had just arranged a marriage for his son, who turned it down. Perturbed, the father asked (much like Jenny Treibel): "You don't want to fall in love, do you? That's not appropriate in our circles."[178] It was not, but it increasingly came to be. Within three decades this family had moved from a traditionally arranged marriage to a modern love marriage (with some guilt feelings toward the older generation).

The *Kur*, a spa for recuperation or vacation, was another very popular place for meeting a future spouse. Designed ostensibly for one's health and one's nerves, spas in Germany, France, and England provided real antidotes to spinsterhood[179]: "no one was really sick, such a trip served . . . to meet new people and 'last but not least' to present daughters on the marriage market [*Heiratsmarkt*]."[180] One drank the waters and regained one's vigor while engaging in flirtation, gossip, and the pursuit of eligible men. This was a familiar enough theme to be taken up in Max Brod's novel *Jüdinnen*.[181] Needless to say, these national marriage markets also drew legions of young men in search of dowries.

Family gatherings, particularly weddings, provided other opportunities to introduce young people to each other. A bachelor's *Tischdame*, the woman seated next to him at dinner, was carefully selected by the hosts. Even when these events took place in distant cities, parents considered them important enough that, if the entire family could not afford to attend, they would send the member of the family of marriageable age to represent the rest. Many couples first met at friends' or relatives' weddings.[182]

Even when families no longer had the power to impose partners on their offspring, they often instigated their children's search or introduced "acceptable" young people to each other. As late as 1920, we read of a man of about thirty who first thought of marriage when his father suggested it, and who then met a young woman through his sister's intercession. He initiated an exchange of letters, and they announced their engagement.[183] Also in 1920, a young Berlin woman who would have married the young man of her choice had he not died, consented to meet a man introduced to her by a family friend. They met "by coincidence" in a restaurant and, for about a half year, he called on her at home. When they decided to marry, their families were delighted with the "good match" (*gute Partie*): a substantial dowry for a successful professional. The couple felt real affection for each other as well.[184] Such marriages entailed a bit more volition and initiative by the individu-

Double wedding portrait of two arranged marriages between the Rosenfelder family of Nördlingen and the Heimann family of Oberdorf, August 17, 1909. *David Heimann Collection. Courtesy of the Leo Baeck Institute, New York.*

als than traditionally arranged marriages. They often involved people who might have met a partner on their own. But, prior to World War I, arranged marriages and cover-ups still predominated.

Love Within Bounds

That is not to say that love relationships did not exist. One can uncover traces of such marriages even prior to the Imperial period. As early as 1853 we have evidence of a young couple who met and agreed to arrange their own marriage as soon as the man could provide for the woman. This was unusual, both for the times and for the individuals involved. Married, they proceeded to live a very traditional life, raising a family of ten children.[185] In the 1890s, when one middle-class man married a woman without a dowry, he was the only one in a large family to marry for love.[186] Most spontaneous decisions to marry, particularly those that involved no dowry, can be found only after 1900. Female university students and women involved in youth movements tended to choose their own partners and to reject the "tragedy of arranged marriages . . . based on money, income, or position."[187] This may be explained partly by the independence it took to enter academia or join the youth movement, either of which implied resistance to traditional parental values or the acceptance of exceptional social behavior by parents, and partly by the female students' exposure to more single males. In such cases, companionate marriages based on complementary interests followed. These couples (and, not infrequently, their parents) thought mutual concerns and activities, rather than traditional considerations of finance, to be the basis for a good marriage.[188] Yet, then as now, choices almost always fell within parameters set by parental expectations and childhood and adolescent socialization. Also, these couples sought their parents' blessings.[189] If the young couple had met all the social, financial, geographical, health, and educational preconditions, parents might give their consent, even if they did not particularly like their child's selection.[190]

Dowries were not vital to love relationships. In earlier eras the couple would wait until the groom had saved enough to manage a family. One such couple who met in 1890 had to wait seven years before the village teacher could support a wife.[191] Another couple had to wait three years until the woman's older sisters had been married off: she had fallen in love "out of turn" and could not embarrass her older sisters by preceding them to the altar. In this case, the postponement also allowed the groom to build up his finances.[192] In these partnerships, then, the emphasis was on "love" and the groom's ability to earn, rather than on the bride's wealth. This does not mean, however, that couples or their families ignored dowries entirely. In 1912, for example, neighbors in a small town agreed to marry after a seven-year courtship. Even though the bride and groom were "in love," their parents initiated financial discussions. The bride's father, a cigar merchant, and the groom's father, a cattle dealer, decided on the woman's dowry—15,000 Marks plus a house. Parents often insisted upon dowries as a contribution to the new household or as an indication of the status of the bride and her family.[193] In sum, even love matches which ignored the traditional formalities of arrangement and financial inquiry often included optional, rather than compulsory, dowries.

Urban working-class Jews were the only Jews who did not formally arrange their marriages either for property, status, or religious reasons. While the lack of substantial property is obvious, religious motivations are more obscure. Compared to the urban middle class, urban workers married out of the faith more frequently.[194] Most likely, property provided a cudgel to keep middle-class offspring within the familial and communal fold, and the lack of property allowed—or forced—poorer Jews to marry out. Dowries (or the threat of losing them, if one intermarried against parents' desires) thus maintained intergroup solidarity. However, interfaith marriage was not only a function of economics, since poor rural Jews intermarried less than their urban counterparts; it was also a function of culture and milieu. The more cohesive rural Jewish community and family were also more religious and restrictive. Isolated from many modern challenges—although not from migration—they attempted to guide their young firmly in traditional ways. Urban society, on the other hand, being more open and secular, offered its young workers more personal freedom, an income, and greater opportunities to meet potential spouses.

Peer groups became the focal point of social activity for young women, whether they lived alone or with their families. Factory jobs, and white-collar work in retail shops, government offices, private business, and industry, presented opportunities unavailable to the cloistered bourgeois *höhere Tochter* or the rural cattle dealer's daughter. For example, after attending trade school and working at a white-collar job for several years, Toni Sender (born in 1888) informed her mother that she did not want or need a dowry, which was in part a way of giving notice that she would also find her own marriage partner. Her mother "was surprised at first, but then did not take my remark seriously. 'Again, one of your crazy ideas,' was her response."[195] Casual meetings at work and at social clubs did lead to liaison and marriage. Eyeing her working-class sisters with some envy, one bourgeois woman (born in 1905, Berlin) recalled that she had been taught, "Love is nothing. That comes later." Yet "poor people fell in love. But I was not in that circle."[196] While this rose-colored version of working-class marriage is exaggerated, it suggests that propertyless marriages[197] allowed women relatively more choice—within the limits set by class and gender—than marriages in which property and status were the primary considerations.

Marriages Between Cousins

On the spectrum between the extremes of traditionally arranged marriages between utter strangers and those initiated by individual choice, lay marriages between relatives (*Verwandtenehen*), usually cousins. Jewish tradition accepted cousin marriages. In fact, in medieval Jewish society cousins had priority over strangers. Marrying daughters "out" for the sake of creating useful family connections was common, but relatives "had more rights."[198] In the Imperial era, parents arranged some of these unions in a traditional manner; individuals who had known each other for many years initiated others; and still others arose as a result of carefully planned family events. Families could dispense with brokers, since each side knew about the health, wealth, and character of the partners. Often young people had met at family occasions in distant cities, had visited each other's homes for vacations or when traveling or studying, and had heard of each other through family correspondence. To meet through family networks was not unusual, since it was typical of Jewish families, even those of very modest means, to send their children on family visits. As marriage age drew near, young people sometimes took advantage of a family gathering to observe each other as potential partners. For some, this opportunity may have been preferable to the impending introduction to a total stranger, although sometimes the cousins were relative strangers themselves. Still, a sense of familiarity, of shared backgrounds, may have made a marriage decision somewhat easier for both. And occasionally the cousins were old friends. (One couple had known each other so long that the wife remembered her husband helping her with her school essays.)[199]

Families strengthened their bonds through these marriages. One set of parents arranged that their three daughters marry three brothers who were also their cousins. The offspring of one of those marriages later married her cousin from another one of the marriages.[200] While this triple arrangement was unusual, it was common for cousins to win parental approval of their marriages. In 1901, at the age of seventeen, Toni Cassirer was sent from Vienna to Berlin, accompanied by her brother, to attend a family wedding. There she was introduced to Ernst, her mother's favorite nephew. Needless to say, her subsequent engagement met general endorsement.[201] Marriages between relatives had advantages besides familiarity, friendship, or family consolidation; there were financial causes and motivations as well. Cousin marriages were a recourse employed, in particular, by small-town Jews with little or no means at their disposal. Without money or wide-ranging social networks, they looked to the family for mates. Their wealthier Jewish neighbors, with wider business and social contacts, resorted to these marriages less frequently.[202] When wealthier cousins did marry, observers generally thought that they were trying "to keep the money in the family."[203] Since Jews engaged in business and commerce, marital alliances could potentially consolidate such enterprises and expand markets. This was no doubt the case in extreme for the Rothschild family: sixteen out of eighteen matches made by the grandchildren of Mayer Amschel Rothschild were contracted between first cousins. Moreover, the Rothschilds went on marrying within the extended family through the following generations.[204]

According to German civil law, marriages between first cousins, uncles and nieces, or aunts and nephews were not illegal (compared, for example, to the United States today, where two-thirds of the states do not allow first cousins to marry). Of such marriages, the overwhelming majority were between cousins, and they were not extraordinary. In *Jenny Treibel*, for example, the professor preferred his nephew rather than the wealthy Treibel heir for his only daughter. None of the characters even remarked on the issue of a union between cousins.

Jews were the religious denomination most disposed to such relationships. In Prussia between 1872 and 1875, for example, 14 per 1,000 marriages among Protestants, 10 per 1,000 among Catholics, and 23 per 1,000 among Jews were between two relatives.[205] In general, Jewish demographers agreed that marriages between Jewish relatives were more common than between non-Jews, and that this was particularly the case in rural areas.[206] By the early 1920s, they noticed that the number of such marriages had increased in small towns and rural villages as a result of Jewish migration from such places. Compared to non-Jewish rural populations, the percentage of Jews in marriages to first cousins was far higher.[207] Eugenics specialists in "racial hygiene" (*Rassenhygiene*) journals assumed this was because the general population understood the eugenic harmfulness of cousin marriages better than Jews. This is unlikely. Jewish demographers and leaders, aware of the potential dangers of such close marriages, continually apprised the Jewish population of their concerns.[208] It is far more likely that cousin marriages were a strategy that was frequently unavoidable and often appealing for a minority intent on preserving its religious distinctiveness. Unlike Christians, for whom the marriage pool was substantial, it was occasionally necessary for Jews to marry relatives because other choices were limited. Also, unlike Catholics, who needed special Church dispensation,[209] Jewish society accepted cousin marriages; there was no censure by the religion or the culture.[210] Despite the genetic dangers, Jews detected potentially more rewards for entering such marriages and greater punishments (not marrying) for forgoing them than did non-Jews.

The primacy of property in marriage decisions would be successfully challenged only after World War I. Then the economic, geographic, and social mobility, and the concomitant increase in personal decision making of a modern market economy—already discernible in the Imperial era but not fully developed until later—contributed to more independent marriage decisions. Furthermore, successive waves of war, inflation, and depression hurt the savings of middle-class families. Very few daughters had dowries to offer. Finally, and significantly, women's independent earnings and earning potential began to replace dowries. In Imperial Germany, however, traditional patterns persisted. Property exchanges and arrangements were uncommon only among the poorest members of society.

For Jews, the picture was complicated by religious, regional, and class factors. Marriage had symbolic and religious meaning, since marriage was one of the few crucial turning points where one affirmed or rejected one's group affiliation. Jews exerted great energy in pursuit of endogamy, resisting absorption into the Christian majority. But marriage was also an opportunity to improve or maintain economic status. Thus Jewish practices reflected the continued importance of property in the middle-class marriage bargain, despite changing ideologies regarding love. As the rhetoric of romance proceeded apace in the early twentieth century, both urban and rural Jews attempted to accommodate to the dominant culture and avoid criticism by covering up arranged marriages. The lengths to which they went in order to make "coincidence" out of preplanned arrangements indicated their recognition of the imbalance between social ideology and Jewish practice. Further, it reflected their desire to mitigate anti-Semitic accusations and to fit into what they believed to be a general consensus on marriage. However, as much as they may have preferred to adapt to changing social ideology and social norms, their minority status, religious beliefs, and economic profile made such adjustments difficult and often impossible.

4

The Labor of Leisure

Conscious that home and family life represented "the success of the enterprise," the German-Jewish writer Lina Morgenstern reminded her readers: "Family life is the sphere in which the extent of our economic success is presented. No one should control this sphere more than the wife."[1] This assignment, however, required a delicate balancing act. Women were expected to reflect the status and wealth of their husbands in the way they organized their own and their families' leisure time, in the friends they made, and in the entertainment they chose. Yet they had to avoid frivolity and ostentation in order to negate frequent charges of excessive materialism made by anti-Semites. The stock figure of the Jewish woman as a haughty, vulgar, status-flaunting cultural boor found in popular humorous journals[2] haunted the emergence of a substantial Jewish leisure class, causing increased tension within an already hypersensitive acculturating Jewish community. Thus Jewish women had to "smooth things over," exhibiting the tokens of new wealth while avoiding all conspicuous consumption and parvenu behavior.

Leisure time was largely a family affair in Imperial Germany, and women, particularly married women, choreographed the main type of leisure activities, family events. In addition, an abundance of primarily—though not exclusively—female circles beckoned to women with time to spare. Before exploring the rich leisure-time opportunities available to Jewish women to pursue their own interests or enhance their husbands' reputations, a brief discussion of what is meant by "leisure" for women is essential.

What Does "Leisure" Mean to Women?

Our dictionaries describe leisure as "time off" or "free, unoccupied time," "not work." In German, it is neatly called *Freizeit* (free time). As long as "leisure" is what takes place in opposition to, or as a complement to, or outside of paid work, it defines an important part of *men's* daily lives—as can be seen in the recent studies of nineteenth-century working-class male leisure, for example. For middle-class women, this definition may confuse rather than explain their experiences, since they were not acknowledged as "working" in the first place. In the nineteenth century neither females nor males considered women's housework (characterized as "love," "duty," or a "natural propensity"), or women's attention to the maintenance of bourgeois culture in the living room or concert hall, as "work." In fact, their very success as bourgeois women depended on just how convincingly they gave the impression that they did not work at all, whether at housework or at leisure. If women did not "work," then when did they have "time off"?

A further issue to be considered is that the definition of leisure has changed over time. In preindustrial Europe both men and women associated leisure time with religious holidays and communal events. Since home and workplace were usually combined, unstructured time off—more diffuse, less-defined—took place within the home or as an extension of it. Industrialization took paid work out of the home, so that locations of work and play separated—at least for men. Rigid lines between public (work) and private (play) could increasingly be drawn for those men who worked outside the home. At home, however, this line could not be drawn. How did women in a job without boundaries perceive leisure? That problem even remained for those with domestics. Woman's work was, in actuality, "never done." Middle-class women remained predominantly within the private sphere, closer to the preindustrial pattern of both women's and men's lives. Housework and leisure blended into each other, each encompassing duties not clearly demarcated. For women, leisure time did not alleviate housework, it only redefined it as pleasure.

Germans regarded leisure as an intimate, private affair. Nevertheless, leisure activities were of utmost importance in reaching out beyond the private sphere. Women nurtured connections which brought the immediate, nuclear family into touch with networks of social and business relations. Conversely, leisure also provided the opportunity, and the family the site, at which cultural osmosis, from the public to the private, took place. Today middle-class women who work outside the home can more readily identify the differences between paid work and housework: leisure is time off from both. Yet, much as for nineteenth-century men, leisure refurbishes, revitalizes, and "re-creates" these women for their work, often furthering their class and professional status in the process. It is precisely the change in the definition of leisure and its multiple ambiguities for women that is significant and problematic for women's historians.

Leisure was (and is) related to social structure. The concept was crucial in distinguishing the middle from the lower classes. The "leisured," or "leisured classes," consumed both time and goods to a far greater extent than those beneath them on the social ladder. Moreover, varied styles of leisure reflected the social differences which existed within the middle class. The actual labor of leisure for upper-middle-class and wealthier women was not physically strenuous, assisted as they were by domestic help. They allotted much of their time to urban cultural events and performed more conspicuous social duties to maintain or enhance their class standing. Lower-middle-class and middle-class women spent more physical energy organizing their own and their families' recreation, much of which took place in the home. Women were the symbols and reality of the leisured class: while bourgeois men exhausted themselves in the competitive, all-consuming world of business and professions, it was their women who gave their families the gloss of leisure. Hence leisure had an important social function. What one did with one's leisure contributed to bourgeois class formation and the maintenance of social standing.

Associated with the problem of the definition, timing, and location of leisure and its social function is the issue of pleasure. Was leisure time fun time? This leads into a conundrum: what is fun for someone may be misery for someone else. Well-trained bourgeoises may have enjoyed, while others may have claimed to enjoy, what perhaps seem to us to be dreadful social situations. Also, work can be pleasurable, too. Important distinctions between work and play, which, as already noted, can more easily be detected in men's lives—the spatial and temporal distinctions between the office and the parlor—are invisible in women's lives. Is reading a bedtime story to a child work or play or both? In women's history, the boundaries between duty and pleasure, as between work and free time, are uniquely permeable.

A final quandary: if we could interview bourgeois women at the turn of the century about their leisure, our perceptions would differ from theirs. Whereas we might define leisure as disposable time over which we have control, they would have pointed to time away from (the work of) running the household (although a dinner party involved increased housework), or (the work of) diapering the baby (although strolling through a park pushing a baby carriage was a maternal duty). From our perspective their leisure was, at best, a change of pace. Although we might remain at odds over what leisure was, we could agree on its functions and difficulties. Pressed by our leading questions, nineteenth-century women would have concurred that leisure, even when thoroughly enjoyable, like a concert or spa vacation, was goal-oriented, class-conscious, and often taxing. What was called leisure time for women was serious work: within the family it was an extension of housework; outside the family it was the careful work of forming the *Bildungsbürgertum*—a phenomenon unthinkable without the "cultured" woman.

For Jews, the time and energy women spent away from housework also strengthened bonds within the Jewish subgroup, reaffirming family connections. Further, leisure encompassed careful social navigation in a non-Jewish world, one which frequently defined itself in snobbish rejection of Jews. In attempting to analyze the leisure time of the German-Jewish bourgeoise, I hope to expose the problem of definition and provide a tentative vocabulary for the discussion of that problem. It is important that we ask new questions about the function of leisure activities and seek new sources to answer them. We must reshape the way we conceptualize "leisure," investing the word with new meaning and using other terms, such as "female sociability," to refer to those activities formerly and uncritically called "leisure."

Home and Family: Domestic Ideals and the Goals of Leisure

A combination of social and economic developments saw the role of Jewish women, like that of bourgeois women in general, change from business partners and producers to housewives and consumers in the decade before, and at the beginning of, the Imperial period. During the Imperial years the rapid economic mobility of Jews, their use of birth control, and their desire to acculturate into the German bourgeoisie as rapidly as possible, affected the role and needs of the family. Jewish bourgeois families required wives and mothers who could organize leisure activities in the home in such a way as to act as a social and cultural mediator between the family and society at large.

Families spent most nonworking hours together in the home, acknowledged to be woman's domain. Married women's activities involved clear-cut duties, even when this was not obvious at first glance. As their leisure time expanded, it became more complex, and women had to fill it in a class-, age-, generation-, and gender-appropriate manner. This involved a wide spectrum of activity, from the self-indulgent and relaxing spa vacation to the anxiety of arranging and conducting a dinner party, from the mentally exhilarating to the physically arduous. It was women in their middle years, mothers of young or unmarried children, who provided a forum for their own nuclear family and for elderly (grand)parents and unmarried siblings. In comparison to wives (or mothers), married men (or fathers), being separated from their business or office, found leisure time more recreational (although for them, too, it had a social function). The time spent with children was a reward (and excuse) for their labor, not an extension of it, as was the case for women. In fact, men's time at home was understood by all as relaxation, whether a quiet evening or a festive event. One woman recalled: "Father, who worked very hard, wanted to have peace and quiet in the family. Mother was not allowed to come to him with complaints about the children [or] servants. . . . 'I have enough problems at work,' he would say."[3] Men consulted, participated, passively cohosted, and sometimes even initiated family time, but women ran it.

Jewish men worked long hours, often traveling out of town as well, and enjoyed far less time for sociability. That which they did have, focused on the family. There they expected wives to imitate the form and substance of the bourgeoisie, to adapt to social situations, to be intelligent and entertaining, to speak French and play the piano. Men's memoirs frequently list these attributes, when they describe the woman they finally chose to marry. Although this may be seen as a general bourgeois phenomenon—one need only recall those wonderful Daumier prints of tired husbands sleeping through concerts or plays, and irate wives trying to waken them—Jews were extraordinarily conscious of it. To exaggerate for a minute: while Jewish men pursued business and careers, the new bourgeois individuals—cultivated and "leisured"—were their wives.

In the guise of entertainment (although, of course, it could also be fun), women were active agents in the circulation and generational transfer of social values and culture. They not only physically reproduced the next generation, but they engaged in social reproduction. This they did, not only as part of regular child-rearing responsibilities, but also in free time. As was noted earlier, they read German fairy tales and bedtime stories to children, and mothers and children amused one another by taking parts in German plays.[4] Especially in Jewish families, the collected works of Goethe and Schiller—those mainstays of German middle-class respectability and *Bildung*—had a vaunted place in the family repertoires.[5] Jews played out, quite literally, their special attachment to what they defined as enlightened German culture. Indeed, their intense engagement with and (possibly conspicuous) display of these classics may be read as an "overadaptation," reflecting the history as well as actual experiences of discrimination.[6]

Women took to their role as cultural mediators with alacrity. Educated to entertain others and to discuss, albeit superficially, literature and art, they became eager consumers of the growing mass market in books and avid users of the newly founded circulating libraries.[7] Cultivation and culture, symbols of virtue and constancy, were almost as tangible as their overstuffed furniture, their home decor, and the sailor suits in which they patriotically and stylishly dressed their children on holidays.

In the creation of bourgeois domesticity, Jewish housewives furthered the process of acculturation to German bourgeois standards. Nowhere is this clearer than in the German-Jewish female romance with the piano. German bourgeois women were expected to play the piano and to entertain their husbands and children. Without gramophones (introduced into wealthier homes only in the first decades of the twentieth century), families—or at least women—made their own music. Their efforts at the piano fit into the more general expectation of how women were to spend their leisure time: they had been educated to discuss literature, to sing, and in general to be entertaining. They were to keep up a conversation, understand when the topic was becoming too serious, and be able to change that gracefully. In sum, women had to organize pleasant, but not intense, familial or social events. The piano was a perfect helpmate in amusing others. The Jewish bourgeoisie was quick to emulate its counterpart. One woman, who learned to play the piano belatedly, at her fiancé's request, performed regularly for her family.[8] "Piano lessons were taken for granted" in urban Jewish circles, but even rural Jews provided pianos and lessons for their daughters. It was not at all incongruous for a cattle dealer to own a piano so that his wife and daughter could play.[9] In fact, it was precisely this kind of women's activity which gave rural Jews the image and reality of a bourgeois lifestyle. Music provided *standesgemäss* and enjoyable activity for young women, but it could also be taken seriously. "The atmosphere at home was not very stimulating, apart from my mother's piano playing," recalled Nora Rosenthal. She enjoyed playing duets with her mother. "In order to get to know the classical literature of symphonies and concertos . . . my mother and I first played them before the concert and again after the performance."[10]

A welcome result of their music education was that some women developed a serious and lasting interest in music. Minding the shop five days a week and doing most of her own housework did not prevent one woman from participating in her weekly chamber music group. She also sang in the synagogue choir and eventually supported her family as a music tutor during World War I.[11] Also, some families developed enough serious talent to form their own quartets and to play with and for one another regularly. When memoir writers describe their mothers' musical talent, they are not only underlining their own bourgeois upbringing; they are also emphasizing the centrality of their mothers in their personal introduction to, as well as their lasting appreciation of, the world of music. Peter Gay has argued perceptively that "the charge, however familiar, that these accomplishments were mere bait that young girls on the marriage market dangled before eligible bachelors was largely a canard." He suggests that middle-class girls were "often talented and serious pianists."[12] Memoirs indicate that even when such talent was lacking,[13] a lasting music appreciation enriched the lives of bourgeois Jews.

The role of cultural mediator complemented an equally serious responsibility. Women preserved Jewish kin and friendship networks. As was already noted in chapter 2, they maintained and enhanced family systems to proclaim both their Germanness and their Jewishness. Moreover, these networks were often essential to economic and social survival. Enlarged networks of relatives created a field for reciprocity and obligation. Economic historians have noted the significant economic asset of the closely knit Jewish family and the social solidarity, mutual confidence, and support among Jews.[14] The survival of this Jewish social tradition should be seen not merely negatively, as a reaction to hostile surroundings, but also positively, as—to a large part—Jewish women's contribution to the social and economic enhancement of their kin and ethnic community. Thus women's "leisure" work had important economic and social repercussions.

On weekends and holidays, mothers prepared favorite dishes, many of which were identified as "Jewish" foods, and organized and ran parties and gatherings. These were most often spent with the extended family. Families enjoyed playing card and board games, with men and women often playing different games in different rooms. "Even we children sat in another room and played cards as well."[15] Women also prepared picnic lunches which the family shared while hiking in nearby woods or parks, enjoying, like many other Germans, a deep and lasting romance with their physical countryside.[16] Whether they were still fighting a stereotype which depicted Jews as denatured strangers to the German soil and soul, or whether they had simply adopted this pursuit with the same verve and engagement with which they emulated other German habits, is hard to say. But it is clear that Jewish families, with rucksacks on their backs, enjoyed hiking and walking in the parks and woods near their homes. One woman described her family's routine wanderings in the Taunus mountains, stopping for their picnic lunch, nourished by a later break at a wonderful pastry shop. All returned home "healthily tired," having reinforced their German consciousness and their family ties.[17]

For those who observed the Sabbath, this was an occasion for formal family "visits," most often arranged by the women, to other family members and friends. The same women who had chatted informally earlier in the week paid a formal "visit" on Saturday afternoons. The difference was the religious meaning of the day and the presence of husbands. There were formal rules as to how long one stayed and how much one ate; they also decreed that the visit would be reciprocated in due time. Generally, in both rural and urban areas, housewives prepared for guests to drop in, unless they themselves planned to visit others.[18] In southern Germany Jewish families would patronize coffee houses on Saturday afternoons. In the evenings, families met at local open-air restaurants. Mothers packed picnic foods and the family bought beer and lemonade. Families exchanged homemade deserts and the children played in the vicinity. Other towns had other Sabbath rituals including long walks with family and friends.[19] Sundays replaced the Sabbath for secular Jews, but they too kept Sundays as a family day. "Sundays we would often come together with the whole family," recalled one woman.[20]

Jewish holidays brought immediate as well as extended family together. The religiously observant planned parties and dances to commemorate the festive holidays. Purim was a time for masquerade balls, Simchas Torah an occasion for a dance. Even when Jews ignored religious ceremonies, or kept them to a minimum, most were conscious of the Jewish calendar and the tradition of particular rituals and foods on holidays. Women took special care in the arrangements for these holidays, particularly the meals, finer tableware, candles, special clothing, and invitations to family members. For secular Jews, family togetherness on holidays often replaced the original meaning of the religious holidays.[21] For religious Jews, women's endeavors at home complemented men's prayer and synagogue attendance. Since Jewish observance, more than that of other religions, took place in the home, women played a prominent role in shaping the milieu in which both secular and religious Jews commemorated the holidays.

Vacations also provided important opportunities to renew family ties. Women were not only hostesses, but most often initiators of family visits, particularly of cousin exchanges among their children, which might lead to cousin marriages. Although it remains to be proven, it seems that Jews traveled to visit each other far more than other Germans did. Perhaps these ties were so assiduously sustained in an attempt to reinforce family networks stretched by higher rates of migration and urbanization than among other Germans. Jews were a disproportionately mobile population as well as a small minority lacking social integration. They moved in the direction of larger and larger urban centers, with different generations settling along the various way stations.

Probably Jews also traveled internationally far more than other Germans, because many Jews had family abroad. "We had relatives in Brussels, Hungary, and England. How nice it had always been to visit each other! One got to know other lands, one maintained family ties."[22] These ties reinforced family business relations as well. An economic historian has noted that young Jews heard far more about life and conditions abroad than their non-Jewish contemporaries. "Many families had relatives abroad in France, England and the United States. . . . No wonder that the young Jew was ready to go abroad on his own sooner—as an apprentice or on a business trip."[23] With the increasing international connections of the German economy, familial links abroad provided advantages to Jewish business endeavors as well as to Jewish vacationers.

Vacation time offered the opportunity to satisfy the German passion for fresh air by taking advantage of the greener grass surrounding less mobile relatives settled in more rural areas.[24] Conversely, visits to city relatives during the rest of the year gave *höhere Töchter* something to do and offered them the opportunity to obtain some cultural polish as well. In general, girls left home in order to maintain family connections, whereas boys left home for an apprenticeship or the university, each preparing for an adult role.

Women often headed vacation households in rented rooms or cabins at the seashore or in nearby mountains. This was another opportunity for the extended family (often one of women, children, and grandparents) to reunite. Sometimes they rented rooms in a kosher pension or they shared a house. At other times they rented places near one another, spending the day together. Often husbands did not spend the entire vacation with their wives or families, only stopping at the resort between business trips or for short periods.[25]

Women were also responsible for preparing family journeys. The most expensive type, an extended trip abroad, was not widespread among Jews, unless they visited relatives. Even the daughter of a banker (1870s—1880s) recalled that her circles were not yet familiar with summer vacations (*Reisen*).[26] One spent one's vacation at home, with intervals of small outings. Still, there were those who

Rudolf and Pauline Altschüler-Westerland at the beach with their children, August 1898. *Altschüler Family Collection. Courtesy of the Leo Baeck Institute, New York.*

ventured abroad, and for women these were arduous journeys. One woman remembered they had to pack "linens, blankets and everything that went along with that," including all cooking utensils and plates, if the family was kosher.[27] Another family visited English relatives every year: "but, what a journey! what luggage! we had to provide our own meals (kosher), huge baskets, including chamber pots and all the rest."[28]

The *Kur*, a yearly ritual of the Jewish (and non-Jewish) middle and upper middle classes, is a more obvious example of the confluence of family vacation and family strategy. The *Kur*, recommended for one's health, provided recuperation from strenuous city life in the fresh air and the rigorous regimen it offered. Few writers admit to going to a spa for a vacation. Instead, one young woman and her mother "recovered" from a "bitterly cold" winter at a fancy hotel.[29] Childbirth, whooping cough, rheumatism, a catarrh, and even a broken engagement sent middle-class women packing for a *Kur*.[30] Observing the spa she patronized, the troubled heroine of *Aus guter Familie* wondered if the Empire had been built with the "blood and iron" of countless young women. These resorts hosted a populace ostensibly worried about its health. In imitation of rich Europeans, the upper middle class participated in "the annual overhauling of the machinery, the great cleansing of the body."[31] In a thrift- and work-oriented society, the middle classes welcomed a medical excuse to pamper themselves. For women, whose assorted migraines and nervous stomachs may have been ways to assert themselves negatively against their roles and environment, concentrating on feeling good was a luxurious notion. One could rejuvenate in the vicinity of the rich and powerful—*Kur* hotels regularly announced which princesses or nobles were in attendance—or at the simpler resorts in the company of friends and relatives.[32] The "anemic" or "nervous" could indulge in the healthy outdoors and a steady diet of concerts, dancing, casinos, and socializing. Even if the *Kur* did not eliminate a specific disorder, it provided a "general feeling of well being."[33] The *Kur* was a favorite vacation, because it provided those who needed an excuse with a perfect one.

Some spas catered mostly to young girls and women.[34] Resembling a women's retreat, *Kur* life provided a brief respite from male domination, daily cares, and boredom. It encouraged a certain amount of independence in women accustomed to submitting to their husbands' schedules and demands. It allowed daughters, in particular, more freedom of movement. One mother took her doctor's advice to take a vacation with her daughters, lest they become hypochondriacs from too much embroidering and sitting around the home. Upon returning home, they became depressed and complained of their cloistered life.[35] Also, there was little or no housekeeping or household responsibility, since most stayed in hotels or pensions. At worst, mothers and daughters may have had to care for small children, and some took maids along for that. Older children, unbound by city constraints, gave their mothers free time as they explored the park and garden complexes, watched the cows being milked, and listened to concerts. Not a few enjoyed the festive meals, which "stood in great contrast to the puritanical ones at home."[36] Trained to serve others and to put their own needs last, mothers may have taken extraordinary pleasure in such self-indulgence.

The *Kur* also reinforced female kin and friendship networks. Women frequently visited such spas with another female relative.[37] One woman and her mother returned to the same spa every year. There they "walked every morning through the gently ascending Kurpark . . . drinking the waters of the famous spring. . . . These were recommended as a cure for rheumatism, anemia, liver complaints and other ailments. To complete the 'cure' we took a pine needle bath twice weekly." The two women also took climbing tours which ended with coffee, cherry tarts, and whipped cream. It is difficult to judge the medicinal value of the pastries, but it was clear that the women enjoyed their stay; in fact, the *Kur* represented the high point in the relationship of mother and daughter. The young woman recalled that her mother "became a different person on these holidays. She came to life."[38]

The work of such vacations, the hidden agenda, came easily. The very act of visiting a spa was a status symbol, since spas announced the type of clientele they served. Although a majority of spas were integrated, Jews knew where they were welcome—and unwelcome. (Some spas even advertised their kosher kitchens to attract a particular clientele.) While it was possible to befriend non-Jews and build long-term relationships from these acquaintances,[39] the Jewish bourgeoisie tended to meet other Jews. This was not only the case at spas, but on vacations in general. "Even when we went on holidays—a few weeks in the mountains, or . . . at the sea—we only came together with other Jewish people. There was a strong Jewish bond."[40] Mothers directed their children to the "right" kind of playmates and, as we have seen (chapter 3), kept a careful watch for the perfect spouse—or desirable in-laws—for their grown children. Meeting the "right" people could also provide new business or professional contacts for husbands, and women made new female friends as well. Thus the serious motive of class consolidation lay behind the frivolity of baths, mineral waters, hikes, casinos, concerts, and whipped-cream tarts.[41] The Jewish bourgeoisie, like its Christian counterpart, tried to solidify and perpetuate itself. Vacations—and particularly spas—provided perfect opportunities to do this, and women most often took the lead. Their labor, clearly part of the duties of the German-Jewish bourgeoise, was certainly enjoyable, although not without its tensions.

Beyond the Family: The Female World of Sociability

Cultural mediation and the preservation of kin networks and class status aside, the social role of leisure had further implications for a minority group. Leisure time was an opportunity for social integration not only into the Jewish, but also into the rest of the German bourgeoisie. And for women, it also provided an opportunity to develop their own space and their own support groups and bonds.

Women played a preponderant role in social activities, since Jewish men in business and the professions spent long hours at work and often traveled away from home. Still, Jewish men did develop Jewish social groups during their nonworking hours. The most famous of these was the B'nai Brith, founded in 1882 (with over 100 chapters and 12,000 members by 1937). Further, it was Jewish men who ran the *Gemeinde* and organized the Central Verein Deutscher Staatsbürger Jüdischen Glaubens (1893), the main Jewish defense organization. Jewish men also participated in non-Jewish organizations, from political parties to the rural local fire brigade and *Stammtisch*. But in a society in which the *Männerbund* became legendary, they could not integrate into the beer-drinking, card-playing, boisterous camaraderie of their neighbors. Nor were they particularly welcome in the old boys' network. As student corps became more and more nationalistic, militaristic, and anti-Semitic,[42] fraternity brothers complemented the slashes and cuts they so generously meted out to each other in imitation of aristocratic manners with the social snubbing, or cutting, of Jews.[43] Moreover, each town had its elite social clubs which barred Jews and, often, Christians who had married Jews. In Sonderburg, for example, the social elite founded a private recreational club in the late nineteenth century and never admitted the wealthiest family in town because it was Jewish.[44]

The type of social and charitable organizations just described (excepting the *Stammtisch*) were often seen by male participants as an extension of "business as usual," or business-by-other-means, a place to pursue political and economic goals, not leisure. Women's communal and social activity, on the other hand, while frequently aspiring to and achieving similar results, was seen by men and women in a deprecatory way as part of women's leisure-time activities. In order to treat such communal activities equally seriously for both men and women, I shall only mention them here, and will focus on women's communal activities separately in chapter 7. Here I will examine private or local forms of sociability.

For Jewish women, time outside the family was segregated by ethnic or religious and gender identities. Jews agreed that, in general, Jews had to turn to one another for social life.[45] For most Jewish women, private and informal gatherings with Jewish female friends and relatives provided their primary activity beyond housework, and probably not at all a new one. Perhaps the only difference was that the female world of sociability was a more open and fluid one for single women than the arena of family leisure. Family leisure focused upon the nuclear family, encompassing young women and single adults (both unmarried and widowed) who were related to one another. The female world offered single women slightly more leeway in enriching their own lives outside the family. In both cases there was a relationship between leisure, gender, and generational roles. As will be shown, housewives carried the greatest burdens of representation, but daughters too had to perform certain tasks.

In small towns and villages, Jewish women met in one another's homes to exchange gossip, to discuss current events, business, and child rearing, to trade recipes and health cures. Women maintained their life-long connections despite familial duties. Clara Geismar's mother visited her girlfriend, a woman whose seventeen births had left her with only three live children, almost every day. Both women shared a deep attachment to each other. They eagerly discussed current events "not, as it often happens today, because it is the style, because one needs an educated appearance for 'society,' but because it was a . . . necessity of life."[46] Eventually, the women married two of their children to each other. Phil Landau recalled how her mother, who worked in the family store (Worms, 1870s, 1880s), stole away to visit her girlfriends. "Often, especially during the late afternoons, mother disappeared suddenly . . . in search of diversion, she went to visit a neighbor. . . . After a while her absence was noticed." When the children heard their father calling for their mother, and particularly when he began to call her by her full name instead of her nickname, one of them would race around to find her. "I can still hear and see her running through the store . . . trying with cheerful excuses to make her . . . excursions plausible to father."[47]

Jewish women participated in *Spielkränzchen*, where they played card games, and their daughters imitated them with play or reading circles of their own.[48] Inside their homes, Jewish women of varying degrees of wealth were more likely to associate with one another than seek the friendship of non-Jewish women of equivalent wealth.[49] This was particularly so in villages where connections among Jews of different classes were closer than those among Christians or among Jews in more urban environments. In part, this resulted from the fact that rural Jews attended the same synagogue and participated in local *Gemeinde* activities together. Also, the differences within the Jewish middle class, even at its extremes, were not as great as the span between classes of other Germans.

Nevertheless, small towns provided some public opportunities for friendliness between Jewish and other German women, and villages encouraged neighborliness. In some small towns, Jewish women associated with the wives of civil servants, who may have found more in common with women of their own class, even if they were Jews.[50] Even in larger towns, the "women's *Stammtisch*" of a popular restaurant included Jews "whose husbands belonged to similar career or professional circles" as those of the other women.[51] Yet this was never carried "too far." In one exemplary case, non-Jewish women invited the Jewish wife of a wealthy manufacturer to kaffeeklatsches in their homes, but never gave her the honor of belonging to their exclusive women's organization. They also allowed her to work for their Red Cross activities, but barred her from their social and recreational functions. She remained permanently disappointed that her work for the group was never appreciated enough to overcome prejudice.[52]

Housewives' organizations attracted numbers of Jewish women from smaller towns. They attended lectures on the scientific management of the kitchen or discussed general themes in home economics while they knitted or sewed. They could also take courses in cooking and handicrafts. In rural areas during winter, members regularly attended a *Vorsetz* or spinning bee.[53] They would visit one another's homes, knit and crochet and enjoy homemade cookies or fruit. They traded conversation, recipes, or old stories. The *Vorsetz* occurred on a larger scale as well: one local housewives' club would invite a sister group from another town and would rent a hall for the joint meeting. Thus Jewish women maintained friendly relations with other German women within public organizations. They even visited one another's homes under the auspices of these organizations. Still, none of this necessarily translated into one-on-one friendships.

In villages, where the German peasantry lived in proximity to a Jewish lower middle or middle class, these types of gatherings were less common. Still, informal public, social, and recreational contact between the faiths occurred most frequently among women. Although Jewish families participated in village celebrations (including national, school, and children's festivals) and local dances, it was Jewish women who socialized with, rather than did business with, their neighbors. Holidays, for example, presented an opportunity for ritualized friendliness. Passover was a time for Jewish women to send their children to Christian neighbors with gifts of matzos, just as Easter was the time to receive colored Easter eggs from them. And many a Jewish child helped to decorate a Christmas tree. Jewish and Christian women visited and congratulated one another on the occasion of a birth, marriage, confirmation, or anniversary. It was women who noted the dates of such events and presented gifts, sometimes with their children or husbands in tow. Neighbors also shared grief over the death of a family member, frequently attending funerals. Christian women and children often aided observant Jews with their Sabbath chores, such as lighting the stove or turning on the lights.[54]

Work and relaxation often flowed together in villages, almost indistinguishably. Women broke up their day with a chat in front of their homes. They found time to bring food to sick neighbors, to lend a baby carriage. There was even a Jewish woman who breast-fed her neighbor's baby.[55] The exhausting task of getting water from the well provided "daily recreation and gossiping time." When modern plumbing came to one village in 1919, a Jewish woman complained that she no longer saw anyone or found out what was going on.[56] With wealth and modern technology came privatization and the further delimiting of women's public space and public interactions. These had been all the more important because there were no informal, private home visits between Jewish women and their non-Jewish counterparts in the village. Jewish and other German women interacted in public space, stepping into private interiors only on formal occasions. Very few could overcome the social distances produced by class and ethnic or religious difference in the private sphere. While Christian and Jewish men had business relationships, women had more chances to be friendly to one another, but still not friends.[57]

Whereas the village allowed informal, neighborly contacts, and the small town provided some public places where Jews and other Germans of the same class could mingle on limited occasions, cities—where the majority of Jews lived in 1910—confronted Jewish women with different responsibilities and opportunities. There, formal "visits" (*Visiten* or *Kaffeevisiten*) to other women's homes were the norm in "good" bourgeois society. Acting as extensions of their husbands and families, women visited the wives of their husbands' professional or business contacts and other women whose social connections they sought. Sometimes they even visited relatives. One woman spent her entire first year of marriage paying formal calls on her husband's many relatives.[58]

These visits were seen as women's duties and were extremely ritualized. Women called on one another at a particular time on a particular afternoon. They spoke about "appropriate" topics for an "appropriate" length of time and then took their leave. Memoirs describe the boredom and sheer horror of such visits for some women. Many were delighted when the person they dropped in on was not home, since then they only had to leave their formal, embossed calling card on a table intended for just such items. Others seem to have enjoyed these visits. Female leisure solidified business interests or created potential ones. In small cities this included formal visits between Christian and Jewish women. For example, in Constance the wives of all the lawyers in town extended invitations to the wife of the only Jewish lawyer when she moved there. Over a cup of coffee she "quickly discovered that it was not appropriate to discuss anything beyond apartments, servants or household."[59]

The picture of Jewish-Christian relations in this area is still unclear. Did such visits absolve class responsibilities alone or serve to further friendships as well, or both? With some exceptions, the opportunity for female sociability did not bring Jews closer to a smooth or relaxed social integration. The visits do indicate formal Jewish social integration. Contact between wives, although often for business reasons, went beyond the realm of pure business, inching toward social acceptance. That is why, for example, non-Jewish women were averse to inviting Jewish women to their homes. Käte Frankenthal recalled how a Christian family excluded her from their daughter's birthday party, even though the girls were best friends (Kiel, 1900). Since the hostess had invited the mothers of all the little girls, the Jewish child's mother would have had to be included. The hostess had no intention of entertaining a Jewish woman, so she omitted the daughter, too, from the guest list.[60] By the time she was a teenager, Frankenthal "shared . . . all the mistrust and all the insecurities of Jewish circles."[61] She described her family's life as "pretty secluded. As a result of my childhood experiences, I understood and approved completely."[62] Arnold Zweig tells an illustrative tale in *Die junge Frau von 1914*. A Berlin Jewish banker and his wife suffered terribly from the snubs of *haut bourgeois* Christian women. Not only had they refused her invitation to have tea in her home, they had also ignored her when they organized their own *Damenkränzchen*. Luckily for the couple, World War I provided the opportunity for (probably temporary) integration. To her delight, the Jewish woman was accepted into the ranks of the elite Frauenhilfe (Women's Aid Society).[63]

Mixed-sex visits—that is, couple visits—were even less likely to occur, being taken as a still greater indication of social acceptance. "I can hardly remember a non-Jewish person among the many guests at our home," Freud's son Martin wrote, referring to the early 1900s.[64] Gershom Scholem recalled that only his father's Christian male colleagues attended a reception at his home. Had they brought their wives along, it would have been necessary to invite the Scholem women in return, an obligation these guests clearly rejected.[65] Thus most Jewish women remained primarily dependent upon their families and other Jewish friends, particularly women. A highly acculturated woman doctor noted: "The family is a circle, turning round on itself with little room for friendships. Jewish families were . . . a closely knit community. . . . Friendships with other Jews were redolent of pleasant family ties but on a rather casual level, and contact with non-Jews did not go further than acquaintanceship."[66] Leisure time may have, in fact, helped harden the lines between majority and minority.

Besides women's visits, the ritual extravaganza of the dinner party would be another area in which to test Jewish integration into German society. By the turn of the century the more casual *Gastfreiheit* of the earlier era had given way to formal dinner parties where couples fulfilled social obligations and demonstrated their financial and social status.[67] At least twice a year women of the upper and "comfortable" middle classes prepared huge dinner parties for business associates and friends. Some twenty guests dined on ten or more courses (etiquette demanded a minimum of six). Along with the preparations and refurbishing of rooms and furniture, the hostess concentrated on the mix of guests and the variety and originality of the menu.[68]

The guest list itself announced the family's location in the social hierarchy. Introduced by their titles—Herr Doktor or Frau Geheimrat—everyone immediately understood the social pecking order. Seating arrangements also indicated rank.[69] Moreover, the very wealthy gave dinner parties, quite consciously, for political or business reasons. Department store owners Betty and Oscar Tietz held large parties or concerts almost every other week. These occasions afforded Oscar the possibility to discuss, "in a quiet corner, business or political matters."[70]

The Tietz family, active in Jewish communal affairs, entertained both Jews and non-Jews. That there was some mixing at other "fashionable" dinner parties may be deduced from the frequent, sarcastic comments about Jewish parvenus in the press. Satirical jibes at status-flaunting, social-climbing Jews attest to disdain for Jewish entry into previously restricted social circles, whether this entry was imagined or real.[71]

Dinner parties exhibited a woman's "feminine" prowess: her imagination, cooking skills, and talent for organization and administration (over the servants and sometimes caterers). Dinners displayed her capacity for picayune detail as well. Jewish advice literature, for example, described six different methods of folding dinner napkins: "One must be careful to keep the corners sharp and to keep each fold exact." (The "swan variation" was "only complete with a tiny bouquet in its beak.")[72] Such events also created an opportunity to reflect well on a woman's family of origin by displaying the treasures from her trousseau. And while women were particularly punctilious regarding preparations, men too were keenly aware of the class standards of a dinner party. A Jewish businessman who considered himself "not rich, but well-situated" (living on an annual income of 12,000 Marks between his marriage in 1906 and the outbreak of World War I), recalled saving money, because he and his wife lived more modestly than others in their circle. He was able to make this statement by describing their dinner parties as "less extravagant than was customary in our circles." Hence the dinner party was a rare opportunity to contrast one's style of life with others of one's class, to make judgments on the personal lives and manners of others, while rating oneself alongside them.[73]

Carefully prepared food and shining glassware and silver made an impression, not scintillating discussion. In fact, advice literature sternly warned against yawning during a conversation, alerting readers to the level of discourse they should expect and foster. Yawning "insults the social gathering about half as much as falling asleep."[74] Most important, the hostess's manner—the aura of calm she created—was her highest achievement. In his novel *Jenny Treibel*, Theodor Fontane made his (non-Jewish) heroine into the epitome of bourgeois aplomb—and pretentiousness:

> Frau Jenny presented herself in full glory, and in her appearance the very last trace of her origins in the little shop on Adlerstrasse had been obliterated. Everything seemed rich and elegant; but the lace on her violet brocade dress, it must be said, did not do it alone, . . . no, more than anything else it was the sure calmness with which she sat enthroned among her guests that lent her a certain refinement. Not a trace of agitation . . . revealed itself.[75]

Jewish advice literature insisted on a similar performance: "If one has prepared everything in advance and has instructed the servants, only a light wink from the housewife will be necessary. . . . Agitation . . . does not improve the service and only disturbs the atmosphere . . . . It is better to let a small mistake occur, apparently unnoticed, and make up for it the next time."[76] Many years after the event, a guest to a dinner party told Marie Munk that what impressed her most about Munk's mother was the calm with which she witnessed her waitress drop a huge platter of venison on the floor in front of twenty-four people.[77] Responsible for the smooth functioning of these events, women absorbed much of the tension and anxiety in order to present themselves and their families in the best light. Jewish women, like other German bourgeoises, attempted to give the impression that there was experience and confidence—class—behind parties the like of which most had, in fact, never experienced in their parents' homes.

In anticipation of similar duties, daughters received some training in poise and decorum at the dance lessons that constituted part of a young woman's cultural education. Afternoon dance lessons provided an occasion for meeting potential marriage partners.[78] Indeed, as a result of parental efforts to encourage endogamy, Jewish adolescents may have attended lessons organized specifically for Jews relatively more than their non-Jewish peers attended similar functions. In 1901, for example, a woman recalled ten to twelve Jewish couples attended lessons in ballroom dancing in her hometown of Nuremberg: "Young men between eighteen and twenty years of age asked young girls between the ages of sixteen and seventeen to be their partners, usually upon suggestions by their mothers. This custom was more widely adhered to in our Jewish society than in society at large. . . . Each weekly lesson was a social affair with chaperones and a visit to a cafe after the lesson."[79] A male participant described a similar scene in Breslau around 1904:

> Students and young business people, almost all from Jewish middle class "good families" [attended]. After a few hours, the first joint lesson with the "ladies" took place. . . . We had to take our street shoes off and wear patent leather shoes, white cummerbunds, and white kid gloves. . . . [As the young men walked into the room,] the young ladies sat along two opposite walls and curtsied their greetings repeatedly. . . . At first, I saw nothing but a cloud of white, pink and blue. . . . There always had to be more men, so that no young woman would be a wallflower.

Mothers situated themselves against the wall directly opposite the young men.[80]

The dance lessons led to formal balls, which mothers chaperoned. There was no escaping these events for a young bourgeois woman. Begging her father not to make her attend yet another ball, the heroine in *Aus guter Familie* is told: "My dear child . . . you have responsibilities . . . toward society and toward the position of your father. . . . As a representative of the government, I have to present myself to the public. What would people think if I left my daughter at home?"[81] Rigid dance rules regulated the young women's every movement and demanded their passivity. One Jewish woman who began attending such events at the age of eighteen recalled: "My path as an advocate for women's interests proceeded, paradoxically, across a ballroom floor. It was prescribed that a young woman had to keep all of her knowledge to herself and let any man take precedence over her. Always cheerful, ready for a light flirtation, alluring in her surface appearance . . . that was all one expected from a girl."[82] The four daughters of Julius Bleichröder took dancing lessons. He considered it their duty to attend the ensuing balls, to depart from the event at 10 p.m. promptly, and to appear at breakfast the following morning at 8 a.m. sharp. Anything short of this provoked his annoyance.[83] Thus, in the guise of engaging in frivolous activities, young women too performed their duties, particularly those of family representation.

Urban women shared less formal and, probably, more pleasant moments as well. Jewish women met regularly in cousins' clubs and charity circles, at lectures, and in women's organizations. Jewish girls participated in sewing circles, where they read classical plays to one another while they sewed gifts for friends and family or clothing for poor children.[84] Early on, they experienced some of the same frustrations that their mothers had encountered, sensitizing them for the future. Marie Munk described her *Kränzchen* of four girls. It consisted of herself (baptized as a small child), her Jewish friend, and two non-Jews, one with a "von" in her last name. In time, she was shocked to learn that the Jewish girl had not been invited to her aristocratic friend's home. Then she sensed that she, too, was "a little out of place and not entirely welcome" there. She discussed the situation with her friend, the daughter of a high-ranking officer, with the result that she no longer went to her friend's home, but her friend still visited her.[85] She remained in close contact with the members of her *Kränzchen* all her life, but also remained conscious of the compromise that lay beneath the surface.

By the 1890s more and more bourgeois women had opportunities to engage in newly expanding urban cultural and social activities—activities beyond the family. Jewish women, in greater proportion than other German women, were situated in both location and class to enjoy the fruits of urban life. Those who had the time and money could take advantage of theaters, cafés, and concerts. The urban environment also offered the opportunities to create or join the rapidly multiplying variety of women's groups focusing on cultural, charitable, or housewives' interests. Jewish women organized and attended "ladies evenings," small salons, and lecture series for women. As we shall see, some also joined the emerging women's movement. By the 1890s more and more women engaged in social and cultural activities beyond the family. Women began to "escape the authority of father or husband" as a result of these extrafamilial lures.[86]

In general, Jews were overrepresented in theater and concert audiences, sometimes using the occasion to meet friends and relatives there.[87] As at the spa, men frequently accompanied women, but it was perfectly acceptable for mothers and daughters, or two female friends, to attend the theater or a concert together without male escorts. Many concerts, in fact, took place during the day, and so were geared to women and children. In Lübeck, for example, "on Wednesday afternoons all the mothers would make a pilgrimage to the garden concert with their spic and span children."[88] In Kassel, women and children attended garden concerts and in the evenings sat "under Italian lights" at outdoor restaurant concerts.[89] In Frankfurt, Nora Rosenthal and her mother attended the Sunday afternoon concerts. Since many Jews would not go to the fancier Friday evening concerts, which interfered with the Sabbath, the Sunday events were known for the large number of Jews in attendance, "out of all proportion to the rest of the public." [90] Jewish women not only mediated culture in the home, but also consumed it in public. This too served the interests of a newly arrived bourgeoisie: to aspire to cultural and hence class integration.

Eventually, around the turn of the century, women graduated from being mere passive participants to becoming active ones. Young women began to study music professionally, entering conservatories to train as singers, musicians, and music teachers.[91] This too gave them some independence from their fathers (who paid the bills) and future husbands. It allowed some of them to support themselves if they never married. An unforeseen but welcome aspect of their musical and theatrical interests was the fact that in the the consumption of culture—much like in their other consumer functions—women could move with relative autonomy and possibly gain considerable independence.

For Jewish women, expanding leisure time served several functions. It afforded Jews the opportunity to maintain family bonds and to build a sense of Jewish community. More leisure time also offered Jewish women the chance to mold families that belonged to an educated and leisured German bourgeoisie. On the surface, a modicum of wealth and time allowed Jewish women, through the display of their homes, housewifery, and manners, to help their families acculturate to the *Bildung* and *Besitz* of the German bourgeoisie. Thus this intensely busy leisure time allowed Jews to partake of bourgeois culture; to make a double statement that Jews were integrated in terms of class and nation; and to blend in—at least superficially.

Jewish women also benefited as women, even from the incomplete returns of their leisure investments. In particular their ties to other women, begun early in life, underlined that women were not just extensions of their husbands or families (a function they also served), but had their own identities. Women could marry and still be their own person, maintaining ties to their family of origin and to their own circles of female friends.

II

JEWISH WOMEN REDEFINE THEIR "PLACE"

5

Jewish Women Confront Academia

Only in the first decade of the twentieth century did German universities officially admit women, years behind other Western industrial nations.[1] Despite Jewish and German patriarchal traditions which considered too much education "unfeminine," when the doors of higher education finally opened to women, the proportion of German-Jewish women students was high, although their actual numbers were small. In an era which saw the beginning of the mass university and the concomitant entry of women into this male bastion, German-Jewish women were drawn to the high schools and universities. Why was this the case? And what were their experiences with regard to the sexist and racist stereotypes and discrimination they encountered?

While we can only speculate on why individuals decided to be pioneers and brave societal suspicion or hostility—and there were probably as many unique reasons as there were women—certain circumstances permitted Jewish women to aspire to higher education. In general, historians have noted, "Jewish students combined the advantages of wealth, mobility, modernity, previous study, and cosmopolitanism."[2] Specifically, Jewish women benefited from the predominantly bourgeois socioeconomic profile of German Jews, which allowed the latter the "luxury" of supporting a daughter's education. Further, the Jewish population was concentrated in urban areas, where most universities were situated. Since indirect costs—lodging and meals—proved more formidable than tuition, it was economical for some Jewish women to live at home or with relatives while attending classes.[3] Also, Jews aspired to the social status accorded to those who excelled in German education, those who acquired *Bildung*.[4] Moreover, in this period the improving socioeconomic situation of Jews and their tendency toward late marriage and relatively small families reinforced each other. After finishing their schooling at age sixteen, Jewish girls of the upper bourgeoisie faced six to ten years of uselessness before they would be ready to marry. Discouraged from earning a living because of their parents' status consciousness, it is no wonder that some prevailed upon their parents to let them pursue an education beyond dancing and tennis lessons. And with fewer mouths to feed, it is also not surprising that many of their parents could afford the costs of that education. Finally, traditional Jewish veneration for learning likely influenced those who consented to their daughter's enterprise, including Orthodox Jews.

Biases Against Women Students

Jewish women's integration into higher education proceeded at a faster rate than that of non-Jewish women. German-Jewish girls attended *Lyceen*, *Oberlyceen*, *Mädchengymnasien*, and *Studienanstalten* which led to university study.[5] Between 1897 and 1906 in Berlin, where Jews made up about 4% of the population, an average of 20% of girls in public and private *Höhere Mädchenschulen* were Jewish (this included 32% of girls in the public *Höhere Mädchenschulen* preferred by Jewish families).[6] The most qualified students prepared for the *Abitur*, or certificate of maturity, which permitted entry to a university. As of 1901 in Prussia, 30% of the young women who had attempted the *Abitur* were Jewish. At the preparatory course leading to that exam in Frankfurt in 1906, 41% of the students were Jewish.[7] In Germany in 1911, 11.6% of girls in *Mädchengymnasien* (2,567 girls) and 11.9% of *Abiturientinnen* (those who took the final exams) were Jews.[8]

That same year, with Jews constituting 1% of the total population, Jewish women made up over 10% of women students at Prussian universities.[9] In 1913/14, they were 12.9% of the women at German universities and 21.7% of the women studying in Berlin.[10] Jewish women were also proportionately better represented in comparison to their male coreligionists than were other German women. The latter were 2.2% of the university population in 1909, 4.4% in 1910, and 6% in 1913/14. In contrast, Jewish female students made up 10% of Jewish students in 1911/12. Even compared with Jewish men, whose university attendance was about five times greater than the Jewish percentage of the general population, Jewish women were almost twice as well represented.[11]

Social acceptance, unlike matriculation statistics, did not come as easily. Jewish female students remained outsiders, both as women and as Jews. Memoirs often allude to the burden of being a Jew—a reaction to the increasing racial anti-Semitism infecting the universities—but the antifemale biases of professors, parents, and male counterparts had the most stinging effects. Contemporary feminist scholarship has shown how sexism and racism are mutually reinforcing and difficult, if impossible, to extricate. Nevertheless, in the first decade in which women enrolled in the universities, Jewish women were keenly conscious that sexism, rather than anti-Semitism, was the predominant obstacle in their paths. It was clear to them that their teachers and professors did not approve of women's aspirations. After passing her *Abitur* in 1907, one woman learned that "on the day before my exam the director of the Ministry of Education declared repeatedly that he would make sure that no woman would ever pass the *Abitur* in Pomerania."[12] The director of a Frankfurt *Gymnasium* "annually urged his female graduates to return to cooking and knitting and to become good mothers and housewives."[13]

Along with petty annoyances such as bureaucratic insistence that only "students" (*Studenten*)—that is, men—could receive tram or rail discounts, or that official university documents were stamped "Herr" despite a female name, women faced more serious insults as well as indirect obstacles intended to preserve male hegemony.[14] Some professors continued to address their mixed classes as "gentlemen" (*meine Herren*) throughout the war years, when female enrollment reached

Henny Simonis (x), born 1859, with her cousin, Jenny Hirsch Meyer (xx), at boarding school in Holstein, 1873. *Simonis Collection. Courtesy of the Leo Baeck Institute, New York.*

approximately 10 percent of the total student body. Others tried to discourage women from taking their courses. Addressing her as "child" (*Kindchen*), one such gentleman told Rahel Straus (born 1880, studied at Heidelberg) that she should consider majoring in something easier than medicine. Later, after she had successfully completed two and a half years of course work, he again warned her in front of her male colleagues: "I know women, none of them can endure this!" Noticing the smirks on the men's faces, she responded: "Yes, you know women, but mostly when they are sick!" These insults only heightened Straus's resolve to attain her degree: "I wanted to show him, to show all men, that one could achieve one's chosen profession."[15] Another professor told Julie Vogelstein (born in 1883): "I must protect myself from my dear female neighbors from the *Tiergartenstrasse* and the area around it, otherwise masses of them will come to my lectures."[16]

Ida Hyde, the first woman to receive a doctorate at Heidelberg (1894), and later the first woman to do research at the Harvard Medical School (1896), recounted her reception by a distinguished Strassburg physiologist as she prepared to ask him for permission to work in his laboratory: "He appeared followed by a fierce-looking bull dog that greeted me with growls and terrifying barks. The stern, dignified professor . . . apologized for the animal's behavior by informing me that the dog disliked women."[17]

Unluckily, Hyde had chosen medicine as her field, thus challenging a notorious antifemale academic bastion. Based on allegedly "scientific" facts, leading professors of anatomy denied women's rights to study "on the basis of the anatomical and physiological differences between man and woman."[18] Directly prior to her arrival at Heidelberg, her future professor had announced in a public lecture that women's place was in the home and that he would never allow "skirts" to enter his lecture hall or lab. Hyde had to study for her exams by borrowing lecture notes. When she passed, despite the obstacles placed before her, she was told by one examining professor that she had deserved *summa cum laude*, but that the Dean of the Medical Faculty had objected to giving a woman that honor.[19] Hyde's story is not unique. Rahel Straus recalled that the man who was to be her professor of anatomy also declared that no woman would enter his lecture hall as long as he lived. Luckily for her, he got sick and retired during the semester (1900) that she began her studies.[20]

A study done in 1897 showed doctors to be the leading opponents of women's university education, with lawyers in second place. Humanists and social scientists displayed less hostility toward women. This may have been related to a very practical consideration: until 1908 about half of all women students chose to study medicine. This same argument, however, is not sufficient to explain the lawyers' reaction, since women could not practice as lawyers until the Weimar Republic, and therefore could not compete. Still, both medicine and law degrees led to specific—mostly independent—careers where men might fear competition. The humanities were much broader and the institutions for which they prepared men, including teaching and the civil service, were respectively biased against or mostly closed to women. While individual doctors or lawyers might one day suffer from female competition, the male bureaucracy and the organizations of male teachers had a long history of successfully limiting the entry and controlling the condition of women's work in their fields.[21]

In 1897 a Berlin journalist surveyed over 120 university professors on their attitudes toward women as students. Responses ranged from rejection to skepticism, from grudging respect to condescension and ridicule. Otto von Gierke, the legal historian who would later solicit a dissertation from a Jewish woman student for his publication series, declared, "The German people has something better to do than to engage in risky experiments with women students." Above all, he was concerned "that our men remain men!"[22] In 1899 in Berlin, the first woman graduated with a degree in physics. The newspaper reported: "The Dean of the University alluded in his speech to the importance of this day, which saw the first female doctoral candidate within the walls of the University of Berlin. Even though a woman should primarily be the high priestess of the domestic hearth (thundering applause), scientific learning would not interfere with that."[23] Most academics agreed that women belonged in the home and should not compete with men. Quite openly, a Breslau historian conceded his worst fear: "if we allow women their say . . . we are declaring a permanent revolution."[24] As Peter Gay so aptly concluded, these professors demonstrated "how elaborately men at ease with words could disguise their most primitive anxieties. In the anguished and inconclusive debate over woman's true place, the fear of woman and the fear of change met and merged."[25]

The posture of male students matched that of their professors. Young men trivialized women by placing them on a pedestal, lecturing them, and belittling them. As the only woman in the medical lab, one pioneer had her lab preparations delivered to her by various fawning young men. She later learned that the men who happened to sit next to her during lectures had not arrived there by coincidence, but by fraternity pecking order. The Freistudentenschaft, an association of liberal men who claimed "unanimous sympathy for the aspirations of female students" and passed a resolution in 1906 in favor of women's full admission to the university, were the only ones to invite academic women to participate in their activities.[26] Those women who accepted such invitations could listen to their ostensibly sympathetic male colleagues' "scientific" monologues on how women students would ultimately deteriorate intellectually, emotionally, and also physically.[27] Jewish fraternities also took note of the "female students of today" (1912). Their newsletter remarked: "We find wonderful dancers and brilliant ice skaters among them."[28] With time, some women noticed that the atmosphere became more tolerable: "There was no longer any hostility, but no particular consideration either—quite to the contrary. . . . Often enough one saw a male and female in a race for an empty seat [in the lecture hall]. The victor . . . was visibly elated if he could grab the seat from the woman in the nick of time."[29]

The preconceptions of parents also discouraged young women. German bourgeois parents expected to exert themselves financially and in other ways for their son's class-appropriate education. Widows and daughters, too, strained to send the young men of the family to the university.[30] Parents considered daughters' educations, on the other hand, far easier to realize. If they stayed home after finishing middle school, helping their mother and participating in occasional social events, their education could be deemed complete. In fact, in Jewish homes parents stressed extracurricular activities like singing, music, and drawing, and social obligations like dance lessons, to such a degree that school grades may have suffered.[31] Further, for all girls their dowry, not their academic achievement, carried the greatest weight.

Thus girls' education stood in a clearly secondary position to that of their brothers. In fact, in many families it seems to have been absolutely acceptable for a daughter to replace one of the servants, so that money could be saved for the son's education. As Germans began to limit their family size, women's chances improved. Nevertheless, even by the turn of the century Karen Horney (who was not

Jewish) experienced a situation typical of her cohort. Between December 1900 and January 1901 she confided to her diary:

> I wanted to go right away to the *Gymnasium* for girls, in my thoughts I was there already, but I had not taken Father into account. My "precious Father" forbade me any such plans once and for all. Of course, he can forbid me the *Gymnasium*, but the wish to study he cannot. . . . Once Father has digested the monstrous idea of sending his daughter to the *Gymnasium*, Mother will talk with him further. . . . Why can't Father make up his mind a little faster? He, who has flung out thousands for my stepbrother Enoch . . . first turns every . . . penny he is to spend for me ten times in his fingers. . . .
>
> He would like me to stay at home now, so we could dismiss our maid and I could do her work. He brings me almost to the point of cursing my good gifts.

With the intercession of her mother, Horney finally received the paternal permission (and financial support) necessary to enter the *Gymnasium*, the path toward the medical career she so desired.[32]

Other daughters, too, received grudging parental approval. Bourgeois parents displayed extraordinary ambivalence regarding their daughters' aspirations. Increasing apprehension about the fate of unmarried women tempered the distaste of some for daughters with university degrees. Still, the fear lingered that educated daughters would educate themselves right out of the marriage market. In fact, these parents had some cause for concern, although proof was not yet available. By 1917, just 346 (or 32 percent) of the 1,078 women who had matriculated in Prussian universities between 1908 and 1912 had married.[33] Despite parental doubts, 39 percent of women students came from the academically educated bourgeoisie (*Bildungsbürgertum*), twice as many as among male students. Also, it was predominantly these fathers who petitioned the Prussian ministry to allow their daughters to study well before the universities officially admitted women.[34]

The prejudices and anxieties of even those parents who supported their daughters' aspirations left a lasting impression. "It took a long time until I overcame my prejudice against female students," recalled one Jewish woman. Her father's pronouncement upon meeting a cousin who was studying at the University of Zurich, "a horrible female" (*ein grässliches Frauenzimmer*), rang in her ears for many years.[35] The intellectual and progressive Rabbi Heinemann Vogelstein was saddened and depressed when, in the first decade of the twentieth century, his daughter decided to continue her education.[36] The family doctor warned Toni Sender that if she kept asking her father for permission to go to the university, she would ruin his health.[37] A Berlin judge confronted his daughter with the objection that her career would take away a salary from someone who needed it, when she declared her intent to enter the university (about 1908).[38]

Parents rarely offered their daughters advice or guidance in their academic careers. One woman, who later became a member of the Berlin Superior Court, arrived there by way of detours through teacher training seminars, volunteer social work, special courses to prepare for the *Abitur* (for which her schooling had not readied her), and a semester studying economics. "I had to search my mind and to make inquiries about the possibilities of future rewarding work. I did not get any counseling . . . from my father or from any other source."[39] (She later wrote the first pamphlet on "Women in the Law" used by high-school career counselors.)

Some parents actually suffered social ostracism after reluctantly agreeing to their daughter's desires. One woman who began her medical studies in 1914 recalled: "I was the only girl in the *Gymnasium*. That made a terrible stir. The priest in my home town, who had for years been my father's game partner, told him: 'Mr. Einstein, I'm very sorry, I can't play cards with you anymore, because you are sending Herta to the boys' school and thus aiding and abetting immorality.' "[40]

Parents who belatedly approved of their daughter's academic career had often resisted at first. One woman doctor (born in 1901) recalled how her parents "wanted us [daughters] to have the best possible schooling and to go to university if we wished." From her experience, she generalized: "Many Jewish families had the same approach, and it was not surprising that a great number of female university students were Jewish." Only much later in her memoir did she admit that at one time her parents had wanted her to give up her medical studies and become a secretary.[41] Käte Frankenthal, who became a doctor, and later, an SPD delegate to the Berlin Stadtrat and the Prussian Landtag, wrote that her parents became indignant at the thought of an "emancipated female" (*emanzipiertes Frauenzimmer*): "that was out of the question in our milieu [Kiel, ca. 1908]. At that time I knew only one female student, who, to be sure, . . . was the embodiment of the bluestocking. This woman was often held up to me as a warning precedent." Much to her family's distress, she declined to participate in the "normal" girls' activities of parties and balls, and began to study for the *Abitur* on her own. "Finally, my father mockingly told his friend, a *Gymnasium* teacher, what I was up to, and asked him to test if anything had come of it. The teacher tested me as thoroughly as he could. Then he went to my father with an expression like a doctor who had to impart sad news: his diagnosis was, with help she would pass easily in one year." After she had completed her medical exams, her parents honored her achievement, and friends who had previously mocked her treated her "as though I had won the Nobel prize."[42]

Choices: Turning Liabilities into Assets

Gender, ethnic/religious identity, and class largely determined the subjects in which Jewish women majored. By 1908, when Prussian universities opened their doors to women, a majority of women majored in the traditionally "female" humanities, those subjects for which they had been prepared in the lower schools. According to a scholar of higher education, the humanities (arts and sciences) "were the true melting pot of the university, blending a few academic children with sons of the plutocracy and especially of the old and new middle class."[43] This held true for the mingling of males and females as well, for it was in the humanities that most women matriculated. There was a particular irony in women's "selections," because by the time the doors opened to women, a general devaluation of the *Geisteswissenschaften* (humanities) and a concomitant increase in popular respect for *Naturwissenschaftliches—technisches Wissen* (scientific-technological fields) had taken place.[44] Thus, as Germany's rapid technological and industrial development proceeded, women would remain marginal. Further, even as they succeeded in pursuing the social status that an academic education promised, this status itself underwent a change. With the gradual professionalization of new fields such as teacher training and higher technical or business education, *Bildung*, or classical education and cultivation—the much-sought-after pedigree of the German bourgeoisie—gave way to *Ausbildung*, or professional training.[45] Whereas elite men could boast of their *Bildung* in a previous generation, those who entered the university belatedly—women along with the new and old lower middle classes—frequently had to settle for an *Ausbildung*.

Specifically, women registered for philosophy, history, and philology. There they could pursue what was commonly called a *Brotstudium* (study to earn one's bread), a course of study which would let them become high-school teachers (*Oberlehrerin*).[46] Jewish women, in numbers far disproportionate to other German women, studied science, math, and medicine.[47] At a time when medicine was still seen as an "unfeminine, even immoral" career for women[48] (in sharp contradistinction to the traditional stereotype of woman as healing and nursing agents), Jewish women, for a variety of reasons, persevered in their medical curricula. In Prussian universities in 1908/09, 34% of Jewish women students, compared to 15% of other German women, studied medicine. If one combines medicine (including dentistry), science, and math majors, then 59% of Jewish women would be encompassed, compared to 37% of their female colleagues.[49] In 1911/12 in Prussia, 40% of Jewish female students, compared to 11% of Protestant and 9% of Catholic women, enrolled in the medical faculty. During a semester in which 14% of female students were Jewish, 39% of women medical students and 50% of dentistry students were Jews.[50] This may in part have been due to class background. Whereas a significant proportion of women students were former elementary school teachers embarking on an academic course of study to become *Oberlehrerinnen*, this does not seem to have been the case for Jewish women. Jewish women tended to enter their studies without previous teaching or job experience.[51] While the *Oberlehrerin* lived on past savings and private tutoring fees,[52] most Jewish women relied entirely on their families. When the daughter of a judge tried to earn a few marks by tutoring, in order to be less dependent on her father, he responded furiously: "'You must give it up at once, or I won't allow you to continue your studies.' It was repugnant to him that his daughter would earn tutoring money, small as it was."[53] Such parents could obviously afford to educate their daughters. Those Jewish women who worked often did so for pocket money; the basics came from their immediate, or extended, family. They could also choose not to work. Rahel Straus, for example, received tuition and upkeep from her uncle. She tutored Latin, Greek, science, and Jewish history in order to earn an extra thirty to forty Marks a month, but stopped all part-time work during her clinical semesters.[54]

A comparison of the class origins of Jewish women students and their non-Jewish counterparts would probably reveal patterns similar to those of male students: the fathers of Jewish men were, generally, well-to-do merchants or members of the free professions. Other male students came from a broader and more diverse middle class, which included a large minority of lower-level civil servants, noncommissioned officers, teachers, and propertied peasants.[55] For these groups, the university was a path for upward mobility. In Prussia in the 1870s, the percentage of students whose parents were doctors or lawyers stood at 37 percent. It had fallen to 20 percent by 1911.[56] University education became more inclusive of the new and lower middle classes, so that after 1900 almost half of all students came from the lower middle class.[57] This trend placed Jews in even sharper contrast. Although we do not have statistical evidence on the parental occupations of Jewish female students, recent studies have indicated that women in general came from wealthier families than their male counterparts. Over half came from the upper strata of society, perhaps over one-third from academic circles.[58] This is probably because only those with sufficient means could support their daughters' educations after their (more important) sons' educations had been paid for. It is likely that most Jewish women came from these upper echelons and that the *Oberlehrerinnen* came from the poorer middle classes. Jewish parents could probably also afford the extra expenses of a medical education better than many other middle-class families.[59] As already mentioned, since the Jewish bourgeoisie had, on the average, smaller families than its Christian counterpart, there were fewer children to support in the first place,[60] and thus a greater likelihood that a daughter's medical education—the longest and most expensive course of study after 1901—could be supported.

More significantly, while teaching was considered a *Brotstudium* by most women, it was the reverse for Jews. Jewish women faced job discrimination as women, but even more pronouncedly as Jews, when they applied for positions in state or private schools (see chapter 6). Thus preparation for teaching would in fact have been preparation for unemployment or for low-status tutoring or governess positions. One Jewish woman switched to medicine, although she had intended to major in philosophy and literature, because it would give her "a livelihood."[61] So Jewish women followed Jewish men into what Germans call the "free" professions, notably medicine and also, for men, law. Barred by an officially sanctioned anti-Semitism from the civil service and from university careers, and by an unofficial but widespread aversion to hiring "non-Christians" in teaching positions and private industry, many Jewish men chose law or medicine as their academic major.[62] These careers gave individuals the opportunity to provide service on their own and to avoid discriminatory hiring practices. A comparison of Jews and the general population for 1882 indicates that 90% of Jews in medicine and 80% of Jews in the legal fields (which included the civil service) had independent practices, compared with 56% and 14%, respectively, of other Germans.[63] Of the two fields, medicine was not only more popular, but had historically been an important profession for Jews. Since the eighteenth century, medicine had offered Jews a career opportunity without having to convert.[64] It had the aura of the freest of the liberal professions and therefore attracted a mixed student body. Sons of doctors or apothecaries mixed with those of wealthier bourgeois and some lower-middle-class children, and Jews too could find a place.[65] Thus an overwhelming preponderance of Jewish men chose the medical faculties. In 1886, close to 60% of Jewish men (compared to 28% of the general student population) majored in medicine, and although this interest waned considerably, as late as 1911 over one-third of Jews continued to do so.[66] In contrast, law was everywhere the most exclusive and the most prestigious faculty. It attracted the nobility or the wealthy patriciate as well as some children of academics.[67] In 1886 only 16% of Jewish men (the same as 16% of the general student enrollment) enrolled in law school. However, their interest (and opportunities) skyrocketed, so that by 1899 32% and by 1911 41% of Jews (compared to 30% and 23%, respectively, of the student population) registered for law.[68]

Jewish women, excluded from the bar like all women until the Weimar Republic, overwhelmingly preferred medicine.[69] It is therefore not surprising that Jewish names figure prominently among recipients of the degree of medical doctor. In 1901 Irma Klausner, from a well-to-do Berlin Jewish family, was one of the first four women to pass the medical *Staatsexamen* (state medical boards).[70] In 1904, four of the nine women to receive a medical degree were Jewish. Two of these, Paula Philippson and Rahel Hirsch, were the granddaughters of the renowned rabbis Ludwig Philippson and Samson Raphael Hirsch, founders of Liberal Judaism and modern Orthodoxy, respectively. (Rahel Hirsch was the first woman to be given the title of "Professor" in Germany in 1913.)[71] The irony cannot escape us that, in this case, the persistent and vicious anti-Semitism of the German school systems actually prompted a significant proportion of Jewish women to avoid the pitfalls of a liberal arts degree. While many of their female counterparts faced the hardships of the teaching profession—a bad job market; low pay and no power compared to male teachers; antifemale colleagues and administrators; and statutory celibacy[72]—Jewish women doctors pursued careers in private and public practice (see chapter 6). Thus whereas class and gender determined most women's entrance into the university and their choice of career paths, racial/religious discrimination forced a large percentage of Jewish women to turn a liability into an asset.

Student Life

After women struggled with parents, professors, and male students, and after they chose their curricula, even more arduous tasks began. In contrast to the carefree and convivial stories that men have told of their student years, women's experiences were more serious and often more solitary. Having rejected a traditional mode of life, they determined to achieve success in their new role and worked diligently to do so. Men could enjoy the "classical epoch of student corporatism," indulging in the elitism, drinking, and rowdiness of their fraternities or in the social and political activities of independent student associations.[73] "They could fully enjoy their academic freedom. That meant, they could waste their time, ruin their health, and run up bills in their fathers' names," commented one of their female counterparts.[74]

Newcomers to the university, women had fewer organizations to make them feel welcome and none to rival the camaraderie and frivolity of the fraternities. Also, since German students changed universities two or three times during their studies (and men could always contact fraternity brothers at their new university), women, probably less itinerant, may still have found themselves in new surroundings which were unprepared for them. Further, German female students tried to distinguish themselves by their proper and ladylike behavior in order to counter charges of being antifemale and "unnatural," a favorite accusation of antifeminists. They had to be nonconformist in their decision to fight popular prejudices against women students and frequently rebellious in confrontations with family and friends. In contrast, as students most felt constrained to act as proper bourgeois ladies, uninterested in attacking women's broader oppression through their own behavior or their organizations. They shrank from the popular stereotype of the Russian female student, who was portrayed as radical both politically and personally. One German-Jewish woman recalled how perplexed she was about whether or not to accept an invitation from male students to go tobogganing one winter.[75] Another insisted, despite her degree and her professional status, that "woman's personality could not develop outside of marriage."[76] Smoking was taboo and dress was respectable. Nowhere do we read of the smoke-filled cafés and radical or feminist political discussions so prominent in novels of the period.[77] Reflecting on her female counterparts during her university days, one Jewish woman noted

> an unbridgeable gap between male and female students, from what different perspectives they view love and life. For male students this period of study is a precious thing in and of itself. They are delighted. . . . They enjoy every day. . . . Nothing very serious is demanded of them except a bit of cramming in the last semesters. . . . Love is a pleasant intermezzo. . . . Marriage is out there. . . . And in this way, in enjoying the moment at hand, they are ahead of all female students. The women students that I have met [are] earnest and conscientious . . . Their student years are not the golden time of freedom, but only a transition period to reach their goals.[78]

During World War I hunger, cold, and fear exacerbated the psychological and intellectual burdens of student life. A medical student recounted that Heidelberg, which had become "a girls' boarding school," lost its merry atmosphere.

> Among twenty or thirty girls sat one unhappy male, usually a soldier on leave . . . instructors were also in uniform. . . . In the laboratories the relationship between students and instructors was difficult because the uniforms intensified their traditional conflict. Our lives were constantly in danger. . . . Emergency sirens chased us into cellars, and soon we became so worn out that we simply didn't bother to go and, instead, tried to sleep on. . . . What we lived from at that time is incomprehensible to me today. . . . Mornings we had a slice of coal black bread . . . with turnip jelly and substitute coffee. At noon . . . the student cafeteria . . . served a horrible mixture of turnips and cabbage with small pieces of meat or a thick soup of undefinable content. . . . Occasionally our soldier colleagues gave us commissary bread and dried meat from their rations. . . . Heated rooms were a dream.[79]

Despite the overriding seriousness of their pursuits, women enjoyed pleasant moments and interests beyond the academic. For some, a stay at a distant university was their first independent step: "This was my first taste of freedom which I used to the fullest. My friend and I made many excursions to the beautiful Black Forest."[80] Women sought relationships on individual bases, since so few university organizations accepted them. A law student recalled that landladies did not like to rent to female students, because they enjoyed studying with friends and therefore brought more company home.[81] Often women took advantage of the opportunities available to them in the cities in which they studied. One young woman filled her student days in Munich (ca. 1912) not only with course work, but with visits to her parents' friends and relatives. These people introduced her to artistic, literary, and political circles as well as to Zionist organizations. On occasion, she also enjoyed spending the Sabbath eve with religious friends.[82] A student at Heidelberg participated in Jewish youth activities in nearby Mannheim. There she developed a sense of confidence in her public speaking abilities. Hiking, a perennial favorite German pastime, offered women brief respites from their studies. One woman took great pride in her ability to be "one of the boys" during these weekend adventures. Her relationship with her hiking comrades, like those of many female students and their male colleagues, was congenial and sisterly.[83]

Platonic relationships were the rule, probably the result of female and male sexual repression. As already mentioned, these women were intent upon achieving their academic goals and guarded their moral reputations. This was particularly difficult in a charged atmosphere where men greatly outnumbered women and where rumors flew. The day after an ice-skating excursion with a male colleague, her male friends warned a young female student, "Never again with only *one* . . . !"[84] Men were ambivalent about intimate relationships with female students. Friendships and some love relationships with female students notwithstanding, most men turned either to neighboring town women of the lower classes or to prostitutes for sex.[85] For marriage, they were loath to wed a professional who might try to juggle a career, husband, and household.

There were, of course, exceptions. Käte Frankenthal, a nonconformist in every way, described several boyfriends. There were also romantic moments with professors, as well as student–teacher relationships which culminated in marriage.[86] A number of student liaisons probably led to "student marriages" (that is, cohabitation) and some, ultimately, to legal ones. Elisabeth Bab, who married in 1905, wrote that "we were a curiosity, because we were the first married student couple in the annals of Berlin University." The lot of the student wife was an extremely difficult one. Both partners worked at other jobs besides pursuing their studies. When their child arrived, "a bedroom for my husband was set up in the kitchen so that he would not be disturbed by the baby, since I had to bathe and care for the child before I went to school in the mornings." Her husband was not responsible for child care: "My mother cared for the child in the mornings. Oh! was I often tired when I had to feed the baby and get ready for school."[87] Thus there was an intellectual and social life outside the classroom, but one that could not emulate the exaggerated conviviality or even the leisure of male students.

Anti-Semitism in the University

Ultimately more threatening than the sexism and gender-related differences of university life was the extent of anti-Semitism in society at large as well as among university faculty and students. The anti-Semitic pamphlets of the 1870s denounced the intellectual "domination" of Germans by Jews. In his anti-Semitic speeches Adolf Stöcker, one of the fathers of modern political anti-Semitism, decried the "disproportionate onslaught on institutions of higher education" by Jews (1879) and "the Judaization of girls' grammar schools" (1890).[88] By the end of the 1870s, more and more fraternities excluded Jews, some by statute and others by "selective reception."[89] As anti-Semitism mushroomed, becoming a social norm on German campuses, the theme of "Jewish competition" cropped up. Particularly during the severe crisis in the academic labor market of the 1880s, students complained; "[The Jews inhabit] our universities in vast numbers and so Jewish doctors push out Christians, Jewish mouths disproportionately emit jurisdiction and law."[90] The large percentage of Jewish women in the medical courses could not have gone unnoticed. At Leipzig, for example, the medical faculty objected to "undesired Russians" who were almost "almost entirely Jewish women," and male students protested their "personal appearance." It seems, therefore, that the animus of male doctors and students against women also contained a significant element of anti-Semitism, more or less camouflaged by conventional misogyny.[91]

By the 1890s the organized German student body was by and large anti-Semitic, espousing an uneven mixture of nationalism, hatred of "Jewish" liberalism, and racism. In 1886, as a result of their exclusion from student life, Jewish men formed the first Jewish fraternity. The Viadrina, as it was called, was intended to cultivate a sense of Jewish identity and to practice self-defense. In 1896 Jewish men founded a national association of Jewish fraternities, the Kartell Convent. By the turn of the century, Jewish men could choose between Jewish fraternities and liberal, nonsectarian associations, such as the Freie Wissenschaftliche Vereinigung, which were in fact made up almost entirely of Jews.[92]

Jewish women thus entered an arena already divided into opposing camps. Their original experiences, however, were not as alienating as those of Jewish men of their cohort. The first women students at Heidelberg, for example, suffered from extraordinary gender discrimination: "Almost all had reached their current path after heavy battles against a thousand prejudices, against family and society." Opposed to any strict or formal sorority requirements, they insisted upon their autonomy from men's organizations. Their club (*Verein*) invited women of all faiths to join. Its chairperson, a Jewish woman, recalled evenings among "the most interesting women . . . participating in building a new woman's existence."[93] Between 1900 and 1906 other women formed all-inclusive women's organizations which coalesced into the Verband der Studierenden Frauen Deutschlands. Open to all confessions and "neutral" in its professed politics, the group attempted to discuss and solve the problems of female students. In 1915 it affiliated with the middle-class German women's movement, the Federation of German Women's Associations (Bund Deutscher Frauenvereine). By 1916 the Verband der Studentinnenvereine Deutschlands, as it was now called, had grown to twenty local chapters.

Yet within a relatively short time, women formed sororities (*Verbindungen*) which excluded Jews. Infected by an environment hostile to Jews, eager to appropriate the attitudes of "insiders"—that is, the fraternities—and perhaps jealous of the economic advantages of Jewish women, many female students became openly anti-Semitic. As early as 1905, a new generation of women in the Heidelberg club voted to become a sorority. They rejected all "foreigners," including German Jews. The original organizers of the Heidelberg group resigned, renaming themselves the

"Alt-Heidelbergerinnen." The new generation was well on its way to aping the worst elements of its male counterparts.[94] In 1909—one year after Prussian universities were formally opened to women—the Verein Studierender Frauen in Berlin split over accepting an invitation from an anti-Semitic male club. Its anti-Semitic members formed the Deutsch-akademischer Frauenbund, a "Christian–national" organization. Its more liberal members bemoaned the split in the academic women's organization. A liberal spokesperson noted: "This incident must be painful for all those who sympathize with the progress of the women's movement. In any case, it is not easy to understand whose interests the aforementioned women's group is pursuing. . . . What woman can expect from reactionaries, that. . . they should finally have learned."[95]

By 1913 one Jewish woman wrote that "the blossom of German youth, male and now also female students, regard no Jew . . . as their equal."[96] In 1914 the anti-Semitic women's group had enough university branches to form a national organization, the Deutscher Verband Akademischer Frauenvereine. With affiliates in Bonn (1905), Berlin (1909), Münster (1909), and Göttingen (1912), the organization encouraged its members' activity in student affairs while it promoted the women's movement and "national questions." By 1917 two new affiliates had joined the effort to cultivate *Deutschtum* (Germanness, or German exclusivity) among the female student population. Honoring the motto, "Remember that you are a German woman," they barred Jews.[97]

Individual Jewish female students, most of whom entered the university after 1908, found few organizations to choose from and, at some universities, none. Unlike Catholic women, another minority group which began to organize in 1911 and joined four affiliates into a national association in 1913, Jewish women did not form their own organizations. While some remained completely unaffiliated, others joined liberal women's organizations and still others sought community outside the academic environment. One can speculate as to why Jewish women did not organize their own association. First, they were few in number: in 1908, there were only 135 Jewish women studying at Prussian universities. Also, they were divided between German citizens and "foreign" students.[98] The latter, about one-fourth of all Jewish women, either were of Eastern European origin (but had resided in Germany for many years) or were actually foreign students.

Foreign women felt especially isolated. One of their male colleagues wrote of the loneliness suffered by these women. They remained outside German society as well as the communities established by men from their countries of origin. Germans ridiculed them: "You did not really come to study. What need has a woman for scholarship? What does one have to do with the other? You are up to no good—not at all what is becoming for a woman."[99] Russian-Jewish women, most of whom studied medicine, came in for the most serious attacks. They faced the hostility of anti-Semitic students and professors who complained of an influx of Jews and radicals. German women were no more friendly toward their Russian-Jewish colleagues, being anxious lest professors exclude all women so as not to be swamped by Russians. In 1901 one German woman wrote, "The foreigners overwhelm us with their numbers."[100] Finally, German-Jewish men added insult to injury, perpetuating unfavorable stereotypes of the Russian female student while trivializing all female students: commenting on the clothes of female students, the Jewish fraternity newspaper suggested that one could practically tell which faculty one was in by the attire of the women.

> We still meet the strangest appearances in the medical faculties, perhaps because they are mostly attended by Russian women. Here we sometimes still meet the type of woman who for a long time represented the female student. Here we note a certain desired laxness in dress, poorly groomed hair, and a stance which says: nothing matters to me but science. In the humanities, in contrast, the "student lady" reigns: elegant young ladies who in no way . . . differ from ladies from the world outside.[101]

As for German-Jewish women, ethnic divisions and small numbers alone do not sufficiently explain their lack of group cohesion. There were, in fact, fewer Catholic women students in Prussia in 1908 than Jewish women. As was (and is) so often the case with minority women in racist societies, Jewish women were forced to choose between their gender and their "race." While some entered the ranks and leadership of liberal women's associations, others supported male-led Jewish organizations. It was as much the ubiquitous anti-Semitism of the era as their gender identification which propelled Jewish women to strengthen the ranks of liberal, nonsectarian women's organizations. These were stronger bases from which to challenge or ignore racism than a small sectarian women's group would have been. At the same time, the desire to "fit in," which is hard to disentangle from an atmosphere of anti-Semitism, probably also played its part. Women who had to struggle against gender discrimination may have sought relief from their "otherness," preferring to merge with liberal women rather than acknowledge and confront their Jewish identity. Nevertheless, there were some whose sense of religious or national identity directed them toward religious or Zionist activities in neighboring communities. Here, too, heightened anti-Semitism may have caused university women to join men in common cause. As the Imperial era drew to a close, increasing numbers of Jewish women faced "German national"—that is, anti-Semitic—women's organizations. Further, some experienced in their classrooms and from their teachers the more rabid anti-Semitism that resulted from wartime chauvinism. Immediately after the war one woman recorded that "there were professors who made yellow marks on their Jewish students' cards."[102] Certainly these men had not had a sudden change of heart in 1918. Many of their female students had sensed their racism much earlier.

In the first decade and a half (1894–1909) in which women entered the universities, sexism rather than anti-Semitism affected Jewish women immediately, making their acceptance into the educated echelons of society much more difficult than that of Jewish men. Later, however, as life became somewhat easier for women students, particularly after their formal admission to Prussian schools, anti-Semitism—never absent from the universities—became a discomfiting, sometimes distressing element in the university careers of Jewish women. Yet in contrast to the tension-filled universities of the Weimar Republic, those of the Second Reich appear relatively hospitable. For example, membership in the anti-Semitic Deutscher Verband Akademischer Frauenvereine increased by 75 percent between 1917 and 1928, while the liberal Verband der Studentinnenvereine Deutschlands lost twelve affiliates between 1916 and 1927.[103]

6

Double Barriers, Double Burdens: Women's Employment

The stereotype of the bourgeois "lady" and the idle *höhere Tochter* notwithstanding, Jewish women worked in a variety of ways, and often without remuneration. A significant minority of them—about 18 percent in 1907—worked outside the home and appeared in the censuses. Others who ran the family shop, delivered goods, kept records, peddled wares, managed a small business, or "helped out" in the household—"family helpers," as they were called in the 1907 statistics—remain invisible, but for our purposes have to be uncovered. Not surprisingly, when we do find women doing unacknowledged labor, they appear in positions similar to other officially employed women.

Jewish women faced a job market riddled with anti-Semitism and sexism. Their skewed job profile—a heavy emphasis on trade and commerce—resulted from their ethnic and religious identities. Their lower job status was a consequence of their gender. The increasing numbers of working Jewish women suggest that Jewish affluence could no longer be taken for granted in Imperial Germany, and that there was not only a gap between some wealthier German Jews and the Eastern European immigrants, but also a gender gap within the German-Jewish working community.

Recognized and Unrecognized Work

In order to reveal the types of jobs Jewish women held and the extent to which they worked, we need to analyze census data and probe for all kinds of hidden, unpaid, or unrecognized work. What statistics do not reveal is almost as important as what they do. They do not, for example, offer an age breakdown, which would disclose a decreasing number of working wives and an increasing number of working daughters in this era. Nor do they reveal what percentage of Jewish working women were immigrants, a figure estimated as high as 25 percent in certain occupations and areas. Further, they do not distinguish between upper-middle-class and middle-class women: the *höhere Tochter* who wanted to work and the daughter who had to work. In addition, statistics are most suggestive when compared to census surveys of non-Jewish Germans. For example, when we compare women's status, we note that the gender gap among Jews, male and female, was less extreme than among other Germans. This was due to a variety of causes which will be discussed below and which offer insight into the economic situation of Jewish families. Finally, we must also be cautious about generalizing on the basis of Reich statistics. Regional and urban censuses may offer better bases for comparison. For example, although the job profile of Jewish women, like that of Jewish males, was skewed, it was less so in large cities. There, Jewish women made job choices more similar to those of other women.

For the Imperial era, employment statistics categorized by religion are available for Prussia and other provinces for 1882, 1895, and 1907. For Germany as a whole, there are censuses from 1895 and 1907. We must therefore assume that the employment of Jewish women in the first decade after their final legal emancipation looked much like their job profile in the 1882 statistics. Before 1907, however, *mithelfende Familienangehörige*—family members who aided the main entrepreneur—did not appear in the census at all, nor were they usually paid. One-fourth of all Jewish working women in 1907 (12,123 out of 48,976)[1] belonged to this group. It is almost certain that the actual number and the percentage of such "family helpers" was even higher in the 1870s as Jews continued to work their way toward middle-class status, and that many more Jewish women worked than showed up in the 1882 statistics. Further, traditional historical sources like census data perpetuate inaccurate information about women's actual unpaid and paid work experiences. Undervaluations and underestimations by census takers as well as the perceptions of women themselves overlook many forms of work such as seasonal employment, home work (music lessons, sewing, taking in boarders, etc.), peddling, or "helping out" in a relative's home or shop. Also, class pretensions or aspirations played a part in obscuring women's "work" experiences. Thus when we look at women's work we must enlarge our definition of "work" (for example, to include family helpers even before 1907), read carefully between the lines of memoirs or diaries to uncover it, and use statistical sources critically.

Examples of unrecognized work abound. In the era before the 1882 census and probably thereafter, the most commonly unrecognized work among Jewish women—that is, unpaid and usually scarcely mentioned in passing—was helping out in the family shop. Wives and daughters took this work for granted. In small towns, daughters generally assisted in the shop or did the bookkeeping for their parents until they married.[2] Even in cities, daughters worked in the shop or in the business—as already mentioned—often behind the scenes. Before the typewriter became commonplace, Anna Ettlinger recalled how she and her sisters copied their father's legal briefs for him, saving him secretarial costs. Wives also worked full-time in their husbands' shops and businesses, often running them on their own. In bakeries, wives shared the same grueling hours and routines.[3]

> Every Thursday night . . . our mother . . . helped braid the Sabbath breads [*Berches*] and sprinkle them with poppy seeds, while father . . . slid them into the oven. . . . With this night of labor finished, mother faced a Friday morning . . . serving customers, . . . giving handouts to the local beggars who appeared . . . for the weekly donation, . . . and preparing for the dignified reception of the . . . Sabbath.[4]

This woman bore ten children as well. Another woman ran a small inn while her husband maintained a traveling sales business. With the help of one sister-in-law, she also managed her household, including twelve children. The inn opened at 5 a.m. She served drinks and meals and kept several rooms for overnight guests. If customers became rowdy, she had to intervene herself: "There were frequent brawls. Then mother intervened in her energetic voice. Sometimes . . . she gave one of those half pints a slap—in any case, the guests respected my mother."[5] Other wives took charge of their husbands' bookkeeping, shipping, or correspondence.[6] Some wives administered their husbands' businesses singlehandedly, because the husbands were not good businessmen. They took no credit for their role and the businesses remained officially in the husband's name. For example, after the failures of his fabric store and brewery, Benno Meidner's wife began to manufacture flowers. Her business grew and thrived with the help of her sons, while her husband "was more of a bother than a help." She managed to recoup their losses and maintain the family in his name.[7]

Women worked in other—even more hidden—areas. Some took in wash, were seamstresses, or did weaving for "private customers."[8] Others accommodated summer "guests," that is, boarders.[9] Even less obvious was the work of girls sent to relatives' homes to "help out" with the children or learn to run a household. They often stayed as long as a year. Neither the young women nor their hosts considered their work to be "domestic service," yet this is exactly what they did. A widower with eight children sent his oldest daughter, aged fifteen, to her aunt for a year, to learn to be a *Hausfrau* and to care for her younger siblings. Her "home economics training" with her aunt involved all but the heaviest domestic labor.[10] Other girls assisted recently widowed relatives, sisters, or aunts who had just had another baby.[11] One young woman ran her widowed aunt's home while the aunt and her sons managed their business.[12] Parents also sent daughters to strangers' homes for slightly more formal "household training." They expected that their daughters would be accepted as part of the family rather than be paid. A plethora of advertisements to this effect could be found in Jewish newspapers: "respected, very religious family . . . wishes to give its daughter to a good family, for household and social training, no pay but complete integration into the family expected." A Jewish girl looking for a job in a Jewish home so as to learn household duties wrote, "salary is not demanded, but family togetherness [is]."[13] This strategy had precedents that reached back to the medieval nobility.[14] Seen as temporary, and intended to prepare a woman for her own marriage and household, or possibly for work as a "household helper" (*Stütze der Hausfrau*) in someone else's home, such work by women was viewed as "training" or "helping out." Sometimes these positions offered the added enticement of learning about life in a bigger town. Moreover, they most likely involved the assistance of a domestic servant. Thus participants and observers could avoid recognizing these positions as work, since the most menial tasks could be delegated.

Even women who stayed home contributed to the family economy beyond the housework that most accomplished. The daughter of a wealthy banker (1880s—1890s) designed and tailored all of her four sisters' clothes. They rarely bought a piece for themselves; one sister recalled the purchase of one new silk blouse for her dancing lessons when she had turned seventeen. Probably the family's seamstress neither saw herself in that role nor was given particular recognition for it.[15] In general, most people saw this kind of work as an extension of woman's proper sphere, so it could easily be discounted as labor. Still, women's labor helped maintain and improve the family's standard of living. Finally, there were cases where women and their families acknowledged their work but hid it, either from government officials or from their neighbors. One woman collected kerosene containers from various shops and delivered them back to the suppliers in order to support her blind father.[16] Another sold dyes from her own home.[17] Others supplemented family incomes by teaching piano. One woman supported her whole family as a piano teacher when her husband sold his business upon being drafted.[18]

A comparison with other German women suggests that many middle-class women shared certain kinds of hidden work, particularly "household training." The differences, however, were significant. Since a large percentage of middle-class Jewish men worked in business and commerce, one finds proportionately more Jewish women in shops and offices, serving behind the counters or doing extra bookkeeping or correspondence. Other middle-class German men filled the growing cadres of the civil service. Their wives or daughters could not "help out" in municipal or state offices. To find the same extent of hidden work in the non-Jewish population, one would have to turn to the vast agricultural sector. There, the wives and daughters of poor as well as wealthier peasants cared for the gardens, livestock, and farm hands. Only a minority of Jews lived in rural areas, and they tended to be shopkeepers or horse and cattle dealers. Hence fewer Jewish women performed hidden agricultural work. Finally, with a proportionately larger proletarian population as well, non-Jewish women tended to take in more homework, or what we call sweated labor, than did Jewish women.

When one analyzes recognized work, that which was revealed by the census data, other precautions are in order. Statistics do not distinguish between the more middle-class German-Jewish population and Eastern European working-class Jewish immigrants. Therefore it is necessary to keep in mind that the "worker" category (categories c, 2–5, in the *Reichstatistik*) probably contained relatively fewer German Jews and more Jewish immigrants. Further, the occupational status categories of the census—"independent," "employee," and "worker"—need some clarification. Frequently, census takers described women working in offices or stock rooms in industrial branches as "workers," when they actually filled white-collar positions and should have been described as "employees." Also, since most Jews were middle-class and urban, it would be instructive to compare them to a similar group of non-Jews. This is not possible with the existing data. Thus with one exception (statistics for cities with populations of over 100,000), the contrast is between a distinctive bourgeois minority and a majority population made up of large percentages of agricultural and industrial laborers. Moreover, the statistics compare an increasingly urban Jewish population with a predominantly rural one. Furthermore, by the 1880s an aging Jewish population experiencing a birth decline is presented alongside the general population with its more traditional age distribution and, hence, more people of working age.

In the case of women, a comparative perspective has special relevance. In the rural population, for example, the incidence of women's work was particularly high. (In 1895, 2,730,000 German women worked in agriculture, and in 1907, 4,558,000.) This was not the case for Jewish women (1895: 1,208; 1907: 3,746), because far fewer Jews lived in rural areas, and those who did belonged to the rural bourgeoisie. Their middle-class composition made it less imperative for rural Jewish women to work for pay. In urban areas, on the other hand, if we compared German-Jewish with other urban middle-class German women, we would probably find relatively similar patterns with some differences. Studies of middle-class German families suggest that housewives rarely worked outside the home.[19] This holds for Jewish families as well. Yet, since even within the bourgeoisie Jews leaned more heavily toward trade than other Germans, when Jewish women worked, it was most likely in the family shop. Other middle-class women could take jobs in the civil service (practically closed to Jews) and in other middle-class occupations away from their families. The census takers could, therefore, note the work of non-Jewish women more easily than that of Jewish women (whose work in the family concern was easier to overlook), making it seem as if Jewish women worked for pay proportionately less than their non-Jewish peers. Still, in the Reich in general, the overall middle-class status of Jews probably allowed more Jewish women to avoid officially recognized work. Jewish girls spent more time in school, attending the *höhere Töchterschule* rather than the briefer *Volksschule*. Therefore, if they worked at all, they usually began later than others and devoted a shorter span of their lives to their jobs. Finally, an aging Jewish population included a large percentage of widows, women who lived from pensions or savings and who also did not appear as active workers in the censuses.

Even when class and age are taken into account, Jewish women still worked for pay less often than their similarly situated non-Jewish cohorts.[20] This may point to a Jewish cultural trait. Some demographers have suggested "Jewish family customs" as a possible explanation.[21] Demographers have also commented on the comparatively higher rate of infant survival among Jewish working-class families. They attribute this to the fact that Jewish working-class mothers breast-fed their babies and stayed home with them to a far greater extent than other immigrant working-class women.[22] Thus familial and cultural traditions may have influenced even proletarian Jewish women to remain at home more than other women of their class and community.

Despite the statistical problems that occur when "Jews" are compared to "Germans," it is still useful to turn to those 11 to 18 percent of Jewish women officially classified as "employed" between 1882 and 1907, to see what they did and what their status was.

Working Population

The first comprehensive employment statistics of 1882 indicated that 11% (or 20,102) of all Jewish women in Prussia—where most Jews lived—compared to 21% of other German women, were employed.[23] By 1895 a German census counted 39,427 Jewish working women (of whom 38,089 lived in Prussia). These figures include category "G" of the census, live-in domestics.[24]

Twelve years later, in 1907, the German census showed a 36% increase to 53,747 (or 18% of the whole). As was already noted, the 1907 census included "family helpers," for the first time, which partially explains the rapid increase in the number of working Jewish women between the two censuses. Further, the number of Eastern European immigrants increased from 20,000 in 1890 to 70,000 in 1910. Thus the 1907 census (after the 1903 and 1905 Kishenev pogroms in Russia) may include as many as 6,500 Jewish immigrant women.[25] Still, even in 1907 the national statistics indicated that a greater percentage of non-Jewish than Jewish women (31% vs. 18%) were gainfully employed.[26]

Those women who ventured out despite their affluence and cultural conditioning, or because of economic need, confronted anti-Semitism. Whereas growing numbers of middle-class women entered the world of work in the late nineteenth century, anti-Semitism closed the doors of many of the new "women's careers" to Jews.[27] The civil service, for example, opened to women (telegraph operators) as early as 1873. Other civil service possibilities before World War I included positions in the post, railroad, and state offices. Intended as a respectable branch of business for ladies of the middle class, the daughters of officials (*Beamten*) and officers,[28] these positions—like those in the male civil service—were generally closed to Jews. Furthermore, there was rampant discrimination against women in the civil service. Despite the promise of tenure, most women did not achieve it before the war. They also had to quit their jobs and lost their rights to their pensions if they married.[29] Thus those Jewish women who did enter the job market often found their opportunities severely limited by a mixture of anti-Semitism and misogyny.[30] They remained, therefore, in traditional "Jewish" sectors of the economy and often within family businesses.

Occupational Profiles

Although their occupational profile more nearly approximated that of the overall population than did the profile of Jewish men, Jewish women did not adapt to a "German" job distribution. Like Jewish men, Jewish women found employment most often in commercial sectors. They were thereby segregated by occupation, an isolation which—as is the case with most minorities—further hindered their integration into the majority society.

A rough comparison of the three major fields of employment in 1895 is shown in table 6.1 (see chapter appendix, tables 1 and 3, for details). Jewish women's

Table 6.1. Jewish Employment, 1895

	Jewish Women (%)	Jewish Men (%)	General Population (%)
Trade/Commerce	48.5	69.0	10.0
Industry	26.0	22.0	36.0
Agriculture	3.0	1.0	36.0

SOURCE: *ZDSJ*, January/March 1919, p. 2.

participation in industrial work (10,363) was concentrated in certain branches determined by their Jewish, urban, and female status. Jews in general worked in "typically Jewish" sectors, and women in "typically female" ones. Specifically, Jews worked in textiles and clothing, and slightly less in the food, beverage, and tobacco industries.[31] Non-Jewish urban women also clustered in the garment industry. In Berlin, women formed about 70 percent of all workers in the clothing industry in 1907. Most engaged in mass (unskilled) production, sewing women's and children's clothes, underwear and linen. One quarter of all fully occupied women in Berlin worked in this sector. This was also the case, only somewhat less so, for Hamburg and other major cities.[32] Thus over 75 percent of Jewish women in industry labored in the clothing and cleaning branches in typically "female" positions such as sewer, seamstress, and trimmer. Other Jewish women worked in the food industry, mostly in a *Konditorei* or in butcher shops as personnel. Eastern Jewish immigrants, who made up about one quarter of Jewish women industrial workers,[33] nearly all worked in the garment or tobacco industries.[34] The fact that so many Jewish women clustered in clothing and textiles or in small shops probably meant that they sought employment among other Jews or in firms owned or run by Jews.

The largest proportion of Jewish women—49%—could be found in the category of "trade and commerce" (19,123 Jewish women), where almost 70% of their male counterparts worked as businessmen and shopkeepers. Over 85% of these women owned or worked in shops (40% were owners). Twelve percent of women fell into the next largest category, inns and taverns (*Gast und Schankwirtschaft*), of whom, again, 40% owned the enterprise.[35] Further, 16% (or 6,298) of Jewish women found employment as domestic servants.[36]

By 1907, Jewish women's employment had shifted slightly, as seen in table 6.2 (see chapter appendix, table 1, for details). There was an approximately 36% increase in Jewish working women in total, or 47% if we focus on "major jobs," omitting live-in servants.[37] These increases of about 15,000 women resulted, for the most part, from the inclusion of "family helpers" and immigrants in the census, but also reflected an earlier trend. More Jewish women had to work for pay. Alluding to the Great Depression of 1873–96, commentators noted, "Perhaps the Jewish population has met with economic adversity, that has to be compensated for by the employment of its dependents." They acknowledged that Jewish women worked in

Table 6.2. Jewish Employment, 1907

	Jewish Women		Jewish Men	General Population
	(%)	(No.)	(%)	(%)
Trade/Commerce	51.8	(27,846)	64.1	11.5
Industry	27.7	(14,906)	26.0	37.0
Agriculture	4.0*	(2,175)	0.8	33.0
Free professions	5.6	(3,056)	8.6	6.0
Domestic service	8.8	(4,771)	0.03	2.0

SOURCE: *ZDSJ*, July/August 1911, pp. 97–112.

*This is an increase of 75% or 900 Jewish women, a result of the 1907 census' inclusion of *mithelfende Familienangehörige*, family helpers.

greater numbers, even though the number of unemployed dependents shrank. The Jewish press interpreted this to mean that "here too, Jews no longer differ from Christian Germans."[38]

Jewish women were particularly visible in the lower paid categories. They increased their representation by fivefold in the "employee" branches of the commercial and industrial sectors of the economy, and they saw 45 to 48 percent increases in the lowest categories (workers and family helpers combined) in industry, commerce, and day labor. These statistics indicate that Jewish women in general entered the job market because they had to.[39] Whereas the memoir literature describes the frustrated upper-middle-class daughter who deeply desired a worthwhile occupation, the statistics allow us to uncover those women who needed to work. While their upper-middle-class cohort could be observed in the free professions in modest but rapidly growing numbers (1,303 women, a 74% increase), lower-middle-class and working-class women congregated in shops and in the textile, clothing, and food industries.

A quickly expanding number of Jewish women staffed the offices of industrial and commercial enterprises in what began to be called the "New Woman" careers, those of secretaries, stenotypists, and sales. Ironically, such "New Woman" work may not have been so new to these young women. These jobs carried on the kind of work some of their mothers or grandmothers had always done: they "helped out" in the shop or office, often in family enterprises. Only now the younger generation worked for pay, exchanging a mentality of *höhere Tochter* for one of working girl (hopefully, only until marriage). In fact, by the time offices and stores began to be seen as "normal" women's workplaces in the last decades of the nineteenth century,[40] as many as 40 percent of Jewish women could already be found there.[41] Thus at a time when most women still worked in agriculture or industry, Jewish women were at the forefront of modern urban life in their "traditional" jobs, leading the way into careers that were later considered the prototypes of "new" female occupations.[42] They also held prominent positions among the founders of the organization of female employees (Verein für Weibliche Angestellte) and made up about 20 percent of its members in 1893.[43]

Immigrant Eastern European Jewish women had a different occupational profile from German Jews. In Berlin, for example, where one-fifth of Jewish immigrants lived, close to half (48%) of Jewish women worked in industry, nearly twice as many as in commerce. Almost two-thirds of them could be found in the garment industry. Immigrant men were nearly equally divided between industry and commerce.[44] In industry women tended to work in family concerns, whereas in commerce they tended to be self-employed. In Berlin, half worked for themselves. They often owned and ran hostels and restaurants, or they worked as peddlers, hawking eggs and secondhand merchandise. Recalling his mother's venture into the peddling business, one man wrote:

> When I close my eyes, I can still see my mother's first steps. . . . She had sat on the bed for hours, with her pack in her hands . . . unable to move herself. . . . Suddenly tears filled her eyes . . . my young soul clearly felt the bitterness and senselessness of this life. . . . A half hour later I accompanied her to the train. . . . Finally she returned. She cried a lot that night. . . . She described how her

> heart beat every time she knocked on a strange door, how she ran away when she heard someone about to open it. . . . In one place the maid did not even let her in, at another place she sold a dozen handkerchiefs. . . . [After some time she] had gotten used to peddling and did not cry so much anymore.[45]

Domestic service provided another major source of employment for immigrant women. In Berlin about 14 percent of immigrant Jewish women found employment in this field, probably in the homes of German Jews.[46]

Sharp regional and local variations occurred, both in the percentage of Jewish women who worked at all and in the sectors of the economy in which they found employment. In Prussia we find the greatest percentage of Jewish working women in the environs of Berlin, in Westphalia, and in the Rhineland. These areas employed clerks and office help in their industrial and commercial enterprises. The fewest employed women appear in Brandenburg, where some of the wealthiest Jews lived.[47] Further, a smaller percentage of Jewish women worked in southern rural communities than in Munich. This was probably the result of a combination of hidden work as well as greater Orthodoxy, and hence larger families and more traditional roles in the villages.[48] In a comparison between Prussia and Bavaria, we see an example of the variation in sectors: in industrial Prussia (1895) only 2% of Jewish women worked in agriculture, whereas in rural Bavaria 11% did so. In Berlin, a manufacturing center, 45% of Jewish women could be found in the industrial sector, whereas in Bavaria only 15% worked there.

In large cities Jewish women's work profile most closely approximated that of non-Jewish women. Since such cities offered broader industrial and professional opportunities, Jewish women's employment, like that of Jews in general, slanted least sharply toward commerce there.[49] The 1907 census (see table 6.3) showed approximately 35% of Jewish women in cities with over 100,000 inhabitants engaged in industry compared to 28% nationally, and 44% in commerce compared to 52% nationally (see chapter appendix, table 2, for details).[50]

Regional censuses delineate the variety behind the general categories (see table 6.4). From these statistics we can note that the most visible segment of Jewish working women labored in shops. Less numerous, and far less visible, were Jewish female domestics. Further, as already indicated, a significant percentage of women in industrial jobs, particularly seamstresses, were of Eastern European Jewish ori-

Table 6.3. Employment of Women in Cities over 100,000 in 1907

	Non-Jewish Women (%)	Jewish Women (%)
Agriculture	1	0
Industry	39	35
Commerce	21	44
Day labor	8	2
Free professions and civil service	5	8
Domestics (live-in)	25	11

SOURCE: *Statistik des deutschen Reichs,* #211, Grossstädte.

Table 6.4. Employment of Jewish Women in Hesse, 1905

Commerce		Domestics		Industry and Crafts	
owners	409	maids	143	dressmakers	
shop assistants (*Ladnerin*)	185	housekeepers	44	independent	124
apprentice shop assistants	32	cooks	36	dependent	24
clerks (*Kontoristin*)	37	companions, apprentices, governesses	18	milliners	
				independent	66
				dependent	11
				factory workers	20
				seamstresses	17
				day laborers	7
				hair dressers	7
				rag collectors	5
				washer women	4
				embroiderers	3
				ironers	2
TOTALS	663		241		290

SOURCE: *ZDSJ*, April 1908, p. 54.

gin. Therefore German-Jewish women were probably even more highly represented in commerce than seems apparent from these statistics.[51]

Yet another way of looking beyond the national census data is to analyze job placement results published by Jewish social welfare bureaus. In Berlin, for example, reports of the Berliner Arbeitsnachweise disclosed a tenfold jump in the number of female job applicants between 1896 and 1913.[52] Women applicants were younger than their male counterparts: 60% of the women were under twenty, but only 42% of the men.[53] Most of these women sought positions in commerce (84%), domestic service (10%), and handicrafts (6%). In the commercial trades they worked as bookkeepers, clerks, salesgirls, stenotypists, warehouse clerks, and dispatchers. (It was as clerical employees in industry that the census often listed Jewish women as working in "industry," when in fact they performed commercial tasks.) Finally, while Berlin was certainly an exceptional city (17% of job applicants were recent immigrants), it was a salient indicator of the work preferences among Jewish women since almost one third of all Jews lived there.[54]

In sum, Jewish women found themselves in a traditionally "Jewish" job category. Both Jewish and non-Jewish observers—the former looking for prospective careers for themselves or their daughters, and the latter often critical of Jewish economic activities—could hardly fail to notice the large representation of Jewish women in the "commerce and trade" sector of the economy. Jews, about 1% of all employed people in Prussia, made up 15% of Prussians in commerce and trade in 1882.[55]

Anti-Semites attacked this concentration as parasitic, and even Jewish leaders often criticized an "unhealthy job distribution." To counteract this imbalance, Jewish leaders urged girls to consider "household careers," a term which was both a euphemism for domestic service as well as a general description for institutional management, social work, and related fields. This was part of an older, broader effort reaching as far back as the era of the German Enlightenment, when both Jews and other Germans had argued that it was only natural that people seeking to normalize their civil rights should attempt to achieve a job distribution similar to that of the majority. Jews had to prove that they contributed to the fatherland rather than exploited it as unproductive middlemen. In the nineteenth century this meant moving into agriculture and crafts, and Jews founded societies to further these fields. However, by the time Jews had been granted the rights to own land or to join a craft or guild, they would have been foolish to do so. A growing capitalist economy encouraged them to remain in or expand their businesses, and the same edicts that accorded Jews civil rights also lifted commercial and trade restrictions on them. Many Jews preferred to utilize the new opportunities in their traditional occupations and fields of expertise, and took the occasion to move to cities which had formerly banned them or limited their numbers. Thus they adapted previously acquired skills and predilections to modern socioeconomic trends, rather than heed those leaders who would have turned them into farmers. In the process, however, the victims and critics of capitalism often vilified Jews, and anti-Semites reviled their "parasitism." They considered Jewish involvement in trade even in an advanced phase of capitalist development as proof of low moral character, and a broad spectrum of society labeled the commercial trades "judaicized" (*verjudet*).[56]

In the face of increased anti-Semitism, some Jewish leaders suggested that Jewish organizations adopt official policies of vocational retraining. They argued that the acquisition of civil rights created both the opportunity and the obligation to integrate into a "German" job profile, and that social integration could proceed more easily if Jews did this. Ignoring the fact that anti-Semitism often excluded Jews from a broader variety of occupations, Jewish leaders once again urged young people to acquire skills useful in industry, crafts, or agriculture. And in fact, Jews seemed to make an effort in that direction, also taking advantage of the growth of German industry. In 1861, for example, 21 percent of employed Jews labored in industry and handcrafts. This figure rose to almost 30 percent by 1907.[57]

Still, Jews remained to a large extent in commerce—even in commercial positions within industry. When the depression hurt internal trade and the consumer goods industry,[58] Jews nevertheless maintained their preference for these sectors. Their adherence to commerce was probably a result of various constraints affecting them as a minority.[59] It was still better for Jews to work among other Jews, often among relatives, so as to enhance familial enterprises or those of the Jewish community more generally, avoid anti-Semitism, and (in the case of Jewish religious Jews) uphold the Sabbath. In sum, they remained within a social and familial tradition rather than venture out. And Jewish women were no more daring than the men. If one compares, for example, the 1907 figures, 52 percent of Jewish women and 64 percent of Jewish men remained in commerce. The lower percentage for women does not indicate an interest in new sectors of the economy (even if those who pushed for Jewish "integration" applauded such endeavors). Women with the fewest skills, and hence choices, entered domestic work (9%) and agriculture (4%). Had the domestics and farm hands had their way, they too would have preferred shops and offices.

Thus the predominance of Jewish women in commerce was closely related to the historical position of Jews in Germany. Jewish men worked in some form of trade and commerce, and family businesses provided jobs for female relatives and untold numbers of acquaintances. The census classified fully 30 percent of Jewish women in commercial enterprises as "family helpers."[60] Widows too reflected the Jewish commercial proclivity, running the businesses that their husbands left behind.[61] This was the case for some of the businesswomen listed in the West Prussian censuses of the 1860s through the 1880s.[62] Memoirs describe widows who not only ran their husbands' businesses, but improved upon them. In one case a widow with five children continued her husband's bakery after his early death; she not only baked the goods and delivered them to her customers in neighboring villages, but also ran a lively Passover matzo business.[63] Left with ten children, the matriarch of the Hadra family invested money in fertilizer and later bought some land. She sold the former for vast profits, and the latter turned into rich mining territory.[64] Other widows embarked on industrial ventures entirely on their own. In 1865, in a Rhineland town of about 3,000 people, Sara Miller, the mother of nine children, began knitting stockings in her home to support her family. Shortly, she bought a manual knitting machine and began producing large quantities of stockings. She built a factory and mill in 1875, and the business continued to grow until it employed over 800 workers.[65]

Women's preference for commercial positions also reflected the geographic situation of Jews as well as the position of women in Jewish and German societies. The majority of Jews lived in cities where trade or office jobs in industry offered young women opportunities for employment. Furthermore, lower-middle-class parents who, by the turn of the century, accepted the idea that their unmarried daughters should earn part of their upkeep, were very conscious of class-appropriate jobs for their offspring. White-collar work was acceptable, although the prestigious civil service, closed to Jews, would have been preferred. Also, most working Jewish women were unmarried, as were most working women in Germany in general, and many saw jobs as only a stage before marriage. The "division of labor according to sex and, amongst women, between the single and the married, was characteristic of the urban economy in Wilhelmine Germany."[66] In Berlin, for example, in 1916 there were about 25,000 economically independent, unmarried Jewish women (*jüdische Mädchen*) between the ages of twenty and fifty. About 70 percent of the total 35,000 working women in Berlin were thus single.[67] Many of these unmarried women needed to sustain themselves financially only until they married. Clerical jobs as well as shop-girl positions demanded a minimum of training—but still more than unskilled factory work, hence maintaining class divisions—and a minimum of commitment. Thus Jewish women flocked to commercial careers. Also in rural areas, and even among the Orthodox, daughters of poor families chose clerical positions or "homemaking" as a stage before marriage. In Baden between 1908 and 1911, for example, the parents of a large family of twelve children had to decide upon their daughters' futures. The father earned a tiny salary as the town's Jewish teacher. Father, mother, and the oldest son, by then a teacher, made the decisions. One daughter became a private teacher, another worked in a store owned by relatives, and a third worked as a household employee. The last was to become a piano teacher and teach in "better Jewish homes," though she had not yet taken even one piano lesson! It was never intended that they would work outside the home after they married, nor did they.[68]

Job Status

Job status was gender-related. Within their respective fields of work, Jewish women, like other German women, held positions inferior to those of men (see chapter appendix, tables 3 and 4). In 1907, while one-third of Jewish working women were still "independents" (including homeworkers), two-thirds belonged to the lowest status categories.[69] For men, the reverse pattern obtained. For example, in 1907 in agriculture, where females outnumbered males (2,175 to 1,571), only 15% of the women were "independent proprietors" compared to 43% of the men (see table 6.5). In the industrial sector, women worked in similarly subordinate positions: whereas 45% of men were owners or managers, only 27% of women belonged to this privileged group. Considering that the "independent" category of the German census included independent seamstresses as well as industrialists, women's status was appreciably lower than even these statistics indicated.[70] In the poorest paid and least respected jobs, household employment and day labor, 99% and 74% respectively of Jews in these categories were women.[71]

Jewish women's lower status followed a general female pattern of decreasing "independents" between 1895 and 1907. This decrease—of 13 percent—was all the more significant because the population increased 19 percent in the same period. Economists attributed this to "increases in large-scale concerns [*Grossbetriebe*] which, first of all, reduce women's independent status."[72] Lower status could also be attributed to the general female pattern of increases in "family assistants." This was, as already mentioned, the result of a statistical fluke (they were first counted in 1907), but it also reflected an absolute and relative increase.[73] Among Jews, three-fourths of all family helpers in 1907 (12,123 out of 16,573) were women. As already noted, women preferred not to spend more time and money than necessary in learning a trade or job, since they expected to stop working after marriage, and their parents for the same reason chose to invest their limited resources in their sons' careers. With minimal training, women could apply only for the less remunerative and lower status jobs.

In his comprehensive research on Jews in the German economy, Avraham Barkai has reflected upon the occupational profile of and economic divisions among Jews. He noted that the job profile of Jews was significantly influenced by East European Jewish immigration and the overaged German-Jewish population.[74] Fur-

Table 6.5. Jewish "Independent" Workers, 1907

	Jewish Men (%)	Jewish Women (%)
Agriculture	43	15
Industry	45	27
Commerce	58	32

SOURCE: *ZDSJ*, January/March 1917, pp. 2–4.

ther, he has speculated that such immigration (of mostly working-class Jews) led to deeper economic divisions among Jews.[75] A gender analysis of Jewish participation in the economy can also be applied to the areas of job profile and economic divisions. Women's entrance did not challenge Jewish job preferences for trade and commerce, despite their slightly greater representation than men in the industrial and agricultural sectors. Even in industry 18 percent worked in offices, and 46 percent were found in the top two job categories (independents and employees); observers insisted that even among those classified as "workers," many worked in offices and sales. Women's entry into the economy did, however, affect the overall job status of Jews and lead to economic divisions among Jews—by sex. As already stated, women made up the overwhelming majority of Jewish day laborers and all domestics; constituted three-fourths of all family helpers; and consistently held lower positions than their male colleagues, even among the most elite professional groups. Thus when Barkai posits the inflexibility of "Jews" in maintaining independent positions in their work life—which may have affected them adversely (as a result of increases in competition and in giant concerns)—and notes that between 1852 and 1907 the percentage of independents (male and female) dropped only from 71 to 60 percent, he is actually referring to Jewish *men*. Since 21 percent of working Jews were female in 1907[67], and their status was significantly lower, they, and not their male coreligionists, represent the lion's share of the drop in independents.

This sexual division of status had other implications. Job discrimination and lack of training caused a serious economic division among Jews, male and female, at the workplace and in the pocketbooks of individuals. Female subordination was completely apparent in the workplace, so obvious that contemporaries found it barely worth noting. However, for German-Jewish women, at least, financial inferiority could be compensated at home. Their standard of living generally equaled that of their fathers, brothers, or husbands. In this way they were more fortunate than Eastern European immigrants, for whom charity was the only recourse. Still, the lower status and hence lower income of Jewish women may have been not only the result of economic uncertainties in the middle class, but a cause of them as well. In his economic history of the Jews, Arthur Prinz concluded that the Jewish minority as a group was more homogeneous in its income and wealth in 1860 than it was thirty or forty years earlier or later. He suggested that the 1870s may have witnessed a widening economic gap separating a new, numerically tiny, but visible handful of industrialists and a significant group of proletarian Jews (of Eastern European origin).[77] A gender analysis indicates a serious and more hidden—because it was in part ignored and in part compensated—division among Jews: that between male and female incomes and job status.

Despite the gender inferiority of Jewish women compared to men, their job status was still higher than that of other German women (see chapter appendix, table 2). For example, in 1907 in cities of over 100,000 population, Jewish women swelled the ranks of "independents" and "employees": in industry 28% of non-Jewish women and 52% of Jewish women were found in these combined categories, while in commerce and trade 41% of non-Jewish women and 55% of Jewish women could be found in them.[78] Within a major city, Hamburg for example, employment conditions favored Jewish women even more.[79] Whereas 60% of all employed people in Hamburg were "workers," the exact reverse held for Jews: 57% of Jewish women (and 72% of Jewish men) were found in the echelons of the "independents" or "employees."[80] This was the result of the predominantly middle-class origins of Jews and their concentration in trade and commerce, but for women, ironically, it was also a result of their status as family assistants (the same status which caused their inferiority vis-à-vis Jewish men). In Germany in 1907, half of all female "workers" (*Arbeiterinnen*) in industry, commerce, and agriculture (12,123 out of 24,705) were actually family members. In the case of trade and commerce, where most Jewish women congregated, their status was even higher (although still inferior to Jewish men) than the 1907 statistics indicated at first glance. First, 53% of these "workers" (8,242 out of 15,412) consisted of family members who helped out in the store, including wives and daughters, some of whom presumably were coowners. Second, "workers in commerce and trade tended to be shop girls whom German census takers classified as "workers," although their social status and class identity equaled that of white-collar employees (*Angestellte*).[81] Almost all the Jewish women classified as "workers" were shop personnel, and therefore "employees" in reality.

Significantly, German-Jewish working women for the most part did receive some training. Their parents could support minimal preparation, even if they could not afford to subsidize them for a lifetime or provide a generous dowry. Also, wealthier relatives often took on the expenses of job training. In addition, Jewish organizations, communities, and individuals provided courses, scholarships, and loans, so that even those without the means to acquire job training could do so. For example, private Jewish foundations like the Paulinenstift in Hamburg provided orphans with job training for careers as seamstresses, kindergarten teachers, or florists.[82] Also family legacies, like the Handwerker und Dienstboten Stiftung in Leipzig, helped to train Jewish boys as craftsmen and Jewish girls as cooks or domestics.[83] In twenty-eight of the larger Jewish communities, loan funds established during the nineteenth century allowed needy Jews to borrow without interest in order to establish themselves in a business or train for a job. Some, such as the Deutsch Israelitische Darlehnskasse für Frauen und Jungfrauen, aimed to assist young women.[84] Finally, Jewish women's organizations also supported the career aspirations of young women, often promoting careers that more traditional leaders found superfluous: the Orthodox newspaper *Laubhütte*, for example, criticized women's groups for encouraging girls to become teachers, educators, or bookkeepers rather than maids or cooks, "an efficient service class."[85]

For all these reasons, when Jewish women earned income outside the home, they tended to enter as semiskilled or skilled employees rather than unskilled laborers.[86] Even when they worked in industry, it was predominantly (65%) in white-collar, independent, or family-helper positions.[87] The benefits of class for the majority, and of Jewish communal support for the minority, partly compensated gender inequality. Nevertheless, inequalities of gender and the specificities of Jewish occupational trends continued to confront and predetermine Jewish women's work life.

The increase in female employment, even when the statistical changes concerning the category of family helper are taken into account, reflected on the economic well-being of the Jewish community. By 1911 Jewish observers noted: "The intensity of their entry into the economy, the rapid development of Jewish women's participation in the economy, startles us, makes us worry."[88] The Jewish press commented that this may have been a sign of economic problems among the Jewish population.[89] In a society which valued women's enforced idleness, the increase in working daughters suggests at least a relative decline in the wealth of certain sectors of the Jewish community, attributed to the increasingly precarious budgets of lower-middle-class families and the wave of proletarian immigration. It seems likely that, increasingly, some breadwinners could no longer earn enough to support their dependents, and some of these dependents worked for their own livelihoods.[90] Other observers pointed to increased standards of living among Jews, complaining that "Jewish simplicity, that sense of frugality and modesty in life-style, is vanishing." The blame, they concluded, lay with women who had to go out to earn more, since they wished to consume more. Some argued that the emphasis on dowries forced women to enter the work force. Many Jewish parents could no longer afford ample dowries. So young women worked either in order to save up for marriage or because they did not have sufficient resources with which to compete in the prevailing marriage market.[91] Finally, some observers suggested that women no longer found housework fulfilling either in terms of time spent, since they no longer produced anything, or in terms of satisfaction—an ever-so-slight reference to the women's movement. Certainly younger women no longer found fulfillment at home and some, not most, displayed an interest in the women's movement. Whatever the reasons for individual women, it is clear that they constituted a general trend toward the greater participation of women in the work force, not only in Germany but in other Western industrializing societies.

For Jewish women, their class of origin presupposed a proclivity for better job training and a more bourgeois job status than other women. Yet the double burden of being both women and Jews plagued them. Discrimination against them as Jews continued to influence their choice of jobs and careers, and rigid sex-role stereotypes continued to affect their job status, as compared to men. Most found themselves in a ghetto within a ghetto: a lower-paid, lower-status enclave within a "Jewish" sector of the economy.

Attitudes Toward Middle-Class Women and Work

By the late nineteenth century the status aspirations and commercial success of German Jewry allowed most women an entirely domestic role. "The sexual division of labor was at the root of respectability,"[92] and Jewish families clung to it perhaps even more than other Germans. Jewish men, whether wealthy or still aspiring to become solidly bourgeois, considered it beneath their dignity, a sign of financial failure, if their wives or daughters worked for wages.[93] Poorer families, too, and even poor widows, attempted to keep their daughters at home in order to avoid any loss of family prestige. Networks of relatives would step in to aid a family ready to send its daughter to work, in order to preserve the family's reputation. As one contemporary noted: "Daughters from poor and simple families . . . worked in shops as . . . bookkeepers, secretaries, and salesgirls—as long as richer relatives did not offer them patronage."[94] Also, in an era in which women's work indicated a sure sign of familial need, many may have thought that keeping their daughter at home would enhance her marriage chances. She might be poor, with a token dowry, but she was still "respectable," if untouched by the workaday world. Those women who demanded jobs or careers (and there were always some who did) precipitated family crises.[95]

Comfortable middle-class families of all religions considered public employment unladylike and improper for their daughters. Further, for a bourgeoisie attempting to deny its own concerns with financial matters, it was important that women not talk about, earn, or even know about money. Women, at least, had to remain "pure" so as to cleanse the male image of the money-making capitalist. For Jews, women's naiveté in these matters may have been even more important as they hastened to contradict anti-Semitic stereotypes depicting Jews as capitalists par excellence. "We were not allowed to know the slightest thing about financial matters," recalled one memoirist.[96] Uncontaminated by base materialism, women nevertheless remained important status symbols and were expected to assume consumption patterns which reflected the wealth and enhanced the prestige of their husbands and fathers.

Prestige, tradition, and class standing took precedence, even when daughters demanding useful work reached a compromise with fathers insisting on the preservation of their "name." When the daughters (born in the 1870s in Mainz) of a wealthy banker insisted on helping out in his bank, their father reluctantly agreed. But they had to hide in a back office, since "it would have hurt the reputation of the firm [for them] to be seen there."[97] Another woman recalled how desperately she wanted to work but how her father, a cigar factory owner, would not let her. "My parents had a good name, a certain standing in the community, and they were very keen to keep it." Finally her father agreed that she could work for a friend of his, a hatmaker, but she could not accept a salary or work on the Sabbath. He made her quit when she mentioned that she had been sent on an errand to the post office—something he, not she, found degrading. Thereafter he allowed her to work in her brother-in-law's fur shop for no pay.[98] In 1905 two daughters of a well-to-do businessman from Nuremberg received their teaching certificates. The father was strongly opposed, but the mother convinced him it would be their "nest egg" in case they could not get married. However, the girls had to promise that they would never take a paid position as long as they lived with their parents. They never did practice their profession.[99] Whenever parents gave in to their daughter's wishes, they enforced career choices perceived as appropriate to their status. A wealthy widow finally allowed her daughter to become a teacher, but the young woman would have preferred nursing, which was unacceptable to middle-class parents in the 1870s and 1880s.[100] In only a few families did "pioneers of a modern idea . . . succeed in convincing their wealthy parents that they could take jobs as secretaries."[101]

Since a *paid* career, not a career per se, was the ultimate bugaboo,[102] many families accepted voluntary social work as an answer. Marie Munk's father, who presided over the superior court of Berlin, made it clear "that I should not prepare for a job in which I would get a salary. . . . It had to be 'genteel' work, suitable for the daughter of a judge." This was not simply a social dictate, but had legal force:

wives and daughters needed the consent of the male head of household to hold a job.[103] This young woman joined the Girls' and Women's Groups for Social Service Work led by Alice Salomon (see chapter 7). Founded in 1893, the Groups thrived in an era when young women of the upper bourgeoisie sought meaningful, systematic work on a professional level but had to compromise with their parents, who still hesitated to let them earn a living.

Despite the taboo against paid positions, other parents agreed to stopgap paid employment for restless daughters. That is, parents accepted a position that all saw as temporary, one that would not interfere with a young woman's primary responsibility to prepare for marriage, at which point her concentration would shift to the household and family, where it belonged. Voluntary social work and stop-gap paid employment shared a common assumption: both presumed women's work would occupy their time only until they married.

Careers, as opposed to temporary jobs or volunteer work, implied serious and dedicated commitment. As such, they presented a more serious—but often unconscious—threat to prevailing bourgeois norms than a paycheck. Bourgeois marriage depended on both parties' putting the husband's career first. His career created the framework for the marriage, its economic and social basis, even its physical location.[104] A potential two-career household implied serious conflicts or compromises. On the one hand, it raised basic questions about whose career would take precedence. It was far safer to prepare a daughter for housekeeping and far more risky—to the girl, her future marriage, and bourgeois gender hierarchy[105]—to further her professional aspirations. On the other hand, parents may have presumed their daughter would simply compromise for her marriage and drop her hard-earned career at the sound of wedding bells. Consequently, why support such an expensive endeavor? When compromises like unpaid work or volunteer social work appeared impossible, young women either submitted to their parents' wishes or, in a few cases, defied them. Nora Rosenthal, a piano teacher, fought with her father, a wealthy manufacturer, who did not want her to accept pay: "it was not done." But, with her teachers on her side, she prevailed.[106] Toni Sender, later a leader of the SPD women's movement, described her ordeal: her parents, and then a whole string of relatives, tried to dissuade her: "I would disgrace the whole family, because I worked to support myself." She described her new friends as young people "from the middle class, who wished to work not for economic necessity, but to become useful members of society."[107] Unfortunately for Sender and others, their parents' lack of interest or adamant hostility toward their careers had made the difficult job of preparing for a career nearly impossible. Marie Munk described her efforts at several careers in teaching and social work as "gropings" en route to her final destination as a judge.[108] As late as 1918 a sixteen-year-old girl, the only one in her class who went on to a higher education, including a doctorate of economics, could write: "Career, what is a career? For us there are no careers. For us, because we feel no 'calling,' [*da wir uns auch wirklich zu nichts berufen fühlen*], the best we can hope for is a specialty that we seize, and in which we do our best, so maybe—no, hopefully—we can find some fulfillment."[109]

In this context, Jewish female professionals present an interesting contradiction. As just noted, most bourgeois Jewish parents reacted negatively to their daughters' unusual decision to earn their own living when they did not have to do so. In fact, battles between daughters who wanted to work and parents who refused to let them do so may have been particularly intense in Jewish families. A certain amount of wealth had provided extra schooling for daughters and had made their housework superfluous, hence their interest in further education and careers. Determined to maintain a newly achieved bourgeois respectability at all costs, their parents opposed them vigorously. Notwithstanding these struggles, many of these daughters ultimately prevailed against their parents' original disinclination. Jewish women were highly visible in the professions and, in general, their fathers paid the bills.[110] Class background goes a long way toward explaining who had the time and money to prepare for elaborate careers. Still, Jewish parents also acquiesced out of respect for education as well as a serious regard for their daughters' desires.[111] Anna Ettlinger remembered her parents' first reaction to her ambition to become a teacher. Her mother cried. Her father replied, "I will not oppose your aspirations, but you are swimming against the current, and that is not easy."[112]

But these were the exceptions. Most German men of the middle class placed women beyond the competitive crush of the outside world to preserve for themselves an island of serenity. One woman echoed the prevailing mentality in her observations about life in Posen in the late 1870s:

> In my youth, no one thought of giving a girl a career as her purpose in life [*Lebensinhalt*]. Aside from artistic endeavors most women's careers were considered . . . inferior, not appropriate to our class. . . . It would have been easy for my father to give me an excellent commercial education, but he would have totally rejected the thought of educating me. His daughter belonged at home, she was to look attractive and to cheer him and others by her joyful nature.[113]

This attitude and the economic privilege to maintain it obtained for most Jews and deeply affected the majority of Jewish women. Thus gender discrimination (as well as class pretensions) made it unlikely that most Jewish women would avail themselves of the public world of work that was increasingly opening to them. Yet a significant minority of women not only worked outside the home, but did so in professional positions. They provide us with a view into the work lives of educated bourgeois women.

Professional Career Women

The surge in employment among middle-class daughters and single women resulted, in part, from shifts in economic and demographic conditions. As the century progressed, advances in the food and consumer industries began to limit homemaking tasks. Also, it was easier to care for smaller families and the limited interiors of city residences. So the wife, a domestic, and perhaps one daughter would suffice to run the household. Other daughters and maiden aunts became superfluous. Yet these women could not count on marriage for their sustenance. The much vaunted *Frauenüberschuss*—oversupply of women—meant that not every woman could marry. In fact, the situation was worse for Jewish women: a larger proportion of them either remained single or married later than other German women.[114] Further, the rising standard and cost of living as well as a dowry inflation meant that some daughters, despite parental dismay, had to contribute to the family income. New types of jobs were needed as the old class-appropriate standbys of governess, household helper (*Stütze der Hausfrau*), companion, or "disgraceful," hidden homework (*verschämte Heimarbeit*) no longer sufficed. Notwithstanding their increasing need, women seeking new careers faced hostility and recalcitrance from governments, educational institutions, and potential male colleagues.

It took a mass movement to open up professions to women in Germany. By the 1860s national as well as local women's organizations urged the German government and local communal authorities to improve girls' education. Women demanded a say on school and communal boards and participated in social welfare projects. The General German Women's Association (Allgemeiner Deutscher Frauenverein), founded in 1865, focused on the economic independence of women. Jewish women figured prominently in its efforts. Henriette Goldschmidt, one of its three cofounders and the wife of a rabbi, also established a women's institute of higher education (Hochschule für Frauen, 1911) and founded training centers for teachers. The Lette Society for the Furthering of the Employment of the Female Sex (Verein zur Förderung der Erwerbsfähigkeit des Weiblichen Geschlechts), established in 1866, was a second organization favoring careers for bourgeois women. Its institutes taught new occupations, and its employment bureaus placed women in positions as kindergarten teachers, governesses, bookkeepers, and other appropriately middle-class careers. Its founder, Adolf Lette, saw such jobs as extensions of women's motherly or housewifely functions—he insisted, "What we do *not* want, and never, even in the most distant centuries, wish nor aim for, is emancipation and equal rights for women"—yet his closest associate and the first woman on the board of directors, Jenny Hirsch, supported women's suffrage in principle.[115] Before associating with Lette, Hirsch had received permission to found her own elementary school, "even though she was Jewish," from the provincial authorities of Anhalt. A career in journalism, novel writing, and women's movement politics (which included translating John Stuart Mill's *On the Subjection of Women*) complemented her years in the Lette Society.[116]

The kindergarten movement was a third major force in demanding and furthering careers for women. Feminists—with Jewish women noticeable among them—played a role in popularizing Friedrich Fröbel's radical approach to child development. He believed that women's maternal inclinations made them ideally suited to teaching. Moreover, he insisted that boys *and* girls receive serious instruction. Further, in a society in which Church and State were indivisible, his theory was a profoundly secular one, hence even more attractive to Jewish women. Lina Morgenstern, who as the daughter of a wealthy Jewish family had become involved in social work, served as president of the kindergarten association in Germany and established kindergartens in Berlin and an institute for kindergarten teachers (see chapter 7). In Leipzig, Henriette Goldschmidt organized kindergartens and the Society for Familial and Popular Education to further Fröbel's teachings. Kindergartens would be a boon to female employment and education.

The prominence of Jewish women in these movements, observed by Jews and other Germans as well as by anti-Semites, can be explained, in part, by their attitudes toward education.[117] Jewish women—very much like Jewish men—linked education with emancipation. This had been the experience of Jews in Germany: Germans had demanded the education and assimilation of Jews before they had granted them full emancipation. Jewish women assumed that, once again, they would also have to prove their worth, only now as women. German women, too, stressed their duty to society rather than their "rights." It is no wonder, then, that Jewish women proved doubly eager to contribute to the German state and culture, demonstrating their usefulness, rather than "selfishly" demanding equality. Furthermore, like Jewish men, they felt at ease in a tradition which valued education. Thus they persevered in insisting on education and careers as a path toward women's and Jewish emancipation.

In turning to the more popular or visible middle-class professions selected by Jewish women—medicine, teaching, and law—we can examine how gender and ethnic factors influenced their choices and their relative successes or failures. Female physicians achieved the most prestige and the highest visibility. Germany was the last major European country to admit women to the medical profession.[118] In 1899, after a decade of uninterrupted feminist agitation, the government agreed to allow qualified women to take the medical certification exams. Most of these women had studied abroad, since German universities still refused to admit them. In 1907 only 195 female doctors (compared to 29,763 male doctors) practiced in all of Germany.[119] By 1915 their number had risen to 233 (compared to 33,000 men.)[120] Their minuscule showing in no way affected the extraordinary hostility showered upon them by their male colleagues.[121]

As we have seen from the university statistics, a relatively high percentage of Jewish women students—over one-third—studied medicine.[122] Consequently, a similarly high percentage of women in medicine were Jewish. In 1908/09, for example, 34 percent of all women enrolled in the medical faculties in Prussian universities were Jewish,[123] and by 1911/12 that had risen to 39 percent.[124] These figures mounted steadily before the war and nearly doubled during it, with the proportion of Jewish women remaining about the same.[125]

Jewish graduates were notable among recipients of the medical degree (see chapter 5).[126] Although exact graduation figures by religion are not available, we do know that 80 percent of women students (compared to 72 percent of male students) finished their requirements in the regulation five years.[127] It is likely that Jewish women finished, in proportion to their percentage in the student body, since few had financial difficulties. Thus we can conclude that a significant number of female doctors practicing toward the end of the Imperial era were Jewish: I would estimate about one-third.[128] In the same period Jewish men never exceeded 6 percent of all male doctors, although, like most Jews, they congregated in large cities where their proportion of the medical population was therefore significantly higher.[129] It has been estimated that two-thirds of women doctors lived in large cities,[130] hence Jewish women would have been greatly overrepresented among women doctors and highly visible in the cities.

Women doctors tended to work in general practices.[131] By 1915 about 10 percent had specialized, and these preferred pediatrics and gynecology.[132] The latter had provided one of the more successful excuses for women's entry into the profession: that feminine modesty required female physicians to treat women.[133] Further, fewer women than men continued for the doctorate beyond the medical degree (a two-step process in Germany). Women were rarely offered prestigious research posts conducive to further publications and, until 1919, universities also barred them from the *Habilitation*, the postdoctoral stage qualifying them for an academic career. Many had family responsibilities which precluded further study. While men went into profitable private practices, women doctors more often sought employment in clinics, hospitals, municipalities, and public health insurance systems. It was easier financially to work for these institutions than to lay out the capital to set up one's own practice. Moreover, one did not have to confront antifemale prejudices which could have threatened the livelihood of an individual practitioner. Also, such work involved limited hours, an important issue for married women. In 1912, 37 percent of women doctors were widowed or married, and over half of these were or had been married to other doctors.[134] Women who refused to make house calls at all hours or who wanted to preserve a set segment of time for themselves chose such employment. Further, with less preparation and possibly less self-confidence, some women preferred working with other colleagues. Finally, many enjoyed working in a collective enterprise for its sociability and its collaboration between social workers and medical practitioners. Employed by Berlin's Public Health Insurance (Krankenkasse), Charlotte Wolff summarized her experiences as a welfare doctor:

> I clearly needed a medical supervisor at my elbow whom I could consult when my own knowledge failed me. . . . The medical side was only half the job. We were concerned with the women's social condition, and those who were in need of help were referred to the Welfare Officer who worked next door. . . . The two of us collaborated closely. . . . I had the good fortune to have well-trained and intelligent social workers attached to me. . . . Our six-hour day suited me well, and after I had finished my work, I could start a different life. My responsibilities had been shared and discharged without fear. . . . I was freed from anxiety, the curse of many physicians who have to stand on their own feet. The status of employee became my ideal.[135]

The memoirs of Jewish doctors point to the solitary nature of a profession in which few women and an abundance of male enmity prevailed; to the pioneering spirit that they all felt when embarking on their university and medical careers; to a sense of public duty and social consciousness that they did not witness in their more elite university professors; and, for those who combined work and family, to the conflicting loyalties that their choice incurred.

Käte Frankenthal had just finished her doctoral thesis and was working in a hospital when World War I broke out. She noticed that the number of female doctors was "unusually large" in the Kiel hospital in which she practiced.[136] Many of the male doctors had joined the army, leaving numerous vacancies for recently graduated women. The war opened opportunities that otherwise would have eluded women for decades.[137] Frankenthal was no exception. She accepted a village post vacated by a man for twice the salary she earned at the hospital. There she experienced the life of a rural doctor (*Landarzt*). Barely out of medical school, she was thrown on her own devices. She could consult no specialists and had to handle cases of enormous variety. The only other professionals in the village were a pharmacist, a teacher, and a judge, all elderly men. Out of sheer boredom, she began to visit the local pub where they and the previous doctor had their *Stammtisch*. Her desire to share a pitcher of beer and some companionship provoked a sensation in the small town: "at first they did not seem averse to throwing me out. But this would have been too strenuous for rural *Gemütlichkeit*, and so they tolerated me."[138] She had few female contacts, aside from her patients and a childhood acquaintance who regaled her with cooking recipes, advice she normally shunned.

Both her desire to leave this rural environment and her awareness of the dire need for military doctors convinced her to apply for a position as an army doctor. Given the extraordinary needs of the times—the army used medical students to cover the urgent demand for doctors—she was quite shocked to learn that the German military would hire her only as a nurse, a profession for which she felt entirely unsuited. The army rejected her services, because military doctors held the rank of officers and "a German man could not serve under a woman since this would hurt discipline."[139] The Austrian army did not share these prejudices and accepted her immediately: "after all, I was not trying to direct battles. The discipline of the Austrian army did not seem to suffer."[140] Even though the Austrian army was eager to hire her, she never saw another female doctor the entire time she remained with it. Moreover, her male colleagues often confused her profession with her gender. As soon as she arrived at her first army post, she was asked to take charge of the kitchen. She announced, to general disappointment, that she knew nothing about cooking. She was able to earn the gratefulness of the other officers only when she treated the wounds of a good cook. She shared quarters with the other officers, the only woman in the barracks.[141] Professionally, these years offered her more intense experiences and greater expertise than she would have acquired in normal times. She dealt not only with the wounded, but with the lice and diseases rampant among men in the trenches. Further, she had to decide which men feigned illness and which could return to duty, even while being a firm opponent of the war in the first place. She also toured the front lines as an expert in disease control: "in the war one advanced quickly to 'expert.' Under normal circumstances I would still have been a very young assistant in a hospital."[142] As a result, she developed a sense of competence and efficiency.

Shortly before the end of the war, Frankenthal accepted a position in a Berlin hospital. The economic situation in Germany had deteriorated to such an extent that she had to establish a private practice in order to survive on her hospital pay. Without funds to set up a practice, she rented two rooms in an apartment and bought the most minimal amount of instruments. As the war drew to a close, Frankenthal witnessed actual starvation conditions in Germany. She dreaded her office hours, because there was so little she could do for her patients.[143] After the war she continued her hospital work and maintained a private practice, until she decided to work for the city.

Like others of her generation, Frankenthal made a conscious decision not to marry. In a survey taken in 1912, over 60 percent of the female doctors who responded had not married.[144] During the first flurry of postwar marriages, she reflected upon her future: she was neither lonely nor unfulfilled. Her practice, her friends, and her political involvement in the SPD kept her busy and happy. She was also satisfied with her sex life. What she really needed was a housekeeper. A husband "would not have relieved me of the small difficulties of daily life, he would have increased them."[145] Further, she feared that children would have totally restructured her life. "Many career women of my generation held similar attitudes on these questions."[146]

Rahel Straus, on the other hand, decided to marry and have children, but never to give up her career. After working in clinics and completing her doctorate, Straus set up her practice in Munich in 1908. Her choice of becoming a general practitioner was typical of the women of her generation. She was one of three women doctors in the city at that time. Besides seeing her patients in her office and on house calls, she worked for the public health insurance. She was acutely conscious that gender roles rigidly prescribed her professional and personal life. Professionally, for example, she was quick to notice that male and female doctors treated obstetrical patients very differently. Recalling Aristotle's dictum that an audience watching a tragedy had to feel fear and sympathy—fear for themselves and sympathy for the heroes—she remarked of the male doctors: "In women's clinics, there is only the second, only sympathy, never fear for oneself, which actually evokes and deepens sympathy."[147] Midwives, on the other hand, impressed her. She learned from their practical knowhow, and in giving them refresher courses also provided them with their first experience of a woman doctor.

Personally, she saw her career limited by family considerations. She always felt a nagging regret that she did not go on to specialize beyond her doctoral thesis. "There were thousands of things I would have loved to learn."[148] Straus worked throughout all her pregnancies and her child-rearing years. In 1909 she had her first child. With full-time household help and child care, she maintained a busy medical career. Still, children changed her life entirely: her time, the way she divided her schedule, "her joys and her worries." She attended to many of the children's basic needs herself. Her first baby's playpen stood next to her desk.[149] She scheduled several hours during the day to be with the child. "It took endless amounts of energy, a great deal of love for my profession, to attempt to manage everything."[150] She recalled being invited to a lecture for young women who hoped to become doctors. The lecturer, the future Frau von Ludendorff, suggested that it would be easy to combine motherhood and professional responsibilities. Straus argued that it was important to tell young women the far more complex truth: this was a choice which demanded energy, will power, and good health. Moreover, she recognized the importance of a "financial base" from which to work; one needed paid help for the house, kitchen, and children. Also, she underscored the importance of the husband's attitudes: he had to view his wife as an equal companion who had a right to her own life and her own development, and who was not there for his convenience. This kind of mate was rare, to be sure. Even her own husband, an attorney supportive of her career, had once told her, "No one can marry a woman doctor."[151] He seemed to adjust well, but of course neither mate questioned the fact that she absorbed the entire burden of running the household. It was she who filled in when the cook was sick, and she who took primary responsibility for the children's physical and emotional well-being. Despite her regret at not having become a specialist, Straus took great pride in surmounting her double duties at home and at work. She emphatically denied that she might have been happier devoting herself entirely to her career. "I would never have renounced my career or my happiness as a wife and mother. But I was always conscious that it was a difficult . . . art to combine both."[152]

Like many of the first generation of women doctors, Straus was called upon by women's organizations (including both German and German-Jewish feminists), by student groups, by Jewish organizations, and even by state health organizations who suddenly found it convenient to have a woman discuss certain topics. For example, the Munich child welfare bureau sent her to speak to peasant women about the importance of breast-feeding. In northern Bavaria Straus, an urban woman who had nursed all of her own babies, found herself in the strange position of encouraging rural women, usually the last to take up new trends, to go back to breast-feeding.[153]

Like so many of her female colleagues, Straus had embarked upon her career in a society which encouraged women to marry a doctor rather than become one.[154] Many of her friends expressed shock and repulsion. They labeled female doctors "unwomanly, even immoral."[155] She had to come to her decision without any encouragement and with the explicit discouragement of prominent professors. Nevertheless, in looking back, she "never regretted [her] decision for a minute."[156] Her statement attests to the spirit of the early women doctors and is representative of the general satisfaction they expressed.

The legal profession was far more frustrating for women. In a society in which most lawyers were civil servants and most upper-level civil servants were lawyers, it seemed impossible to crack both barriers at once. "The probability of women gaining access to legal careers was so small that male physicians, when they feared that the government was about to allow women into their ranks, tried to prevent this by insisting that all professions be treated the same, knowing full well that law would remain closed."[157] A few German women studied law in Zurich before the Prussian universities admitted women in 1908. Thereafter only a handful enrolled in law courses, since states still barred women from becoming lawyers or judges.

Nevertheless, by 1917 there were 45 female doctors of jurisprudence—a significant step beyond the law degree—and an organization of female lawyers, the German Women Lawyers' Society (Deutscher Juristinnenverein), with 28 members. Moreover, 119 female law students had risked matriculating for the degree.[158] Some had entered in the hope and belief that the legal profession would soon open to women as had the medical and teaching professions. Aware of male hostility, they knew the prejudices that stood in their way: that women were not objective enough to judge; that a woman could not represent the authority of the state as well as a man; that women would not trust other women with their cases.[159] Yet there was cause for some optimism. Each state could define its own requirements as to who could take the state examination. In 1912 Bavaria permitted women to take the first exam, the equivalent of the Prussian *Referendar*, or junior barrister exam. However, they could not call themselves *Referendarin* or take the second state exam, the one that allowed them to become a probationary lawyer (*Assessor*). The women's movement, including several Jewish women lawyers (Margarete Berent and Margarete Meseritz), petitioned the various states to allow women to take all necessary exams. By 1918 they had not met with success. Thus even women who had gone beyond the original law degree to earn their doctorates in law could not become fully acknowledged lawyers until the Weimar Republic.

Jewish women were heavily represented among lawyers as they were among doctors. Even though their actual numbers amounted to very little, over a quarter (28%) of the female law students in Prussia in 1911/12 were Jewish.[160] Many Jewish women belonged to the German Women Lawyers' Society: at least five of the seven members of its board of directors, including its chairperson, were Jewish or of Jewish origin.[161] Why law, when the profession still practically barred women? Here too, Jews showed a disproportionate proclivity toward the "free" professions. In part, this resulted from a lack of choices. Not everyone showed a talent for medicine, and the situation for Jewish women teachers, as will be seen, was even worse. Further, law had shown itself hospitable to Jewish men. In 1907, about 15 percent of Germany's lawyers were Jewish. Having watched their fathers and brothers prosper in this field, Jewish women might expect that, with some energy and flexibility, they too could experience an interesting professional life.[162]

The career of Margarete Berent, treasurer of the German Women Lawyers' Society, illustrates the varied career of many women lawyers of her era. The daughter of a Berlin businessman, she passed the *Staatsexamen* in 1906 and taught for four years at middle- and upper-grade girls' schools. While teaching, she also prepared for the university entrance exam. She studied law for three years, receiving the doctorate magna cum laude in 1913. Her dissertation discussed an issue of concern to the women's movement as well as to the legal profession: "The Community of Earnings of Husband and Wife." It was later published in a prestigious legal history series edited by Otto von Gierke, one of Germany's leading legal scholars.[163] (Von Gierke is the same professor who responded to an inquiry on female students in 1897 by agreeing he might admit a few women to his lectures to help them in "decking themselves out in the degree of doctor of law." He saw no possible career for women in law.)

Berent would continue to write articles for legal and professional journals throughout her career. She passed the first law exam in Bavaria, but this is where her path began to diverge from that of her male peers. Being a woman, she could not take the second exam and was therefore barred from the required official apprenticeship. Instead, she worked for various lawyers in Berlin, substituting for some who were ill, for others who were drafted. At the same time (from early 1914 until September 1915) she worked at the Legal Aid Office for Women (Rechtsschutzstelle für Frauen) and, for a short period, led the Adoption Office of the Youth Welfare Bureau (Deutsche Zentral für Jugendfürsorge). From 1914 until 1917 she also taught commercial law at the Victoria School for Girls, and courses in family and youth law at Alice Salomon's School of Social Work (Soziale Frauenschule), two renowned educational institutions for women. Somehow she also found time to volunteer for the war effort. From 1915 to 1917 she worked as an administrator and a "legal helper" (*juristische Hilfsarbeiterin*) for the electrical industry (AEG, Berlin). This type of position was typical for women lawyers by 1917. Despite male opposition to women in the profession, during the war women participated in the same manner as other *Referendare* in private, communal, and legal organizations, even in courts, though officially they had lower professional status and different titles.[164]

While her early career path was characteristic of that of other women lawyers, Berent may have been atypical in her outspoken feminism and activism. She was a cofounder of the German Academic Women's Society (Deutscher Akademikerinnenbund) (1926); president of the German Women Lawyers' Society; president of the International Organization of Women Lawyers (Internationale Organisation Weiblicher Anwälte); and a member of the advisory council (*Beirat*) of the Federation of German Women's Associations (Bund Deutscher Frauenvereine), and of the board of directors of the League of Jewish Women (Jüdischer Frauenbund). Further, she had a keen appreciation of feminist issues as they pertained to the law. She argued that women lawyers had two special concerns beyond their general legal duties. The first was to counsel those women who might prefer talking to another woman. The second was

> to influence laws, which have until now been made by men, and . . . have considered the needs and viewpoints of men. . . . The needs of women should also be expressed in the shaping of laws. This means not only regulations concerning the position of wives and mothers, but also considerations regarding the particular status of women in society. . . . (A socially conscious law [*ein soziales Recht*] will not only take the views and living conditions of men in varying social circles into consideration, but also the legal views and sentiments [*Rechtsanschauungen und Rechtsempfinden*] of women. . . .) It will be the special responsibility of women lawyers to recognize these needs and to try to give them expression in the interpretation and formulation of the law.[165]

Like many women of her generation, Berent had begun with a teaching background, worked as a legal "adviser" or "helper" rather than as a credentialed lawyer, and taught law at women's schools and schools of social work. She was ultimately admitted to the Prussian Bar during the Weimar Republic, one of the first four women to gain entry. And at the age of sixty-two she was admitted to the New York State Bar—no longer representative of German women lawyers, but of the relatively few Jewish lawyers who managed to start over again after their forced emigration.[166] Marie Munk, the first woman law student at the University of Bonn and later the first woman judge in Prussia, followed a similar career path. Keeping her expectations to a minimum and her hopes high, she wrote:

> Although the full practice of law was still closed to women, I reasoned that with a Doctorate of Law or Jurisprudence I could use my knowledge in Legal Aid Clinics, which were private organizations and had many female clients, . . . also in the legal services which some large newspapers supplied to their subscribers. . . .I would also be able to do some teaching, particularly in Schools of Social Work, lecturing, and writing. Actually, I did all of these later on.[167]

During the war Munk directed a project for the Department of Public Welfare in Munich. Only belatedly was she transferred to the city's Legal Department.[168] Eventually she was the first woman to sit on the Berlin Superior Court. Her career, too, was cut short in Germany. Forced to emigrate, she supported herself by teaching at various colleges in the United States.

Like Berent and Munk, most women juggled a combination of careers in their attempt to remain in the legal profession. A survey of lawyers in 1917 found that of 33 respondents with the doctorate, 27 had worked or were still working in social work. At least 14 found employment with legal aid clinics and 12 with private lawyers. Most had also held positions at one time or another in journalism (2), industry and business (4), communal administration (9), or the army or war administrations (8), and one was a full-time legal scholar. Women lawyers tended to change jobs frequently, as a result, in part, of the war and the availability of positions vacated by men. Also, banned from formal apprenticeships, women had to patch their legal experiences together and create their own apprenticeships: they inclined toward leaving a position once they achieved competence in that particular area of the law. Moreover, they often held more than one job at a time. Most did some writing, editing, or teaching to supplement their regular—and obviously inadequate—salaries. Some did all of these. Women never achieved the automatic prestige that the Doctor of Jurisprudence bestowed upon men.[169]

Still, these are the "success" stories. Other women never actually practiced law. Margarete Meseritz, for example, became a journalist and continued to give lectures about and petition for women's entry into the legal profession during the Imperial era.[170] She maintained her writing career in emigration. Less fortunate were those legal graduates whose advertisements in the "jobs wanted" pages sought office work, offering their foreign language skills as extra inducements.[171]

Their numbers being so small, and scattered as they were among many jobs and careers, it is difficult to trace the personal life choices of women lawyers. Marie Munk, however, may serve as an example not only of a legal professional, but of those early career women in general—probably a majority—who decided not to marry. Although she was courted, she

> felt instinctively . . . that my quest for knowledge and for leading a useful life would hardly be fulfilled by being a wife, a housekeeper, and even a mother. I needed other outlets. I had a passion for freedom and could not have taken any restrictions in my friendships with men and women. . . . An unhappy or dissatisfied wife and mother is not a good companion and does not fill her role. On the other hand, I also knew that I was not strong enough—few women are—to combine the responsibilities of wife and mother with those of an exacting job. I would have had a feeling of guilt, had I neglected one or the other. . . . Actually, many of my friends . . . who were very attractive and did not lack opportunities, remained unmarried or married late.[172]

Teaching was one of the few careers that parents grudgingly accepted as appropriate to their social status, when daughters insisted on working or had to earn their keep. As early as 1837, Prussia instituted the first teaching exam for women, allowing women to teach in the lower grades, in the *Volksschule*. Secular women flocked there in particular during the anti-Catholic repression of the 1870s, when the state dismissed nuns from the lower schools.[173] The more prestigious profession of teacher in a middle or high school (girls' *höhere Mädchenschule*, also called *höhere Töchterschule*, and boys' *Gymnasium*, respectively) remained closed to them, the result of an alliance between male teachers and the state. Not only, as we have seen, did Prussia manage to keep women out of the universities until 1908, thereby withholding the necessary education and certification exams required to qualify for teaching in the highest grades, but most states also hesitated to support public middle schools for girls. Between 1800 and 1870, governments set up only 115 such middle schools (*Mädchenschulen*) in all of Germany. This limited not only educational opportunities for girls and possible employment for women, but also the potential population of female teachers. Women had to graduate from these middle schools in order to teach in the lower schools. By 1878 about 1,500 women taught in the Prussian public lower schools, and 6,000 in the public and private middle schools for girls.[174] Ten years later, only 10 percent of Prussian teachers (elementary as well as secondary) were female, compared to 54 percent in France and 69 percent in England.[175]

Women had to struggle to become educators. An organized women's movement lobbied and petitioned legislators and administrators, as did individual female applicants. Not surprisingly, teachers played a key role in the women's movement.[176] In the late 1860s women, many Jews among them, began to set up teacher-training seminars to take girls through the last stages before entry to universities. The most famous of these was the Victoria School for Girls in Berlin, founded in 1868 by an Englishwoman and supported by the Crown Princess. Many leaders of the feminist movement studied or taught there. Women activists approached education holistically: their overall design included teacher-training seminars, kindergartens, extension courses, and eventually university admission.[177]

The Prussian government reacted slowly and grudgingly to women's initiatives and demands. By 1874, as a result of the myriad schools and courses set up to train female teachers, and bending, no doubt, to women's protests and to the increasingly apparent need for middle-class women's employment,[178] it decreed that women's exams should be the equivalent of men's. This granted women the same legitimacy as men in the higher, but not the highest, grades. For the latter, teachers needed university training. Then, as *Oberlehrerinnen* (upper-level teachers), they could teach at the preuniversity level. In 1894 Prussia created an *Oberlehrerinnen* exam which certified women who had five years of teaching experience and three years of university study (Prussian universities were still officially closed to women until 1908), to teach the highest grades in the public middle schools for girls (*höhere Mädchenschulen*). They were still barred from the *Gymnasium*, the elite boys' (university preparatory) high school.

Overall delaying tactics persisted before the turn of the century. The Prussian ministry, for example, required that female teachers of academic subjects (*wissenschaftlich geprüfte Lehrerinnen*) be certified in needlework and gym after they passed their first exam.[179] Also, male colleagues continued to accuse women of physical, mental, and emotional inferiority. Nor was popular opinion much more favorable. There was a general disdain for women in positions of authority. Still, by 1900, after two decades of considerable unemployment among female teachers, their numbers had grown rapidly to about 15 percent (or 22,000 out of 144,000) of *Volksschule* teachers.[180] In 1908 the Prussian government at last permitted women to enter the university en route to their career as *Oberlehrerinnen*. Doggedly reaffirming male privilege, it stipulated that at least one-third of the personnel in all higher schools for girls had to be male.[181] Female teachers found themselves in difficult straits. Good positions were hard to get. Advancement for women was much slower than for men. There were almost no opportunities at the top levels in public education, and salaries remained between one-third and one-half of men's through the 1920s.[182]

Numerically, more Jewish women prepared for the teaching profession than for either medicine or law. Yet here they experienced a double disadvantage: not only did they suffer from antifemale biases and strictures, but they also experienced anti-Semitism far more profoundly than in the other fields. Unlike the free professions, where Jewish women encountered male hostility but could set up their own practices or find individual employers willing to hire them, entire anti-Semitic school systems, not to mention principals and teaching staffs, all but closed the profession to them. As one Jewish newspaper said of the Jewish woman teacher, "with few exceptions, private schools, communal and higher public schools are off limits to her."[183] In 1886 only 94 Jewish women taught in Prussia and not all of them held full-time positions: 53 taught in the public *Volksschulen* and 30 in private middle schools for girls. Five years later, this figure had risen by only ten. By 1901, although over 1,000 Jewish women sought positions,[184] only 115 had found regular teaching posts.

Surprisingly, over a quarter of these women taught at the highest level permitted to women at the time, the *höhere Mädchenschule*. Their relative advantage on this level (compared to 18% of other women and 1% of Jewish men) resulted from their overwhelming disadvantage at lower levels: non-Jewish women or Jewish men had far greater opportunities to teach at lower grade levels where the grade-school teacher also served as the religious instructor. Since lower schools were primarily denominational, that is, Catholic or Protestant, and the school systems forbade Jews from teaching Christianity, Jewish women found few available posts. Non-denominational schools, too, avoided hiring Jews. In 1913 the Jewish teachers' organization claimed only 112 out of 1,568 such schools (known as *Simultanschulen*) in Prussia had Jews on their faculties.[185] Finally, even Jewish schools balked at hiring women. These schools, facing declining enrollment, preferred male teachers who could combine the role of grade-school teacher and Jewish religion teacher. In small towns and villages, male teachers also served as professional communal religious leaders, performing pastoral, life-cycle, liturgical, and sometimes cantorial functions.[186] As a result of traditional religious discrimination, Jewish women could not fulfill these duties. They could only serve as substitute teachers, replacing some men during World War I.[187] In those areas of the Empire where discrimination against Jews forced Jewish teachers to teach in exclusively Jewish schools,[188] Jewish women faced an insuperable problem. At best, they could move to bigger cities to avoid the preference for Jewish males in small towns, and aim for middle or higher school employment to avoid religious proscriptions at the *Volksschule* level.[189]

Jews worked in private rather than public schools. Of her experience as a pupil in the public middle school for girls in Kiel (ca. 1900), Käte Frankenthal recalled: "It was inconceivable . . . that a Jewish teacher would have been hired."[190] In 1901 in Prussia, for example, 3% of male and female teachers at private middle schools were Jewish, compared to well under 1% at most public schools.[191] Private middle schools tended to be more hospitable to female teachers. In the mid–1890s, for example, women comprised 75% of the teachers in the private girls' schools, compared to 33% in the public schools at that level.[192] Therefore those Jewish women who found employment at all most likely taught in the private sector: in 1901, 47 out of 59 Jewish women middle-school teachers taught in private institutions.[193]

As teachers, Jews of both sexes faced a concerted effort to ban them from the extensive field of public education. German education, once characterized as "practical Christianity for the masses," emphasized religious and moral instruction as the foundation of elementary school education. The curriculum stressed religion, reading, writing, arithmetic, and discipline.[194] The same narrow goals applied to the selection of teachers. The director of a teacher-training school acknowledged to his class: "The authorities have not chosen you for your deep scholarly attainments. . . . No, but because you . . . have shown yourselves humble and true believing Christians."[195]

Jewish women faced an additional obstacle. Ironically, the subjects that the women's movement had dubbed "women's" topics—religion, German, and history, the *Gesinnungsfächer* (courses which promoted convictions or ways of thinking)—were precisely those that anti-Semites used against Jewish women. Typically, the German women's movement had stressed the need for patriotic education: it demanded women "attuned to the fatherland" (*vaterländisch gesinnte Frauen)*, "genuinely German women," to bring a new spirit to the girls' schools.[196] Arguing that Jews could hardly convey the essence of the German language or the history of the nation or *Volk*, anti-Semites within and outside the Prussian ministry of education (Provinzialschulkollegium) pushed to limit Jewish women to Jewish religion classes.[197] Further, they insisted that small children should not remain under the influence of a Jewish classroom teacher for the (normal) four-year term. School inspectors also worried about whether Jewish teachers should teach handwriting, for fear of influencing the content, and suggested that Jewish children be taught history by Christian teachers. Conservatives lobbied against the further "Judaization of the Christian *Volksschule*," pushing and supporting the Prussian ministry in its anti-Jewish discrimination.[198]

The Prussian government obligingly hindered the hiring of Jewish women. Jewish organizations, aware of behind-the-scenes pressure, reported that one of the reasons directors of middle and higher schools did not hire Jewish women—even when they did not require religion to be taught—was because they feared official reprimands.[199] The state also sought to limit practice teaching positions for Jews to slots in which a Jewish teacher already taught, thus keeping the number of future Jewish women teachers static, and presumably discouraging young women from entering the field.[200] One Jewish newspaper began its article on the situation of such women with the caption: "Jewess-Teacher-Prussia—a Tragedy." It emphasized how impossible it was to accuse the state of illegality, because government officials covered up the real reason for rejecting Jewish women, namely, their religion.[201]

Prussia was not unique in its treatment of Jewish women. In Baden, for example, a city council report revealed that the school superintendent (*Oberschulrat*) of Karlsruhe had informed a female teacher that she could not count on a position in the public schools because she was Jewish. Another woman received an appointment shortly after she was baptized. Jewish organizations observed that the states pushed Jews toward conversion to improve their career chances, encouraging not only apostasy, but unprincipled behavior as well.[202]

Government anti-Semitism influenced the private sector as well. When the government heard of a Jewish woman teaching the highest grade in a private girls' school, the Prussian Minister of Education wrote: "It is noticeable that . . . a large portion of the curriculum is the responsibility of a Jewish teacher. . . . It is absolutely necessary that the arrangements in private teacher-training institutes be the same in all essential aspects as those in public establishments."[203] By 1909 the situation had become so difficult that the Central Verein, the Jewish defense organization, initiated a formal inquiry with the Prussian government, asking if a regulation existed forbidding Jewish women from being hired to teach German or history in state, local, or private schools in Prussia. The government denied such a ruling.[204]

Prussia and Bavaria carefully observed and controlled the number and character of candidates allowed into the teachers' colleges, concerned lest there be either a surplus or a shortage of males. The state also responded to pressure groups, the parties, the churches, the many associations. In the case of female teachers, the state reacted to the pressure of male teachers and their spokesmen; in the case of Jews, to anti-Semitic pressure groups; in the case of Jewish women, to all of these.[205] Effectively locked out of the lower schools, where (Christian) religion had to be taught, they were shunted away from the upper schools by government hostility.

Even when Jewish women trained as teachers attempted to find other employment, anti-Semites stood in their way. In Breslau, for example, four out of five librarians in the local library and reading room—positions which led to civil service status—were Jewish. The editor of the anti-Semitic *Morgen Zeitung* raised the issue of financial waste at a city council meeting. He argued that these positions should be an extracurricular duty of regularly employed teachers, or that there should be "parity" (that is, equal religious representation) in hiring librarians. Jewish papers quickly pointed out that these Jewish librarians had not found teaching jobs in the city's confessional schools because of anti-Semitism; no one had raised the issue of parity in teaching for them.[206]

Other trained teachers eked out an existence by giving lessons or tutoring. Jewish newspapers often ran ads placed by teachers. They offered various courses to other women. In the same columns as ads for cooks and cleaning women, these young "educators" (*Erzieherinnen*) listed the famous professors with whom they had studied and the subjects they could teach.[207] Having passed their teaching exams, they could also offer private lessons. Many Jewish women took this route for granted. Around 1900, for example, Henriette Hirsch opted to become a private tutor, because "Jewish women could not be hired as public school teachers in Prussia."[208]

Teachers could also seek positions as governesses. As late as 1899, over a quarter of women teachers in Germany found employment in this manner.[209] Among Jewish women this may have been closer to half. The job-wanted ads evinced some trepidation: "*Erzieherin* seeks a position with a respectable family. Good treatment is more important than a high salary." Such women preferred posts at girls' schools, but would settle for "an honorable family" if they had to.[210] The position of governess, with its status incongruities, presented many problems. Governesses as well as feminists described the difficulties inherent in such employment.[211] One (non-Jewish) woman reported that she had to teach two children while their mother ordered her around like a servant. Further, she had to tolerate the advances of their father. Although these did not go beyond some kisses, she left the position swearing that she would never again be a governess. Luckily for her, she did not meet with the religious discrimination facing Jewish women and did not have to enter private service again.[212] The plight of the Jewish governess became a topic of short serial stories and dramas in Jewish newspapers. The plot usually involved an unhappy young woman whose family had scrimped in order to send her to teacher-training seminars. Her degree in hand, she faced anti-Semitic school systems, rebuffs from the snobbish mistress of the house, and disrespect from her small charges. Sometimes the young woman rescued herself from her misery by marrying a rich old widower. These stories both described the difficult conditions facing young governesses and prescribed marriages to widowers. And surely some young women must have felt rescued by such unions. Other stories of this genre simply concentrated on the unfairness of anti-Semitism and the disappointment of the female teacher.[213]

Notwithstanding gloomy job prospects and rampant discrimination, Jewish parents continued to support teacher training for daughters who desired or needed careers. In fact, even those parents who objected to any paid employment seem to have made an exception for teaching.[214] Daughters, too, preferred to prepare for a teaching career even with the odds so terribly against them. It was the path of least familial resistance; a way of perhaps attaining respectable status; a chance to procure some amount of higher education; and at the very least, a useful background for an educated mother. Further, Jewish communities and welfare societies provided scholarships for teacher training. The Israelite Society to Further Education in East Prussia (in Königsberg), for example, assisted young women who wanted to be teachers (*Lehrerinnen*) or educators (*Erzieherinnen*)—which in this case meant governesses.[215] By 1911, despite the well-known difficulties that lay ahead, the majority of Prussian Jewish female students took subjects leading to teaching careers.

As more women entered the field—by 1907 there were 1,128 Jewish women teachers—they pressed for acceptance in the school systems.[216] In the early twentieth century they organized interest groups in Breslau and Berlin with the help of the League of Jewish Women.[217] Although their pleas and remonstrations were ignored, they may have gained a sense of collegiality from meeting other women in their situation. They supported local information bureaus for teachers[218] and also met with male colleagues for professional exchanges.[219] Further, the Jewish community began to follow the lead of nonsectarian teacher groups which had founded retirement homes for women teachers as of the mid-1890s.[220] Almost every German state required celibacy of its female teachers, precluding husbands' or childrens' contributions toward their sustenance after retirement.[221] Moreover, as already noted, most Jewish women teachers could not depend on pensions, since discrimination practically barred them from the school systems. Many of these women feared aging without a steady income. In 1899 the first retirement home for Jewish teachers opened in Berlin. Subsidized by Jewish community funds and private donations, it had support groups in sixteen other cities. A Jewish woman, herself a private tutor, had succeeded in pressing communities to plan for the over 1,000 teachers already at work, 90 percent of whom were governesses or private tutors who would have neither state pensions nor savings to secure their old age.[222] A second retirement and convalescence home opened in Frankfurt in 1908.[223] These homes by no means sufficed for the numbers of needy women, but they indicated communal acknowledgment of the plight of women teachers.

The career of Anna Ettlinger (born 1841, died 1934) offers an example of how some teachers molded their own employment opportunities. In 1870 Ettlinger convinced her parents, who wanted her to marry and settle down, that she preferred a career. She left home to study in the newly opened Victoria School for Girls in Berlin. The school offered courses by guest professors and served as a limited substitute for *Gymnasium* and university study. The director, Miss Archer, expected that her courses would stimulate further interest and studies among her students. She was instrumental in encouraging them to continue to educate themselves. Ettlinger majored in literature and passed the teachers' exam in 1872. The school system being a dead end, she gave private lessons in literary history and lived with her family. When her father died and she needed to earn more, she began to give lectures to small groups of women who paid a fee to take her "course." The courses met twice a week and lasted from September until the end of March. After the lectures, some of the students stayed for tea. Beyond these courses, Ettlinger accepted speaking engagements from women's groups throughout the country and even from men's organizations. She recalled her first invitation from the local Karlsruhe chamber of commerce: "The lecture was a success and, so, I forgot the horrible anxiety I had gone through. If it had not gone well, they would not have simply blamed me, but would have placed the burden on woman in general, since I was the first woman who had ever spoken there in public."[224] In fact, right before that lecture her niece had come home astounded by her teacher's declaration that it was not at all respectable for a woman to give a public lecture. That was in 1882.[225]

As a private tutor who supplemented her income with lecture tours, Ettlinger was sensitive to discrimination against women teachers. She realized that she had been asked to substitute for a male teacher at far below his salary only because she was a woman. Also, she recalled not being offered a position in one school, because the director worried lest people think the school was trying to save money by hiring a woman. Still, Ettlinger found satisfaction and success in her varied career. The *Frankfurter Zeitung* reprinted some of her lectures. She enjoyed her travels, assisted her two unmarried sisters who worked as translators, and made time to pursue her interest in literary history. She seems not to have encountered financial stress, sharing the family home with her sisters. Further, she realized how important she had become to her students: "If I had to suffer . . . from the disadvantages . . . of my profession, . . . because I was a woman, I also received acknowledgements that a man might not have. . . . After every public lecture and at the end of every course, people tried to show their extra appreciation by sending flowers, poems, books and a mass of cakes, even though I protested."[226] Satisfaction could be achieved, but most Jewish women teachers never practiced their chosen career.

Teachers at the Jakob Loewenberg School in Hamburg, a private school for girls, around 1896. Both students and teaching staff were predominantly Jewish. *Jakob Loewenberg Collection. Courtesy of the Leo Baeck Institute, New York.*

In Imperial Germany a significant minority of Jewish women worked in income-earning positions. In the early decades of the Reich, wives and daughters did unacknowledged labor in the family shop or business. Toward the turn of the century, single women—daughters who needed or wanted to work outside the home—entered the labor market. They found themselves in the forefront of modern urban careers: shop girls, typists, clerks. At the same time, Jewish women professionals joined the fields of medicine and law in numbers disproportionate to their share in the population and persisted in the teaching field against overwhelming odds. Jewish women in the professions—similar to other Jewish working women—made choices within the limits affecting them as women and Jews. They needed to find careers that were approachable, if not friendly, to women and to Jews.

Appendix Table 1. Jewish Women's Employment in Germany, 1895 and 1907, by number and percent

Career Branch	Status	1895	All Working Jewish Women (%)	1907	All Working Jewish Women (%)	Women among all Working Jews (%)	Increase or Decrease, 1895–1907
A. Agriculture	a. Independents	419		324			− 95
	b. Employees	3		14			+ 11
	c.1. Family helpers c.2–5. Workers	786		1,688 149			+1,051
	Total	1,208	3	2,175	4	57	+ 967
B. Industry	a. Independents	4,796		4,748			− 48
	b. Employees	537		2,702			+2,165 (+503%)
	c.1. Family helpers c.2–5. Workers	5,030		2,193 5,263			+2,426 (+ 48%)
	Total	10,363	26	14,906	28	23	+4,543
C. Trade and commerce	a. Independents	7,836		9,099			+1,263
	b. Employees	683		3,335			+2,652 (+480%)
	c.1. Family helpers c.2–5. Workers	10,604		8,242 7,170			+4,804 (+ 45%)
	Total	19,123	49.5	27,846	52	19	+8,743
D. Daily labor		682	2	993	2	74	+ 311 (+ 45%)
E. Public service and free professions	a. Independents	1,421		2,087			+ 366 (+ 47%)
	b. Employees	45		322			+ 277

	c. Family helpers	287		647			+ 360
	Total	1,753	4	3,056	5	16	+1,303 (+ 74%)
F. Live-in servants		6,298	16	4,771	9	99	−1,527 (− 24%)
	Totals	39,427		53,747			
Totals	a. Independents	14,472		16,258			
	b. Employees	1,268		6,373			
	g. Live-in servants	6,298		4,771			
	c.1. Family helpers	16,707		12,123			
	c.2–5. Workers			13,229			

SOURCE: *ZDSJ*, July/August 1911, pp. 97–112.

Category

A. Agricultural independents down 95, workers up 1,051. 77% are family helpers.

B. Industrial independents down, employees up fivefold; workers up 48%. 24% are family helpers. Probably three times more "b" jobs (and fewer "c" jobs) than appears to be the case, since Jewish women worked in offices and sales. 65% in top three categories.

C. Commercial employees increased fivefold. Workers increased 45%. 30% are family helpers. Most "c" jobs are really "b" jobs here. Women increased their representation in commercial fields from 48% (1895) of all working Jewish women to 52%; men decreased from 69% of all working Jewish men to 64%.

D. Women make up 74% of all Jewish day laborers in 1907.

E. Women in the professions increased from 12% of all working Jews to 16%.

F. Jewish women servants decreased from 16% of all Jewish working women to 9%.

Totals: about a 36% increase in number of Jewish working women (+14,320).

By 1907, almost one-third of Jewish working women were "independent," compared to 50% of all Jews and 22% of the German population.
12% of Jewish working women were "employees."
47% of Jewish working women were in the "c" category, including family members, but many of these jobs were probably "b" types.
40% of Jewish working women were in "New Woman" professions: categories B, b and C, b and c, i.e., sales and office work (21,449).
23% of Jewish working women were family helpers.

Appendix Table 2. Jewish and Non-Jewish Women's Employment in 1907 in Cities with over 100,000 Population, by number and percent

	Jewish		Non-Jewish	
	(No.)	(%)	(No.)	(%)
Agriculture				
a. Independents	10	(28)	2,097	(12)
b. Employees	4	(11)	251	(1)
c. Workers	22	(61)	16,060	(87)
	36	100	18,408	100
Industry				
a. Independents	2,711	(29)	142,056	(23)
b. Employees	2,240	(24)	37,143	(6)
c. Workers	4,486	(47)	448,144	(71)
	9,437	100	627,343	100
Commerce				
a. Independents	3,711	(32)	87,000	(26)
b. Employees	2,710	(23)	51,799	(15)
c. Workers	5,359	(45)	201,135	(59)
	11,780	100	339,934	100
Free professional and civil service	9,445		466,310	
TOTALS:	30,698		1,451,995	

SOURCE: *Reichstatistik,* 1907, vol. 207, table 3, pp. 581–82.

1. In the industrial sector 28% of non-Jewish women and 52% of Jewish women are found in categories "a" and "b."
2. In commerce 41% of non-Jewish women and 55% of Jewish women are found in categories "a" and "b."
3. A conservative estimate of "New Woman" jobs (only "b" and "c" in Commerce) indicates 26% of Jewish women and 17% of non-Jewish women engaged in such work. If one includes category "b" from Industry, then 33.5% of Jewish women (or 10,309 Jewish women) and 19.9% of non-Jewish women can be found there.

Appendix Table 3. Jewish Women Compared to Jewish Men, 1895, by percent and number

	Jewish Women per Sector		Jewish Men per Sector		Total German Population per Sector
	(%)	(No.)	(%)	(No.)	(%)
Agriculture	3.0	(1208)	1.3	(2,163)	37.5
Industry	26.0	(10,363)	21.5	(35,630)	37.5
Commerce	49	(19,123)	69.0	(114,328)	10.6
Free professions	4	(1,753)	7.8	(12,888)	6.4
Live-in servants	16	(6,298)	.1	(73)	8.0

SOURCES: V. O. Schmelz, "Die demographische Entwicklung der Juden in Deutschland," *Zeitschrift für Bevölkerungswissenschaft* 8 (January 1982), p. 64; *ZDSJ,* July/August 1911, p. 105.

Appendix Table 4. Jewish Women Compared to Jewish Men, 1907, by percent and number

	Jewish Women per Category a–c (%)	Absolute Numbers	Working Jewish Women (%)	Jewish Men per Category a–c (%)	Absolute Numbers	Working Jewish Men (%)	Large Cities: Jews	Large Cities: Non-Jews
Agriculture								
a. Independents	15	(324)		44	(687)			
b. Employees	0	(14)		3	(56)			
c.1. Family helpers	78	(1,688)		26	(408)			
c.2–5. Workers	7	(149)		27	(420)			
	100	2,175	4	100	1,571	0.8	0.2	1.3
Industry								
a. Independents + homeworkers	32	(4,045) + (703)		45	(21,479) + (740)			
b. Employees	18	(2,702)		23	(10,773)			
c.1. Family helpers	15	(2,193)		1	(422)			
c.2–5. Workers	35	(5,263)		31	(14,675)			
	100	14,906	28	100	(47,349)	26	32	52
Commerce								
a. Independents	32	(9,099)		59	(69,297)			
b. Employees	12	(3,335)		17	(19,566)			
c.1. Family helpers	30	(8,242)		3	(3,620)			
c.2–5. Workers	26	(7,170)		21	(25,277)			
	100	27,846	52	100	117,760	64	55	26
Day labor		(993)	2		(357)	0	—	—
Professions and civil service		(3,056)	5		(15,792)	9	9	9.6
Live-in servants		(4,771)	9		(26)	0	0	11.3

SOURCES: Schmelz, "Die demographische Entwicklung," p. 167; *ZDSJ*, March 1919, p. 8.

Among Jews, 75% of family helpers were women (12,123 women out of 16,573 family helpers); 99% of live-in servants were women; 74% of day laborers were women.

In commerce and industry combined, where 80% of Jewish women were found, 61% were in low-level jobs and 39% were independent. Among men, 90% were in commerce and industry combined, and 55% were independent.

7

Her Sister's Keeper: Women's Organizations from the *Chevra* to Feminism

The extraordinary involvement of Jewish women in charitable and social welfare organizations reflected a combination of deeply held Jewish traditions as well as social transformations within Imperial Germany. Among the latter, the evolution of women's role in the public arena is prominent. For many women, it was the religious social welfare context from which their feminist perceptions and movement grew. Indeed, excluded until 1908 from most political involvement, women's social service activism can be interpreted as a form of women's politics, a way in which women created their own power structures alongside the political and business spheres dominated by men. After the founding of the German Empire, the complex interaction between state and private welfare and the Jewish minority also affected the involvement of Jewish women in voluntary social welfare. Further, social welfare was a form of minority self-help and self-protection in an era of increased anti-Semitism. It was also a form of liberal, bourgeois politics vis-à-vis those of a lower social class: specifically, German Jews tried to alleviate the conditions of Eastern European immigrant Jews and help them acculturate to German society.

Traditions and Social Change

Jewish women's voluntarism was part of a more general secularization: a transformation of religious values into social welfare. This was easily done, since Judaism incorporated social welfare into the heart of its theology. The extensive social welfare network that Jews created and the communal bonds that they forged provided the post-Emancipation Jewish community with a modern, secular Jewish identity. Women were crucial to this process. In sharp contrast to their prescribed social passivity, women were the real "movers and shakers" of Jewish welfare work, hence the real shapers of a modern Jewish identity.

The Religious Legacy

Charity is central to traditional Judaism and can be documented in countless examples in the Bible and the laws. Often it is broken down into two related concepts: *tzedakah* and *gemilut chessed*. The former is translated as "charity," but actually derives from the Hebrew term for "justice." *Tzedakah* was seen as an important lesson to the benefactor and a means to ensure social justice. Although intended primarily to benefit the poor, *tzedakah* encouraged the poor to give to those in even greater destitution. Aid was to be given graciously, preferably anonymously, so that the recipient did not experience shame. Through *tzedakah* the poor would avoid impoverishment, and the wealthier would be ennobled by their good deeds. In the twelfth century Maimonides delineated levels of charity: the highest were loans or employment that would allow a person to become financially solvent; the lowest, alms that did not alleviate but only perpetuated poverty. *Gemilut chessed*, translated as "loving-kindness," implied personal participation in the fate of the needy, an attempt to feel with and for them. This depended less on the amount one gave than on how it was given. It was judged on love and "empathy with the feelings of the oppressed and persecuted."[1] *Gemilut chessed* was often a service in kind: for example, visiting the sick, inviting a stranger to dinner, preparing corpses for burial, or supporting Torah scholars, orphans, or the elderly.

Charity was so important that Jewish law emphasized *tzedakah* as one of the three significant duties of a "worthy daughter of Israel."[2] Moreover, the daily male study routine—the highest ideal for personal and communal life, because learning was considered the key to Jewish survival—could be interrupted only to perform a charitable act or bury the dead.[3] Charity was not simply a lofty ideal, but had very practical purposes in Jewish history. Before the nineteenth century, German-speaking lands tolerated Jews only in certain localities, and then only in restricted neighborhoods or ghettos. This kind of corporate autonomy gave Jews the opportunity to maintain their religion and to control educational processes, judicial action, and social welfare. Thus in the early modern period they elected their own leaders, collected taxes, and set up their basic institutions: synagogues, houses of study, schools for poor children, and various charities. The last were critical, since Christian rulers granted Jews residence permits but declined to perform any social services for them. Thus self-preservation forced an already tight-knit community to care for itself. The burial society or "holy society" (*chevra kaddisha*) held a special position among social services. It often became a major philanthropic agency, dispensing other forms of aid to the poor, and sometimes actually formed the nucleus of a Jewish community.

Superstition, too, reinforced religious prescripts. Wealthier families often acted as if charity would compensate for their own self-indulgence. Rich German Jews of the seventeenth and eighteenth centuries contributed liberally to supporting the needy or the learned. Popular views held that it was a good omen to befriend and give charity to the poor, that charitable acts would assure well-being, that they could ward off "evil spirits."[4] By the seventeenth and eighteenth centuries, "visiting the sick" associations provided doctors and nurses for the needy and prayed for speedy recoveries. Some communities sponsored a society to "welcome visitors," to accommodate scholarly and "respectable" travelers. Most supported organizations which provided for dowerless brides, gave ritual objects to the poor, educated poor children, and provided "loans of grace"—loans for little or no interest—to small business people and artisans. Jews had to give charity not only when the need arose, but on regular occasions such as the Sabbath and holidays as well. On Fridays the poor obtained funds to provide for their Sabbath needs. Giving food to those in need was women's responsibility.[5] During Saturday morning services, people pledged contributions to the charitable fund.[6] Purim was the most prominent of the charity-giving holidays.[7] Much later, in the Imperial era, Purim parties and Purim masquerade balls continued to be major fund-raising activities.

Women contributed to and participated in many charitable activities in medieval and early modern times. From their position in the home, they played hostess to traveling strangers and the needy. Glückl von Hameln (1646–1724), a Jewish businesswoman and mother of thirteen, observed several such cases in her memoirs, although she typically credited the patriarchal household: "And whoever came hungry to my father's house went forth fed and satisfied."[8] She recalled that when Jews fled Vilna in 1648, ten of them, destitute and diseased, found refuge in her home. She wrote: "my father took [them] under his charge," but added that her grandmother tended them until she became infected and died.[9] Proud that hospitality and caring were family traditions, Glückl remarked about one of her daughters: "One and all were received with welcome and respect at her table, charity guests as well as invited guests."[10]

Women's burial society activities continued from medieval times through the Imperial era, lasting even longer in rural towns and villages. Despite women's participation, men led most charitable enterprises. Sometimes several "honorary ladies" (*Ehrendamen*) sat in on executive board meetings but had no vote. Similar to Christian groups of this type, even organizations made up entirely of women and concentrating on women's issues frequently had male leadership. Among the earliest organizations consisting exclusively of women were the Women's Society (*Frauenverein*) in Worms (1609); the Women's Burial Society of Mainz (1650–93); the Dowering Society of Mainz (1724); and the Pious Women, founded in Berlin in 1745.[11]

The French Revolution and its ensuing ideological and political repercussions prepared the way for Jewish Emancipation in the German states. Emancipation offered Jews gender-specific improvements in their legal status and occupational opportunities. The increased affluence resulting from these openings enabled Jews to support social welfare, but they lost their intense communal ties. Although we have evidence of charities which managed to sustain themselves—for example, the Israelite Association for Sick Care and Burial (Königsberg, 1704–1904)[12]—the ghetto's social service structure evolved into loosely organized communal activities.

Women's and men's volunteer organizations played a significant role in reestablishing an elementary social service network in early nineteenth-century Germany. Like their Christian counterparts, these organized Jewish charities, along with private philanthropists, attempted to minister relief to the poor on an ad hoc basis. In the early period of Emancipation they set up credit bureaus, scholarship funds, vocational training for the handicrafts, and home economics schools to encourage Jews to take advantage of their new freedom and to channel some into "acceptable" careers in line with the job profile of the rest of the population. Local groups continued the traditional Jewish charitable work of caring for the sick, the traveling poor, and indigent mothers, as well as attending to burials, supporting the education of children, and providing dowries to women who needed them. Most of the charitable institutions and organizations operated as volunteer groups. Toward the end of the nineteenth century, it appears that the local *Gemeinden* (Jewish communities—see p. 12) took on more of these responsibilities, but when and how and to what extent they supplemented public welfare, and to what extent they provided very basic support, remain topics for another investigation. Throughout the nineteenth century and until 1938, volunteer groups continued to thrive. In fact, with the founding of the B'nai B'rith (1882), the League of Jewish Women (Jüdischer Frauenbund or JFB 1904), and other similar national organizations, the role of voluntary agencies increased around the turn of the century.

Women's increasing activism in Jewish organizational life challenges customary conclusions about German Jews: that they were simply Germans "of the Jewish persuasion"; that they abandoned most Jewish religious loyalties and disaffiliated as well from ethnic customs. In fact, women's communal work suggests that Jews created and maintained the structures which held them together and provided a separate social identity. Parallel with the growing Reform movement in Judaism, which emphasized moral conduct rather than ritual acts, Jews transformed religious values into social commitments. Charitable institutions, in fact, embodied Jewish moral principles for many Liberal Jews. [13] Jewish women and men turned to myriad associations engaged in helping other Jews, causing one observer to remark: "The more women and men. . . participate in organization life, the more people remain interested in Jewish matters, . . . [the more] their joy in belonging, [the more] their feelings of solidarity are strengthened."[14]

Social Transformations and Challenges

The sheer number of Jewish women's organizations, their increase over time, and their tendency toward broader goals and more modern methods can be best understood in the context of the transformation of German social policy and increasing Jewish needs. In Germany, the era of unification (from the 1860s through 1871) stimulated a reconsideration of poor relief and social insurance policies. In an attempt to organize and discipline the poor and rationalize social services, a quasi-scientific "social welfare" approach, as well as state and local regulation of the poor, replaced previous relief methods for the poor.[15] The so-called Elberfeld system of poor relief, begun earlier in the century, spread to most large municipalities by 1914. This system ostensibly "decentralized" and "individualized" relief.[16] In practice, this meant that an increased army of poor-relief guardians judged their clients' needs and set out to monitor and reform recipients.

In the face of an Imperial government which abdicated responsibility for the relief of poverty to local administrations, and the resulting bankruptcy of many public programs, private charities, mostly focusing on single issues, responded. The crash of 1873 and the ensuing unemployment, transiency, and social unrest spurred the growth of church charities and private associations. They "shot out of the earth, all over, like mushrooms."[17] In 1880 a group of lawyers, political economists, government bureaucrats, and poor-relief officials proposed the founding of a national association whose empirical studies would allow it to recommend legislation on the "social question." The era of centralization and scientific inquiry commenced. Looking to cut costs by organizing relief, the German Association for Poor Relief and Charity (DVAW, 1881) encouraged rational, scientific inquiries into public and private relief. It attempted to wean the public away from indiscriminate almsgiving; centralized information bureaus for charity organizations in various large cities; established links among local communities to discuss policy innovations; and above all proposed concrete programs for public poor relief and private charities at a time when social unrest posed serious problems.[18] Toward the turn of the century, as men became less eager to occupy the increasing number of honorary poor-relief-agent positions, the DVAW provided an opening for some middle-class women. The women's movement, which had demanded social welfare jobs for women as early as 1868, played an important role in educating middle-class women for these posts and in pushing for their acceptance.[19] Many became volunteers and, after World War I, others trained as professional social workers.

Several Christian and nonsectarian central organizations—some of them founded earlier, others responding to immediate economic stress—grew rapidly in the last quarter of the century. The Central Committee for the Inner Mission, established in 1848, increasingly coordinated and furthered Protestant charitable organizations and cooperated closely with government agencies.[20] The Caritas Association for Catholic Germany, established in 1897, worked from within the church and at more distance from the state. It too sought to centralize local Catholic charities. Finally, the Red Cross (1859) and the Patriotic Women's Association of the Red Cross (1866) supported centralized emergency aid as well as poor relief, nurses training, and schools. Women's volunteer work played a major role in all these organizations, being seen sometimes as a religious duty and at other times as a counterpart to men's military service.[21]

Thus Jewish social work developed in a context of Jewish culture and philanthropy, economic depression, the rationalization of state poor relief, and a large variety of centralizing, modernizing Christian and secular charities. Simultaneously it responded to specifically Jewish concerns, primarily the need of a minority to be as unobtrusive as possible, to keep its own house in order. While most Jewish organizations had worked on an isolated, local basis, some limited central charitable agencies existed as early as 1838 (i.e., the Berlin Support Association). By the end of the century many local organizations began to combine for fund raising and to coordinate some services. National agencies came about at a slower pace, generally as a by-product of German unification. The year 1869 saw the founding of the Deutsch-Israelitischer Gemeindebund (Association of German-Israelite Communities). In tandem with its campaign against anti-Semitism, it expanded social welfare efforts, particularly its coordination of relief services for "the wandering poor" (*Wanderarmenfürsorge*). Its Berlin office supervised hospitals, orphanages, homes for the aged, the blind, and the deaf, and other such institutions through its state branches, and aided local organizations by exchanging information on philanthropic undertakings. It also provided pension funds for employees of Jewish organizations and stipends for rabbinical students and educational and vocational trainees. Moreover, it supported poor *Gemeinden* in their efforts to maintain social and educational services.

In the 1880s German Jews faced an immense influx of Jewish refugees. In Eastern Europe the final decades of the nineteenth century witnessed the most massive anti-Semitic persecution of the pre-Nazi era. In Russia a policy aimed at driving Jews into pauperism accompanied "spontaneous" violence and climaxed in the pogroms of 1903 and 1905. In Austria-Hungary and Romania, anti-Jewish riots coincided with the systematic exclusion of Jews from professions and schools. In 1901 German Jews established a national organization, the Hilfsverein der Deutschen Juden (Relief Association of German Jews), to aid Jews in Eastern Europe and help transmigrants from those lands. Not surprisingly, Germany appeared a safe haven to the oppressed Jews of Eastern Europe. Hundreds of thousands passed through Germany. Some hoped to start a new life there, while others saw it as a way station en route to the United States. However, the Eastern European immigration with its attending social and economic problems coincided with a new wave of anti-Semitism in Germany, too. For German Jews this meant fighting anti-Semitism in its new, more virulent form, while absorbing foreign coreligionists who often stood out because of their dress, poverty, and occupations.

Inhospitable German state governments possessed a powerful means of getting rid of "troublesome" (*lästig*) populations: expulsion. Beginning in the 1880s and lasting through 1914, the states (Prussia, in particular) expelled tens of thousands of Jewish immigrants. Sensing that the "vulnerability of foreign Jews raised questions about the security of all Jews in Imperial Germany,"[22] German Jews interceded politically and launched massive charitable efforts to aid the refugees, to help some move on, and to give the government no "cause" to expel them. Jewish organizations and communities set up job-counseling centers, "committees to aid alien Jews," schools for adult education, girls' clubs, reading rooms, kindergartens, child-care centers, and vocational schools, to name a few.

The number of charitable organizations and activities grew rapidly in the Imperial era, with women providing the overwhelming majority of volunteers and sponsoring a large percentage of organizations as well. Despite significant household responsibilities, Jewish middle-class women turned to charitable endeavors which they fit into their household schedules and which, they believed, benefited from their domestic experience and skills. Moreover, women's participation in these activities brought respect and recognition to their families. By differentiating themselves from those below them, they avowed their bourgeois status as well as their claim to a German identity.

By the 1890s there was no Jewish community of size without one or more women's organizations. For example, in a hundred towns in Hesse, many of them with only a few Jewish families, there were forty-two women's charities (either run by women or, in a few cases, created for women) and eight dowry clubs.[23] In Munich a 1910 survey found that seven out of twenty Jewish clubs with social purposes were organized exclusively by or for women. Women of course took part in most of the other Jewish associations and some general ones as well.[24] In 1905 the League of Jewish Women, which did not by any means encompass all Jewish women's groups, counted 72 affiliated clubs of 100 to 600 members each; by 1913 this figure had jumped to 160 affiliated clubs representing about 32,000 members. For a population of 615,000 Jews (1910), this is an exceptionally high rate of affiliation.[25]

Jewish social welfare attempted to relieve social tensions between German middle-class and Eastern working-class Jews. The Toynbee Halls, for example, in imitation of the British settlement house, were designed so that "the rich [could] meet the poor, the educated. . . the uneducated, to seek a common ground."[26] In effect, the programs of the Halls aimed to acculturate foreign Jews and instill middle-class values in them.[27] These institutions may have dissolved some intra-Jewish tensions, but, just as likely, they may have highlighted new sources of friction. Moreover, they did not soften class boundaries or alleviate cultural biases. When German-Jewish women volunteers described an evening with working-class Eastern European women as ending with *nette Jargonlieder* (nice songs in "jargon," that is, Yiddish), a certain distance and feeling of superiority were evident.[28]

Still, Jewish women were not for the most part "ladies bountiful" acting in the spirit of noblesse oblige. They came from all strata of the middle class, convinced of the urgency for Jews to help one another and of the necessity for middle-class women to help ameliorate the situation of needy women and children. Their endeavors followed the pattern set by other middle-class women, intent on alleviating poverty but not on disputing the social or political status quo. Although their benevolence pointed to social issues, they remained untouched by the matter of whether or not the class structure and economic order caused the poverty and sexual inequality which they fought. They offered, instead, an ethnic/religious consensus among Jews and won some supporters among working-class recipients. Ultimately it served class as well as ethnic interests to help Eastern European immigrants acculturate to German middle-class norms as quickly as possible. Finally, middle-class women in general displayed their own social status as they served the destitute. It was fitting that the wife of a professor would direct a citywide war relief effort.[29] In fact, such activities led to intermingling between Jews and other Germans, and probably to some social climbing within the Jewish middle classes as well.

Jewish charity, like its Christian counterpart, had assumed new forms by the turn of the century. "Social welfare" or "social service" ideology superseded the idea of "charity." In large part the result of the women's movement (see below), social work shifted from an overt emphasis on protecting society from the poor to a social–ethical perspective: attempting to provide social justice and valuing the happiness of the individual. This differed, as well, from previous religious charity approaches. An ideology of love and pity lost its centrality to poor relief. Far more, and in line with the rationalized poor-relief efforts outlined above, female social workers attempted to study the needs of the poorer classes and to seek general social reform.[30] Lengthy studies of the facts and causes of distress, and investigation and control of the administration of aid, replaced casual lay activity. Welfare became secularized and relatively more impersonal; ethnic loyalty and civic duty worked in tandem with religious duty; and long-range remedies or preventive steps replaced momentary relief. In conjunction with an expansion of welfare services (youth homes, homes for the retarded and blind, vacation colonies, children's convalescent homes, day care [*Horte*] and kindergartens, orphanages, transient care, etc.), came a revision of welfare ideology and a reorganization of welfare associations. Nevertheless, only the devastating impact of World War I brought into being a nationwide central agency designed specifically for the purpose of social welfare, the Central Welfare Agency of German Jews (Zentralwohlfahrtsstelle der deutschen Juden), founded in 1917.

From Charity to Social Work

The evolution of traditional Jewish women's charities from mutual-aid and relief societies employing narrow, stopgap approaches to the beginnings of modern social work was an odyssey in attitudes and behaviors. Although most Jewish women remained unpaid volunteers, the younger generation began to see opportunities open up as social work became professionalized in the early twentieth century. Furthermore, even sectors of the older generation came to acknowledge the need for improved training and methods, and full-time commitment secured by a salary. However, none viewed social work as a radical departure from traditional women's concerns or duties. Even those who focused their efforts on secular welfare, and later on feminist enterprises, remained within a long tradition of Jewish women's social services.

From an assortment of remaining fragments, including protocols of conferences, organizational statutes, and the memoirs or biographies of participants, we can gather that Jewish women's voluntary work followed three separate paths: (1) traditional religious charities, like the burial or dowering association, which maintained their tried and true ways; (2) volunteer organizations willing to modernize their approach to social issues and broaden their areas of concerns; and (3) modern social work which depended upon paid social workers. Significantly, religious charities continued to exist alongside the newer types. Indeed, the same women often participated in several different organizations at once, traditional as well as modern, Jewish as well as secular. Thus enthusiastic amateurs and professional relief workers frequently joined forces and influenced each other and the organizations they supported. In Berlin, for example, a 1909 survey found that, whereas about 10,000 Jews belonged to only one Jewish charitable organization, over 7,000 belonged to two, and 1,100 to three.[31] Also, the names of women involved in Jewish communal affairs often appear in secular organizations from Ethical Culture to feminist groups as well. Overlap was common.

Traditional Charity

Female burial societies played an essential role in German-Jewish communities. Members attended the dying, sewed shrouds, performed the ritual ablutions, stood watch over the female corpse, and accompanied it to the cemetery. They nursed the sick and aided the impoverished. Made up entirely of untrained volunteers, these societies provided an ad hoc approach to social problems within the predominantly middle-class Jewish community. They promoted social integration within the middle class, providing a safety net for people generally like themselves whose status could become precarious upon a business failure, the death of the main breadwinner, or serious illness. Finally, local social life often centered on charitable institutions; these traditional organizations provided sociability to the community.

The Israelite Women's Association founded in Bayreuth in 1900, was typical of women's religious burial societies. Its statutes describe its primary function as assisting in cases of sickness, death, and poverty. The club welcomed all women in the vicinity to join at four Marks a year and waived dues for those who could not afford them. The statutes encouraged members' personal participation. "Active" members visited and aided the sick: they worked three-hour shifts before midnight, and six-hour shifts thereafter (members over the age of sixty did not have to fulfill this duty).[32] The board of directors sewed and delivered shrouds for the deceased, refusing payment from the needy. Two members at a time held watch over the corpse until its burial, or paid to have two women (at least one of whom had to be Jewish) guard it. The club demanded a large turnout of its membership at funerals: "a member can only be relieved of this duty under the direst circumstances." Also, it required some members to stay with the deceased's family during the funeral. Keeping the names of donors and recipients a secret, the group also supported needy families and the traveling indigent. Finally, it was in charge of beautifying the synagogue. In 1910 it claimed seventy-eight members.[33] A minority of similar organizations included men on their board of directors, particularly as treasurers.[34]

Another such religious group in Alzenau, originally organized by the community's (male) Jewish teacher in 1905, encompassed twenty-six female members. As few as six regularly attended general assemblies, but commitment, as measured by dues, visits to the sick, and attendance at burials, remained high—and compulsory. The group fined members for reneging on sick calls and required them to give substantial extra donations to charity when their families celebrated Bar Mitzvahs (five Marks), engagements (five Marks), marriages (ten Marks) or a woman's leaving childbed (five Marks). The minutes of meetings, written by the Jewish teacher (a nonvoting member of the executive committee), brimmed with thanks to God as well as loyalty to the fatherland and to local royalty. In 1908 the club unanimously agreed to repair the community's *mikveh* (ritual bath) to the cost of one-fourth of its entire budget. In 1917, amid the club's war efforts, it donated some of its funds to congratulate King Ludwig III of Bavaria on his golden wedding anniversary. By 1918 the club could boast twenty-eight members, from every Jewish family in town.

It was organizations such as this one which provided not only social services but especially social solidarity to small communities. While the synagogue brought men (and sometimes women) together, these women's groups maintained an equally crucial form of neighborliness among women (and, through women, among men as well).[35] The Israelite Women's Association, founded in Münster in 1843, was also a traditional ladies' charity, but went one step beyond the traditional burial society. In a report dated January 1911–January 1914, we learn that the club consisted of eighty-three women who participated in helping the "poor and needy." This group was run exclusively by women for general welfare purposes. They expected their own members to inform them of crises so that they could "lend a helping hand." They concentrated on supporting unemployable people (*erwerbsunfähige Leute*) and sending sickly children for recuperative vacations. For this they depended on the Patriotic Women's Association, a German patriotic women's organization which allowed the children to spend time at its vacation home. Although Jewish women belonged to patriotic organizations, and the Patriotic Women's Association, included at least one Jewish woman in its leadership, this cooperation was certainly significant.[36] Jews could not assume friendship on the part of "patriotic" associations, since this adjective frequently implied considerable anti-Semitic feeling. Jewish women raised funds at Hanukkah and also accepted goods in kind, including clothing, material, and toys. They bought linens, foods, clothing, and shoes with their funds and distributed these to the appropriate families. Further, they received major financial donations from businesses and individuals, so that their yearly budget stood at 7,223 Marks in 1914, compared to 5,180 Marks in 1897. These budgets excluded the monetary equivalent of volunteers' services, but we should make a note of this as well. Although the extent of their know-how seemed limited to doling out necessary supplies to destitute families that came to their attention, the sum of money collected and distributed was substantial, amounting to the salary of an upper-level civil servant.[37] This was not an insignificant amount for women with little or no business experience.[38]

These organizations consciously harked back to ancient Jewish customs, making no pretense at contemporary methods or motivations. They not only supported the sick materially, but also insisted on personal commitment, the "duty of friendship and love." They urged anonymity in order to avoid humiliating the recipients of charity. A self-help principle further alleviated embarrassment: if a member who had served the club ever needed aid for herself or her family, she would only be receiving her due.[39] Religious traditions, such as decorating the synagogue or designating Purim (or in other cases Hanukkah or Simchat Torah) as the occasion for a fund-raising event, were purposely maintained.[40] Through small-scale fund raising, such groups sometimes supported other charitable ventures, for example, orphanages.[41] Also, they attempted to streamline payment procedures to prevent overpayment or fraud. Stipends were limited, doctors often had to verify the seriousness of an illness, and members themselves testified to the neediness of recipients.[42]

These groups—as well as their more modern variants—not only lent social cohesion but also continuity over time to their communities. All welcomed every female member of the *Gemeinde*. Local historians of these women's groups assumed every woman participated in them.[43] Except for big cities, where some Jews took advantage of the Prussian Law of Secession of 1876 allowing them to officially withdraw from the Jewish Community, local communities would have included every Jew in the vicinity, and most women would have participated in a women's group—at least passively. Even where this may not have been entirely the case, most women's participation was taken for granted. Although Jews were a geographically highly mobile population and the minutes of club protocols frequently report members "moving to Berlin," it is nonetheless striking to observe the continuities. The names of members appear and reappear on lists, with little change, for decades. Eulogies recall members' devotion to the cause over their entire adult lifetimes. These people were deeply rooted in their local Jewish communities. Their organizations provided the ties that held them together in the face of disruption as well as providing an anchor to newcomers.

***One Woman's* Mitzvah.** Many individual women spent a regular portion of their time in charitable endeavors that brought relief and cohesion to their communities. They not only helped out needy families or individuals on a spontaneous, informal level, but also administered private charities. Jacob Rosenheim, the founder of the Orthodox Agudat Israel, described his mother's volunteer activities in the 1890s in conjunction with the philanthropy of the Frankfurt Rothschilds:

> Visiting hours began at 8 a.m. . . . during which my dear parents, particularly my mother, received countless petitioners of all ages and both sexes, giving them smaller donations from the means at their disposal or . . . preparing the way for an interview with Baron Wilhelm von Rothschild. . . . Every evening my father went to the Baron's office . . . to personally present him with a list carefully prepared by my mother, with 20 or 30 requests . . . from all over the Jewish world.

Before the Baron dispensed large amounts of money, he required some verification from rabbis in the vicinity regarding the people or charities asking for help. Rosenheim's mother managed all this correspondence.

> So my dear mother corresponded in lively Hebrew and Judeo-German with all the well-known rabbis of Eastern Europe without any of them knowing—unless he happened to discover this to his surprise in a personal visit to Frankfurt—that "E. Rosenheim" was a woman. . . . The colossal amount of paper work connected with this *tzedakah* increased . . . before the holidays. Then my mother sat at her large desk till late into the night.[44]

Placing crisis intervention above rehabilitation, and religious tradition over a rationalized social welfare system, Rosenheim's dedicated volunteer work as an individual mirrored the approach of the traditional charities in both its strengths and weaknesses.

Modernizing Charities: The Shift Toward Social Work

Jewish welfare societies predated the Imperial era, but more of them with broader goals and more modern approaches came into being after the founding of the German Empire. This pattern followed a general German trend. More than half of all women's organizations in existence in 1908, whether social, charitable, professional, or quasi-political, had been founded after 1900.[45] Since women's political organizations were generally forbidden until 1908, religious and social groups frequently benefited from women's desire and increased ability to participate in community life.

Jews also affiliated rapidly. Jewish sources estimated that there were about

5,000 clubs (including primarily welfare organizations but also educational and self-defense groups) in Germany in 1906. Of these, 42 percent had been founded in the last quarter of the nineteenth century.[46] The organized leadership began to develop programs and associations to centralize the distribution of charity. In 1897 the Federation for Jewish Welfare Work was established for this purpose in Berlin. Other major cities followed suit.

On the local level, Jewish groups saw the need for new projects and began to expand the type of aid they offered and to revise their philosophy of giving. While individual German-Jewish families continued to show hospitality to Jewish beggars and other itinerants from Eastern Europe, causing Jewish organizations to criticize the spontaneous generosity of individual women—"our women still have not been able to let . . . beggars pass by . . . without giving them a donation"[47]—women's groups began to provide an organized approach reminiscent of developments in the German poor-relief system. Some women's organizations augmented their burial/sickness/poverty associations, usually intended solely for members of the *Gemeinde*, to include transmigrants. In Lautenberg, West Prussia, for example, the local women's charity gave "Poles in Transit" cards directing Polish Jews to a member who had volunteered her hospitality. The group maintained a ledger noting the name, situation, and hometown of the recipient and the name of the donor.[48] This system spread the responsibility over as wide a network of families as possible and endeavored to avoid random begging. Most likely, it also identified "repeat" recipients and helped to limit the assistance available to them. Another attempt at rationalizing poor relief can be observed from the same group's efforts to divide the town into four sections, each with a "district lady" (*Bezirksdame*) who would recommend needy cases to the board of directors.[49]

Other women's organizations responded to immediate pressing needs in their communities. They broadened their scope of activities supported by heavy donations of personal labor and contributions. For example, in Mannheim the Jewish Women's Association responded to the diverse requirements of the increasing number of Eastern European Jews in the city by organizing a kindergarten, an employment service, and a sewing circle. The latter provided clothing at Hanukkah and Purim for the kindergarten children. Forty women donated their considerable sewing talents as well as material in a weekly effort to keep the children properly clothed.[50]

Comparing the concerns of the Kissingen women's charity in 1878 and 1919 gives us an example of the transformation of one local women's group. In 1878 the group still invited men to its general assembly. Some years later its inventory consisted of shrouds for men and women, protocol books, and ledgers to note visits to the sick and burial responsibilities. By 1919 the group supported a broader range of social services and had joined the League of Jewish Women, whose feminist goals and leaders were well known.[51] The Lautenberg group similarly expanded from traditional concerns to supporting a girls' home in Germany and a soup kitchen in Jerusalem (1912–13). Some groups began to offer educational lectures or courses for their members as well as other interested women. Themes dealt with Jewish history—including that of famous Jewish women—as well as contemporary concerns.[52] Even when these charities branched out beyond the narrowly religious to extend humanitarian aid in broader fields, most of their institutions remained kosher, their agencies respected the Sabbath, and their organizations adhered to rituals and holidays.

Innovations and Individuals. The social engagement of two individuals shows how women transformed their traditional charitable endeavors into more modern social welfare activities. Rosa Vogelstein (born in 1846), the wife of a well-known rabbi, and Lina Morgenstern (born in 1830), best known for her devotion to secular causes, provide us with models of women whose persistence and innovativeness provided new social services for their communities. Their class status also allowed them the time, funds, and connections to make a difference in the field of social work. And their religious culture encouraged these activities, offering them an approved alternative to boredom and endorsing the exercise of considerable female independence. They are representative of a new breed of Jewish women who ventured in a sustained and successful manner into the public domain on a local and sometimes national level. However, they are decidedly not representative of the average Jewish charity lady. We know of them precisely because they reached beyond the *Gemeinde*, offering their initiative and skills to Jews and non-Jews alike.

Rosa Vogelstein began with traditional Jewish charities and ended up as one of the founders of modern social welfare and feminist organizations. The wife of the rabbi of Stettin, she met her fiancé when she was sixteen. Heinemann Vogelstein became one of the leaders of the Liberal movement in Judaism. Although she had attended university lectures with her fiancé in the 1860s—when women were barely tolerated in the universities and could not matriculate—she became a typical rabbi's wife after marriage. Between 1870 and 1883 she had five children and participated in the activities of her congregation. As chair of the Israelite Women's Association, the local Jewish ladies' charity, she sent anonymous donations of money (in envelopes without return addresses) to those in financial distress. She and her husband also spent much of their own time, energy and resources on personal giving. During the Russian pogroms, both of them met Jewish refugees at the train station early in the morning, guided and helped them during the day, and accompanied them to their special shelters at night. This continued for months, exhausting them, but rewarding them with thank-you notes from America for years thereafter. The couple also received supplicants of all religions in their home: "Why didn't they turn to their pastors or priests?" their daughter wondered, then recalled: "Many avoided the unsympathetic manner in which they were told to accept their fate."[53] Personal giving, in the tradition of *gemilut chessed* and without regard to religious afflilia-tion, continued throughout Rosa Vogelstein's life, long after she joined and organized social welfare and educational institutions. Even as a widow she accepted the guardianship of the illegitimate baby of a young Catholic woman.[54]

This kind of personal, spontaneous charity did not satisfy her. During the 1880s she considered other manners of dealing with poverty. Accompanying her husband on a trip to Sweden, she toured Swedish welfare institutions. At home she succeeded in forming a branch of the German women's movement (1894) in an attempt to organize social welfare and education projects. With the help of Auguste Schmidt, her former school principal and one of the leaders of the Federation of

German Women's Associations, as well as the occasional visits of other luminaries of the women's movement (Helene Lange, Marie Stritt, Käthe Schirmacher, Jeanette Schwerin), she received support for her local projects. These women stayed in her home when they came to Stettin, becoming acquainted with the rabbi and the family as well. Her daughter reported that the rabbi, politically liberal, was open to his wife's guests, though a bit put off by Schirmacher's "man-hating."[55] With the backing of the federation, Vogelstein initiated a legal aid office, a Bureau for Home Care, and several day-care centers.

Her efforts at arranging after-school care for children of working mothers reveals the amount of individual energy such an effort took. She personally approached every school principal whose building she hoped to use to allow her to do so—and returned to inform the more recalcitrant ones that other colleagues had given their permission, and urged them to change their minds. (They often did.) She then had to convince each member of the city council to allow these children to use the gyms, playgrounds, and classrooms of the school buildings. Once her program was established, she prevailed upon a private citizen who owned boats to take the children on biweekly excursions. Aware that the children needed medical attention, she convinced young doctors to volunteer their expertise on a regular basis. She encouraged the daughters of friends and acquaintances to volunteer their services to aid the professional day-care directors. Finally, she took charge of finding vocational training for children who "graduated" from these programs. It took patience and optimism to steer these various initiatives through the city bureaucracy and to secure sufficient help to run them. The experience she gained from this venture helped her in her next major project, to further the education of women.

In the same personal and single-handed manner, she organized lectures on history, literature, biology, physics, and philosophy for women. Again she turned to individual professors, convincing them of the importance of this venture even when she could not guarantee how many women might show up for the first set of lectures. She required serious lectures, opposing "a stroll through the garden of culture." She made all the arrangements for renting lecture halls and wrote all the invitations by hand. The lectures soon turned into adult education courses (*Fortbildungskurse*) which lasted several decades. Her successes emboldened Vogelstein to broaden these offerings and to inaugurate high-school courses (*Gymnasialkurse*) for young women. Upon her husband's death in 1911, the mayor of Stettin attended the funeral and asked to accompany the family to the burial. En route, he shared his fear with the family that Rosa would leave the city—a second irreplaceable loss for Stettin.[56]

Vogelstein's work exemplifies the progression from old-fashioned charities to modern social institutions. Moreover, it illuminates the ways in which women recast the public sphere to reflect their needs. Also, it demonstrates how this kind of activity could lead to reaching beyond the immediate Jewish community into the secular—in this case, feminist—world. Still, Vogelstein remained committed to the Jewish community both privately and in public. Even though her daughter referred to her as a "one-person central organizing committee for education,"[57] and she was a board member of the Stettin Women's Association and Committee for Continuing Education and Day-Care Centers, she nevertheless managed to remain active in her local Jewish women's group.[58] Among the founders of the newly established League of Jewish Women, she took an active part at national gatherings as well as representing her local group.[59]

Vogelstein's course, I suspect, was representative of that of other Jewish activists. Although most Jewish women remained in Jewish organizations, many of them found no contradiction in supporting Jewish and non-Jewish social welfare activities, particularly those related to the women's movement. Rahel Straus, among others, divided her time between Jewish and general women's organizations, gaining experience and support from both sides. Ottilie Schönewald and Henriette Fürth managed to work for both concerns and, after 1908, to participate in political parties as well as previously all-male Jewish associations.

Significantly, it was through these welfare endeavors (many with feminist values and goals) that Jewish women met with and often befriended other German women. The Vogelsteins regularly entertained numerous non-Jewish guests and friends in their home. As a result of her social commitment and the continuing education lectures and courses (in which her husband taught Greek philosophy), the Vogelsteins met many people outside the Jewish community, welcoming them into the family's social circle.[60] Her work relationship with one Christian woman turned into a deep friendship. When the woman and her husband paid a friendly (formal) visit to the Vogelsteins, the latter learned to their surprise that the husband was the new police commissioner (*Polizeipräsident*) of Stettin. Thereafter, the police department sent Vogelstein all confiscated foods and other useful products for her welfare projects.[61] Her daughter, too, made friends with girls who had attended her mother's courses or listened to her father's lectures.[62] She described the "big crowd, about sixty to eighty people, separated by neither religion nor profession," who met in her home. She remarked on the character of these gatherings, which was not really that of a salon but seemingly a neutral space: "On such occasions, people showed themselves differently than in their narrower circles."[63] It is in the area of volunteer work that one might continue a fruitful exploration of the relationships between Jews and other Germans. For, although some societies were clearly "off limits" to Jews, and Vogelstein herself experienced at least one anti-Semitic incident, many volunteer organizations, especially those with feminist content, provided a potential arena for cowork, mutual respect, and sometimes even friendship.

More speculatively, as a result of the women's movement and the liminal space it created in which Jews and other Germans could mingle, it may have been easier for Jewish women than men to achieve a modicum of integration. At the very least, and despite the occasional volunteer fire brigade or male bowling club, women's voluntary social organizations, as opposed to the requisite business associations more readily available to men, offered a less constrained atmosphere for acquaintances or friendships based on mutual interests rather than business opportunities. The experience of Rosa Vogelstein, as unusually energetic and imaginative as she may have been, suggests that contacts and friendships with other Germans could and did take place—and without alienation from the Jewish community.

"Soup kitchen Lina" was one of the best-known figures of late-nineteenth-century Berlin, recognized in the rest of the country as well as a founder of the German women's movement and myriad social welfare organizations and institutions. The daughter of a wealthy Jewish family, Lina Morgenstern was born in Breslau in 1830. She grew up in a household in which the tradition of charity was not only respected but furthered. Conceiving of the charitable function as one of amelioration rather than social change, her father, a factory owner, built living quarters for his workers, and her mother and sisters worked with "morally endangered young women."[64] Her education included the normal *höhere Mädchenschule* and religious instruction with the famous Liberal rabbi Abraham Geiger. The boring and unfulfilling life of a *höhere Tochter*, some music lessons, housework, and astronomy, came to a sudden end with the Revolution of 1848. From that point on, the young woman insisted on doing social charity work and, with her mother, founded the Penny Club to Support Poor School Children, an organization which was to last eighty years. She led the group until 1854, when she married and moved to Berlin.

Soon involved in bringing up a family of five, Morgenstern engaged in activities to support Friedrich Fröbel's kindergarten movement. Fröbel's attractiveness to Jewish women stemmed not only from their shared liberal outlook, but also from his views on religion. He hoped to awaken a religious feeling in children, but unlike other educators as well as school systems, he avoided a Christian emphasis. He welcomed children of all faiths in his kindergartens.[65] Given the hostile climate of the public school system toward Jews, they may have been particularly grateful for this kind of acceptance. The Prussian government actually banned these kindergartens for over a decade as centers of socialism, atheism, and other types of destructive progressivism. Morgenstern nevertheless managed to found the Society for the Promotion of Fröbel Kindergartens (1859) and write a handbook explaining Fröbel's ideas (which went through seven editions by 1905). She also organized an institute to train caretakers of young children (Kinderpflegerinnen Institut) and participated in the Jewish Association for People's Kindergartens in the Eastern Section of Berlin (Verein für Volkskindergärten im Osten Berlins) which provided free care for needy children.

Morgenstern set up her famous soup kitchen during the war of 1866, and the idea spread rapidly.[66] Responding to a practical necessity by feeding those impoverished by war, she also hoped to bridge class differences through charitable endeavors and provide useful volunteer work for women eager to escape the confines of their homes. She founded the Society of Berlin Soup Kitchens, starting with contributions of 13,000 Marks.[67] In two years she had succeeded in establishing ten such kitchens. She gained the support of well-known men and women, among whom Jews were heavily represented. In the first twenty-five years of the soup kitchens' existence, over a thousand women served voluntarily; Jewish women were overproportionally represented.[68] This should come as no surprise, given the large number of Jews in Berlin in this era (about 25,000 Jews in 1864, or 3 to 4 percent of the entire population), their middle-class status, and their energetic participation in charitable endeavors. In 1892, forty-eight Jewish women's groups existed in Berlin alone.[69]

Morgenstern only began with the kindergartens and kitchens. During her career she was on the board of the General German Women's Association (Allgemeiner Deutscher Frauenverein, 1871–85) and organized the Berlin Housewives' Association (1873), editing its nationally known newsletter, the *Deutsche Hausfrauen-Zeitung*, for thirty years. At the request of the Prussian government, she set up committees to feed soldiers in transit and, later, to care for the wounded during the Franco-Prussian war (for which she received the Iron Cross). Together with Louise Otto-Peters, one of the best-known women's rights advocates in Germany, she founded a club to educate working women and led the club from 1871 to 1874. Having nursed wounded soldiers in the war of 1871, she also entered the fight to allow women to study medicine by writing a book entitled *An Open Word to Professor Waldeyer About the Study of Medicine by Women*. At the formation of the Federation of German Women's Associations, she fought to include working-class women in the organization. Finally, during a period of increasing nationalism and arms buildup in Germany, she joined the executive committee of the League for World Peace (Weltfriedensbund) and popularized the international women's peace movement.[70]

Although she did not maintain rituals in her later life, she felt that Judaism was a "larger, wider family to which I . . . belong." She also coauthored a prayer book for Jewish youth[71] and interceded on behalf of needy Jews. In fact, in 1907, two years before her death, she beseeched Queen Elizabeth of Romania to protect Jews from discrimination. The queen assured her that outsiders had slandered the Rumanian government, which refused to address these charges, but that "when so worthy a woman as you turns to me, I would like to correct your error. . . . With best wishes for the success . . . of your important work for humanity."[72]

Anti-Semites quickly noticed Morgenstern's prominence and, of course, her religion. Writing of her efforts on behalf of the soup kitchens, one man asked: "Why is it necessary that a Jewish women (Lina Morgenstern) has to manage these soup kitchens: why can't Germans do that; does everything have to be left to Jews?"[73]

Believing in the possibility of cooperation between Jewish and non-Jewish Germans, Morgenstern responded to critics by emphasizing that Jews didn't simply enjoy themselves, "but worked, and not only to gather capital, but . . . to help their fellow citizens. . . . We feel like equally entitled citizens, since we conscientiously fulfill all our duties to the throne, fatherland, state, and society."[74] Like many Jewish women who donated their time and resources to secular causes, Morgenstern hoped to mitigate anti-Semitism and challenge racist stereotypes. Moreover, she hoped to transform negative perceptions of Jewish contributions to society while firmly staking her claim as a citizen of that society. Jews contributed to non-sectarian social work, Morgenstern pointed out, *because* they belonged to German society, not in order to belong.

"Social Welfare" at the Turn of the Century

The prewar era saw Jewish organizations expand significantly, often reaching beyond Germany to help Jews in other parts of the world. In their abiding interest in aiding other women, Jewish women successfully established new and substantial institutions "by women for women," frequently extending their services to non-Jews. Finally, like other middle-class women, Jewish women created "invisible careers" for themselves.[75] They established female-led enterprises from which they could exercise public power under the banner of social housekeeping and religion. Moreover, the institutions they created opened employment opportunities for their daughters. A description of several typical organizations can shed light on the development of Jewish women's social welfare work.

In Hamburg the Israelite Humanitarian Women's Society focused on the needs of women, conscious, as a member of the League of Jewish Women, of feminist programs and demands.[76] Its goals included making "women and families employable and economically independent." In 1912 the group subsidized 108 young women studying crafts, tailoring, and hairdressing, and found positions for 215 people through its employment service. It delivered milk to needy families, and its infant care program included a bonus payment for nursing mothers. Although primarily assisting a Jewish population, the group made these services accessible to non-Jewish mothers and children. It also supported several institutions, including a day-care center, a home for girls, and a rest home.[77] In 1914 it planned to increase programs for unwed mothers and found a club for young working women. Although most of the helpers volunteered, the club also hired professional nurses and social workers. The Frauenverein often worked in conjunction with the Hamburg B'nai B'rith and the Zentrale für Jüdische Wohltätigkeit. In 1913 it had 600 members, and in 1914, 972.[78] Its substantial budget, supported by coin boxes, was heavily supplemented by private donations.

Other groups expanded their services, increased their expenditures, hired more professional staff, and considered themselves "modern." In Munich the Women's Aid established a kindergarten, a day-care center, and a Girls' Club in 1904. Starting small—in 1905 it served 30 children—it accommodated 95 children by 1912, of whom about one-fifth were not Jewish. Its budget that year (excluding volunteer help and donations in kind) was 12,819 Marks. The Girls' Club, open daily, provided entertainment, sewing instruction, first-aid courses, reading circles, and foreign-language and stenography lessons. The women's group arranged for the girls to be invited to lectures sponsored by the Association for Jewish History and Literature. They also received free tickets from the Volkstheater and delightedly reported on a performance of Goethe's *Faust*.

The Munich group attempted to enrich the lives of young Eastern European working women, to help them acculturate to German-Jewish mores, and to prevent them from getting into trouble in unfamiliar surroundings. The group also attempted to lessen class and ethnic tensions between middle-class German Jews and working-class Jewish immigrants. During the "Evenings for Mothers" held by the club's kindergarten and day-care committee, German-Jewish volunteers and Eastern European working mothers drank tea, discussed topics of concern, or listened to lectures or music. Often they brought their mending along and received advice and assistance from the volunteers.[79] This attempt to alleviate intra-Jewish class tensions and cultural differences succeeded insofar as regular attendance by both groups continued. However, all involved clearly recognized "volunteers" and "recipients."

Bertha Pappenheim's Women's Welfare (Weibliche Fürsorge) in Frankfurt/Main serves as an example of one of the most modern social welfare organizations of the prewar era. Initiated and organized solely by women in 1902, the group attempted to transcend the "do-good" approach and to merge the concerns of the German women's movement with those of Jewish social work. Although they did not stress social services as a "right" of the recipient as much as a "duty" of the donor, their attitude avoided the sentimentality of other Jewish charitable groups. Moreover, they envisaged broader programs and cooperated with other organizations in a much more systematic and comprehensive manner. Women's Welfare may be seen as one of the first larger, expanded service associations, one which worked regularly with other major groups and tried to centralize and coordinate social services within a particular area.

Pappenheim taught her colleagues new social work techniques including the use of questionnaires and detailed case reports, and set up special committees which researched methods of child care, means of finding foster homes, and ways of providing aid to travelers. The organization cooperated with larger Jewish and women's organizations, including the Jewish community poor-relief fund (Almosenkasten), the Jewish Collective Guardianship (Sammelvormundschaft), the Club to Clothe Schoolgirls and Apprentices, and the Hilfsverein. Not wishing to be overwhelmed by the bigger male-dominated organization, Women's Welfare participated in Hilfsverein work, but insisted that it be represented on the larger associations' board of directors.[80] Its work with the clothing group enabled it to benefit from the latter's research efforts, and also assured that clothing disbursement was carefully coordinated among charity groups.

Women's Welfare set up its own day-care center for over one hundred infants in 1907 and ran an infants' milk kitchen (*Säuglingsmilchküche*). It supported its own employment service for women. Volunteers who met with applicants followed strict guidelines which included handling each case according to individual needs and in a friendly fashion; charging no fees; advising women of safe lodgings; and checking all foreign positions for fraud or white slave traffickers before recommending them.[81] The organization also set up its own Commission to Protect Children. Further, Women's Welfare initiated international outreach programs to help Jews in Eastern Europe. With the financial backing of other Jewish organizations, the women's group supported kindergartens, hospitals, and information centers for women intending to travel or seek work abroad.[82]

By mid-1914, the club had expanded its enterprises considerably and had received several large donations from wealthy women.[83] It increased its services for adolescents, working with the juvenile court (*Jugendgericht*), providing guardians, counseling, and accommodations for young people. The Frankfurt group also supported the general women's movement, attending protest meetings against the establishment of official brothels, and signing petitions to allow women as jurors, to increase women's citizenship rights, and to raise the requirements for compulsory schooling of girls.[84]

The success of Women's Welfare and the need for expanded social services caused Pappenheim and her associates to think bigger: to create a national Jewish women's network to serve the welfare needs of the Jewish community and the specific needs of women. They founded the League of Jewish Women (JFB) in 1904, preferring their own organization because, as Pappenheim put it, the male-led Jewish social service societies "underestimated the value of women's work and trifled with their interest by refusing to admit them as equal partners."[85] She argued that the leaders of Jewish community welfare boards carelessly lost some of the best women, who preferred the independence of the German women's movement. Hers was an attempt not only to create an independent arena for women, but to lure some of these Jewish women back into the fold. She insisted on a women's movement that was equal to and entirely independent of men's organizations, refusing the leadership of the B'nai B'rith's women's auxiliary.

It was clearly their early experience in Women's Welfare which gave these women (and similar organizers from Hamburg, Munich, Berlin, and other cities) the know-how and courage to organize a national movement and to exclude men. At the inception of the League of Jewish Women Pappenheim appealed to women to free themselves from "tutelage" and to reach a "certain independence, especially since in most cases . . . the feelings and understandings of women are more accurate than those of men" (*viel eher das Richtige treffe*). For this reason, men were asked to leave the founding session of the JFB.[86] The JFB welcomed women of all political beliefs and professed religious neutrality vis-à-vis the various branches of Judaism. Representatives of Jewish women's organizations from the United States and England attended the first meeting. A historian has noted: "The early women's movement . . . flourished because of the experiences women had gained from decades of work in single-sex voluntary associations . . . fighting for issues they defined as women's issues."[87] This was certainly true of those groups which founded the League of Jewish Women.

Bertha Pappenheim and Alice Salomon: Leaders of the Women's Movement. The two Jewish women who most characterize this era of modernizing social work were Bertha Pappenheim, born in 1859, and Alice Salomon, born in 1872. Pappenheim belonged to the German and international women's movements, but concentrated her efforts on issues affecting Jewish women and on the Jewish women's movement. Salomon focused entirely on nondenominational women's work and the German and international women's movement. She is credited with being the founder of modern social work in Germany. Although very different in their allegiance to Judaism—Pappenheim remained very observant, while Salomon converted to Christianity in midlife—both are examples of Jewish women for whom social work was a clear path to women's emancipation, and for whom the women's movement provided sustenance in their personal lives.

Intense and energetic, Bertha Pappenheim founded the Jewish feminist movement in 1904 and led it for twenty years, remaining on its board of directors until her death in 1936. She introduced a generation of German-Jewish women to ideas and issues raised by feminism. She was the first person to speak openly of Jewish unwed mothers, illegitimate children, and prostitutes, and she encouraged Jewish women to demand political, economic, and social rights as well as commensurate responsibilities. Born in Vienna to a family of wealthy, religious Jews, she first made history at the age of twenty-one as "Anna O." Her treatment by Josef Breuer and the later discussions of her case by Sigmund Freud marked the beginning of the psychoanalytic age.[88] After a long convalescence, she moved to Frankfurt with her mother. Her entry into Frankfurt social work made a profound difference in her life. Beginning with volunteer work in soup kitchens, she quickly gained the experience

Bertha Pappenheim, founder of the League of Jewish Women. *Pappenheim Collection. Courtesy of the Leo Baeck Institute, New York.*

necessary to organize Women's Welfare. Although she felt she was fulfilling a religious commandment to help those in need (she spoke of social work as a *mitzvah*), she shied away from traditional charity clubs. Instead, she hoped to apply the goals of the German feminist movement, whose literature she had read and whose spokeswomen she admired, to Jewish social work.

Pappenheim's writings, beginning in the 1890s and continuing throughout her lifetime, reflected her feminist and Jewish concerns. By 1899, when she published a play entitled *Women's Rights* and a translation of Mary Wollstonecraft's *A Vindication of the Rights of Women*, she was firmly committed to fighting for women's human rights and their educational advancement. Her pamphlets and books on Jewish life in Eastern Europe expressed her growing alarm at the conditions of life there. She attempted to mobilize Jewish communities to educate young women and to aid the victims of anti-Semitic government policies. Her translations of the *Tsenerene* (a sixteenth-century women's bible), the *Mayse Bukh* (a collection of medieval folktales and biblical and Talmudic stories which had been widely read by women), and the seventeenth-century diary of Glückl von Hameln (a distant relative), can be seen as efforts to retrieve for Jewish women parts of their cultural and historical heritage.

The fact that Protestant and Catholic women had their own national organizations encouraged Pappenheim in her pursuit of a national Jewish women's association. She turned exclusively to women, convinced that "men always and in every situation follow their private interests."[89] She expected women to volunteer their services, because Jewish organizations could not afford to pay for the amount of help they needed, and because volunteer work would enrich what she saw as the empty lives of middle-class Jewish women. She brought the JFB into the largest middle-class feminist organization, the Federation of German Women's Associations. She credited German feminism with giving "the shy, uncertain advances of Jewish women direction and confidence."[90]

Neither Pappenheim nor the movement she founded subscribed to a radical version of feminism: instead, they accepted conventional views that fundamental, natural differences existed between the sexes. Within the Jewish community, however, the JFB's demand for suffrage and equal representation (not only in the nation, but inside the *Gemeinde*), its open discussion of Jewish involvement in the white slave traffic and denunciation of the double standard of morality, its criticism of the "second-class status" of women in Judaism, and its demand for employment opportunities often caused irritation. Antifeminists attacked the JFB, and rabbis ignored it, but it continued to expand to encompass 35,000 women in its first ten years. By 1929 it counted 430 affiliates, 34 of its own branches, 10 provincial alliances, and a total membership of 50,000.[91]

Pappenheim's particular emphasis on women's condition and women's equality gave form and content to what might otherwise be seen as simply social welfare projects. Hers was a "social feminism," practical social reforms to improve the circumstances of women's lives.[92] For example, for Pappenheim, the attempt to end Jewish participation in the white slave traffic had a Jewish social welfare and a distinctly feminist component. In attempting to bring about social welfare reforms, she attended all the major Jewish and secular international conferences on the subject; wrote her best-known book, *Sisyphus Work*, which described the problem of Jewish prostitution and white slavery in Eastern Europe and the Middle East; encouraged the JFB to set up railroad and harbor posts in major cities to aid female travelers; publicized the dangers of white slavery to women; traveled to Eastern Europe to organize Jewish committees to combat white slavery; and set up girls' clubs in Germany as a preventive measure. However, she always brought a feminist analysis to bear on the causes of prostitution. She joined national and international feminist crusades to abolish state regulation of prostitution and condemn the double standard. She also focused on the economic causes of prostitution, arguing that women needed better employment opportunities. Moreover, she assailed women's inferior legal status in Judaism. This, she claimed, resulted in many abandoned wives (*Agunot*) in Eastern Europe, which added to the problem of destitution and white slavery.

The league established job-counseling centers and home economics schools, with Pappenheim encouraging women to seek careers as a means to psychological as well as economic independence. Its most radical effort, probably inspired by the new and radical League for the Protection of Motherhood and Sexual Reform (1904), was its Home for Endangered Girls. "Proper" society—both Jewish and Christian—condemned unmarried mothers with "illegitimate" children. Neither private nor public welfare supported institutions for them at the turn of the century. Only Leipzig had one such public institution.[93] The JFB established its home in Neu-Isenburg in 1907, to protect and educate these women and children and, according to Pappenheim, to save them for the Jewish community. She wanted to establish a "home" for girls, not an institution for inmates, and preferred to be "too good" to the girls by the standards of her society. Divided into family units where mothers took care of their own babies, the residents received job training and ran the home themselves. They cooked according to Jewish dietary laws and celebrated all religious holidays together. "Graduates" were placed in jobs upon leaving.[94]

Pappenheim's most frustrating campaign, to achieve full equality for women within the Jewish community, or *Gemeinde*, was part of the larger struggle for women's suffrage in Germany. Pappenheim personally approached numerous rabbis, seeking favorable interpretations of Jewish law regarding women's rights. Even after receiving a justification from an eminent rabbi, the league had to petition countless individual Jewish communities and organize public meetings and protests. Nevertheless, Jewish women had to wait for a voice in the *Gemeinde* long after they and other German women had attained suffrage in the nation.[95]

Pappenheim's commitment to Judaism and to feminism went hand in hand. She argued that feminism could reinvigorate Judaism in Germany, insisting that Jews were turning away from Judaism because women—the transmitters of culture—were alienated from Jewish customs and communities. Although her analysis resembled that of certain conservative circles—perhaps as a way of masking the radical nature of her demands—she did not blame women the way they did. Instead, she created the Jewish women's movement to fight for women's equality as both a means by which women would return to Judaism and an end in itself. Moreover, she believed that social work for women within the Jewish community offered a form of practical politics that would enhance women's lives. Absorbing some traditional women's charities and building on programs that older groups had pioneered, the JFB offered a new, feminist approach to social welfare institutions as well as a national, coordinated organization to pursue women's interests.

Alice Salomon, a pioneer in the field of modern social work, was born of a well-to-do Jewish family in Berlin in 1872. She experienced her childhood as happy but her adolescence as unbearable, because her formal education ground to a halt by age fourteen. She had wanted to become a teacher, but her family opposed her desires as inappropriate for someone of her social class. Doomed to "feed the canaries and embroider doilies,"[96] with an occasional game of tennis, she eagerly attended the founding meeting of the Girls' and Women's Groups for Social Service Work (Mädchen- und Frauengruppen für Soziale Hilfsarbeit) in 1893. She wrote that her life started at that moment.[97]

Closely tied to the bourgeois women's movement, these groups did not see themselves as yet another women's charity. Seeking to make social work more

Dr. Alice Salomon, founder of the Soziale Frauenschule, Berlin, with her students, around 1915. *Alice Salomon Collection. Courtesy of the Leo Baeck Institute, New York.*

effective, to work "at the right time with the right means,"[98] they emphasized two related goals: to organize bourgeois women's social work and to train and educate bourgeois women to perform their tasks more effectively. The Groups provided volunteers who worked among the poor and, importantly, gave theoretical and practical training to their own members. In their first year, the Groups invited Max Weber to present a series of lectures on modern societal developments. Other lecturers covered private and state welfare in Germany, welfare innovations in England and America, and the basics of hygiene and child care. Members of the Groups met "in the afternoons . . . at tea time" to discuss their activities and exchange information. "Not exactly big-city-like" (*nicht grossstädtisch*), according to Salomon, "in fact, very old-fashioned"—but intimate.[99]

The Groups' approach to social work differed from that of their predecessors. It was neither religious, in the sense of traditional church charities, nor bureaucratic, in step with the German Association for Poor Relief and Charity. Indeed, the women's movement may have invented modern social work as distinct from religion and bureaucracy. The Groups—which were recruiting grounds for the women's movement, although they officially denied this for twenty years—promulgated a new attitude toward the poor, one that stemmed perhaps from the women's movement's own universal appeal to an emancipatory spirit. As Minna Cauer, one of the progressive leaders of the German women's movement, observed, bourgeois women felt a certain solidarity with the underprivileged in society, acknowledging some common disadvantages and goals. Further, these women emphasized the moral responsibility of the bourgeoisie to concern itself with the needy.[100] Moreover, Salomon believed social work should overcome class differences, should bridge the chasm between the "two nations."[101]

For Salomon, the Groups provided a meaningful existence for herself and, by extension, for all middle-class women: "freeing middle-class girls [*höhere Töchter*] from idleness was as important to her as social work."[102] Social work meant "practical politics," not private charity, and direct help from women to women. [103] The Groups saw a clear connection between the "social question" and the "women's question," and hoped to become so important to public welfare that they could no longer be ignored as a political force.[104] Ultimately, they were path-breaking in their approach to social work and in preparing women for public welfare and other communal or state offices as counselors, guardians, welfare workers, factory inspectors, and vocational guidance and employment officials. Their strength lay in having well-trained women at hand to fill positions in the expanding social welfare field.[105]

In 1899 the Groups organized a one-year course to prepare social workers more formally. That year Salomon at age twenty-seven became the director of the Groups upon the death of her mentor, Jeanette Schwerin. Schwerin had been elected to the executive board of the Federation of German Women's Associations in 1896 and had brought the Groups into that organization in 1898.[106] Thus Salomon automatically became part of the leadership of the federation as well. She continued to organize lectures by famous professors of economics, sociology, and politics to stimulate her Groups. Their membership grew from 127 in 1895 to 890 in 1908.[107] By 1912, 140 similar Groups existed throughout Germany.[108]

Salomon audited university courses in Berlin and received her Ph.D. in political economy (*Nationalökonomie*) in 1906, two years before Prussia allowed women to matriculate. Her doctoral thesis analyzed "the causes of unequal pay for men and women." She was also the first woman awarded the honorary doctorate of medicine by the University of Berlin for her publications in the area of health care. Confronted by an increased need for social workers in the city and state bureaucracies, a demand for education by the women's movement, and the continued incompetence of traditional charity workers, Salomon founded the first nondenominational school of social work in Germany in 1908.[109] She became its dean and went on to found the Academy for Social and Educational Women's Work (Deutsche Akademie für Soziale und Pädagogische Frauenarbeit, 1925), which offered continuing education in social work, and the Conference of Schools of Social Work in Germany (1933), as well as to help organize the International Association of Schools of Social Work and become its president.

Her activity did not cease with the successful establishment of the school and, later, the field of social work. In Berlin she helped establish girls' homes (*Mädchenhorte*) and working women's homes and clubs.[110] Her writings focused on issues concerning the working class and the protection of mothers (*Mutterschutz*), including maternity insurance, as well as technical and pedagogical texts on social work. She left over twenty-eight monographs and 250 articles as her contribution to the social politics of her day. Despite these scholarly endeavors, she would have considered herself an activist. She was a board member of the German and international branches of the women's movement, for which she wrote numerous articles and pamphlets. In 1909 she accepted the post of secretary of the International Council of Women.

Salomon focused her entire energies on secular causes, never participating in the Jewish women's movement or the Jewish community. Although her parents had hired a Jewish religion teacher for their children when she was about ten years old, his Orthodox manner alienated the children. At school the children sat in on Christian religion lessons, despite an agreement between the parents and the principal that the children had to attend only those sessions dealing with the Old Testament. At home the family ignored Jewish rituals, although her father was buried by a rabbi in 1885. For a while they celebrated Christmas, but after the death of her sister in 1889 they preferred to practice no religion. Still, Salomon required a religious basis for her social work and found this, at age forty-two, during the bewildering first weeks of World War I, by converting to Protestantism.[111] This was not a cynical move. It in no way enabled her to advance in her field, something she had succeeded in doing with her Jewish identity intact. Indeed, at the end of the war Gertrud Bäumer, the president of the Federation of German Women's Associations, who had hoped to have Salomon replace her, had to agree that, in the anti-Semitic atmosphere of the times, a woman with even a Jewish-sounding name would have split the women's movement.[112]

Salomon is representative of Jewish women who chose to work outside the Jewish community. Several others who were well known to their contemporaries should be briefly mentioned. Jeanette Schwerin (1852–99), one of the founders of the German Society for Ethical Culture, initiated an information bureau for social welfare institutions for that society and founded the Hauspflegeverein in Berlin. She was one of the original four founders of the Groups, directing them from 1897 until her untimely death.[113] Jenny Apolant (1874–1925), a cousin of Walter Rathenau, was prominent in the fight for women's rights to civic (what we would call civil-service) jobs. She established a Central Bureau for Civic Positions for Women (Zentrale für Gemeindeämter der Frau); led the Frankfurt section of the General German Women's Association, sitting on its national board of directors; and wrote numerous articles on women's rights to vote and work.[114] Apolant never denied her Jewishness and in fact belonged to the Central Verein Deutscher Staatsbürger Jüdischen Glaubens. Still, she focused entirely on secular social work.[115] Helene Simon (1862–1947) was the child of a religious Jewish family. Her father, a businessman and banker, gave generously to impoverished Jews in his community, yet she chose a completely nondenominational path. Becoming a social reformer and member of the women's movement, she spent much of her time learning from the English Fabians and relaying their message back home. A Social Democrat, she was active in the Workers' Welfare organization (Arbeiterwohlfahrt) and wrote articles for socialist and feminist organs as well as two major biographies, one of Robert Owen, the other of Mary Wollstonecraft and William Godwin.[116]

What Salomon and women like her shared with Bertha Pappenheim may not be apparent at first glance, but there are common threads. First, compared to their percentage of the population, Jewish women activists seemed disproportionately highly involved in social reform and women's movements. Although the majority of feminist leaders came to the women's movement from education and social welfare, Jewish, non-Jewish, and anti-Semitic observers tended to agree on the prominence of Jewish women activists.[117] Jewish observers worried—with cause—that anti-Semites would label the women's movement "Judaicized" (*verjudet*), a charge the Nazis would repeat decades later. Anti-Semitic papers likened the role of Jewish women in the women's movement to that of Jews in the Social Democratic Party, two movements they despised.[118] Minna Cauer noted that right-wing groups attacked her, the daughter of a pastor, for allegedly changing her name from "Krakauer" so as not to be recognized as Jewish. She added:

> I knew, and so did many others, that the Christian-Social Stöcker party wanted to destroy the women's movement. . . . In order to do that particularly well, they tried to stamp the whole movement, but especially the newer, more progressive current of the late 1880s, as purely Jewish. They believed that they could discredit it [by association] in the flood of anti-Semitism of that era, and thereby demolish it.[119]

Others—Jews and non-Jews—praised such activism. The editor of one Jewish paper commented that, although the majority of the "Jewish" names at the International Council of Women meeting were "only born Jewish," they "spoke with a Jewish spirit and sensitivity."[120] Minna Cauer wrote: "It seems that it became the task of Jewish women to fight for the rights of all women: among them, we note not only the most active, but also the most talented and courageous women. Women, the working classes, and Jews: they are the most oppressed people of this century." Whereas Jewish women pioneered in the fight for rights, Cauer suggested that Christian women may have been inhibited by the directive of St. Paul that women must be silent in the community. She commented on Jewish women's "admirable characteristics, including tenacity in achieving their goals, indefatigable ability to work, keen judgement, and strong powers of observation."[121]

Commonalities among these Jewish women did not simply result from their engagement in social welfare or feminist ventures. We can begin to understand their activism in terms of gender, class and cultural backgrounds, and anti-Semitism. Stifled by their enforced boredom as young middle-class women, they found social work an escape from a trifling and passive existence. All engaged in social work as an acceptable gender- and class-appropriate outlet for their energies. Further, Jews in Imperial Germany, only recently fully emancipated, were eager to catch up. Jewish men focused their energies on business, the professions, and scholarship. Jewish women not only witnessed the pressure for achievement in their husbands, fathers, and brothers, but must have felt these pressures themselves. Yet as we have seen, anti-Semitism limited their options. Thus Jewish women found space to maneuver and excel in the long and honored tradition of social work in Judaism. Nevertheless, middle-class status alone is insufficient to explain Jewish women's disproportionate activism in social reform movements.

Most of these women came from Jewish backgrounds in which their families stressed social service or charity. Even if, by this time, social welfare had become secularized and impersonal, with a sense of civic duty and feminist involvement largely replacing any awareness of Jewish law, Jewish cultural traditions enforced social commitment. When a recent biographer of Alice Salomon wrote that she grew up "like many millions [*sic*] of others as an assimilated Jewish woman" hardly influenced by her Jewish origins, the writer overlooked the subtlety with which those origins manifested themselves. Like so many "non-Jewish Jews," women such as Salomon devoted themselves to the betterment of society in general, but the impetus for this may very well have come from a Jewish cultural background which had emphasized communal organizing and social responsibility.[122] Moreover, for some women social work helped to ease the tensions between religious traditions and secular identity. Women could, consciously or unconsciously, nurture a cultural or religious legacy while becoming "modern": social work was both part of a tradition and the means of going beyond this tradition.

In addition, Jewish defensiveness may have played a role. By their avid participation in general social work, Jewish women could hope to soften anti-Semitic stereotypes of Jews as greedy capitalists who brought harm to the German nation. Lastly, the secular social work of Jewish women may be seen as part of the process of acculturation and (limited) integration. It made Jews "acceptable" and accepted in certain sectors of society, because everyone engaged in a common cause. Social welfare activism provided an entrée into the social world of the bourgeoisie. Whereas men gained access to this world through their businesses or professions, Jewish women approached other German women through their volunteer work.

World War I

World War I seemed to offer women an opportunity for action beyond anything they had previously undertaken. Like German men, most exhibited early enthusiasm for the war effort. They saw the *Burgfrieden*—the domestic peace among classes and parties declared by the Emperor—as an opportunity to become integrated into and respected by society at large. Indeed, the government welcomed them as never before, sponsoring projects they had long sought, well aware that the military front depended on the home front. Jewish women, in organizations and as private individuals, exerted enormous efforts in war relief activities. More than ever before, they were integrated into the general women's endeavor. In fact, war relief became the arena of social interaction for middle-class girls and women, Jewish and Gentile. Still, Jewish women's experiences at home frequently ran parallel to those of their men at the front: they were often physically integrated, but persistent anti-Semitism plagued them and actually increased during the war. The crucible of war and the experiences of Jewish women on the home front give us an opportunity to examine the extent to which Jews "belonged" in Germany: a chance to witness their enthusiasm for the nation, their willingness to engage in a common endeavor, their tenuous acceptance by other Germans, and their intermittent rejection.

On July 31, 1914, a day before Germany officially declared war, Gertrud Bäumer, the head of the Federation of German Women's Associations, organized the National Women's Service (Nationaler Frauendienst). The National Women's Service worked with the Red Cross and the Patriotic Women's Association and consulted with a broad spectrum of other private and governmental welfare organizations. The government supported all kinds of social work projects which women had clamored for before the war,[123] only now for a completely different goal—to win the war. The German women's movement experienced acceptance and solidarity in mobilization. New opportunities opened up for bourgeois women. The military state set up women's employment bureaus (*Frauenarbeitszentrale*) with positions available in countless new areas. One of the leaders of the German and Jewish women's movement commented: "wartime meant the coming to maturity, but also the emancipation of the women's movement."[124] Referring to the usefulness of the women's movement in a period of national danger (and in so doing, justifying its long history), Helene Lange, one of its founders, wrote: "I think we can say, that the women who went through the school of the women's movement . . . can for their part steer our people through this terrible crisis."[125] Bäumer expressed her gratitude that the women's movement, which had been "forced" to defend women's special interests, could be taken up in "this great and momentous drawing together [*Zusammenwachsen*] of all national energies into a powerful common will." With no power to influence the politics of Imperial Germany, these women still felt like "citizens with obligations toward the general public."[126] So long at odds with German politics and society, the bourgeois women's movement seemed to welcome this feeling of blending into the nation or *Volk*.[127]

The war provided a situation in which Jews, too, could work in highly visible positions for the common cause. Like most Germans, Jews believed that their fatherland was in grave danger and that the fight against "czarism" was a righteous one. They participated in the nationalist enthusiasm as soldiers, officers, army chaplains, and, at home, as social workers and volunteers. The war also seemed to offer them the opportunity to feel that they belonged; they seemed to be part of a nation under siege, working together with other Germans for a common cause. Moreover, their labor might also convince the most obdurate anti-Semite of their honesty and generosity. In fact, Jews tended to compare their situation to that of outcast Germany, sometimes likening Germany to the Jewish people as a victim of slander.[128] Pappenheim suggested that Jews, like Germans, knew the feeling of not belonging: "unloved because of our efficiency, our adaptability, a certain prosperity, a certain particular culture."[129]

Jewish feminists hoped to impress anti-feminists as well as anti-Semites. Sidonie Werner, on the board of the League of Jewish Women and head of its Hamburg local, suggested that while men served at the front, women performed social home-front service (*soziale Innendienst*) and argued that when the war came to an end, "we women will have helped in the victory."[130] (The reverse of this statement, that the war would be lost and that women and Jews would be blamed, did not occur to her.) One of the more widely read Jewish newspapers commented: "In the history of this war, the labors of love . . . of Jewish women will be entered in gold letters."[131] More practically, Rahel Straus, one of the leaders of the League of Jewish Women in Munich, noted the group's indebtedness to the women's movement, which had provided members with experience in organizing, fund raising, training personnel, and setting up such institutions as employment bureaus.[132]

Jewish Organizations Join In

Jewish women's organizations, like their German counterparts and often in conjunction with them, geared up for greater exertions than ever before. For the most part, specifically Jewish social work transformed itself into German war relief. Jewish women's groups cooperated on the local and national level with other women's groups and government agencies.[133] Jewish associations, sometimes even the most traditional ones, established soup kitchens as well as kitchens for needy middle-class patrons (who paid a small amount). They expanded their services to mothers and children; initiated countless sewing and knitting groups to provide soldiers with warm clothing and women with jobs; set up *Schreibstuben*, offices where people could send letters or messages to the front, and information bureaus relating to the war effort; and provided volunteers to write for and read to hospitalized soldiers.[134] The Women's Association of Neuweid, for example, a tiny group of eight to fifteen charitable ladies, determined to meet more regularly for the duration of the war. In August 1914 they resolved to subsidize needy families whose men had enlisted in the army, to ask young women (probably their daughters) to work in the day-care center, and to join the National Women's Service.[135] They decided that knitting evenings could include some sociability "in these desolate times." True to their allegiance to *Bildung*, they agreed that, "besides letting the women entertain themselves in as lively and clever a manner as they can, something appropriate should be read aloud for intellectual stimulation." It seems they delivered monthly contributions of earmuffs and approximately fifty pairs of socks and pulse warmers to the Red Cross. Members knitted most items, but even schoolchildren, including boys, contributed hand-knit items.

The League of Jewish Women, with its extensive network and modern institutions, joined the National Women's Service, and its locals not only provided assistance but made their buildings and other facilities available to the war administration. In Berlin, the JFB local offered the rooms of its girls' club as office space to the National Women's Service (as well as to the War Relief Commission of the Berlin Jewish Community), and its members worked with the Service, frequently in leading positions.[136] The Berlin local—like many other JFB locals—collected money for war relief, participating in the Kriegsspende deutscher Frauendank. Members of the local remarked that Jewish women's cooperation "was not repulsed this time, or even just tolerated, but welcomed joyously by all."[137] Other Jewish women also experienced acceptance, even when working with aristocrats or the Empress.[138]

A few further examples will have to suffice to give a picture of Jewish women's wartime social service activities. In Frankfurt/Main the Society for Jewish Nurses (Verein für Jüdische Krankenpflegerinnen zu Frankfurt/Main) turned its own dormitory into an army infirmary.[139] In Stuttgart the Israelite Women's Association (Israelitscher Frauenverein) supported two such infirmaries, a relatively common occurrence in most cities.[140] It also set up a sewing circle for soldiers and refugees while continuing to care for the sick and pay respects to the dead. In Düsseldorf the Israelite Women's Association (Israelitscher Frauenverein) set up a "war kitchen" (*Kriegsküche*) to feed 120 people of all faiths daily.[141] In Breslau the JFB local worked closely with the National Women's Service and the Patriotic Women's Association, establishing sewing circles which employed over six hundred women of all faiths.[142] Reacting to the needs of children whose fathers had fallen in battle and whose mothers needed to work outside the home, the group also established a children's home (*Kleinkinderheim*).[143] Other groups set up day-care centers for the duration, as for example the Kriegskinderstube in Hamburg.[144] In Munich the JFB centralized and organized all sewing and knitting work, employing over five hundred women. They produced shirts, jackets, and mittens for soldiers as well as items for local stores.[145]

Finally, Jewish women's organizations also attempted to give aid to needy Jews, both those at home as well as those caught on the Eastern front, or refugees from that area.[146] In Breslau special day-care centers accepted Jewish children whose fathers had been killed in the war and whose mothers had to work outside the home.[147] In Berlin, women's groups established a home and club for refugee girls.[148] The National Women's Service donated funds to organize a kosher kitchen in Posen. Intended for Jewish soldiers and civilians, it was also open to all faiths. "Ladies from the best circles have joined in to serve the cause," a newspaper noted, mentioning the major's wife and the wives of army commanders.[149] Thus Jews could receive assistance as well as give it.

Volunteering as Individuals

Jewish women volunteered as individuals, joining local Red Cross, National Women's Service, or Jewish women's groups, or serving at the front.[150] At the front they functioned as nurses and helpers. Ostensibly, one Jewish woman even dressed as a man in order to fight.[151] At home they knitted countless pairs of socks and mittens for soldiers and volunteered in hospitals and infirmaries.[152] They set aside rooms in their homes for refugees from East Prussia[153] and interrupted their university studies to volunteer in "war kindergartens" (*Kriegskindergärten*). More enterprising—and far wealthier—women like Agathe Bleichröder established their own small business ventures. She organized a sewing circle, hired a director, acquired materials for free, and paid her employees. She devised this plan after first volunteering in a city counseling center.[154]

Jewish women also led citywide organizations. Margarethe Goldstein, the wife of a professor of philosophy in Darmstadt, codirected the city's Women's Wartime Aid. Among other things, she arranged for shipments to the front of essentials such as clothing and medical supplies; urged private citizens to send packages to soldiers (*Liebesgaben*); set up soup kitchens, employment services, and children's day-care centers and reading rooms; and wrote pamphlets educating the public to change its eating habits and reduce domestic consumption. Concentrating on families of soldiers, her group provided free meals for over 650 children a day; an afternoon children's center for children whose mothers worked; a summer "vacation colony" for these children; invitations for family dinners at the homes of wealthier citizens; and advice on how to deal with state and army bureaucracies. In a letter to a friend, in which she recounted the ceaseless work over the past twenty-one months, Goldstein described a staggering list of the activities of "several hundred" volunteers. Further, her letter exhibited a feeling of belonging, of pulling together in which there was no sense of Jewish isolation (something she might have shared with

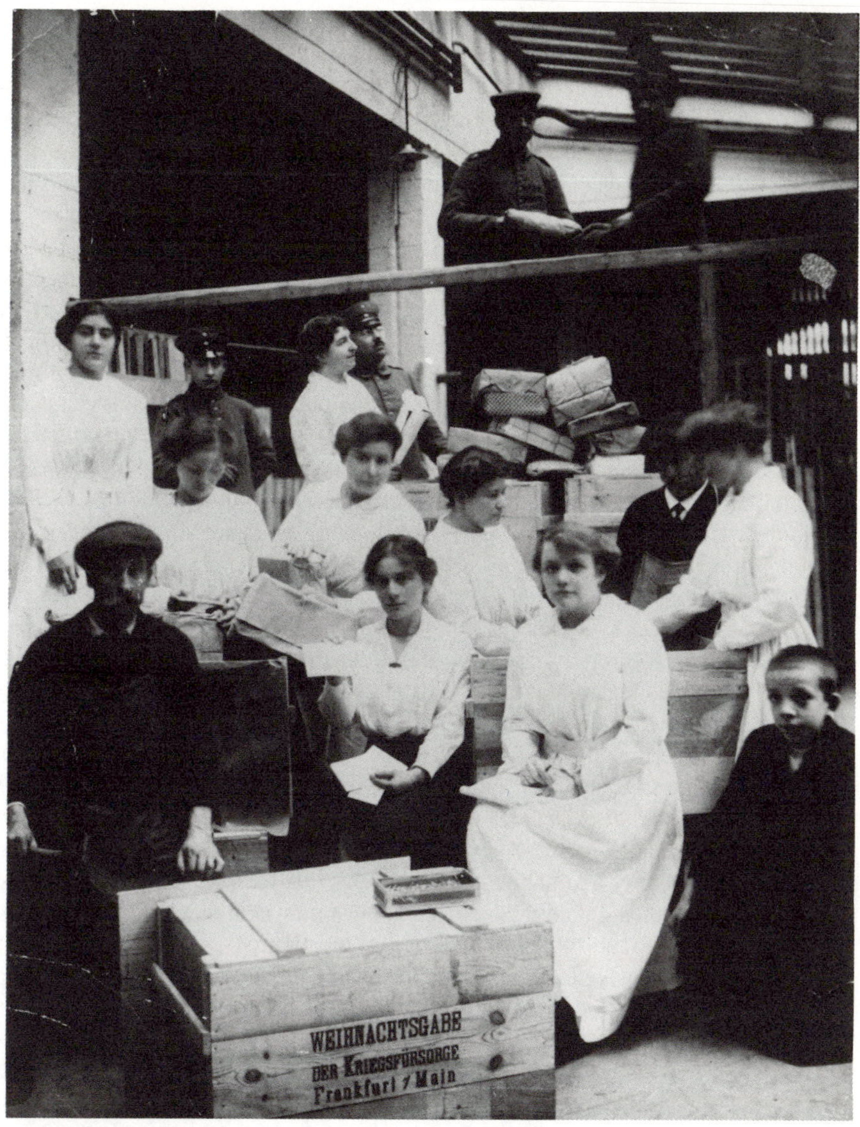

Jewish women participated in joint women's projects during World War I. Here Eva Sommer (second from left in foreground) helps send Christmas packages to the front. *Eva Ehrenburg Collection. Courtesy of the Leo Baeck Institute, New York.*

her Jewish friend): "in this difficult time, we are very . . . close to our sisters [*Mitschwestern*], because we all have our most loved one at the front. . . . Our home army [*Heimarmee*] works . . . with undiminished zeal, punctuality, love and perseverance. . . . We women, too, stand shoulder to shoulder, just like our men in the trenches, and feel the fate of our sisters as if it were our own."[155] This unity, a heady experience for those who had been on the outside, may not have had a permanent impact (on either side of the equation). After the war, Goldstein focused on activities within the League of Jewish Women and worked for the World Union for Progressive Judaism.

Despite escalating shortages of food, clothing, and heating fuel, the increasing severity of rationing and the necessity to "hamster" (to buy or barter on the black market; literally, to collect food like a hamster),[156] Jewish women continued their services and later exhibited great pride in their achievements. They saved the acknowledgments they received from the state (Red Cross certificates and medals; commemorative war medals; the King Ludwig Cross; Cross of Honor), handing them on to their children as part of their legacy.[157] Also, they described their war efforts in the memoirs they left their children, including feelings that "this difficult, mutual experience bound us ever more closely and more intimately" with other Germans.[158] As with Goldstein, it may be that part of this pride had to do with their acceptance in an all-German cause—a first experience for many of them.[159]

Besides their acceptance by other Germans, and of course their abundant patriotism, probably part of the impetus behind the frantic activity of individual women lay in their enforced passivity. The war was a men's war and women, if they were not nurses or doctors or munitions workers, had no place in it. They could send packages and knit warm clothing. They could put tiny flags on maps and hang big flags out their windows. This passivity and the desire to overcome it was only heightened when the fortunes of war began to turn against Germany and morale began to sag. One woman reported: "This passivity, this not-being-there, was even harder to endure, when I began to realize that I had to paste my patriotic feelings on myself." Volunteering at the railroad station canteen, where she watched countless trainloads of wounded and dead return to Germany, she became disillusioned with the war and worked all the harder not to let these feelings show.[160]

Women's unusual commitment was also the result of the simple absence of men. Asked to serve on city and national commissions that had ignored them in normal times, they performed with efficiency and enthusiasm. Ottilie Schönewald, the last president of the League of Jewish Women, told of being drafted to serve on an advisory commission for new public buildings for the province of Westphalia, as well as on an arbitration panel to solve disputes between domestics and their employers for the city of Bochum.[161] There she gained political and administrative experiences which would later make her an attractive candidate for political parties, Jewish (formerly entirely male-led) organizations, and the Jewish women's movement.

Younger women, too, achieved leadership positions that would have eluded them but for the dearth of men. Jewish youth organizations reported that "only girls were left on the board of executives" (in Elberfeld): that 80 percent of the members were at the front (in Aachen); and that some groups had become coed, because not enough men remained to form separate divisions.[162] The girls in these groups sent packages, letters, and Jewish newspapers to clubmembers and others at the front, helped wounded soldiers in their hometowns, volunteered to serve at railroad stations and infirmaries, and even participated in harvests. They accepted responsibility for "the spirit and mood that Germany needs on the home front." Still, they considered their leadership temporary: "The future of the youth organizations will be decided by those who will come back . . . we keep the house in order for them."[163] (One wonders, however, whether their experience of independence made them reluctant to abdicate all power after the war.)

A Flawed Symbiosis

This picture of cooperation, of a German-Jewish social symbiosis (as opposed to the way we usually think of it—an intellectual symbiosis), was a partial one. Even in their integration into war relief efforts, Jews remained relatively separate, their endeavors marred by the fear and reality of anti-Semitism. The reports and records of Jewish associations offer evidence as to Gentile-Jewish cooperation, especially on the organizational level. Obviously Jewish leaders of these various groups met and planned strategies with local and national members of the National Women's Service, the Patriotic Women's Association, and the Red Cross. However, it seems that most, not all, of this volunteer work was still pursued within the Jewish subgroup. Jewish women reached out to national groups in support of the war, provided services for all faiths, and hence made more contacts than previously with the non-Jewish world. Moreover, some joined nondenominational groups established specifically for the war effort. Also, those Jewish women who worked only in secular organizations worked all the more intensively with non-Jews in these years. Countless formal acknowledgments of their contributions to the national community notwithstanding, they did not achieve (should they have so desired) or retain many lasting friendships or social contacts with non-Jews as a result of their wartime teamwork.

Moreover, social contact occurred within a context in which anti-Semitism was a salient factor. With the outbreak of war, anti-Semitism briefly disappeared from public discussion.[164] At the front, despite some anti-Semitic incidents, many Jewish soldiers experienced their first camaraderie with non-Jews.[165] But as the war dragged on and civilian living conditions deteriorated sharply, a renewal of anti-Semitism took hold. The traditional right-wing enemies of the Jews as well as a wide spectrum of conservative interests blamed Jews for "internationalism," shirking, and war profiteering.[166] This prejudice never again abated.

Even in the general euphoria of frantic patriotism in the first year of the war, we can detect a certain pessimism about their own position among Jews. For example, in January 1915, the head of the JFB local in Hamburg (over 1,000 members) gave a lecture in which she warned Jewish women and girls to avoid any "excessive display." "Women and girls can hardly dress simply enough, their entire way of life has to become more modest."[167] The Central Verein, too, reminded parents (mothers, we can assume, since many fathers were no longer at home) to discipline and educate their children. In these times the Jewish child "must behave better than other children."[168] The JFB even suggested that its members use fewer matzos on Passover and that "the Seder be kept modest."[169] The attempt to encourage simplicity in dress reflected the defensive posture of those who hoped discretion in appearance and behavior would mitigate anti-Semitism, would avert any criticism that Jews were "doing well" during the war. It was also a reflex of Jews who had learned over the ages to be inconspicuous for fear of reprisals.

Three examples of individual, organizational, and governmental anti-Semitism are suggestive of the kinds of opposition Jews faced. On the personal level—in the midst of a knitting circle—one Jewish woman recalled her encounter with anti-Semitism. Although she hated knitting, she had volunteered to do it and had become friends with others in the group. To her dismay, one of her friends complained that "Jews avoided the draft." She jumped up to say that she knew many Jewish men at the front, "but a mistrust remained . . . and a certain insecurity in me vis-à-vis Christians."[170] Anti-Semitic organizations lost no time. As early as the autumn of 1914, they accused Jews of undermining the war effort. Some even pointed specifically to Jewish women, reviling them for allegedly preaching pacifism to German youth.[171] The government, too, inflamed anti-Semitic passions. In 1916 the Prussian War Ministry ordered a census of Jews in the armed forces (*Judenzählung*). Ostensibly to suppress rumors that Jews had evaded military service, the order gave anti-Semites cause for celebration. Jewish organizations, including the JFB, protested this singling out of Jews. Individuals, soldiers as well as their families, reacted with shock and anguish.[172] Although the military never published the results, the census cast a shadow over the rest of Jewish war relief efforts.[173] Looking back on her war relief work and her general enthusiasm from the vantage point of 1939, one Jewish woman remarked: "We were patriotic and blind . . . as only Germans could be."[174]

The history of women's social welfare endeavors raises two general issues. It underlines the ambiguity in the meaning of "public" and "private" spheres, affirming that these arenas are not separate, but seamless and often overlapping. Women acted in a "feminine" manner, caring for the sick, nurturing needy children, feeding the hungry, and in a "private" manner, too, maintaining female, domestic roles. They then insisted that their traditional household duties extended, with the blessings of religion, to local and then national benevolent duty, that is, to the public arena. Further, they impressed their views upon male family members and received financial and civic support in their efforts.[175] They introduced a continuity between the private and public: the "female values" of domesticity and religion provided a basis for the "social housekeeping" or "social motherhood" ideology of the feminist movement. Conversely, the home was not an isolated island of domesticity, immune from economic and social change. Women thought about and acted upon issues they confronted in the public realm, whether in the traditional manner of inviting a stranger to dinner or in the more modern mode of arranging household tasks and child care so as to make space for volunteer work.

The history of benevolence and social work suggests another area in which to study women's political involvement. Social welfare work was indeed women's political involvement, particularly in Germany. There, as we have seen, severe restrictions forbade political commitment by women, and women had to wait until the Weimar Republic for suffrage. Thus at the turn of the century, religious groups benefited from the increased ability of middle-class women to join "acceptable" organizations. This may explain the popularity and numerical increase of religious groups, and suggests a conflation of social work, religious motivation, and politics. William II understood this when, in 1910, he declared that women "should learn that their main duty . . . was not in the realm of club and organizational life, but in quiet work in the house and family."[176] With no ballot box at their disposal, women used benevolence, and later social work, to impress their views on male leadership. These tools provided the means to ameliorate conditions of poverty among working-class women, to enhance the career possibilities of working and middle-class women, to provide educational enrichment for all women, and to forge avenues in which to exercise public power. When, after the war, Jewish feminists insisted on the vote in the *Gemeinde* rather than an equal role for women in the synagogue or rituals, it was because that was the arena in which they had already achieved success and the one in which they perceived the action to be.

Conclusion

With his sharp insight and customary insensitivity to women, Karl Marx wrote: "one can measure social progress exactly by the social position of the fair sex (ugly ones included)."[1] Similarly, the situation of Jews has often been seen as a barometer of social harmony or progress. Both groups benefited from, and faced formidable obstacles to, the promises held out by bourgeois society. Jewish men gained civic equality and advanced economically. Women pushed successfully for educational and political reforms, taking advantage of the new white-collar careers slowly opening to them. But both women and Jews struggled to achieve equality and acceptance within narrow limits. Beyond the practical constraints imposed by domestic responsibilities, social and individual demands for "respectability"—for class- and hence gender-appropriate behavior—effectively controlled and limited women's aspirations. "The sexual division of labor was at the root of respectability, as important for social cohesion as the economic division of labor that G. W. F. Hegel and Karl Marx saw as essential for the existence of capitalism."[2] The threat of being labeled "unfeminine" or "unnatural"—a common tactic of those who opposed women's initiatives—made many women hesitate to demand radical changes in the gender system. Jews too strove for respectability, for entrée into the bourgeoisie. They too attempted to shun all forms of distinctive behavior, so as to avoid the "social disdain, moral condemnation and aesthetic disgust" heaped upon them by anti-Semites.[3] In a society unwilling or unable to expand and become inclusive, Jews and women waited on the outside.

Still, Jewish women gained from the progress of women and Jews. But in a society deeply split and anguished by the challenges of secularism and liberalism, they also endured the continued oppression of, as well as backlashes against, women and Jews. For example, as Jews they could live where they wanted, take pride in their husbands' or fathers' political rights, and benefit from their newly acquired wealth. As women they could join myriad societies opening to them, enter the university (mostly after 1908), and enlist in political groups (again, after 1908). However, as women they were denied civic equality with men, watched their property rights diminish upon marriage, faced sex-segregated job markets, while as Jews they confronted social distance or anti-Semitism in their relationships with other Germans. A focus on Jewish women highlights the contradictions and ambivalence of female and Jewish "progress" in the Imperial era.

Instead of focusing on the history of ideas, high culture, or the public politics of

Jewish-German relations, this study has concentrated on the politics of social relations, of the family, and of women's social and educational endeavors, and has accented the ways in which women negotiated and revised gender roles within the family and community. Moreover, it has defined culture broadly to include the tastes and manners of the bourgeoisie. In this way it has shown the intricate and intimate nature of Jewish cultural and social responses to modern German society.

For Jews, the home symbolized not only the transmission of class and ethnic identity but the constancy of gender roles as well. I have stressed the pivotal role of Jewish housewives and mothers in creating domesticity as the centerpiece of family life and as the hallmark of the Jewish bourgeoisie. Confined by ideology and custom to the private sphere, they venerated domesticity and used it to enhance their own and their families' status. However, their obvious dissatisfaction with total submersion in the cult of the home was evident in the eagerness with which they sought a variety of ways out. Using the traditional rhetoric of the self-sacrificing, devoted, and charitable Jewish woman—the "woman of valor"—Jewish women justified and disguised their activities in the broader world. Leisure-time activities, for example, required painstaking and conscientious adherence to the tasks of social representation and cultural mediation in order to promote the family's best interests. Nevertheless, such activities frequently fostered female networks and helped to expand women's spatial and social boundaries. Women reached out into public space and maintained female ties, increasingly experiencing their own agency and autonomy.

It was social work, in particular, which allowed Jewish women an arena in which to display their enterprising talents and assert their priorities. A rich and varied organizational life offered an opportunity to meet a broader circle of women, provided friendships beyond the formal "visits" forced upon the bourgeoise, and hence improved the quality of women's lives.[4] In taking on communal responsibilities, women derived a sense of gender consciousness and a personal sense of value and social usefulness. They developed considerable power in their own circles on their own behalf, ultimately emerging as public actors. Pushing past the boundaries that had restrained them, they challenged public assumptions about their position in society. Even among the most traditional groups who performed relief work requiring no new understanding of women's roles, women experienced limited autonomy and leadership within the community. Also, as many of these groups took on additional tasks, their members began to break out of old, dependent molds into newer ones of energy, competence, and efficiency. In popularizing woman-oriented projects and showing what women could do, these groups helped women to assert their own rights, both as individuals who needed meaningful (paid or unpaid) work outside the home and, later, as members of organizations which pursued feminist goals. Charitable activities, which merged with traditional notions of Jewish womanhood, liberated them from an exclusive preoccupation with the home and offered a path for developing gender consciousness. Indeed, as openly feminist an organization as the League of Jewish Women preferred to stress domestic imagery and its Jewish social service heritage. Religious zeal and social welfare were legitimate means of enhancing women's lives and public roles; protesting male authority was not.

A dialectical relationship existed between the public and the domestic, a division which was an expression not only of gender, but of class and religion as well. Changes in the public realm affected women's personal lives, just as private constraints influenced their public behavior. For example, as public religious observance waned, women preserved certain forms of religious practices in the family. In doing so, they secured their religious role and class status but also acquiesced in a hardening of the bourgeois definition of "women's place" at precisely the time when structural changes would open the public sphere to them. This did not stop those who had to work outside the home from doing so—although it placed a formidable obstacle in their path. It simply underlined the significance of the family to women who traversed both the private and public spheres.

This confluence of private and public shaped men's worlds, too. Although this book does not focus on the domestic as a central point for studying the history of men, as the recent work of Leonore Davidoff and Catherine Hall does for the English middle class, it underscores the importance of the domestic world in shaping middle-class economic affairs.[5] Men depended upon their wives for running the household, displaying rank, making personal contacts, producing heirs and personnel for the business, supplying money (dowries) for, and sometimes participating in, the enterprise. Thus women's role in their "husbands'" economic affairs highlights the convergences between public and domestic.

These tensions and intersections between public and private not only reveal their mutual dependency but emphasize the fact that "womanhood" itself was a contested site. Jewish women and men engaged in ongoing, often frustrating, renegotiations of gender divisions and power relations similar to those taking place in the broader German context. While some women submitted to the constraints of "womanhood," others succeeded in broadening its meaning and hence in giving themselves more room for maneuver. Consequently women often walked a precarious tightrope between change and custom, paving the way for their families, inching toward new definitions of their own "place," and absorbing many of the strains inherent in such acrobatics.

In presenting the sources of power and weakness in Jewish women's lives, I have stressed how their multiple identities interacted to shape their choices and attainments. In assessing women's paid work, for example, it was noted that their occupational profile mirrored that of their ethnic group: a result of traditional Jewish employment patterns and a reaction to anti-Semitism. Their job status, too, resulted from both the negative impact of anti-Semitism as well as the positive one of familial and communal support. The matter of job status highlighted the convergence of ethnicity with gender and class identities. Gender expectations gave most Jewish women little preparation for or support of higher ambitions. Over one quarter remained "family helpers," with about half encompassed within the low-status category of "workers and family helpers." In no way could women's status compare to that of men. They served as support staff for their fathers, uncles, and brothers. This gender discrepancy could be found among other Germans as well, even more so. That is, Jewish women's position vis-à-vis Jewish men was inferior, but it was privileged compared to Christian women. Thus Jewish women's experiences in the world of work, much as in other areas, was rife with contradictions. On the one hand, they benefited from their background by receiving better training and refuge in family firms, while on the other hand, anti-Semitic and sexist stereotypes limited their aspirations and achievements.

This study has emphasized the importance of Jewish women's role—and that of bourgeois women in general—in class formation and representation. Gender and class functioned together. Davidoff and Hall noted this for the English middle class as well, arguing that "consciousness of class always takes a gendered form." Even "the language of class formation was gendered."[6] Women's roles, even the definition of femininity, changed as the bourgeoisie attempted to establish itself. The "lady of leisure"—whether she hid her work or never lifted a finger—proclaimed her husband's social identity. Moreover, as the bourgeoisie attempted to enhance its position in society through consumption, "women, in their association with consumption, [were] often seen as creators as well as the bearers of status."[7] Their needs, desires, and pleasures came to define their families' positions in society.

Parallel with their consumption functions, and even more fundamental to their existence, were women's housekeeping and social skills. Men's status and the family economy depended upon them. A good *Haushalt* equaled a good "house" and a respectable family, one that evinced *Bildung* and *Besitz*. Even among lower-middle-class Jews, notions of respectability and correctness derived from the more affluent. This demonstrated the cohesiveness of middle-class ideology, the desire of even poorer Jews for integration into the bourgeoisie. It also accentuated the dilemma of housewives who had to accomplish this. Women mediated class values and class practice. In so doing, they played a leading—if unrecognized—role in the creation and maintenance of *Bildung*. Bourgeois women fulfilled their mission to create the family of *Bildung* at home, at "leisure," even in the paid employment they pursued.

In addition to class values, the German-Jewish bourgeoise had a special task to perform. She had to introduce German culture (both high and popular) to her children and also had to instruct them in the comportment, manners, and style of their German counterparts. Jews rapidly took on the clothing, education, cultural forms, and habits they saw around them in the group closest to their financial status (or aspirations) and in their (mostly) urban surroundings. Rural and poorer Jews, too, aspired to such behavior and customs. In fact—as alluded to in the discussion of the piano—Jews helped to introduce urban furniture and women's fashions as well as bourgeois habits into the small villages. On a day-to-day basis, it was the Jewish housewife and mother who carried the responsibility of shaping a family whose decent and correct behavior demonstrated that it was at one with other middle-class Germans. Ultimately, under her meticulous tutelage, a harmonious family life and polite, decorous children provided the tangible signs of Jewish acculturation to the German bourgeoisie.

Unlike their rapid and complete integration into the language and literature of Goethe, Jews' social integration remained incomplete. Emancipation shifted the "Jewish problem" from the civic to the social field. Over fifty years ago Jacob Katz wrote: "Jews have not assimilated into the German people, but into a certain layer of it, the newly emerged middle class."[8] More recently, he added that the entry of Jewry meant the "creation of a separate subgroup, which conformed to the German middle class in some of its characteristics."[9] A social history of German-Jewish women offers a more nuanced picture: Jews were more "Jewish" and less integrated than many have argued, but they were not separate either. Group solidarity need not be confused with segregation.

Although most Jewish women remained comfortably within familial and communal boundaries, these became increasingly permeable. Neighbors who exchanged Easter eggs and matzos, schoolmates who visited each other's homes, and friendships made at the university or office allowed Jews and Christians to penetrate the borders that separated them. Also, increasing numbers of intermarriages reflected not only a legal blending of the two groups, but expanded opportunities for meeting and befriending each other. Such mingling was even more apparent in voluntary organizations. Many Jewish women reached out to join feminist or secular women's groups. Moreover, some of the very same women who worked in Jewish organizations also participated in secular ones. Recall the rabbi's wife who arranged major civic and feminist projects for women and children, and the large number of Jewish women who belonged to or led secular women's organizations. Attracted by the universal appeal of the women's movement, they joined with other German activists to contribute new ideological and practical approaches to social work. Even when working in typically "Jewish" jobs in commerce and trade, Jewish women could be found in the German union of female white-collar workers in numbers well beyond their portion of the work force. Jewish women's activism in the Berlin soup kitchens, the Girls' and Women's Groups for Social Service Work, and unions, to recall only a few areas, indicated communication and cooperation between Jews and other Germans.

Yet limits existed. Jews "lived in a twilight of favor and misfortune and knew with certainty only that both success and failure were inextricably connected with the fact that they were Jews."[10] The "Jewish question" continued to haunt their social lives. Jewish efforts during World War I, for example, signified the extent to which Jews desired to "join in," as well as the boundaries set by other Germans. Jewish women's prominence in many German women's organizations testified to their integration, but the very fact that they frequently stood out or apart indicated an acknowledgment of "difference" from the Jewish and Christian sides alike. In spite of these limits, communication and involvement did exist between Jewish and other German women. It was this which gave hope to the vision of a German-Jewish symbiosis that would reach beyond a mere intellectual affinity.

Women's experience has also shed light on the processes by which Jews preserved or transformed traditional religious customs. Publicly flaunted Germanness and a drop in (essentially male) synagogue attendance need not be the only relevant criteria for judging the adherence of Jews to their community or faith. Focusing on women permits a more complicated picture than the usual "modernization" analysis of nineteenth-century German-Jewish history to emerge. It allows us to recognize the private and more traditional attitudes and institutions that persisted in dynamic tension with the forces of secularization. It underlines the tension between the lure of acculturation and the tenacity of tradition.

Throughout the book one could ask, "What was German about these women, what was Jewish about them?" The answer is clear: they were both. Their dress, furnishings, housewifery, speech, love of the German landscape and German classics, "leisured" behavior, adherence to bourgeois norms of respectability, and participation in the war effort, to name only a few examples, reveal the depth of their adaptation to German bourgeois society and culture.

Yet Jewish women tended to refract ideas, cultural trends, even new opportunities in characteristically Jewish prisms rather than simply mirroring them. Their cultivation of Jewish friends, their marriage choices, their residential concentration, and their rigorous adherence to the spirit and letter of *Bildung* were unique to them.[11] So were their early use of birth control, their education and job profiles, the extent of their voluntarism, perhaps even the interactions between husband and wife, parents and children. Jewish child-rearing practices appear more tolerant, patriarchal authority less formidable. Moreover, the closeness of the Jewish family stands out. This may have been, in part, a result of minority status and uncertainty, a situation in which kin were valued as economic and social resources. Anthropologists have noted that different cultures have distinctive ways of relating familial affection to the social organization of survival.[12] Such relationships "might be *more*, rather than less, tender or intense *because* relations are . . . critical to mutual survival."[13] Significantly, this closeness was not only compatible with German bourgeois values; Jewish identity, too, "was linked to family pride."[14]

As strict religious observance declined, Jews, like other bourgeois Germans, looked toward the family for celebrations and wider purpose to their lives. Family holidays, like the growth of national holidays in place of some religious ones, seem to have come about as secular substitutes for religious holidays in the German and Jewish bourgeoisies alike during this period. The family and national holidays provided meaning and centrality that had once been the domain of "religion." Public celebration in synagogue and church became private celebrations *en famille*. The family was a way of explaining a rapidly changing universe to themselves: it was a "reservoir of resistance to the complete dehumanization [*Entseelung*] of the world."[15] Through the mediation of women, the family itself increasingly provided a replacement for religion. For Jews, it also served as a mainstay of ethnic culture.

Even more was at stake for Jews. In the desire to maximize opportunities for their children, they relied on extended family networks for business and cultural reasons as well as for contacts to ensure the possibility of endogamy. Where relatives were unavailable, the Jewish community served as extended kin, providing the economic or social assistance necessary. It was as much cohesion within their own group as exclusion by the wider society which kept Jews from being completely absorbed by the mainstream. This becomes particularly clear when the focus shifts to women's lives.

Observing women in their private world and public, communal role suggests that there was no one-way street of emancipation leading to the dead end of assimilation. Ultimately, a gender analysis supports the hypothesis that "Jewishness," the interaction of Jews with each other and their sense of affiliation with the community, continued to thrive in the Imperial era even as Jews adapted to their modern surroundings. No longer residing in ghettos or attending synagogue with either the regularity or passion they once displayed, Jews created new forms of group cohesion. Such an analysis rejects the conclusion of those who have argued that "Judaism," defined as the values, beliefs, rituals, ceremonies, and behavior patterns of

Jews, declined.[16] Measured in synagogue attendance, this has some resonance. But values, beliefs, sentiments, and rituals cannot be measured so simply. Moreover, they evolved over time and blended with "Jewishness." Religion became a form of "ethnic encounter,"[17] in which ritual and ceremonies formerly attached to specific religious practice developed into family occasions and community events.

Thus Jewish consciousness was reinforced by educational, occupational, and demographic patterns. It was further augmented by women's dedication to familial and communal life as well as to familial forms of religion. In addition, women's extensive Jewish social service endeavors reflected an ardent commitment to, and determined identification with, the Jewish community. If one adds to these characteristics the solidarity evidenced and reinforced by ethnic politics, which have been described so well in other studies of Jewish communities and defense organizations,[18] a comprehensive portrait of German Jews' attachment to their origins and community emerges. Only a portrait which includes women's history can provide an all-encompassing definition of "Jewishness."

Jewishness—the modernized practice of their religion as well as a strong sense of solidarity with other Jews—defined the identity of the vast majority of German Jews more than has been recognized by historians and more than they themselves may have realized. As time went on, it was the Jewish family and the Jewish community, rather than the strict observance of traditional religion, which provided a vehicle for Jewish identity in Germany. Women played a crucial role in creating and maintaining these bonds. Keepers of tradition and bearers of modernity, they nurtured and recast Jewish customs in the home while shaping a modern secular Judaism in their public endeavors. They were central to the formation of a modern Jewish identity.

NOTES

Preface

1. See Renate Bridenthal, Claudia Koonz, and Susan Stuard, eds., *Becoming Visible: Women in European History*, 2nd ed. (Boston, 1987).

2. Claudia Koonz, *Mothers in the Fatherland: Women, the Family and Nazi Politics* (New York, 1987), and Rita Thalmann, *Etre femme sous le IIIe Reich* (Paris, 1982).

3. Monika Richarz's masterful collection of memoirs depicting German-Jewish social history is the outstanding exception to this statement. Her skilled choice of documents highlights the role of women as well as their viewpoints and has been invaluable to me. See *Jüdisches Leben in Deutschland*, vol. 2, *Selbstzeugnisse zur Sozialgeschichte im Kaiserreich* (Stuttgart, 1979).

4. For examples, see Charlotte Baum, Paula Hyman, and Sonya Michel, *The Jewish Woman in America* (New York, 1976); Elizabeth Ewen, *Immigrant Women in the Land of Dollars: Life and Culture on the Lower East Side, 1890–1925* (New York, 1985). A recent exception to this statement is Deborah Hertz, *Jewish High Society in Old Regime Berlin* (New Haven, Conn., 1988). See also Judith Baskin, ed., *Jewish Women in Historical Perspective* (Detroit, Mich., forthcoming).

5. See Bonnie G. Smith, *Ladies of the Leisure Class: The Bourgeoises of Northern France in the Nineteenth Century*, (Princeton, N.J., 1981); Joan Burstyn, *Victorian Education and the Ideal of Womanhood* (London, 1980); Ute Frevert, ed., *Bürgerinnen und Bürger: Geschlechterverhältnisse im 19. Jahrhundert* (Göttingen, 1988); Mary Ryan, *Cradle of the Middle Class: The Family in Oneida County, New York, 1780–1865* (London and New York, 1981).

6. Jacob Toury, *Soziale und Politische Geschichte der Juden in Deutschland, 1848–1871* (Düsseldorf, 1977), p. 114. The statistics are for 1871–74.

7. With some significant exceptions—Hansjoachim Henning, Rolf Engelsing, and the Bielefeld Center for Interdisciplinary Study—most scholars of Germany have concentrated on working-class social history in the Imperial era. See Hansjoachim Henning, *Das westdeutsche Bürgertum in der Epoche der Hochindustrialisierung, 1860–1914: Soziales Verhalten und Soziale Strukturen*, vol. 1, *Das Bildungsbürgertum in den Preussischen Westprovinzen* (Wiesbaden, 1972); Rolf Engelsing, *Zur Sozialgeschichte deutscher Mittel- und Unterschichten* (Göttingen, 1973); Jürgen Kocka, ed., *Bürger und Bürgerlichkeit im 19. Jahrhundert* (Göttingen, 1987); J. Kocka, ed., *Das Bürgertum im 19. Jahrhundert: Deutschland im europäischen Vergleich* (Munich, 1988); and Frevert, ed., *Bürgerinnen und Bürger*. The last three volumes are the results of a research program entitled "Bürger, Bürgerlichkeit und Bürgerliche Gesellschaft. Das 19. Jahrhundert im Europäischen Vergleich," sponsored by the Center for Interdisciplinary Research under the directorship of Jürgen Kocka at the University of Bielefeld. Peter Gay's massive study of the European bourgeoisie is essential reading for its general insights as well as its specific reflections on the German bourgeoisie: *The Bourgeois Experience: Victoria to Freud*, vol. 1, *Education of the Senses* (New York, 1984), and vol. 2, *The Tender Passion* (New York, 1986). See also Eric Hobsbawm, *The Age of Empire* (New York, 1988).

8. Up to the end of the 1870s, Jewish voters supported the National Liberals. After 1890 Jewish voters tended to support progressive parties. By the last years of the Empire, about

two-thirds of Jewish voters supported the Progressive Party, while half of the remainder supported the Social Democratic Party. Ernest Hamburger and Peter Pulzer, "Jews as Voters in the Weimar Republic," *Leo Baeck Institute Year Book*, 1985, p. 4.

9. Toni Cassirer, "Aus meinem Leben mit Ernst Cassirer," memoirs, Leo Baeck Institute, New York (hereafter LBI), p. iii.

10. Henriette Hirsch, "Erinnerungen an meine Jugend," memoirs, LBI, p. 1.

11. This is clearly an area for further research, one that could supplement recent works on the history of these immigrant groups and on working-class women's history. See Jack Wertheimer, *Unwelcome Strangers: East European Jews in Imperial Germany* (New York, 1987); Steven Aschheim, *Brothers and Strangers: The East European Jew in German and German-Jewish Consciousness, 1800–1923* (Madison, Wis., 1982); and Trude Maurer, *Ostjuden in Deutschland* (Hamburg, 1987). For working-class women's history, see R. Beier, *Frauenarbeit und Frauenalltag im deutschen Kaiserreich: Heimarbeiterinnen in der Berliner Bekleidungsindustrie, 1880–1911* (Frankfurt/Main, 1983).

12. In 1910 the Zionist movement in Germany counted only 6,800 members. Michael Meyer, *Response to Modernity: A History of the Reform Movement in Judaism* (New York, 1988), p. 210. See Jehuda Reinharz, *Fatherland or Promised Land: The Dilemma of the German Jew, 1893–1914* (Ann Arbor, Mich., 1975); Stephen M. Poppel, *Zionism in Germany, 1897–1933: The Shaping of a Jewish Identity* (Philadelphia, 1977). The Women's Zionist Organization of America, or Hadassah, was founded three years later, in 1912, by Henriette Szold.

13. Because I found so little material, and because Zionism and Orthodoxy were movements supported by only a small minority of German Jews, these movements remain areas for future study.

Introduction

1. Henriette Hirsch (born 1884, Berlin), "Erinnerungen an meine Jugend," memoirs, Leo Baeck Institute, New York (hereafter LBI).

2. Betty Lipton, "At Home in Berlin," in *Community of Fate: Memoirs of German Jews in Melbourne*, ed. John Foster (Sydney, 1986), pp. 23–25.

3. Gertrud Catts, "A Portable Career," ibid., pp. 36–37.

4. In fact, I will argue in chapter 2 that they felt less conflict between being Germans and Jews than did Jewish men.

5. The intellectual and political history of German Jewry has been documented in the work of the Leo Baeck Institute (its *Bulletin*, *Yearbook*, and monograph series) as well as by many independent scholars.

6. Gayle Rubin, "The Traffic in Women: Notes on the 'Political Economy' of Sex," in *Toward an Anthropology of Women*, ed. Rayna R. Reiter (New York, 1975), p. 179.

7. Peter Gay has written, "Whether *grand* or *petit*, old or new, bourgeois tried to live decently, educate their children, decorate their houses, and leave property." *The Bourgeois Experience*, vol. 1, *Education of the Senses* (New York, 1984), p. 24.

8. A similar pattern can be seen in other countries among the middle classes. Leonore Davidoff and Catherine Hall, *Family Fortunes: Men and Women of the English Middle Class, 1780–1850* (London, 1987).

9. The constitution of the North German League annulled all discriminatory residence laws in 1867. Two years later, religious discrimination was forbidden. Also, the Imperial Citizenship Law of 1871 eliminated special demands regarding Jewish applications.

10. Reinhard Rürup, "Emanzipation und Krise: Zur Geschichte der 'Judenfrage' in Deutschland vor 1890," in *Juden im Wilhelminischen Deutschland, 1890–1914*, ed. Werner E. Mosse (Tübingen, 1976), p. 21.

11. There is no complete social history of Jews in Imperial Germany. Monika Richarz's introduction to the memoirs she edited is comprehensive and imaginative; to date it is the best source we have. See *Jüdisches Leben in Deutschland*, vol. 2, *Selbstzeugnisse zur Sozialgeschichte im Kaiserreich* (Stuttgart, 1979), pp. 7–64. Avraham Barkai reminds us that between 1871 and 1910 about 50,000 to 60,000 Jews emigrated from Germany and suggests that emigration had significant demographic repercussions. "German-Jewish Migration in the Nineteenth Century, 1830–1910," in *Leo Baeck Institute Year Book* (hereafter *LBIYB*), 1985, pp. 309–10.

12. Jack Wertheimer, *Unwelcome Strangers: East European Jews in Imperial Germany* (New York, 1987), p. 83. This comprehensive study traces the absorption of Eastern Jews into Germany, focusing on government policy and on the interrelationships between German Jews and Eastern Jews. For a detailed social history, see Trude Maurer, *Ostjuden in Deutschland* (Hamburg, 1987).

13. Usiel O. Schmelz, "Die demographische Entwicklung der Juden in Deutschland von der Mitte des 19. Jahrhunderts bis 1933," in *Zeitschrift für Bevölkerungswissenschaft* 1 (1982): 42–43. See chapter 3, n. 109, for details comparing Jewish women's marriage patterns to other German women and to Jewish men.

14. Schmelz, "Die demographische Entwicklung," p. 44.

15. Ibid., p. 55.

16. Richarz, *Jüdisches Leben*, vol. 2, p. 16. This figure does not include the increasing number of Jews who left their faith but chose not to convert to another religion.

17. Ibid., p. 17. Schmelz argues that, given a Jewish population under 1% of the total population, the intermarriage rate indicates a tendency toward *en*dogamy. If marriage partners had been chosen based on pure coincidence, the intermarriage rate would have been far higher. Schmelz, "Die demographische Entwicklung," p. 53.

18. "Bürgerlich gesichert," according to Jacob Toury, *Soziale und politische Geschichte der Juden in Deutschland, 1847–1871* (Düsseldorf, 1977), pp. 100–114.

19. Avraham Barkai, *Jüdische Minderheit und Industrialisierung* (Tübingen, 1988), p. 5.

20. This was particularly the case in medicine and law. Papers by Konrad H. Jarausch, "Jewish Lawyers in Germany, 1848–1938: The Breakdown of a Professional Symbiosis," and Geoffrey Cocks, "Anti-Semitism, National Socialism, and the Medical Profession in Germany," delivered at the American Historical Association meeting in San Francisco in December 1989 (forthcoming in *LBIYB*, 1991).

21. Barkai, *Jüdische Minderheit*, pp. 20–21.

22. Barkai, "German-Jewish Migration," p. 301.

23. In contrast, non-Jewish migration consisted of young, single farmhands seeking work in industry, mining, or domestic service. Ibid., p. 304.

24. For a comprehensive definition and discussion of the German bourgeoisie, or *Bürgertum*, see Jürgen Kocka, "Bürgertum und bürgerliche Gesellschaft im 19. Jahrhundert: Europäische Entwicklungen und deutsche Eigenarten," in *Bürgertum im 19. Jahrhundert: Deutschland im europäischen Vergleich*, ed. Jürgen Kocka and Ute Frevert (Munich, 1988), pp. 11–78. Kocka defines the attributes of the *class* as well as those of bourgeois *culture* and *society*. He notes that only about 5–15% of German society could be called bourgeois in the nineteenth century, and that this group consisted of the academically educated (the core of the bourgeoisie, or *Bildungsbürger*, only about 3–4% of the entire population) as well as business people. Some were independent, others were civil servants or upper-level employees. As

much as they differed, they shared certain values and politics in their attempt to carve out a place for themselves distinct from the nobility and the working classes. See also Jürgen Kocka, "Bürgertum und Bürgerlichkeit als Probleme der deutschen Geschichte vom späten 18. zum frühen 20. Jahrhundert," in *Bürger und Bürgerlichkeit im 19. Jahrhundert*, ed. Jürgen Kocka (Göttingen, 1987), pp. 21–63.

25. Owing to severe restrictions, only 3% of Jews were doctors or lawyers before 1871. See Monika Richarz, *Jüdisches Leben in Deutschland*, vol. 1, *Selbstzeugnisse zur Sozialgeschichte, 1780–1871* (Tübingen, 1976), p. 41. Jewish economic development was uneven. Most Prussian Jews had achieved middle-class incomes by 1848, but progress was slower in the southern and southwestern rural areas.

26. Zygmunt Bauman, *Modernity and the Holocaust* (Ithaca, N.Y., 1989), p. 49.

27. "When Thomas Mann, as late as 1918, praised the *Bürger* and denigrated the bourgeois, he was working in a rhetorical tradition at least a century old." Gay, *Bourgeois Experience*, vol. 1, p. 18.

28. George L. Mosse, *German Jews Beyond Judaism* (Bloomington, Ind., 1985), p. 11. See also George Mosse, "German Jews and Liberalism in Retrospect: Introduction to Year Book XXXII," *LBIYB*, 1987, p. xiv.

29. Mosse, *German Jews*, p. 69.

30. I prefer the term *Bildung*, used by German Jews to describe themselves or their aspirations, to the term "cultivation." Although *Bildung* can be translated as "cultivation," the German term ties in more closely to the German Enlightenment tradition held in such high regard by Jews. Nevertheless, Peter Gay's contention that "the claim to cultivation is probably more characteristic of more bourgeois than any other of their cultural habits," and that this claim "is a piquant and useful ingredient in a possible definition of the bourgeoisie," certainly applies to Jews. *The Bourgeois Experience*, vol. 1, pp. 28–29.

31. Fritz Ringer emphasized the importance of "evaluative insight" (*Weltanschauung*) and the experience with texts in his paper "The German Professionals and Their Jewish Colleagues: Academics in Germany," delivered at the American Historical Association meeting in San Francisco in December 1989 (forthcoming in *LBIYB*, 1991).

32. David Sorkin, "The Genesis of the Ideology of Emancipation, 1806–1840," *LBIYB*, 1987, p. 19.

33. David Sorkin, *The Transformation of German Jewry, 1780–1840* (Oxford and New York, 1987), p. 15. Sorkin analyzes the Jewish ideology of emancipation and the subculture that propounded it.

34. Mosse, "German Jews and Liberalism," p. xiii. Humboldt was the chief of Prussian education in the years 1809–10. A close friend of Schiller and Goethe, he aimed at making the humanism of Weimar the basis of the educational system.

35. Ute Frevert, "Bürgerliche Meisterdenker und das Geschlechterverhältnis: Konzepte, Erfahrungen, Visionen an der Wende vom 18. zum 19. Jahrhundert," in *Bürgerinnen und Bürger: Geschlechterverhältnisse im 19. Jahrhundert*, ed. Ute Frevert (Göttingen, 1988). p. 29.

36. Ringer, "German Professionals."

37. Peter Gay described Mabel Loomis's attitudes, particularly "because money was not abundant" in her home, as insistent on these characteristics. *Bourgeois Experience*, vol. 1, p. 74. For German examples, see Wilhelm H. Riehl, *Die Naturgeschichte des Volkes als Grundlage einer deutschen Social-Politik*, vol. 3, *Die Familie,* (9th ed. Stuttgart, 1882).

38. George L. Mosse, "The Secularization of Jewish Theology," in *Masses and Man: Nationalist and Fascist Perceptions of Reality*, ed. George L. Mosse (New York, 1980), p. 258.

39. Mosse, *German Jews*, p. 4.

40. On the importance of dropping Yiddish in favor of the German language in the pursuit of *Bildung*, see Shulamit Volkov, "Die Verbürgerlichung der Juden in Deutschland: Eigenart und Paradigma," in *Bürgertum im 19. Jahrhundert*, ed. Jürgen Kocka, pp. 351–56.

41. Mosse, *German Jews*, p. 4.

42. Ibid., p. 11.

43. Gershom Scholem, "On the Social Psychology of the Jews in Germany," in *Jews and Germans from 1860 to 1933: The Problematic Symbiosis*, ed. David Bronsen (Heidelberg, 1979), p. 17.

44. Charlotte Wolf, *Hindsight: An Autobiography* (London, 1980), p. 6.

45. Michael Meyer, *Response to Modernity: A History of the Reform Movement in Judaism* (New York and Oxford, 1988), p. 187.

46. Michael R. Marrus, "European Jewry and the Politics of Assimilation: Assessment and Reassessment," *Journal of Modern History* 49 (1977): 89–109.

47. Shulamit Volkov has cautioned against a simple, linear formulation of Jewish assimilation, pointing to a new self-understanding among Jews in the 1890s and to the family as a locus for both integration and the maintenance of group identity. While I agree with her critique of assimilation, I find "the family" too vague a concept and prefer, where possible, to find the male and female actors in the family in order more clearly to understand motivation and observe behavior. See Volkov, "Erfolgreiche Assimilation oder Erfolg und Assimilation: Die deutsch-jüdische Familie im Kaiserreich," in *Wissenschaftskolleg zu Berlin: Jahrbuch* (Berlin, 1982/1983), pp. 373–77.

48. This unconscious Jewish feeling may have had nothing to do with religion, although Jews preferred to "emphasize the exclusively religious nature of the differences with non-Jews": Scholem, "On the Social Psychology," p. 20.

49. This definition was used by Larry D. Nachman in "The Question of the Jews: A Study in Culture," in *Salmagundi*, no. 44/45 (Spring/Summer 1979), pp. 166–81.

50. Marion Berghahn, *German-Jewish Refugees in England* (London, 1984), p. 45.

51. Ibid., pp. 36, 44.

52. Ibid., p. 12, referring to Nathan Glazer and Daniel Patrick Moynihan, eds., *Ethnicity: Theory and Experience* (Cambridge, Mass., 1975), pp. 3ff.

53. Uriel Tal, *Christians and Jews in Germany: Religion, Politics, and Ideology in the Second Reich, 1870–1914* (Ithaca, N.Y., 1975), p. 290.

54. I have found the work of Milton Gordon helpful in delineating the processes of acculturation and assimilation. His formulation of "ethclass" has been very useful. He suggests that people share a sense of "peoplehood" and behavioral similarities with others of their same ethnic group and same social class. (With a person of the same class but different ethnic group, one shares behavioral similarities; with a person of the same ethnic group but different class, one shares historical identification.) Only with a member of the same "ethclass" does one share a sense of "consciousness of kind." Milton Gordon, *Assimilation in American Life: The Role of Race, Religion and National Origins* (New York, 1964).

55. See Calvin Goldscheider and Alan S. Zuckerman, *The Transformation of the Jews* (Chicago, 1984), pp. 187, 235, where they stress structural forces as crucial to survival (rather than shared values or Jewish desires to survive as a group).

56. After 1876 Jews could formally leave the *Gemeinde*, but few did. Peter Honigmann, *Die Austritte aus der jüdischen Gemeinde Berlin, 1873–1941* (Frankfurt/Main, Bern, New York, 1988); Robert Liberles, *Religious Conflict in Social Context: The Resurgence of Orthodox Judaism in Frankfurt am Main, 1838–1877* (Westport, Conn., 1985), chapters 6 and 7.

57. Meyer, *Response to Modernity*.

58. Peter Gay, *Freud, Jews and Other Germans: Masters and Victims in Modernist Culture* (New York, 1978), p. 19.

59. "From Hitler to Bismarck: 'Third Reich' and Kaiserreich in Recent Historiography," in *Rethinking German History: Nineteenth-Century Germany and the Origins of the Third Reich*, by Richard Evans, (London, 1987), pp. 55–93.

60. See Richard Levy, *The Downfall of Anti-Semitic Parties in Imperial Germany* (New Haven, Conn., 1975); Shulamit Volkov, *The Rise of Popular Anti-Modernism in Germany: The Urban Master Artisans, 1873–1896* (Princeton, N.J., 1978); Jacob Katz, *From Prejudice to Destruction: Anti-Semitism, 1700–1933* (Cambridge, Mass., 1980); Peter J. G. Pulzer, *The Rise of Political Anti-Semitism in Germany and Austria* (New York and London, 1964; rev. ed., Cambridge, Mass., 1988); Paul Massing, *Rehearsal for Destruction* (New York, 1949); George Mosse, *The Crisis of German Ideology: Intellectual Origins of the Third Reich* (New York, 1964).

61. Shulamit Volkov has done this for the master artisans; see *The Rise of Popular Antimodernism in Germany.* In the future, I would like to see analyses of Jewish-Christian interactions as well as of the thoughts and beliefs of nonpolitical groups, women, and families.

62. In 1871 about 70% of German Jewry lived in Protestant Prussia, and 24% in the more Catholic southern and southwestern states such as Bavaria and Baden. Parts of the Rhineland and Württemberg were also Catholic.

63. Herta Natorff, memoirs, LBI, p. 2.

64. Julie Braun Vogelstein related a peculiar but not atypical incident. She met an attractive woman on her vacation and hoped to pursue their friendship in the future. "We had grown fond of each other, understood each other in artistic as well as simple human terms. She was going back home. Now the time seemed right to me to tell her that I was a Jew. . . . She was taken aback for a moment." Their friendship continued. *Was niemals stirbt: Gestalten und Erinnerungen* (Stuttgart, 1966), p. 227.

65. Peter Pulzer, "Why Was There a Jewish Question in Imperial Germany?" *LBIYB*, 1980, pp. 133–46. (This quote is from p. 142.)

66. Pulzer, "Jewish Question," pp. 138, 142.

67. Wertheimer, *Unwelcome*, pp. 31–34, 60–63.

68. The Anti-Semitic Petition of 1882 distributed to government and business leaders had 225,000 signatures and demanded that Bismarck restrict Jewish immigration, maintain a "Christian" character in the schools, prevent Jews from holding administrative offices, and renew a religious census.

69. The Antisemitische Volkspartei.

70. For German-Jewish negative attitudes about Eastern European Jews, see Steven Aschheim, *Brothers and Strangers: The East European Jew in German and German-Jewish Consciousness, 1800–1923* (Madison, Wis., 1982).

71. Wertheimer, *Unwelcome*, p. 31.

72. See Ismar Schorsch, *Jewish Reactions to German Anti-Semitism, 1870–1914* (New York, 1972).

73. They are also often not the same for lower-class men as for the elites. Joan Kelly challenged assessments of historical epochs based on only half a population. See her article "Did Women Have a Renaissance?" in *Becoming Visible: Women in European History*, ed. Renate Bridenthal and Claudia Koonz (Boston, 1987), pp. 175–202.

74. For urban, middle-class Americans in the 1880s, the family ("little islands of propriety"—Theodore Dreiser) also became the social focus of men's lives after work. See Richard Sennett, *Families Against the City* (Cambridge, Mass., 1970), pp. 47–53. For Germany, see Rolf Engelsing, *Zur Sozialgeschichte deutscher Mittel- und Unterschichten* (Göttingen, 1973), pp. 225–61.

75. Riehl, *Die Familie*, p. 80.

76. Karin Hausen, "Family and Role Division: The Polarisation of Sexual Stereotypes in the Nineteenth Century—An Aspect of the Dissociation of Work and Family Life," in *The German Family*, ed. Richard J. Evans and W. R. Lee (London, 1981), p. 66.

77. Ute Frevert, *Women in German History: From Bourgeois Emancipation to Sexual Liberation* (Oxford, Hamburg, New York, 1989), pp. 108–9.

78. Ibid., p. 136.

79. Ibid., pp.118–20.

80. Ibid., p. 114.

81. In Prussia the *Vereinsgesetz* forbade women and minors any engagement in politics. Passed in 1851, it was finally dropped in 1908. Similar laws in Bavaria and Saxony were even stricter.

82. See my study of the Jüdischer Frauenbund for further details: *The Jewish Feminist Movement in Germany: The Campaigns of the Jüdischer Frauenbund, 1904–1938* (Westport, Conn., 1979).

83. For a general background, see Richard Evans, *The Feminist Movement in Germany, 1894–1933* (London, 1976); John Fout, ed., *German Women in the Nineteenth Century* (New York, 1984); Ute Gerhard, *Verhältnisse und Verhinderungen: Frauenarbeit, Familie und Rechte der Frauen im 19. Jahrhundert* (Frankfurt/Main, 1978); Barbara Greven-Aschoff, *Die bürgerliche Frauenbewegung in Deutschland, 1894–1933* (Göttingen, 1981); Ruth-Ellen Joeres and Mary Jo Maynes, eds., *German Women in the Eighteenth and Nineteenth Centuries* (Bloomington, Ind., 1986); and Ute Frevert, *Women*.

84. Joan Scott, *Gender and the Politics of History* (New York, 1988), pp. 20–21.

85. Joan Kelly, "The Doubled Vision of Feminist Theory," *Feminist Studies* 5: 1 (Spring 1979): 216–27; Marilyn Boxer and Jean Quataert, *Connecting Spheres: Women in the Western World* (New York, 1987).

86. Scott, *Gender*, p. 24.

87. Ute Frevert notes this in her introduction to *Bürgerinnen und Bürger*, pp. 14–15.

88. Scott, *Gender*, pp. 20–21. Scott has cautioned that the history of women is recovered at the risk of isolating them again, and so reproducing the very divisions that women's historians have questioned.

Chapter 1

1. Stefan Zweig, *Welt von Gestern: Erinnerungen* (Frankfurt/Main, 1970), p. 13.

2. Henriette Hirsch (born 1884, Berlin), memoirs, LBI, p. 9.

3. Sophie Diamant (born 1879, Mainz), memoirs, LBI, p. 5.

4. Semi Moore (born ca. 1882, Randegg), "The History of the Family Moos," memoirs, LBI, p. 46.

5. Esther Calvary (born ca. 1855, Eisenstadt, Austria), memoirs, LBI, p. 1.

6. Sibylle Meyer, *Das Theater mit der Hausarbeit: Bürgerliche Repräsentation in der Familie der wilhelminischen Zeit* (Frankfurt/Main, 1982).

7. Edmund Hadra (describing his mother, who married in 1853 at the age of seventeen), memoirs, LBI, p. 89.

8. Urban Orthodox women faced similar situations. Like age and geography, religion made an important difference in women's lives. The wealthy urban Orthodox woman could differ substantially from her more secular Jewish neighbors, similar incomes notwithstanding.

9. Memoirs of "Tante Emma" (born ca. 1860, Poemsen), in Max Gruenewald collection, LBI.

10. Edmond Uhry (born 1874, Ingwiller, Alsace), memoirs, LBI, p. 46.

11. Ibid., p. 86.

12. Ibid., p. 21.

13. Ibid., p. 21.

14. Jacob Picard, "Childhood in the Village," *LBIYB*, 1959, pp. 273–93 (1880s).

15. Monika Richarz, ed., *Jüdisches Leben in Deutschland*, vol. 2, *Selbstzeugnisse zur Sozialgeschichte im Kaiserreich* (Stuttgart, 1979), pp. 158–59.

16. Conrad Rosenstein (born 1910, Berlin), memoirs, LBI, p. 19.

17. Richarz, *Jüdisches Leben*, vol. 2, p. 171.

18. Ibid., pp. 243–45. See chapter 2 for details on kosher kitchens.

19. Margarete Freudenthal uses such account books in her study *Gestaltwandel der städtischen, bürgerlichen und proletarischen Hauswirtschaft unter besonderer Berücksichtigung des Typenwandels von Frau und Familie* (Würzburg, 1934). Almanacs and pocket calendars for women included attractive pictures, texts, and formulas for maintaining a household budget. See Karin Hausen, "'. . . eine Ulme fur das schwanke Efeu': Ehepaare im deutschen Bildungsbürgertum," in *Bürgerinnen und Bürger*, ed. Ute Frevert (Göttingen, 1988), p. 104.

20. Freudenthal, *Gestaltwandel*, p. 38.

21. Diamant, memoirs, p. 5.

22. Jonas Frykman and Orvar Löfgren, *Culture Builders: A Historical Anthropology of Middle-Class Life* (New Brunswick, N.J., 1987), pp. 30–31.

23. *Deutsche Hausfrauenzeitung*, January 10, 1886, p. 1.

24. Hansjoachim Henning, *Das westdeutsche Bürgertum in der Epoche der Hochindustrialisierung, 1860–1914: Soziales Verhalten und Soziale Strukturen*, vol. 1, *Das Bildungsbürgertum in den Preussischen Westprovinzen* (Wiesbaden, 1972), p. 344.

25. W. A. Riehl, *Die Naturgeschichte des Volkes als Grundlage einer deutschen Social-Politik*, vol. 3, *Die Familie*, 9th ed. (Stuttgart, 1882), p. 80.

26. Gerda Lerner, *The Majority Finds Its Past: Placing Women in History* (New York, 1979), p. 132.

27. Anna Kronthal, *Posner Mürbekuchen: Jugend Erinnerungen einer Posnerin* (Munich, 1932), p. 10. That this was a general bourgeois phenomenon can be seen in a study of Sweden in the same era: Frykman, *Culture Builders*, p. 120.

28. L. v. Stein (1886), quoted by Jürgen Zinnecker in *Sozialgeschichte der Mädchenbildung* (Weinheim/Basel, 1973), pp. 116, 118.

29. Peter Gay, *The Bourgeois Experience*, vol. 1, *Education of the Senses* (New York, 1984), p. 17.

30. Utz Jeggle, *Judendörfer in Württemberg* (Tübingen, 1969), p. 165.

31. Ibid., p. 223. See also Beate Bechtold-Comforty, "Jüdische Frauen auf dem Dorf—zwischen Eigenständigkeit und Integration," *Sozialwissenschaftliche Informationen* 18:3 (September 1989): 160–62.

32. For anti-Semitic reactions, see Uwe Westphal, *Berliner Konfektion und Mode, 1836–1939: Die Zerstörung einer Tradition* (Berlin, 1986), pp. 24–27. Memoirs and interviews suggest that many Jewish women approached clothing fashion with a sense of understatement, since they believed that Germans saw fashion as something "foreign" and anti-Semites attacked fashion as something Jewish. Jeggle also pointed out the "understatement." In his interviews, John Foster noted the same regarding furniture (conversation with the author).

33. Hirsch, memoirs, pp. 35–36.

34. Ernst Herzfeld (born 1874, Grätz in Posen), memoirs, LBI, pp. 43, 49.

35. Jeggle, *Judendörfer*, pp. 220, 226.

36. Elfie Labsch-Benz, *Gemeinde Nonnenweier: Jüdisches Leben und Brauchtum in*

einer badischen Landgemeinde zu Beginn des 20. Jahrhundert (Baden/Württemberg, 1980), p. 30.

37. Urbanization occurred even in rural areas. See Alice Goldstein, "Urbanization in Baden, Germany: Focus on the Jews, 1825–1925," *Social Science History*, 801 (Winter 1984): 43–67.

38. Gay, *Bourgeois Experience*, vol. 1, p. 28.

39. Rosenstein, memoirs, p. 4.

40. Arendt, *The Origins of Totalitarianism* (Cleveland and New York, 1958), p. 61.

41. German housewives were similar to their Scandinavian counterparts, whose household manuals warned; "If a housewife lacks a sense of order she must work with all her might to attain it": Frykman, *Culture Builders*, p. 245.

42. Mrs. Sidgwick, *Home Life in Germany* (New York, 1912), pp. 113, 129, 136.

43. Jeggle, *Judendörfer*, p. 221. See also Moore, memoirs, p. 52.

44. Margarete Weinberg, *Die Hausfrauen der deutschen Vergangenheit und Gegenwart* (Mönchen Gladbach, 1920), pp. 43, 46.

45. Henning, *Bürgertum*, p. 248.

46. Barbara Beuys, *Familienleben in Deutschland* (Reinbek bei Hamburg, 1980), p. 441.

47. See Ute Gerhard, *Verhältnisse und Verhinderungen: Frauenarbeit, Familie und Rechte der Frauen im 19. Jahrhundert* (Frankfurt/Main, 1978), pp. 282–310.

48. *Schweizer Frauenheim*, May 25, 1895, pp. 291–92, in Eleanor Riemer and John Fout, eds., *European Women: A Documentary History, 1789–1945* (New York, 1980), p. 155.

49. Heidi Müller, *Dienstbare Geister: Leben und Arbeitswelt städtischer Dienstboten* (Berlin, 1981), p. 152.

50. Müller, *Dienstbare*, p. 153. "Blitzblank und rein,/Soll immer deine Küche sein."

51. See Müller, *Dienstbare*, p. 150, for a proposed schedule; also Gerhard, *Verhältnisse*, pp. 295–99.

52. Judith Hauptman, "Images of Women in the Talmud," in *Religion and Sexism*, ed. Rosemary Radford Ruether (New York, 1974), p. 187.

53. Mark Zborowski and Elizabeth Herzog, *Life Is with People: The Culture of the Shtetl* (New York, 1952), p. 292. For dietary and holiday rituals, see chapter 2. To be seen as a *baleboste*, or religiously observant and good housewife, was a compliment for Eastern European Jewish housewives: Tamar Somogyi, *Die Scheinen und die Prosten* (Berlin, 1982), p. 81.

54. Salomon Carlebach, *Ratgeber für das jüdische Haus: Ein Führer für Verlobung, Hochzeit und Eheleben* (Berlin, 1918), p. 8.

55. Müller, *Dienstbare*, picture, p. 215.

56. Nora Rosenthal (born 1892, Frankfurt/Main) "Opus One," memoirs, LBI, p. 11.

57. Moore, memoirs, p. 52 (1880s, 1890s).

58. *Illustriertes Unterhaltungsblatt* 3:5 (February 1, 1904): 37. German writers also stressed the connection between the housewife's consumer functions and orderliness and the national economy. See L. v. Stein, "Die Frau auf dem Gebiete der Nationaloekonomie," in Gerhard, *Verhältnisse*, pp. 311–24.

59. Frykman, *Culture Builders*, p. 166.

60. Steven Aschheim, *Brothers and Strangers: The East European Jew in German and German Jewish Consciousness, 1880–1923* (Madison, Wis., 1982), p. 60.

61. *Der jüdische Selbsthass* (1930), in Aschheim, *Brothers*, p. 109.

62. Paul Tachau, "My Memoirs," LBI, p. 275.

63. These attitudes toward garlic were expressed not only in interviews with women born

in Imperial Germany, but also among German Jews who grew up in the Weimar Republic. See for example Charles Hannam, *A Boy in Your Situation* (London, 1977), p. 58. Verifying a prejudice is a difficult business, but German-Jewish cookbooks proved useful. An analysis of popular books from the Imperial era came up, predictably, with salt as the most commonly used spice. Other seasonings, like pepper, vinegar, onions, and cloves, may be found in recipes less often. Bay leaves, ginger, nutmeg, parsley, and shallots have their place now and then. Garlic is totally absent in one book (Henny van Cleef, *Die Israelitische Küche*, 3rd ed. [Leipzig, 1898]); appears with a goulash dish (a Hungarian recipe) and one other dish in a 371-page cookbook (Bertha Gumprich, *Vollständiges, praktisches Kochbuch für die jüdische Küche*, 7th ed. [Frankfurt/Main, 1914], p. 81); and generally shows up once or twice (in some wurst recipes) in other books.

64. Müller, *Dienstbare*, p. 26. In 1882 there were 1,324,924 servants, and in 1907 the census registered 1,264,755. See also Dorothee Wierling, *Mädchen für Alles: Arbeitsalltag und Lebensgeschichte städtischer Dienstmädchen um die Jahrhundertwende* (Berlin, 1987).

65. In Hamburg, for example, servants in the population dropped from 10.8% in 1852 to 4.3% in 1890.

66. Rolf Engelsing, *Zur Sozialgeschichte deutscher Mittel- und Unterschichten* (Göttingen, 1973), p. 238.

67. Müller, *Dienstbare*, pp. 96, 103. About 37% of domestics were between the ages of fifteen and twenty. Domestics were the most mobile workers at the turn of the century: Wierling, *Mädchen*, p. 67.

68. Müller, *Dienstbare*, p. 28. See also Heidi Rosenbaum, *Formen der Familie* (Frankfurt/Main, 1982), pp. 341–42.

69. Letter from Dora Edinger to the author, New York, February 25, 1976.

70. Richarz, *Jüdisches Leben*, vol. 2, p. 24.

71. Werner Mosse, *Jews in the German Economy: The German-Jewish Economic Elite, 1820–1935* (Oxford, 1987), p. 13.

72. Jeggle, *Judendörfer*, p. 224.

73. Clara Geismar (born 1845, Eppingen), memoirs, LBI, p. 20. In 1895 there were 6,298 Jewish maids in Germany (16% of all Jewish working women), but this number dropped to 4,771 in 1907 (9% of all Jewish working women). Jakob Segall, *Die berufliche und soziale Verhältnisse der Juden in Deutschland* (Berlin, 1912), p. 80.

74. *Zeitschrift für Demographie und Statistik der Juden* (hereafter *ZDSJ*), April 1905, pp. 1–2. In 1895 in Hamburg there were only 214 Jewish maids, and 178 in 1907. *ZDSJ*, May/July 1919, pp. 88–89.

75. Uhry, memoirs, p. 88 (referring to the 1870s and 1880s).

76. Engelsing, *Sozialgeschichte*, pp. 239–41.

77. Rosenstein, memoirs, p. 8.

78. Phillipine Landau, *Kindheitserinnerungen: Bilder aus einer rheinischen Kleinstadt des vorigen Jahrhunderts* (Dietenheim, 1956), p. 55; Müller, *Dienstbare*, pp. 116, 156.

79. Müller, *Dienstbare*, p. 156.

80. Jeggle, *Judendörfer*, p. 224.

81. Ibid.

82. Müller, *Dienstbare*, p. 144.

83. Carlebach, *Ratgeber*, p. 8.

84. *Israelitisches Familienblatt* (hereafter *IF*), March 28, 1908, p. 11.

85. Jack Wertheimer, *Unwelcome Strangers: East European Jews in Imperial Germany*, (New York, 1987), p. 101 (ca. 1897).

86. *IF*, March 19, 1908, p. 11.

87. *Israelitisches Gemeindeblatt*, January 10, 1908, p. 11.

88. Johanna Meyer Loevinson (born 1874, Berlin), memoirs, LBI, p. 37.

89. Jeggle, *Judendörfer*, p. 225.

90. Ibid.

91. Hilda Albers Frank (born ca. 1901, Cologne), memoirs, LBI, p. 6.

92. Eva Ehrenburg, *Sehnsucht—mein geliebtes Kind* (Frankfurt/Main, 1963), p. 33.

93. Richarz, *Jüdisches Leben*, vol. 2, p. 336.

94. Meyer Loevinson, memoirs, p. 17.

95. Freudenthal, *Gestaltwandel*, p. 176, quoting from "Der Frauen Natur und Recht," Berlin, 1876.

96. Freudenthal, *Gestaltwandel*, as well as the memoir literature of the time.

97. Diamant, memoirs, p. 7.

98. Marie Munk (born 1880s, Berlin), memoirs, I, 10. Helene Lange archives, Institut für Sozialwissenschaft, Berlin.

99. Müller, *Dienstbare*, pp. 162–65, and Meyer Loevinson, memoirs, p. 30, for details of the "great wash."

100. Munk, memoirs, I, 10.

101. Ibid., I, 13A.

102. Ibid.

103. Ibid., I, 11A.

104. Meyer Loevinson (referring to the 1880s and 1890s), memoirs, p. 17.

105. Alice Ottenheimer (born 1893, Hochberg am Neckar), memoirs, LBI, p. 3.

106. Bruno Stern, *Meine Jugenderinnerungen an eine württembergische Kleinstadt und ihre jüdische Gemeinde* (Stuttgart, 1968), p. 66.

107. Ibid., p. 80.

108. Ibid., pp. 52, 64, 70, 80.

109. Hirsch, memoirs, passim.

110. Gerda Lerner, *The Creation of Patriarchy* (New York, 1986), pp. 10, 171.

111. John Knodel, *The Decline of Fertility in Germany, 1871-1939* (Princeton, N.J., 1974), pp. 136–47, 246–63. See also James Woycke, *Birth Control in Germany: 1871–1933* (London, 1988), pp. 2–5.

112. Lawrence Schofer, "Emancipation and Population Change," in *Revolution and Evolution: 1848 in German-Jewish History*, ed. Werner Mosse, Arnold Paucker, and Reinhard Rürup (Tübingen, 1981), pp. 79–80.

113. *Israelitisches Gemeindeblatt*, February 6, 1903, p. 53. From the 1880s on, Eastern European Jewish immigrants helped offset the general decline of fertility among German Jews. See Wertheimer, *Unwelcome*, pp. 85–86.

114. Schofer, "Emancipation," p. 81; Jacob Toury, *Soziale und politische Geschichte der Juden in Deutschland, 1847–1871* (Düsseldorf, 1977), p. 22.

115. *Israelitisches Gemeindeblatt*, February 6, 1903, p. 53; Usiel Schmelz, "Die demographische Entwicklung der Juden in Deutschland von der Mitte des 19. Jahrhunderts bis 1933," in *Zeitschrift für Bevölkerungswissenschaft* 1 (1982): 44–45; Schofer, "Emancipation," p. 79.

116. S. Lowenstein, "The Pace of Modernization," *LBIYB*, 1976, pp. 41–56, and "Voluntary and Involuntary Limitation of Fertility in Nineteenth Century Bavarian Jewry," in *Modern Jewish Fertility*, ed. by Paul Ritterband (Leiden, 1981), pp. 94–111.

117. Knodel, *Decline*, p. 260.

118. Henning, *Bürgertum*, p. 478.

119. Knodel, *Decline*, p. 252. See also Chapter 5, note 60.

120. Knodel, *Decline*, p. 138. Rural Jews, more traditional and more religious, had larger families, although their fertility rates also fell below rural standards. Lowenstein, "Voluntary."

121. David Feldman, *Marital Relations, Birth Control and Abortion in Jewish Law* (New York, 1974), pp. 298–301. Shulamit Volkov has argued that Jewish traditions regarding the laws of *niddah*, which regulated sexual encounters according to a woman's menstrual cycle, may have predisposed Jews to accepting "restraint" (although at different times during the cycle). "Erfolgreiche Assimilation oder Erfolg und Assimilation: Die deutsch-jüdische Familie im Kaiserreich," in *Wissenschaftskolleg zu Berlin: Jahrbuch* (Berlin, 1982/1983), p. 386.

122. Quoted by Wertheimer, *Unwelcome*, p. 39.

123. Reich statistics on Eastern European Jewish fertility do not exist. However, on the basis of limited data for some localities, the following evidence is available: in Berlin in 1910, Eastern European women had an average of 2.9 children compared to 1.2 for German Jews. In Munich in 1910 there were 1.4 children for foreign Jewish women, compared to 0.7 for native Jewish women. Wertheimer concludes that Jewish families from the East were larger than German-Jewish families, but he wonders whether their fertility decreased once they lived in Germany: *Unwelcome*, p. 85. A class analysis might also indicate that their fertility decreased once they had gained an economic foothold.

124. Arthur Prinz, *Juden im deutschen Wirtschaftsleben*, ed. Avraham Barkai (Tübingen, 1984), p. 77.

125. Knodel, *Decline*, pp. 140–41.

126. Ann Taylor Allen, "Sex and Satire in Wilhelmine Germany: 'Simplicissimus' Looks at Family Life," in *Journal of European Studies* 7 (1977): 38.

127. See *ZDSJ*, May 1914, p. 72, on Hesse, 1901–12.

128. Alice Goldstein, "Some Demographic Characteristics of Village Jews in Germany: Nonnenweier, 1800–1931," in *Modern Jewish Fertility*, ed. Paul Ritterband (Leiden, 1981).

129. Jews attended Germany's higher schools (those leading to a university education) by six times their proportion of the population. Jewish girls were represented by seven times their proportion of the population in these same schools. Statistics for 1914 in Prussia:

Female Students in Prussian School

	Prot.	Cath.	Jews	Other	Total
Lycéen	100,380 (68%)	35,930 (24%)	10,509 (7%)	317 (0.2%)	147,136 (100%)
Upper Lycéen	6,019 (64%)	3,258 (34%)	223 (2%)	2 (0%)	9,502 (100%)
College Prep Schools (*Studienanstalten*)	2,758 (62%)	1,133 (26%)	526 (12%)	17 (0.4%)	4,434 (100%)
TOTAL	109,157 (68%)	90,321 (25%)	11,258 (7%)	336 (0.2%)	161,072 (100%)

SOURCE: *ZDSJ*, July–September 1915, p. 82.

In 1912 the Prussian population consisted of 61% Protestants, 36% Catholics, and 1% Jews.

On the higher marriage ages of Jewish women, see Schmelz, "Die demographische Entwicklung," p. 43; Schofer, "Emancipation," pp. 82–87; and for Berlin, *ZDSJ* September–October 1914, pp. 131–32.

130. For a discussion of birth control among Jews as a "social pathology," see H. L.

Eisenstadt, "Die Sozialpathologie der Juden und ihre Lehren," in *Soziale Medizin und Hygiene* 5 (1910): 22, 29–31.

131. Adolf Riesenfeld (born 1884, Breslau), memoirs, LBI.

132. Conversation with Dora Edinger, New York, 1986.

133. For an example of the former, see Sammy Gronemann, memoirs, LBI, p. 234; for the latter, see Arnold Zweig, *Junge Frau von 1914* (Berlin, 1931).

134. Riesenfeld, memoirs.

135. Stefan Behr, *Der Bevölkerungsrückgang der deutschen Juden* (Frankfurt/Main, 1932), p. 96. Ninety percent of the married general population used withdrawal, and others either condoms or the Mensinga Pessary: Behr, p. 92. Jewish demographers based their assertions on criminal statistics: in 1904–10 in Germany, 1.5 Christians and 0.6 Jews out of 100,000 people (*ZDSJ*, June 1913, p. 93), and in 1916, in absolute numbers, 6 Jews and 1,204 Christians, or 0.9 and 1.8 out of 100,000 women, were convicted on charges of having had an abortion (*Im deutschen Reich*, February 2, 1911, pp. 77–81).

136. Charlotte Hamburger-Liepmann, memoirs, LBI, p. 111.

137. Stern, *Jugenderinnerungen*, p. 116; Uhry, memoirs, p. 52; Gerhard Wilke and Kurt Wagner, "Family and Household: Social Structures in a German Village Between the Two World Wars," in *The German Family*, ed. Richard Evans and W. R. Lee (London, 1981), p. 129.

138. Picard, "Childhood," p. 280, and Uhry, memoirs, p. 111.

139. Riesenfeld, memoirs.

140. Hirsch, memoirs, p. 50.

141. Straus, *Wir lebten in Deutschland: Erinnerungen einer deutschen Jüdin* (Stuttgart, 1962), p. 201.

142. Klinik weiblicher Ärzte. Elisabeth Bab, memoirs, LBI, p. 102.

143. Herzfeld, memoirs, pp. 24, 51. In 1869 Mrs. Herzfeld's mother helped her with her first infant, and in 1894 Mrs. Herzfeld rushed to help her daughter with her first baby.

144. "Ferien und Erholungsreise" (between 1851 and 1861); in Jacob Rosenheim, *Erinnerungen, 1870–1920* (Frankfurt/Main, 1970), p. 11.

145. Stern, *Jugenderinnerungen*, p. 116.

146. Riesenfeld, memoirs, book 2, p. 138.

147. Geismar, memoirs, pp. 185–86. See also Antoinette Kahler (born 1862, Bruenn), memoirs, LBI, p. 33.

148. Jenny Apolant collection, Archives of the City of Frankfurt/Main.

149. Straus, *Wir lebten*, p. 196.

150. John Knodel and Hallie Kintner, "The Impact of Breast Feeding Patterns on the Biometric Analysis of Infant Mortality," *Demography*, no. 4 (November 1977), pp. 391–409.

151. Knodel and Kintner, "Impact," p. 399. In Berlin in 1885, 68% of legitimate children were still breast-fed. In southern and eastern Bavaria, areas of high infant mortality, 75% of infants were not breast-fed (1904–06), whereas in Oberfranken, with less mortality, about 85% were breast-fed (Knodel and Kintner, p. 401). Rahel Straus (*Wir lebten*, p. 145) claimed that the lack of breast-feeding in Upper Bavaria came from the Church's influence. The Church found breast-feeding *unsittlich*; 33% of infants died.

152. Knodel and Kintner, "Impact," p. 405. Patterns of several decades before 1900 are representative of the first years of the twentieth century, too: Knodel and Kintner, p. 400, and Kintner, "Trends and Regional Differences in Breastfeeding in Germany from 1871 to 1937," *Journal of Family History* 10:2 (1985): 163–82.

153. In Hesse, in 1903–06, for example, 75 Jewish infants and 148 non-Jewish infants died for every 1,000 born (*ZDSJ*, March 1908, p. 47). See also U. O. Schmelz, *Infant and*

Early Childhood Mortality Among the Jews of the Diaspora (Jerusalem, 1971), pp. 19–21, 26; Schmelz, "Die demographische Entwicklung," pp. 40, 45, 154.

154. Rates of Illegitimacy in Prussia

	Christian	Jewish
1900–1904	7.11	3.36
1910	7.87	4.59
1912	8.23	5.84
1914	8.65	5.44

Rates of Illegitimacy in Bavaria

	Christian	Jewish
1910	12.21	2.37
1912	12.7	3.33
1914	13.49	3.58

SOURCE: *ZDSJ*, April 1906, pp. 61–62, and April–June 1916, p. 31.

Even in large cities, where illegitimacy rates were higher, Jewish rates were lower than those of non-Jews. For example, in 1904 in Berlin, the Jewish rates of 5.5% was almost one third of the Christian rate which was 16.7% (*ZDSJ*, March 1906, p. 47). For Frankfurt/Main a similar ratio holds: in 1906, 4.93% of Jewish babies were illegitimate, compared to 13.93% of Christian babies (*ZDSJ*, May 1908, p. 77). The rate of Jewish illegitimacy was only 23% of the non-Jewish rate in 1821. By 1861 it had grown to about 45% of the rate of the general population. By 1902 the Jewish rate was about 53% of the general figure. *ZDSJ*, July 1910, p. 104.

155. Schmelz, *Infant Mortality*, pp. 46, 50, 78, 81.

156. Mention of breast-feeding can be found in Julie Kaden, memoirs, LBI; Antoinette Kahler, memoirs, in Kahler collection, LBI; Gertrud Hirsch, memoirs, LBI, p. 15. These are by no means the only memoirs which discuss breast-feeding.

157. Julie Braun-Vogelstein, *Was niemals stirbt: Gestalten und Erinnerungen* (Stuttgart, 1966).

158. Geismar, memoirs, p. 161.

159. Engelsing, *Sozialgeschichte*, p. 234. In mid-eighteenth-century Hamburg, with a population of 100,000, there were 4,000 to 5,000 wet nurses.

160. Henriette Hirsch, (1880s, 1890s), memoirs, p. 9; Regina Elbogen (born ca. 1883, Hamburg), memoir, in Ismar Elbogen collection, LBI; William Kober (1890s), memoirs, LBI, p. 16; Kahler, memoirs, p. 43.

161. Herzfeld, memoirs, pp. 23, 25.

162. Hamburger-Liepmann (1898–99, Berlin), memoirs, pp. 116, 125.

163. See also Kaden (1895), memoirs, p. 20.

164. Theodor Fontane (Berlin, 1893), p. 211.

165. Kaden, memoirs, p. 21.

166. Emil Sander (his mother was born in 1856 in Darmstadt), memoirs, p. 10.

167. Ibid., p. 11.

168. Margarete Sallis-Freudenthal, *Ich habe mein Land gefunden* (Frankfurt/Main, 1977), p. 37, and Charlotte Wolff, *Hindsight: An Autobiography* (London, 1980), p. 2.

169. *Eselsmilch*. In Kaden (1895), memoirs, p. 22.

170. Müller, *Dienstbare*, p. 130.

171. Regina Elbogen (1890s), memoir, Ismar Elbogen collection, LBI, p. 6.

172. Wolff, *Hindsight*, p. 2.

173. *Israelitisches Wochenblatt*, January 12, 1912, p. 28.

174. Flora Goldschmidt (born 1853, Breslau), memoirs, LBI.

175. *Bürgerliches Gesetzbuch*, paragraphs 1354, 1627, 1634, 1649. See also Ute Gerhard, "Die Rechtsstellung der Frau in der bürgerlichen Gesellschaft des 19. Jahrhunderts: Frankreich und Deutschland im Vergleich," in *Bürgertum im 19. Jahrhundert: Deutschland im europäischen Vergleich*, vol. 1, ed. Jürgen Kocka (Munich, 1988), pp. 452–57.

176. *Gesetzbuch*, paragraph *1687*. Even against her will she might have to accept counsel. See also *Vormund*, paragraph 1782.

177. See Jeggle's *Judendörfer* for examples.

178. Marcia Guttentag, *Too Many Women? The Sex Ratio Question* (Beverly Hills, Calif., 1983), chapter 4. This chapter discusses the fact that there were (and are) more male than female children born to Orthodox Jews as a result of the ritual purity laws. These regulations (coincidentally) restrict the sex act to precisely the time when it is more likely to conceive sons. The authors argue, convincingly, that this ratio gave women a higher status than they might otherwise have had.

179. Olwen Hufton also noted the effects of men's absences: "Women and the Family Economy in Eighteenth-Century France," *French Historical Studies* 9 (1975): 1–22.

180. Kronthal, *Posner*, p. 10.

181. Quoted by Estelle Roith in *The Riddle of Freud: Jewish Influences on His Theory of Female Sexuality* (London, 1987), p. 121.

182. For an exception, see Theodor Lessing in Beuys, *Familienleben*, p. 433.

183. Wagner and Wilke, "Family and Household," pp. 136–37; Helmut Moeller, *Die kleinbürgerliche Familie im 18. Jahrhundert* (Berlin 1969), pp. 75–88, on "Obrigkeit." See also Yvonne Schütze, "Mutterliebe-Vaterliebe: Elternrollen in der bürgerlichen Familie des 19. Jahrhundert," in *Bürgerinnen und Bürger*, pp. 118–33.

184. Gabrielle Reuter, *Aus guter Familie*, 17th ed. (Berlin, 1908), p. 128.

185. Jeggle, *Judendörfer*, pp. 165, 224.

186. Marianne Berel, memoirs, LBI, p. 51.

187. Lucy Maas-Friedmann (born 1870s, Baden), memoir, LBI, p. 7. Schütze has discovered that fathers do not devote much space to children in their memoirs either: "Mutterliebe," p. 126.

188. Toni Sender, *Autobiographie einer deutschen Rebellin* (translated from the American version, 1939; Frankfurt/Main, 1981), pp. 29–30.

189. Ehrlich, memoirs, pp. 12, 29.

190. Straus, *Wir lebten*, p. 142.

191. Ibid., p. 195.

192. Schütze, "Mutterliebe," p. 125. Fanny Lewald is an example of this. See Juliane Jacobi-Dittrich, "Growing up Female in the Nineteenth Century," in *German Women in the Nineteenth Century*, ed. John Fout (New York, 1984), pp. 199–204.

193. Ingeborg Weber-Kellermann, *Die deutsche Familie* (Frankfurt/Main, 1974), p. 108.

194. *Im deutschen Reich*, September 1914, p. 225; Friedrich Blach, *Die Juden in Deutschland: Von einem jüdischen Deutschen* (Berlin, 1911), p. 19.

195. John Murray Cuddihy, *The Ordeal of Civility: Freud, Marx, Lévi-Strauss, and the Jewish Struggle with Modernity* (New York, 1974), pp. 12–14.

196. Joseph Wortis, *Fragments of an Analysis with Freud* (New York, 1954), p. 145, cited by Cuddihy, *Ordeal*, p. 36.

197. Wertheimer, *Unwelcome*, pp. 28–29 (1879–80).

198. Ascheim, *Brothers*, p. 9.

199. George Mosse, *German Jews Beyond Judaism* (Bloomington, Ind., 1985), pp. 74–75.

200. Mosse, *German Jews*, p. 69, using Ismar Schorsch's "Art as Social History: Oppenheim and the German-Jewish Vision of Emancipation," in *Moritz Oppenheim: The First Jewish Painter* (Jerusalem, 1983).

201. Mosse, *German Jews*, p. 69.

202. Rosenstein, memoirs, p. 34.

203. Hirsch, memoirs, p. 48.

204. Kronthal, *Posner*, p. 17; Sender, *Autobiographie*, p. 31.

205. Sender, *Autobiographie*, p. 31.

206. For a similar situation in England, see Leonore Davidoff, "Class and Gender in Victorian England," in *Sex and Class in Women's History: Essays from Feminist Studies*, ed. Judith Newton, Mary Ryan, and Judith Walkowitz (London and Boston, 1983), p. 27.

207. Meyer Loevinson, memoirs, p. 17. See also Clara Sander (born ca. 1871, Frankfurt/Main), memoirs, p. 51 (on skating, biking, and chaperoning); Ottenheimer, memoirs, p. 5 (on bathing, sledding); Nora Rosenthal, "Opus One" (unpublished memoir, archives of the city of Frankfurt/Main), pp.12–13 (on hikes); Kronthal, *Posner*, p. 23 (on building healthy bodies).

208. Jenny Apolant collection, Archives of the city of Frankfurt/Main.

209. Berel, memoirs, p. 51. "Chilly doses of fresh air" seem to have been the British middle-class answer to child care as well. Ellen Ross, "Working-Class Mothers and Their Children: London, 1870–1918," paper presented to the University Seminar on Women and Society, New York, January 1987.

210. *Im deutschen Reich*, November 1909, p. 654.

211. Geismar, memoirs, p. 57.

212. Jeggle, *Judendörfer*, p. 275.

213. Conversation with Ilse Blumenthal-Weiss (born 1900, Berlin), Queens, New York, June 1984. See also Braun-Vogelstein, *Was niemals stirbt*, p. 184.

214. Mosse, *German Jews*, p. 14.

215. Ibid., p. 45.

216. Fontane was a favorite author of Jews: Ernest Bramsted, *Aristocracy and the Middle Classes in Germany* (Chicago, 1964), pp. 262–68. Meyer Loevinson, memoirs, p. 37; Ilse Blumenthal-Weiss, conversation, June 1984.

217. Ehrlich, memoirs, p. 24.

218. Ilse Blumenthal-Weiss, conversation, June 1984.

219. Geismar, memoirs, p. 57; Picard, "Childhood," p. 285.

220. Müller, *Dienstbare*, p. 130; Hirsch, memoirs, p. 2. Sender discovered cartons of the *Gartenlaube* in her attic: *Autobiographie*, p. 32.

221. Picard, "Childhood," p. 257; Jeggle, *Judendörfer*, p. 164.

222. Berel, memoirs, p. 50.

223. Weber-Kellerman, *Familie*, p. 112; Ottenheimer, memoirs, p. 4; Bertha Katz, memoirs, LBI, p. 13.

224. Kahler, memoirs, p. 20.

225. Katz, memoirs, p. 13.

226. Hirsch, memoirs, p. 2.

227. *Israelitischer Jugendfreund*, I (1895), p. 294.

228. Ibid., p. 171.

229. Ibid., p. 142.

230. Meyer Loevinson, memoirs, p.41; Gertrud Catts in *Community of Fate: Memoirs of German Jews in Melbourne*, ed. John Foster (Sydney, 1986), p. 37.

231. Ibid., 1898, p. 184.

232. Ibid., 1895, p. 17.

233. Ibid., 1898, p. 18.

234. Mary Ryan, "Femininity and Capitalism in Antebellum America," in *Capitalist Patriarchy and the Case for Socialist Feminism*, ed. Zillah R. Eisenstein (New York, 1979), p. 161.

235. Braun-Vogelstein, *Was niemals stirbt*, p. 32; *Israelitisches Gemeindeblatt* (Köln), (January 15, 1892), pp. 21–22.

236. Munk, memoirs, I, 11a–b.

237. Goldschmidt, memoirs, p. 3.

238. Fritz Stern, *Gold and Iron: Bismarck, Bleichröder, and the Building of the German Empire* (New York, 1977), p. 479.

239. Sender, *Autobiographie*, p. 31.

240. Meyer Loevinson, memoirs, p. 3.

241. Ibid., p. 4.

242. Ibid., p. 28.

243. Max Grunwald, *Beruria: Gebet- und Andachtsbuch für jüdische Frauen und Mädchen* (Vienna, 1907), pp. 310–13.

244. Goldschmidt (1860s), memoirs, p. 3.

245. Hamburger-Liepmann (1860s, 1870s), memoirs, p. 14.

246. Kronthal (1860s, 1870s), *Posner*, p. 5.

247. Hamburger-Liepmann, memoirs (on Agathe Bleichröder); Apolant, diary and letters; Katz, memoirs.

248. Zweig (Berlin, 1931), p. 150.

249. Salomon Carlebach, *Sittenreinheit: Ein Mahnwort an Israels Söhne und Töchter, Väter und Mütter* (Berlin, 1917), pp. 19, 21. It has been suggested that, in supervising their children's sexuality, middle-class parents were fighting their own sexuality as well as upholding "social order" in the face of flagging self-control and disorder. Frykman, *Culture Builders*, pp. 243–44.

250. Hamburger-Liepmann, memoirs, p. 117.

251. Elbogen, memoirs; emphasis added.

252. Frankenthal, *Der dreifache Fluch: Jüdin, Intellektuelle, Sozialistin: Lebenserinnerungen einer Ärztin in Deutschland und im Exil* (Frankfurt/Main, 1981), p. 3.

253. Bab, memoirs, p. 15.

254. Reuter, pp. 41–42.

255. Heinrich Mann, *Man of Straw (Der Untertan)* (Middlesex, Eng., 1984), pp. 5–6.

256. Wolfgang Paulsen, "Theodor Fontane— the Philosemitic Antisemite," *LBIYB*, 1981, p. 317.

257. Ibid., pp. 303–22.

258. *Im deutschen Reich*, May 1908, p. 289.

259. *Hindsight*, p. 11 (Riesenburg, 1901).

Chapter 2

1. David Leimdorfer, *Ein Wort zu unserer Frauenfrage* (Berlin, 1900), p. 3.

2. Examples abound. See *Jüdisher Volksbote* (Frankfurt/Main), November 1909, pp. 48–

52; *Der Freitagabend* (Frankfurt/Main), 1859, p. 61; *Israelitisches Gemeindeblatt* (Cologne) October 12, 1892, p. 1; May 15, 1903; August 21, 1903; July 24, 1908, p. 1; and *Schlemiel* January 1, 1904, p. 3. In the United States, rabbis and male leaders also blamed women for religious decline. See Norma Fain Pratt, "Transitions in Judaism: The Jewish American Woman Through the 1930s," in *American Quarterly* 3:5 (Winter 1978): 694–95.

3. *Die Laubhütte* (Regensburg), July 18, 1895, p. 335.

4. Paula Hyman, "The Other Half," in *The Jewish Woman*, ed. Elizabeth Koltun (New York, 1976), pp. 105–13. Jewish feminists have recently challenged this tradition, with the result that women's role in religious ritual has increased. Women may now be ordained as rabbis in the Reform (1972) and Conservative (1983) movements.

5. Rachel Biale, *Women and Jewish Law* (New York, 1984).

6. Hyman, "Other Half," p. 107.

7. Robert Redfield, *Peasant Society and Culture* (Chicago, 1956). See especially chapter 3, "The Social Organization of Tradition."

8. Martha Ackelsberg, "Introduction," *The Jewish Woman*, ed. Koltun, p. xv.

9. The *Brandspigl* was first written in 1596 and includes chapters such as "how the modest woman should conduct herself in the home," "who is a good wife and who is a bad wife," etc.: Herman Pollack, *Jewish Folkways in Germanic Lands (1648–1806)* (Cambridge, Mass., 1971), p. 51. See Chava Weissler, "The Religion of Traditional Ashkenazic Women: Some Methodological Issues," *Association for Jewish Studies Review* 12:1 (Spring 1987): 73–94.

10. Pollack, *Jewish Folkways*, p. 156.

11. Chava Weissler, "Religion of Ashkenazic Women," and "The Traditional Piety of Ashkenazic Women," in *Jewish Spirituality*, ed. Arthur Green (New York, 1987). As late as the twentieth century, the *Tsenerene* was translated from Judeo-German into German by Bertha Pappenheim as well as Salomon Goldschmidt. The latter published yearly editions from 1911 through 1914. Observers of rural life mention the importance of the *Tsenerene* and the *tkhines* into the Weimar era. See Herman Schwab, *Jewish Rural Communities in Germany* (London, 1956), p. 49.

12. See also Judith R. Baskin, "Jewish Women in the Middle Ages," in her volume *Jewish Women: Historical Essays* (Detroit, Mich., forthcoming).

13. Deborah Hertz, *Jewish High Society in Old Regime Berlin* (New Haven, Conn., 1988).

14. Jacob Katz, *Out of the Ghetto: The Social Background of Jewish Emancipation* (Cambridge, Mass., 1971), p. 84.

15. Mordechai Eliav, *Jewish Education in Germany in the Period of Enlightenment and Emancipation* (in Hebrew) (Jerusalem, 1960), chapter 11 and pp. 271–79.

16. Clara Geismar (born 1844, Eppingen), memoirs, LBI, p. 73.

17. Monika Richarz, ed., *Jüdisches Leben in Deutschland*, vol. 2, *Selbstzeugnisse zur Sozialgeschichte im Kaiserreich* (Stuttgart, 1979), p. 232.

18. In the 1880s in Hamburg, the girls' school of the Jewish community offered four hours a week of religion, Biblical history, and Hebrew (out of a thirty-five-hour schedule). Israelitische Mädchen—Realschule (formerly Israelitische Töchterschule), "Lehrplan," 1884, pp. 2–6, 31–50, 57, Hamburg State Archives, "Jüdische Gemeinde," #538n. By 1910 the girls' school in Frankfurt offered only three hours of religion, including Hebrew, which was optional. Philanthropin. Real und Höhere Mädchenschule der Israelitischen Gemeinde zu Frankfurt a. M, "Programm, Ostern 1911," Central Archives, Jerusalem, TD 908, pp. 8–19.

19. In the 1870s the religion school of the Jewish community in Kassel, for example, offered boys and girls four hours of instruction in Hebrew and biblical history from the ages

of six until ten. Then, boys took five hours of instruction a week and girls continued with four. Rudolf Hallo, *Geschichte der jüdischen Gemeinde Kassel*, vol. 1, (Kassel, 1931), p. 171.

20. The *Israelitische Wochenschrift*, Magdeburg, discussed a German translation of the Hebrew services and encouraged women to spend an hour in synagogue reading this, rather than "desecrating [the time] with profane and disturbing chatter": 24:36 (September 1893): 282.

21. Charlotte Wolff, *Hindsight: An Autobiography* (London, 1980), p. 47.

22. Nora Rosenthal (born 1892, Frankfurt/Main), "Opus One," unpublished memoir, Stadtarchiv Frankfurt/Main, p. 10.

23. Anna Kronthal, *Posner Mürbekuchen: Jugend Erinnerungen einer Posnerin* (Munich, 1932), p. 27; Richarz, *Jüdisches Leben*, vol. 2, p. 427.

24. "Die Stellung des weiblichen Geschlechtes in dem Judenthume unserer Zeit," in *Wissenschaftliche Zeitschrift für jüdische Theologie* 3 (1837): 6, 13–14.

25. Breslau Commission recommendations, found in David Philipson, *The Reform Movement in Judaism* (New York, 1967), p. 218. The blessing is intended to show gratefulness for the (male) obligation of reading the Torah and studying Jewish law.

26. Michael Meyer, *Response to Modernity: A History of the Reform Movement in Judaism* (New York, 1988), p. 140.

27. Ibid.

28. Isaac Asher Francolm, "Simplicity Not Pomp," from *Das rationale Judentum* (1840), translated and excerpted by W. Gunther Plaut, *The Rise of Reform Judaism: A Sourcebook of Its European Origins* (New York, 1963), p. 174.

29. Ibid.

30. The Hamburg Temple (Reform) had established confirmation for girls and boys as early as 1822, as had a few smaller ones in Berlin. These were group ceremonies held on Shavuot. David Rudavsky, *Emancipation and Adjustment: Contemporary Jewish Religious Movements, Their History and Thought* (New York, 1967), p. 160. For the later period, see *Allgemeine Zeitung des Judentums* (hereafter *AZDJ*), January 30, 1914, p. 4. See also Jakob Brandeis, *Ruth: Deutsches Gebet und Erbauungsbuch* (Breslau, 1908), pp. 153–55, for prayers to be said by girls on the day of their confirmation.

31. Joseph Aub, "One or Two Wedding Rings?" in Gunther Plaut, *The Growth of Reform Judaism: American and European Sources Until 1948* (New York, 1965), p. 218.

32. Philipson, *Reform Movement*, p. 310; Meyer, *Response to Modernity*, p. 190.

33. Meyer, *Response to Modernity*, p. 190.

34. Carlebach Archives, LBI, #413, part 2. Letter from Oberrabbiner Hirsch.

35. Plaut, *Growth*, p. 68.

36. Segregated seating continued well into the 1930s in Germany, although the opaque wall between the women's and men's sections was frequently modified.

37. *Im deutschen Reich*, May 1908, pp. 288–89; December 1908, p. 718.

38. Historians have noted that religion became more familial just as men detached themselves from the family. "With the beginning of industrialization the focal point of religious life often changed from the church to the family, from which men increasingly distanced themselves." Hugh McLeod, "Weibliche Frömmigkeit—männlicher Unglaube? Religion und Kirchen im bürgerlichen 19. Jahrhundert," in *Bürgerinnen und Bürger: Geschlechterverhältnisse im 19. Jahrhundert*, ed. Ute Frevert (Göttingen, 1988), p. 140.

39. Hermann Greive, "Zionism and Jewish Orthodoxy," in *LBIYB*, 1980, p. 188.

40. Meyer, *Response to Modernity*, p. 210.

41. In the 1830s most Jewish children had attended separate Jewish schools, but by 1886 only 318 such schools still existed in Prussia. This number dropped to 219 in 1911. Of 247

Jewish *Volksschulen* in Germany in 1913, 94 had less than 10 pupils. This drop was in part the result of the decline in the Jewish birth rate, as well as the state's refusal to grant funds to poor Jewish communities whose populations were migrating to the cities. But it was also the result of German Jews' desire to enter the secular mainstream and their financial ability to do so. By 1901 only 37% of Jewish *Volksschule* pupils in Germany went to Jewish schools. (And only 43% of Jewish children went to a *Volksschule* at all: most attended secular, higher schools.) Geoffrey G. Field, "Religion in the German Volksschule, 1890–1928," *LBIYB*, 1980, p. 68. In the higher schools, statistics for Breslau indicated that only 10% of the children received Jewish instruction: *Israelitische Wochenschrift*, March 14, 1905, p. 151. Of course this varied by region, with rural Hesse, for example, showing 50% of Jewish children attending a Jewish *Volksschule: Zeitschrift für Demographie und Statistik der Juden* (hereafter *ZDSJ*), February 1914, pp. 30–31.

42. S. D. Goitein, *A Mediterranean Society*, vol. 3, *The Family*, viii, B, 1, p. 54.

43. Sydney Weinberg, *The World of Our Mothers* (Chapel Hill, N.C., 1988), p. 17 (discussing Eastern European immigrant Jews in the United States).

44. Men's relationship would be measured by synagogue attendance, by observance outside the home (e.g., not working on the Sabbath), and only lastly by ritual in the home. While I am stressing the familial context of women's religious observation, I would agree with Chava Weissler's point that women actually participated in *two* religious worlds. Like men, they prayed from the prayer book and observed the Sabbath and holidays, but they had another set of religious concerns focusing on the family and home. She also notes: "the fact that women were situated in certain social roles influenced all of their religious life. . . . The two worlds were forged into one." I would simply add, "with a heavier emphasis on the familial." "Traditional Piety of Ashkenazic Women," pp. 251–52.

45. For the Responsa, see Isadore Epstein, "The Jewish Woman in the Responsa, (900 CE–1500 CE)," in *Response*, 1973, p. 24. On religion teachers, see Heinrich Berger, *Methodik des jüdischen Religionsunterrichtes* (Leipzig, 1911), p. 15. Ironically, Jewish law makes it incumbent upon the father to teach his son religion (*Kiddushin* 29a, "to teach the son Torah": Biale, *Women*, p. 30). Yet in memoirs, literature, and sentimental and polemical writings we constantly encounter the popular image of the traditional Jewish woman as the one who passes, or was supposed to pass, the heritage to her children. Her ostensible "failure" to do so provoked the wrath of the writers quoted earlier.

46. The case of Julius Bleichröder is illustrative. His wife felt fewer ties to the religion than he. "Although Julius felt very close ties to Judaism, he was unable to transmit this enthusiasm to even one of his children." Charlotte Hamburger-Liepmann, "Geschichte der Familien Liepmann und Bleichröder," memoirs, LBI, p. 67. Sydney Weinberg discovered in her interviews that, for women, rituals in the home—almost always connected with a mother or grandmother—were more enduring than attendance at synagogue. Weinberg, *The World*, p. 18 (interviews of Eastern European Jewish women in the United States).

47. "Die Hausfrau und die Köchin," from *Die Laubhütte*, July 18, 1895, 334–37.

48. "On the Social Psychology of the Jews in Germany," in *Jews and Germans from 1860 to 1933: The Problematic Symbiosis*, ed. David Bronson (Heidelberg, 1979), p. 12. Adele Rosenzweig (born 1867, Ahlen; moved to Kassel in 1872) recalled that her family kept a kosher kitchen until her mother died. At that point her grandmother refused to visit their home because it was no longer kosher. "Jugenderinnerungen," ed. Rivka Horwitz, *LBI Bulletin*, 16/17:53/54 (1977/1978): 144.

49. Joelle Bahlout, "Foodways in Contemporary Jewish Communities: Research Directions," *Jewish Folklore and Ethnology Review* 9:1 (1987): 2.

50. Ibid., p. 5.

51. Ibid., p. 4.

52. Charlotte Wolff, *Hindsight*, pp. 6, 21.

53. Barbara Kirshenblatt-Gimblett, "Recipes for Creating Community: The Jewish Charity Cookbook in America," *Jewish Folklore and Ethnology Review* 9:1 (1987): 8.

54. Ibid., p. 8.

55. Barbara Kirshenblatt-Gimblett, "The Kosher Gourmet in the Nineteenth-Century Kitchen: Three Jewish Cookbooks in Historical Perspective," *Journal of Gastronomy*, 2:4 (Winter 1986/87): 74.

56. Kirshenblatt-Gimblet, "Recipes," p. 12, n. 2.

57. Kirshenblatt-Gimblet, "Hearth, Laboratory, Social Experiment, Sanitarium, Sanctuary, or Museum: The Jewish Kitchen as Seen Through Cookbooks, 1815–1987," paper delivered at the 59th Annual YIVO Conference, New York, April 6, 1987.

58. Witwe Joseph Gumprich, *Vollständiges praktisches Kochbuch für die jüdische Küche* (7th ed.; Frankfurt/Main, 1914). (The first edition was published in 1888.) The winners of these international competitions were Witwe Marie Kauders, *Vollständiges israelitisches Kochbuch* (4th ed., Prague and Breslau, 1903), who between 1894 and 1900 won awards at these competitions in Paris, Prague, and various German cities; and Marie Elsasser, *Ausführliches Kochbuch für die einfache und feine jüdische Küche*, (4th ed.; Frankfurt/Main, 1930), who between 1905 and 1929 won various awards, including the Gold Medal. (Elsasser's book was first published in 1900.)

59. Samuel Krauss, "Aus der jüdischen Volksküche," *Mitteilungen zur jüdischen Volkskunde* 18:1–2 (1915): 1–40; A. Berliner, "Jüdische Speisetafel," *Jahrbuch für jüdische Geschichte und Literatur* 13 (1910): 201–11.

60. Ibid.; Max Grunwald, "Aus dem jüdischen Kochbuch," *Menorah* 6:9 (September 1928): 518–20.

61. Elsasser, *Ausführliches*, p. 6, and Gumprich, *Vollständiges*, foreword. (*Palmin* appeared around 1900.)

62.

> Schalet, schöner Götterfunken,
> Tochter aus Elysium!
> Also klänge Schillers Hochlied
> Hätt' er Schalet je gekostet.
> . . . .
> Schalet ist des wahren Gottes
> Koscheres Ambrosia.

These verses can be found in the "Princess Sabbath" in Heine's *Hebrew Melodies*. Probably unbeknown to him, Heine was part of a tradition which hailed the *Schalet* or *Kugel*. In Galicia, oral tradition passed on songs about this favorite Sabbath food in rhymed dialectical Yiddish. Weissler, "Traditional Piety," p. 257.

63. Rebekka Wolf stressed "thrift" in *Kochbuch für Israelitische Frauen* (Berlin, 1875). International recipes appeared in Gumprich, *Vollständiges*, and Kauders, *Vollständiges*. The parenthetical notation to milk products implied that the reader was interested in kosher rules (in Kauders, index).

64. Wolf, *Kochbuch*; Elsasser, *Ausführliches*. One book described elaborate dinner parties of at least forty people and included seating arrangements, the number of servants necessary, and table decorations (including a bouquet at each lady's place). Porging is the removal of the sinew from the hind leg of kosher slaughtered animals.

65. Kauders, *Vollständiges*, pp. 325–32, 336–43.

66. Max Dessauer, *Aus unbeschwerter Zeit*, p. 124, quoted by Jeggle, *Judendörfer in Württemberg* (Tübingen, 1969), p. 223.

67. Beate Bechtold-Comforty, "Jüdische Frauen auf dem Dorf—zwischen Eigenständigkeit und Integration," *Sozialwissenschaftliche Informationen* 18:3 (September 1989): 159.

68. Ibid., p. 160. This included chicken soup, roast chicken or veal with vegetables, wine, *Berches*, cake, and coffee.

69. Henny van Cleef, *Die israelitische Küche*, 3rd ed. (Leipzig, 1898).

70. Elisabeth Schiff Hirsch, "Jenny's Cookbook," *Jewish Folklore and Ethnology Review* 9:1 (1987): 26–27.

71. Jeggle, *Judendörfer*, pp. 222–23.

72. Rahel Straus, *Wir lebten in Deutschland: Erinnerungen einer deutschen Jüdin, 1880–1933* (Stuttgart, 1962), p. 42.

73. See Richarz, *Jüdisches Leben*, vol. 2, pp. 158–59.

74. Bruno Stern, *Meine Jugenderinnerungen an eine württembergische Kleinstadt und ihre jüdische Gemeinde* (Stuttgart, 1968), p. 93.

75. Esther Calvary, memoirs, LBI, p. 11; Geismar, memoirs, pp. 20–23, 42–44.

76. Hugo Mandelbaum, *Jewish Life in the Village Communities of Southern Germany* (New York, 1985), pp. 75–76; See also Henriette Hirsch, memoirs, LBI, p. 9.

77. Stern, *Jugenderinnerungen*, p. 106.

78. Picard, "Childhood in the Village," *LBIYB*, 1959, pp. 285–86.

79. Johanna Meyer Loevinson, memoirs, LBI p. 23.

80. Esther Goody, *Contexts of Kinship* (Cambridge, 1973), quoted by Hans Medick and David Sabean, "Interest and Emotion in Family Kinship Studies: A Critique of Social History and Anthropology," in *Interest and Emotion: Essays on the Study of Family and Kinship*, ed. Hans Medick and David Sabean (Cambridge, Eng., 1984), p. 14.

81. Having stressed the family as a replacement for a religious void, I should acknowledge, however, that there were also those for whom the growing German idealization of the family and the increasing German tendency toward family celebrations (from birthday parties to Sedan Day festivities) provided a means of leaving religion behind and integrating into the secularized Protestant mainstream more quickly. Such desires notwithstanding, these Jews, too, helped maintain the very same family ties which had more religious or ethnic meanings to others.

82. George Mosse, "The Secularization of Jewish Theology," in *Masses and Man: Nationalist and Fascist Perceptions of Reality*, ed. George Mosse (New York, 1980), p. 258.

83. Ibid.

84. Hansjoachim Henning, *Das westdeutsche Bürgertum in der Epoche der Hochindustrialisierung, 1860–1914: Soziales Verhalten und soziale Strukturen*, vol. 1, *Das Bildungsbürgertum in den Preussischen Westprovinzen* (Wiesbaden, 1972), p. 479. Henning suggests that the lack of interest of academically educated German bourgeois men in religion had to do with the new critical spirit in which they had been educated. The more they saw their existence as rationally determined, the more they loosened their commitment to the church.

85. Ingeborg Weber-Kellermann, *Die deutsche Familie: Versuch einer Sozialgeschichte*, 4th ed. (Frankfurt/Main, 1978), pp. 112–13.

86. Catherine Prelinger, letter to author dated January 20, 1988.

87. Henning, *Bürgertum*, pp. 302, 345–46, 393, 488–89. *Jettchen Gebert*, written in 1906, went into its ninetieth reprinting in 1920.

88. For example, the contrasts between male and female Protestants were greater in the cities than in rural areas, where men retained religious feelings longer. McLeod, "Weibliche Frömmigkeit," p. 136.

89. Men's scientific and women's more religious approach are also highlighted by Bonnie G. Smith in *Ladies of the Leisure Class: The Bourgeoises of Northern France in the Nineteenth Century* (Princeton, 1981).

90. Karin Hausen, "Family and Role Division," in *The German Family*, ed. Richard Evans and W. R. Lee (London, 1981), p. 56.

91. Wilhelm Riehl, *Die Familie*, 9th ed. (Stuttgart, 1882).

92. Picard, "Childhood," p. 287.

93. John Foster, ed., *Community of Fate: Memoirs of German Jews in Melborne* (Sydney, 1986), p. 28. Born in 1905, the memoirist Mrs. Lipton was married in 1930. Her upbringing was typical of traditional Jews in Imperial Germany, and thus the question of control over the domestic sphere is representative of an earlier era as well. Her experience with a less religious husband is also typical.

94. McLeod, "Weibliche Frömmigkeit," p. 140.

95. Ibid., p. 143, for Christian families.

96. Calvary, memoirs, p. 19.

97. "Comments on the Papers of Ismar Schorsch, Vernon Lidtke and Geoffrey G. Field," *LBIYB*, 1980, p. 73.

98. Richarz, *Jüdisches Leben*, vol. 2, pp. 298–99.

99. Semi Moore, The History of the Family Moos," memoirs, LBI, p. 65. (She was from the town of Randegg near Lake Constance.)

100. Richarz, *Jüdisches Leben*, vol. 2, p. 362.

101. *Hindsight: An Autobiography* (London, 1980), pp. 6, 21.

102. Toni Ehrlich, memoirs, LBI, pp. 6, 9–10, 61.

103. Foster, *Community*, p. 28.

104. Kronthal, *Posner*, p. 27.

105. Antoinette Kahler (born 1862, Bruenn), memoirs, LBI, p. 53. Examples of this time lag are available in many memoirs. See those of Ernst Herzfeld (born 1874, Grätz) about his parents; Doris Davidsohn; and Josef Jaschuwi (on poor rural Jews) at the LBI.

106. "Memoirs of a Grandmother," in *The Golden Tradition: Jewish Life and Thought in Eastern Europe*, ed. Lucy Dawidowicz (New York, 1967), p. 164.

107. Quoted by David Aberbach, "Freud's Jewish Problem," *Commentary*, June 1980, p. 37.

108. Weinberg, *World*, p. 107.

109. Lucy Maas-Friedmann (born 1886, Baden), memoirs, LBI, p. 19.

110. In fact, whereas about two-thirds of Jews lived in Prussia, two-thirds of the *mikvehs* were located in the southern states and Alsace. Arthur Ruppin, *Die jüdischen Gemeinden und Vereine in Deutschland* (Berlin, 1906), pp. 17–18. The closeness of rural Jewish communities sustained the continued use of the *mikveh*. In the small town of Ingwiller (Alsace), for example, the due dates of each user were publicly recorded, hardly an encouragement for those who felt like missing their turn! Edmond Uhry (born 1874), memoirs, LBI, p. 46.

111. In Bavaria, two-thirds of the Jewish communities had working *mikvehs*. Ibid., p. 18, and *ZDSJ*, August/September 1910, p. 131. See also, Mandelbaum, *Jewish Life*, p. 80; Central Archives, Akten und Archivalien der Gemeinde Unterfranken Rep WR, Landkreis Ochsenfurt 446: Das Ritualbad. See also the fund-raising notice in *Das jüdische Blatt* for *new* ritual baths in the Rhineland on June 26, 1914, p. 13.

112. For grandmothers, see Kronthal, *Posner*, p. 6; Picard, "Childhood," pp. 285–86. For ads, see *Frankfurter Israelitisches Familienblatt*, April 3, 1908, p. 8, or March 18, 1910, p. 15. Orthodox dismay can be found in Salomon Carlebach, *Ratgeber für das jüdische Haus: Ein Führer für Verlobung, Hochzeit und Eheleben* (Berlin, 1918), p. 12.

113. Jeggle, *Judendörfer*, p. 273, for the town of Affaltrach.

114. Max Weinreich preferred to write of the "fusion of beliefs and practices" and pointed out that the Jewish baby-naming ceremony took on the German pagan image of [Frau] Holle, while the German image of Holle was also affected by the Jewish myth of Lilith. Holle was a

good–evil creature that could protect children but also steal them, particularly newborns. Lilith, mentioned in the Talmud, was thought in legends to attack newborns. Weinreich suggested that neighbors shared fears and ideas about the supernatural, and that the Holekrash came from such a "climate of cross fertilization." For further information on Holekrash (Holekreisch or Holkrasch) see Weinreich, "Holekrash: A Jewish Rite of Passage," in *Folklore International: Essays in Traditional Literature, Belief, and Custom in Honor of Wayland Debs Hand*, ed. D. K. Wilgus (Hatboro, Pa., 1967), pp. 243–53; A. Landau, "Holekreisch," *Zeitschrift des Vereins für Volkskunde*, 1 (1899): 72–73. Holekrash was performed mostly in what is today central and southwestern Germany and, in certain regions, only for girls: Steven Lowenstein, "Results of Atlas Investigations among Jews of Germany," in *The Field of Yiddish: Studies in Language, Folklore, and Literature*, vol. 3, ed. Marvin Herzog et al. (London, 1969), pp. 27–30. For memoirs of these events, see Jacob Picard, "Childhood in the Village," *LBIYB*, 1959, p. 280; Uhry, memoirs, LBI, p. 111; Stern, *Jugenderinnerungen*, pp.116–18; Phillipine Landau, *Kindheitserinnerungen: Bilder aus einer rheinischen Kleinstadt des vorigen Jahrhunderts* (Dietenheim, 1956), pp. 90–91.

115. Most likely, these death rituals were maintained throughout the Imperial period, particularly in the villages. It is unclear when Jewish women began to abdicate to "professional" death watchers and preparers. It is known that in small Protestant villages, *Totenfrauen*, women who washed and dressed the body, were replaced by the gravedigger in the 1920s: Gerhard Wilke and Kurt Wagner, "Family and Household: Social Structures in a German Village Between the Two World Wars," in *The German Family*, eds. Richard Evans and W. R. Lee (London, 1981), p. 141.

116. Richarz, *Jüdisches Leben*, vol. 2, p. 346. It was Walter Benjamin's mother, from a Reform Jewish family, and not his father, of Orthodox background, who bought their Christmas tree: *Berliner Kindheit um Neunzehnhundert* (Frankfurt/Main, 1950), p. 116.

117. *ZDSJ* October 1906, p. 159; January–February 1924, p. 25; October 1930, p. 54. These statistics tell us how many men and women were willing to marry out of their faith, not how many of these people married *converted* Jews. Such a breakdown, if possible, would spotlight a group of only partly assimilated Jews and might also offer evidence on gender preferences in such alliances. The percentages in Prussia were:

Percentage of Mixed Marriages Contracted by Jewish Grooms and Brides in Prussia

	Jewish Grooms	Jewish Brides
1875–79	4.3	4.4
1880–84	5.0	4.9
1885–89	6.1	5.6
1890–94	6.0	5.9
1895–99	8.3	7.3
1900–04	9.3	8.3
1905–09	12.4	10.4
1910–14	17.1	12.9
1915–19	24.0	17.2
1920–24*	19.8	12.9
1925–29	25.9	16.9
1930–33	29.6	17.7

SOURCE: Data computed from the official statistics and communicated to me by Prof. U. O. Schmelz, Institute of Contemporary Jewry, The Hebrew University, Jerusalem.

*Borders of Prussia contracted after World War I.

118. These statistics are for Frankfurt/Main for 1914: *ZDSJ*, February–March 1915, pp. 52–54. See also Felix A. Theilhaber, *Die Schädigung der Rasse durch soziales und wirtschaftliches Aufsteigen bewiesen an den Berliner Juden* (Berlin, 1914), pp. 87–88. His statistics show that of 563 Jewish women marrying Jews, 359 (or 63%) had never worked for a living. Of 116 Jewish women entering a mixed marriage, 37 (31%) had never been employed.

119. Max Marcuse, *Über die Fruchtbarkeit der Christlich-jüdischen Mischehe* (Bonn, 1920), p. 16.

120. Ibid., p. 12.

121. Arthur Ruppin, *Die Juden der Gegenwart* (Berlin, 1918), p. 162. *Simplicissimus*, among others, called attention to the alliance between the wealthy Jewish woman and the Prussian aristocrat or officer and made it an object of scorn. In one caricature, an old Jewish mother-in-law reproaches her tall, blond son-in-law: "Well, my dear son-in-law, what would you have been today if we hadn't married you?" See for examples: "Der Heiratsvermittler," 2:36 (1896–98): 284; "Mesalliance," 2:36 (1897–98): 285 (for the preceding quote); "Adelige Weltanschauung," 5:9 (1900–01): 69; and 5:47 (1900–01): 377. See also Eduard Fuchs, *Die Juden in der Karikatur: Ein Beitrag zur Kulturgeschichte* (Munich, 1921), p. 226.

122. In these cases, however, the actual numbers were extremely low: in Baden, for example, an average of 6 women (and 2 men) intermarried annually between 1888 and 1897; in Bavaria, for the four consecutive years in which women outnumbered men (1877–80), a yearly average of 8 women (and 5 men) intermarried; and in Hesse an average of 4 women (and 3 men) intermarried annually between 1871 and 1901. *ZDSJ*, August 1905, p. 7; June 1906, p. 82.

123. Arthur Ruppin, *Die Juden im Grossherzogtum Hessen*, Veröffentlichung des Bureaus für Statistik der Juden, vol. 6 (Berlin, 1909), p. 24. In Bavaria, for example, 3.3% of Jewish women and 5.1% of Jewish men intermarried in 1904, compared to 9.1% of Jewish women and 11% of Jewish men in Prussia in 1904.

124. Jacob Segall, *Die Entwicklung der jüdischen Bevölkerung in München, 1875–1905*, Veröffentlichungen des Bureaus für Statistik der Juden, vol. 7 (Berlin, 1910), pp. 7, 10.

125. *ZDSJ*, October 1906, p. 159.

126. *Israelitisches Gemeindeblatt* (Cologne), May 8. 1908, p. 186; *ZDSJ*, October 1911, p. 150.

127. Intermarriages produced fewer offspring than marriages of partners of the same religion. In Prussia, for example, by 1904–06, Jewish couples had 2.5 children and mixed marriages between Jews and non-Jews produced only 1.1 children. The reasons for this range from the later age at which intermarriages took place to the greater frequency of divorce. Further, couples willing to break with their religious or ethnic past may have been more likely to forgo traditional large families. See Marcuse, *Fruchtbarkeit*, p. 5. See also Stefan Behr, *Der Bevölkerungsrückgang der deutschen Juden* (Frankfurt/Main, 1932).

128. Marcuse, *Fruchtbarkeit*, p. 12.

129. *Israelitisches Gemeindeblatt* (Cologne), May 8, 1908, p. 186. Under one-fourth of children of mixed marriages remained Jewish. In a survey taken in 1900, of 2,242 mixed marriages of Jewish men, 27.7% of the children remained Jewish, compared to 20% of the children of 1,810 mixed marriages in which the woman was Jewish: *ZDSJ*, July 1906, pp. 107–8. This is despite the ruling in Jewish law whereby the mother's faith determines the Jewishness of the child.

130. Marcuse, *Fruchtbarkeit*, p. 16.

131. *ZDSJ*, January 1908, p. 13.

132. Toury suggests that in all of Germany, approximately 11,000 Jews converted between 1800 and 1870. Thereafter, between 1870 and 1900, another 11,500 conversions took place. Jacob Toury, *Soziale und politische Geschichte der Juden in Deutschland, 1847–1871* (Düsseldorf, 1977), p. 60. See also *Im deutschen Reich*, August 1913, pp. 339, 342.

133. *Im deutschen Reich*, August 1913, pp. 339, 342; *Israelitisches Gemeindeblatt* (Cologne), November 3, 1905, pp. 439–40. See also Peter Honigmann, *Die Austritte aus der jüdischen Gemeinde Berlin, 1873–1941* (Frankfurt/Main, 1988), especially p. 141.

134. See chapters 4–7 for the ways in which women redefined their roles in private and public life.

135. *The Origins of Totalitarianism* (New York, 1966), p. 28.

136. Rahel Straus, "Ehe und Mutterschaft," in *Vom jüdischen Geiste: Eine Aufsatzreihe*, ed. Der Jüdische Frauenbund (Berlin, 1934), p. 21.

137. An extreme example, but a suggestive one, is a set of divorce statistics (Berlin, 1909) for Jewish women and men. Ten times as many Jewish men as women were divorced as a result of adultery *(Ehebruch)*, compared to two times as many Gentile men as women. See chapter 3, note 17, for a brief discussion of these divorces. As marriages neared divorce, there is evidence that Jewish women tried harder to save them. For example, women initiated 60% of the formal attempts at reconciliation in district courts in Berlin and its suburbs in 1907–08: *ZDSJ*, October 1911, p. 150; survey in *ZDSJ*, May 1908, pp. 86–87. Jewish divorce rates, particularly among those who had intermarried, increased during the Imperial era: *ZDSJ*, May 1905, pp. 9–10, and July–September 1915, p. 83. By the 1920s the Jewish divorce rate was higher than that of the general population in Prussia. In Berlin, however, where close to a third of all Jews lived, it was lower than that of the rest of the population: Usiel O. Schmelz, "Die demographische Entwicklung der Juden in Deutschland von der Mitte des 19. Jahrhunderts bis 1933," in *Zeitschrift für Bevölkerungswissenschaft*, 1 (1982): 43.

138. See Edmund G. Hadra, memoirs, LBI, p. 89 (on family networks); Julie Braun Vogelstein, *Was niemals stirbt: Gestalten und Erinnerungen* (Stuttgart, 1966), p. 53 (on helping family members); Simon Bischheim, memoirs, LBI, p. 4 (on parents living with married children); and Geismar, memoirs, pp. 30–40 (on family visits).

139. Eva Ehrenburg, *Sehnsucht—mein geliebtes Kind* (Frankfurt/Main, 1963), p. 24 (born 1891, Frankfurt/Main).

140. One of these young women, who had turned down a good job abroad in order to stay with her aging father (ca. 1900, Berlin), told her sister: "One has to sacrifice with a smile": Hirsch, memoirs, p. 65. Sophie Diamant (born 1879, Mainz) lived with her aging mother well after her five brothers and sisters left home. At thirty-one she married, and her mother moved into her home shortly thereafter: "Familiengeschichte Schlesinger," memoirs, LBI. See also "Tante Emma," Max Gruenewald collection, archives of LBI; and Manfred Sturmann, memoirs, LBI, pp. 22–23 (on Tante Trude).

141. See Adele Rosenzweig, "Jugenderinnerungen" (on learning household skills from a distant aunt); Jacob Rosenheim, *Erinnerungen, 1870–1920* (Frankfurt/Main, 1970) (on learning household skills from distant relatives); Geismar, memoirs (on visiting relatives in a big city and helping out in their home).

142. Arthur Prinz, *Juden im Deutschen Wirtschaftsleben*, ed. Avraham Barkai (Tübingen, 1984), p. 7.

143. Ricki Burman, "'She Looketh Well to the Ways of Her Household': The Changing Role of Jewish Women in Religious Life, 1880–1930," in *Religion in the Lives of English Women, 1760–1930*, ed. Gail Malmgreen (Bloomington, Ind., 1986), p. 253. In her study of Eastern European Jews in Manchester, Burman's findings parallel my own.

Chapter 3

1. Lawrence Schofer, "Emancipation and Population Change," in *Revolution and Evolution: 1848 in German-Jewish History*, ed. Werner E. Mosse et al. (Tübingen, 1981), p. 83.

Since the topic of love and marriage is a sensitive one, some people who gave interviews preferred to remain anonymous. I have used an initial, instead of a name, where this was the case.

2. Peter Gay, *The Bourgeois Experience: Victoria to Freud*, vol. 2, *The Tender Passion* (New York, 1986), p. 3.

3. Despite the notorious, but relatively few, marriages between wealthy Jewish women and impecunious nobles, we can assume that most intermarriages were not arranged by Jewish parents. Conversely, the low rate of intermarriage points to the likelihood of careful arrangements. As late as 1916, when commenting upon the small number of Jewish women involved in mixed marriages, Jewish demographers suggested the reason for this was the "usual way of getting married among the Jews, namely brokered marriages [*Ehevermittlung*]": *Zeitschrift für Demographie und Statistik der Juden* (hereafter *ZDSJ*), April/June 1916, p. 56.

4. Elise Polko, *Unsere Pilgerfahrt von der Kinderstube bis zum eigenen Herd* (Leipzig, 1863), pp. 128, 133.

5. Ann Taylor Allen, "Sex and Satire in Wilhelmine Germany: 'Simplicissimus' Looks at Family Life," *Journal of European Studies*, 7 (1977): 29.

6. *Die Frau und der Sozialismus*, 10th ed. (Stuttgart 1891), pp. 90–93.

7. Hans Medick and David Sabean write: "When the peasant expresses himself in a concrete form ('I love the woman with 40 acres'), analysis should not stop with the notion that here only instrumental values are in play and that emotions and feelings are stunted." See their article "Interest and Emotion in Family and Kinship Studies: A Critique of Social History and Anthropology," in *Interest and Emotion: Essays on the Study of Family and Kinship*, ed. Hans Medick and David Sabean (Cambridge, Eng., 1984), pp. 12, 22, and 27, n. 71.

8. In France, for example, propertied families from the aristocracy to the peasantry viewed economic concerns as primary in marriage considerations. "When the young women of the Nord married, they did so without illusions of love and romance": Bonnie Smith, *Ladies of the Leisure Class: The Bourgeoises of Northern France in the Nineteenth Century* (Princeton, N.J., 1981), p. 57. See also Erna Hellerstein et al., eds., *Victorian Women: A Documentary Account of Women's Lives in Nineteenth-Century England, France, and the United States* (Stanford, Calif., 1981), pp. 140-42; F. M. L. Thompson, *The Rise of Respectable Society: A Social History of Victorian Britain, 1830-1900* (Cambridge, Mass., 1988), pp. 102–4, 110.

9. *Encyclopaedia Judaica*, vol. 6 (Berlin, 1930), pp. 237–38.

10. Diane Owen Hughes, "From Brideprice to Dowry in Mediterranean Europe," in *The Marriage Bargain: Women and Dowries in European History*, ed. Marion Kaplan (New York, 1985), p. 29; Susan Mosher Stuard, "Dowry Increase and Increments in Wealth in Medieval Ragusa (Dubrovnik)," *Journal of Economic History*, 10 (December 1981): 795–812.

11. Sometimes the terms *Mitgift*, *Aussteuer*, and *Ausstattung* were used interchangeably. It is necessary to examine the context in which they appear, to see if they mean wealth and property or linen and furniture.

12. David Sabean, "Verwandtschaft und Familie in einem württembergischen Dorf 1500 bis 1870: einige methodische Überlegungen," in *Sozialgeschichte der Familie in der Neuzeit Europas*, ed. Werner Conze (Stuttgart, 1976), p. 244. A surplus of embroidered linens was a sign of both wealth and diligence: an indication of the bride's leisure time and of her industriousness.

13. Jewish families invited neighbors in as well. One woman recalled the display of her sixty-four hand-embroidered pillow cases along with embroidered sheets, blanket covers, towels, and handkerchiefs. Interviews with Anna Hamburger (born 1888, Württemberg),

New Jersey, June 1981, March 1982. The custom of displaying the trousseau seems common in other societies, too. See Jane Lambiri-Dimaki, "Dowry in Modern Greece: An Institution at the Crossroads Between Persistence and Decline," and Jane Schneider, "Trousseau as Treasure: Some Contradictions of Late Nineteenth-Century Change in Sicily," both in Kaplan, *Bargain*.

14. Toni Ehrlich, memoirs, LBI, p. 62.

15. Describing a middle-class trousseau of the 1890s, Toni Ehrlich recalled dozens of bedroom linens, tablecloths, and household linens. The latter included special towels for dishes, glasses, knives, silver, bathrooms, windows, and combs. Memoirs, p. 62. As late as World War I, women took great pride in their embroidered linens, but already by the 1890s some were purchasing their trousseaus from stores. Clara Sander recorded that her sister's trousseau (Frankfurt/Main, 1892) was store-bought and that her mother's had been entirely handmade twenty-five years earlier. Clara Sander, memoirs, LBI, p. 64.

16. To understand the cost of a 2,000- to 3,000-Mark trousseau, it is useful to know that a middle-class family of six spent that annually on food between 1900 and 1905. Margarete Freudenthal, *Gestaltwandel der städtischen, bürgerlichen und proletarischen Hauswirtschaft unter besonderer Berücksichtigung des Typenwandels von Frau und Familie* (Würzburg, 1934), p. 140. For trousseau ads, see *Israelitisches Gemeindeblatt* (Cologne), September 8, 1905, p. 362, and February 16, 1912, p. 74. For a complete description of a *standesgemäss* (class- or status-appropriate) trousseau, see the list from *Das Blatt gehört der Hausfrau* (1901) in Ingeborg Weber-Kellermann, *Die deutsche Familie: Versuch einer Sozialgeschichte* (Frankfurt/Main, 1974), pp. 113-14.

17. Wilhelm Riehl, *Die Naturgeschichte des Volkes als Grundlage einer deutschen Social-Politik*, vol. 3, *Die Familie*, 9th ed. (Stuttgart, 1882), p. 180.

18. Schofer, "Emancipation," p. 83.

19. Some of these exceptions included the marriages of the Berlin salon women in the late eighteenth century.

20. *The Memoirs of Glückl of Hameln*, trans. Marvin Lowenthal (New York, 1977), p. 96. The quote is from the Talmud, *Sota*, 2-a.

21. By 1794 the Allgemeines Preussisches Landrecht codified what had perhaps already become common behavior: parents could not force children to marry a particular partner, and both parties had to give their free consent. Ute Gerhard, *Verhältnisse und Verhinderungen: Frauenarbeit, Familie und Rechte der Frauen im 19. Jahrhundert* (Frankfurt/Main, 1978), p. 86. As of 1875, the Prussian law allowed women over the age of twenty-four to marry without parental permission. The German Civil Code of 1896 eliminated penalties for a broken engagement. Before this, laws had made engagements binding, and a betrothal was taken as seriously as a marriage ceremony.

Jewish custom had also viewed the betrothal as binding. At least until the eighteenth century, each party had to pay a heavy penalty, generally half the marriage payment, and accept a "ban of the *kehillot*," if the engagement was broken. Jacob Katz, "Family, Kinship, and Marriage Among Ashkenazim in the Sixteenth to Eighteenth Centuries," *Jewish Journal of Sociology* 1 (1959): 5–6.

Recent researchers have argued that love was never entirely absent from marriage even when parental and societal strictures prevailed. See David Biale, "Love, Marriage and the Modernization of the Jews," in *Approaches to Modern Judaism*, ed. Marc Lee Raphael (Chico, Calif., 1983), pp. 1–17. Nathan Hurvitz argues that even in the shtetl, "romantic love was not unknown." See "Courtship and Arranged Marriages Among East European Jews prior to World War I as Depicted in a *Briefenshteller*," in *Journal of Marriage and Family* (1975), pp. 422–30.

Nevertheless, Pat Jalland's observation that most of the marriages among the late-nineteenth-century English bourgeoisie involved "love inspired by judgement rather than passion," probably holds for the arranged marriages I have described as well. Jalland, *Women, Marriage and Politics, 1860–1914* (Oxford, 1986), p. 75. See also John Gillis, *For Better, for Worse: British Marriages, 1600 to the Present* (New York, 1986).

22. Quoted in Alice Berend, *Die gute alte Zeit: Bürger und Spiessbürger im 19. Jahrhundert* (Hamburg, 1962), pp. 122–23. Deborah Hertz has found that the average age for Jewish brides between 1780 and 1790 in Berlin was twenty-four years. For *salonnières*, the average was eighteen. *Jewish High Society in Old Regime Berlin* (New Haven, Conn., 1988), pp. 196–97.

23. Rahel Straus, *Wir lebten in Deutschland: Erinnerungen einer deutschen Jüdin, 1880–1933* (Stuttgart, 1962), p. 104.

24. Sander, memoirs, p. 5.

25. Lucy Maas-Friedmann (born 1886), memoirs, LBI, pp. 8, 10, 18.

26. Flora Goldschmidt, memoirs, LBI, p. 17.

27. Jacob Rosenheim, *Erinnerungen, 1870–1920*, ed. Heinrich Eisenmann and Herbert N. Kruskal (Frankfurt/Main, 1970), pp. 66–67.

28. Straus, *Wir lebten*, p. 104.

29. Clara Geismar, memoirs, LBI, p. 112.

30. Charlotte Hamburger-Liepmann, "Geschichte der Familien Liepmann und Bleichröder," memoirs, LBI, n.p.

31. Josef Lange, unpublished memoirs, LBI, p. 4.

32. See *General Anzeiger für die gesamten Interessen des Judentums* (Berlin), March 19, 1903, supplement, and *Handwerk und Gewerbe* (Berlin), June 1915, back cover.

33. Simon Bischheim (born 1886, Frankfurt/Main), memoirs, LBI, p. 4.

34. Alice Goldstein, "Some Demographic Characteristics of Village Jews in Germany: Nonnenweier, 1800–1931," in *Modern Jewish Fertility*, ed. Paul Ritterband (Leiden, 1981). This may have been a pattern among non-Jews and in different countries as well. See Ernestine Friedl, *Vasilika: A Village in Modern Greece* (New York, 1962).

35. Isidor Hirschfeld memoirs in Monika Richarz, ed. *Jüdisches Leben in Deutschland*, vol. 2, *Selbstzeugnisse zur Sozialgeschichte im Kaiserreich* (Stuttgart, 1979), pp. 248–49.

36. Hermann Schwab, *Jewish Rural Communities in Germany* (London, 1956), p. 15.

37. Perles collection, LBI, #ARB 414, 4884, pp. 25, 38–39. I would like to thank Ismar Schorsch for calling my attention to this collection.

38. Herman Pollack, *Jewish Folkways in Germanic Lands (1648–1806)* (Cambridge, Mass., 1971), p. 31.

39. Gustav Jacoby collection, LBI, #ARC 1120, 2943.

40. *Im deutschen Reich*, May, 1909, p. 305, comments on an ad placed by a broker in which officers appeared ready to "sell" their status and name to rich Jewish women.

41. Ads such as "Wanted: Broker, well-known in better circles . . . " can be found in *Israelitisches Gemeindeblatt*, October 27, 1905, ad page; *Das jüdische Blatt* (Ansbach/Strassburg), September 22, 1911, p. 17; and *General Anzeiger*, January 25, 1904, ad page.

42. *Handwerk und Gewerbe*, January 1915, p. 129. *Israelitisches Gemeindeblatt*, October 13, 1905, p. 409.

43. Pinkus collection, LBI, box 5, folder 7. The letter was dated June 20, 1910.

44. Utz Jeggle, *Judendörfer in Württemberg* (Tübingen, 1969), p. 281.

45. Salomon Andorn, memoirs, LBI, #414, p. 13. Andorn writes of the 1870s. He lived in Gemünden an der Wohra, a village of 1,200 people in Hesse.

46. William Wertheimer, *Zwischen zwei Welten: Der Förster von Brooklyn (Lebenserinnerungen des ehemaligen jüdischen Lehrers in . . . Baden)* (Passau, 1966), p. 24. See also Andorn, memoirs, #413, pp. 4–5.

47. Andorn, memoirs #414, pp. 13–14. This was the case among Eastern European Jews as well. In their study of the shtetl, researchers note that brokers were the butt of many jokes. Mark Zborowski and Elizabeth Herzog, *Life Is with People: The Culture of the Shtetl* (New York, 1952), pp. 271–73.

48. Hannelore Hahn, *On the Way to Feed the Swans* (New York, 1982), p. 21.

49. *Frankfurter Israelitisches Familienblatt*, October 18, 1907, p. 13.

50. Fabius Schach in *Israelitisches Wochenblatt* (Berlin), January 19, 1912, p. 2.

51. *General Anzeiger*, June 27, 1904, ad page. Although these samples run only as high as 100,000 Marks, there were advertisements in general papers, such as the *Frankfurter Zeitung und Handelsblatt*, in which Jews also advertised, that ran as high as 300,000. See papers from July 1914. For purposes of comparison, it should be noted that in 1904 a higher civil servant (*Justizbeamter*) could earn about 8,700 Marks a year: Freudenthal, *Gestaltwandel*, p. 132.

52. *General Anzeiger*, March 21, 1904, supplement. It was not uncommon for more to be promised "at a later date." Fathers promised money at the marriage, and more after their deaths as part of the inheritance. See Graetz, letter to Perles, 1884, regarding his daughter-in-law's marriage settlement: 200,000 at the wedding and 300,000 upon her father's death: Perles collection, LBI. Also, among the very wealthy there were those who gave a generous sum and then yearly stipends. See Ehevertrag, Hans Sachs collection, LBI, 2566, II/25 (1880).

53. Interview with Mrs. B. (born ca. 1900, Berlin), New York, June 1981.

54. Mrs. Lipton (born 1905, Berlin) in *Community of Fate: Memoirs of German Jews in Melbourne*, ed. John Foster (Sydney, 1986), p. 25. The idea of marrying for a good home was certainly not unique to Jews, but was a matter of course for most European bourgeois families. The grandmother's advice was remarkably similar to that given by the *Family Herald* (London, 1856) to a governess who had received a proposal from a man forty years her senior: "It is merely a question of expediency, as marriage in general is: it is 'Can I do better—would it be better to accept a home of this kind than to run the risk of having none at all?' Women all reason thus, and so do men. The ideal of love is never realized . . . if it is, danger awaits it, for perfect satisfaction is of short duration on this planet." Sally Mitchell, "The Forgotten Woman of the Period," in *A Widening Sphere: Changing Roles of Victorian Women*, ed. Martha Vicinus (Bloomington, Ind., 1977), p. 46.

55. *General Anzeiger*, May 30, 1904.

56. Ibid.

57. Freudenthal, *Gestaltwandel*, pp. 138–39; *General Anzeiger*, January 29, 1903, p. 4.

58. *General Anzeiger*, May 30, 1904.

59. For example, a craftsman might accept 7,000 Marks with a woman who was also enterprising (*geschäftstüchtig*). *General Anzeiger*, June 20, 1904; January 29, 1903, p. 4; March 19, 1903, supplement.

60. *General Anzeiger*, March 21, 1904, supplement.

61. *General Anzeiger*, January 13, 1907.

62. See Felix A. Theilhaber, *Die Schädigung der Rasse durch soziales und wirtschaftliches Aufsteigen bewiesen an den Berliner Juden* (Berlin, 1914), pp. 87–88; *ZDSJ*, February–March 1915, pp. 52–54. Among Jews, the very richest and the very poorest probably intermarried relatively more than those in the middle. Among the richest, families paid dearly in order to enter Gentile high society (see p. 102, "A Christian is more expensive than a Jew"). For the poorest women, intermarriage may have been the only option, since Jewish men, in short supply, preferred women with dowries. It would be worth investigation to see if the decline of dowry was related to an increase in intermarriage. For information on the "surplus" of women, see note 109.

63. Interview with Bruno Stern, (born 1912, Niederstettin, Wiirttemberg), New York, November 1980.

64. Adolf Riesenfeld collection, LBI, diary, p. 98. We should distinguish the groom's "worth," that is, his own money or value, from the bride-price. The latter was an economic exchange tendered to the woman's kin. In both cases the man had to show something of value, but in industrial societies he kept it himself and promised only to maintain his wife.

65. *Frankfurter Israelitisches Gemeindeblatt*, October 18, 1907, pp. 3, 13.

66. *General Anzeiger*, January 15, 1903, supplement.

67. *Das jüdische Blatt*, February 28, 1914, p. 14.

68. Andorn, memoir #413, p. 2. In Breslau in 1850, a printer earned about 175 Thaler a year. Freudenthal, *Gestaltwandel*, p. 78.

69. Schwab, *Jewish Rural*, p. 82. Interview with Anna Hamburger, married in 1912.

70. *Das jüdische Blatt*, June 26, 1915, and *Israeltisches Gemeindeblatt*, October 13, 1905, p. 409, respectively.

71. *General Anzeiger*, December 4, 1902, supplement.

72. Hannelore Hahn, *On the Way*, p. 32.

73. The examples and conclusion were offered by Bruno Stern during an interview held in New York in November 1980.

74. Jeggle, *Judendörfer*, p. 281. In this same period the migration of Christian German women was linked to marriage or to the demand for domestic servants, whereas men migrated in response to modern labor market conditions. John Knodel and Mary Jo Maynes, "Urban and Rural Marriage Patterns in Imperial Germany," *Journal of Family History*, 1 (1976): 144.

75. Theilhaber, *Schädigung*, pp. 88–89. Jack Goody has suggested that the later marriage age of European women may have been connected to the necessity of accumulating dowries. Jack Goody and S. J. Tambiah, *Bridewealth and Dowry* (Cambridge, 1973), p. 10. Karin Hausen notes that between 1850 and 1899, 57% of German women married under the age of twenty-five. "'. . . eine Ulme für das schwanke Efeu': Ehepaare im deutschen Bildungsbürgertum," in *Bürgerinnen und Bürger: Geschlechterverhältnisse im 19. Jahrhundert*, ed. Ute Frevert, (Göttingen, 1988), p. 95. Based on church marriage records, Jürgen Kocka has observed that the marriage age of poorer women was generally older than that of wealthier ones (hence, similar to the Jewish case). See "Family and Class Formation: Intergenerational Mobility and Marriage Patterns in Nineteenth Century Westphalian Towns," *Journal of Social History* 17:3 (Spring 1984): 422. In explaining the late age at marriage of Jews, demographers have usually pointed to men's need to establish businesses or careers. It is also likely that dowry accumulation delayed marriage.

76. *General Anzeiger*, December 4, 1902, supplement.

77. Choices for single women were very limited. Until the turn of the century, women had no education which would have enabled them to earn their own living. As late as 1907 there were only 150,000 white-collar jobs available to middle-class women: Werner Conze, "Sozialgeschichte, 1850–1918," in *Handbuch der deutschen Wirtschafts-und Sozialgeschichte*, ed. Hermann Aubin and Wolfgang Zorn (Stuttgart, 1976), p. 635. Many ended up as governesses. See Elberfeld, 1890s, in Hamburger-Liepmann, memoirs, p. 74. On the plight of dependent spinsters, see Rolf Engelsing, *Zur Sozialgeschichte deutscher Mittel- und Unterschichten* (Göttingen, 1973), p. 41; and Aimée Duc, *Sind es Frauen*? (Berlin, 1903), quoted in translation in Lillian Faderman and Brigitte Eriksson, *Lesbian-Feminism in Turn-of-the-Century Germany* (Weatherby Lake, Mo. 1980), p. 11. See also Max Brod's novel *Jüdinnen* (Berlin, 1911), p. 175. His characters dread being "left behind" and fear becoming burdens on their families.

78. See Steven Lowenstein, "Results of Atlas Investigations among Jews of Germany," in

The Field of Yiddish: Studies in Language, Folklore and Literature, vol. 3, ed. Marvin Herzog et al. (London, 1969), p. 24. Memoirs and interviews also point this out.

79. This was the case among propertied peasants as well. See Sabean, "Verwandtschaft," p. 242.

80. Marcel Mauss, *The Gift: Forms and Functions of Exchange in Archaic Societies* (New York, 1967).

81. Conrad Rosenstein (born 1910, Berlin), memoirs, LBI, p. 12.

82. Interview with Anna Hamburger (born 1888, Pflaumloch, Württemberg), New Jersey, 1978.

83. *Brockhaus' Conversations-Lexikon*, 13th ed., vol. 11 (1885), p. 771, and 14th ed., vol. 11 (1902), p. 935. In one case the husband demanded the dowry in return for his consent to a Jewish ritual divorce after the marriage had been nullified in civil court. Riesenfeld diary, ca. 1905–08.

84. B. Katz, ca. 1900, memoirs, LBI, p. 8.

85. Karl Ettlinger, *Moritzchens Tagebuch* (Berlin, 1908), pp. 138–39. The events took place in the first decade of the twentieth century.

86. See Ehevertrag, Elkan Family collection, LBI, #ARC 700/1960, #17. Contract from 1867. Collection includes the official receipts for the dowry and the trousseau signed by the groom. In the Catalog of Assets (*Vermögensbuch*) of the Pinkus family firm, a 100,000-Mark entry in the profits column for 1885 reads: "dowry for Max Pinkus, junior partner." Thanks to John Foster for this reference from Warsaw: W.A.P. Opole, Oddziat Zysa: Collection S. Fraenkel Werke, Neustadt O/S: Vermögensbuch, 1889.

87. See Ehevertrag, Sinn Family collection, LBI, #ARC406/1163, IV, #l. Contract from 1867.

88. Ibid.

89. See Elkan collection, and Walter Harold collection, LBI, #ARC 4156, II, #20. Contract from 1872. I am grateful to Erika Grossmann and my mother, Grete Weinberg, for helping me decipher these marriage documents. Contracts were not the only official documents. A letter from Dr. Albert Mosse to his daughter on July 24, 1916, notifying her of the amount and disposition of her dowry, concludes by asking her "for the sake of good order" to verify the receipt of the money in writing. Mosse Family collection, LBI, section D.1.

90. For example, in 1884 Heinrich Graetz asked his friend Perles to state in writing that Graetz's son's father-in-law had formally told Perles the extent of his daughter's inheritance. It seems that the father-in-law wished to disinherit his daughter, because she was keeping a kosher household. Graetz hoped to avert this by asking the original witness to testify to the father's spoken promise. By this time, then, spoken promises may have begun to replace written contracts, with the understanding that the spoken word was as binding as the written one. Perles collection, pp. 71–72.

91. Richarz, *Jüdisches Leben*, vol. 2, p. 249.

92. Marie Maas (born 1855, Breslau), memoirs, LBI, pp. 40–48. At the turn of the century, a highly placed civil servant paid 300 Marks a year for this insurance: Freudenthal, *Gestaltwandel*, p. 137.

93. Geismar, memoirs, p. 97. In eighteenth-century Hamburg the Jewish community insisted that relatives help the needy: Pollack, *Jewish Folkways*, p. 32.

94. Hughes, "From Brideprice," p. 284.

95. Pollack, *Jewish Folkways*, p. 32.

96. Jacobson collection, LBI, II, #42.

97. Aron Hirsch Heymann, memoirs, LBI, pp. 168, 225, 299.

98. Hamburg and Altona: Hamburg Staatsarchiv, "Jüdische Gemeinde," 522-1, Ehesachen; Würzburg: records of the Feist Hirsch Berg'schen Aussteuer Stiftung, Central Ar-

chives for the History of the Jewish People, Jerusalem, Rep. WR, #909–972; Lübeck: Central Archives, GAII/541. These clubs were also found in smaller towns and villages. See Israelitisches Brautausstattungsverein zu Lorsch, statutes of 1901, founded in 1812, Central Archives GAII/544, or Verein zur Unterstützung Bedürftiger Bräute (Halberstadt), statutes of 1896, Central Archives, TD 1044.

99. For example, the Verein zur Ausstattung Jüdischer Bräute (Cologne) agreed to give a 3,000-Mark dowry to brides nominated by its members. This club had a membership of 130, annual income from dues of 1,103 Marks, and fixed assets. Other clubs gave less. *Israelitisches Gemeindeblatt*, March 1, 1912, p. 92.

100. Jack Wertheimer, *Unwelcome Strangers: East European Jews in Imperial Germany* (New York, 1987), pp. 45, 83, and 214, n. 7.

101. Geismar, memoirs, p. 112. She was referring to the 1860s and 1870s.

102. L. Stern, in Monika Richarz, ed., *Jüdisches Leben in Deutschland*, vol. 3, *Selbstzeugnisse zur Sozialgeschichte, 1918–1945* (Stuttgart, 1982), pp. 168–71. These examples add further evidence to the hypothesis that Jewish emigrants were poor and came from villages and small towns, whereas wealthier Jews moved to cities. For non-Jews, the opposite seemed to hold: the better-off emigrated and the poorer moved to industrial centers. Avraham Barkai, "The German Jews at the Start of Industrialisation: Structural Changes and Mobility, 1835–1860," in *Revolution and Evolution*, ed. Mosse et al., pp. 135–36.

103. Wertheimer, Zwischen, p. 25.

104. Rosenstein, memoirs, p. 2. This was in Berlin in 1870.

105. Marie Maas, memoirs, p. 63. This was in Breslau in the 1870s. Unless they were wealthy, widows with children did not remarry as easily as widowers. This can be seen, in part, by the fact that children of widows were more likely to be found in orphanages than those of widowers. The latter could choose from a pool of widows as well as among marriageable young women. For orphanages, see Staatsarchiv Königsberg, Rep 2, II, #3 194, p. 59, Geheimes Staatsarchiv Preussischer Kulturbesitz, Berlin.

106. Sander, memoirs, p. 24. This took place in the 1870s.

107. Riesenfeld, diary entry of May 11, 1916, referring to Breslau in the 1890s, LBI.

108. *Israelitisches Gemeindeblatt*, June 24, 1892, pp. 204–7.

109. Statistics for the nineteenth century indicate that, when comparing Jews and non-Jews of marriageable age, fewer Jews did indeed marry. Later the, statistics available for 1925 indicate proportionally more single Jews of both sexes: in Prussia, 15.5% of Jewish women between the ages of forty-five and forty-nine were single, compared to 10.5% of non-Jewish women. Usiel O. Schmelz, "Die demographische Entwicklung der Juden in Deutschland von der Mitte des 19. Jahrhunderts bis 1933," in *Zeitschrift für Bevölkerungswissenschaft* 1 (1982): 43. In order to discover the extent to which Jewish women were actually "left behind," we would have to examine population, intermarriage, and conversion statistics, and marriage frequency. Where possible, it would then be useful to compare these statistics to those of the general population.

At the turn of the century, Germany, like most West European countries, had a population in which there were more women than men: in 1900, 1,033 women to 1,000 men. Their distribution, however, was varied: the greatest disproportion was found in the large cities and in the rural countryside. Although statistics for the Reich did not separate population by religion, surveys by the states indicate that in 1900 there were 6,384 more Jewish women than men in Prussia, a ratio similar to that of the general population: Jacob Segall, *Die Entwicklung der jüdischen Bevölkerung in München, 1875–1905* (Berlin, 1910), p. 7.

Among Jews, too, the size of the city mattered: the smallest towns and biggest cities (excepting Berlin and Cologne) had the greatest "surplus" of women (Segall, ibid). By 1907, statistics demonstrated that there were 1% more Jewish women than men in Germany (compared to 2% more non-Jewish women than men): *Israelitisches Familienblatt* (hereafter *IF*), October 2, 1919, p. 10. In 1910 in Prussia, there were 1,031 Jewish women to every 1,000 Jewish men (compared to 1,026 non-Jewish women to 1,000 men). The ratios of Jewish women to 1,000 Jewish men in several other areas were: 1,086 in Charlottenburg (1910); 1,056 in Hesse (1905); and 1,048 in Baden (1890). In Saxony (863 in 1905), Bavaria (989 in 1905), and Württemberg (1,001 in 1905), the overall ratios were even, or seemed to benefit women: *ZDSJ*, February 1906, p. 24, and December 1913, p. 179. However, this may be deceptive, for as in the case of Württemberg, there were far more women in rural areas than men. In the cities, where the numbers of men and women were even, there were greater opportunities for interfaith marriage or conversion, and greater business or career incentives for men to postpone marriage.

Jewish men intermarried and converted (particularly during marrying years, age twenty to forty) more than Jewish women, leaving fewer available Jewish husbands: *ZDSJ*, June 1909, pp. 88–89.

If one then examines the frequency of Jewish marriages, preliminary conclusions also indicate that Jewish women were being "left behind" compared to non-Jewish women. For example, in 1903 fewer Jews married relative to their population than non-Jews. Only 70 per 10,000 Jews (including those in intermarriages) married, compared to 82 per 10,000 Christians: *ZDSJ*, April 1905, p. 8. In 1906, 82 per 10,000 Christians and 74 per 10,000 Jews married. Since Jews had a relatively greater marriage-age population than non-Jews, the Jewish population married even less frequently than these percentages indicate: *ZDSJ*, December 1908, p. 189. For 1905—86 per 10,000 Christians and 74 per 10,000 Jews—see *ZDSJ*, May 1907, p. 79.

In Berlin in 1910, 64% of Jewish women between twenty and thirty (compared to 59% of women in the general population), and 26% of Jewish women between thirty and forty (compared to 22% of women in the general population) remained unmarried: *ZDSJ*, September/October 1914, p. 131. There were cities like Frankfurt where more Jewish women were married (44%) than non-Jewish women (40%), but in general, it appears that Jews married later and relatively less frequently than non-Jews. (For Frankfurt in 1880, see *ZDSJ*, October 1910, p. 144. For age statistics, see *ZDSJ*, September/October 1914, p. 131.) This was most accentuated in rural areas. In Hesse, for example, in the first decade of the twentieth century, for every 1,000 women, 248 non-Jews and 282 Jews over the age of twenty were single: Arthur Ruppin, *Die Juden im Grossherzogtum Hessen* (Berlin, 1909), p. 46. It remains the task of demographers to discover the number of Jewish and Gentile women remaining single at given ages throughout the Imperial era, before we can substantiate these observations.

Finally, *in comparison to Jewish men*, it seems that more Jewish women married. Partial statistics for Hesse, Frankfurt/Main, and Berlin indicate that more Jewish men than women remained single, and that more Jewish women than men were married: Ruppin, ibid., p. 45, for Hesse, 1900; *ZDSJ*, October 1910, p. 144, for Frankfurt/Main, 1880; *ZDSJ*, September/October 1914, p. 131, for Berlin, 1910.

110. Gerald-Elsas, memoir of his mother, LBI, p. 4.

111. *Allgemeine Zeitung des Judentums* (hereafter *AZDJ*), April 9, 1849, pp. 203–5.

112. *Die Laubhütte* (Regensburg), July 18, 1895, p. 336.

113. Ibid., March 26, 1903, supplement, p. 1.

114. *IF*, July 31, 1919, p. 10.

115. Sidonie Werner in *Im deutschen Reich*, February 1914, pp. 53–54.

116. *ZDSJ*, July 1907, p. 110; December 1907, p. 187.

117. *ZDSJ*, October 1911, p. 150. The article discusses the causes of divorce in Berlin in 1909. Of all divorces, 57% resulted from adultery. This was the same for Jewish as for non-Jewish divorces. Hence, in large cities temptations were the same for Jews and non-Jews.

However, whereas Christian men were twice as likely, Jewish men were ten times as likely as their wives to be adulterous. This may have had something to do with a greater emphasis on arranged marriages among Jews—and, of course, with all men's greater freedom. Jewish women had fewer opportunities than their husbands to wander away from the marriage and less financial recourse if they did. On the other hand, it may also have been a result of the more frequent use of birth control in Jewish families—withdrawal or abstinence—which men could ameliorate by looking elsewhere for sexual intimacy. For efforts at marital reconciliation, see chapter 2, n. 137.

118. *Gedichte und Scherze in jüdischer Mundart* (Berlin, n.d.), pamphlet 18.

119. Ibid., pamphlet 23.

120. Ibid., pamphlet 7, pp. 8–10.

121. *Jettchen Gebert* describes a Jewish family in 1839–40 in Berlin. It is a sentimental depiction of Jewish integration into German society with all its trials and tribulations. It went through 166 reprintings and new editions and was made into a play, a film, and a musical between 1913 and 1928.

122. Georg Hermann, *Henriette Jacoby* (Berlin, 1915), p. 22.

123. Ettlinger, *Moritzchen*, pp. 123–24.

124. Georg Hirschfeld, *Agnes Jordan* (Berlin, 1898).

125. Arthur Landsberger, *Millionäre* (Berlin, 1913), pp. 326–27.

126. Richarz, *Jüdisches Leben*, vol. 2, p. 224.

127. Jeggle, *Judendörfer*, p. 165.

128. Henry Wassermann, "The *Fliegenden Blätter* as a Source for the Social History of German Jewry," *LBIYB*, 1983, p. 115.

129. *Simplicissimus*, 2:36 (1897–98): 284–85; 5:9 (1900–01): 69, and 5:47 (1900–01): 377.

130. See Hans Joachim Henning, *Das westdeutsche Bürgertum in der Epoche der Hochindustrialisierung, 1860–1914* (Wiesbaden, 1972), p. 301, for the middle class. See also Jürgen Kocka, "Family and Class Formation," pp. 411–34. He discusses family marriage strategies among the nobility, lower strata, and peasantry and finds similar interest in maintaining class standing and financial resources. A famous (non-Jewish) literary example is Toni Buddenbrooks' dowry in Thomas Mann's *Buddenbrooks*.

131. Alan Robinson, "Problems of Love and Marriage in Fontane's Novels," in *German Life and Letters* 5 (1952): 279–85.

132. Theodor Fontane, *Jenny Treibel*, trans. Ulf Zimmermann (New York, 1976), pp. 148–49. The novel appeared in 1893.

133. Gordon Craig, *Germany: 1866–1945* (New York, 1978), p. 453.

134. Jalland, *Women, Marriage and Politics*, p. 54. In Sweden, too, these ideas predominated: Jonas Frykman and Orvar Löfgren, *Culture Builders: A Historical Anthropology of Middle-Class Life* (New Brunswick, N.J., 1987), p. 96.

135. Berend, *Die gute alte Zeit*, p. 66.

136. *Frankfurter Zeitung und Handelsblatt*, July 26, 1914, p. 3; July 30, 1914, p. 5; August 2, 1914, p. 3.

137. Ibid., August 2, 1914, p. 3; from *Berlin Lokalanzeiger* (May 13, 1909), reprinted in *Im deutschen Reich*, June 1909, p. 389.

138. *Allgemeine Zeitung München*, April 18, 1885, p. 1576.

139. *Frankfurter Zeitung und Handelsblatt*, July 26, 1914, pp. 7, 12. *Berliner Illustrierte Zeitung*, January 18, 1914, p. 41.

140. *Frankfurter Zeitung und Handelsblatt*, August 2, 1914, p. 3.

141. Berthold Auerbach, *Barfüssele* (Berlin, 1912).

142. Riehl, *Die Familie*, p. 13.

143. Robert Lee, "Family and 'Modernisation': The Peasant Family and Social Change in Nineteenth-Century Bavaria," in *The German Family*, ed. Richard Evans and W. R. Lee (London, 1981), p. 95.

144. Gerhard Wilke and Kurt Wagner, "Family and Household Social Structures in a German Village Between the Two World Wars," in *The German Family*, ed. Evans and Lee, p. 137. Most likely, the matchmakers in question were Jews. Jews were heavily involved in the rural economy as cattle dealers (25,000 of Germany's 40,000 cattle dealers in 1917 were Jews), and Jeggle's findings for Württemberg, that Jews were brokers for Christian marriages, probably holds for other rural areas as well. (On Jewish cattle dealers, see Monika Richarz, "Emancipation and Continuity: Jews in the Rural Economy," in *Revolution and Evolution*, ed. Mosse et al., p. 106.) In fact, Jews may have continued this occupation into the 1930s. On July 6, 1938, the Nazis forbade Jews from acting as brokers for "Aryan" marriages. They were limited to arranging marriages between two Jews or between "first degree *Mischlinge* [those of mixed origin]." Joseph Walk, *Das Sonderrecht für die Juden im NS Staat* (Heidelberg, 1981). See Gesetz zur Änderung der Gewerbeordnung für das Deutsche Reich.

145. Richarz, *Jüdisches Leben*, vol. 2, p. 162.

146. Wilke and Wagner, "Family," p. 139.

147. Jeggle, *Judendörfer*, pp. 220, 225–26.

148. This continued well into the 1920s in some of the smallest towns. Interview with Liesl Stern (born 1922, Weikersheim, Württemberg), New York, December 1982.

149. Henry Mayhew, "German Life and Manners as Seen in Saxony at the Present Day" (London, 1865), quoted in Priscilla Robertson, *An Experience of Women: Pattern and Change in Nineteenth-Century Europe* (Philadelphia, 1982), p. 81. See also Heidi Rosenbaum, *Formen der Familie* (Frankfurt/Main, 1982), pp. 332–38.

150. Karen Horney, *The Adolescent Diaries of Karen Horney* (New York, 1980), pp. 61–62.

151. *Akademisch gebildeten Beamten* ranged from *Referendar* to *Oberpräsident*. Henning, *Bürgertum*, pp. 294, 331.

152. Ibid., p. 383.

153. Ibid., p. 274, and Karin Hausen, "Die Polarisierung der 'Geschlechtscharaktere'—Eine Spiegelung der Dissoziation von Erwerbs- und Familienleben," in Conze, *Sozialgeschichte*, p. 384.

154. Henning, *Bürgertum*, pp. 432, 460–61.

155. Ibid., pp. 393, 454, 460. The desire to save for substantial future dowries may have been another cause for the decline in Jewish fertility in this period.

156. Claudia Hahn, "Der öffentliche Dienst und die Frauen—Beamtinnen in der Weimarer Republik," in *Mutterkreuz und Arbeitsbuch: Zur Geschichte der Frauen in der Weimarer Republik und im Nationalsozialismus*, ed. Frauengruppe Faschismusforschung (Frankfurt, 1981), p. 51.

157. After World War I, dowries and the arrangements that went with them became much less common in Germany. Jews, in contrast to non-Jews, may have clung longer to arranged marriages in order to assure endogamy in a small pool of available partners. Also, as a result of their participation in business and commerce, many Jews continued to demand dowries throughout the 1920s. In the 1920s Ruppin remarked that the dowry was much less common among Christians than among Jews. Arthur Ruppin, *Soziologie der Juden* (Berlin, 1930), p. 221. This does not, however, imply that love matches ignored financial issues. In 1952, 65% of a sample of German women claimed to have brought a dowry into their marriages: William J. Goode, *World Revolution and Family Patterns* (New York, 1970), p. 34.

158. F. M. L. Thompson, *The Rise of Respectable Society*, p. 102.

159. Hughes, "From Brideprice," p. 288.

160. Fritz Stern, *Gold and Iron: Bismarck, Bleichröder, and the Building of the German Empire* (New York, 1977), p. 462.

161. Henning, *Bürgertum*, p. 334.

162. Max Weber quoted by Stern, *Gold*, p. 468.

163. This does not mean that Jews were unaware of upward social mobility within their *own* community. However, Jewish and non-Jewish *perceptions* differed here: outsiders were unlikely to recognize marriage to another Jew, no matter what her or his family's position, as an increase in *social* status, since it was not a marriage into the German Christian elite.

164. Gay, *The Bourgeois Experience: Education of the Senses*, and *The Bourgeois Experience: The Tender Passion.*

165. Jacob Katz, paper delivered at the National Jewish Family Center of the American Jewish Committee, March 18, 1982.

166. Examples of *Brautbriefe* are those between Sigmund and Martha Freud. See also the letters of Agathe Bleichröder (born 1871) in Hamburger-Liepmann, memoirs.

167. Riesenfeld diary, book 2, pp. 69–70. He became engaged around 1907 in Breslau.

168. *The Diaries, 1910–1923*, trans. Max Brod (New York, 1949).

169. This pretense of spontaneity was sometimes followed by a pretense of ignorance regarding financial matters. Marianne Weber (born 1870) recalled that dowries were important, but girls were not supposed to know about them. Robertson, *An Experience*, p. 81. Some in fact, did not.

170. Jacob Epstein, memoirs, LBI, p. 31. This took place in Frankfurt/Main in 1881.

171. Riesenfeld, diary, book 2, pp. 134–35.

172. Marianne Berel, "Family Fragments," memoirs, LBI, p. 48.

173. Bruno Stern, *Meine Jugenderinnerungen an eine württembergische Kleinstadt und ihre jüdische Gemeinde* (Stuttgart, 1968), p. 122. He described the period up to 1933.

174. Louis Boehm, *Lieder eines fahrenden Chossid: Humoristische Dichtungen für jüdische Geselligkeit* (Frankfurt/Main, 1922), pp. 17–18.

> [the uncle]
> "Meine werten Tischgenossen":
> Sagt er laut und streicht den Bart,
> "Amor hat es heut beschlossen,
> dass die Beiden sich gepaart.
>
> Nur Gott Amor durfte fügen
> Diesen Ehebund auf Ehr'
> Denn der Chozzen konnte kriegen
> Siebenhundert Taler mehr."
>
> [the broker]
> "Ja," der Schadchen denkt sich heute,
> "Mühe hat's genug gemacht,
> Eh' ich diese beiden Leute
> Glücklich hab zusamm'n gebracht."

175. Richarz, *Jüdisches Leben*, vol. 2, p. 227. This occurred around 1905.

176. According to William Goode, since love is potentially disruptive of lineages and class strata, it must be controlled before it appears. There are several patterns by which parents achieve this: child marriage, social segregation of adolescents, formal and informal

parental initiatives. The formal pattern permits love to emerge, and the informal pattern actually encourages love relationships. "The Theoretical Importance of Love," *American Sociological Review* 24:1 (February 1959): 38–46. See also Jalland, *Women, Marriage and Politics*, p. 46.

177. Rahel Straus, *Wir lebten*, pp. 19–20, 101–5.

178. Ibid., p. 105.

179. By the mid-eighteenth century, major watering places like Bath had become marriage markets for a wealthy clientele. By the mid-nineteenth century, "hordes of mothers and daughters in search of husbands" descended on Vichy. See Lawrence Stone, *The Family, Sex and Marriage in England, 1500–1800* (New York, 1979), p. 213, and Theodore Zeldin, *France, 1848–1945*, vol. 2 (Oxford, 1977), p. 93.

180. Phil Landau, *Kindheitserinnerungen: Bilder aus einer rheinischen Kleinstadt des vorigen Jahrhunderts* (Dietenheim, 1956), p. 30.

181. Published in 1911.

182. Toni Cassirer, memoirs, LBI, pp. 12–13. See also Max Gruenewald collection, LBI. His father's memoirs describe how he met his future wife at a family wedding in 1890.

183. Edwin Landau (born 1890, Deutsch-Krone, West Prussia), memoirs, LBI.

184. Interviews with Mrs. B. held in New York in June 1981 and January 1982.

185. Edmund Hadra, memoirs, LBI, p. 88. In previous centuries love relationships occurred infrequently. When they did, parents who consented to the union would employ a matchmaker after the fact "for appearance's sake." Customary negotiations took place, and betrothal documents were signed by both sets of parents. If a young couple fell in love against their parents' wishes, rabbis usually ruled in favor of the parents. Katz, "Family, Kinship," pp. 9–10. For the late eighteenth and the nineteenth centuries, I am purposely excluding the love relationships of untraditional women such as the participants in the Berlin salons or early feminists.

186. Ludwig Guttman, memoirs, LBI, p. 123.

187. Straus, *Wir lebten*, p. 129. The author attended the University of Heidelberg and married in 1905.

188. Ibid. See also Charlotte Landau-Muehsam, memoirs, LBI, p. 41. She married in Lübeck in 1908 after meeting her spouse in the Zionist movement.

189. Anna Kronthal, *Posner Mürbekuchen: Jugend Erinnerungen einer Posnerin* (Munich, 1932), pp. 90–93.

190. Hadra, memoirs, p. 200. This marriage took place in Berlin around 1900.

191. Gruenewald, memoirs. This took place in a small town in Westphalia.

192. Bertha Katz, memoirs, LBI, p. 8. Also, Mrs. Lipton in Foster, *Community*, p. 26. The third sister in her family had to forgo "lots of opportunities to marry when she was 18 or 19 . . . because the elder sisters were not yet married. So she had to wait, and she was very unhappy." More than sisterly solicitude, the cases of women marrying in birth order indicate the extent of parental control even when there were no dowries.

193. Interview with Anna Hamburger.

194. Theilhaber, *Die Schädigung*.

195. Toni Sender, *Autobiographie einer deutschen Rebellin* (Frankfurt/Main, 1981), p. 38. This incident took place around 1905.

196. Mrs. Lipton in Foster, *Community*, p. 25.

197. This does not mean that workers had no trousseaus. See Heilwig Schomerus, "The Family Life-Cycle: A Study of Factory Workers in Nineteenth-Century Württemberg," in *The German Family*, ed. Evans and Lee, p. 189. It remains to be seen whether working-class Jewish women brought some savings into marriage. They did marry at a later age (twenty-five to twenty-six for those marrying craftsmen, and twenty-six for those marrying workers) than

their propertied sisters and may have been saving up for marriage. Theilhaber, *Die Schädigung*, pp. 88–89, a study of women in Berlin, 1909.

198. S. D. Goitein, *A Mediterranean Society: The Jewish Communities of the Arab World as Portrayed in the Documents of the Cairo Geniza*, vol. 3, *The Family* (Berkeley and Los Angeles, 1978), part viii, B, I, pp. 55–56.

199. Sander, memoirs, p. 62 (born in Frankfurt, married ca. 1894); Landau-Muehsam, referring to her sister, memoirs, p. 31 (in Lübeck, sister married in 1896); Henriette Hirsch in Richarz, *Jüdisches Leben*, vol. 2, pp. 79–80 (met in Halberstadt, married ca. 1880).

200. M. Michael, memoirs, LBI, p. 1. The first set of marriages took place in Hamburg in the 1860s; the second pair married in the 1880s.

201. Cassirer, memoirs. See also Ernst Herzfeld, memoirs, LBI, pp. 15–18.

202. Wilhelm Reutlinger, "Über die Häufigkeit der Verwandtenehen bei den Juden in Hohenzollern und über Untersuchungen bei Deszendenten aus jüdischen Verwandtenehen," *Archiv für Rassen und Gesellschaftsbiologie* 14 (1922): 303.

203. Interview with L. Stern, (born 1922, Weikersheim, Württemberg), New York, March 1982.

204. Anka Muhlstein, *Baron James: The Rise of the French Rothschilds* (New York, 1982), p. 76.

205. Ruppin, *Soziologie*, p. 201; *ZDSJ*, March/April 1924, p. 53. In Hungary, Ruppin shows that Jews requested twice as many dispensations (required by the Hungarian government) for marriages between relatives than did non-Jews. In Alsace-Lorraine between 1872 and 1876, there were 23 per 1,000 such marriages among Jews, compared to 10 per 1,000 among Catholics (pp. 200–201). According to Jacob Katz, Jews prohibited marriage only within the innermost circle of relatives, such as between sister and brother or aunt and nephew (not uncle and niece). Katz, "Family, Kinship," p. 14.

206. In Hohenzollern, for example, the Jewish population had declined by 41% between 1890 and 1922. An earlier generation of 164 married couples (married in the second half of the nineteenth century, and one or both of whom were dead by 1922) evinced an 11% rate of marriage with relatives. First cousins were found in 5% of the cases, second cousins in 2%, and third cousins in 4%. A generation later (both partners still alive in 1922), 22% of 117 couples consisted of relatives: 16% were first cousins, 3% were second cousins, and 3% were third cousins. In one town, Haigerloch, 27% of the 82 Jewish couples were relatives, of which 18% were first cousins. Reutlinger, "Verwandtenehen," pp. 301–3.

207. In the two Hohenzollern towns, for example, 18% of Jews in Haigerloch and 11% of Jews in Hechingen were married to first cousins. In similar towns in Württemberg—two Catholic towns and one Protestant—marriages between first cousins in the non-Jewish population were 0.7%, 2.7%, and 2.5% respectively. Reutlinger, "Verwandtenehen," pp. 301–3.

208. See "Die Krankheiten der Juden," in *Im deutschen Reich*, April 1911, pp. 201–5; *ZDSJ*, April 1911, p. 63, and April 1924, pp. 52–53; H. L. Eisenstadt, "Die Sozialpathologie der Juden und ihre Lehren," *Soziale Medizin und Hygiene* 5 (1910): 3. These writers worried about the possibility of increased cases of mental retardation and epilepsy among the offspring of cousin marriages. Clearly, some Jews were aware of the health risks. Margarete Sallis-Freudenthal and her cousin restrained themselves from a more intense relationship because "of the danger of cousin marriages": *Ich habe mein Land gefunden* (Frankfurt, 1977), p. 35.

209. The Church discouraged cousin marriages; couples had to request special dispensation for them up to the fourth degree of relationship. Such dispensations, however, were not uncommon. Jack Goody, *The Development of the Family and Marriage in Europe* (Cambridge, 1983), pp. 55–57, 134–46, 181–87.

210. The theme of *Verwandtenehe* appeared frequently in Jewish novels and magazines.

See "Zum Seder," in *Der Freitagabend, eine Familienschrift* (Frankfurt/Main), 1859, or *Jettchen Gebert*. It also appeared in non-Jewish literature: Gabrielle Reuter, *Aus guter Familie*, 17th ed. (Berlin, 1908).

Chapter 4

1. Lina Morgenstern, *Deutsche Hausfrauenzeitung* (Berlin), January 10, 1886, p. 14.

2. Henry Wassermann, "The Fliegende Blätter as a Source for the Social History of German Jewry," *LBIYB*, 1983, p. 120.

3. Anna Kronthal, *Posner Mürbekuchen: Jugend Erinnerungen einer Posnerin* (Munich, 1932), p. 10.

4. Clara Geismar (born 1844, Eppingen), memoirs, LBI, p. 182.

5. Sidney Bolkosky, *The Distorted Image: German Jewish Perceptions of Germans and Germany, 1918–1935* (New York, 1975).

6. It was Heine who—early on—pointed out that no one was more "German" than a German Jew. Thanks to Alf Lüdtke for coining "overadaptation" in a letter to the author (December 9, 1988).

7. Jürgen Zinnecker, *Sozialgeschichte der Mädchenbildung* (Weinheim, 1973). Most Jewish girls attended a private or public *Volksschule* (elementary school), and an increasingly and disproportionately high percentage—approximately 42% of Jewish girls in Prussia in 1901, compared to 3.7% of non-Jewish girls (though these percentages would be modified, if we could factor in class)—went to a *höhere Töchterschule* (approximately through the age of sixteen): *Zeitschrift für Demographie und Statistik der Juden* (hereafter *ZDSJ*), September 1909, p. 141.

8. Clara Sander (born ca. 1871, Frankfurt/Main), memoirs, LBI, p.3.

9. Interviews with Anna Hamburger (born 1888, Württemberg), New Jersey, June 1981, March 1982. For urban attitudes, see Toni Ehrlich (born ca. 1880, Breslau), memoirs, LBI, p. 32.

10. Nora Rosenthal (born 1892, Frankfurt/Main), memoirs, Stadtarchiv Frankfurt/Main, p. 18.

11. Conrad Rosenstein, memoirs, LBI, pp. 19–23. His mother married at twenty-one in 1870 and lived in Berlin.

12. *The Bourgeois Experience: Victoria to Freud*, vol. 1, *Education of the Senses* (New York, 1984), pp. 28–29.

13. Toni Ehrlich wrote that Jews sent daughters "with or without talent" for piano lessons. Memoirs, LBI, p. 32.

14. See David Landes, "The Bleichröder Bank," *LBIYB*, 1960, p. 203; Werner Mosse, *Jews in the German Economy: The German-Jewish Economic Elite, 1820–1935* (Oxford, 1987), p. 168.

15. Interview with Mrs. Lipton in *Community of Fate: Memoirs of German Jews in Melbourne*, ed. John Foster (Sydney, 1986), p. 24.

16. Nora Rosenthal described weekend walks in the Taunus, the "lovely narrow paths through pine woods." Writing in 1973, she remarked, "I must say that the Taunus is the *only* thing I hanker for, as far as Germany is concerned and my former life there": memoirs, p. 12. See also Margarete Sallis-Freudenthal, *Ich habe mein Land gefunden* (Frankfurt/Main, 1977), p. 23.

17. Bertha Katz, memoirs, LBI, p. 26.

18. Henriette Hirsch, memoirs, LBI, p. 3.

19. Utz Jeggle, *Judendörfer in Württemberg* (Tübingen, 1969), p. 240; Bruno Stern,

Meine Jugenderinnerungen an eine württembergische Kleinstadt und ihre jüdische Gemeinde (Stuttgart, 1968), p. 97. Rudolf Hallo, *Geschichte der jüdischen Gemeinde Kassel*, vol. 1 (Kassel, 1931), p. 117.

20. Mrs. Lipton in *Community of Fate*, p. 24.

21. See chapter 2. See also: Marion Kaplan, "Priestess and Hausfrau: Women and Tradition in the German-Jewish Family", in *The Jewish Family: Myths and Reality*, ed. Steven Cohen and Paula Hyman (New York, 1986).

22. Henriette Necheles, unpublished memoirs, "Reminiscences of a German-Jewish Physician," p. 6, courtesy of Atina Grossmann.

23. Arthur Prinz, *Juden im deutschen Wirtschaftsleben, 1850–1914*, ed. Avraham Barkai (Tübingen, 1984), pp. 9–10.

24. Toni Sender, *Autobiographie einer deutschen Rebellin* (Frankfurt/Main, 1981), p. 32.

25. Ehrlich, memoirs, pp. 18–19.

26. Sophie Diamant, "Familiengeschichte Schlesinger," memoirs, LBI, p. 5.

27. Kronthal, *Posner*, p. 29; also H. Hirsch, memoirs, p. 41.

28. Rosenthal, memoirs, p. 6.

29. Sallis-Freudenthal, *Ich habe*, p. 52.

30. Geismar, memoirs, p. 185; Sallis-Freudenthal, *Ich habe*, p. 52; Ernst Herzfeld (born 1874, Grätz), memoirs, LBI, pp. 37, 39, 41, 60–61; Marie Mass (born 1855, Breslau), memoirs, LBI, pp. 37, 52; Rosenthal, memoirs, p. 25.

31. Fritz Stern, *Gold and Iron: Bismarck, Bleichröder, and the Building of the German Empire* (New York, 1977), p. 483.

32. Rosenthal, memoirs, pp. 13–14. See also *Die Dame*, advertisements, May/June 1916, pp. 52–53.

33. Herzfeld, memoirs, p. 45.

34. Rosenthal, memoirs, p. 13.

35. Antoinette Kahler (born 1862, Bruenn), memoirs, Kahler collection, LBI, p. 64. See also Max Brod, *Jüdinnen* (Berlin, 1911).

36. Phillippine Landau, *Kindheitserinnerungen: Bilden aus einer rheinischen Kleinstadt des vorigen Jahrhunderts* (Dietenheim, 1956), p. 125.

37. Marie Maas, memoirs, p. 37.

38. Charlotte Wolff, *Hindsight: An Autobiography* (London, 1980), p. 23.

39. Interview with Ilse Blumenthal-Weiss (born ca. 1900, Berlin), New York, 1982.

40. Mrs. Lipton in *Community of Fate*, p. 24.

41. Kronthal, *Posner*, p. 54; Rosenthal, memoirs, pp. 13–14.

42. In 1886, as a result of their exclusion from student life, Jewish men formed the first Jewish fraternity, the Viadrina.

43. Heinrich Mann gives particularly vivid examples of this in *Der Untertan* (1918), translated as *Man of Straw* (London, 1984).

44. Frances Henry, *Victims and Neighbors: A Small Town in Nazi Germany Remembered* (South Hadley, Mass., 1985), p. 58. Sonderburg is a fictitious name.

45. Solomon Andorn, memoirs, #414, LBI, p. 15.

46. Geismar, memoirs, p. 18, referring to her mother's activities in the 1850s and 1860s.

47. Landau, *Kindheitserinnerungen*, p. 55.

48. Andorn, memoirs, #414, p. 15; Hallo, *Geschichte*, p. 117; Ehrlich, memoirs, pp. 14–15.

49. Jeggle, *Judendörfer*, p. 227.

50. Andorn, memoirs, #414, p. 15.

51. Hallo, *Geschichte*, p. 119.

52. Henry, *Victims*, pp. 58–59.

53. These were also called *Spinnstuben*. See Gerhard Wilke and Kurt Wagner, "Family and Household: Social Structures in a German Village Between the Two World Wars," in *The German Family*, ed. Richard J. Evans and W. R. Lee (London, 1981), pp. 133, 139.

54. On Catholic/Jewish neighborliness in the village of Rexingen (Württemberg), see Beate Bechtold-Comforty, "Jüdische Frauen auf dem Dorf—zwischen Eigenständigkeit und Integration," *Sozialwissenschaftliche Informationen* 18:3 (September 1989): 157–62. For the exchange of matzos and eggs, see Stern, *Jugenderinnerungen*, p. 102; Jeggle, *Judendörfer*, pp. 260–61.

55. Memoirs of Tante Emma, p. 14, Max Gruenewald collection, LBI.

56. Stern, *Jugenderinnerungen*, p. 79.

57. Henry, *Victims*, p. 65.

58. Sallis-Freudenthal, *Ich habe*, p. 8.

59. Geismar, memoirs, p. 156.

60. Käte Frankenthal, *Der dreifache Fluch: Jüdin, Intellektuelle, Sozialistin* (Frankfurt/Main 1981), p. 4.

61. Ibid., p. 5.

62. Ibid., p. 5.

63. Arnold Zweig, *Junge Frau von 1914* (Berlin, 1931; reprint, Frankfurt/Main, 1970), pp. 36–37.

64. Dennis Klein, *Jewish Origins of the Psychoanalytic Movement* (Chicago, 1985), p. 72.

65. Scholem, "On the Social Psychology of the Jews in Germany: 1900–1933," in *Jews and Germans from 1860 to 1933: The Problematic Symbiosis*, ed. David Bronsen (Heidelberg, 1979), p. 19.

66. Wolff, *Hindsight*, p. 6.

67. Margarete Freudenthal, "Gestaltwandel der städtischen, bürgerlichen und proletarischen Hauswirtschaft unter besonderer Berücksichtigung des Typenwandels von Frau und Familie," diss. (Würzburg, March 1934), pp. 92–93. See also Heidi Rosenbaum, *Formen der Familie* (Frankfurt/Main, 1982), pp. 371–72.

68. Sibylle Meyer, *Das Theater mit der Hausarbeit: Bürgerliche Repräsentation in der Familie der wilhelminischen Zeit* (Frankfurt/Main, 1982).

69. Ibid., p. 51.

70. Georg Tietz, *Hermann Tietz: Geschichte einer Familie und ihrer Warenhäuser* (Stuttgart, 1965), p. 148, as quoted by Werner E. Mosse, "Terms of Successful Integration: The Tietz Family, 1858–1923," *LBIYB*, 1989, p. 151. Throughout this article Mosse describes Betty Tietz as excessively ambitious. He writes that she "revelled in large-scale entertaining," while her husband "did not like this in the least" (p. 138). Mosse appears to have taken her son Georg's obviously hostile and critical reports completely at face value. He fails to recognize the importance of this kind of female activity to her husband, Oscar. His economic and political status benefited from her "ambition." Moreover, Oscar—and later Georg—may have found it psychologically convenient to "blame" Betty for performing exactly those social functions—entertaining, insisting on the "right" schools for her son, acquiring an elegant home, and aspiring to the "right" social circles—that they expected of her.

71. Wassermann, "The Fliegende Blätter," pp. 117, 120, 126, 131, 137–38.

72. Bertha Gumprich, *Vollständiges praktisches Kochbuch für die jüdische Küche*, 7th ed. (Frankfurt/Main, 1914), pp. 362–64.

73. Leo Lippmann, *Mein Leben und meine amtliche Tätigkeit: Erinnerungen und ein Beitrag zur Finanzgeschichte Hamburgs* (Hamburg, 1964), p. 76.

74. Meyer, *Das Theater*, p. 51.

75. Fontane, *Jenny Treibel*, translated by Ulf Zimmermann in *Theodor Fontane: Short Novels and Other Writings*, ed. Peter Demetz (New York, 1982), p. 155.

76. Gumprich, *Kochbuch*, p. 361. See also Sibylle Meyer, "Die mühsame Arbeit des demonstrativen Müssiggangs: Über die häuslichen Pflichten der Beamtenfrauen im Kaiserreich," in *Frauen suchen ihre Geschichte*, ed. Karin Hausen (Munich, 1983), p. 180.

77. Marie Munk (born ca. 1888, Berlin), memoirs, Helene Lange Archives, Berlin, I, 11a.

78. Scholem, "On the Social Psychology," p. 19.

79. Stephanie Orfali, *A Jewish Girl in the Weimar Republic* (Berkeley, 1987), pp. 17–18.

80. Adolf Riesenfeld, diary, LBI, entry of November 3, 1917 (referring to 1904).

81. Gabrielle Reuter, *Aus guter Familie: Leidensgeschichte eines Mädchens*, 17th ed. (Berlin, 1908), p. 231.

82. Olly Schwarz, memoirs, LBI, pp. 15–16.

83. Charlotte Hamburger-Liepmann, memoirs, LBI, p. 67 (referring to the 1870s and 1880s).

84. Ehrlich, memoirs, pp.14–15; Munk, memoirs, II, 4.

85. Munk, memoirs, V, 18–19.

86. Ann Taylor Allen, "Sex and Satire in Wilhelmine Germany: 'Simplicissimus' Looks at Family Life," *Journal of European Studies* 7 (1977): 34.

87. Jacob Katz, "German Culture and the Jews," in *The Jewish Response to German Culture: From the Enlightenment to the Second World War*, ed. Jehuda Reinharz and Walter Schatzberg (Hanover, N.H., 1985), pp. 86–90.

88. Charlotte Landau-Muehsam, memoirs, LBI, p. 27.

89. Hallo, *Geschichte*, p. 117 (referring to 1870s, 1880s).

90. Rosenthal, memoirs, p. 18.

91. For singers, musicians, etc., see Siegmund Kaznelson, ed., *Juden im deutschen Kulturbereich* (Berlin, 1959). See also Erna Magnus collection, LBI, box III.

Chapter 5

1. Women could audit courses if the professor and the Ministry of Education gave their assent. Thus before the first state, Baden, officially allowed women to matriculate in 1901, individual women sat in on lectures and took exams. Munich, Erlangen, and Würzburg let women enter in 1904, Tübingen in 1905, and Leipzig in 1907. Prussia, the last state, allowed women to matriculate in 1908.

2. Konrad Jarausch, *Students, Society and Politics in Imperial Germany: The Rise of Academic Illiberalism* (Princeton, N.J., 1982), p. 96.

3. For example, in cities with large Jewish populations like Frankfurt/Main and Berlin, we find a disproportionately high representation of Jewish women (21% in 1908 and 22% in 1913/14, respectively), compared to their general representation in German universities as a whole. *Preussen: Statistik der Landesuniversitäten*, #223, 1908/09, pp. 28–29.

4. Hansjoachim Henning, *Das Westdeutsche Bürgertum in der Epoche der Hochindustrialisierung, 1860–1914: Soziales Verhalten und Soziale Strukturen*, vol. 1, *Das Bildungsbürgertum in den Preussischen Westprovinzen* (Wiesbaden, 1971), pp. 477, 484.

5. For an excellent description of the varieties of women's schools, see James Albisetti, "The Reform of Female Education in Prussia, 1898–1908: A Study in Compromise and Containment," *German Studies Review* 8 (February 1985): 11–41.

6. *Zeitschrift für Demographie und Statistik der Juden* (hereafter *ZDSJ*), August 1909, p. 117.

7. James C. Albisetti, *Schooling German Girls and Women* (Princeton, N.J., 1988), p. 216. I want to thank James Albisetti for generously sharing parts of his manuscript with me before its publication.

8. *Mädchengymnasium* statistics available in *ZDSJ*, April 1913, p. 61. *Abiturientinnen* statistics from *ZDSJ*, February 1914, p. 31. James Albisetti suggests that Jewish representation can be explained, in part, by where Jews lived. "That the three German cities with the largest Jewish populations—Berlin, Frankfurt, and Breslau—were sites of *Abitur* courses for girls helps to explain the high percentage of Jewish *Abiturientinnen*" (*Schooling*, p. 217). However, Jewish *Abiturientinnen* percentages were even higher in rural areas than in Germany as a whole. In Hesse, for example, between 1909 and 1913, 15.7% of the *Abiturientinnen* were Jewish (*ZDSJ*, February 1914, p. 31). Thus class and culture probably played a greater role than urban location. For men, an *Abitur* opened paths in the middle ranks of the civil service and allowed them to take various higher state exams. Fritz Ringer reminds us that the number of students who successfully completed the *Abitur* was much less than the enrollment figures in relation to the age group, generally just under a third: Fritz K. Ringer, *Education and Society in Modern Europe* (Bloomington, Ind., 1979), pp. 34, 56.

9. Of the 266 Jewish women, 189 were German Jews and the other 77 were of foreign origin, mostly Eastern Europeans. Together, they made up 14% of women students. *ZDSJ*, July–September 1915, p. 83, and *ZDSJ*, 2:2 (1925): 33. The statistics are for the winter semester of 1911/12.

10. Albisetti, *Schooling*, p. 290.

11. Jews made up 5.6% of the male student population. *ZDSJ*, June 1914, pp. 86–87; *Blätter des Jüdischen Frauenbunds* (hereafter *BJFB*), September 1933, pp. 10–11; *KC Blätter* (*Zeitschrift des Kartell Convents der Verbindungen Deutscher Studenten Jüdischen Glaubens*), February 1, 1914, pp. 120–21. By 1924, the 389 Jewish women at Prussian universities still accounted for 11% of the total female student population and had climbed to 20% of the Jewish student population. At this time German women (including Jewish women) accounted for 11% of the entire student population, while Jewish men made up only 6% of male students. *ZDSJ*, 2:2 (1925): 33. These postwar statistics include foreign students, although "foreign" by German standards could include people who had been born or raised in Germany, but whose parents did not have citizenship (see n. 47). See also *Preussen Statistik: Statistik der Landesuniversitäten und Hochschulen*, #279, Winterhalbjahr 1924/25, pp. 2–3.

12. Julie Braun-Vogelstein, *Was niemals stirbt: Gestalten und Erinnerungen* (Stuttgart, 1966), p. 222.

13. Margarete Sallis-Freudenthal, *Ich habe mein Land gefunden: Autobiographischer Rückblick* (Frankfurt/Main, 1977), p. 27.

14. Rahel Straus, *Wir lebten in Deutschland: Erinnerungen einer deutschen Jüdin, 1880–1933* (Stuttgart, 1962), p. 86.

15. Ibid., pp. 88–89.

16. Braun-Vogelstein, *Niemals*, p. 219. This remark may have been tinged with anti-Semitism as well, since the Berlin neighborhoods he mentioned were ones in which many Jews resided, although they were not the majority.

17. Ida H. Hyde (née Heidenheimer), "Before Women Were Human Beings," *Journal of the American Association of University Women* 31:4 (June 1938): 226.

18. Quoting Wilhelm Waldeyer (Berlin). Professors who were particularly alarmed at the thought of women studying obstetrics and gynecology used similar arguments. Laetitia Boehm, "Von den Anfängen des akademischen Frauenstudiums in Deutschland," *Historisches Jahrbuch* 77 (1958): 309; James Albisetti, "The Fight for Female Physicians in Imperial Germany," in *Central European History*, 15:2 (June 1982): 99–123.

19. Hyde, "Before Women," pp. 231–32, 234. She later became a professor of physiology at the University of Kansas. Jacob Marcus, *The American Jewish Woman, 1654–1980* (New York, 1981), p. 72.

20. Straus, *Wir lebten.*, p. 90.

21. See Boehm, "Von den Anfängen," p. 309; Albisetti, "The Fight for Female Physicians," pp. 99–123. Konrad Jarausch has suggested that the theologians were even worse than the medical faculties, even though less threatened by competition. Letter to author, February 17, 1982.

22. Peter Gay, *The Bourgeois Experience*, vol. 1, *Education of the Senses* (New York, 1984), p. 223.

23. Agnes Zahn-Harnack, *Die Frauenbewegung, Geschichte, Probleme, Ziele* (Berlin, 1928), p. 185.

24. Ute Frevert, *Frauengeschichte: Zwischen Bürgerlicher Verbesserung und Neuer Weiblichkeit* (Frankfurt, 1986), p. 122.

25. Gay, *Experience*, vol. 1, p. 225.

26. Konrad H. Jarausch, "Students, Sex and Politics in Imperial Germany," *Journal of Contemporary History* 17:2 (April 1982): 296. See also p. 149.

27. Straus, *Wir lebten*, p. 96. This occurred in 1902.

28. *KC Blätter*, April 1, 1912, p. 141.

29. Käte Frankenthal, *Der dreifache Fluch: Jüdin, Intellektuelle und Sozialistin: Lebenserinnerungen einer Ärztin in Deutschland und im Exil* (Frankfurt/Main, 1981), p. 30.

30. Karin Hausen "'. . . eine Ulme für das schwanke Efeu': Ehepaare im Bildungsbürgertum. Ideale und Wirklichkeiten im späten 18. und 19. Jahrhundert," in *Bürgerinnen und Bürger*, ed. Ute Frevert (Göttingen, 1988), p. 101.

31. In 1904 a study of 176 Jewish and 492 Christian girls in a *höhere Mädchenschule* in Berlin indicated that Jewish girls tended to achieve more middling grades than their Christian schoolmates, who clustered more at the top and bottom of the grade levels. This was particularly the case in the higher grades, when, Jewish observers noted, Jewish girls had more social activities that they attended. These same observers pointed out that Jewish parents showed little interest in their daughters' progress, compared to that of their sons. (Of course this would be the case for non-Jewish families as well.) *ZDSJ*, August/September 1906, pp. 129–135.

32. Karen Horney, *The Adolescent Diaries of Karen Horney* (New York, 1980), second diary, 1900–1902, pp. 19–26. Horney's dilemma, but not its resolution, was typical of many women of her day.

33. Albisetti, *Schooling*, p. 290.

34. Claudia Huerkamp, "Frauen, Universitäten und Bildungsbürgertum: Zur Lage studierender Frauen, 1900–1930," in *Bürgerliche Berufe: Zur Sozialgeschichte der freien und akademischen Berufe im internationalen Vergleich*, ed. Hannes Siegrist (Göttingen, 1988), pp. 202–3.

35. Anna Kronthal, *Posner Mürbekuchen: Jugend Erinnerungen einer Posnerin* (Munich, 1932), p. 70.

36. Braun-Vogelstein, *Niemals*, pp. 207, 212, 220.

37. Toni Sender, *Autobiographie einer deutschen Rebellin* (Frankfurt/Main, 1981), p. 40 (this occurred ca. 1905).

38. Marie Munk, unpublished memoirs, Helene Lange Archives (Berlin), III, 1. Munk was the first woman judge on the Berlin Superior Court. She had been baptized as a child.

39. Munk, memoirs, VI, 2.

40. Interview with Herta Natorff by Atina Grossmann, held in New York in 1980. I would like to thank Atina Grossmann for sharing her notes with me.

41. Charlotte Wolff, *Hindsight: An Autobiography* (London, 1980), pp. 26, 82.

42. Frankenthal, *Dreifache*, pp. 13, 32.

43. Konrad Jarausch, "Higher Education and Social Change: Some Comparative Perspec-

tives," in *The Transformation of Higher Learning, 1860–1930: Expansion, Diversification, Social Opening and Professionalization in England, Germany, Russia and the United States*, ed. Konrad Jarausch (Stuttgart, 1983), p. 30.

44. Klaus Vondung, "Zur Lage der Gebildeten in der wilhelminischen Zeit," in *Das wilhelminische Bildungsbürgertum: Zur Sozialgeschichte seiner Ideen*, ed. Klaus Vondung (Göttingen, 1976), p. 30.

45. Jarausch, "Higher Education and Social Change," p. 34.

46. Elisabeth Bab (born 1880, Berlin), "Aus zwei Jahrhunderten: Lebenserinnerungen," memoir, LBI, p. 75.

47. These statistics include citizens as well as foreigners (*Ausländer*). Where statistics separate students by citizenship, German-Jewish women's humanities profile is closer to, but not as high as, that of non-Jewish women: *ZDSJ*, July–August 1913, p. 115. This is because a large percentage of Russian women students (many of whom were Jewish) majored in medicine; when they were counted into the general statistics, it raised Jewish representation in medicine. Consolidated statistics of foreign and German Jews are used, because a clear breakdown of foreign students by religion is unavailable. Also, some of the "foreign" Jews were probably second-generation Eastern Jews who had been born in or resided in Germany. Germany had extraordinarily complicated naturalization procedures which required ten years' residency and the approval of all state governments. These regulations kept tens of thousands of Eastern Jews from becoming citizens, although many were born in Germany and, in the case of men, may have even served in the German army. See Donald L. Niewyk, *The Jews in Weimar Germany* (Baton Rouge, La., 1980), pp. 15–16, 119; Jack Wertheimer, *Unwelcome Strangers: East European Jews in Imperial Germany* (New York, 1987).

48. Straus, *Wir lebten.*, p. 87.

49. The numbers are: 135 Jewish women students, of whom 46 majored in medicine; 12 in dentistry; 1 in pharmacy; 7 in chemistry (*Chemie*); and 13 in mathematics and science (*Mathematik und Naturwissenschaften*). Of the 46 Jewish women in medicine, 21 (or 45%) were Jews of "foreign" origin. Protestants and Catholics had the following enrollments: Of 437 Protestants, 63 majored in medicine, 12 in dentistry, none in pharmacy, 6 in chemistry, and 72 in math/science. Of 60 Catholics, 16 majored in medicine and 16 in math/science. *Preussen: Statistik der Landesuniversitäten*, #223, 1908/09, Anhang: Die Studierenden Frauen im Winterhalbjahr 1908/09, pp. 70–71.

50. Eight out of 16 female dental students and 109 out of 282 medical students were Jewish. *ZDSJ* 2:2 (1925): 33. By 1924/25, Jewish women, who were 11% of the female student population, were 18% of the women enrolled in the medical faculty. Whereas 46% of Jewish women continued to major in medicine and dentistry (30% together) and math and sciences (16% together), 36% of non-Jewish women majored in medicine (17%) and math and science (19%). *Preussen: Statistik*, #279, pp.2–3.

51. It is also likely that Jewish women were, on the average, younger than non-Jewish women, since many of the latter had worked for several years before entering the university. In 1899 Rahel Straus noted that, at nineteen, she was much younger than the other women who wanted to be high-school teachers and had already taught. For several years she remained the youngest woman at the university, although she was the "oldest" (first) female student at Heidelberg.

52. *KC Blätter*, April 1, 1912, p. 141. See also Bab, memoirs.

53. Munk, memoirs, III, 4.

54. Straus, *Wir lebten*, p. 97 (ca. 1899–1905).

55. These were areas from which Jews had been traditionally excluded.

56. Ringer, *Education*, pp. 85–87, 91.

57. Konrad H. Jarausch, "Liberal Education as Illiberal Socialization: The Case of Stu-

dents in Imperial Germany," *Journal of Modern History* 50:4 (December 1978): 615. See also Albisetti, *Schooling*, p. 289.

58. Konrad H. Jarausch, "Frequenz und Struktur: Zur Sozialgeschichte der Studenten im Kaiserreich," in *Bildungspolitik in Preussen zur Zeit des Kaiserreichs*, ed. Peter Baumgart (Stuttgart, 1980), p. 140. Albisetti states that 40% of women students in 1911 came from academic backgrounds: *Schooling*, p. 289.

59. Norbert Kampe suggests that, "unlike most male Jewish students, the Jewish women appear to have been of upper-class origin." From reading the memoir literature, I would suggest that Jewish women describe themselves as coming from the upper middle class, not upper class. Kampe, "Jews and Antisemites at Universities in Imperial Germany: (I) Jewish Students: Social History and Social Conflict," *LBIYB*, 1985, p. 374, n. 53.

60. According to Henning, the academically educated bourgeoisie who worked as civil servants had an average of three children between 1860 and 1890. This figure was slightly—but insignificantly—lower for the period after 1890. Those in the free professions had between two and three children before 1890 and only two thereafter. Jews seem to have regulated their fertility rate at least a generation before other Germans. Before 1907, the majority of Jews limited their families to one or two children, whereas the "two-child system" had made few inroads into Gentile families. See chapter 2. See also Henning, *Bürgertum*, pp. 297, 422, 478; Erich Rosenthal, "Jewish Population in Germany," *Jewish Social Studies* 6 (1944): 270; Lawrence Schofer, "Emancipation and Population Change," in *Revolution and Evolution: 1848 in German-Jewish History*, ed. Werner Mosse et al. (Tübingen, 1981), pp. 79–80.

61. Wolff, *Hindsight*, p. 50.

62. In 1909, Jewish university graduates who intended to help one another find jobs established the Arbeitsamt Jüdischer Akademiker. A survey of theirs concluded that "a frighteningly large number of government offices and private firms, . . . must be viewed as clear of Jews (*judenrein*)." In 1912, of 169 members from 42 cities, only one female name can be ascertained. *Arbeitsamt für jüdische Akademiker: Bericht für die Jahre 1910/12*, Central Archives for the History of the Jewish People, TD/353, p. 3.

63. Avraham Barkai, *Jüdische Minderheit und Industrialisierung* (Tübingen, 1988), pp. 48–50, and Table II.24, p. 133.

64. Monika Richarz, *Der Eintritt der Juden in die akademischen Berufe: Jüdische Studenten und Akademiker in Deutschland, 1778–1848* (Tübingen, 1974).

65. Jarausch, *Students, Society*, pp. 87, 145.

66. Barkai, *Jüdische Minderheit*, p. 50.

67. Jarausch, *Students, Society*, pp. 142–43, and "Higher Education and Social Change," p. 30.

68. Barkai, *Jüdische Minderheit*, Table II.26, p. 134, from Norbert Kampe, "Bildungsbürgertum und Antisemitismus im Deutschen Kaiserreich," diss., Technical University, Berlin, 1983, pp. 211, 492. Kampe notes that Jewish law students tended to be wealthier and from more elite circles than those who studied medicine. Kampe is quoted by Barkai, p. 50. Even though medicine was the longer and more expensive course of study, it was the law faculty which required proof of *standesgemäss* support for five years and offered very little financial aid: Jarausch, *Students, Society*, p. 143.

69. Nevertheless, a number of Jewish women did major in law, in the hope that the bar would soon open, or with the understanding that teaching, in any case, was closed to them. (See chapter 6.) Only in 1922 were women permitted to function as full-fledged lawyers. Berent collection, LBI, II, #19–20.

70. Charlotte Landau-Muehsam, memoirs, LBI, p. 41. Of the four daughters of the publisher M. A. Klausner, one became a doctor, one became one of the first female lawyers

in Germany, another was a sculptress, and the fourth, with a Ph.D., became a delegate to the Landtag. They were all educated in the first decade of the century.

71. *General Anzeiger für die gesamten Interessen des Judentums*, August 8, 1904, supplement. Rahel Hirsch collection, LBI, ARC 2610, #4.

72. Doris Kampmann, "'Zölibat—ohne uns!' Die soziale Situation und politische Einstellung der Lehrerinnen in der Weimarer Republik," in *Mutterkreuz und Arbeitsbuch: zur Geschichte der Frauen in der Weimarer Republik und im Nationalsozialismus* (Frankfurt/Main, 1981), pp. 79–85.

73. Jarausch, "Liberal Education," pp. 621–22.

74. Frankenthal, *Dreifache*, p. 23.

75. Straus, *Wir lebten*, p. 98.

76. Else Croner, *Das Tagebuch eines Fräulein Doktor* (Stuttgart, 1908), p. 208.

77. For example, see the café scenes in Aimée Duc, *Sind es Frauen?* (Berlin, 1903).

78. Croner, *Tagebuch*, pp. 11–13.

79. Henriette Necheles, "Reminiscences of a German-Jewish Physician," unpublished memoirs, pp. 8–9, courtesy of Atina Grossmann.

80. Munk, memoirs, VI, 8.

81. Ibid., VI, 8.

82. Bertha Badt-Strauss, "Studententage in München, 1912–13," in *Von Juden in München*, ed. Hans Lamm (Munich, 1958), p. 144.

83. Nathorff interview.

84. Straus, *Wir lebten*, p. 98.

85. Konrad H. Jarausch, "Students, Sex and Politics in Imperial Germany," in *The Journal of Contemporary History* 17:2 (April 1982): 289–91.

86. Croner, *Tagebuch*, pp. 10, 209; Sallis-Freudenthal, *Ich habe*, pp. 52–53.

87. Bab, memoirs, pp. 95–97.

88. Kampe, "Jews and Antisemites," p. 374, n. 54.

89. Detlef Grieswelle, "Antisemitismus im deutschen Studentenverbindungen des 19. Jahrhunderts," in *Student und Hochschule im 19. Jahrhundert*, vol. 12 of *Studien zum Wandel von Gesellschaft und Bildung im Neunzehnten Jahrhundert*, ed. Otto Neuloh and Walter Rüegg (Göttingen, 1975), p. 375; Manfred Studier, "Der Corpsstudent als Idealbild der Wilhelminischen Ära," diss., University of Erlangen-Nürnberg, 1965, p. 173.

90. Norbert Kampe, "Jews and Antisemites at Universities in Imperial Germany: (II) The Friedrich-Wilhelms-Universität of Berlin: A Case Study on the Students' 'Jewish Question,'" *LBIYB*, 1987, p. 59.

91. Albisetti, *Schooling*, p. 245; Jack Wertheimer, "The 'Ausländerfrage' at Institutions of Higher Learning: A Controversy over Russian–Jewish Students in Imperial Germany," *LBIYB*, 1982, pp. 185–217.

92. Straus, *Wir lebten*, p. 93; Jarausch, *Students, Society*, pp. 271–72.

93. Straus, *Wir lebten*, pp. 94, 96.

94. Ibid., p. 96.

95. *Im deutschen Reich*, August 1909, pp. 447–48; October 1909, p. 588.

96. Johanna Simon-Friedenberg, *Gegenwartsaufgaben der jüdischen Frau* (Berlin, 1913), p. 12. Anti-Semitism was not unique to German universities. By 1917 there were five Jewish national sororities in the United States, since non-Jewish women kept Jews at a social distance. Jacob R. Marcus, *The American Jewish Woman, 1654–1980* (New York, 1981), pp. 68–69.

97. *KC Blätter*, August 1, 1914, p. 258; Michael Doeberl, ed., *Das akademische Deutschland*, vol. 2 (Berlin, 1931), pp. 591–92. By 1931 the organization was describing itself as "standing on Aryan principles" (Doeberl, p. 659).

98. *Preussen: Statistik*, #223, pp. 70–71. For a discussion of "foreign", see n. 47.

99. Zalman Gordon on the plight of these women, quoted by Jack Wertheimer, "Between Tsar and Kaiser: The Radicalization of Russian Jewish University Students in Germany," in *LBIYB*, 1983, p. 337, n. 17.

100. Albisetti notes that at least two Jewish women were among the German protesters. See *Schooling*, p. 246. See also Wertheimer, *Unwelcome*, pp. 63–71, on the general situation of Russian students.

101. *KC Blätter*, April 1, 1912, pp. 140–41.

102. Necheles, memoirs, p. 15.

103. Doeberl, *Das akademische Deutschland*, pp. 589, 591–92.

Chapter 6

1. Jakob Segall, *Die berufliche und soziale Verhältnisse der Juden in Deutschland* (Berlin, 1912), p. 81.

2. Elfie Labsch-Benz, *Die jüdische Gemeinde Nonnenweier: Jüdisches Leben und Brauchtum in einer badischen Landgemeinde zu Beginn des 20. Jahrhunderts* (Baden-Württemberg, 1980), p. 33.

3. For Ettlinger, see Monika Richarz, ed., *Jüdisches Leben in Deutschland*, vol. 1, *Selbstzeugnisse zur Sozialgeschichte, 1780–1871* (Stuttgart, 1976), p. 385. For other examples, see pp. 171, 335, 339. See also Ludwig Frank, memoirs, LBI, pp. 1–29.

4. Richarz, *Jüdisches Leben*, vol. 1, p. 199.

5. Monika Richarz, ed., *Jüdisches Leben in Deutschland*, vol. 2, *Selbstzeugnisse zur Sozialgeschichte im Kaiserreich* (Stuttgart, 1979), p. 243.

6. Richarz, ed., *Jüdisches Leben*, vol. 1, p. 246.

7. Ibid., p. 332.

8. Heinrich Grünfeld, memoirs, LBI, p. 47; Richarz, *Jüdisches Leben*, vol. 1, p. 283.

9. Julius Frank, memoirs, LBI, p. 44. (He was born in 1889 and described his mother's work.)

10. Jacob Rosenheim, *Erinnerungen, 1870–1920* (Frankfurt/Main, 1970), p. 66.

11. Clara Geismar, memoirs, LBI, pp. 166–67.

12. Bertha Katz, memoirs, LBI, p. 8.

13. *Israelitisches Familienblatt* (hereafter *IF*), October 18, 1907, p. 13; *Israelitisches Gemeindeblatt*, February 12, 1892, p. 56.

14. Bonnie Anderson and Judith Zinsser, *A History of Their Own: Women in Europe*, vol. 1 (New York, 1988), pp. 293–94.

15. Sophie Diamant (born 1879, lived in Mainz), memoirs, LBI, p. 10.

16. Richarz, *Jüdisches Leben*, vol. 1, p. 158.

17. Ibid, p. 242.

18. Richarz, *Jüdisches Leben*, vol. 2, p. 67.

19. Margarete Freudenthal, "Gestaltwandel der städtischen, bürgerlichen und proletarischen Hauswirtschaft unter besonderer Berücksichtigung des Typenwandels von Frau und Familie" diss. (Würzburg, 1934).

20. *Zeitschrift für Demographie und Statistik der Juden* (hereafter *ZDSJ*), January/April 1923, p. 17.

21. Usiel O. Schmelz, "Die demographische Entwicklung der Juden in Deutschland von der Mitte des 19. Jahrhunderts bis 1933," *Zeitschrift für Bevölkerungswissenschaft* 8 (January 1982): 62.

22. Usiel O. Schmelz, *Infant and Early Childhood Mortality Among the Jews of the*

Diaspora (Jerusalem, 1971). Of course, if they worked at home, this would have gone unnoticed.

23. Here are the percentages and numbers for Prussia in 1882:

	Jewish Women	Non-Jewish Women
Employed in "major" jobs	9.0	15.5
Servants	2.0	6.1
TOTAL NUMBERS	20,102	3,017,702

SOURCE: *ZDSJ*, May 1911, pp. 79–80.

In the 1890s, Prussian Jewish working women made up 68% of all German-Jewish working women and can therefore be used as a sample of German-Jewish women: *ZDSJ*, May 1911, pp. 79–80. My 11% figure (see text) differs from that of 16% given by most demographers of Jews, because they also included anyone who "earned an independent income," that is, "independents without a career" (*Beruflose Selbstständige*). See n. 24.

24. *ZDSJ*, August 1911, pp. 104–5; *ZDSJ*, May 1911, p. 80. Stefan Bajohr, *Die Hälfte der Fabrik* (Marburg, 1979), p. 18, says that 25% of German women were employed in 1895. German "employment" statistics included *Ohne Beruf*, category F, people who were financially "independent" and did not work for a living. This included university students who no longer lived at home; those in jail or institutionalized; and those on welfare or living from their own savings or pensions. About 35% of all Jewish women in the overall employment statistics (compared to about half of that for non-Jewish women), fell into this category. Among Jewish women this figure was often as high as 50%. Most of them were widows surviving on pensions. Jakob Segall, *Die Entwicklung der jüdischen Bevölkerung in München* (Berlin, 1910), p. 34; *ZDSJ*, April 1905, p. 1. In this study I refer only to women actually working, excluding category "F" of the census.

25. See n. 33 for a discussion of the numbers of Jewish immigrant women.

26. *ZDSJ*, January–March 1919, p. 3. In 1910, 11% of Jews in Germany were immigrants. Therefore it is fair to assume that a substantial number of these Jewish women were immigrants of proletarian, Eastern European origin, thus making the percentage of German-Jewish women employed even smaller.

27. This is not to imply that there were no Jewish female teachers or nurses. For teachers, read on in this chapter. By 1916, there were enough Jewish nurses to form a national association consisting of thirteen local nurses' organizations. These women may have come from poorer families, since the comfortable middle class considered nursing "beneath" their status. On Jewish nurses, see: Claudia Prestel, "Erschliessung neuer Erwerbszweige für jüdische Frauen: Das Beispiel der Krankenschwester," *Vierteljahresschrift für Sozial- und Wirtschaftsgeschichte* (forthcoming).

28. See Eleanor S. Riemer and John C. Fout, eds., *European Women: A Documentary History, 1789–1945* (New York, 1980), pp. 40–41, on telegraph operators. Jakob Lestschinsky noted that as late as 1925 Jews represented less than one-half of 1 per cent (0.45%) of civil servants in Prussia. This means that only about 2% of Jews were civil servants. *Das wirtschaftliche Schicksal des deutschen Judentums* (Berlin, 1932), pp. 106–07.

29. Claudia Hahn, "Der öffentliche Dienst und die Frauen—Beamtinnen in der Weimarer Republik," in *Mutterkreuz und Arbeitsbuch*, ed. Frauengruppe Faschismusforschung (Frankfurt/Main, 1981), pp. 50–52.

30. See *ZDSJ*, January–March 1919, p. 4; *IF*, April 28, 1910, p. 13.

31. Avraham Barkai, "The German Jews at the Start of Industrialisation: Structural

Change and Mobility 1835–1860," in *Revolution and Evolution: 1848 in German-Jewish History*, ed. Werner Mosse et al. (Tübingen, 1981), p. 142; and "Sozialgeschichtliche Aspekte der deutschen Judenheit in der Zeit der Industrialisierung," in *Jahrbuch des Instituts für deutsche Geschichte*, vol. 11 (1982), p. 246.

32. Robyn Dasey, "Women's Work and the Family: Women Garment Workers in Berlin and Hamburg before the First World War," in *The German Family*, ed. Richard J. Evans and W. R. Lee (London, 1981), p. 235. From 35% to 40% of women in the clothing industry worked from home, in particular married women (Dasey, p. 235).

33. One quarter is a rough estimate obtained by working backward from the 1910 statistics. Although there were only half as many immigrants in 1895, their proportional occupational distribution was similar to later. There were about 70,000 Eastern European immigrant Jews in Germany in 1910, of whom 45% (31,500) were women. If even a quarter of these women earned an income (the figure for Berlin, where about one-fifth of immigrant Jews lived, was 27%: *ZDSJ*, January/April 1923, p. 17), that would only amount to 7,875 people, less than half of whom (48%, or about 3,780) worked in industry. Thus of the 14,906 Jewish women found in industrial jobs in 1907, about one quarter were Eastern European immigrants: Jack Wertheimer, *Unwelcome Strangers: East European Jews in Imperial Germany* (New York, 1987), pp. 100–01. Owing to their recent arrival, they probably filled the ranks of "family helpers" and "workers" out of proportion to their numbers.

34. By 1913 Eastern Jews—mainly women and older men—represented 20% of the work force in Berlin's large cigarette factories. Wertheimer, *Unwelcome*, p. 95.

35. ZDSJ, May 1911, p. 108 (for 1895 statistics).

36. *ZDSJ*, May 1911, pp. 79–80.

37. *ZDSJ*, July/August 1911, pp. 97–112.

38. *Im deutschen Reich*, September 1897, p. 405. It should be noted that the increase in "family assistants" may not always have exactly reflected the increase in the actual number of working women: some family members may have been included on the payroll for tax purposes without actually working. However, the inclusion of some extra women who may have "padded the payroll" probably did not begin to make up for the family assistants who had previously worked and been excluded from the census plus the newly working family members. Further, some of these "family assistants" were undoubtedly wives who actually ran the business. The job profile of Jewish women did not shift significantly during the rest of the Imperial era and into the 1920s. See Lestschinsky, *Das wirtschaftliche Schicksal*, pp. 132–37.

39. Segall, *Die berufliche*, p. 78. In fact, between 1882 and 1907, a twenty-five-year period, the number of Jewish working women had more than doubled.

40. Ute Frevert, *Frauen-Geschichte: Zwischen Bürgerlicher Verbesserung und Neuer Weiblichkeit* (Frankfurt/Main, 1986), p. 75.

41. This includes category "b" under Industry and categories "b" and "c" under Commerce. Jewish statisticians claimed that some of the women in category "c," worker in industry, were really doing office work, therefore the overall total may be closer to half of Jewish women.

42. Frevert, *Frauen-Geschichte*, p. 172.

43. Letter from Ursala Hagen, Berlin, December 16, 1979.

44. Berlin had about 130,000 Eastern Jews in 1910. Steven Aschheim, *Brothers and Strangers: The East European Jew in German and German-Jewish Consciousness, 1800–1923* (Madison, Wis., 1982), p. 44. Wertheimer, *Unwelcome*, pp. 100–01; *ZDSJ*, January/June 1920, pp. 17–21.

45. Salomon Dembitzer, *Aus engen Gassen* (Berlin, 1915), pp. 21–23, 26, 32.

46. *ZDSJ*, January/April 1923, p. 16; Wertheimer, *Unwelcome*, p. 101. On the other

hand, Donald Niewyk contradicts this. He reports that there were antagonisms between German Jews and Eastern Jews, quoting one memoir: "It was well known that neither wealthy German Jews nor refugee Jewish domestics were comfortable together, preferring to serve or be served by non-Jews." Niewyk, *The Jews in Weimar Germany* (Baton Rouge, La., 1980), p. 118.

47. *ZDSJ*, April 1905, pp. 4–5.

48. Paula Weiner-Odenheimer, *Die Berufe der Juden in Bayern* (Berlin, 1918), pp. 41, 96.

49. Segall, *Die berufliche*, p. 63.

50. *ZDSJ*, July 1911, p. 105; *Statistik des deutschen Reichs*, #211, Grossstädte; *ZDSJ*, April 1905, p. 2.

51. For Bavaria, see Weiner-Odenheimer, *Die Berufe*, pp. 70–81. For example, 55% of the Jews in tailoring (*Schneiderei*) and the clothing industry (*Kleiderkonfektion*) came from Eastern Europe, where many of them had practiced these skills before.

52. In 1896, 14% (or 93 applicants) were female; in 1913, 47% (or 996 applicants) were female. *ZDSJ*, February/March 1915, pp. 17–30.

53. Thirty percent of female job seekers were between twenty-one and thirty, after which the drop was precipitous. For men, 38% looked for work between twenty-one and thirty. They continued the job hunt into their late thirties. Men also participated in training programs that kept them out of the job market longer, while many women worked to tide them over until they married. The age averages are for 1905–12.

54. Richarz, *Jüdisches Leben*, vol. 2, pp. 21–22; *ZDSJ*, February/March 1915, pp. 17–30, for employment bureau statistics of 1896–1913.

55. Schmelz, "Die demographische," p. 65. In 1895 in Hesse, they were about 2% of all employed people and made up 13% of those in commerce and trade. Arthur Ruppin, *Die Juden im Grossherzogtum Hessen* (Berlin, 1909), p. 52.

56. Barkai, *Jüdische Minderheit und Industrialisierung* (Tübingen,1988), p. 39.

57. Schmelz, "Die demographische," p. 63.

58. Barkai, "Sozialgeschichtliche Aspekte," p. 253. See also Barkai, *Jüdische Minderheit*, pp. 43–44. Barkai hypothesizes that although the increase in Jewish income kept pace with the general increase in income, its "tempo" may have slowed down (*Jüdische Minderheit*, p. 72).

59. These constraints affect most minorities. Simon Kuznets has described these as (1) "affiliation constraints": Jews' preference for jobs that would not interfere with their religion; (2) "heritage equipment constraints": their traditional, historical know-how in areas of trade and commerce; (3) "recent-entry constraints": the tendency of immigrants and migrants to enter fields or work with people they already know; (4) "majority-bias constraints": the positive and negative prejudices of the majority as to where the minority person should work; and (5) "economic growth constraints": the way the economy favors or hinders a minority's ability to put their job experience to practice. Barkai, "Sozialgeschichtliche Aspekte," pp. 258–60.

60. *ZDSJ*, April 1905, p. 2.

61. William Kober, memoirs, LBI, pp. 3–4.

62. Geheimes Staatsarchiv Preussischer Kulturbesitz, Regierung Danzig, Reps. 180–81.

63. Semi Moore, memoirs, LBI, p. 52.

64. Edmund G. Hadra, memoirs, LBI.

65. Francis Henry, *Victims and Neighbors: A Small Town in Nazi Germany Remembered* (South Hadley, Mass., 1984), p. 21. The author changed the names of her respondents.

66. Dasey, "Women's Work," p. 232.

67. *ZDSJ*, July–September 1916, p. 86.

68. William Wertheimer, *Zwischen zwei Welten: Der Förster von Brooklyn* (Passau, 1966), p. 29.

69. *ZDSJ*, July 1911, p. 107.

70. Segall, *Die berufliche*, p. 85. One-sixth to one-seventh of all "independent" seamstresses (*Näherinnen*) and dress makers (*Schneiderinnen*) worked at home. Other employed seamstresses and dressmakers usually eked out a living by relying on private customers in slow seasons and on shop or homework in better times. Sometimes they worked at all three together. Dasey, "Women's Work," p. 240.

71. *ZDSJ*, January/March 1919, p. 2–4.

72. J. Silbermann, "Die Frauenarbeit nach den beiden letzten Berufszählungen," *Schmollers Jahrbuch für Gesetzgebung* 35 (1911): 219.

73. Silbermann, "Die Frauenarbeit," p. 213.

74. Barkai, "Sozialgeschichtliche Aspekte," p. 249.

75. Ibid., p. 256.

76. *ZDSJ*, January/March 1919, p. 31.

77. Arthur Prinz, *Juden im deutschen Wirtschaftsleben*, ed. Avraham Barkai (Tübingen, 1984), pp. 188–89.

78. *Statistik des deutschen Reichs, 1907*, vol. 10, #211.

79. Here are the percentages for Hamburg in 1907:

	Jewish Women	Non-Jewish Women
Independents	42	28
Employees	25	9
Workers	31	62

SOURCE: *ZDSJ*, May–July 1919, p. 108.

80. *ZDSJ*, January–March 1919, p. 2.

81. Only office personnel came under the rubric *Angestellte*.

82. Staatsarchiv Hamburg, Paulinenstift folder 487, pp. 22–23.

83. *Mittheilungen vom Deutsch Israelitischen Gemeindebund*, #24 (Berlin, 1889).

84. *ZDSJ*, April/June 1915, p. 41–48.

85. "eine tüchtige dienende Classe"; *Laubhütte*, July 18, 1885, p. 337.

86. Segall, *Die berufliche*, p. 81.

87. *ZDSJ*, January–March 1919, p. 2.

88. *ZDSJ*, July–August 1911, p. 102.

89. *Im deutschen Reich*, September 1897, p. 405.

90. Ibid. See also Prinz, *Juden*, pp. 188–89.

91. Segall, *Die berufliche*, pp. 78–79.

92. George Mosse, "Jewish Emancipation: Between *Bildung* and Respectability," in *The Jewish Response to German Culture*, ed. Jehuda Reinharz and Walter Schatzberg (Hanover, N.H., 1985), p. 12.

93. *Israelitisches Gemeindeblatt*, August 9, 1912, p. 347.

94. Richarz, *Jüdisches Leben*, vol. 2, p. 230.

95. Lucy Maas-Friedman, memoirs, LBI, p. 7.

96. Ibid.

97. Diamant, memoirs, LBI, p. 8.

98. John Foster, ed., *Community of Fate: Memoirs of German Jews in Melbourne* (Sydney, 1986), p. 26. (This woman was born in Berlin in 1905.)

99. Stephanie Orfali, *A Jewish Girl in the Weimar Republic* (Berkeley, Calif., 1987), p. 21.

100. Diamant, memoirs, p. 11. In Germany, nursing probably also appeared to be a "Christian" profession, since nuns and deaconesses had dominated the field in its early years.

101. Richarz, *Jüdisches Leben*, vol. 2, p. 230.

102. Ibid.

103. After 1900 a wife could contract for a job without her husband's permission, but he could nullify her work contract until 1957. My thanks to Ute Gerhard and Bob Moeller for deciphering these laws for me. See also Ute Gerhard, "Die Rechtsstellung der Frau in der bürgerlichen Gesellschaft des 19. Jahrhunderts: Frankreich und Deutschland im Vergleich," in *Bürgertum im 19. Jahrhundert: Deutschland im europäischen Vergleich*, vol. 1, ed. Jürgen Kocka (Munich, 1988), pp. 448–52.

104. Karin Hausen, "'. . . eine Ulme für das schwanke Efeu': Ehepaare im Bildungsbürgertum: Ideale und Wirklichkeiten im späten 18. und 19. Jahrhundert," in *Bürgerinnen und Bürger*, ed. Ute Frevert (Göttingen, 1988), pp. 109-10.

105. In his introduction to a collection of essays on gender relationships and bourgeois society, Jürgen Kocka asks whether gender inequality is fundamental (*konstitutiv*) to bourgeois society. See *Bürgerinnen und Bürger*, ed. Frevert, p. 9. If one used as a case study the resistance to women's careers, a positive response would be in order.

Where a certain degree of gender equality within the couple was required in order for the woman to fulfill extrafamilial duties, men (and women) met such aspirations with enormous enmity. Bourgeois society as constituted in the nineteenth century could not envision women with public lives equal to those of men. And no one even dreamed of questioning the gender division within the household: even the most progressive women simply assumed they would juggle the double burden of career and family or, as we shall see, gave up family life for a career. Men never faced such burning dilemmas.

106. Nora Rosenthal (born 1892, Frankfurt/Main), memoirs, Stadtarchiv Frankfurt/Main, pp. 23–24 (1914–15).

107. Toni Sender, *Autobiographie einer deutschen Rebellin* (Frankfurt/Main, 1981), p. 35.

108. Marie Munk, memoirs, Helene Lange Archives, Berlin, III, 3a; VI, 3. Munk spent some time in Alice Salomon's Groups.

109. Emmy Livneh (born Frankfurt/Main, 1902), memoirs, LBI, p. 1.

110. Eric Hobsbawn, "Kultur und Geschlecht im europäischen Bürgertum, 1870–1914," in *Bürgerinnen und Bürger*, ed. Frevert, p. 178.

111. In families without sons, daughters sometimes benefited from their parents' inclination toward education. See Herta Natorff, memoirs, LBI, p. 1.

112. Richarz, *Jüdisches Leben*, vol. 2, p. 348.

113. Anna Kronthal, *Posner Mürbekuchen: Jugend Erinnerungen einer Posnerin* (Munich, 1932), p. 73.

114. See chapter 3 on dowries. Statistics in Schmelz, "Die demographische," p. 43.

115. A few years after Lette's death in the 1870s, Hirsch announced her support for suffrage, but considered it premature. This was still decades before the Federation of German Women's Associations advocated suffrage.

116. Anna Plothow, *Die Begründerinnen der deutschen Frauenbewegung* (Leipzig, n.d., ca. 1906 or 1907), pp. 57–58, 130.

117. Catherine Prelinger, *Charity, Challenge, and Change: Religious Dimensions of the Mid-Nineteenth Century Women's Movement in Germany* (Westport, Conn., 1987).

118. James Albisetti, "The Fight for Female Physicians in Imperial Germany," *Central European History* 15:2 (June 1982): 99–123.

119. *Statistik des deutschen Reichs, 1907*, vol. 211, p. 272.

120. Judith Herrman, *Die deutsche Frau in akademischen Berufen* (Leipzig and Berlin, 1915), p. 47.

121. Albisetti, "The Fight for Female Physicians."

122. In 1908/09, for example, 34% of Jewish women students in Prussia (46 out of 135), compared to 14% of Gentile women, enrolled in the medical faculty. *Preussen: Statistik der Landesuniversitäten*, #223, 1908/09, pp. 70–71. In 1911/12, 41% of Jewish women (109 out of 266) studied medicine, compared to only 10% of Protestant and 9% of Catholic women. See chapter 6 for comparisons with Jewish men.

123. *Preussen: Statistik*, #223, pp. 70–71. Thirty-four percent of Jewish women (see previous note) meant 46 out of 132 women enrolled.

124. In absolute numbers, this meant 109 out of 282 women were Jewish.

125. In Germany in 1908, 702 women in all were enrolled in medicine; in 1913/14, 859; and in 1918, 1,765. *K.C. Blätter* (Berlin), May/June 1918, p. 1089.

126. *General Anzeiger* (Berlin), August 8, 1904, supplement.

127. Albisetti, "The Fight for Female Physicians," p. 122, on completion rates. In 1909/10, 47 degrees (*Promotionen*) were received; in 1911/12, 79; in 1914, 70: Herrmann, *Die deutsche Frau,* p. 48.

128. It is likely that close to half of all women dentists were Jewish, given that 47% of all women dental students between 1908/09 and 1911/12 were Jewish. In 1907 there were 165 women dentists in Germany. *Statistik des deutschen Reichs*, vol. 211, 1907, p. 272. See also Herrmann, *Die deutsche Frau*, p. 43.

129. Richarz, *Jüdisches Leben*, vol. 2, p. 33.

130. Herrmann, *Die deutsche Frau*, p. 47.

131. Atina Grossmann estimated that 70% of women doctors in the 1920s were general practitioners: "Berliner Ärztinnen," in *Unter allen Umständen: Frauengeschichte(n) in Berlin*, ed. Christiane Eifert and Susanne Rouette (Berlin, 1986), p. 189. In the Prussian census of 1925 there is a noticeable shift toward independent status. The number of "independent" Jewish women doctors (206) was greater than those "employed" (124): Lestschinsky, *Das wirtschaftliche Schicksal*, p. 138.

132. Herrmann, *Die deutsche Frau*, p. 47.

133. Albisetti, "The Fight for Female Physicians," pp. 108–09.

134. Albisetti, "The Fight for Female Physicians," p. 122. Thanks to James Albisetti for informing me of the ban on the *Habilitation* for women until 1919.

135. Charlotte Wolff, *Hindsight: An Autobiography* (London, 1980), pp. 97–98. I would guess that accessibility to panel practice was more difficult for women than for men, although Michael Kater notes that women faced heavier obstacles during the 1920s than earlier, when women were still a curiosity: *Doctors under Hitler* (Chapel Hill, N.C., and London, 1989), p. 90.

136. Käte Frankenthal, *Der dreifache Fluch: Jüdin, Intellektuelle, Sozialistin* (Frankfurt/Main, 1981), p. 53.

137. See also Herta Natorff, memoirs, p. 3. As a result of the war, she too was appointed to a very responsible position just as she was finishing her medical studies at the University of Heidelberg.

138. Frankenthal, *Der dreifache*, p. 55.

139. Ibid., p. 57.

140. Ibid., p. 58.

141. Ibid., p. 72.

142. Ibid., p. 71.

143. Many of them subsisted on the rations of the period: in Berlin in June 1918, three

pounds of potatoes were allowed per person per week; by July this had sunk to one pound of potatoes and one kilo of bread per person per week (ibid., p. 79).

144. Of the 125 female doctors who responded, 42 were married and 5 were widowed. See Albisetti, "The Fight for Female Physicians," p. 122.

145. Frankenthal, *Der dreifache*, p. 110.

146. Ibid., p. 110.

147. Rahel Straus, *Wir lebten in Deutschland: Erinnerungen einer deutschen Jüdin* (Stuttgart, 1962), p. 137.

148. Ibid., p. 143.

149. Ibid., p. 196.

150. Ibid., p. 143.

151. Ibid., pp. 87, 141.

152. Ibid., p. 143.

153. Ibid., p. 145.

154. See Wilhelmina von Hillern, *Only a Girl: A Physician for the Soul, a Romance*, trans. A. L. Wister (Philadelphia, 1870).

155. Straus, *Wir lebten*, p. 87.

156. Ibid., p. 88.

157. James Albisetti, "Women and the Professions in Imperial Germany," in *German Women in the Eighteenth and Nineteenth Centuries*, ed. Ruth-Ellen Joeres and Mary Jo Maynes (Bloomington, Ind., 1986), p. 95.

158. Margaret Edelheim Mühsam collection, LBI, II, 14, 720. By 1914, 25 women had enrolled in the law faculties of Prussian universities. This number increased to 74 by 1917. Deutscher Juristinnenbund, ed., *Juristinnen in Deutschland* (Munich, 1984), p. 5.

159. *Die Frau der Gegenwart*, November 1, 1917, pp. 153–54, in Margarete Berent collection, LBI, II, #2; also interview with Margaret Edelheim Mühsam, New York, October 1974.

160. This amounted to 5 out of 18 women: Herrmann, *Die deutsche Frau*, p. 42. Margarete Meseritz's married name was Edelheim Mühsam.

161. In 1919 the Board of Directors consisted of Margarete Meseritz, chair; Marie Munk, cochair (baptized as a child); Margarete Berent, treasurer; Alice Eisner, secretary; and three others, including Elisabeth Hamburger. Although names are a risky means of identifying religious background, at least 21% of the eighty-five members appeared to be Jewish. This agrees with the proportion of Jews matriculated in the law faculties some years earlier.

162. Richarz, *Jüdisches Leben*, vol. 2, p. 33. Konrad Jarausch found that in 1904 the proportion of Jewish attorneys practicing as advocates (*freie Advokatur*) in Prussia was as high as 27%. This resulted from discrimination against Jewish lawyers in academic and administrative positions. "Jewish Lawyers in Germany, 1848–1938: The Breakdown of a Professional Symbiosis," paper delivered at the American Historical Association convention, San Francisco, December 29, 1989.

163. *Untersuchungen zur deutschen Staats- und Rechtsgeschichte*, vol. 123. Her dissertation was entitled "Die Zugewinstgemeinschaft der Ehegatten." Berent collection, LBI, #63. On von Gierke, see Peter Gay, *The Bourgeois Experience*, vol. 1, *Education of the Senses* (New York, 1984), pp. 222–23.

164. *Die Frau der Gegenwart*, Berent collection, pp. 153–54; *Juristinnen in Deutschland*, p. 4. Berent wrote on legal issues touching the lives of women, children, and adolescents. See for example "Schutz von Frauen und Kindern im Entwurf zum Strafgesetzbuch," *Monatsschrift deutscher Aerztinnen* 8:9 (1929); and "Jugendschutz im Strafgesetzentwurf," *Zentralblatt für Jugendgericht und Jugendwohlfahrt* 18:10 (1927).

165. *Die Frau der Gegenwart*, Berent collection, p. 157.

166. Berent collection, #70. See also Frank Mecklenburg, "Deutsche Juristen im Amerikanischen Exil," forthcoming.

167. Munk, VI, 5. See also *Juristinnen in Deutschland*, p. 14.

168. Munk, VIII, 5, and VIII, 11. She received the King Ludwig Cross, the Bavarian counterpart of the Iron Cross, for her work at the center.

169. Munk, VI, 5; Mühsam collection, LBI, II, 15.

170. Mühsam collection, II, 14, 720.

171. *Frankfurter Zeitung und Handelsblatt*, July 26, 1914, p. 10.

172. Munk, V, 16–17. For marriage statistics, see chapter 5; see also James Albisetti, *Schooling German Girls and Women* (Princeton, N.J., 1988), p. 290.

173. Nuns returned in Bavaria, where they retained slightly under half of the female teaching posts until the turn of the century. See Catherine Stodolsky, "Missionary of the Feminine Mystique: The Female Teacher in Prussia and Bavaria,1880–1920" (Ph.D. diss., State University of New York at Stony Brook, 1987), p. 419.

174. Margrit Twellman-Schepp, *Die deutsche Frauenbewegung: Ihre Anfänge und erste Entwicklung, 1843–1889* (Meisenheim, 1972), p. 104. Only in Berlin could one find a broader offering of schools: in 1878, 47 middle schools for girls, of which 46 were private.

175. Pricilla Robertson, *An Experience of Women* (Philadelphia, 1982), pp. 400–401.

176. Twellmann-Schepp, *Die deutsche Frauenbewegung*, p. 99.

177. For more details, see Barbara Greven-Aschoff, *Die bürgerliche Frauenbewegung in Deutschland, 1894–1933* (Göttingen, 1981), pp. 51–58, 72–78; James Albisetti, "The Reform of Female Education in Prussia, 1899–1908: A Study in Compromise and Containment," *German Studies Review* 8 (February 1985); Ilse Brehmer, ed., *Lehrerinnen: Zur Geschichte eines Frauenberufes* (Munich, 1980). Among the women educators were several active Jewish women: Henriette Goldschmidt, Lina Morgenstern, Ulrike Henschke, Gertrud Pappenheim, Johanna Goldschmidt, Marie Friedlander, Jenny Asch, Margarete Henschke, Helene Simon, Anna Edinger. See Siegmund Kaznelson, ed., *Juden im deutschen Kulturbereich* (Berlin, 1959).

178. It is estimated that, around 1890, 16–25% of upper-class and middle-class women could not marry: Brehmer, *Lehrerinnen*, p. 81.

179. Elisabeth Bab, memoirs, LBI, p. 48, and Brehmer, *Lehrerinnen*, p. 85.

180. By 1911, 21% of *Volksschule* teachers (39,000) were female. Werner Conze, "Sozialgeschichte, 1850–1918," in *Handbuch der deutschen Wirtschafts- und Sozialgeschichte*, vol. 2, ed. Hermann Aubin and Wolfgang Zorn (Stuttgart, 1976), p. 678. See also Doris Kampmann, "'Zölibat—ohne uns!' Die soziale Situation und politische Einstellung der Lehrerinnen in der Weimarer Republik," in *Mutterkreuz und Arbeitsbuch: Zur Geschichte der Frauen in der Weimarer Republik und im Nationalsozialismus* (Frankfurt/Main, 1981), p. 83; Albisetti, "Women and the Professions," p. 98. By 1905, 15% of Prussian teachers and 18% of Bavarian teachers were women.

181. Further, in Prussia only men could serve as directors of girls' schools, whereas females were not hired in boys' schools: thus the state, in collusion with male teachers, both preserved female inferiority and limited the number of positions available to them. See Brehmer, *Lehrerinnen*.

182. See also Kampmann, "Zölibat," p. 86, who states that women teachers received 50% of male salaries on the average. This salary ratio persisted, despite a Prussian edict of 1885 setting women's salaries at 75–80% of men's: Brehmer, *Lehrerinnen*, p. 103.

183. *Allgemeine Zeitung des Judentums* (hereafter *AZDJ*), September 1, 1914, p. 414.

184. Central Archives of the Jewish People, TD 980, p. 4.

185. Marjorie Lamberti, *Jewish Activism in Imperial Germany and the Struggle for Civil Equality* (New Haven, Conn., 1978), p. 163.

186. Werner Weinberg, *Wunden, die nicht heilen dürfen* (Freiburg, 1988), pp. 54–55.

187. Moses Sonn, "Schulgeschichtliche Aufzeichnungen über die israelitische Volksschule Buttenwiesen," *Leo Baeck Institute Bulletin* 12:48 (1969): 221–52.

188. Ernst Hamburger, *Juden im öffentlichen Leben Deutschlands: Regierungsmitglieder, Beamte und Parlamentarier in der monarchischen Zeit, 1848–1918* (Tübingen, 1968), pp. 55–64; Peter Pulzer,"Why Was There a Jewish Question in Imperial Germany?" *LBIYB*, 1980, p. 144.

189. Arthur Ruppin and Jakob Thon, *Der Anteil der Juden am Unterrichtswesen in Preussen* (Berlin, 1905), p. 48. There may be one positive reason why Jewish women could be found at the highest ranks: since they were overrepresented in the first generation of university women, they would have been available early on as *Oberlehrerinnen* and may have been hired to fill the early vacancies in the growing number of girls' schools after the 1870s—at least until the dearth of *Oberlehrerinnen* was over: *IF*, April 28, 1910, p. 13.

190. Frankenthal, *Der dreifach*, p. 12.

191. Of 100 teachers in Prussian Schools in 1901:

	Male Jewish Teachers	Female Jewish Teachers
Public *Volksschule*	0.44 (338)	0.44 (56)*
Public Middle School	0.03 (1)	0.39 (3)
Public *Höhere Mädchenschule*	2.04 (21)	0.83 (9)
Private Middle School	3.16 (23)	2.99 (16)
Private *Höhere Mädchenschule*	1.52 (3)	0.88 (31)

SOURCE: Ruppin and Thon, *Der Anteil*, p. 49. *Of these 56 women, 42 taught in Berlin.

192. Albisetti, "Women and the Professions," p.98.

193. Ruppin and Thon, *Der Anteil*, p. 48. See also *ZDSJ*, July/September 1915, p. 83. Within the private school network, Jewish men were more often employed in Jewish schools and Jewish women in nonsectarian ones. In 1901 in Prussia, 47 Jewish women taught at nonsectarian schools compared to 9 who taught at Jewish ones. Jewish men found themselves in the opposite situation: 48 in nonsectarian schools and 307 in Jewish schools. Ruppin and Thon, *Der Anteil*, p. 49. This was more likely the result of antifemale discrimination in Jewish schools than of positive inducements to Jewish women in nonsectarian schools.

194. Geoffrey Field, "Religion in the German Volksschule, 1890–1928," *LBIYB*, 1980, p. 42.

195. Quoting F. Nyssen, "Das Sozialisationskonzept der Stiehlschen Regulative und sein historischer Hintergrund," ibid., p. 43.

196. Greven-Aschoff, *Die bürgerliche*, p. 52.

197. *Im deutschen Reich*, September 1895, p. 135. Jewish women were forbidden to teach German for a time in 1895, but Berlin female teachers and the *Vossische Zeitung* protested: *Im deutschen Reich*, November 1895, p. 255; *Allgemeine Israelitische Wochenschrift* (Berlin), December 23, 1898, pp. 816–18; *Allgemeine Israelitische Wochenschrift*, September 15, 1899, p. 586. See also *Im deutschen Reich*, August 1895, p. 87, which reports a city councillor's questioning whether Jewish women should be allowed to teach at all in Berlin.

198. *Im deutschen Reich*, September 1895, p. 185.

199. *IF*, April 28, 1910, p. 13. See also *Allgemeine Israelitische Wochenschrift*, April 21, 1905, p. 220.

200. *Im deutschen Reich*, April 1896, pp. 233–37.

201. *IF*, April 28, 1910, p. 13.

202. *Im deutschen Reich*, April 1906, p. 233. *Im deutschen Reich* frequently reported on schoolteachers who received a job as soon as they converted: see October 1896, p. 505. Also, since it was common for a non-Jewish woman to pass her state exams and have a job within three months, while Jewish women searched in vain, Jews could draw their own conclusions rather easily. *KC Blätter*, October 1, 1911, p. 10.

203. Thanks to Catherine Stodolsky for sharing the following document found in the Deutsches Zentralarchiv, Merseburg, Prussian archives for the Ministry of Education: a letter from the Minister der Geistlichen und Unterrichts Angelegenheiten to the Provinzialschulkollegium, October 18, 1917.

204. *Im deutschen Reich*, March 1910, p. 185. A year later the Jewish press wondered why the Prussian government had not simply decreed that Jewish women were barred from teacher-training seminars, since it was obvious that Prussia felt Jewish women would harm *Volksschule* children: *IF*, April 28, 1910, p. 13. Of course Jewish women were discriminated against in state teacher-training institutes as well. *Im deutschen Reich*, April 1908, pp. 227–28, an article discussing a Berlin *Lehrerinnenseminar* where the director refused to admit Jewish girls. As late as 1919, Jewish newspapers warned women of rampant discrimination in teaching: *ZDSJ*, January/March 1919, p. 4. In an interview with Christl Wickert, Berta Jordan, a leading SPD woman, said that Jewish women could not get teaching jobs in state or city schools throughout the 1920s. My thanks to Christl Wickert for sharing this information.

205. On the situation of women teachers, see Stodolsky, "Missionary of the Feminine Mystique."

206. *IF*, April 29, 1909, p. 11; *Im deutschen Reich*, May 1909, p. 304.

207. See *Das jüdische Echo*, December 8, 1916, p. 476; April 19, 1918, p. 187.

208. Henriette Hirsch, memoirs, LBI, p. 74.

209. Albisetti, "Women and the Professions," p. 97.

210. *AZDJ*, January 3, 1871, p. 15.

211. See *Neue Bahnen* 7:5 (872): 33–35; Louise Otto, "Die Bonne," in Ute Gerhard, *Verhältnisse und Verhinderungen: Frauenarbeit, Familie und Rechte der Frauen im 19. Jahrhundert* (Frankfurt/Main, 1978), pp. 278–81. For similar situations in England, see M. Jeanne Peterson, "The Victorian Governess: Status Incongruence in Family and Society," in *Suffer and Be Still: Women in the Victorian Age*, ed. Martha Vicinus (Bloomington, Ind., 1972), pp. 3–19.

212. Bab, memoirs, p. 54.

213. *Israelitisches Gemeindeblatt*, June 24, 1892, pp. 204–07; *General Anzeiger*, March 12 and March 19, 1903, both in the supplement.

214. Richarz, *Jüdisches Leben*, vol. 2, p. 230. See also statistics for Hesse in *ZDSJ*, March 1913, p. 46.

215. Geheimes Staatsarchiv Preussischer Kulturbesitz, Dahlem, Regierung Königsberg, Rep. II, #3467, pp. 87–88 (1877–1920).

216. *ZDSJ*, January/March 1919, p. 4.

217. *AZDJ*, September 1, 1911, p. 414.

218. *AZDJ*, June 27, 1913, supplement.

219. See "Statuten der Vereinigung israelitischer Lehrer und Leherinnen in Frankfurt/Main," 1914, in Central Archives, TD 1125.

220. Albisetti, "Women and the Professions," p. 102.

221. Ibid., p. 103; Kampmann, "Zölibat"; Brehmer, *Lehrerinnen*, pp. 95–96.

222. The woman was Pauline Munchhausen. See *Dreissig Jahre Verein Israelitisches Lehrerinnenheim, 1899–1929*, in Central Archives, TD/980; *General Anzeiger*, May 11,

1903, supplement; *Jahresbericht des Vereins Israelitischen Lehrerinnenheims zu Berlin, e.V., 1910*, vol. 12 (Berlin, 1910); *General Anzeiger*, July 16, 1905, p. 5; *General Anzeiger*, September 26, 1904, supplement; *Lehrerinnenheim, Berlin* in Central Archives, TD/980 and TD/112 (annual reports for 1906 and 1908).

223. S. Grünebaum, *Bericht des Vereins Israelitischen Lehrerinnenheims*, 1908, Central Archives, TD/980.

224. Richarz, *Jüdisches Leben*, vol. 2, p. 352.

225. Ibid., p. 350.

226. Ibid., p. 352.

Chapter 7

1. *Jüdisches Lexikon*, vol. 5 (Berlin, 1930), under "Wohltätigkeit."

2. The other two were domestic duties and modesty: Rachel Biale, *Women and Jewish Law* (New York, 1984), p. 38.

3. Herman Pollack, *Jewish Folkways in Germanic Lands (1648–1806)* (Cambridge, Mass., 1971), pp. 67; 246, n. 116.

4. Pollack, *Jewish Folkways*, pp. 55; 238, n. 31; 322, n. 90.

5. Elizabeth Ewen notes this for shtetl women as well: *Immigrant Women in the Land of Dollars: Life and Culture on the Lower East Side, 1890–1925* (New York, 1985), p. 42.

6. Also, according to the Talmud, no Sabbath meal was complete unless a needy stranger was present: Pollack, *Jewish Folkways*, p. 162.

7. Special Purim funds were set up. Everyone was expected to present two gifts to a neighbor (including foods, drink, or spices). Frequently, Purim meals were another opportunity to invite the poor. Ibid., pp. 179–80.

8. *The Memoirs of Glückel of Hameln*, trans. Marvin Lowenthal (New York, 1977), p. 6.

9. Ibid., pp. 19–20.

10. Ibid., p. 266.

11. Arthur Ruppin, *Die Juden im Grossherzogtum Hessen* (Berlin, 1909), pp. 122–23. For the Berlin group, see *Encyclopedia Judaica* (Jerusalem, 1971), vol. 5, p. 347.

12. *Israelitischer Verein für Krankenpflege und Beerdigung (Königsberg, 1704–1904)*, a pamphlet in honor of its 200th anniversary, Central Archives, TD926; *Gesellschaft zur Verbreitung des Handwerks und des Ackerbaus unter den Juden* (Prussia, 1812–1912), Central Archives, TD 804, TD 872.

13. This was the case for Moritz Lazarus, ethnologist and philosopher, whose *Ethics of Judaism* (1898) became a guide for Liberal Jews: Michael Meyer, *Response to Modernity: A History of the Reform Movement in Judaism* (New York, 1988), p. 204.

14. Goldschmidt, 1919, as quoted by Rolf Landwehr, *Das jüdische Armen- und Wohlfahrtswesen von 1812–1939* (Berlin, forthcoming), chapter 5, section 1. Thanks to Rolf Landwehr for sharing his work-in-progress with me.

15. Ibid., chapters 1 and 2.

16. Christoph Sachsse and Florian Tennstedt, *Geschichte der Armenfürsorge in Deutschland: Vom Spätmittelalter bis zum Ersten Weltkrieg* (Stuttgart, 1980); Florian Tennstedt, "Fürsorgegeschichte und Vereinsgeschichte: 100 Jahre Deutscher Verein," *Zeitschrift für Sozialreform* 27 (1981): 77.

17. Rüdeger Baron, "Die Entwicklung der Armenpflege in Deutschland vom Beginn des 19. Jahrhunderts bis zum Ersten Weltkrieg," in *Geschichte der Sozialarbeit*, ed. Rolf Landwehr and Rüdeger Baron (Weinheim and Basel, 1983), p. 30.

18. Christoph Sachsse, *Mütterlichkeit als Beruf: Sozialarbeit, Sozialreform und Frauenbewegung, 1871–1929* (Frankfurt/Main, 1986), pp. 30–31; 314, n. 19. For a general overview of the development of German social work, see Sachsse and Tennstedt, *Geschichte*.

19. For why men lost interest and the role of women, see Rüdeger Baron and Rolf Landwehr, "Von der Berufung zum Beruf: Zur Entwicklung der Ausbildung für die soziale Arbeit," in *Sozialarbeit und Soziale Reform: Zur Geschichte eines Berufs zwischen Frauenbewegung und öffentlicher Verwaltung*, ed. Rüdeger Baron (Weinheim and Basel, 1983), pp. 2–3. DVAW stands for Deutschër Verein für Armenpflege und Wohltätigkeit.

20. Gerhard Buck, "Die Entwicklung der freien Wohlfahrtspflege von den ersten Zusammenschlüssen der freien Verbände im 19. Jahrhundert bis zur Durchsetzung des Subsidiaritätsprinzips in der Weimarer Fürsorgegesetzgebung," in Landwehr, *Geschichte*, pp. 142–43.

21. Sachsse and Tennstedt, *Geschichte*, p. 233.

22. Jack Wertheimer, *Unwelcome Strangers: East European Jews in Imperial Germany* (New York, 1987), p. 7.

23. Ruppin, *Die Juden im Grossherzogtum Hessen*, pp. 126–37. This contrasts with non-Jewish women in Hesse, where researchers noted that as late as the 1920s women took no part in local club life or in church administration. These are limited, local studies, however; more research is needed before we can generalize about Jewish and non-Jewish women's public participation. Gerhard Wilke and Kurt Wagner, "Family and Household: Social Structures in a German Village Between the Two World Wars," in *The German Family*, ed. Richard Evans and W. R. Lee (London, 1981), p. 136. On the other hand, Ute Frevert described a highly developed women's organizational life in such middle-sized cities as Elberfeld by 1914: *Frauen-Geschichte: Zwischen bürgerlicher Verbesserung und neuer Weiblichkeit* (Frankfurt/Main, 1986), p. 112.

24. *Das jüdische Echo: Bayrische Blätter für die jüdischen Angelegenheiten*, February 12, 1915, pp. 43–44. See also: Claudia Prestel, "Weiblíche Rollenzuweisung in Jüdischer Organisationen. Das Beispiel der Bnei Briss," *Leo Baeck Institute Bulletin* (forthcoming).

25. In 1910 about 79,000 foreign Jews lived in Germany—about 12.8% of all Jews. The rate of affiliation was therefore even higher among German Jews, since most of these clubs were predominantly German-Jewish.

26. Wertheimer, *Unwelcome*, p. 154.

27. Ibid., p. 155.

28. *Frauenhilfe: Israelitischer Verein für Kindergarten, Kinderhort und Mädchenheim*, sixth annual report (Munich, 1911), p. 5.

29. Julius and Margarethe Goldstein collection, LBI. He was a professor of philosophy in Darmstadt. While he served at the front, his wife became a leading member of the Women's Wartime Aid. See text.

30. Baron and Landwehr, "Von der Berufung," p. 4.

31. 550 belonged to four and 350 to five such groups: *Zeitschrift für Demographie und Statistik der Juden* (hereafter *ZDSJ*), May 1909, p. 77.

32. Attending the sick was a common requirement in many of these groups. For example, the Mildthätigkeits-Verein der Frauen in Köln declared, "every active member is duty bound . . . to personally participate in watching over the sickbed." *Statuten des Mildthätigkeits-Verein der Frauen in Köln*, archives, LBI. The burial society of Hammelburg (Würzburg) listed the death-watch service of its active members, including the exact times of their two-hour shifts and who went to the funeral: Central Archives, WR/99. In Lautenberg the club mandated that two women at a time attend night shifts for the sick, making the long stretch between 10 p.m. and 6 a.m. more bearable. *Israelitischer Frauenverein, Lautenberg, W. Pr.*, Central Archives, GAII/546, report of activities between 1898 and 1913.

33. *Israelitischer Frauen-Verein*, Central Archives F/VIa, 3 (Oberfranken).

34. See Lautenberg report; see also *Bad Kissingen, Israelitischer Wohltätigkeitsverein für Frauen*, Central Archives, WR 367.

35. *Protokolle über die Gründung und General Versammlungen des Israelitischen Frauenvereins Alzenau-Wasserlos (Gemeinde Würzburg)*, Central Archives, WR/4.

36. Frau Kommerzienrätin Eva Levy was a leading member of the Women's Patriotic Association in 1904: *General Anzeiger*, June 13, 1904, supplement.

37. Margarete Freudenthal, "Gestaltwandel der städtischen, bürgerlichen und proletarischen Hauswirtschaft unter besonderer Berücksichtigung des Typenwandels von Frau und Familie" (diss., Würzburg, 1934), p. 132.

38. Central Archives, GAII/538, pp. 1–4.

39. *Statuten des Lübecker Frauen-Krankenvereins*, 2nd ed. (Lübeck, 1883), Central Archives, GAII/542.

40. *Statuten des Israelitischen Frauenvereins, Lautenberg, W. Pr.*, 1908, Central Archives, GA II/546.

41. 93rd *Jahresbericht des Israelitischen Waisenhauses . . . zu Königsberg in Preussen, 1899*, Geheimes Staatsarchiv Preussischer Kulturbesitz, Regierung Königsberg, Rep 2, #3194, vol. 2, p. 7.

42. In Lautenberg the chair of the club visited recipients to "convince herself of their indigence." *Statuten des Israelitischen Frauenvereins*, 1908, Central Archives, GA.II/546. Widows and orphans would be supported "until they had forged a new livelihood." *Statuten des jüdischen Frauenvereins Kolberg*, 1876, reprinted in 1902 (club founded in 1848), Central Archives, GAII/563.

43. Lautenberg, *Statuten*, 1908, Central Archives, GAII/546.

44. Jacob Rosenheim, *Erinnerungen, 1870–1920* (Frankfurt/Main, 1970), pp. 60–61.

45. *Statistik der Frauenorganisationen im deutschen Reich* (Berlin, 1909), pp. 18–66.

46. Arthur Ruppin, *Die jüdische Gemeinden und Vereinen in Deutschland* (Berlin, 1906), pp. 60–61.

47. Quote from "Bericht über die Verhandlungen der Delegierten Versammlung Israelitischer Gemeinden," 1894, in Rolf Landwehr, *Das jüdische Armen-und Wohlfahrtswesen*.

48. Lautenberg, Central Archives, GAII/546. The Deutsch Israelitischer Gemeindebund instituted this system of registration throughout Germany before World War I. See Landwehr, *Das jüdische Armen- und Wohlfahrtswesen*.

49. This method was obviously based on the Elberfeld System, in which well-to-do bourgeois men (and later women) attested to the poverty in their districts. Baron, "Die Entwicklung," pp. 22–26.

50. *Das jüdische Blatt*, February 28, 1913, p. 7.

51. *Protokoll des Israelitischen Wohltätigkeitsvereins für Frauen (Landkreis Kissingen)*, 1878–1923, Central Archives, WR 367.

52. *General Anzeiger*, November 10, 1907, supplement; *Israelitische Wochenschrift* (Berlin), November 2, 1900, p. 697.

53. Julie Braun-Vogelstein, *Was niemals stirbt: Gestalten und Erinnerungen* (Stuttgart, 1966), p. 70.

54. Ibid., p. 93.

55. Ibid., p. 80.

56. Ibid., p. 91.

57. Ibid., p. 95.

58. Julie Braun-Vogelstein collection, box 4, folder 2, documents regarding the Israelitischer Frauenverein, LBI.

59. *General Anzeiger*, June 20, 1904. In 1910 she delivered a lecture on "Charity and Welfare" at a general assembly meeting of the League: *Israelitisches Familienblatt* (hereafter *IF*), January 19, 1911, p. 12.

60. Braun-Vogelstein, *Was niemals*, p. 75.

61. Ibid., p. 83.

62. Ibid., p. 81.

63. Ibid., p. 80.

64. Maya I. Fassmann, "Die Mutter der Volksküchen: Lina Morgenstern und die jüdische Wohltätigkeit," in *Unter allen Umständen: Frauengeschichte(n) in Berlin*, ed. Christiane Eifert and Susanne Rouette (Berlin, 1986), pp. 34–35.

65. Catherine M. Prelinger, *Charity, Challenge, and Change: Religious Dimensions of the Mid-Nineteenth-Century Women's Movement in Germany* (Westport, Conn., 1987), pp. 88–95, 140–43, 168–69. Individual kindergartens may not always have respected Fröbel's nonsectarian perspective. In 1906 in Königsberg, for example, the Jewish community argued for a Jewish kindergarten because "even the Fröbel schools . . . educate the children in a Christian spirit." Central Archives, Königsberg, (Kn II), Folder III, #4.

66. Within a short time, soup kitchens opened in over thirty German cities, as well as in Vienna and Stockholm. Many Jewish women, including Morgenstern's sister and daughter, participated in their founding.

67. Fassmann, "Die Mutter," p. 42.

68. Ibid., p. 48.

69. Ibid., p. 38.

70. Daniela Weiland, *Geschichte der Frauenemanzipation in Deutschland und Österreich*, Hermes Handlexikon (Düsseldorf, 1983), pp. 173–77.

71. Fassmann, "Die Mutter," p. 35.

72. Lina Morgenstern, Vilna Collection on Germany, folder 1, #1, YIVO Institute for Jewish Research.

73. Carl Paasch, quoted by Fassmann, "Die Mutter," p. 50.

74. Fassmann, "Die Mutter," p. 56.

75. Arlene Kaplan Daniels, *Invisible Careers: Women Civic Leaders from the Volunteer World* (Chicago, 1987).

76. *Allgemeine Zeitung des Judentums* (hereafter *AZDJ*), March 8, 1912, supplement.

77. Ibid.

78. *AZDJ*, March 16, 1914, supplement, p. 3.

79. "Frauenhilfe" Israelitischer Verein für Kindergarten, Kinderhort und Mädchenheim, second, third, fourth, sixth, eighth, and ninth annual reports (Munich, 1907–9, 1911, 1913, 1914).

80. *IF*, January 20, 1910, p. 10.

81. They served 147 infants in 1910. *IF*, January 19, 1911, p. 12.

82. *AZDJ*, April 17, 1908, supplement, p. 3.

83. The organization received 30,000 Marks from one woman alone, and property from another. *AZDJ*, May 1, 1914, supplement.

84. *AZDJ*, May 1, 1914, supplement. See also Helga Heubach, *Das Heim des Jüdischen Frauenbundes in Neu-Isenburg, 1907 bis 1942* (Neu-Isenburg, 1986), pp. 17–21.

85. Ottilie Schönewald, memoirs, LBI, p. 16.

86. *General Anzeiger*, June 20, 1904, pp. 5–6. See also June 27, 1904, p. 3.

87. Carroll Smith-Rosenberg, "Politics and Culture in Women's History," *Feminist Studies* 6:1 (1980): 62.

88. For further information on "Anna O," see Sigmund Freud and Josef Breuer, *Studies on Hysteria*, trans. James Strachey (New York, 1966); Max Rosenbaum and Melvin Muroff,

eds., *Anna O: Fourteen Contemporary Reinterpretations* (New York, 1984); Lucy Freeman, *The Story of Anna O* (New York, 1972); Marion Kaplan, *The Jewish Feminist Movement in Germany: The Campaigns of the Jüdischer Frauenbund, 1904–1938* (Westport, Conn., 1979).

89. Bertha Pappenheim collection, LBI, #331, (9).

90. *Blätter des Jüdischen Frauenbunds* (hereafter *BJFB*), July 1936, p. 8.

91. For samples of rabbinical opinions and antifeminist comments, see *Jeshurun* 6 (1919): 262–66, 515–19; *BJFB*, February 1928, p. 2, and June 1932, pp. 4–6. For more details on the JFB, see Kaplan, *The Jewish Feminist Movement*.

92. For comparisons with U.S. social feminism, see J. Stanley Lemons, *The Woman Citizen: Social Feminism in the 1920's* (Urbana Ill., and Chicago, 1973), or William O'Neill, *Everyone Was Brave: The Rise and Fall of Feminism in America* (Chicago, 1969).

93. Baron, "Die Entwicklung," p. 55. The Deutsch Israelitischer Gemeindebund set up a home for "wayward girls" in Berlin-Plötzensee in 1902, but restricted it to girls who were past school age. Landwehr, *Das jüdische Armen-und Wohlfahrtswesen*.

94. Heubach, *Das Heim*, pp. 36–37 and passim.

95. Kaplan, *The Jewish Feminist Movement*, chapter 5.

96. Dora Peyser, "Alice Salomon, ein Lebensbild," in *Alice Salomon: Die Begründerin des Sozialen Frauenberufs in Deutschland*, ed. Hans Muthesius (Cologne and Berlin, 1958), p. 18.

97. See her autobiography, *Charakter ist Schicksal: Lebenserinnerungen*, translated from an English manuscript by Rolf Landwehr, ed. Rüdeger Baron and Rolf Landwehr (Weinheim and Basel, 1983), p. 30. See also Monika Simmel, "Alice Salomon: Vom Dienst der bürgerlichen Tochter am Volksganzen," in *Jahrbuch der Sozialarbeit* 4 (1981): 369–402; Joachim Wieler, *Er-Innerung eines zerstörten Lebensabends: Alice Salomon während der NS-Zeit (1933–37) und im Exil (1937–48)* (Darmstadt, 1987), chapters 1 and 2; Marlis Dürkop, "Alice Salomon und die feministische Sozialarbeit," in Baron, *Sozialarbeit und Soziale Reform*, pp. 52–80; and Muthesius, ed., *Alice Salomon: Die Begründerin*.

98. Simmel, "Alice Salomon," p. 374.

99. Birgit Sauer, "Den Zusammenhang zwischen der Frauenfrage und der sozialen Frage begreifen: Die 'Frauen- und Mädchengruppen für soziale Hilfsarbeit' (1893–1908)," in *Unter allen Umständen*, ed. Eifert and Rouette, p. 83.

100. Landwehr, *Das jüdische Armen- und Wohlfahrtswesen*. I am grateful to Rolf Landwehr for discussing the impact of the women's movement on social work with me. See also Baron and Landwehr, "Von der Berufung," pp. 2–6.

101. Salomon quoted Disraeli: *Charakter*, p. 45.

102. Hedwig Wachenheim, *Vom Grossbürgertum zur Sozialdemokratie: Memoiren einer Reformistin* (Berlin 1973), p. 28. The memoirs of Agathe Bleichröder testify that such work liberated young women from daily boredom. She volunteered at Jeanette Schwerin's Ethical Culture social service group, attended lectures on social and political issues, and generally felt more useful than she had with her art lessons. Charlotte Hamburger-Liepmann, memoirs, LBI, pp. 90, 154.

103. Sauer, "Den Zusammenhang," p. 88.

104. Ibid.

105. Peyser, "Alice Salomon," p. 44.

106. Sauer, "Den Zusammenhang," pp. 80–86.

107. Ibid., p. 83.

108. Peyser, "Alice Salomon," p. 46; Baron and Landwehr, "Von der Berufung," p. 4.

109. In 1905 the German Evangelical Frauenbund had set up a school for Christian

charity within the framework of the Innere Mission in Hannover: Simmel, "Alice Salomon," p. 377.

110. Hilde Ottenheimer, "Soziale Arbeit," in *Juden im deutschen Kulturbereich*, ed. Siegmund Kaznelson, pp. 852–53.

111. Salomon, *Charakter*, pp. 139–43.

112. Peyser, "Alice Salomon," p. 85.

113. Sachsse, *Mütterlichkeit als Beruf*, pp. 122–25.

114. Dorothee von Velsen, "Jenny Apolant," *Die Frau* (Berlin), August 1925, p. 337, Jennny Apolant collection, Stadtarchiv, Frankfurt/Main.

115. Eulogies: "Eine deutsch-jüdische Frau," Jennny Apolant collection, Stadtarchiv, Frankfurt/Main.

116. Sabine Klöhn, *Helene Simon: Deutsche und britische Sozialreform und Sozialgesetzgebung im Spiegel ihrer Schriften und ihr Wirken als Sozialpolitikerin im Kaiserreich und in der Weimarer Republik* (Frankfurt/Main, 1982).

117. The well-known Jewish women activists and their contributions to German social work and feminist organizations can be found in Hilde Ottenheimer, "Soziale Arbeit" and "Pädagogik und Sozialpädagogik," in *Juden im deutschen Kulturbereich*, ed. Kaznelson. Also, the pages of the *Blätter des jüdischen Frauenbundes* regularly presented profiles of Jewish women involved with the German women's movement from Fanny Lewald, Hedwig Dohm and Henriette Goldschmidt to contemporary activists. See *BJFB*, March 1927, pp. 1–2. See also Meyer Kayserling, *Die jüdischen Frauen in der Geschichte, Literatur und Kunst* (Leipzig, 1879).

118. "Jüdische Frauen in der deutschen Frauenbewegung," *General Anzeiger*, June 13, 1904, p. 5. See also *AZDJ*, December 26, 1913, supplement, which comments on an article in the anti-Semitic *Staatsbürgerzeitung*. The latter called for the founding of more anti-Semitic women's organizations, because the "Jewess" and "rabbi's wife" Henriette Goldschmidt was winning too much influence over the female youth of Leipzig. See also: *Im deutschen Reich*, September 1909, p. 531; December 1909, p. 696.

119. *Im deutschen Reich*, October 1911, pp. 566–69.

120. *General Anzeiger*, July 4, 1904, supplement. While his statistics and perceptions were no doubt exaggerated, non-Jewish activists made similar observations.

121. Minna Cauer, *Die Frau im 19 Jahrhundert* (Berlin, 1898). Catherine Prelinger has noted that Jewish names were conspicuous in the membership list of interconfessional reform groups in the mid- and late nineteenth century: *Charity, Challenge, and Change*. The Verein für Weibliche Angestellte (VWA, or Association for Women Employees), founded in Berlin in 1889, which fought to improve working conditions for women in offices and sales jobs, had a heavy representation of Jewish names among its leadership and members. Rosa Cohn, one of its founders, worked for the VWA until her death in 1910. Gertrud Israel wrote and lectured on the bourgeois women's movement and social questions and represented the VWA to other women's organizations and at women's conferences. In an 1893 survey of VWA members, 190 of 965 members in Berlin gave their religion as Jewish. Letter to author from Ursala Hagen, Davis, Calif., December 16, 1979.

The role of Jewish women in non-Jewish social welfare and feminist organizations cannot be covered in this chapter, and should be the topic of another research endeavor. This may also be the case for Jewish men active in general social welfare organizations, such as Emil Münsterberg and Paul Levy. See Sachsse and Tennstedt, *Geschichte*, pp. 232–33.

122. Quote from Simmel, "Alice Salomon," p. 369. Paula Hyman similarly connects the prominent role of Jewish women in American secular political and volunteer organizations with their gender, class and cultural backgrounds. See "Culture and Gender: Women in the

Immigrant Jewish Community," in *The Legacy of Jewish Migration*, ed. David Berger (Brooklyn, 1983), pp. 157–68.

123. *BJFB*, April 1927, pp. 3–4.

124. Henriette Fürth, *Die deutschen Frauen im Kriege* (Tübingen, 1917), pp. 51–52.

125. From *Die Frau*, September 1914, in Ursula von Gersdorf, *Frauen im Kriegsdienst* (Stuttgart, 1969), p. 16.

126. Frevert, *Frauen-Geschichte*, p. 147 (for original German version, which includes the expression "Zwang ihrer Sonderbestrebungen"); also Frevert, quoting Marie Bernays on "citizens," in *Women*, p. 152.

127. Frevert, *Women*, p. 152.

128. *LBI News* (New York), Winter 1988, p. 2.

129. *AZDJ*, April 28, 1916, supplement, p. 1.

130. *Israelitisches Wochenblatt*, January 15, 1915, p. 20.

131. *AZDJ*, June 4, 1915, p. 266.

132. *Das jüdische Echo: Bayrische Blätter für die jüdischen Angelegenheiten*, January 15, 1915, p. 13.

133. Ernestine Eschelbacher, "Die Arbeit der jüdischen Frauen in Deutschland während des Krieges," *Ost und West* 19:5/6 (May/June, 1919): 138–50.

134. *AZDJ*, June 4, 1915, p. 266.

135. Protocols 79 and 81, Protokollbuch des Frauenvereins, Neuweid, 1906–38, Central Archives, NW/881.

136. *AZDJ*, January 21, 1916, supplement, p. 2.

137. Ibid.

138. *Israelitisches Wochenblatt*, February 12, 1915, p. 54; also Marie Munk, memoirs, Helene Lange Archives (Berlin), VII, 4.

139. *Im deutschen Reich*, January 1916, p. 33.

140. Rechenschaftsbericht des Israelitischen Frauenvereins von den Jahren 1912, 1913, 1914, Stuttgart, Central Archives, TD/126.

141. *AZDJ*, January 18, 1915, supplement, p. 2.

142. *AZDJ*, June 25, 1915, supplement, p. 2.

143. *AZDJ*, November 10, 1916, supplement, p. 2.

144. The Israelitischer Humanitärer Frauenverein in Hamburg gave its sanatorium and home economics school buildings to the army command for infirmary use. It also fed up to 1,000 people a day in its soup kitchen, employed over 300 women, and voted that all its funds go to the war effort. See *AZDJ*, September 18, 1914, supplement, p. 3; *AZDJ*, February 19, 1915, supplement, pp. 2–3; *AZDJ*, February 26, 1915, supplement, p. 2; *Israelitisches Wochenblatt*, March 21, 1916, p. 85.

145. *Das jüdische Echo: Bayrische Blätter für die jüdischen Angelegenheiten*, January 15, 1915, p. 13.

146. See Stuttgart: Israelitisches Frauenverein, Central Archives, TD 126. For Breslau see *AZDJ*, June 25, 1915, supplement, p. 2.

147. *AZDJ*, November 10, 1916, supplement, p. 2.

148. *AZDJ*, May 28, 1915, supplement, p. 2; *AZDJ*, February 9, 1917, supplement, p. 2.

149. *AZDJ*, March 23, 1917, supplement, p. 2.

150. See the memoirs of Mally Dienemann, LBI, pp. 2–3, for National Women's Service; Franz Rosenzweig's mother's diaries for Patriotic Women's Association, Kassel, 1917–19, LBI; Alice Salomon collection, LBI, for her work with the Red Cross; Elsa Oestreicher collection, LBI, ARA 152/328 (II, 37), for work with the Red Cross; Frieda Wunderlich collection, LBI, I, 2–3, for the National Women's Service. This is only a sampling of the available material.

151. See Rosel Landshut in Klaus Loewald collection, LBI; also Katharina Perl collection, LBI, #3143 (48), for a young woman who served as a nurse at the front for four years and then brought her own gold to the bank to "strengthen Germany's financial reserves." The woman who dressed as a man is mentioned in the *Israelitisches Wochenblatt*, January 22, 1915, p. 29.

152. Interview with Anna Hamburger, Newark, N.J., 1979; Marie Munk memoirs, VII, 3–4. Marie Munk received the King Ludwig Cross (the Bavarian equivalent of the Prussian Iron Cross) for outstanding contributions by civilians.

153. Hamburger-Liepmann, memoirs, p. 159; Charlotte Levinger, memoirs, LBI, pp. 4–6.

154. Hamburger-Liepmann, memoirs, p. 159.

155. Goldstein collection, Box 8, folder 5. See Box 8 in general for Frauenhilfe materials.

156. For descriptions of the black market, see Bruno Stern, *Meine Jugenderinnerungen an eine württembergische Kleinstadt und ihre jüdische Gemeinde* (Stuttgart, 1968), p. 63; Hilda Albers, memoirs, LBI, p. 13; Marie Munk, memoirs, VIII, 14; Nora Rosenthal, memoirs, Stadtarchiv, Frankfurt/Main, p. 24; Stephanie Orfali, *A Jewish Girl in the Weimar Republic* (Berkeley, 1987), p. 74.

157. See such medals and certificates in the LBI collections: Hans Eltzbacher (#42); Alfred Eliassow (folder 1, #6); Hildegard Boehme (#13); Katharina Perl; Marta Fraenkel, #AR4348 (35); Sinn collection, ARC406, 1163, IV (17). See also Marie Munk, memoirs.

158. Monika Richarz, ed., *Jüdisches Leben in Deutschland*, vol. 2, *Selbstzeugnisse zur Sozialgeschichte im Kaiserreich* (Stuttgart, 1979), p. 235.

159. See Arnold Zweig's *Junge Frau von 1914* for a Jewish woman's delight at being invited to work with non-Jewish women of the upper middle class (Berlin, 1931; reprint, Berlin, 1970), pp. 36–37.

160. Margarete Sallis-Freudenthal, *Ich habe mein Land gefunden* (Frankfurt/Main, 1977), pp. 38–39.

161. Schönewald, memoirs, pp. 11–12.

162. *Mitteilungen des Verbandes der jüdischen Jugendvereine Deutschlands* (Berlin), November 1916, p. 80, and July 1917, pp. 87–88; *Blau Weiss Blätter*, December 1914, pp. 20–21, and August 1914, special issue.

163. *Mitteilungen des Verbandes der jüdischen Jugendvereine Deutschlands*, November 15, 1916, pp. 80–81.

164. Ruth Pierson, "Embattled Veterans—The *Reichsbund jüdischer Frontsoldaten*," *LBIYB*, 1974, p. 141.

165. For camaraderie despite "occasional anti-Semitic . . . excesses," see Sammy Gronemann in Richarz, *Jüdisches Leben*, vol. 2, pp. 413–14. For examples of anti-Semitism at the front, see the memoirs of Kurt Joseph (in the air force), Paul Tachau (an army surgeon), and Friedrich Solon (a noncommissioned officer) at the LBI.

166. Werner Jochmann, "Die Ausbreitung des Antisemitismus," in *Deutsches Judentum in Krieg und Revolution, 1916–1923*, ed. Werner Mosse and Arnold Paucker (Tübingen, 1971), pp. 409–45.

167. *Israelitisches Wochenblatt*, January 15, 1915, p. 20.

168. *Im deutschen Reich*, September 1914, p. 350.

169. *Israelitisches Wochenblatt*, February 12, 1915, p. 53.

170. Charlotte Stein-Pick, memoirs, LBI, p. 9.

171. *Im deutschen Reich*, July/August 1916, p. 172. When pressed, the accusers could furnish no further information.

172. *AZDJ*, February 19, 1917, supplement. p. 2; Pierson, "Embattled," p. 142.

173. Jews later made their own survey, setting up a Committee for War Statistics. They discovered that about 12,000 men had died in action and that 100,000 had served in the war (out of a Jewish population of 550,000); 18% of Jews and 20% of Gentiles had served, and 2.1% of Jews and 2.9% of Gentiles had died. See Jakob Segall, *Die deutschen Juden als Soldaten im Krieg, 1914–1918* (Berlin, 1922); Werner T. Angress, "The German Army's 'Judenzählung' of 1916—Genesis, Consequences, Significance," in *LBIYB*, 1978, pp. 117–38. See also Adolf Asch, memoirs, LBI, p. 1 .

174. Richarz, ed., *Jüdisches Leben*, vol. 2, p. 235.

175. Hugh McLeod has written: "when women in Rochester [N.Y.] engaged in campaigns against slavery, prostitution and alcoholism, they could rely on three resources that their husbands, brothers or fathers provided to them: legitimation, money and political goodwill. There were close ties between benevolent [*wohltätigen*] women and powerful people from the church, press, economy and politics." "Weibliche Frömmigkeit—männlicher Unglaube? Religion und Kirchen im bürgerlichen 19. Jahrhundert," in *Bürgerinnen und Bürger: Geschlechterverhältnisse im 19. Jahrhundert*, ed. Ute Frevert (Göttingen, 1988), p. 144.

176. From *Die Gleichheit* 20:25 (1910): 386, quoted by Ulrike Bussemer in "Bürgerliche und proletarische Frauenbewegung (1865–1914)," in *Frauen in der Geschichte*, ed. Annette Kuhn and Gerhard Schneider (Düsseldorf, 1979), p. 43.

Conclusion

1. Quoted by Jürgen Kocka in the Foreword to *Bürgerinnen und Bürger*, ed. Ute Frevert (Göttingen, 1988), p. 8. Karl Marx, *Letters to Dr. Kugelmann* (New York, 1934), p. 83.

2. George Mosse, "Jewish Emancipation: Between *Bildung* and Respectability," in *The Jewish Response to German Culture: From the Enlightenment to the Second World War*, ed. Jehuda Reinharz and Walter Schatzberg (Hanover, N.H., 1985), p. 12. Mosse also suggested that the sexual division of labor was used against Jews and shows how racists accused them of being "feminine" and a menace to respectablity: *Nationalism and Sexuality: Respectability and Abnormal Sexuality in Modern Europe* (New York, 1985).

3. Zygmunt Bauman, *Modernity and the Holocaust* (Ithaca, N.Y., 1989), p. 46. Bauman argues that Jews were the prime target of resistance to modernism, particularly to its capitalist form.

4. This appears to have obtained in Christian groups as well. Hugh McLeod, "Weibliche Frömmigkeit—männlicher Unglaube? Religion und Kirchen im bürgerlichen 19. Jahrhundert," in *Bürgerinnen und Bürger*, ed. Ute Frevert, p. 145.

5. Leonore Davidoff and Catherine Hall, *Family Fortunes: Men and Women of the English Middle Class, 1780–1850* (London, 1987).

6. Ibid., p. 450.

7. Ibid., pp. 29–30.

8. *Die Entstehung der Judenassimilation in Deutschland und deren Ideologie* (Frankfurt/Main, 1935), p. 32, quoted by Katz in his essay "German Culture and the Jews," in *The Jewish Response to German Culture*, ed. Reinharz and Schatzberg, p. 85. See also Eva Reichmann, *Hostages of Civilization* (Boston, 1951), pp. 22–30.

9. Katz, "German Culture," p. 85.

10. Hannah Arendt, *The Origins of Totalitarianism* (Cleveland and New York, 1958), p. 67.

11. In evaluating the eagerness with which Jews supported *Bildung* (in this case, high culture), Jacob Katz wrote: "The difference between German and German-Jewish cultural behavior is, first of all, quantitative. Jews were more intensively involved in the cultivation of their *Bildung* than were their Gentile counterparts." He also noted that in the early nineteenth century Jewish women stood out among audiences attending productions of Goethe's plays. "German Culture," p. 87.

12. Hans Medick and David Warren Sabean, referring to research by Esther Goody, in the introduction to *Interest and Emotion: Essays on the Study of Family and Kinship*, ed. Medick and Sabean (Cambridge, 1984), pp. 5–6.

13. Medick and Sabean, quoting E. P. Thompson, in "Family and the Economy of Emotion," *Interest*, p. 23.

14. Mosse, "Jewish Emancipation in *The Jewish Response*, ed. Reinharz and Schatzberg p. 8.

15. M. Horkheimer as quoted by Karin Hausen, "Family and Role-Division: The Polarisation of Sexual Stereotypes in the Nineteenth Century: An Aspect of the Dissociation of Work and Family Life," in *The German Family*, ed. Richard Evans and W. R. Lee (London, 1981), p. 65.

16. I have found the following studies useful in articulating the "survivalist"/"assimilationist" debates among sociologists: Calvin Goldscheider, *Jewish Continuity and Change* (Bloomington, Ind., 1986); Charles Silberman, *A Certain People* (New York, 1985); and Charles S. Liebman, "The Debate on American Jewish Life: A 'Survivalist's' Response to Some Recent 'Revisionist Works,'" in *Studies in Contemporary Jewry* 4 (1988): 174–84.

17. Phyllis Albert, "L'Intégration et la persistence de l'ethnicité chez les Juifs dans la France moderne," *Le Devenir des Juifs de France entre universalisme et particularisme, 1789–1989*, ed. Pierre Birnbaum (Paris, 1991).

18. See Ismar Schorsch, *Jewish Reactions to German Anti-Semitism, 1870–1914* (New York, 1972); Marjorie Lamberti, *Jewish Activism in Imperial Germany: The Struggle for Civil Equality* (New Haven, Conn., 1978); Jack Wertheimer, *Unwelcome Strangers: East European Jews in Imperial Germany* (New York, 1987).

SELECTED BIBLIOGRAPHY

Books

Albisetti, James C. *Schooling German Girls and Women: Secondary and Higher Education in the Nineteenth Century*. Princeton, N.J., 1988.

———. *Secondary School Reform in Imperial Germany*. Princeton, N.J., 1983.

Anderson, Bonnie, and Judith Zinsser. *A History of Their Own: Women in Europe from Prehistory to the Present*. Vol. 2. New York, 1988.

Aschheim, Steven. *Brothers and Strangers: The East European Jew in German and German-Jewish Consciousness, 1800–1923*. Madison, Wis., 1982.

Autorinnengruppe Uni Wien. *Das ewige Klischee: Zum Rollenbild und Selbstverständnis bei Männern und Frauen*. Vienna, 1988.

Bajohr, Stefan. *Die Hälfte der Fabrik: Geschichte der Frauenarbeit in Deutschland*. Marburg, 1979.

Barkai, Avraham. *Jüdische Minderheit und Industrialisierung*. Tübingen, 1988.

Baron, Rüdeger, ed. *Sozialarbeit und soziale Reform: Zur Geschichte eines Berufs zwischen Frauenbewegung und öffentlicher Verwaltung*. Weinheim and Basel, 1983.

Behr, Stefan. *Der Bevölkerungsrückgang der deutschen Juden*. Frankfurt/Main, 1932.

Berend, Alice. *Die gute alte Zeit: Bürger und Spiessbürger im 19. Jahrhundert*. Hamburg, 1962.

Berger, Heinrich. *Methodik des jüdischen Religionsunterrichtes*. Leipzig, 1911.

Berghahn, Marion. *German-Jewish Refugees in England*. London, 1984.

Beuys, Barbara. *Familienleben in Deutschland*. Reinbek bei Hamburg, 1980.

Biale, Rachel. *Women and Jewish Law*. New York, 1984.

Blackbourn, David, and Geoff Eley. *The Peculiarities of German History: Bourgeois Society and Politics in Nineteenth Century Germany*. Oxford and New York, 1984.

Boxer, Marilyn, and Jean Quataert, eds. *Connecting Spheres: Women in the Western World, 1500 to the Present*. New York, 1987.

Brandeis, Jakob. *Ruth: Deutsches Gebet- und Erbauungsbuch für israelitische Mädchen*. Breslau, 1908.

Brehmer, Ilse, ed. *Lehrerinnen: Zur Geschichte eines Frauenberufes*. Munich, 1980.

Breuer, Mordechai. *Jüdische Orthodoxie im deutschen Reich, 1871–1918*. Frankfurt/Main, 1986.

Bridenthal, Renate, Claudia Koonz, and Susan Stuard, eds. *Becoming Visible: Women in European History*. 2nd ed. Boston, 1987.

Bronsen, David. *Jews and Germans from 1860 to 1933: The Problematic Symbiosis*. Heidelberg, 1979.

Carlebach, Salomon. *Ratgeber für das jüdische Haus: Ein Führer für Verlobung, Hochzeit und Eheleben*. Berlin, 1918.

———. *Sittenreinheit: Ein Mahnwort an Israels Söhne und Töchter*. Berlin, 1917.

Caspary, Gerda. *Die Entwicklungsgrundlagen für die soziale und psychische Verselbständigung der bürgerlichen deutschen Frau um die Jahrhundertwende*. Heidelberg, 1933.

Cauer, Minna. *Die Frau im 19. Jahrhundert*. Berlin, 1898.

Conze, Werner. *Sozialgeschichte der Familie in der Neuzeit Europas*. Stuttgart, 1976.

Cuddihy, John Murray. *The Ordeal of Civility: Freud, Marx, Lévi Strauss, and the Jewish Struggle with Modernity*. New York, 1974.

Davidoff, Leonore, and Catherine Hall. *Family Fortunes: Men and Women of the English Middle Class, 1780–1850*. London, 1987.

Deutscher Juristinnenbund, ed. *Juristinnen in Deutschland*. Munich, 1984.

Dormitzer, Else. *Berühmte jüdische Frauen in Vergangenheit und Gegenwart*. Berlin, 1925.

Edinger, Dora. *Bertha Pappenheim: Leben und Schriften*. Frankfurt/Main, 1963.

Eifert, Christiane, and Susanne Rouette, eds. *Unter allen Umständen: Frauengeschichte(n) in Berlin*. Berlin, 1986.

Elsasser, Marie. *Ausführliches Kochbuch für die einfache und feine jüdische Küche*. 2nd ed. Frankfurt/Main, 1911.

Engelsing, Rolf. *Zur Sozialgeschichte deutscher Mittel- und Unterschichten*. Göttingen, 1973.

Evans, Richard J. *The Feminist Movement in Germany, 1894–1933*. London, 1976.

Evans, Richard J., and W. R. Lee, eds. *The German Family*. London, 1981.

Feldman, David. *Marital Relations, Birth Control, and Abortion in Jewish Law*. New York, 1974.

Foster, John, ed. *Community of Fate: Memoirs of German Jews in Melbourne*. Sydney, 1986.

Fout, John, ed. *German Women in the Nineteenth Century: A Social History*. New York, 1984.

Franzoi, Barbara. *At the Very Least She Pays the Rent: Women and German Industrialization, 1871–1914*. Westport, Conn., 1985.

Freudenthal, Max, ed. *Religionsbuch für den israelitischen Religionsunterricht an der Oberklassen der Gymnasien und Töchterschulen*. Nuremberg, 1912.

Frevert, Ute, ed. *Bürgerinnen und Bürger: Geschlechterverhältnisse im 19. Jahrhundert*. Göttingen, 1988.

———. *Frauen-Geschichte: Zwischen bürgerliche Verbesserung und neuer Weiblichkeit*. Frankfurt/Main, 1986 (translated as *Women in German History: From Bourgeois Emancipation to Sexual Liberation*. Oxford and New York, 1989).

Frykman, Jonas and Orva Löfgren. *Culture Builders: A Historical Anthropology of Middle-Class Life*. New Brunswick, N.J., 1987.

Fuchs, Eduard. *Die Juden in der Karikatur: Ein Beitrag zur Kulturgeschichte*. Munich, 1921.

Fürth, Henriette. *Die deutschen Frauen im Kriege*. Tübingen, 1917.

Gay, Peter. *The Bourgeois Experience: Victoria to Freud*. Vol. 1, *Education of the Senses*. New York, 1984.

———. *The Bourgeois Experience*. Vol. 2, *The Tender Passion*. New York, 1986.

———. *Freud, Jews and Other Germans: Masters and Victims in Modernist Culture*. New York, 1978.

Gerhard, Ute. *Verhältnisse und Verhinderungen: Frauenarbeit, Familie und Rechte der Frauen im 19. Jahrhundert*. Frankfurt/Main, 1978.

Gersdorff, Ursula von. *Frauen im Kriegsdienst*. Stuttgart, 1969.

Glatzer, Nahum N., ed. *Leopold and Adelheid Zunz: An Account in Letters, 1815–1885*. London, 1958.

Goldscheider, Calvin, and Alan S. Zuckerman. *The Transformation of the Jews*. Chicago, 1984.

Goody, Jack. *The Development of the Family and Marriage in Europe*. Cambridge, 1983.

Goody, Jack, and S. J. Tambiah. *Bridewealth and Dowry*. Cambridge, 1973.

Greven-Aschoff, Barbara. *Die bürgerliche Frauenbewegung in Deutschland, 1894–1933*. Göttingen, 1981.

Grunwald, Max. *Beruria: Gebet- und Andachtsbuch für jüdische Frauen und Mädchen*. Vienna, 1907.

Gumprich, Bertha (Witwe Joseph). *Vollständiges praktisches Kochbuch für die jüdische Küche*. 7th ed. Frankfurt/Main, 1914.

Hallo, Rudolf. *Geschichte der jüdischen Gemeinde Kassel*. Vol. 1. Kassel, 1931.

Hamburger, Ernst. *Juden im öffentlichen Leben Deutschlands: Regierungsmitglieder, Beamte und Parlamentarier in der monarchischen Zeit, 1848–1918*. Tübingen, 1968.

Handbuch der jüdischen Gemeindeverwaltung und Wohlfahrtspflege. Berlin, 1909.

Hausen, Karin, ed. *Frauen suchen ihre Geschichte*. Munich, 1983.

Henning, Hansjoachim. *Das westdeutsche Bürgertum in der Epoche der Hochindustrialisierung, 1860–1914: Soziales Verhalten und soziale Strukturen*. Vol. 1, *Das Bildungsbürgertum in den Preussischen Westprovinzen*. Wiesbaden, 1972.

Henry, Frances. *Victims and Neighbors: A Small Town in Nazi Germany Remembered*. South Hadley, Mass., 1985.

Herrmann, Judith. *Die deutsche Frau in akademischen Berufen*. Berlin, 1915.

Hertz, Deborah. *Jewish High Society in Old Regime Berlin*. New Haven, Conn., 1988.

Honigmann, Peter. *Die Austritte aus der Jüdischen Gemeinde Berlin, 1873–1941*. Frankfurt/Main, 1988.

Jahres-Bericht der jüdischen Toynbee-Halle der Berliner Bnei Briss Logen, 1912/13. Berlin, 1913.

Jalland, Pat. *Women, Marriage, and Politics, 1860–1914*. Oxford, 1986.

Jarausch, Konrad. *Students, Society and Politics in Imperial Germany: The Rise of Academic Illiberalism*. Princeton, N.J., 1982.

Jeggle, Utz. *Judendörfer in Württemberg*. Tübingen, 1969.

Joeres, Ruth-Ellen, and Mary Jo Maynes. *German Women in the Eighteenth and Nineteenth Centuries*. Bloomington, Ind., 1986.

Kaplan, Marion. *The Jewish Feminist Movement in Germany: The Campaigns of the Jüdischer Frauenbund, 1904–1938*. Westport, Conn., 1979.

———, ed. *The Marriage Bargain: Women and Dowries in European History*. New York, 1985.

Karpeles, Gustav. *Die Frauen in der jüdischen Literatur*. Berlin, 1889.

Katz, Jacob. *Out of the Ghetto: The Social Background of Jewish Emancipation*. Cambridge, Mass., 1971.

Kauders, Marie. *Vollständiges israelitisches Kochbuch*. 4th ed. Prague and Breslau, 1903.

Kayserling, Meyer. *Die jüdischen Frauen in der Geschichte, Literatur und Kunst*. Leipzig, 1879.

Kaznelson, Siegmund, ed. *Juden im deutschen Kulturbereich*. Berlin, 1959.

Knodel, John. *The Decline of Fertility in Germany, 1871–1939*. Princeton, N.J., 1974.

Kocka, Jürgen, ed. *Bürger und Bürgerlichkeit im 19. Jahrhundert*. Göttingen, 1987.

———, ed. *Bürgertum im 19. Jahrhundert: Deutschland im europäischen Vergleich*. Munich, 1988.

Koltun, Elizabeth, ed. *The Jewish Woman*. New York, 1976.

Labsch-Benz, Elfie. *Die jüdische Gemeinde Nonnenweier: Jüdisches Leben und Brauchtum in einer badischen Landgemeinde zu Beginn des 20. Jahrhundert*. Baden-Württemberg, 1980.

Lamberti, Marjorie. *Jewish Activism in Imperial Germany: The Struggle for Civil Equality*. New Haven, Conn., 1978.

Lamm, Hans, ed. *Von Juden in München: Ein Gedenkbuch*. Munich, 1958.

Landsberger, Julius. *Religion und Liebe: Ein kleiner Katechismus für die israelitische Jugend*. Berlin, 1883.

Landwehr, Rolf, and Rüdeger Baron, eds. *Geschichte der Sozialarbeit*. Weinheim and Basel, 1983.

Lasker-Schüler, Else. *Dichtungen und Dokumente*. Edited by Ernst Ginsberg. Munich, 1951.

Leimdorfer, David. *Ein Wort zu unserer Frauenfrage*. Berlin, 1900.

Lerner, Gerda. *The Majority Finds Its Past: Placing Women in History*. New York, 1979.

Lestschinsky, Jakob. *Das wirtschaftliche Schicksal des deutschen Judentums*. Berlin, 1932.

Levi, Abraham. *Die Pflichten der jüdischen Frau: Für Bräute und Frauen*. Frankfurt/Main, 1903.

Levy-Rathenau, Josephine. *Die deutsche Frau im Beruf: Praktische Ratschläge zur Berufswahl*. 4th ed. Berlin, 1915.

Lewin, Adolf. *Geschichte der badischen Juden*. Karlsruhe, 1909.

Liberles, Robert. *Religious Conflict in Social Context: The Resurgence of Orthodox Judaism in Frankfurt am Main, 1838–1877*. Westport, Conn., 1985.

Mandelbaum, Hugo. *Jewish Life in the Village Communities of Southern Germany*. New York, 1985.

Marcuse, Max. *Über die Fruchtbarkeit der Christlich-jüdischen Mischehe*. Bonn, 1920.

Maurer, Trude. *Ostjuden in Deutschland*. Hamburg, 1987.

Medick, Hans, and David Sabean, eds. *Interest and Emotion: Essays on the Study of Family and Kinship*. Cambridge, Eng. 1984.

Meyer, Michael. *Response to Modernity: A History of the Reform Movement in Judaism*. New York, 1988.

Meyer, Sibylle. *Das Theater mit der Hausarbeit: Bürgerliche Repräsentation in der Familie der wilhelminischen Zeit*. Frankfurt/Main, 1982.

Möller, Helmut. *Die kleinbürgerliche Familie im 18. Jahrhundert*. Berlin, 1969.

Mosse, George L. *German Jews Beyond Judaism*. Bloomington, Ind., 1985.

———, ed. *Masses and Man: Nationalist and Fascist Perceptions of Reality*. New York, 1980.

Mosse, Werner. *Jews in the German Economy: The German-Jewish Economic Elite, 1820–1935*. Oxford, 1987.

———, ed. *Juden im Wilhelminischen Deutschland, 1890–1914*. Tübingen, 1976.

Müller, Heidi. *Dienstbare Geister: Leben und Arbeitswelt städtischer Dienstboten*. Berlin, 1981.

Müthesius, Hans, ed. *Alice Salomon: Die Begründerin des sozialen Frauenberufs in Deutschland*. Cologne and Berlin, 1958.

Niewyk, Donald. *The Jews in Weimar Germany*. Baton Rouge, La., 1980.

Nossig, Alfred, ed. *Jüdische Statistik*. Berlin, 1903.

Perrot, Michelle, ed. *A History of Private Life*. Vol. 4, *From the Fires of Revolution to the Great War*. Translated by Arthur Goldhammer. Cambridge, Mass., 1990.

Plaut, W. Gunther. *The Growth of Reform Judaism: American and European Sources until 1948*. New York, 1965.

———. *The Rise of Reform Judaism: A Sourcebook of Its European Origins*. New York, 1963.

Plothow, Anna. *Die Begründerinnen der deutschen Frauenbewegung*. Leipzig, n.d. (ca. 1906 or 1907).

Polko, Elise. *Unsere Pilgerfahrt von der Kinderstube bis zum eigenen Herd*. Leipzig, 1863.

Pollack, Herman. *Jewish Folkways in Germanic Lands (1648–1806)*. Cambridge, Mass., 1971.

Poppel, Stephen M. *Zionism in Germany, 1897–1933: The Shaping of a Jewish Identity*. Philadelphia, 1977.

Prelinger, Catherine. *Charity, Challenge, and Change: Religious Dimensions of the Mid-Nineteenth Century Women's Movement in Germany*. Westport, Conn., 1987.

Prinz, Arthur. *Juden im deutschen Wirtschaftsleben*. Edited by Avraham Barkai. Tübingen, 1984.

Pulzer, Peter. *The Rise of Political Anti-Semitism in Germany and Austria*. New York, 1964. Rev. ed. Cambridge, Mass., 1988.

Reinharz, Jehuda. *Fatherland or Promised Land: The Dilemma of the German Jew, 1893–1914*. Ann Arbor, Mich., 1975.

Reinharz, Jehuda, and Walter Schatzberg, eds. *The Jewish Response to German Culture: From the Enlightenment to the Second World War*. Hanover, N.H., 1985.

Richarz, Monika. *Der Eintritt der Juden in die akademischen Berufe: Jüdische Studenten und Akademiker in Deutschland, 1778–1848*. Tübingen, 1974.

———, ed. *Jüdisches Leben in Deutschland*. Vol. 1, *Selbstzeugnisse zur Sozialgeschichte, 1780–1871*. Stuttgart, 1976.

———, ed. *Jüdisches Leben in Deutschland*. Vol. 2, *Selbstzeugnisse zur Sozialgeschichte im Kaiserreich*. Stuttgart, 1979.

———, ed. *Jüdisches Leben in Deutschland*. Vol. 3, *Selbstzeugnisse zur Sozialgeschichte, 1918–1945*. Stuttgart, 1982.

Riehl, Wilhelm. *Die Naturgeschichte des Volkes als Grundlage einer deutschen Social-Politik*. Vol. 3, *Die Familie*. 9th ed. Stuttgart, 1882.

Ringer, Fritz K. *Education and Society in Modern Europe*. Bloomington, Ind., 1979.

Rosenbaum, Heidi. *Formen der Familie*. Frankfurt/Main. 1982.

Rozenblit, Marsha. *The Jews of Vienna: Assimilation and Identity, 1867–1914*. Albany, N.Y., 1983.

Rudavsky, David. *Emancipation and Adjustment: Contemporary Jewish Religious Movements, Their History and Thought*. New York, 1967.

Ruppin, Arthur. *Die Juden der Gegenwart*. Berlin, 1918.

———. *Die Juden im Grossherzogtum Hessen*. Berlin, 1909.

———. *Die jüdischen Gemeinden und Vereine in Deutschland*. Berlin, 1906.

———. *Soziologie der Juden*. Berlin, 1930.

Ruppin, Arthur, and Jakob Thon. *Der Anteil der Juden am Unterrichtswesen in Preussen*. Berlin, 1905.

Sachsse, Christoph. *Mütterlichkeit als Beruf: Sozialarbeit, Sozialreform und Frauenbewegung, 1871–1929*. Frankfurt/Main, 1986.

Sachsse, Christoph, and Florian Tennstedt. *Geschichte der Armenfürsorge in Deutschland: Vom Spätmittelalter bis zum Ersten Weltkrieg*. Stuttgart, 1980.

Schmelz, Usiel. *Infant and Early Childhood Mortality Among the Jews of the Diaspora*. Jerusalem, 1971.

Schorsch, Ismar. *Jewish Reactions to German Anti-Semitism, 1870–1914*. New York, 1972.

Schwab, Herman. *Jewish Rural Communities in Germany*. London, 1956.

Scott, Joan. *Gender and the Politics of History*. New York, 1988.

Segall, Jakob. *Die beruflichen und sozialen Verhältnisse der Juden in Deutschland*. Berlin, 1912.

———. *Die Entwicklung der jüdischen Bevölkerung in München, 1875–1905*. Berlin, 1910.

Sidgwick, Mrs. *Home Life in Germany*. New York, 1912.

Silbergleit, Heinrich. *Die Bevölkerung und Berufsverhältnisse der Juden in Deutschland*. Berlin, 1930.

Simon-Friedenberg, Johanna. *Gegenwartsaufgaben der jüdischen Frau*. Berlin, 1913.

Smith, Bonnie. *Ladies of the Leisure Class: The Bourgeoises of Northern France in the Nineteenth Century*. Princeton, N.J., 1981.

Somogyi, Tamar. *Die Scheinen und die Prosten*. Berlin, 1982.

Sorkin, David. *The Transformation of German Jewry, 1780–1840*. Oxford and New York, 1987.

Stern, Fritz. *Gold and Iron: Bismarck, Bleichröder, and the Building of the German Empire*. New York, 1977.

———. *The Politcs of Cultural Despair: A Study in the Rise of the Germanic Ideology*. Berkeley, Calif., 1961.

Stillich, Oscar. *Die Lage der weiblichen Dienstboten in Berlin*. Berlin, 1902.

Tal, Uriel. *Christians and Jews in Germany. Religion, Politics, and Ideology in the Second Reich, 1870–1914*. Ithaca, N.Y., 1975.

Theilhaber, Felix A. *Der Untergang der deutschen Juden*. Munich, 1911.

———. *Die Schädigung der Rasse durch soziales und wirtschaftliches Aufsteigen bewiesen an den Berliner Juden*. Berlin, 1914.

Thompson, F. M. L. *The Rise of Respectable Society: A Social History of Victorian Britain, 1830–1900*. Cambridge, Mass., 1988.

Toury, Jacob. *Soziale und politische Geschichte der Juden in Deutschland, 1848–1871*. Düsseldorf, 1977.

Twellman-Schepp, Margrit. *Die deutsche Frauenbewegung: Ihre Anfänge und erste Entwicklung, 1843–1889*. Meisenheim, 1972.

van Cleef, Henny. *Die israelitische Küche*. 3rd ed. Leipzig, 1898.

Vicinus, Martha, ed. *Suffer and Be Still: Women in the Victorian Age*. Bloomington, Ind., 1972.

Volkov, Shulamit. *The Rise of Popular Anti-Modernism in Germany*. Princeton, N.J., 1978.

Vondung, Klaus, ed. *Das wilhelminische Bildungsbürgertum: Zur Sozialgeschichte seiner Ideen*. Göttingen, 1976.

Weber-Kellermann, Ingeborg. *Die deutsche Familie: Versuch einer Sozialgeschichte*. 4th ed. Frankfurt/Main, 1978.

Weinberg, Margarete. *Die Hausfrauen der deutschen Vergangenheit und Gegenwart*. Mönchen Gladbach, 1920.

Weinberg, Werner. *Die Reste des Jüdischdeutschen*. Stuttgart, 1969.

Weiner-Odenheimer, Paula. *Die Berufe der Juden in Bayern*. Berlin, 1918.

Weinryb, Sucher. *Der Kampf um die Berufsumschichtung: Ein Ausschnitt aus der Geschichte der Juden in Deutschland*. Berlin, 1936.

Werner, Joachim. *Die Heiratsannonce: Studien und Briefe*. Berlin, 1908.

Wertheimer, Jack. *Unwelcome Strangers: East European Jews in Imperial Germany*. New York, 1987.

Wierling, Dorothee. *Mädchen für Alles: Arbeitsalltag und Lebensgeschichte städtischer Dienstmädchen um die Jahrhundertwende*. Berlin, 1987.

Wolf, Rebekka. *Kochbuch für Israelitische Frauen*. 6th ed. Berlin, 1875.

Woycke, James. *Birth Control in Germany: 1871–1933*. London, 1988.

Zahn-Harnack, Agnes. *Die Frauenbewegung—Geschichte, Probleme, Ziele*. Berlin, 1928.

Zborowski, Mark, and Elizabeth Herzog. *Life Is with People: The Culture of the Shtetl*. New York, 1952.

Zentralwohlfahrtsstelle der deutschen Juden. *Führer durch die Jüdische Wohlfahrtspflege in Deutschland*. Berlin, 1929.

Zinnecker, Jürgen. *Sozialgeschichte der Mädchenbildung*. Weinheim and Basel, 1973.

Articles

Albisetti, James C. "The Fight for Female Physicians in Imperial Germany." *Central European History* 15:2 (June 1982).

———. "The Reform of Female Education in Prussia, 1899–1908: A Study in Compromise and Containment." *German Studies Review* 8 (February 1985).

———. "Women and the Professions in Imperial Germany." *German Women in the Eighteenth and Nineteenth Centuries*. Edited by Ruth-Ellen Joeres and Mary Jo Maynes. Bloomington, Ind., 1986.

Allen, Ann Taylor. "Sex and Satire in Wilhelmine Germany: 'Simplicissimus' Looks at Family Life." *Journal of European Studies* 7 (1977).

———. "Spiritual Motherhood: German Feminists and the Kindergarten Movement, 1848–1911." *History of Education Quarterly* 22 (1982).

Angress, Werner T. "The German Army's 'Judenzählung' of 1916—Genesis, Consequences, Significance." *LBIYB*, 1978.

Bahlout, Joelle. "Foodways in Contemporary Jewish Communities: Research Directions." *Jewish Folklore and Ethnology Review* 9:1 (1987).

Barkai, Avraham. "German-Jewish Migration in the Nineteenth Century, 1830–1910." *LBIYB*, 1985.

———. "The German Jews at the Start of Industrialisation: Structural Changes and Mobility, 1835–1860." *Revolution and Evolution: 1848 in German-Jewish History*. Edited by Werner Mosse, Arnold Paucker, and Reinhard Rürup. Tübingen, 1981.

———. "Sozialgeschichtliche Aspekte der deutschen Judenheit in der Zeit der Industrialisierung." *Jahrbuch des Instituts für deutsche Geschichte* 11 (1982).

Baron, Rüdeger. "Die Entwicklung der Armenpflege in Deutschland vom Beginn des 19. Jahrhunderts bis zum Ersten Weltkrieg." *Geschichte der Sozialarbeit*. Edited by Rolf Landwehr and Rüdeger Baron. Weinheim and Basel, 1983.

Baron, Rüdeger, and Rolf Landwehr. "Von der Berufung zum Beruf: Zur Entwicklung der Ausbildung für die soziale Arbeit." *Sozialarbeit und Soziale Reform: Zur Geschichte eines Berufs zwischen Frauenbewegung und öffentlicher Verwaltung*. Edited by Rüdeger Baron. Weinheim and Basel, 1983.

Bechtold-Comforty, Beate. "Jüdische Frauen auf dem Dorf—zwischen Eigenständigkeit und Integration." *Sozialwissenschaftliche Informationen* 18:3 (September 1989).

Berliner, A. "Jüdische Speisetafel." *Jahrbuch für jüdische Geschichte und Literatur* 13 (1910).

Biale, David. "Love, Marriage and the Modernization of the Jews." *Approaches to Modern Judaism*. Edited by Marc Lee Raphael. Chico, Calif., 1983.

Boehm, Laetitia. "Von den Anfängen des akademischen Frauenstudiums in Deutschland." *Historisches Jahrbuch* 77 (1958).

Burman, Ricki. " 'She Looketh Well to the Ways of Her Household': The Changing Role of Jewish Women in Religious Life, 1880–1930." *Religion in the Lives of English Women, 1760–1930*. Edited by Gail Malmgreen. Bloomington, Ind., 1986.

Bussemer, Herrad-Ulrike. "Bürgerliche und proletarische Frauenbewegung (1865–1914)." *Frauen in der Geschichte: Frauenrechte und die gesellschaftliche Arbeit der Frauen im Wandel*. Edited by Annette Kuhn and Gerhard Schneider. Düsseldorf, 1979.

Cahnmann, Werner. "A Regional Approach to German-Jewish History." *Jewish Social Studies* 5 (1943).

Epstein, Tilly. "38 Jahre Lehrerin am Philanthropin." *Das Philanthropin zu Frankfurt am Main*. Kommission zur Erforschung der Geschichte der Frankfurter Juden. Frankfurt/Main, 1964.

Eschelbacher, Ernestine. "Die Arbeit der jüdischen Frauen in Deutschland während des Krieges." *Ost und West* 19:5/6 (May/June, 1919).

Fassmann, Maya. "Die Mutter der Volksküchen: Lina Morgenstern und die jüdische Wohltätigkeit." *Unter allen Umständen: Frauengeschichte(n) in Berlin*. Edited by Christiane Eifert and Susanne Rouette. Berlin, 1986.

Field, Geoffrey. "Religion in the German Volksschule, 1890–1928." *LBIYB*, 1980.

Frevert, Ute. "Bürgerliche Meisterdenker und das Geschlechterverhältnis: Konzepte, Erfahrungen, Visionen an der Wende vom 18. zum 19. Jahrhundert." *Bürgerinnen und Bürger: Geschlechterverhältnisse im 19. Jahrhundert*. Edited by Ute Frevert. Göttingen, 1988.

Gerhard, Ute. "Die Rechtsstellung der Frau in der bürgerlichen Gesellschaft des 19. Jahrhunderts: Frankreich und Deutschland im Vergleich." *Bürgertum im 19. Jahrhundert: Deutschland im europäischen Vergleich*, vol. 1. Edited by Jürgen Kocka. Munich, 1988.

Goldstein, Alice. "Some Demographic Characteristics of Village Jews in Germany: Nonnenweier, 1800–1931." *Modern Jewish Fertility*. Edited by Paul Ritterband. Leiden, 1981.

———. "Urbanization in Baden, Germany: Focus on the Jews, 1825–1925." *Social Science History* 8:1 (Winter 1984).

Goode, William. "The Theoretical Importance of Love." *American Sociological Review* 24:1 (February 1959).

Greive, Hermann. "Zionism and Jewish Orthodoxy." *LBIYB*, 1980.

Grieswelle, Detlef. "Antisemitismus im deutschen Studentenverbindungen des 19. Jahrhunderts." *Student und Hochschule im 19. Jahrhundert*. Edited by Otto Neuloh and Walter Rüegg. Göttingen, 1975.

Grünewald, Max. "The Jewish Teacher." *LBIYB*, 1974.

Grunwald, Max. "Aus dem jüdischen Kochbuch." *Menorah* 6:9 (September 1928).

Hahn, Claudia. "Der öffentliche Dienst und die Frauen—Beamtinnen in der Weimarer Republik." *Mutterkreuz und Arbeitsbuch*. Edited by the Frauengruppe Faschismusforschung. Frankfurt/Main, 1981.

Hausen, Karin. "'. . . eine Ulme für das schwanke Efeu': Ehepaare im Bildungsbürgertum. Ideale und Wirklichkeiten im späten 18. und 19. Jahrhundert." *Bürgerinnen und Bürger: Geschlechterverhältnisse im 19. Jahrhundert*. Edited by Ute Frevert. Göttingen, 1988.

———. "Family and Role Division: The Polarisation of Sexual Stereotypes in the Nineteenth Century: An Aspect of the Dissociation of Work and Family Life." *The German Family*. Edited by Richard Evans and W. R. Lee. London, 1981.

———. "Technical Progress and Women's Labour in the Nineteenth Century: The Social History of the Sewing Machine." *The Social History of Politics: Critical Perspectives in West German Historical Writing Since 1945*. Edited by George Iggers. Leamington Spa, Eng., 1985.

Huerkamp, Claudia. "Frauen, Universitäten und Bildungsbürgertum: Zur Lage studierender Frauen, 1900–1930." *Bürgerliche Berufe: Zur Sozialgeschichte der freien und akademischen Berufe im internationalen Vergleich*. Edited by Hannes Siegrist. Göttingen, 1988.

Hurvitz, Nathan. "Courtship and Arranged Marriages Among East European Jews Prior to World War I as Depicted in a *Briefenshteller*." *Journal of Marriage and Family* 37 (1975).

Hyman, Paula. "Culture and Gender: Women in the Immigrant Jewish Community." *The Legacy of Jewish Migration*. Edited by David Berger. Brooklyn, 1983.

———. "The Other Half: Women in the Jewish Tradition." *The Jewish Woman*. Edited by Elizabeth Koltun. New York, 1976.

Kampe, Norbert. "Jews and Antisemites at Universities in Imperial Germany: (I) Jewish Students: Social History and Social Conflict." *LBIYB*, 1985.

———. "Jews and Antisemites at Universities in Imperial Germany: (II) The Friedrich-Wilhelms-Universität of Berlin: A Case Study on the Students' 'Jewish Question.'" *LBIYB*, 1987.

Katz, Jacob. "Family, Kinship, and Marriage Among Ashkenazim in the Sixteenth to Eighteenth Centuries." *Jewish Journal of Sociology* 1 (1959).

———. "German Culture and the Jews." *The Jewish Response to German Culture: From the Enlightenment to the Second World War*. Edited by Jehuda Reinharz and Walter Schatzberg. Hanover, N.H., 1985.

Kirshenblatt-Gimblett, Barbara. "The Kosher Gourmet in the Nineteenth-Century Kitchen: Three Jewish Cookbooks in Historical Perspective." *Journal of Gastronomy* 2:4 (Winter 1986/87).

Knodel, John, and Mary Jo Maynes. "Urban and Rural Marriage Patterns in Imperial Germany." *Journal of Family History* 1 (1976).

Kocka, Jürgen. "Family and Class Formation: Intergenerational Mobility and Marriage Patterns in Nineteenth Century Westphalian Towns." *Journal of Social History* 17:3 (Spring 1984).

Krauss, Samuel. "Aus der jüdischen Volksküche." *Mitteilungen zur jüdischen Volkskunde* 18:1–2 (1915).

Landes, Ruth, and Marc Zborowski. "Hypotheses Concerning the Eastern Jewish Family." *The Psychodynamics of American Jewish Life*. Edited by N. Kiell. New York, 1967.

Loewenberg, Jakob. "Schule und Haus: Ein Wort an die Eltern meiner Schülerinnen." *Geheime Miterzieher: Plaudereien*. Edited by Jakob Loewenberg. Hamburg, 1906.

Marcuse, Max. "Die christlich-jüdische Mischehe." *Sexual-Probleme: Zeitschrift für Sexualwissenschaft und Sexualpolitik*, October 1912.

Marrus, Michael. "European Jewry and the Politics of Assimilation: Assessment and Reassessment." *Journal of Modern History*, no. 49 (1977).

McLeod, Hugh. "Weibliche Frömmigkeit—männlicher Unglaube? Religion und Kirchen im bürgerlichen 19. Jahrhundert." *Bürgerinnen und Bürger: Geschlechterverhältnisse im 19. Jahrhundert*. Edited by Ute Frevert. Göttingen, 1988.

Mosse, George L. "German Jews and Liberalism in Retrospect: Introduction to Year Book XXXII." *LBIYB*, 1987.

———. "The Jews and the German War Experience, 1914–1918." *Masses and Man: Nationalist and Fascist Perceptions of Reality*. Edited by George L. Mosse. New York, 1980.

———. "The Secularization of Jewish Theology." *Masses and Man: Nationalist and Fascist Perceptions of Reality*. Edited by George L. Mosse. New York, 1980.

Nachman, Larry. "The Question of the Jews: A Study in Culture." *Salmagundi*, no. 44/45 (Spring/Summer 1979).

Pulzer, Peter. "Jews as Voters in the Weimar Republic." *LBIYB*, 1985.

———. "Why Was There a Jewish Question in Imperial Germany?" *LBIYB*, 1980.

Rand-Schleifer, Betty. "Lern- und Lehrjahre, 1908–38." *Das Philanthropin zu Frankfurt am Main*. Kommission zur Erforschung der Geschichte der Frankfurter Juden. Frankfurt/Main, 1964.

Reutlinger, Wilhelm. "Über die Häufigkeit der Verwandtenehen bei den Juden in Hohenzollern und über Untersuchungen bei Deszendenten aus jüdischen Verwandtenehen." *Archiv für Rassen und Gesellschaftsbiologie* 14 (1922).

Richarz, Monika. "Emancipation and Continuity: Jews in the Rural Economy." *Revolution and Evolution: 1848 in German-Jewish History*. Edited by Werner Mosse, Arnold Paucker, and Reinhard Rürup. Tübingen, 1981

Rosenthal, Erich. "Trends of the Jewish Population in Germany, 1910–1939. " *Jewish Social Studies* 6 (1944).

Rürup, Reinhard. "Emancipaton and Crisis: The 'Jewish Question' in Germany, 1850–1890." *LBIYB*, 1975.

Sauer, Birgit. "Den Zusammenhang zwischen der Frauenfrage und der sozialen Frage begreifen. Die 'Frauen-und Mädchengruppen für soziale Hilfsarbeit' (1893–1908)." *Unter allen Umständen: Frauengeschichte(n) in Berlin*. Edited by Christiane Eifert and Susanne Rouette. Berlin, 1986.

Schmelz, Usiel O. "Die demographische Entwicklung der Juden in Deutschland von der Mitte des 19. Jahrhunderts bis 1933." *Zeitschrift für Bevölkerungswissenschaft* 1 (1982).

Schofer, Lawrence. "Emancipation and Population Change." *Revolution and Evolution: 1848 in German-Jewish History*. Edited by Werner Mosse, Arnold Paucker, and Reinhard Rürup. Tübingen, 1981.

Scholem, Gershom. "On the Social Psychology of the Jews in Germany." *Jews and Germans from 1860–1933: The Problematic Symbiosis*. Edited by David Bronsen. Heidelberg, 1979.

Schütze, Yvonne. "Mutterliebe-Vaterliebe: Elternrollen in der bürgerlichen Familie des 19. Jahrhunderts." *Bürgerinnen und Bürger: Geschlechterverhältnisse im 19. Jahrhundert*. Edited by Ute Frevert. Göttingen, 1988.

Sorkin, David. "The Genesis of the Ideology of Emancipation, 1806–1840." *LBIYB*, 1987.

Stelzner, Helenefrederike. "Der weibliche Arzt." *Deutsche medizinische Wochenschrift*, nos. 26/27 (1912).

Stern, Baruch. "Die Stellung der Juden im öffentlichen Volksschulwesen in Preussen in ihrer Entwicklung vom Beginne der Emanzipation bis Heute." *Festschrift für Jacob Rosenheim*. Edited by Heinrich Elsemann. Frankfurt/Main, 1931.

Stone, Lawrence. "Family History in the 1980's." *Journal of Interdisciplinary History* 12:1 (Summer 1981).

Straus, Rahel. "Ehe und Mutterschaft." *Vom jüdischen Geiste: Eine Aufsatzreihe*. Edited by Der Jüdische Frauenbund. Berlin, 1934.

Tennstedt, Florian. "Fürsorgegeschichte und Vereinsgeschichte: 100 Jahre deutscher Verein." *Zeitschrift für Sozialreform* 27 (1981).

Toury, Jacob. "The 'Jewish Question': A Semantic Approach." *LBIYB*, 1966.

Volkov, Shulamit. "Erfolgreiche Assimilation oder Erfolg und Assimilation: Die deutsch-jüdische Familie im Kaiserreich." *Wissenschaftskolleg zu Berlin. Jahrbuch*. Berlin, 1982/1983.

Wassermann, Henry. "The *Fliegenden Blätter* as a Source for the Social History of German Jewry." *LBIYB*, 1983.

Weissler, Chava. "The Religion of Traditional Ashkenazic Women: Some Methodological Issues." *Association for Jewish Studies Review* 12:1 (Spring 1987).

———. "The Traditional Piety of Ashkenazic Women." *Jewish Spirituality*. Edited by Arthur Green. New York, 1987.

Wertheimer, Jack. "The '*Ausländerfrage*' at Institutions of Higher Learning: A Controversy over Russian-Jewish Students in Imperial Germany." *LBIYB*, 1982.

———. "Between Tsar and Kaiser: The Radicalization of Russian Jewish University Students in Germany." *LBIYB*, 1983.

Wilke, Gerhard, and Kurt Wagner. "Family and Household: Social Structures in a German Village Between the Two World Wars." *The German Family*. Edited by Richard Evans and W. R. Lee. London, 1981.

Published Memoirs

Badt-Strauss, Bertha. "Studententage in München, 1912–13." *Von Juden in München*. Edited by Hans Lamm. Munich, 1958.

Benjamin, Walter. *Berliner Kindheit um Neunzehnhundert*. Frankfurt/Main, 1950.

Braun-Vogelstein, Julie. *Was niemals stirbt: Gestalten und Erinnerungen*. Stuttgart, 1966.

Croner, Else. *Das Tagebuch eines Fräulein Doktors*. Stuttgart, 1908.

Ettlinger, Anna. *Lebenserinnerungen für ihre Familie*. Privately printed, n.d. (written ca. 1915–20), Leipzig. LBI.

Frankenthal, Käte. *Der dreifache Fluch: Jüdin, Intellektuelle, Sozialistin: Lebenserinnerungen einer Ärztin in Deutschland und im Exil*. Frankfurt/Main, 1981.

Hahn, Hannelore. *On the Way to Feed the Swans*. New York, 1982.

Hameln, Glückel of. *The Memoirs of Glückl of Hameln*. Translated by Marvin Lowenthal. New York, 1977.

Horney, Karen. *The Adolescent Diaries of Karen Horney*. New York, 1980.

Hyde, Ida H. "Before Women Were Human Beings." *Journal of the American Association of University Women* 31:4 (June 1938).

Kronthal, Anna. *Posner Mürbekuchen: Jugend Erinnerungen einer Posnerin*. Munich, 1932.

Landau, Phillipine. *Kindheitserinnerungen: Bilder aus einer rheinischen Kleinstadt des vorigen Jahrhunderts*. Dietenheim, 1956.

Natorff, Herta. *Das Tagebuch der Herta Natorff*. Edited by Wolfgang Benz. Frankfurt/Main, 1988.

Orfali, Stephanie. *A Jewish Girl in the Weimar Republic*. Berkeley, Calif., 1987.

Picard, Jacob. "Childhood in the Village." *LBIYB*, 1959.

———. *Erinnerungen eigenen Lebens*. Berlin, 1938.

Rosenheim, Jacob. *Erinnerungen, 1870–1920*. Frankfurt/Main, 1970.

Rosenzweig, Adele. "Jugenderinnerungen." Edited by Rivka Horwitz. *LBI Bulletin* 16/17: 53/54 (1977/1978).

Sallis-Freudenthal, Margarete. *Ich habe mein Land gefunden*. Frankfurt/Main, 1977.

Salomon, Alice. *Charakter ist Schicksal: Lebenserinnerungen*. Translated from the English manuscript by Rolf Landwehr. Edited by Rüdeger Baron and Rolf Landwehr. Weinheim and Basel, 1983.

Sender, Toni. *Autobiographie einer deutschen Rebellin*. Frankfurt/Main, 1981. Translated from the English publication, *Autobiography of a German Rebel*. New York, 1939.

Straus, Rahel. *Wir lebten in Deutschland: Erinnerungen einer deutschen Jüdin*. Stuttgart, 1962.

Wachenheim, Hedwig. *Vom Grossbürgertum zur Sozialdemokratie: Memoiren einer Reformistin*. Berlin, 1973.

Wassermann, Jakob. *Mein Weg als Deutscher und Jude*. Berlin, 1921.

Wertheimer, William. *Zwischen zwei Welten: Der Förster von Brooklyn (Lebenserinnerungen des ehemaligen jüdischen Lehrers in Eubigheim und Buchen in Baden)*. Passau, 1966.

Wolff, Charlotte. *Hindsight*. London, 1980.

Unpublished Memoirs

Albers, Hilda. LBI.

Andorn, Salomon. #413 and #414. LBI.

Asch, Adolf. LBI.

Bab, Elisabeth. "Aus zwei Jahrhunderten: Lebenserinnerungen." LBI.

Berel, Marianne. "Family Fragments." LBI.
Bischheim, Simon. LBI.
Calvary, Esther. LBI.
Cassirer, Toni. "Aus meinem Leben mit Ernst Cassirer." LBI.
Davidsohn, Doris. "Erinnerungen einer deutschen Jüdin." LBI.
Diamant, Sophie. "Familiengeschichte Schlesinger." LBI.
Dienemann, Mally. LBI.
Ehrlich, Toni. LBI.
Elsas, Gerald. LBI.
Epstein, Jacob. LBI.
Flersheim, Ernst. "Lebenserinnerungen." LBI.
Frank, Julius. LBI.
Frank, Ludwig. LBI.
Geismar, Clara. LBI.
Goldschmidt, Flora. "Jugenderinnerungen." LBI.
Gova, Sabina. "Fanny Lewald." LBI.
Gronemann, Sammy. LBI.
Grünfeld, Heinrich. LBI.
Guttman, Ludwig. LBI.
Hadra, Edmund. LBI.
Hamburger-Liepmann, Charlotte. "Geschichte der Familien Liepmann und Bleichröder." LBI.
Herzfeld, Ernst. LBI.
Heymann, Aron Hirsch. LBI.
Hirsch, Gertrud. LBI.
Hirsch, Henriette. "Erinnerungen an meine Jugend." LBI.
Jaschuwi, Joseph. LBI.
Joseph, Kurt. LBI.
Kaden, Julie. "Der erste Akt meines Lebens." LBI.
Katz, Bertha. LBI.
Kober, William. LBI.
Landau, Edwin. LBI.
Landau-Muehsam, Charlotte. LBI.
Lange, Josef. "Mein Leben, 1855–1935." LBI.
Levinger, Charlotte. "My First Fifty Years." LBI.
Livneh, Emmy. LBI.
Maas-Friedmann, Lucy. LBI.
Maas, Marie. LBI.
Meyer Loevinson, Johanna. LBI.
Michael, M. LBI.
Moos-Moore, Semi. "The History of the Family Moos." LBI.
Munk, Marie. Helene Lange Archives.
Natorff, Herta. LBI.
Necheles, Henriette. "Reminiscences of a German-Jewish Physician." Courtesy of Atina Grossmann, New York.
Ottenheimer, Alice. LBI.
Rosenstein, Conrad. LBI.
Rosenthal, Nora. "Opus One." City Archives, Frankfurt/Main.
Sander, Clara. LBI.
Sander, Emil. LBI.

Schönewald, Ottilie. LBI.
Schwarz, Olly. LBI.
Solon, Friedrich. LBI.
Stein-Pick, Charlotte. LBI.
Sturmann, Manfred. "Grossvaters Haus." LBI.
Tachau, Paul. "My Memoirs." LBI
Uhry, Edmond. LBI.

Archives

Archives of the City of Frankfurt/Main
  Collections:
    Jenny Apolant
    Nora Rosenthal
Central Archives for the History of the Jewish People, Jerusalem
  Collections:
    Alzenau-Wasserlo
    Bad Kissingen
    Bamberg
    Bayreuth
    Charlottenburg
    Collection of Caricatures on German Jewry
    Cologne
    Danzig
    Ehesachen
    Ems
    Frankfurt/Main (TD108)
    Grünstadt
    Halberstadt
    Halle
    Hammelburg
    Israelitisches Lehrerinnenheim zu Berlin, e.V.
    Kissingen (Landkreis Kissingen)
    Kolberg
    Königsberg
    Lautenberg, West Prussia
    Leipzig
    Lorsch
    Lübeck
    Mainz
    Münster
    Neuweid
    Oberfranken
    Prussia
    Stuttgart
    Vereinigung Israelitischer Lehrer und Leherinnen in Frankfurt/Main
    Verein Israelitisches Lehrerinnenheim
    Würzburg

Geheimes Staatsarchiv Preussischer Kulturbesitz, Berlin
Collections:
Staatsarchiv Königsberg
Staatsarchiv Hamburg
Collections:
Jüdische Gemeinde: Ehesachen; Paulinenstift; Statistisches Material; Heiratskontrakte; Israelitischer Brautausstattungsverein von 1840; Frauenverein zur Unterstützung Armer Witwen
Polizeibehörde Hamburg, Abteilung IV (Politische Polizei): Israelitischer Frauenverein für Krankenpflege; Israelitische Haushaltungschule; Israelitischer Humanitärer Frauenverein
Hauptstaatsarchiv Düsseldorf, Schloss Kalkum
Collections:
Synagogengemeinde in Duisburg
Institut für Sozialwissenschaften, Berlin
Helene Lange Archives
Leo Baeck Institute, New York
Collections:
Berent, Margarete
Boehme, Hildegard
Braun-Vogelstein, Julie
Carlebach Collection (microfilm)
Edelheim Mühsam, Margaret
Elbogen, Ismar (for Regina Elbogen memoirs)
Eliassow, Alfred
Elkan family
Eltzbacher, Hans
Eschelbacher, Ernestine
Fraenkel, Marta
Frauenbewegung
Frisch, Fega
Goldstein, Julius and Margarethe
Gruenewald, Max (for memoirs of "Tante Emma" and his father, Simon Gruenewald)
Harold, Walter
Hirsch, Rahel
Jacobson, Jacob
Jacoby, Gustav
Kahler, Antoinette (memoirs)
Keibel family
Magnus, Erna
Meyer Loevinson, Johanna (collection and memoirs)
Mildtätigkeitsverein der Frauen in Köln
Mosse family
Muehsam, Margarete
Oestreicher, Else
Pappenheim, Bertha
Perl, Katharina
Perles, Joseph
Pinkus family

Riesenfeld, Adolf (diary)
Sachs, Hans
Salomon, Alice
Sinn family
Wunderlich, Frieda
YIVO Institute for Jewish Research
Collections:
Vilna collection on Germany

Government Publications

Statistik des Deutschen Reiches
Statistisches Jahrbuch für das Deutsche Reich
Statistisches Jahrbuch für den Preussischen Staat
Statistisches Jahrbuch der Stadt Berlin

Dissertations

Freudenthal, Margarete. "Gestaltwandel der städtischen, bürgerlichen und proletarischen Hauswirtschaft unter besonderer Berücksichtigung des Typenwandels von Frau und Familie." Johann Wolfgang Goethe University, Frankfurt/Main, 1934 (printed in Würzburg, 1934; rpt. Frankfurt/Main, 1986).

Hackett, Amy. "The Politics of Feminism in Wilhelmine Germany, 1890–1918." Columbia University, New York, 1976.

Kampe, Norbert. "Bildungsbürgertum und Antisemitismus im deutschen Kaiserreich." Technical University, Berlin, 1983.

Stodolsky, Catherine. "Missionary of the Feminine Mystique: The Female Teacher in Prussia and Bavaria: 1880–1920." State University of New York at Stony Brook, 1987.

Newspapers and Periodicals

Allgemeine Zeitung des Judentums (*AZDJ*) (Berlin).
Blätter des jüdischen Frauenbundes (*BJFB*) (Berlin).
Blau Weiss Blätter (Berlin).
Die Frau der Gegenwart (Breslau).
Frauen-reich: Deutsche Hausfrauenzeitung (Berlin).
Der Freitagabend (Frankfurt/Main).
Frankfurter Israelitisches Familienblatt.
Frankfurter Israelitisches Gemeindeblatt.
General Anzeiger für die gesamten Interessen des Judentums (Berlin).
Handwerk und Gewerbe: Offizielles Organ des Zentralverbandes selbstständiger jüdischer Handwerker Deutschlands (Berlin).
Im deutschen Reich: Zeitschrift des Centralvereins deutscher Staatsbürger jüdischen Glaubens (Berlin).
Israelitische Wochenschrift (Berlin).
Israelitische Wochenschrift (Magdeburg).
Israelitischer Jugendfreund (Berlin).
Israelitisches Familienblatt (*IF*) (Hamburg).

Israelitisches Gemeindeblatt (Cologne).
Israelitisches Wochenblatt: Zentral-Organ für die gesamten Interessen des Judentums (Berlin).
Das jüdische Blatt (Ansbach/Strassburg).
Das jüdische Echo: Bayrische Blätter für die jüdischen Angelegenheiten (Munich).
Jüdischer Volksbote (Frankfurt/Main).
K.C. Blätter (Zeitschrift des Kartell Convents der Verbindungen deutscher Studenten jüdischen Glaubens, Berlin).
Die Laubhütte (Regensburg).
Mitteilungen des Deutsch-Israelitischen Gemeindebund (Berlin).
Mitteilungen des Verbandes der jüdischen Jugendvereine Deutschlands (Berlin).
Neue Bahnen (Leipzig).
Ost und West (Berlin).
Preussische Jahrbücher (Berlin).
Schweizer Frauenheim (Zurich).
Simplicissimus (Munich).
Zeitschrift für Demographie und Statistik der Juden (*ZDSJ*) (Berlin).

Interviews

Blumenthal-Weiss, Ilse (born 1900, Berlin). New York. June 1981, January 1982.
Edinger, Dora (born 1890, Berlin). New York. 1986.
Hamburger, Anna (born 1888, Württemberg). New Jersey. June 1978, June 1981, March 1982.
Stern, Bruno (born 1912, Württemberg). New York. November 1980.
Stern, Liesl (born 1922, Württemberg). New York. March and December 1982.

Novels and Plays

Auerbach, Berthold. *Barfüssele*. Berlin, 1912.
Brod, Max. *Jüdinnen*. Berlin, 1911.
Duc, Aimé. *Sind es Frauen?* Berlin, 1903. Translated by Lillian Faderman and Brigitte Eriksson in *Lesbian-Feminism in Turn-of-the-Century Germany*. Weatherby Lake, Mo., 1980.
Ettlinger, Karl. *Moritzchens Tagebuch*. Berlin, 1908.
Fontane, Theodor. *Jenny Treibel*. Berlin, 1893.
Hermann, Georg. *Henriette Jacoby*. Berlin, 1915.
———. *Jettchen Gebert*. Berlin, 1906.
Hillern, Wilhelmina von. *Only a Girl: A Physician for the Soul, a Romance*. Translated by A. L. Wister. Philadelphia, 1870.
Hirschfeld, Georg. *Agnes Jordan*. Berlin, 1898.
Landsberger, Arthur. *Berlin ohne Juden*. Hannover, 1925.
———. *Millionäre: Ein Berliner Roman*. Munich, 1913.
Mann, Heinrich. *Der Untertan*. Berlin, 1918.
Reuter, Gabrielle. *Aus guter Familie: Leidensgeschichte eines Mädchens*. 17th ed. Berlin, 1908.
Tergit, Gabriele. *Effingers*. Frankfurt/Main, 1982.
Zweig, Arnold. *Junge Frau von 1914*. Berlin, 1931. Reprint. Frankfurt/Main, 1970.

INDEX

N.B.: Italic numbers refer to illustrations.